CRY HAVOC

ALSO BY JOSEPH MAIOLO

Joseph Maiolo, Kirsten Schulze, Jussi Hanhimaki and Antony Best,
An International History of the Twentieth Century
(2nd ed. rev. 2008)

Joseph Maiolo and Robert Boyce, eds.,
*The Origins of World War Two:
The Debate Continues* (2003)

Joseph Maiolo,
*The Royal Navy and Nazi Germany, 1933–1939:
Appeasement and the Origins of
the Second World War in Europe* (1998)

CRY HAVOC

How the Arms Race
Drove the World to War
1931–1941

JOSEPH MAIOLO

BASIC BOOKS
A Member of the Perseus Books Group
New York

Joe Maiolo acknowledges the support of the Arts and Humanities Research Council during
the preparation of *Cry Havoc*.

 Arts & Humanities
Research Council

Library of Congress Cataloging-in-Publication Data
Maiolo, Joseph A.
    Cry havoc : how the arms race drove the world to war, 1931-1941 / Joseph Maiolo.
        p. cm.
    Includes bibliographical references and index.
    ISBN 978-0-465-01114-8 (alk. paper)
    1. World War, 1939-1945—Causes. 2. Arms race—History—20th century. I. Title.

D741.M26 2010
940.53'11—dc22

                                                                              2010005533

10 9 8 7 6 5 4 3 2 1

To my teacher
Donald Cameron Watt

Cry "Havoc," and let slip the dogs of war . . .

—MARK ANTONY,
in Shakespeare, *Julius Caesar*, Act III, Scene 1

Our Legions are brim-full, our cause is ripe.
The enemy increaseth every day;
We, at the height, are ready to decline.
There is a tide in the affairs of men,
Which, taken at the flood, leads on to fortune;
Omitted, all the voyage of their life
Is bound in shallows and in miseries.
On such a full sea we now afloat,
And we must take the current when it serves,
Or lose our ventures.

—MARCUS BRUTUS,
in *Julius Caesar*, Act IV, Scene 3

CONTENTS

ILLUSTRATIONS

Illustration credits: © akg-images: 2 above left, 3 above. © Bettmann/Corbis: 1 above left, 5 above, 7 above, 7 below, 8 above, 8 below. © Corbis: 1 below right. German Resistance Memorial Center: 1 below left. © Getty Images: 4 below, 5 below, 6 below. © Hulton-Deutsch Collection/Corbis: 2 above right. © Kyodo News: 1 above right. © Popperfoto/Getty Images: 2 below, 3 below left, 3 below right. © Roger Viollet/Getty Images: 4 above left. © Time & Life Pictures/Getty Images: 4 above right, 6 above.

MAPS

ACKNOWLEDGMENTS

Thanks first and foremost to my literary agent, Peter Robinson, without whose constant encouragement and guidance I would not have written this book. At Basic Books I am indebted to Lara Heimert, Norman MacAfee, Robert Kimzey, Kay Mariea, Alex Littlefield and Ross Curley.

I am deeply grateful to Rolf Tamnes, the Director of the Norwegian Institute for Defence Studies, who invited me to spend the 2005–6 academic year in Oslo to work on the book, and to the Arts and Humanities Research Council of the United Kingdom, which awarded me a research leave grant in 2008–9 to finish it. I also benefited from the enthusiastic help of three terrific librarians: Irene Kulblik of the Norwegian Institute for Defence Studies, Anne C. Kjelling of the Norwegian Nobel Institute, and Geoffrey Bellringer of King's College London.

Peter Jackson, Antony Best, James Harris, Sven Holtsmark, Massimiliano Fiore, Marcus Faulkner and Steve Casey generously shared their time, expertise and collections of documents with me. John Gooch and Adam Tooze graciously allowed me to read their draft manuscripts. Bob Davies, Robert Self and Evan Mawdsley helpfully answered my questions. I am indebted to Barrie Paskins and Anthony Best for reading the chapters as I wrote them, and to Beatrice Heuser, David Stevenson and Philip Bell for reading the final draft. I am also extremely grateful to Catherine Keen, Mary Keen, Julia Davinskaya, Peter Busch, Alan James, Sam Copeland, Caroline Martin, Stafford Ward, Talbot Imlay, Ksenia Gerasimova, Ksenia Skvortsova, Murielle Cozette, Vivienne Jabri, Helen Fisher, Richard Mason, David Wardle, Martin Collins, Douglas Matthews, Ian Paten, Bernard Dive, Caroline Westmore, Jeffrey Ward, Therese Klingstedt and Alessio Patalano. Last but not least I am grateful to my students over the years at King's College London for sharpening my ideas.

Finally a note on the text. For the sake of readability I have generally avoided using foreign terms. For Japanese and Chinese names, I have followed the practice of those cultures and placed the family name first. I have not distinguished between grades of senior military ranks: thus, rear admirals and brigadier generals are simply admirals and generals. Fascism refers to the Italian political movement, and fascism for the political phenomenon in general. To devote my time and energy to less accessible sources, where an adequate translation of a source was available (Ciano's diary, for instance), I have quoted from it.

THE GREAT POWERS, 1936

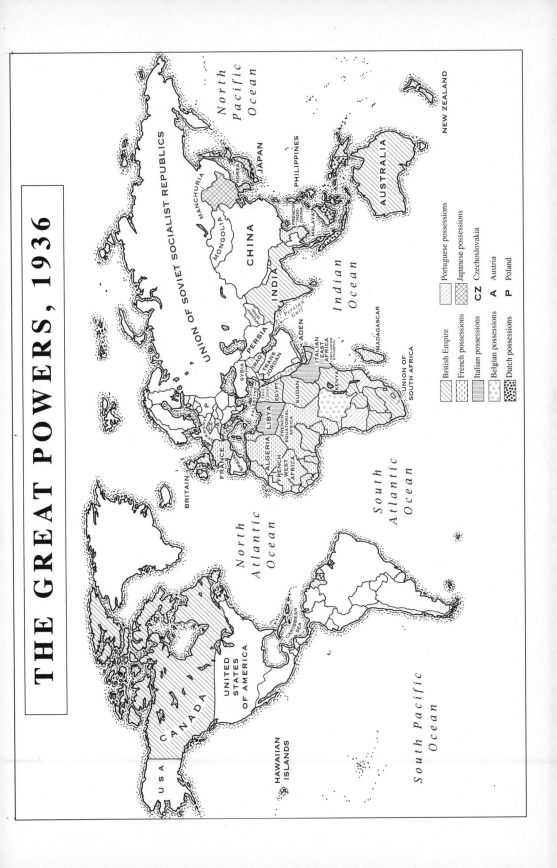

British Empire

French possessions

Italian possessions

Belgian possessions

Dutch possessions

Portuguese possessions

Japanese possessions

CZ Czechoslovakia

A Austria

P Poland

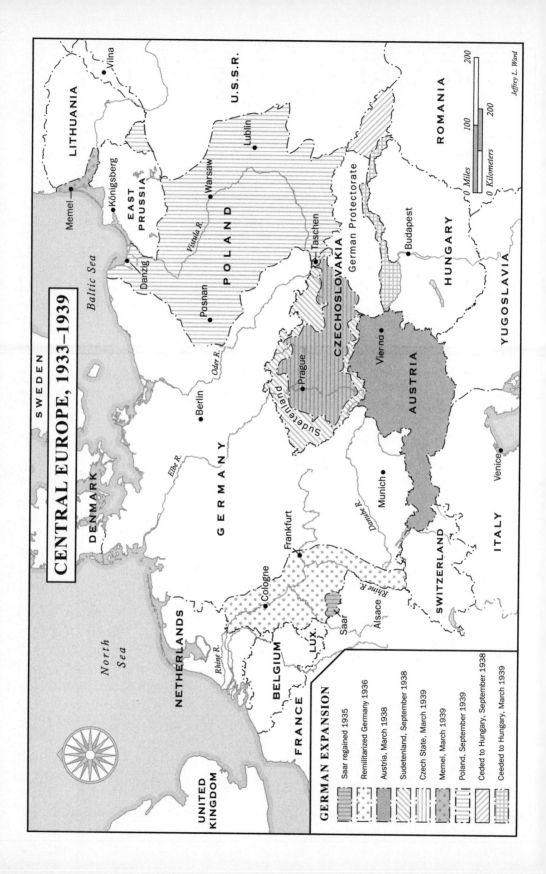

CENTRAL EUROPE, 1933–1939

Jeffrey L. Ward

SWEDEN

LITHUANIA

U.S.S.R.

ROMANIA

Vilna

Memel

Königsberg

EAST PRUSSIA

Lublin

Warsaw

POLAND

Vistula R.

Danzig

Posnan

Oder R.

Baltic Sea

Taschen

German Protectorate

Budapest

HUNGARY

CZECHOSLOVAKIA

Vienna

Prague

Sudetenland

AUSTRIA

YUGOSLAVIA

Berlin

Elbe R.

GERMANY

Munich

Venice

Danube R.

Frankfurt

Cologne

Rhine R.

Saar

Alsace

SWITZERLAND

ITALY

NETHERLANDS

Rhine R.

BELGIUM

LUX.

FRANCE

North Sea

UNITED KINGDOM

DENMARK

0 Miles   100   200

0 Kilometers   200

GERMAN EXPANSION

Saar regained 1935

Remilitarized Germany 1936

Austria, March 1938

Sudetenland, September 1938

Czech State, March 1939

Memel, March 1939

Poland, September 1939

Ceded to Hungary, September 1938

Ceeded to Hungary, March 1939

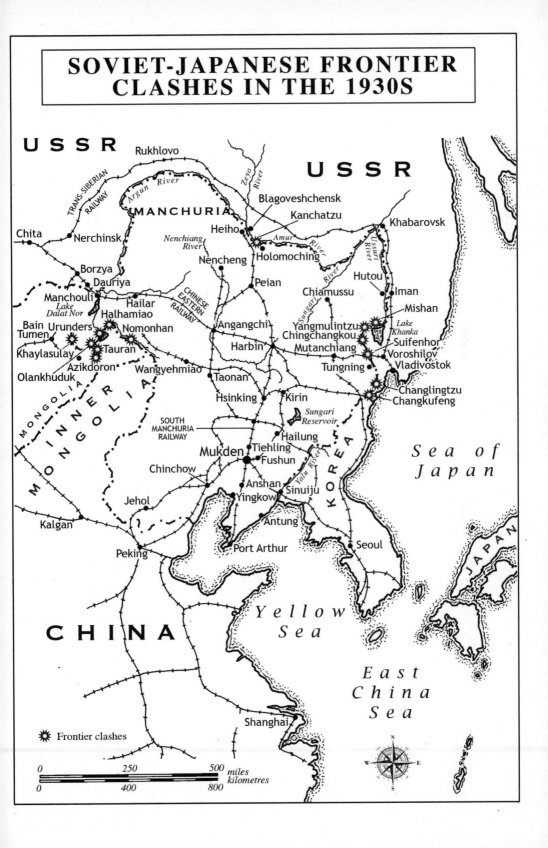

SOVIET-JAPANESE FRONTIER CLASHES IN THE 1930S

USSR

Rukhlovo

USSR

TRANS-SIBERIAN RAILWAY

Argun River

Zeya River

MANCHURIA

Blagoveshchensk

Kanchatzu

Heiho

Khabarovsk

Chita

Nerchinsk

Nenchiang River

Amur River

Ussuri River

Nencheng

Holomoching

Borzya

Peian

Hutou

Dauriya

Chiamussu

Iman

Manchouli

Lake Dalat Nor

Hailar

Halhamiao

Mishan

Sungari River

Ussuri River

Bain Urunders

Nomonhan

Angangchi

Yangmulintzu

Lake Khanka

Tumen

Chingchangkou

Khaylasulay

Tauran

Harbin

Mutanchiang

Suifenhor

Voroshilov

Azikdoron

Wangyehmiao

Vladivostok

Olankhuduk

Taonan

Tungning

MONGOLIA

INNER MONGOLIA

Hsinking

Kirin

Changlingtzu

Sungari Reservoir

Changkufeng

Sea of Japan

SOUTH MANCHURIA RAILWAY

Hailung

Mukden

Tiehling

KOREA

Chinchow

Fushun

Yalu River

Anshan

Sinuiju

Jehol

Yingkow

Antung

JAPAN

Kalgan

Port Arthur

Seoul

Peking

CHINESE EASTERN RAILWAY

Yellow Sea

CHINA

East China Sea

⊛ Frontier clashes

Shanghai

| 0 | 250 | 500 | *miles* |

| | | | *kilometres* |

| 0 | 400 | 800 | |

N W E S

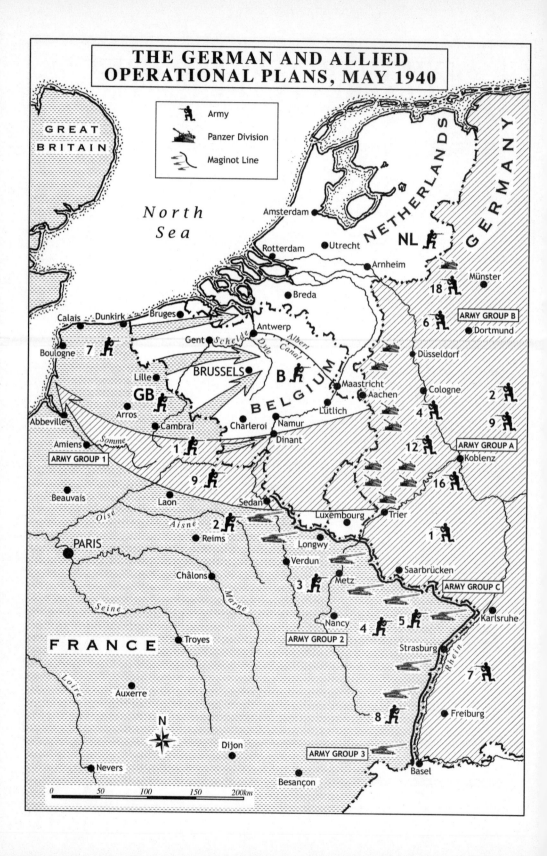

THE GERMAN AND ALLIED OPERATIONAL PLANS, MAY 1940

Army

Panzer Division

Maginot Line

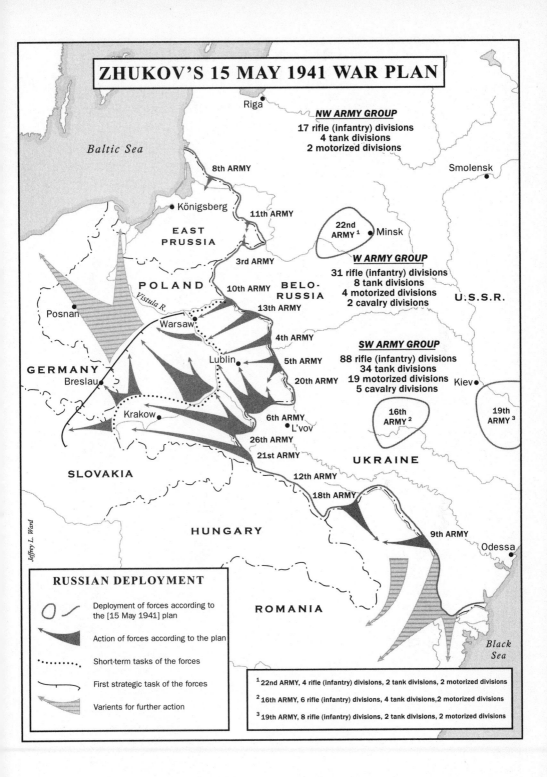

ZHUKOV'S 15 MAY 1941 WAR PLAN

Riga

Baltic Sea

Smolensk

8th ARMY

Königsberg

11th ARMY

NW ARMY GROUP
17 rifle (infantry) divisions
4 tank divisions
2 motorized divisions

EAST PRUSSIA

22nd ARMY [1] • Minsk

3rd ARMY

POLAND

Vistula R.

10th ARMY

BELO-RUSSIA

13th ARMY

W ARMY GROUP
31 rifle (infantry) divisions
8 tank divisions
4 motorized divisions
2 cavalry divisions

U.S.S.R.

Posnan

Warsaw

4th ARMY

GERMANY
Breslau

Lublin

5th ARMY

20th ARMY

SW ARMY GROUP
88 rifle (infantry) divisions
34 tank divisions
19 motorized divisions
5 cavalry divisions

Kiev •

16th ARMY [2]

19th ARMY [3]

Krakow

6th ARMY
• L'vov

26th ARMY

21st ARMY

UKRAINE

SLOVAKIA

12th ARMY

18th ARMY

HUNGARY

9th ARMY

Odessa

ROMANIA

Black Sea

Jeffrey L. Ward

RUSSIAN DEPLOYMENT

Deployment of forces according to the [15 May 1941] plan

Action of forces according to the plan

Short-term tasks of the forces

First strategic task of the forces

Varients for further action

[1] 22nd ARMY, 4 rifle (infantry) divisions, 2 tank divisions, 2 motorized divisions

[2] 16th ARMY, 6 rifle (infantry) divisions, 4 tank divisions, 2 motorized divisions

[3] 19th ARMY, 8 rifle (infantry) divisions, 2 tank divisions, 2 motorized divisions

INTRODUCTION

In the summer of 1914, the major European powers plunged into war with offensive plans for quick victories. By the winter those plans had come to naught. The elusive short war of maneuver turned into a long one of trenches and grinding industrial attrition. During 1915, Europe's political leaders and general staffs soon discovered that they lacked the deep reserves of men and munitions to wage what would be called "total war."[1]

As the battles raged on, governments scrambled to turn whole economies and societies into gigantic war machines. Raising the vast quantities of men, money and munitions demanded industrial and popular regimentation on an unprecedented scale. Peacetime government structures creaked and groaned under the mounting pressure. Existing bureaucracies swelled, and new hydra-like mobilization agencies sprang up as powerful emergency instruments of state control and central planning. While wartime leaders diverted ever larger percentages of national resources into producing war materiel, prewar patterns of trade and financial practices became distorted and market forces were curbed. Those who lived through the war experienced it as a titanic siege fought between economies and societies racing toward all-out mobilization.

Naturally, the cataclysm made an indelible imprint on the minds of those who survived it and who came of age after it. For many officials, soldiers, statesmen, scholars and industrialists of all political shades, the war had opened up the awe-inspiring possibility that in the future technocratic elites could rationally plan and manage entire industrial economies and societies to realize grand political aspirations. In the years just after the conflict, however, the overwhelming political impulse among the victors was not to perfect the wartime practices of centralized state control but to put into reverse the political, economic and social distortions generated by total war.

During the 1920s one of the major feats of this demobilization project was the restoration of the pre-1914 mechanism of international currency stabilization and exchange known as the gold standard. By adhering to the gold standard, all the capitalist states not only promoted the smooth flow of trade and capital across frontiers but also locked themselves into a strict budgetary discipline that would inhibit massive arms build-ups. Among the major capitalist nations, the onset of the Great Depression from 1929 onward broke the trend toward demobilization. The industrial slump, the spectacular failure of markets to self-correct and the breakdown of the gold-standard system helped to propel into positions of power many cohorts of eager scholars, bureaucrats, soldiers and politicians who dreamed of salvation through the exercise of advocated state control over aspects of national life, especially markets.[2]

The economic crash also coincided with what was supposed to be the finale of another postwar exercise in demobilization, the opening in early 1932 in Geneva of the World Disarmament Conference. While officials squabbled over a deal on global levels of weaponry, to the shock of military men, many of whom were already reeling from slashed budgets, the slump cut huge swathes through the heavy industries and engineering firms that would be needed to maintain existing armaments and, of course, to expand them. This process began to crank into reverse once the Geneva talks closed in 1934 and the recently installed Nazi regime started to arm Germany at full throttle. And with that, for the second time in twenty years, another gigantic, bureaucracy-breeding, market-crushing power bonanza of an arms race was on.

This book tells the story of that arms race. It explains how arms rivalry among the great powers—the Soviet Union, Japan, Germany, Great Britain, France, Italy and the United States—contributed to the outbreak and expansion of war in 1939–41.

The two decades before the Second World War are usually remembered as constituting an abject lesson in the hazards of shunning arms races. During the 1920s—so runs the cautionary tale—the democracies recklessly encouraged challenges by neglecting their defenses. During the 1930s the democratic nations compounded that error by failing to arm fast enough to stop Axis aggression. That account of the arms race is firmly fixed in popular mythology as the story of how wicked dictators (chiefly Adolf Hitler) out-armed and out-smarted naïve "appeasers" (above all Neville Chamberlain).

The trouble with the conventional view is that it reduces everything to simple choices (to arm or not) and ignores the role of the arms race as an independent, self-perpetuating and often overriding impersonal force that shaped events. My aim in this narrative study is to correct the orthodoxy by telling the more complex tale of how politicians and military men the world over struggled to cope in vain with the arms race as an underlying dynamic, the supreme wrecker of all master plans.[3]

To tell the story in all its complexity, I have tried to combine the political, diplomatic, military and economic elements of arming into one international history. One of the arguments of this book is that the arms race can only be understood from a large-scale perspective. Arms races are like waves of action and reaction that ripple through the international system. In periods of acute political tension, one state races ahead to win a military edge over its rivals, who in turn respond to the menace by arming too, and a perilous cycle of actions and reactions ensues, which ends either in war or in some sort of uneasy political-military stalemate. Before 1914, for instance, the European great powers raced against each other by building ever more powerful battleships and by equipping mass conscript armies that could be mobilized for attack faster than their competitors. During the Cold War the superpowers spurred each other on to stockpile nuclear weapons far beyond the point of overkill.[4]

During the 1930s, surges of action-reaction among the great powers sped up the making of ships, tanks, guns and aircraft. Diverting ever more money, factories imported raw materials and labor to the mass production of munitions at the cost of profitable exports, and living standards placed tremendous strains on each nation and each nation's rivals. In the shorthand of the day, arming diverted production from butter to guns—or in the case of Japan, from rice to guns. To do so the competitors found themselves imposing, or under mounting political, economic and competitive pressure to impose, state control over economic and social life. Entering the arms race was not a politically neutral act. The symptoms of escalating arms growth—swelling bureaucracies, multi-year industrial plans and social regimentation—proclaimed a new order to come. As the race spiraled out of control, it was no coincidence that "future war" became interchangeable with "totalitarian war." Planning trampled freedom: an efficient war economy was irreconcilable with parliaments, free markets and social progress. Arming meant turning entire nations into tightly integrated war machines that were self-sufficient (autarkic) in food and industrial raw materials. That was the universal military-political lesson of 1914–18 and the compelling emulate-or-capitulate logic that drove the arms race forward.[5]

Not everyone reacted to that competitive pressure to conform in the same way. Some embraced it; others resisted. Everywhere military men saw disciplined societies and state-managed economies as the logical necessity of modern warfare and the arms race. Sometimes they met opposition from industrialists and state officials; sometimes they allied with like-minded entrepreneurs and ambitious civil servants to lobby hard in the budding bureaucratic power bonanza for industrial concentration, autarky and technocratic rule. The new revolutionary movements that secured power after 1914–18—Bolshevism, Fascism and National Socialism—were profoundly marked by that conflict and by a belief in the need to prepare for future total wars that would demand sweeping mobilization. During the 1930s, once the arms race heated up and another big war loomed, it was widely accepted that the states that had already gone totalitarian had a head start in the race toward all-out social and economic mobilization. Confounded by runaway German rearmament, the liberal democracies struggled with the problem of how to arm themselves against the escalating threat of total war without succumbing to totalitarianism. Some predicted that the Nazi regime would eventually run out of steam; others thought that the only answer to the threat was to accelerate the arms race by redirecting ever more national resources into armaments; and others hoped to buck the relentless totalizing trend by arming just enough to deter Hitler.

In what follows I hope readers will be struck by the similarities between the internal political debates and organizational processes over arming that occurred at different times and in different places. Though expressed in different tongues, conceptions of the arms race, its logic and the measures it required, varied little. No matter what type of regime or its military starting point, the race sent everyone down the same totalitarian track. In the general effort to turn ideas into reality, similar technical, economic, political and military problems came up repeatedly. Everywhere the internal debates had a marked tendency toward rhetorical absolutes with a sharp political edge. Air force zealots untiringly oversold the capabilities of bombing to win bigger budgets. Intelligence was prone to inflation or (much less often) deflation of foreign threats to advance the goals of its advocate. And, as one exasperated economist noted at the peak of the race, disputes about economic organization flew off into fantasy. "Much nonsense has been talked in some countries about planning," he shrewdly remarked, "and much ink spilt in defence or attack of economic freedom that never existed and equally of patchwork intervention that was never logically planned." Still, however detached from reality some of the debates may have been, narrating them in parallel, as I do here, reveals much about how the arms race acted as an agent and a rationale for action.[6]

Although the arms race takes center stage in this book, its story will be told from the vantage points of leading politicians (Stalin, Mussolini, Roosevelt, Hitler, Chamberlain, Churchill and others) and some less well-known military men, officials and businessmen. The way in which the race prompted decision makers to adjust to changing circumstances and to recalculate the element of time is compelling drama. Like all historical processes, arms races occur over time. Once they get under way, there is no way to erase the unintended consequences of early actions and restore initial conditions. Escalating competition erodes the pacesetter's advantages. Time itself becomes a real player, working for some and working against others.

As we shall see, first in Berlin, then in Rome and finally in Tokyo, the ebb and flow of arms competition compelled leaders to make now-or-never decisions about war. Still, the tidal-like effects of arms racing did not force anyone to choose war. In Rome and Tokyo we can imagine alternative choices being formulated. What made a great European conflict inevitable was Hitler's determination to wage one. Yet, as scholars have often noted, Hitler did not get the big war against the Soviet Union backed by Britain and Italy that he had originally wanted. Instead he provoked one against France and Britain. The explanation for why events unfolded in that way lies in the arms race. Hitler was losing it and he knew it. Refusing to be deterred, he decided to run the risk of an all-out war against a constellation of foes that possessed a crushing level of economic superiority over the flagging Third Reich. As economic historians have shown, the decisive wealth gap between Germany and its enemies was even wider than most contemporary experts believed. In retrospect that makes Hitler's decision to venture into an unwinnable war even more astonishing. That the economic lightweights Italy and Japan followed that path too is doubly astonishing.[7]

While recognizing Germany's pivotal role in the arms race and in causing the Second World War, we should not overlook the much wider forces that converged to make the arms race possible in the first place. The arming of the Nazi regime was as much a symptom as a high-octane accelerant of the underlying dynamic. My goal is to bring those wider forces into much sharper relief and to appreciate the interwar years as a chapter in the tragic history of twentieth-century armaments competition.

CHAPTER 1

DEEP WAR AND RED MILITARISM

O n May 7, 1932, Joseph Stalin wrote a letter of apology. The most
powerful man in the Soviet Union sent carefully measured words
of conciliation to the Red Army's director of armaments, Mikhail
Nikolayevich Tukhachevsky. The episode that prompted this rare
admission of error by Stalin had taken place two years before. On January 11,
1930, Tukhachevsky, then serving as commander of the Leningrad Military
District, had drafted a paper that described his vision of the scale and quality of forces required by the Soviet Union. "As you know," wrote Stalin, "I
subscribed basically to the views of our [military] Staff and expressed myself
extremely negatively about your memorandum, considering it to be the fruit
of bureaucratic maximalism, the result of playing with figures, and so forth. . . .
Now, two years later, when some unclear matters have become clearer for me,
I must confess that my judgement was too sharp, and that the conclusions of
my letter were not correct in all respects."[1]

In his original proposal, Tukhachevsky admitted that his calculations were
rough. From a statistical analysis of the Soviet Union's expanding automobile
and tractor industries, he derived figures for the maximum potential output
of aircraft and tanks. His numbers were staggering: Soviet industry could
churn out in *each* year of a future war 122,500 aircraft and 197,000 tanks. Accounting for losses through combat and wear and tear, and the time lag between manufacture and use, these figures meant that the Red Army could
field approximately 35,000 airplanes and 50,000 tanks. The wartime army
would consist of 250 divisions, ten more than Germany had deployed in the
First World War, and 150 more than the current war plan. Besides the colossal numbers, what really made Tukhachevsky's proposal provocative was the
important questions he left unanswered: How big would the whole army need

to be to field these combat forces? What levels of spending and peacetime industrial readiness did warfare on this scale demand? What about all the artillery, machine guns, transport vehicles, small arms and explosives, not to mention the ammunition, food, fuel, clothing, medical equipment and other stores that Tukhachevsky's projected maximum army would consume?[2]

Boris Shaposhnikov, the chief of staff of the Red Army, ordered his officers to find the answers. After running the numbers, they concluded that Tukhachevsky's army would need eleven million men, or 7.5 percent of the country's population. Simply to mobilize the manpower, every male from fourteen to forty-five would have to be called up. The peacetime spending necessary for Tukhachevsky's plan, sixty billion rubles, was twenty-four times the entire army procurement budget for 1930. Shaposhnikov's staff calculated that mobilizing Tukhachevsky's proposed army "would devour the whole state budget over the last three years and still not be adequately fulfilled."

Kliment Voroshilov, the commissar for defense, a member of Stalin's inner circle and no friend of the ambitious war planner, sent a copy of Tukhachevsky's "super-rearmament" plan and the staff's observations on it to Stalin. "To carry out such a 'plan,'" Stalin replied, "would certainly ruin the economy of the country, and the Red Army: that would be worse than any counter-revolution." He denounced Tukhachevsky's plan as a form of "red militarism," which would lead to the "liquidation of socialist construction."[3]

Stalin's words would have surprised Kremlin watchers. Most foreign observers saw his Five Year Plan (1928–32), to overtake the West in industrial production and technology, as preparation for war, and thus self-evidently red militarism. Stalin's turnaround from admonishing to apologizing to Tukhachevsky can in part be explained by the large volume of hardware churned out by the mushrooming weapons factories in the Five Year Plan. But this peculiar episode in the history of Russian armaments also mirrors a widespread and recurrent pattern of these years. Before the outbreak of the Second World War, time and again, in the capitals of all the major powers, similar disputes erupted over the magnitude of armaments preparations between all-outers, who recognized few if any limits to arming, and their critics, who did.[4]

In the Soviet Union there was of course no dispute about the need to rearm, nor that arming required an industrial economy to fight machine-age war. In 1918, after the German Army had forced the Bolsheviks to sign a punitive peace treaty, V. I. Lenin, the founder of the Bolshevik Party and the first leader of the Soviet Union, bitterly remarked that "the war taught us . . . that those who have the best technology, organization, discipline and the best machines emerge on top. . . . It is necessary to master the highest technology or be crushed."[5]

The lesson was reinforced by the Russian Civil War (1918–20), in which the capitalist powers had intervened against the Bolsheviks. When the Red Army lost the Soviet-Polish War of 1920–21, their defeat checked the spread of the Russian Revolution and endangered the survival of the only socialist state in the unforgiving world of cut-throat capitalism and relentless imperialism.[6]

After Lenin died on January 21, 1924, a struggle developed at the top of the Communist Party over what path to take toward a future workers' utopia. The Party's general secretary, Joseph Stalin, who, with relentless cunning, emerged as Lenin's successor, largely favored the radical direction advocated on the left of the party by his chief rival, Leon Trotsky. Both men favored co-ercive measures to transform the Soviet Union's technologically backward and chiefly rural economy into an industrial powerhouse. But Stalin rejected Trotsky's call for collective leadership at the top and sought to isolate him. Once he had outmaneuvered Trotsky, Stalin turned on his rivals on the right of the party, principally Nikolai Bukharin, who advocated a much slower and more orderly march toward socialism. By the end of the 1920s, Stalin emerged from the power struggle as Lenin's successor, and the supreme leader of the Soviet Union.[7]

Stalin believed that a showdown with the forces of capitalism was in-evitable, but fear of imminent war was also a useful tool to isolate the right and mobilize the party, the officials and the people for a headlong dash to so-cialism in one country. After all, there was little difference between mobiliz-ing for industrialization and mobilizing for war; and even less difference between planning a socialist economy and planning a war economy. In both cases, securing the food supply was essential. In the summer of 1927 a war scare (sparked by a diplomatic quarrel with Britain) and a grain crisis caused by the reluctance of peasants to surrender their harvest provided pretexts for action. To control the harvest for state purposes, Stalin began to wage a class war against resisters among the peasantry, the *kulaks*, and ended the limited free market in foodstuffs that had existed since 1921. Once he had sidelined Bukharin and his allies at the end of 1928, industrialization and the collec-tivization of farming began in earnest. Large-scale, state-run collective farms replaced individual peasant farms. In parallel, the Five Year Plan initiated the swift development of huge state-planned, administered and managed indus-tries, and hastened the growth of a new urban working class. [8]

In the drive to industrialize, Stalin saw the Soviet Union racing to catch up to and overtake the capitalist states in economic and technological

strength. "When we have seated the USSR on an automobile and the peasant on a tractor," he wrote, "let the esteemed capitalists, who boast about their
'civilisation,' try to catch us up then."[9]

Building socialism and defending it were indivisible, and the Soviet leader
kept a close eye on everything: Marxist-Leninist theory, socialist art, archi-
tecture, cinema, literature and of course weapons development. On this last,
as on much else, he was not happy: "Our artillery is insufficient," he scolded
Voroshilov, "scandalously insufficient." "Besides airplanes, tanks, artillery and
ammunition," he told the Politburo, "we must also check on the production
of submarines. The situation with submarines is very bad, their production is
too slow and outrageously bad. We must push this task hard, day after day,
continuously, *without a respite*."[10]

In constructing socialism, Stalin was flexible enough to make tactical re-
treats. In 1932–33, forced collectivization caused food production to plummet.
Millions of peasants were being persecuted as kulaks or dying from famine.
Because many soldiers were peasants themselves, their loyalty was tested. Re-
alizing this, Stalin eased up on de-kulakization and coercive grain requisitions.
In armaments, Stalin also exercised flexibility by making tradeoffs among conflicting goals. Although he dreamed of a magnificent fleet of battleships proudly
flying the Red Banner across the world's oceans, in the early 1930s he cut spending on ships to buy tanks. The same was true for the overall balance of investments in the early days of the first Five Year Plan, which put steel, iron, coal and
especially tractors for farming ahead of artillery, airplanes and tanks. As jarring
as it may seem to put it this way, at the time he called Tukhachevsky a "red militarist," Stalin was a relative moderate when it came to arms.

A TRUE ALL-OUTER, Tukhachevsky was one of the archetypal future war
systematizers of his age. Born in 1893 to an impoverished aristocratic family,
the gifted young Mikhail Nikolayevich Tukhachevsky might have become a
scholar or a composer had his father possessed the means. Instead, he became
an army officer. In 1915 he was wounded and captured by the Germans. In
October 1917 he escaped and joined the Red Army, quickly earning a reputation as a bold field commander. After 1921 he distinguished himself first as
head of the new military academy and then as chief of staff to Mikhail
Frunze, the commissar for defense. A dyed-in-the-wool Bolshevik with an
aptitude for strategy, Frunze indulged his young protégé's cascade of ideas
about wars to come. Tukhachevsky's relations with the rest of the Bolshevik
elite—like those of all the "specialists" retained from the Tsar's army—were

less good. During the war against Poland, Tukhachevsky had quarreled over battlefield operations with numerous swaggering revolutionaries, including Voroshilov and Stalin himself. Even so, Stalin seems to have respected the man. Voroshilov, on the other hand, who replaced Frunze when he died in 1925, thought his new chief of staff insufferable. For his part, Tukhachevsky, a man with a titanic ego, found it hard to conceal his contempt for the new defense commissar's superficial grasp of modern war.[11]

How genuine Tukhachevsky's commitment was to socialism is impossible to know. He certainly knew how to please his masters by composing his theories in the idiom of Marx, Engels and Lenin. The elegant coherence that Marxist-Leninism brought to industrial-age warfare probably appealed to his abstract intellect. Stripped to bare essentials, however, there was not much that was Marxist about his thinking. Tukhachevsky believed that future wars would be decided by the capacity of rival economies to mass-produce tanks, bombers, artillery, gas and rockets and the ability of their armies to move mass divisions of these high-speed weapons through enemy lines, and then to fight "deep" behind the enemy's front. To fight deep would permit the Soviet Union to disrupt the enemy's battlefield command, control, supply and support; at the higher, operational level, to fight deep would allow the Red Army to disrupt an enemy's entire industrial system.[12]

When Tukhachevsky became chief of staff in 1925, the Red Army was incapable of fighting a major war. He saw that without radical industrialization, securing the ammunition for the army's old weapons was difficult and procuring new stocks of modern munitions would be impossible. As one staff officer lamented, "One can say directly that if the craftiest spy had been given the task of disorganising [our arms industry] at its roots, he could hardly have invented greater chaos and worse personnel." Industrial weakness frustrated staff officers because armaments planning boiled down to economic planning. Soviet planners, like their counterparts everywhere, needed to grapple with three different industrial mobilization projections. The first concerned the arms needed in peacetime to equip the standing army (about 600,000 men in 1926) and the several million reservists who would be called up in an emergency. The second involved estimating realistic production targets to supply existing forces and to equip freshly trained men while industry geared up to full speed. And, finally, following those months of intense industrial mobilization, there was the problem of estimating the maximum production targets for each full year of a future war.[13]

Obviously, the arms production capacity required in peacetime was much less than that needed in a long war. Tukhachevsky knew that it made no sense to set aside huge munitions factories fully stocked with machine tools and skilled workers just so they could sit idle until a crisis. The army relied on a core of long-service professional soldiers and short-service conscripts, who received two years of compulsory military training, to build up a large pool of reserves. Now, officials planned to build a core of "cadre" defense plants to meet peacetime demands and to prepare civilian factories for conversion in wartime to weapons production. After all, soldiers and civilians agreed that making tractors, automobiles, transport aircraft and chemicals was not very different from making tanks, bombers, gas and explosives. Where they disagreed was over who should ultimately control these preparations, and whether civilian or military needs should take priority in the distribution of limited resources. Soviet military thinkers repeated emphatically that preparing industry for war must not wreck the economy as a whole. But they could never forget how in 1915 the Tsar's army desperately needed more shells than Russia's factories could produce. Deep down, most soldiers felt that economics was too important to be left to civilians.[14]

The most outspoken was Tukhachevsky. He suffered from the impatience that often comes with a relentlessly logical mind. Deep battle required deep mobilization. In pursuit of this depth, a command economy had the edge over market-driven ones, so long as a central directing authority structured the economy to make a seamless transition from peace to war. "We must learn how to maneuver our resources," he urged, "exactly as we know how to maneuver our army."[15]

Several obstacles prevented the orchestration of the war economy in this way, however. Not least of these was a divided command structure at the top of the Red Army. As chief of staff, Tukhachevsky jockeyed for control of the army with two other bodies with overlapping authority, the administrative and inspectorate branches. Frunze had deliberately set up this divided structure as a check against any future would-be Napoleon who might try to usurp the Revolution, but it was at the cost of efficiency. Coordination between civilian industrial managers and armaments planners was also lacking. Tukhachevsky struggled hard to gain for the military some influence in economic planning. In June 1927, at his initiative, a defense section of the State Planning Commission (Gosplan) was set up to coordinate military-economic preparations. Although this restructuring went a long way toward achieving Tukhachevsky's goal, he was not appointed chairman of Gosplan's defense section.

The details are unclear, but at some point in 1928 frustration with the bureaucratic tangle became too much for the high-strung chief of staff. His relationship with Voroshilov deteriorated. "Your constant phrases: 'The Staff does not calculate with costs,' 'economy does not interest the Staff,' and so on," Tukhachevsky complained, "cannot but undermine the Staff's authority in the eyes of other bodies." Voroshilov retorted, "You insisted on concentrating this enormous power in the Staff of the Red Army. I was categorically against this, because I considered that this task also be accomplished by the civilian authorities and be directed by a government organ." In May 1928 Tukhachevsky resigned to take command of the Leningrad Military District.[16]

His successor as chief of staff, Shaposhnikov, a much more deferential soldier, shared some of Tukhachevsky's views on staff primacy. He too was unhappy about the slow rate of military modernization. What Shaposhnikov did not share was his predecessor's proclivity for poking holes in Voroshilov's inflated sense of self-importance. The defense commissar regarded himself as the Red Army's champion in the fight for resources within the Soviet oligarchy. In the late 1920s arms spending increased, but slowly. In the summer of 1928 Voroshilov exploded when the Soviet premier, Alexei Rykov, an associate of Bukharin, cut the budget. He complained to Stalin: "I don't doubt for a second that someday [in a military crisis] Rykov will announce 'Kliment Efremovich [Voroshilov] is the one responsible for defence,' and wash his hands of the matter, and forget his own helpful work in preparing the Red Army." The political situation began to shift in 1929, with Bukharin's expulsion from the Politburo and the accession the next year of Vyacheslav Molotov, Stalin's lieutenant, to the post of premier. In July, three months after the formal decision to begin rapid industrialization, and while the Red Army clashed briefly with Chinese troops over possession of the Russian-owned Chinese Eastern Railway in Manchuria, the Soviet leadership made its first significant decisions on rearmament within the time frame of the first Five Year Plan.[17]

On July 15, the Politburo adopted a resolution on the condition of Soviet defense. Brimming with the vocabulary of intense military competition, the document described the vulnerable state of the Soviet Union. The Red Army had fallen far behind the capitalist armies in military technology and mobilization planning. Industrial officials should accelerate the expansion of heavy industry most crucial to armaments. To measure future rearmament goals, the Politburo set down two yardsticks. The size of the Red Army should not "lag" behind that of the most likely foe in the main theater of war, and the armed forces should be qualitatively "stronger" than any potential enemy force in two or three types of the most important weapons (aviation, artillery and tanks). The resolution on defense, which bemoaned the inferior quality of

Soviet aircraft, established the target for air force strength at 2,000 first-line machines with 1,500 additional planes in reserve. By the end of the first Five Year Plan (1932), the fully mobilized army would field about three million soldiers, deploy at least 100 combat divisions armed with about 2,000 tanks, and over 10,000 artillery pieces, and be equipped with up to 180,000 motor vehicles. The output capacity of the munitions industries was also to be scaled up to feed this modern force with a steady supply of fresh tanks, aircraft, guns, small arms, machine guns, bullets, bombs and shells.[18]

Expansion on this scale would transform the Red Army into the world's most fearsome war machine, twice the size of the mobilized French Army, which in 1929 was the world's largest. The Soviet Union would possess more combat planes than either the British or French air forces. What made this arms growth practicable was a convergence of aims and interests inside the Soviet Union between military and industrial planners and the political leadership, but what drove the arming forward was fear of the outside world.

Even in the relatively placid years 1926–29, the Soviet leaders saw much to fear beyond their frontiers. The war plans of this period provide a vivid picture of these anxieties. In the Soviet Union the magnum opus of all war plans was *Future War*. Tukhachevsky commissioned it in 1926, and the intelligence directorate of the Red Army staff did much of the detailed work contained in its 750 pages. The final version of July 1928 took readers on a panoramic tour of the coming struggle for survival against the combined forces of global capitalism. "The political purpose of intervention against the USSR will be the liquidation of the Soviet system," the planners began, "the subordination of Soviet influence for the purpose of the use of the Russian market and transformation of Russia into a colony." France and Britain, the Soviet Union's most implacable foes, would be the drivers behind the armed league that would someday try to crush communism. The armies of Poland, Romania, the Baltic states and Finland would bear the burden of the fighting, reinforced with anti-Bolshevik Russian émigrés. Britain, France, Czechoslovakia and Italy would supply their armies with munitions and advanced weapons, aviation, armor and warships, as well as technical aid. Assuming that the war would go well for the attackers, other nations such as Germany, Japan and the United States would throw their lot in with the enemy coalition. The authors of *Future War* legitimized these broad-brush images with page after page of detailed mathematical calculations of the hypothetical size and firepower of the capitalist forces, which made the Red Army's case for swift rearmament and huge investments in the defense industries overwhelming.[19]

The reality was somewhat different than that portrayed in *Future War*. Most French and British officials had no love for the Soviet experiment, but they had no plans to enlist millions of Poles, Romanians, Balts and Finns to unseat the Bolsheviks. Yet the Red Army turned shadows into clear-cut intentions. *Future War* pointed to French agreements with Poland and other east European states to contain Germany as the diplomatic cornerstones of the anti-Soviet military alliance. Regardless of the bewildering array of numbers and oblique facts in *Future War*, the Red Army actually knew little about the military strength of the western powers. Officials complained about the "complete absence" of intelligence on foreign weapons as well as the "unsatisfactory" means of gathering it. The war-making capacity of the Japanese, French, British and U.S. economies was an even greater mystery. For clues, intelligence analysts combed official statements on defense distributed by governments and the League of Nations, as well as foreign newspapers, periodicals and military publications. Unfortunately, the available foreign military literature conveyed an inflated impression of the fighting strength of the capitalist powers. Soviet overestimates were also founded on the belief that their potential foes lied about defense. As Voroshilov said in April 1929, the "capitalist states spend no less than twice as much as their official military budgets."[20]

Between Tukhachevsky's super-rearmament plan of January 1930 and Stalin's apology of May 1932, the hypothetical threats described in *Future War* became all too real. The fracturing of the global economy after the Wall Street crash of October 1929 heralded the crisis of capitalism long predicted by Lenin and his followers. World trade slumped, prices dropped, currencies devalued, banks closed and factories shut. The 1930s wore on with unprecedented levels of unemployment, poverty and social unrest everywhere. No wonder Moscow predicted that the ruling classes in Paris and London would soon face the choice of either class war on their own streets or joining forces to strike a spiteful blow against that beacon of proletarian hope, the Soviet Union.

Danger signs appeared in the West and the East. At the end of 1929 the Red Army defeated Chinese forces in a brief border war. In 1930, a menacing drumbeat of complaints from Washington, London and Paris about Soviet dumping of wheat onto the world's depressed markets coincided with unusually friendly trade talks between Berlin and Warsaw. "The Poles are certain to be putting together (if they have not already done so) a bloc of Baltic states," Stalin warned in September 1930, "in anticipation of a war against the USSR. . . . To repulse both the Polish-Romanians and the Balts, we should prepare to deploy (in the event of war) no fewer than 150 to 160 infantry divisions, that is, (at least) 40 to 50 divisions more than are provided for under our current guidelines."[21]

In January 1931 the Politburo altered its original July 15, 1929 guidelines on defense: it was not enough that the Red Army simply not "lag" too far behind the strength of a capitalist coalition; it must be "superior to our probable adversaries." Some officials now feared that the swift growth in Soviet arms might provoke their foes to strike before it was too late. "From the imperialists' viewpoint," wrote one planner, "a war [against us] in 1931 would have the character of a *preventive war*."[22]

On September 18, 1931, another external jolt triggered even greater efforts in immediate armaments preparations. Japanese troops began the conquest of Manchuria, long a region of conflict between the two powers. The Red Army had defeated the poorly armed Chinese in November 1929, but the Japanese posed a much more serious threat to Russia's sparsely defended 4,000-mile frontier with Manchuria. Intelligence that trouble was brewing had arrived in March: an intercepted message to Tokyo from the Japanese military attaché in Moscow advocated a "speedy war with the Soviet Union."[23]

Was Manchuria just a first step? While Chinese resistance in Manchuria was crushed over the winter months, Stalin sought to dissuade Japan from further aggression in 1932 with concessions and an accelerated arms buildup. Offers to sign a nonaggression pact and to sell Russia's stake in the Chinese Eastern Railway, however, did not cut much ice in Tokyo. In December, to direct measures against the Japanese, Stalin formed a working group that included Molotov, Voroshilov and Sergio Ordzhonikidze, the pugnacious commissar who oversaw the economy. They ordered more tanks, planes and guns. Arms spending doubled. Work on new arms factories began, and civilian plant was switched to military work. Troops, cavalry, armor, aircraft and artillery poured into the Soviet Far East.[24]

This escalation occurred during the height of a major internal crisis caused by the colossal scale of the first Five Year Plan. The magnitude of this economic transformation is difficult to imagine. A doubling of industrial investment and absurdly ambitious production targets drove everything forward at breakneck speed. As factories across Europe and the United States fell silent because of the Great Depression, blast furnaces, steel mills, electric generators, coking and chemical plants, aluminum and other metal works were coming alive in European Russia, the Urals, Siberia and Central Asia. The industrial workforce doubled. But the boom exacted a high price. The consumer-goods sector crashed. Privileged urban workers suffered food shortages, but millions of peasants died of hunger. Inflation drove up manufacturing costs, while raw-material shortages and shoddy workmanship forced constant delays. An adverse balance of trade developed because the world depression reduced the value of Soviet grain exports, which made vital imports of high technology and foreign expertise all the more expensive. Despite all the strains, the Soviet government raised the 1931 investments and output targets to achieve fulfillment of the Five Year Plan in four years. "Either we overtake the advanced countries in ten years," Stalin warned, "or they will do us in."[25]

The 1931 acceleration did not come too soon for the Red Army. In 1929–30, civilian planners often spoke of turning the Soviet Union into an unassailable bastion for waging total war, but in the rush to meet hopeless targets, steel, iron and tractors won out. Shaposhnikov liked to joke that the relations between the military and civilian planners were "as hostile as that between Poland and Russia." Thanks to the aggression of the Japanese Army, however, the balance in this internal struggle over priorities swung in favor of the Red Army. The central economic plan for 1931 projected an astonishing 125 percent increase in military production. In June 1931, Tukhachevsky returned to Moscow from Leningrad to become Voroshilov's deputy and the Red Army's director of armaments. The latter position, created eighteen months earlier to focus armament and mobilization planning within the Red Army staff, assumed even greater importance with the huge resources allotted to arming in 1931. Only a year and a half earlier Tukhachevsky had fallen foul of Voroshilov and Stalin about the magnitude of his "rearmament" plan. Now, the capacity to think big was exactly what the situation called for.[26]

Many of the problems that plagued forced industrialization, however, also frustrated fulfillment of rearmament goals. Not the least of these difficulties was a lack of know-how and experience in the design, development and production of guns, tanks and aircraft. In 1929–30 Soviet officials traveled abroad to undergo training and to negotiate technical transfer agreements with U.S., British, Italian and German firms. The Soviet Union also employed many foreign technicians in design bureaus and on shop floors. During the 1920s, it sought to compensate for the crippling damage done by revolution and civil war to its arms industries by cooperating closely with Germany. But this was an uneasy relationship. Soviet technicians suspected that their German counterparts withheld their most promising innovations. The Berlin connection was also an irritating reminder to the Soviet leaders of their reliance on the willingness of likely adversaries for the import of technology essential to national survival.[27]

In July 1929, the Politburo resolved to leap ahead in aircraft and tank design. "The Politburo and mainly Comrade Stalin," Voroshilov later recalled, "demanded from us: take all measures, spend the money, even large amounts of money, run people to all corners of Europe and America, but get models, plans, bring in people, do everything possible and impossible in order to set up tank production here." In the 1920s, Soviet workers had built small batches of tanks based on early French models. The technical mission now sent abroad to buy advanced prototypes got lucky in Britain and the United States. Vickers-Armstrong, a leader in the global arms trade, sold samples of Vickers 6-ton and Medium tanks, and a machine-gun carrier called the Carden-Lloyd Mark VI. The mission also signed a deal with the American entrepreneur J. Walter Christie, who dreamed of fast tanks and experimented with wheel-track suspension systems to make them go fast. Alarming reports of Polish interest in Christie's design arrived in Moscow, but the Red Army alone adopted the prototype with deep passion. "Only a tank with great power and speed resources for fast attack," gushed the Red Army's director of motor mechanization, "can confuse the enemy's plans, disorganise and demoralise it and destroy the rear of its forces."[28]

On November 7, 1931, Stalin watched as the first Soviet-adapted Vickers and Christie tanks rumbled past Red Square on parade. Mass production was the next step. Defense planners drew up a "great tank program," with a goal to build 2,000 BT tanks (Christie's chassis), 3,000 T-26 tanks (Vickers 6-ton) and 5,000 T-27 (Carden-Lloyd) machine-gun carriers. Such vaulting ambition, so typical of the superoptimistic Five Year Plan, caused industrial chaos and waste. In 1931 industry made 2,000 of the older French models. But the Vickers and Christie models required much more complex motors, gearboxes, chassis, caterpillar tracks, optics, traversing mechanisms, and cast and face-hardened armor plate for the hulls and gun turrets. All these precision-engineered parts needed to be fed into the assembly process on time to ensure a steady flow of finished tanks. Throw into this mix inexperienced managers, bungling engineers, a too narrow range of machine tools and workers inexpert in their use, frequent material shortages—all in a frenzy whipped up by propaganda screaming for "fulfillment"—and the result was breakdown. Converting tractor plants to tank assembly helped to boost output, but as Tukhachevsky and his staff soon discovered, conversion was much easier said than done. In October 1932 Voroshilov boiled with frustration as the Red Army's inspectorate branch confessed that "we still have not completely managed to master the production of tanks on the scale assigned by the government, especially with regard to malleable cast-iron, armour, thermal finishing of parts, and quality of assembly." Production was 4,000 units behind schedule, monthly output was a third what it needed to be to hit the 10,000-tank target, and many of the finished tanks suffered from structural and mechanical flaws and lacked treads, guns and turrets.[29]

The collision of impossible targets with industrial reality, combined with the infusion of foreign technology, intensified the deep-seated Soviet fear of internal enemies. After the revolution, the Bolsheviks had retained many from the bourgeoisie who were specialists in critical professions—military officers, administrators, scientists and engineers. Without this compromise, the revolution would have been bound to fail. However, doubts about the loyalty of bourgeois "specialists" lingered long after. In July 1929, not for the last time, the Politburo decided to root out the specialists in the defense sector. The problem was that some of them, such as the aeronautical engineers, could not be "liquidated" without crippling whole enterprises. Even before the first Five Year Plan, the industry was rife with accusations of "wrecking." A tiny design flaw, a missing bolt or a faulty control cable, and a test flight could end with a burning wreck. Typically, aviation experts came from bourgeois origins and had regular contact with foreign contractors. In 1929–30 dozens were imprisoned to continue their work in an aircraft design gulag run by the secret police near Moscow.[30]

By the end of 1932 mounting inflation, a poor harvest, widespread famine and a decline in industrial output compelled Stalin and his inner circle to re-think their policies. In 1933 modernization slowed down. Investment was reduced, and plans became more realistic. For a brief time, a market in consumer goods was permitted. Specialist baiting was discouraged. After the huge investments in defense in the two previous years, the military budget for 1933 was reduced. Voroshilov complained, but Stalin applied the brakes. He also attacked the Red Army's mobilization plan. It was "outrageously inflated and very burdensome for the state," he wrote. "It must be reworked and *cut back* as much as possible." Stalin was unperturbed about the large shortfalls in arms production: "Concerning tanks and aircraft, industry has obviously not yet sufficiently rearranged itself to (our) tasks. Never mind! We shall press and support it to adapt. The important matter is to keep certain (mainly the defence) industry branches under permanent control. They will adapt and shall fulfil the programme, if not 100 per cent, then 80–90 per cent. Is that really so bad?"[31]

Stalin had good reason to be stoical. In the first six months of 1932, military production had risen by sixty percent over the year before. Tank, aircraft and artillery output saw the biggest gains. In 1929 the army had ninety tanks; in 1933 it had 4,700, with more in production. By 1933 the air force had 5,000 aircraft, with the percentage of newer models steadily rising. The army also now deployed 17,000 artillery pieces and 51,000 heavy machine guns. Work on new barracks, fortifications, naval bases and airfields surged ahead. The quality of weapons was as impressive as the quantity. The BT and T-27 tanks outclassed most of the competititon well into the 1930s. The Red Army was the first to fly huge four-engine bombers. Formations of these TB-3s filling the sky above the Kremlin, with big red stars blazoned on their fuselages, came to symbolize the modernity of Soviet aircraft technology. The French Air Force lavished praise on the quality of Soviet aviation. British intelligence concluded that the Soviet Union possessed "a thorough organisation for planning industrial mobilisation which has already made considerable practical progress." Though he might grumble about spending cuts, Voroshilov still could boast in the summer of 1932 that "the Red Army is capable of victoriously taking on the army of any capitalist country."[32]

Tukhachevsky saw things in a different light. Stalin's apology of May 7 appeared to be something of a vindication. Stalin had even conceded that a mobilized Red Army of six to eight million men might be within economic capacity in three or four years—though he had remarked that a force of eleven million (the staff's projection from Tukhachevsky's "super-rearmament" plan) was still a fantasy. Yet as director of armaments, Tukhachevsky could not be content. Employing the same crude arithmetic projections that had figured so prominently in *Future War* and in every forecast thereafter, his staff erroneously credited the economies of France, Britain and the United States with the wartime capacity to make 24,000 to 60,000 tanks a year. In the Soviet Union, in contrast, the big tank program had fallen well short of its goal. The aviation industry lagged behind in adopting the techniques of mass production. A mobilized army of three million men equipped with only 14,000 trucks could hardly be called "motorized." Tukhachevsky lashed out at boastful civilians who obfuscated about production results: "This evil is not only a betrayal of the party but also one way to avoid implementing the military-industry orders."[33]

The economy could not sustain the industrial effort pictured in the draft mobilization plans. Thousands of officials were now assigned to organize mobilization preparations across the economy—but was the work being done, especially as priorities were swinging back to civilian projects? Almost all the tank and aircraft production in 1931–32 had taken place in dedicated defense factories, not in civilian plants. The switch of tractor factories to tank assembly plants had underscored the need for prewar spending to make such conversions run smoothly in wartime. The dilapidated railways, vital for shifting men, machines and supplies, also cried out for investment. Yet the Politburo had sharply reduced capital investments and slackened the pace of armaments growth.[34]

In early January 1933, the Central Committee of the Communist Party gathered in Moscow. The leaders were in a buoyant mood. Stalin spoke to the assembled audience on January 8: "The successes of the Five Year Plan have mobilised the revolutionary forces of the working classes of all countries." Without the plan, he said, "our position would . . . have been more or less analogous to the position of present-day China, which does not have its own heavy industry, and its own armaments industry, and is nibbled at by anyone who feels like it." In his report to the committee two days later, Ordzhonikidze took up the theme. "Alarms" in the Far East had made it necessary to produce tanks and aircraft in huge numbers. Stalin called out: "And to Tukhachevsky it's all very little." Laughter filled the Kremlin hall. Ordzhonikidze joined in the fun: "Everything is little to him. But we can say to comrade Tukhachevsky the following: when we need to move these weapons to the front, we will give the Red Army as much as it needs." At the next day's plenum Voroshilov too could not resist taking a dig at his deputy. While in his speech he expounded on the technical triumphs of the Red Army, he also produced diagrams showing Soviet armaments growing much faster than those of any other country and joked, "Comrade Tukhachevsky has no grounds to be dissatisfied."[35]

For the first and last time Stalin and his circle felt confident about Soviet armaments. At the end of January, a new chancellor took office in Germany. The slowdown in Soviet defense spending in 1933 was only temporary.

CHAPTER 2

COLONEL ISHIWARA
GOES TO MANCHURIA

Rich in natural resources such as coal, iron ore and timber, Manchuria consists of a large central plain surrounded by low mountain ranges. Its continental climate, which subjects the fertile plain to the extremes of blazing hot summers and freezing cold winters, provides good conditions for the cultivation of soya beans, rice, millet, maize, wheat and other cereals. Historically, the land of the Manchus was divided into three provinces—Heilongjiang to the north, Kirin to the east, and Liaoning (as it was named in 1928) to the south. Between the two world wars, estimates of Manchuria's total area varied because of its ill-defined and disputed frontiers: geographers often equated it to the landmasses of France and Germany combined, or about 380,000 square miles. To the west lay Inner and Outer Mongolia; to the southeast, the Japanese colony of Korea; to the north, the Amur River formed a natural border between Manchuria and the Soviet Union's vast Siberian wilderness.[1]

That Manchuria became the flashpoint between the Soviet Union and Japan in the early 1930s came as little surprise. For the first three decades of the century, Russia and Japan had vied for domination of Manchuria at China's expense. In 1904 they went to war, and Japan won on land and sea. Afterward, Russia retained influence in northern Manchuria, while the south fell to the Japanese. When war came in 1914, Russia and Japan found themselves fighting on the same side. Japanese soldiers captured the German leasehold territory in China at Shantung, and Tokyo exploited the opportunity to demand from the Chinese greater economic and political privileges on the continent. The chaos in Russia during the Bolshevik Revolution in 1917 allowed Japan to advance into northern Manchuria and Siberia. Only in 1925, when

Japan recognized the new Bolshevik government, did the last Japanese soldiers finally leave Soviet soil.[2]

The responsibility for the defense of Japan's railway concessions and growing population of colonists in Manchuria belonged to a detachment of the Japanese Army of about 10,000 men known as the Kwantung army. As so often happens with soldiers stationed on the frontiers of empires, the Kwantung officers developed a taste for freebooting action and a disdain for paper-pushing warriors and weak-kneed civilians back home. They saw across the frontier a land rife with communism and believed they knew best how to deal with the situation. Running networks of agents and informers across northern China, the Kwantung army meddled in the struggle between the Chinese warlords for control of the capital, Peking.[3]

By the end of the 1920s, defending Japan's foothold on the continent became much more difficult. China was reviving from decades of decline and crippling internal turmoil. With military aid from Moscow, the Chinese Nationalist Party, under the leadership of Generalissimo Chiang Kai-shek, became the strongest faction in the civil war for national unification. From 1926 to 1928, in a series of military campaigns known as the Northern Expedition, the generalissimo defeated his rivals in central China and established the Nationalist government in Nanjing. With Chinese popular nationalism directed against the foreign imperialist presence on Chinese territory gaining strength, Chiang aimed to unify the whole of China, including Manchuria.

All the great powers with imperial and commercial stakes in China, including not just Japan but also Britain, France and the United States, reacted to the nationalist upsurge by offering small political and economic concessions. However, it was impossible to reconcile the Chinese dream of national unity with Japan's wish to remain predominant in Manchuria. The inevitable clash came on September 18, 1931. The Kwantung army staged a fake Chinese attack near the city of Mukden in southern Manchuria as a pretext to overthrow the local Chinese warlord. Over the next six months, the Japanese operation expanded to the whole of Manchuria and the fighting spread to central China. In Manchuria the Japanese claimed that they were backing a popular liberation movement. They smuggled Henry Puyi, the young "last emperor" of the defunct Manchu Ch'ing dynasty, out of China and installed him as ruler of the puppet state of Manchukuo. Defying the League of Nations' efforts to mediate, Japan recognized Manchukuo in September 1932 and in 1933 withdrew from the organization altogether. For the moment, the newly established Nationalist government could not afford an all-out war with the Japanese. As China's supreme military and political leader, Chiang had little choice but to accept a truce.

The initiative for the Mukden incident came not from the government or army headquarters in Tokyo, but from a conspiracy of Kwantung army officers, with the sympathy of others in Japan. The conspirators opposed making concessions to Chinese nationalism, which they regarded as a slippery slope to Japan losing its influence in Manchuria and control of its colonies, Korea and Taiwan. The conquest of Manchuria was thus as much a shock to the government in Tokyo as it was to the Chinese. The conspirators had calculated that the establishment of Manchukuo would be so popular in Japan that the government would be forced to endorse it, and they were right. News of the Kwantung army's attack ignited a wildfire of patriotic enthusiasm across Japan, just when the Great Depression, financial scandals and the political deadlock in China had battered the authority of parliamentary government.[4]

The mastermind of the conspiracy was Colonel Ishiwara Kanji. This bookish, forty-two-year-old officer with a serene expression must have appeared out of place on the rough and ready, hard-living frontier. But Manchuria was the place he wanted to be. This was unusual for a staff officer with as brilliant a career as Ishiwara's, who might have been expected to seek a prestigious posting as an attaché in Europe or on the general staff. Yet his whole career was marked by a headstrong individualism. In 1915 Ishiwara first distinguished himself by earning a place at the elite army staff college, and then three years later by finishing second in his class. Apart from a brief tour of duty in China, most of his postings over the next decade were in military education and research. Ishiwara spent three years in Germany, where, all around him, soldiers, scholars and politicians agonized over the catastrophe that had befallen them. Ishiwara then returned to Japan to teach at the army staff college until October 1928, when he joined the Kwantung army as chief of operations.[5]

In his new post Ishiwara took charge of drawing up contingency plans for the Kwantung army. But his imagination soared high above the details of operational movements and missions. Ishiwara had developed a vision of warfare that blended orthodox military theory with an historical determinism worthy of Karl Marx. From history Ishiwara deduced that warfare oscillated in irregular cycles between decisive and continuous wars. Decisive wars (such as Japan's war against Russia in 1904–5) were won by defeating the enemy's army in swift operations. Continuous wars (of which 1914–18 was the supreme example) were won by grinding the adversary down over years to the point of exhaustion. Only limited mobilization of armed forces was needed to wage decisive wars, while continuous wars called for the total mobilization of whole economies and societies. A devotee of the apocalyptic teachings of the Nichiren sect of Buddhism, Ishiwara predicted that the cycles of human warfare would end in one final conflict, fought on a titanic scale with the most terrifying weapons of the machine age, squadrons of city-destroying bombers. In this coming Armageddon, the Japanese were destined to lead Asia against the United States. After Japan's victory, humanity would "enter an era of peace under the guidance of the imperial throne."[6]

One can only guess what his more down-to-earth Kwantung army colleagues made of Ishiwara's "final war" prophecies. Yet his prescription of what needed to be done to prepare for future war appealed to the gung-ho frontiersmen: Japan needed Manchuria, and the only way to get it was through a masterstroke.[7]

COLONEL ISHIWARA went to Manchuria as the standard-bearer of a powerful set of ideas held by many forward-thinking military officers and civilian bureaucrats. True all-outers, these visionary young men rose to prominence after 1931 to build a totalitarian "national defense state," and by doing so drove Japanese rearmament forward.

For the soldiers the defining moment had come in 1918. Germany's defeat troubled Japan's officer corps because it struck at their roots. In 1868 two centuries of feudal rule in Japan known as the shogunate ended. To prevent Japan falling victim to the kind of Western colonization that had befallen Indochina, the Dutch East Indies, the Philippines and China, a small group of reforming barons from the most developed southern regions of Japan established a modern state under the authority of the emperor in a brief civil war known as the Meiji Restoration. With the slogan "Rich Country, Strong Army," Japan adopted advanced technology and established national institutions. Within a short time, the Japanese were making modern armaments and laying down the foundations of an industrial economy. For help with army organization, doctrine and training, Japan turned to Germany. It was a natural choice. In the years before and after the Meiji Restoration, German armies employing the latest implements of land warfare, railways, telegraphs and rifles unified their nation by smashing first the Austrian and then the French armies. Among swaggering German soldiers, Japan's eager-to-learn modern warriors felt right at home. Although in 1914 Japan formally sided with Germany's foes, much of the military elite rooted for their venerated old Prussian tutors.[8]

What went wrong with the German war effort became the preoccupation of the 1920s, debated in countless Japanese Army study groups and periodicals. In the search for an answer, up-and-coming officers like Ishiwara toured Europe and America to meet the men who had waged total war. For those who saw victory wholly as the just reward for individual heroism and the unwavering devotion of the nation to martial values, the answer was shocking: Germany had lost not because its army performed badly but because Germany's economy had failed. The Allies had won because their blockade had cut Germany off from food and raw materials. What was alarming was Japan's own economic vulnerability. As the country's top officers knew, had Russia fought on in 1905, Japan would have gone bankrupt in a few months. In the 1920s the resource-poor home islands lacked the vital commodities—food, raw materials and fuel—to feed its fast-growing cities and supply its heavy industries. Measured against the severe standards of total war, Japan was neither rich nor strong.[9]

For one group of officers, Japan's future capacity to wage a total war started as a seminar topic, became an obsession and finally a mission. In the late 1920s these officers, who had graduated from the academy in the first decade of the century, would gather to dine, present papers and debate. Aspiring leaders now reaching the middle ranks, they resented the monopoly over key positions in the army held by the founding clans of the Meiji era. Bound by a shared purpose, their number included Major Suzuki Teiichi of the general staff; Colonel Tōjō Hideki, the future wartime prime minister; Colonel Nagata Tetsuzan of the Army Ministry, a man consumed by thoughts of industrial mobilization—and Ishiwara Kanji. In its essentials, their crude geopolitical logic would have scored top grades at any war college on the face of the earth. If the Japanese Empire in wartime did not have the resources to feed its soldiers and workers and run its factories, so ran the logic, then Japan was not a great power. Japan must be a great power or someday fall prey to one; Manchuria contained many of the industrial raw materials and the rich farmland that Japan needed for autarky; therefore Japan must take Manchuria. While at the end of the 1920s these total-war officers spoke of autarky and pulled each other up the career structure, events moved ahead that prompted them into action.[10]

On the continent, Chinese nationalism now threatened Japan's foothold in Manchuria. Yet, over the horizon, something much more ominous appeared—the resurgence of Soviet armaments. After the war of 1904–5, Japanese war planners expected that Russia would one day seek revenge. In the early 1920s the threat was only theoretical. True, the Japanese saw the malign hand of Bolshevism behind Chinese nationalism and fretted over Chiang's links to Moscow, but the prospect of the Red Army marching into Manchuria looked a long way off. (At the time Mao Tse-tung's Chinese Communist Party was only a small force, and after 1927 Chiang tried to stamp it out several times.)

All this changed with the Soviet Union's first Five Year Plan (1928–32). A foretaste of what it would do for the Soviet presence in Asia came at the end of 1929, when Red Army air and ground forces swept aside Chinese troops in a railway dispute. Intelligence warned of worse to come. The Army Ministry in Tokyo calculated that one quarter of the budget of the Five Year Plan was devoted to armaments. A Japanese military officer who attended Red Army combined tank and aircraft exercises warned that the Japanese Army could not stop such attacks, and, even if it could, Soviet arms factories would be making these machines in such vast quantities that the Japanese would eventually be wiped out. When would the Soviet Union muscle its way into northern China? "Although Russia probably won't be starting anything for two or three years," predicted the Japanese Army's chief of operations in March 1931, "to say flatly that they won't would be a mistake." Total-war officers such as Suzuki, Nagata and Ishiwara agreed. A Soviet Manchuria would prevent autarky. Without autarky, Japan would fall irreversibly into armaments decline while the Soviet Union's war machine grew stronger and moved closer. With each passing month, the urge to take preventive action grew.[11]

The Five Year Plan provoked horror and fascination. Bolshevism as a political creed disgusted the total-war officers, but they admired the way the Soviets armed. Given the people, space and resources available to Red Army planners, it made perfect sense to Suzuki, Nagata and Ishiwara that the Russians would "plan" their economy. A planned economy was a war economy. And just like their Soviet counterparts, these officers wanted an "economic general staff" to plan in peacetime for a swift transition to all-out war. This drive for domestic modernization encompassed more than a desire for the military to get its hands on the economic levers. Japan was simply not the centralized state that their prophecies of future war required. Under the constitution, sovereignty was invested in the emperor, but he did not rule. Until the 1920s, cabinets dominated by the Meiji oligarchs governed. In 1924 oligarchy gave way to cabinets of party politicians drawn from the elected Parliament. This limited Taishō democracy ushered in a modest liberalization abhorrent to military men. In their eyes, party politicians were greedy and corrupt "degenerates." Foreign ideologies such as pacifism, socialism and communism twisted naïve minds. The political parties were seen as hostile to the military and eager to slash arms budgets, while free-market economics exposed Japan to global booms and busts and encouraged the frivolous pursuit of profits. The remedy to these evils championed by the total-war officers was a new, army-run "national defense state," which would control the economy, distribute resources to maximize armaments and mobilize the nation around the imperial throne.[12]

The total-war officers, however, were not the only ones looking to replace free-market capitalism with a state-run economy. A rising cohort of "reform" bureaucrats shared their outlook. In their youth at the University of Tokyo, in the same years when Lenin and his followers began to make the Soviet state, these future civil servants avidly read Marx and Engels. Many of them absorbed the economics of the German historical school, which claimed that the value of any individual could only be realized through the state. In the 1920s, when they joined state ministries in junior posts, the Japanese economy was reeling from the First World War. During that war, as Europeans turned their factories and farms over to war production and abandoned Asia's markets, Japanese producers stepped in. Japanese manufacturing and agriculture prospered accordingly thanks to the export boom. National income doubled. New steel, machinery and chemical factories sprang up. When peace came, however, the demand for Japanese goods fell, and the country suffered a financial shock, mass bankruptcies and rice riots. The postwar stagnation persisted, punctuated only by another financial panic in 1927, until things got much worse after 1929 with the onset of the Great Depression.[13]

What was wrong with the Japanese economy? The young men of the ministries, especially those working in the newly formed Ministry of Commerce and Industry, came to one conclusion—the free market. Unregulated competition drove a price-and-demand roller-coaster. Market forces favored consumer and export goods and were slow to allocate investments to heavy industries, like steel, iron, chemical and machine tools. The remedy was state control and central planning. Experiments with control took place in the 1920s, when the Ministry of Commerce and Industry promoted industrial concentration and rationalization through formation of self-regulating cartels in industries such as coal, steel, shipbuilding and engineering.[14]

For the reform bureaucrats, this was a step in the right direction, but one step too short. They rejected "self-control" by industrialists and instead wanted state control by technocrats like themselves. Foremost among them was Kishi Nobusuke. Born in 1896, a top graduate of the University of Tokyo, in 1920 Kishi joined what was then the Ministry of Agriculture and Commerce. In the mid-1920s he toured America and Europe to study industrial policy. In the booming United States, he marveled at mass production and consumption; in Germany, he saw state-sponsored industrial cartels. Yet what "shocked and impressed" him most was the Soviet Five Year Plan, which turned him into a planomaniac. During the 1930s Kishi became one of the prime movers behind the alliance of reform bureaucrats and total-war officers. His corporatist vision of Japan's national economic destiny was an ideal conceptual twin for the "national defense state" envisioned by those officers.[15]

In Manchuria, to test-run the ideas of the total-war officers and reform bureaucrats, Ishiwara carved out an enclave bigger than France and Germany combined. What he and his staff planned was as recklessly ambitious as the Soviet Five Year Plan. Manchukuo was a deliberate emulation of Russia's forced industrialization—a reply in kind, one powerful armaments economy to be raised against another.

From the start, army planners imposed their will in Manchukuo. Manchuria would be not simply a fund of resources but a huge military-industrial complex held together by a modern transport network and integrated into the home economy. Industries essential for armaments would get the biggest investments: coal, iron, steel, other metals, chemicals and machine tools. To erect this military-industrial powerhouse, a legion of civil servants, engineers, accountants, managers, clerks, skilled workers and farmers marched in from Japan. Distrustful of Japan's huge banking and industrial combines, the army planned to organize the state-owned enterprises on the principle of "one industry, one firm." Yet Manchukuo cried out for private money to achieve economic take-off. When Kishi Nobusuke became Manchukuo's deputy minister for industrial development in 1935, he reconciled the army to private investment. He also took the army's principle of "one industry, one firm" a step further—"all industries, one firm."[16]

Meanwhile, back in Japan, the creation of Manchukuo helped shift power away from the party politicians to the military-bureaucratic elite. Even before the Mukden incident, civilian-dominated government was teetering. In 1930, against the advice of the admirals and public opinion, the cabinet of Prime Minister Hamaguchi Osachi capped the size of the navy by agreeing to the London Naval Treaty. With the League of Nations World Disarmament Conference due to begin in 1932, everyone expected the army to be next. Reducing arms spending was part of a policy of tight money and balanced budgets. In January 1930, to induce steady industrial growth and competitiveness, the Hamaguchi cabinet pegged Japan's currency to the gold standard. Whatever the merits of fixing the yen to the gold standard, however, the timing was calamitous. During the worst depression ever, the Hamaguchi cabinet clung on, pricing Japanese goods out of the world market. In November 1930 a lone fanatic angry at the naval treaty and the distress of farmers killed Hamaguchi. The new government lasted only until December 1931. The next government under Inukai Tsuyoshi took the yen off the gold standard, yet this too proved damaging. Public outrage over rumors of currency speculators amassing fortunes while ordinary souls lost everything shook the government. In May 1932, ultranationalist naval cadets killed Inukai in a botched coup. Emperor Hirohito then called upon Admiral Saito Makoto to form a national unity cabinet. From now on, Japan's prime ministers would be drawn from a mixed bag of admirals, generals and senior state officials and one from the nobility.[17]

The sort of intense instability experienced by Japan in the early 1930s sometimes confers upon an unlucky few a role that runs contrary to their true motives and values. This was the fate of Takahashi Korekiyo, Japan's finance minister from December 1931 to February 1936. Some see him as the last barrier to militarism, but he did more than anyone else to facilitate a sustained acceleration in Japanese arms spending. When he took up the Finance Ministry for the fifth time at the end of 1931, he was seventy-seven. He was born the illegitimate son of an artist and a housemaid, and his rise from errand boy to head of the Bank of Japan attests to his genius. A product of the Meiji era, he attached much more importance to making the Japanese people rich rather than making the army and navy stronger than he thought they needed to be. Although he believed that the government must in times of trouble intervene in the economy to counteract market forces, he was against permanent state controls.[18]

Takahashi planned Japan's recovery from the Great Depression with his own brand of interventionist economics. His first act was to abandon the gold standard. The yen's value dropped by fifty percent. Although this enriched currency speculators and blackened the image of the government, the new exchange rate also set off a surge in Japanese exports while most of the rest of the world's trade stagnated. To stimulate business investment and growth, he cut interest rates. To fuel demand, Takahashi increased state spending through deficit financing.

Apart from financial relief for Japan's struggling farmers, most of Takahashi's expenditures went to shipbuilders, munitions makers and other defense-related industries. The military budget rose from 462 million yen in 1931 to over one billion yen in 1935. By 1935, seventy-eight percent of the total rise in state spending was in defense. The elderly banker who loathed extravagant defense spending tossed cash at the military to spend his way out of the slump. With no less irony, it was Takahashi who began to erect the type of government controls that one U.S. secretary of state aptly vilified as "economic armament." In July 1932 and again in March 1933, the state imposed central control on foreign currency movements and required all overseas business transactions to be approved by the Ministry of Finance. Takahashi once joked that "it is much harder to nullify the results of an economic conquest than a military conquest." He would live long enough to see the truth of his remark.[19]

Takahashi's largesse played into the hands of the new army minister, Araki Sadao, who was appointed to unify the Japanese Army after the Kwantung army's disobedience. Nicknamed the Tiger, Araki was a fierce spokesman for the Imperial Way faction within the army and much admired among subordinates. Proponents of the Imperial Way emphasized the cultivation of "flesh before steel," that is, what they saw as exceptionally Japanese spiritual qualities above the mere stockpiling of weapons. Araki's faction was formed in opposition to manpower cuts made in the mid-1920s by his predecessor, the then army minister, General Ugaki Kazushige, who had diverted the savings to tanks and aircraft. In his new post, Araki at first showed little favoritism to his own faction and appointed Ugaki's supporters, especially total-war officers such as Suzuki, Tōjō and Nagata, to high posts.[20]

All this changed, however, in June 1933, when Araki convened a meeting of top military planners to decide on policy. He proposed a crash two-year mobilization, expanding the army, stockpiling weapons and ammunition and on the continent building border fortifications and improving rail networks— to be ready to fight the Soviet Union by 1936. Nagata, now a general, was baffled. During the First World War he had reported from neutral Denmark on Germany's economic collapse. No matter what Japan did in the next three years, he knew that it could not fight Russia on an equal footing and would be doomed to suffer Germany's fate. The whole purpose of Manchukuo had been to achieve autarky. Capturing Manchuria's resources without building the factories to convert them into explosives, bullets, bombs, guns, tanks and aircraft was pointless. What was needed, Nagata argued, was a long period of peace to build up the heavy industries necessary to wage total war.

Araki was not ignorant of these considerations. He just did not believe that Japan could win an arms race against the Soviet Union. He also resented the influx into war planning of civilians, who uttered buzzwords like rationalization and scientific management. The idea that 1936 represented some sort of "crisis year" was more a tool for mobilizing ordinary citizens and prying yet more money out of Takahashi than a genuine prediction of future war.

To fire up junior officers, Araki would shout: "If the Soviet Union does not cease to annoy us, I shall have to purge Siberia as one cleans a room of flies." In reality, he negotiated with the navy, the army's most dangerous rival, in the internal struggle for money and steel. He offered to support the navy's policy of denouncing the naval arms-limitation treaties if it backed the army's rearmament program and his plan to introduce ideological indoctrination into schools. Nagata was appalled. Japan could not at the same time win a land-air race against the Soviet Union and a naval race against the United States and Britain. Nagata was also out of the job he loved most. Araki had him transferred out of planning to the command of a regiment.[21]

Nagata's exile was temporary. Araki's purge of senior officers like Nagata and his bombast about the "crisis of 1936" made him unpopular with his fellow generals as well as the cabinet, and in January 1934 he resigned. Under the new army minister, General Hayashi Senjurō, Nagata and others returned to the high command, restoring long-term work on autarky, the industrialization of Manchukuo and the mobilization of Japan. He lobbied the Court and Parliament to endorse his vision of a totalitarian national defense state. In March 1934, in the first of many war-oriented controls, Parliament passed legislation requiring petroleum companies to retain a six-month stock of fuel. In May 1935 the cabinet created a new super-agency, the Cabinet Research Bureau, to coordinate the armaments and mobilization planning work of the armed services and the civilian ministries. Nagata was euphoric. Since the mid-1920s, he and other total-war officers had lobbied for an economic general staff. Now they had one in the making because the Cabinet Research Bureau placed military planners and the reform bureaucrats together at the apex of the state—a prime location to circumvent the formal structures of decision making and to make their influence over policy felt most.[22]

Nagata did not enjoy his success for long. Araki's protégés blamed him and others for conspiring against Imperial Way. On August 10, 1935, a sword-wielding army officer burst into his office and killed him.[23]

Nagata's assassination was a blow to the total-war officers. But just before he died, he appointed some of his own men to the high command, including Ishiwara Kanji. Ishiwara's exploits in Manchuria had made him something of a luminary within the army, and a potentially troublesome one too. Although his Mukden plot had paid off, the army could not reward insubordination. His career therefore followed the routine pattern for an officer of his rank and experience. In 1933 he was given the command of a regiment, where he remained until the summer of 1935, when Nagata had him posted to Tokyo as head of the operations section of the general staff.

Nearly two years' worth of field exercises, training courses and parade-square bashing with his regiment had removed Ishiwara from the big picture of what had taken place on the continent since 1932. When he studied the intelligence on the scale of Soviet forces across the Manchukuo-Siberian frontier, he was shocked. Like so many arms racers before and after, Ishiwara and the other total-war officers assumed that their adversary's speed of arms growth would remain fairly constant, while their own program sped ahead. They had not anticipated that Stalin would accelerate his armaments build-up in the Far East in response to the creation of Manchukuo and the expansion of the Japanese Army.

Before the Mukden incident in September 1931, the Japanese had estimated that the Red Army in the Far East amounted to six rifle divisions with modest aircraft and tank support. By the time Ishiwara had left Manchuria in 1932, the intelligence section of the general staff calculated that the Russian strength had increased to eight rifle divisions and a regiment of cavalry, supported by about 300 aircraft and the same number of tanks. In 1933 Japanese forces began to notice strong defensive positions—wood and wire barricades, watchtowers, pillboxes and other steel and concrete emplacements—springing up on the other side of the frontier. Spies reported that in strategic areas the work extended deep behind the frontier. The Polish Army had told the Japanese about deep fortified zones of this type, and now they were seeing them for themselves. Overflights of Soviet territory revealed that the Russians were improving roads and building airstrips at a startling rate, and double-tracking the trans-Siberian railway, allowing for speedier reinforcement of the Far East.[24]

What the Japanese did not know until they saw the result was that Stalin and Tukhachevsky considered air power the key to deterring the Japanese Army from aggressive war. In the summer of 1932, when Stalin learned that only six of the four-engine TB-3 heavy bombers were heading for the Far East, he said, "We need to send no less than 50–60 TB-3s. And as soon as possible. Without this the defence of the Far East is only an empty phrase." One year later Tukhachevsky reported that the Japanese arms build-up in Manchuria continued unabated and war now seemed imminent. Unlike Araki, who prophesied that 1936 would be the critical year, Tukhachevsky considered 1934 the year of crisis. "If we could deploy, say, 2,000 aircraft," he added, "then a war in 1934 could be considered excluded."[25]

The Japanese got the message. By the end of 1935, Japanese intelligence estimated that the Red Army air forces had 1,200 planes, including 170 twin-engine TB-5 bombers within range of Japan. The Japanese put on a brave face in public. Araki told a British journalist in March 1935 that, so long as they were not "taken by surprise," Japan's air defenses could repulse the "500 planes" stationed at Vladivostok. Soviet officials told foreign correspondents that their bombers could ignite Japan's "paper and matchwood" cities. The ratio of opposing forces between the Kwantung army and the Soviets was no less intimidating. In 1935–36, the total number of Red Army divisions rose to nineteen, including four mechanized and three cavalry, or 300,000 troops, equipped with 1,200 tanks. The Kwantung army had under 200,000 men equipped with 230 planes and 150 tanks. "Although the military power of the Soviet Union in the Far East was originally in a state of balance, only four short years after the Manchurian Incident," one of Ishiwara's subordinates reminded him, "Japanese troop strength in Manchuria is only a fraction of the Soviet forces, and in aircraft and tanks particularly, there is no comparison." Worse still, plans for developing Manchuria's war economy were only just starting to pick up speed; in the Soviet Union the second Five Year Plan (1933–37) was well under way.[26]

Ishiwara concluded that he had to accelerate Japan's drive for arms and autarky. Two obstacles, however, stood in the way. The first was Finance Minister Takahashi's resistance to further arms increases. State spending and the expanding deficit fueled inflation. Overseas purchases of raw materials, machine tools and oil required foreign exchange earned through trade, but imports to keep up the armaments boom were growing faster than exports. In November 1935 the eighty-one-year-old finance minister slugged it out with the army and navy in a twenty-four-hour cabinet meeting. His aides carried the old man home. On February 26, 1936, Takahashi was murdered during another abortive army coup, this time by young supporters of the Imperial Way faction in a last-ditch effort to set Japan on the true path. His successor, Baba Eiichi, caved in to service demands. Arms spending jumped from 2.3 billion yen in 1936 to three billion in 1937. Munitions makers increased imports of raw materials, fuel and machinery. Japan now faced a full-blown balance-of-payments and inflation crisis.[27]

The second obstacle to Ishiwara's plan was the navy. Both services enjoyed near autonomy under the Meiji constitution: the army saw the Soviet Union as the prime threat, whereas the navy's number-one foe was the United States. The erosion of cabinet authority during the 1930s and a lack of coordination intensified their differences. In 1934–35, at the navy's behest, the government demanded, during the international naval arms control negotiations, the right to build a fleet as large as each of the world's two biggest navies, the American and the British. Washington and London rejected the demand. A naval arms race now seemed certain. For the Japanese Army this was a nightmare. Warship building would gobble up huge amounts of money, steel, plant and skilled labor. The army asked the navy to postpone its plans; the navy asked the same of the army. Ishiwara explained to his naval colleagues that Japan must first attain autarky and industrialize Manchukuo. It was a convincing case, just the sort of logic that would justify a freeze on naval construction. The admirals understood this perfectly and continued to draw up plans for the most powerful big-gun warships ever built. In August 1936, at the end of an effort to hammer out a focused strategy, the cabinet endorsed a vague shopping list of aims, the Fundamentals of National Policy. Japan would seek better diplomatic relations and more trade abroad, and stabilize the government at home. The army would get what it wanted to resist the Red Army in the Far East; naval strength would be raised to a point sufficient to fight the U.S. Navy in the western Pacific.[28]

Undaunted, Ishiwara and his team of staff planners continued to work out a five-year plan to prepare Japan-Manchukuo for an all-out slugging match with the Soviet Union. Pressure for a comprehensive plan also came from officials in Manchukuo such as Kishi and Tōjō, who had been appointed to the headquarters of the Kwantung army. Reform bureaucrats in the Cabinet Research Bureau, now inspired by the Nazi regime's economic measures, saw expanding armaments as a vehicle for greater state control over the economy and for more power in the hands of the technocrats. From Manchuria, Ishiwara brought Miyazaki Masayoshi, a top planner employed by the South Manchurian Railway, to Tokyo to supervise the detailed work. Overall, the goal was to be able by 1941 to field a force eighty percent the size of the Red Army deployed in the Far East. To sustain and expand that future army, the various drafts of plans prioritized steep annual increases to the empire's heavy industries: targets for steel, metals, fuel, chemicals, machine tools, vehicles and aircraft. By 1941 Ishiwara wanted Japan to be producing twenty percent of the world's aircraft—or 10,000 a year, of which 3,000 should be built in Manchukuo.[29]

Resistance to these measures and their 3.13 billion yen price tag came from the party politicians, businessmen and cabinet ministers. The corporate elite resented the attack on their managerial rights and profits. The older generation of civil servants who dominated the ministries disliked giving up what was left of their influence over economic and social life to the arch-centralizers of the Cabinet Research Bureau. In November 1936, after months of lobbying by the army, Japan signed an anti-Soviet agreement with Germany, the Anti-Comintern Pact, and the Army Ministry circulated 300,000 copies of a pamphlet to raise support for its arms program. Japan was losing the arms race against the Soviet Union and China, the pamphlet declared, and the only solution was a "national defense state": "The state must be rebuilt on the basis of the Japanese spirit and in accordance with the needs of modern armaments. A state reorganised on a *totalitarian* basis has latent power in time of peace which would prove the decisive factor in time of emergency." In December, amid competing accusations of treason and militarism, the army's program was rejected in Parliament. The government fell.[30]

In 1937 the former army minister and old friend of Nagata, General Hayashi, became prime minister, but even he could not square the burden of the five-year plan with a healthy economy. "If we do exactly as the most powerful of the middle-echelon in the army wish," wrote one minister, the present economic "structure will collapse and lead to chaos." Spending was reduced. Many of the most aggressive state controls contained in the plan were removed. The setback for Ishiwara and his bureaucratic allies, however, was temporary. In June 1937 the popular forty-six-year-old Prince Konoe Fumimaro replaced Hayashi. He supported a controlling "national defense state" and the other goals of the total-war officers. But he wanted arms and autarky to expand in stages and within the limits set by a healthy balance of trade and a vigorously growing economy. Like Ishiwara—and Nagata before him—Konoe knew that Japan needed a long period of peace to prepare for total war.[31]

And then, on July 7, 1937, mere weeks after Konoe took office, fighting spontaneously erupted between Chinese and Japanese patrols around the Marco Polo Bridge near Peking. In Tokyo the cabinet believed that the Nationalist government would cave in after a short, sharp offensive in north China from the Kwantung army. But neither Chiang Kai-shek nor the Chinese people would back down. Only a few months earlier, Chiang's followers had forced him to abandon his war against Mao's communists and instead unite with them against Japan. He was in a good position to do so. Ironically, thanks to training and weapons from Japan's nominal ally, Germany, the Nationalists now commanded an elite force of 400,000 soldiers.[32]

The fighting in China horrified Ishiwara. Japan did not have the resources to fight the Chinese and at the same time arm against the Soviet Union, the British Empire, the United States and the other Pacific powers. China "will be what Spain was for Napoleon," he predicted correctly, "an endless bog."[33]

CHAPTER 3

"REARM AND GET READY"

On the evening of February 3, 1933, the commanders of the German armed forces were invited to dinner at the Berlin home of General Kurt von Hammerstein-Equord. The principal guest was Germany's new chancellor, Adolf Hitler. General Werner von Blomberg, the new defense minister, had arranged the event so that Hitler could speak directly to the top brass. Blomberg was gushingly enthusiastic about the new chancellor, but others, including the host, greeted the National Socialist leader with aristocratic aloofness.

After dinner, Hitler spoke for over two hours. He began by stating that his supreme goal was the recovery of German political power. To achieve this, Marxism, pacifism and democracy had to be stamped out, especially among the young, who would fill the ranks of the future armed forces. The military, as a tool of political power and a mechanism for national integration, was the most important institution of the state. The task of fighting the internal struggle against the forces of Bolshevism would, however, fall to the Nazi Party. Hitler promised he would not attempt to merge the army with the Nazi Party's militia of brown-shirted storm troopers, the SA. As for the economy, Hitler rejected increasing exports as a solution to Germany's army of unemployed workers. A healthy economy, he asserted, could be founded only on greater *Lebensraum* (living space) for the German people. The external purpose of political power would be the conquest of more living space in "the east," which would be "ruthlessly Germanized." The idea that Germany would cap the size of the armed forces according to agreements reached at Geneva was absurd. The military must expand. Meanwhile, the period of initial arms growth would be the most dangerous. If there were any "prudent statesmen" in France, Hitler warned, the French and their allies would strike before Germany rearmed.[1]

Judging from the surviving transcripts, Hitler's audience was most interested in what he had to say about the place of the military in the state. He did
not disappoint. Germany would rearm, and the army would stay out of what
the soldiers regarded as the dirty job of crushing German communism. Ex-
pressing the views of many present, Admiral Erich Raeder, the head of the
German Navy, called the speech "extraordinarily satisfying." Although Hitler
did not present a detailed program for what he intended to do once Germany
rearmed, his talk of living space made his long-range intentions clear enough.
Even those who dismissed his words as the half-baked ranting of a foreign
policy novice did not voice objections. As Blomberg had hoped, the dinner
party initiated an alliance between the military elite and Hitler that would
drive the first phase of all-out German rearmament.[2]

Despite the huge gulf between their social standing, education and experience, the alliance of the German officer corps and the Nazi leader was not
at all surprising. What drew them close together was a powerful set of ideas
about future war and what needed to be done to wage it successfully. The vocabulary and logic of arming for total war were not exclusively German or
Nazi. The developing arms race between the Soviet Union and Japan had
been shaped fundamentally by the same ideas well before Hitler took office.
These all-pervasive ideas belonged to a general effort to understand the First
World War and impose order and meaning on wars to come.

To most Germans, defeat in 1918 had come as a shock. After all Germany
and its allies had advanced deep into France and fought the western alliance
to a stalemate; by 1917 Russia had been beaten. A year earlier Germany's
supreme warlords, Generals Paul von Hindenburg and Erich Ludendorff,
had launched a huge program of social and economic mobilization for one
final maximum effort. That great push came in the summer of 1918, when the
Germans attacked the British, French and growing American forces in the
west. But it failed, and everything fell apart. In November the high command
packed Kaiser Wilhelm off into exile and abdicated responsibility for negotiating peace to a cabinet of social democratic politicians. The navy mutinied,
soldiers' and workers' councils formed and armed revolutionaries took to the
streets. To prevent a Bolshevik revolution, the high command cut a deal with
the government: the army would protect the new republic founded at Weimar
from the revolutionaries, and the republic would respect the command privileges of the officer corps.

After the war, German soldiers raked over these events. On the pages of
military journals, in history books and in countless debates, a single lament
arose: "We won the battles, but our enemies won the war for reasons that had

nothing to do with military operations." Defeat on the home front emerged as the chief explanation. Ludendorff championed this explanation in its most venomous form, the stab-in-the-back—the idea that socialists, democrats, Jews and war profiteers broke the resolve of the German people while the army fought on from victory to victory. This was nonsense. It was in fact the failure of Ludendorff's final offensives of 1918, his realization that Germany's flagging economy could not sustain more total war and the high command's bid to find a face-saving way out of the defeat that sparked the internal collapse. Even so, the larger lesson that Germany lost the war because its economic and social regimentation had not been "total" became a powerful idea. Modern war, so ran the lesson, had become "a terrible competition of production, and victory falls to the competitor who produces faster and more ruthlessly."[3]

During the early 1920s German soldiers remained obsessed with the problem of mobilizing the totality of the nation's resources for war. Some, including the young Blomberg, toyed with the idea of waging a decentralized "people's war" against the victors, but most soldiers agreed that a mass insurgency was likely to end in national disintegration rather than liberation. The peacemakers, meanwhile, had ensured that Germany could not wage a conventional conflict. Under the terms of the Treaty of Versailles of 1919, Germany was limited to a long-service army of 100,000 men. Tanks, artillery, gas and aircraft were banned. Arms factories were disassembled. And Germany's western region, the Rhineland, was vulnerable to a French invasion because the peacemakers had banned the Germans from building fortifications or placing troops there. Despite the difficulties, the army worked with civilian ministers to rearm covertly on a small scale. Most officers saw this accommodation with the republic as temporary. Some began to dream of an all-encompassing mobilization and a new state fit for the task. Foremost among them was Blomberg. The tall, dashing officer who would become Hitler's defense minister was a forward-looking soldier with the type of expansive imagination and impulsive enthusiasm that triggered automatic hostility from colleagues. At age forty-nine, in 1927, he had risen to the position of chief of the army staff. Although he lacked Tukhachevsky's powers of expression and Ishiwara's millenarian outlook, Blomberg's systematizing military mind was no less captivated than theirs by the mechanistic logic of total war.[4]

What fascinated Blomberg was the capacity of the modern state to organize industry and society for grand political purposes. He looked to the Soviet Union and the United States for inspiration. In 1928, at the beginning of the first Five Year Plan, he visited the Soviet Union, was stunned by what he saw and returned joking that he had become a Bolshevik. In 1930 he toured the United States as a guest of the U.S. Army. The "pulsating" hum of American mass production and the U.S. Army's talent for drumming a "healthy" spirit of "militarism" into young reservists left him gushing: "The army, National Guard, organised reserves, and the preparation of war industry are cut out for the creation of an army of millions."[5]

On a more modest scale, German rearmament began in October 1928. By a secret decree, the cabinet approved a four-year program to build up the stocks for a projected field army of twenty-one divisions, or 300,000 men. The German Army's victory here was the cabinet's endorsement of systematic civil-military preparations for this force, including pilot plans to mobilize industry. But there were limits to how much the Weimar state, committed as it was to progressive welfare protection for workers, would and could invest in armaments, even before the shock waves from the 1929 collapse of the American stock market paralyzed the republic's finances. In the 1920s Germany had borrowed heavily to finance its recovery and to pay war reparations. As the Great Depression began to bite, foreign investors called in their loans, most of which were short-term credit from American lenders. In Europe, German industry was the hardest hit. Between 1929 and 1933, unemployment jumped from one to six million. In March 1930, unable to resolve the financial and political deadlock caused by the slump, Germany's last social democratic government fell.[6]

German officers regarded the Weimar Republic with the same venom that their Japanese counterparts reserved for Taishō democracy. It was a social democracy born out of a humiliating defeat, and its politicians valued social reform over military spending. Few if any officers mourned its decline. The way was now in fact opening for an authoritarian national defense state. With this alluring prospect looming, a split opened at the top of the officer corps between all-outers, such as Blomberg, and more cautious men such as General Kurt von Schleicher, the army's most influential and ambitious officer. Blomberg and the other radicals found themselves posted away from Berlin. Schleicher worked with the powerful circle around Hindenburg, who had become president of the Weimar Republic in 1925, to override the German Parliament. Hindenburg exploited his legal powers to appoint a series of presidential chancellors (Schleicher being the last before Hitler) and to set up an authoritarian regime. But, to the frustration of the old elite, Hindenburg's appointees could not mobilize enough public support to claim a credible national consensus. Meanwhile the German Communist Party and especially the National Socialists attracted more and more followers.

A solution to this political problem was needed if Germany were to rearm at all. Expanding the army called for national youth-militia training schemes because the last soldiers trained up to 1918 who were fit for call-up would dwindle after 1931. The industrial predicament was equally pressing. During 1932, while German diplomats in Geneva demanded the right to rearm, German arms planners put the final touches to an enhanced five-year plan to equip the army with tanks, guns and aircraft. At the same time, the Great Depression was wrecking the industries indispensable to rearming. Unless they received token orders or financial subsidies, many small and medium-sized engineering firms would soon shut for good.[7]

It was in this context that on January 30, 1933, with the approval of the army, Hindenburg appointed Hitler chancellor. The Nazi leader offered the conservatives the mass base of popular support that they lacked, and his SA had the potential to provide the cover that the army needed to train Germany's youth. To ensure the army's autonomy, Hindenburg swore in Blomberg as defense minister hours before the rest of the new cabinet.

Historians often remark that it is impossible to think of Nazism, the coming of the Second World War and the Final Solution *without* Hitler. But is it as difficult to imagine a European arms race in the 1930s without Hitler? What if General Schleicher had used the army to install himself as dictator? Under a military dictatorship Germany would have rearmed—less rapidly perhaps, but rearmed nonetheless—and by so doing would have invited military escalation from its neighbors. Grisly scenarios of total wars to come would have induced arms planners across Europe—as they did in the Soviet Union and Japan—to press for more forces and more influence over their national economies. Whether a European arms race without Hitler would have ended in another world war or a cold war is another question.[8]

What we do know is that Schleicher shrank at the thought of a coup d'état, and that Hitler took office instead. And, as Blomberg realized, there was little difference between what the army and the Nazi leader understood by rearmament: 1914–18 had defined them both.

Before the war, Hitler's life was one of failure and isolation. After leaving school in 1907, this resentful son of an Austrian customs official eked out a dismal living as a landscape painter in Vienna. On the streets and in the flophouses of one of Europe's greatest centers of art and learning, the young Hitler absorbed the radical nationalism, social Darwinism and anti-Semitism that would be fundamental to Nazism. Corporal Hitler then saw industrial-age war at the front, thriving on what he and many others experienced as the

fraternity of the trenches. He was decorated for bravery and wounded just before Germany's collapse. After Hitler recovered, the army employed him as a
political agitator and informer. In 1919 he joined the small, nationalist German
Workers' Party and quickly stamped his own vision upon it. In 1923, during
the turmoil brought about by the French occupation of the Rhineland, Hitler,
along with Ludendorff and other right-wingers, led a failed coup in Munich.
After a brief stay in prison, during which he dictated his book *Mein Kampf*,
Hitler reasserted his charismatic leadership over his party and sought power
through mass politics.[9]

In his speeches and writings the Nazi leader spoke of arms, autarky and a
new people's community. For Hitler, history was a story of racial competition. To flourish, a race had to preserve its biological purity and seize more
living space. The Treaty of Versailles, which had left the Germans stripped of
their weapons and confined within reduced frontiers, jeopardized the survival of the race. Hitler too pinpointed the cause of the defeat of 1918 in the
sabotage by Jews, Marxists, pacifists and other internal enemies. He felt that
destiny had ordained him to be Germany's savior. Hitler intended to erase
the peace settlement and destroy the most dangerous foe, the Jews. In his
eyes, Jews were parasites who plotted on a global scale to enslave some races
with Bolshevism, such as the Slavs, and to destroy others, especially the Germans. To expand, Germany needed great armaments and a racially pure, ide-
ologically cohesive home front to preclude another stab in the back.[10]

Hitler's idea of living space should be understood in terms of the same
siege mentality that lay behind the Soviet Union's first Five Year Plan and
Japan's conquest of Manchuria; or, more broadly still, in the widespread rejection of liberal capitalism that accompanied the Great Depression. Reliance
on world trade made Germany vulnerable to market forces and blockade,
while the unfettered pursuit of wealth encouraged Germans to act at the expense of the national community. Germany needed to control its own sources
of food and raw materials to win the big wars to come, and the state needed
to direct resources to national purposes. Autarky, as one Nazi economist put
it, was "the vital right of every people and every nation to organize the economy in such a way that it is like a defensive fortress, where it is safe from
starvation and death from thirst in case of involvement in trade, foreign [cur-
rency] exchange or even military conflicts." The geopolitical reasoning of the
time predicted that the future belonged to continental-sized states. As Hitler
argued in *Mein Kampf*, Germany's living space lay to the east: the wheat fields
of the Ukraine, the material riches of the Urals and the forests of Siberia.

Like so many Europeans, liberal, socialist and fascist, Hitler was impressed by and apprehensive about the rise of the American model of mass industrial production and consumption. The mission of National Socialism, as he saw it, was to prepare the German people to compete on this titanic scale by remaking first Germany and then the Eurasian landmass.[11]

In the first two years of Nazi rule, the alliance between the army led by Blomberg and Hitler as chancellor was cemented. Hitler kept his promises. The Nazis used terror to secure a dictatorship. Political opposition was stamped out. Parliament surrendered its powers. Parallel state and party structures grew. Public associations such as labor unions, the churches and the professions were Nazified. Race laws against Jews and other "non-Germans" were enforced with savagery. Some military officers voiced their distaste at the lawless brutality, but they accepted it.[12]

The only concern for Blomberg and the officer corps was the faction of the Nazi Party that called for the replacement of the army with the Nazi storm troopers, the SA. Chief among them was Ernst Röhm, the leader of the SA. Hitler did not tolerate rivals. He also knew that the army was still in a position to impose a military dictatorship when the question of who would succeed President Hindenburg arose. On June 30, 1934, in what came to be called the Night of the Long Knives, Hitler had Röhm and the rest of the SA leadership massacred. For good measure, he ordered his predecessor as chancellor, General Schleicher, murdered, along with a few other political enemies. Blomberg approved of Hitler's ruthless actions. After Hindenburg died on August 2, 1934, Hitler became chancellor and president. On Blomberg's initiative, the armed forces swore a new oath of "unconditional obedience" to Hitler as Führer of the German people.[13]

Despite some differences about just how close the armed forces should be to the new regime, Blomberg and his fellow officers had good reasons to be pleased. Germany was undergoing the transformation required by their forecasts of future war, the army's position within the state was assured, or so it seemed, and Hitler meant what he said about arming. At the first cabinet meetings in February 1933 he scolded ministers for not spending money fast enough on arms.[14]

Thanks to Hitler, therefore, the armed forces benefited most from the German recovery from the Great Depression. By 1935 they accounted for seventy-five percent of state spending. As a percentage of national income, the military's share from 1933 to 1935 had jumped from one to almost ten percent. No nominally capitalist state had ever before devoted resources on this scale and with such speed to arming in peacetime. Much of the state spending on work creation was also defense related, such as the construction of airfields, barracks, bridges, railways, waterways and highways.[15]

More men, materiel and transport networks, and the money to pay for them, were all items that had been on the army's wish list for years. But the planners had also craved something much deeper. Before the 1930s the job of mobilization planning in the German Army had been a speculative task. Staffers wrote papers, read the technical literature, collected statistics and compiled surveys of industrial plants, but not much more. The most prophetic of these officers was Georg Thomas, the son of an industrialist. At the end of 1927 the thirty-seven-year-old Thomas was posted to the army's arms-procurement office in Berlin. There, he found his calling. In this world of draft production timetables, budget forecasts and macroeconomic abstractions, Thomas, like Nagata Tetsuzan, became an evangelist for the rational pursuit of industrial-age total war. "Modern war," he solemnly declared, "is no longer a clash of armies, but a struggle for the existence of the peoples involved. All the resources available to a warring nation must be pressed into service, not just the population, but also industry and the economy."[16]

By the early 1930s Thomas had coined two concepts that captured the modern military condition: "breadth" and "depth" of armament. Breadth meant all the trained men, materiel and stocks available at the outbreak of war; depth meant the capacity of the economy to mobilize, expand and sustain the fighting forces and itself over a long war. As Thomas knew, the restrictions of the Treaty of Versailles and the years without cycles of orders and technological renewal of the arms industries had left Germany with little breadth or depth. Of course, the armed forces had worked on developing illegal weapons with foreign companies and their Soviet counterparts, but these were sporadic projects and not systematic preparations for all-out production. Some German manufacturers cooperated with covert arms work, especially if cash subsidies were offered. But, to the irritation of the planners, German firms were reluctant to cooperate if the illegal work jeopardized their foothold on the world market. Worse, the few monopoly firms legally authorized to make arms for the army could not produce weapons at low prices without long production runs. The armaments program of 1932 included funds for industrial infrastructure, but to the horror of the planners, the Depression threatened to bankrupt the monopoly weapons makers and many other firms that would be needed for future armaments growth.[17]

In 1934, when Thomas, now a colonel, moved into the Defense Ministry to head the Office for War Economy, money for long production runs was no longer a problem. The problem was building up a properly functioning war economy. Blomberg and Thomas, both apostles of organization and centralization, agreed that the Defense Ministry should coordinate the expansion of the army, air force and navy and that the new regime should restructure the economy so that Germany armed efficiently. To this end, some had spoken of "socializing" German industry, but for now Blomberg and Thomas favored strong state supervision of private producers. While Thomas established a network of regional inspectorates to work with industry on munitions production and mobilization plans, Blomberg took his chair as Hitler's deputy on the new Reich Defense Council—a position from which, among other things, he intended to shape economic policy. As the armed forces started to grow in 1933–34, the jump in armaments spending quickly began to put pressure on the economy. Measures to reorganize industry for large-scale arming were also slow to take hold. Production of equipment lagged behind. Progress on building plants to produce synthetic fuel, oil and rubber was also slow. Raw materials, and the foreign currency needed to buy them, became alarmingly scarce. Calls for the brakes to be applied could now be heard from the economic and finance ministries.[18]

In the spring of 1934, Blomberg and Thomas went on the offensive. In a series of memos to Hitler and his economic advisers, they warned against an arms slowdown. A striking assertion of the Thomas-Blomberg line came from the head of the army's ordinance office in a lecture to senior officers. Word of what was said reached Hitler, and he asked for a transcript. It told a familiar story: modern armies consumed huge quantities of munitions; no army could stockpile all it would need in peacetime; a powerful war economy needed "deep" preparations in peacetime to meet wartime exertions. Germany lacked such depth. And "armed forces which must lay down their weapons after six or eight weeks because of a complete lack of ammunition and fuel are useless to a field commander, and still less useful in the hands of a statesman who wishes to conduct a foreign policy."[19]

Blomberg and Thomas were calling for an economic dictator exercising complete authority over finance, industry, agriculture and trade and ensuring the primacy of arms and autarky. The man they had in mind for the job was the president of the Reichsbank, Hjalmar Schacht. With his stiff collars, dark suits and pince-nez perched on his beak of his nose, he looked every inch the respectable banker he truly was. Schacht had made his reputation for financial wizardry in 1923, when hyperinflation ravaged Germany. As president of the Reichsbank, Schacht helped to negotiate the Dawes Plan, which financed Germany's reparation payments to France and Britain through American loans to Germany. He thus played no small part in embedding Germany in the liberal economic order of the 1920s. Yet deep down he was a strident nationalist who counted the days to Germany's release from its postwar financial and political obligations. By the spring of 1930 he had grown frustrated with cooperation as a way to achieve release. After negotiating a deal on the final reduction and rescheduling of reparation payments devised by the American businessman Owen Young, Schacht bitterly attacked its implementation. He was forced to resign as president of the Reichsbank. By 1932 he saw Hitler as the solution to Germany's ills; in April 1933 Hitler returned Schacht to his former post as Germany's top central banker.[20]

As Hitler's financial wizard, Schacht not only backed Blomberg against any slowdown in military expansion but also developed the system of credit finance that fueled the initial arms boom. Under Schacht, the Reichsbank and four blue-chip industrial firms with a big stake in rearmament set up a dummy company, Metallurgische-Forschungsgesellschaft, or Mefo, which provided a smoke screen to allow the Reichsbank to print more money to pay for the expansion of the armed forces. From 1933 to 1938 Mefo issued twelve billion Reichsmarks' worth of state-guaranteed credit notes to pay arms producers. Cooking the state's books was not his invention, but Schacht took covert deficit spending soaring to new fiscal heights.[21]

Eventually, Schacht would share the fate of Japan's elderly finance minister, Takahashi Korekiyo—powerless to slow an arms boom that he had helped to set in motion. However, unlike Takahashi's situation in Japan, Schacht joined Hitler with his eyes wide open. He willingly became the spearhead of those inside and outside the Nazi Party clamoring for a final break with the liberal economic order. The process had begun earlier under Heinrich Brüning, who in March 1930 had become Hindenburg's first presidential chancellor. Brüning's government stuck to the gold standard to show Germany's creditors that it was making every effort to meet its financial obligations. Adherence to gold forced Brüning to cut spending and imports, and to raise taxes. Severe austerity, so he hoped, would win Germany's release from reparation payments, and a balanced budget would ward off the specter of inflation until the free market restored economic growth. Austerity, however, only made matters worse. During the summer of 1931, in the midst of a spiraling banking crisis, Brüning was forced to take the Reichsmark off the gold standard and to introduce exchange controls to prevent a run on the currency.

Three years later, Schacht wanted to exploit the possibilities opened up by the breakdown of global capitalism and the Nazi regime's accelerating rearmament to assert Germany's economic independence. When Hitler made him economics minister in August 1934 with full dictatorial powers over the economy, Schacht vigorously applied himself to building a state-run economy.

The problem he faced revolved around Germany's balance of payments. The German economy and people could not survive without imports of food and industrial raw materials such as iron ore, rubber and oil. To pay for imports, Germany had to earn foreign exchange by selling goods abroad. Although Britain and France canceled German reparations in July 1932, Germany still owed billions in long-term loans. Servicing that debt consumed nearly a quarter of Germany's foreign earnings. Paying debts thus placed a huge burden on the German balance of payments and limited the volume of imports. What Germans produced also had an impact. Making weapons for the armed forces diverted industry from making profitable goods for export and expanded industry's appetite for costly foreign raw materials. Rising employment, meanwhile, fed a demand for imports of consumer goods. And the Nazi regime's policy of keeping the Reichsmark's value high to avoid inflation added to the problem by making German exports uncompetitive on world markets.

Because of this trade imbalance, by the spring of 1934 Germany's foreign-exchange reserves had fallen to the point where payments were made on a day-to-day basis. A balance-of-payments crisis and a halt to arming were imminent. Schacht's first move was to default on Germany's debts, but this alone did not reverse the trend. Two more options presented themselves. One was to boost exports with state subsidies; the other was to prioritize imports. Which should take priority? Sustaining breakneck rearmament, or promoting a revival in consumer demand and an export-led economic recovery, perhaps coupled with a managed devaluation of the Reichsmark? Hitler had made his views known often enough, and Schacht rolled up his sleeves. Building on Brüning's exchange controls, he erected a powerful bureaucratic mechanism called the New Plan. Launched in September 1934, the New Plan required importers to apply for foreign exchange before placing any orders abroad. Supervisory offices vetted these applications and prioritized those related to armaments or other indispensable commodities. Hand in hand with foreign-exchange controls came a reordering of Germany's foreign trade. Through a series of bilateral barter deals, Schacht broke away from trading goods with the British Empire and the United States, and instead linked Germany's industrial economy to the Balkans and Latin America as secure suppliers of raw materials.[22]

German economists had long promoted the idea that the state should shape economic life, and a whole generation of economists and civil servants, who would later man the barricades of Nazi Germany's economic controls, had been brought up on this idea. During the 1920s and early 1930s German industry organized itself into large cartels to manage overcapacity and protect profits, and the buzzword of "rationalization" that so inspired Japan's reform bureaucrats took hold. In 1934 Schacht took these private alignments of major industries a big step further, with the compulsory imposition of cartels. With imports restricted exclusively to products that could not be made at home, the restructuring of German industry initiated a boom in investment and growth in the heavy industries essential for armaments growth. Schacht's industrial restructuring also launched whole new industries dear to total-war planners like Colonel Thomas. He coerced the coal companies, for instance, to front the money to pay for synthetic oil plants. Businessmen resented the regime barging into the boardrooms. They would have preferred an export-led recovery, but they were happy to get wage and price controls, the shutting down of the unions, protections from foreign rivals and from the ravages of another slump, not to mention whopping great profits.[23]

For a brief time the New Plan restored Germany's balance of payments. Germany continued to arm. Whatever his own motives, Schacht's actions continued to follow the logic of arming for total war, something that could not be accomplished while Germany remained embedded within the liberal economic order.

The same was true of the political situation. Germany could not rearm without provoking some reaction from those powers with a stake in the postwar settlement—Britain, France and France's allies in eastern Europe, Poland and Czechoslovakia. In the first two years of his rule, Hitler cautiously exploited the disunity among the former wartime allies. In December 1932, to salvage the world disarmament talks in Geneva, the great powers had recognized Germany's equality of rights in armaments. In 1933, while professing a love of peace, Hitler demanded that equality of rights be put into practice—Germany should be allowed to arm up to France's level, or to some internationally agreed standard. Britain and France could not agree on a compromise offer on disarmament, but in the end, Hitler had no intention of accepting one. At the urging of Blomberg, Hitler decided to make the breach. In October 1933 Germany walked out of the disarmament talks and the League of Nations too. In January 1934, against the advice of the diplomats, Hitler signed a ten-year nonaggression treaty with Poland, thus estranging France from its strongest ally in eastern Europe.[24]

During 1934, while Hitler consolidated his regime, purged the SA and dealt with the backlash from a failed Nazi coup in Austria, Europe waited for the moment when Germany would openly rearm. In March 1934 the last German military budget to be published in the 1930s showed a huge spending hike. Paris issued warnings; London made inquiries. Berlin blamed the French for blocking a compromise, and many in London were inclined to agree that France was the obstacle. No one doubted that German military expansion was close at hand. With each month, the fear among the German establishment of some sort of preventive military and economic action diminished, but no one doubted that there would be a response and some risk. "In judging the situation we should never overlook the fact that no kind of rearmament in the next few years could give us military security," warned one senior German diplomat: "A particularly dangerous period will be in 1934–35 on account of the reorganisation of the German army. Our only security lies in a skilful foreign policy and in avoiding all provocations."[25]

In 1935 Hitler preferred well-timed provocations. Yet he too understood that they entailed risks. One way of minimizing them was to manipulate the image of the magnitude and direction of German rearmament. The more formidable Germany appeared, the less likely that any of its foes would attack. And in no other sphere was there more scope for this manipulation than in the build-up of the Luftwaffe.

COMBAT AIRCRAFT MADE their debut in the First World War. The ponderous wire-braced, wood-and-fabric machines of the era, with their open cockpits and light payloads, did not turn battles around. However, many people believed that with more time, many more machines and much more daring, aircraft might have proved decisive in support of armies and navies, and as an independent force to strike deep behind enemy lines. Once the armistice came, minds soared. Literary futurologists like H. G. Wells foresaw that the high-tech societies to come would inhabit the skies. Future war, too, belonged to the air. Massed swarms of bombers roaming over Europe's tightly packed cities would wage the apocalyptic wars of the future. Images of air war entered into mass culture and were analyzed by the advocates of "strategic" bombing. Chief among them was the Italian theorist of future war, Giulio Douhet. In 1921 Douhet published his most important and universally influential work, *The Command of the Air*. Parroted by air-war evangelists from the United States to Japan, the book argued that armies and navies were obsolete: in the next war, victory would go to the nation that could dominate the skies. Air war recognized no dividing line between soldier and civilian. It was total war in its purest form. Bombers would target the pillars of national strength, popular morale and industrial production. To strike first, with great ferocity, was the way to win.[26]

Germany was not immune to the dread of bombing, or to its promise. The Nazis used air raid precautions and recreational aviation as forms of national mobilization. From 1933 the idea of an independent German Air Force enjoyed backing from the top, especially from the First World War flying ace Hermann Göring. Blomberg had planned to develop air units as support arms for the army and navy, but Göring, minister for aviation, wanted to make the Luftwaffe his own strategic arm. Both Göring and Hitler reckoned that the emergence of a formidable Luftwaffe would provide them with a deterrent against preemptive strikes, and later a big stick with which to intimidate Germany's neighbors.[27]

The man who gave these ideas coherence was a director of the commercial airline Lufthansa, Robert Knauss. A First World War combat pilot, Knauss, like so many German flyers after 1919, pioneered civilian air travel. A clue about his true ambition comes from the title of a novel he published in 1932: *Air War 1936: The Destruction of Paris*. In May 1933, when Blomberg and Göring began their tug of war over the Luftwaffe, Knauss drafted a memo advocating the construction of a fleet of bombers that was pure Douhetism. Air power alone was capable of winning wars, Knauss wrote, and it had advantages over land and sea arms. During the vulnerable stage of early arming, bombers would deter preemptive war. No state within range of the German air forces would "risk" retaliation against its cities. But, Knauss warned, time was working against Germany. France's new air minister, Pierre Cot, favored the build-up of an independent air force. With the rate of technological change accelerating, Germany must compete or fall hopelessly behind. With the support of the Nazi regime, Knauss concluded, the new Luftwaffe could win for Germany a ten-year "lead" in air armaments.[28]

The urge to take the lead drove the spectacular growth of the Luftwaffe in the early years of the arms race. In 1933–34 the state secretary at Göring's Air Ministry and Knauss's former boss at Lufthansa, the relentless Erhard Milch, initiated the phenomenal rise of the Luftwaffe and the German aircraft industry. In the summer of 1933 Milch finalized an expansion plan that would give Germany 2,000 first-line aircraft by 1935. In January 1933, only two firms, Heinkel and Junkers, could deliver aircraft in significant numbers, and the whole sector only employed 3,000 workers. Very quickly huge investments attracted other firms into making aircraft. Within two years the numbers of workers employed in making planes had jumped to 54,000. Milch ruthlessly cranked up and sought to control production. Unhappy with the way Dr. Hugo Junkers ran his company, Göring and Milch simply expropriated it.[29]

By the beginning of 1935, German rearmament was reaching the point where its scale could not be cloaked in secrecy and diplomatic obfuscation for much longer. The German Navy was assembling U-boats from prefabricated sections and laying down conspicuously large surface warships. Soon the number of aircraft in German skies would suggest to even the most dim-witted of foreign spies that something was up. And, most pressing of all, the army needed to introduce general conscription.

Conscription was essential to expanding the army. It operated like a giant machine, annually churning out hundreds of thousands of trained reservists who would be available to inflate the army to its full wartime strength. In December 1933, Blomberg and the army staff projected a peacetime army of 300,000 men formed into twenty-one divisions, expandable to sixty-three divisions, ready for use by March 1938. To stick to its growth timetable, the army pressed for compulsory military service by the end of 1935. A debate broke out among the army planners about the rate of expansion: some wanted to go at full speed; others wanted to move at a cautious and methodical pace. Even so, the twenty-one-division army was always seen as merely a passing phase. In March 1935 the army's chief of staff, General Ludwig Beck, described what he saw as the army's minimum size, in light of what he regarded as the "very high levels" of arming undertaken the previous year by France and its allies. He now foresaw a peacetime army of thirty-six divisions or 520,000 men capable of expanding to sixty-three divisions of 1.5 million men, a formidable force only 400,000 short of the Imperial German Army that had marched in August 1914.[30]

When to announce conscription was of course Hitler's decision. On February 3, 1935, France and Britain condemned violations of the Treaty of Versailles. Hitler invited British ministers to Germany, but only to divide London from Paris. Military measures in Czechoslovakia and France would supply a pretext for conscription. In December 1934 the Czechs, in order to keep more men in uniform longer, had extended their compulsory military service from one to two years; the French planned to do the same. On March 4, 1935, the British announced hikes in arms spending and drew attention to the anxiety caused by Germany's arms escalation. The German press took offense. Hitler postponed his talks with the British on the diplomatic pretense of having caught a cold. He was in fact buoyant. "The English will have to become accustomed to treating us on an equal footing," he told one of his loyal followers. "In a year, nobody will dare attack us!" Confident of Germany's growing strength, he added, "If we had waited until 1936 to rearm, it would have been too late."[31]

At this point Hitler might have entered into talks and extracted concessions on armaments that would have provided diplomatic camouflage for his plans. But he wanted spectacular faits accomplis. On March 10, Göring caused a political storm by telling a reporter from the London Daily Mail of the existence of the Luftwaffe. For good effect, Göring told the British air attaché that the new force consisted of 1,500 combat aircraft, which was nearly the size of the Royal Air Force (the real figure was 800 combat planes, the rest were trainers). While the European papers shrieked about the horrors of aerial bombardment, Hitler believed he had caught the French and British off guard. He would now do the same thing with conscription. On March 13, while in Munich, Hitler called for his military adjutant, Major Friedrich Hoßbach. From Berlin Hoßbach rushed to Hitler's hotel the next morning. The Führer wanted to announce the commencement of conscription, timed to coincide with the decision of the French Parliament on the extension of their military service. Hitler asked what size German Army was planned. Hoßbach, whose job it was to have details of this sort at hand, said he needed to check, but he thought that thirty-six divisions was the right number. (He was wrong. The army's plan called for twenty-one divisions; thirty-six divisions was a long-range goal under discussion.) Hitler agreed to thirty-six divisions and, revealing something of his true attitude toward his military advisers, he added that he did not want Blomberg or the army staff informed. Hoßbach convinced Hitler otherwise. The next day, in Berlin, Hitler spoke with his advisers. The defense minister was agitated. Blomberg wanted conscription, but to his way of thinking and that of the army planners, the proposed proclamation was too much, too quick and all too likely to provoke a reply in kind from Germany's neighbors.[32]

On March 16, with thirty-six divisions in the offing, Blomberg swallowed his anxiety and lauded Hitler's bold leadership. The announcement was made. Germany would build up a peacetime army of thirty-six divisions. Nine days later, when the British ministers arrived for talks, Hitler bluffed them by saying that the Luftwaffe had reached parity with the Royal Air Force. Hoping to drive another wedge between London and Paris, he suggested that a deal to cap the German Navy was on the table.[33]

On April 11, Britain, France and Italy met at the resort town of Stresa to discuss a diplomatic response to German behavior. All three powers agreed to uphold the 1925 Treaty of Locarno, which guaranteed the Franco-German border and the Rhineland demilitarized zone. Seven days later the League of Nations condemned Hitler's unilateralism. In May, Paris and Moscow signed a mutual assistance pact, which was tied to a qualified Soviet pledge to aid the Czechs if they fell victim to German attack. On May 21, Hitler delivered a foreign policy speech, once again saying he wished for world peace. He also repeated his offer to the British of a deal on naval arms control. Talks opened in London, and on June 18, an Anglo-German Naval Agreement was signed. Hitler was overjoyed. He had always hoped to woo the British and the Italians in order to isolate the French. The deal with London pointed to real success. The capper came in October 1935, when Italy broke with the British and French by invading the small African state of Ethiopia.[34]

The events of 1935 inflated Hitler's faith in his own judgment. He had taken Germany through what he saw as the most perilous period of rearmament without suffering anything more than reprimands. In August, he predicted that wars would soon break out between Britain and Italy and between the Soviet Union and Japan, which would leave Germany free to expand eastward. On October 18, he took up this theme before a gathering of German military officers and other officials. Italy was now at war in Africa and might soon be fighting Britain. This crisis had come too soon. Germany needed three more years of arming to exploit such moments. "Rearm and get ready," Hitler told them. "Europe is on the move again. If we are clever, we will be the winners."[35]

CHAPTER 4

"WE ARE MOVING AMONG GIANTS"

In the early hours of October 24, 1917, in the magnificent Alpine valley cut by the emerald waters of the Isonzo River, artillery suddenly broke the silence. Poison gas and high-explosive shells prepared the way for an infantry attack. Fifteen German and Austro-Hungarian divisions advanced against six divisions from the Italian 2nd Army entrenched in the valley and on the heights above, near the ancient town of Caporetto. Outnumbered, the Italian defenses simply collapsed. Surprised by the speed of their breakthrough, the German and Austrian commanders pushed south toward Venice. There were 30,000 Italians dead or wounded and 280,000 surrendered. Then, after seventeen days and ninety miles of retreat, the Italians, with British and French reinforcements, fought their enemies to a halt along the Piave River.

The battle of Caporetto marked a stunning reversal of fortunes. For two years the Italians had attacked the Austro-Hungarians across the Isonzo eleven times. The strategy of the Italian commander, General Luigi Cadorna, was simple enough. Pound the enemy until he cracked. On the grueling rock and glacier battlefields of the Julian Alps, Cadorna's men fought his war of attrition with courage, enduring casualty rates as high or higher than those suffered in France. By August 1917 both sides were near the breaking point. The Austrian commander knew his troops were too worn out to stop another Italian offensive, and so he appealed to his German allies for reinforcements, while he concentrated his divisions, stores and guns on a narrow front not far from Caporetto.

General Cadorna and his staff failed to pick up on these preparations and also failed to fortify their front. At the time, however, Cadorna blamed his men for the defeat, accusing them of cowardice. "Is it my fault," he asked, "if the Army is full of vermin?"[1]

Benito Mussolini disagreed. The thirty-four-year-old soldier-journalist did not doubt the valor of the men on the Upper Isonzo. Defeat, he thought, came from a more profound source. In the November 9 issue of his newspaper, *Il Popolo d'Italia*, Mussolini wrote that while Britain, France and Germany regimented entire economies and societies, Italy had been half asleep. What had demoralized the men at Caporetto was the gulf between the ennobling experience of the trench and the "frivolities" of civilian life behind the front. "We have had enough of the normality that is leading us to defeat. It is time that the Nation—above all, every civilian—accept and endure the moral discipline of war. . . . If we want to win the war, not a single man must be left free of escaping the sacred duties of national solidarity. Every man, every woman, must be used. . . . *The whole Nation must be militarized.*"[2]

UNLIKE HITLER, who probably would never have emerged from his vagabond existence had it not been for the Great War, Mussolini had had a successful political career before 1914. He was born on July 23, 1883, in the Emilia-Romagna of northeast Italy, a region famous as a hotbed of socialism. His mother, Rosa, was a schoolteacher; his father, Alessandro, a blacksmith and a socialist activist well known to the police. Cunning and ambitious, young Benito had a sensitive regard for his own interests. Marx and Dante sped off his tongue as fast as he could throw a punch. The teenage Mussolini took up his mother's vocation and his father's politics.

In 1902, after an adulterous affair, Mussolini left his first teaching job to emigrate to Switzerland. There, he lived the life of a bohemian intellectual, dabbling in journalism and perfecting his socialism. In 1904 the young radical who bemoaned the seductive powers of imperialism and militarism to distract the toiling masses from the revolutionary struggle returned home to fulfill his obligatory military service. In 1907 he upgraded his teaching credentials at the University of Bologna. But the classroom did not hold his ambitions for long. In the following year Mussolini wrote an anticlerical bodice-ripper called *The Cardinal's Mistress* while editing an Italian socialist paper in Austrian-ruled Trentino until the local authorities expelled him for sedition. A charismatic speaker and astute propagandist, he swiftly rose to the top of Italy's fast growing socialist movement. In 1912 he became the editor of the Italian Socialist Party's newspaper, *Avanti*. In the general elections of 1913, Italy's first with a mass franchise, Mussolini stood for Parliament and lost. Still, few doubted his promise.

When war broke out in July 1914, most Italians wanted no part of it. Their leaders, however, had other ideas. With the blessing of King Victor Emmanuel III, the prime minister, Antonio Salandra, who led a minority conservative government, and Foreign Minister Sidney Sonnino conspired to wage aggressive war. If they had a glorious victory, they could tighten the right's grip on power. Formally, Italy was tied to Austria-Hungary and Germany by the Triple Alliance of 1882, but its adherence to the pact had always been tenuous. Apart from the governing conservative elite, a small but clamorous group of interventionist intellectuals also craved war. Most of them shared little except an almost mystical belief that war would somehow modernize Italy. Mussolini, at that time editor of *Avanti*, was one exceptionally loud voice among the hawks.[3]

In September 1914, Mussolini endorsed his party's call for neutrality. Yet he was restless. A surge of left-wing unrest had swept northern Italy a few months earlier but fizzled out. The fear that history would leave Italy behind unless something decisive happened burned within him. The break came in October. He published a provocative editorial in *Avanti* calling for intervention. True revolutionaries, he argued, could not stand idly by when Europe was about to explode.

Not long afterwards Mussolini resigned from *Avanti* and founded *Il Popolo d'Italia*. To teach Italian workers that revolution would come only through a crusade, he helped to organize and promote a new association of left-wing nationalists. In early May 1915, when the Salandra government nearly fell, Mussolini urged shooting a few dozen antiwar politicians to break the political deadlock. But Salandra, backed by Victor Emmanuel, and Mussolini got their way. On May 24, 1915, Italy declared war on Austria-Hungary.[4]

Mussolini fought his war on two fronts. In August 1915 he joined his unit in the field while still writing for *Il Popolo d'Italia*. As the war dragged on into 1916 and 1917, and the state drafted men, intervened in the economy and crushed civil liberties, the lack of popular support for the war began to trouble politicians, some generals and the editor of *Il Popolo*. General Cadorna gave the masses—and the worries of politicians—little thought. He continued to use the army at great cost as a battering ram and just expected everyone to like it. Meanwhile, living standards fell and discontent with an unwanted war grew. Strikes, food riots and mutinies became common. "It is sad," Mussolini wrote of the antiwar protests, "infinitely sad, that in Italy, while the army, the salt of the nation, fights and wins, in the back lines the parasites attempt to render vain the sacrifice of blood."[5]

In February 1917, a bout of syphilis ended Mussolini's combat service. While on medical leave, he had plenty of time to think and write about Italy's war effort. Images of "internal enemies" became more lurid in his journalism. The revolution in Russia, which both inspired and repelled him, convinced Mussolini that the fault line of the whole war was national cohesion. The warring empires that could maximize their fighting strength without imploding first would win. Where would the next crack appear? In France, Britain and Germany the all-out mobilizations of 1916–17 had peaked. Did the recent mutinies in the French Army foretell that France would collapse next? Then came the shock of Caporetto. In the months that followed, Mussolini's understanding of total war came together. Caporetto was not a military blunder but a verdict on the entire nation. Italy had failed to mobilize the totality of its material, physical and mental resources. This lesson would guide his politics from then on.

ALTHOUGH ITALY ENDED UP on the winning side, psychologically the postwar experience of Italians was closer to that of the war's losers. At the Paris Peace Conference of 1919 Italy secured the territories of Trentino and Trieste at Austria's expense, but Rome's wider colonial ambitions in the Mediterranean, the Balkans and the Red Sea were stymied. Instead of uniting Italians, the war and the postwar economic slump divided them. Radicalized by the Russian revolution, the Italian Socialist Party made huge gains in the 1919 parliamentary elections. During 1920–21, strikes by workers and peasants swept the country.

In this overheated atmosphere of what looked like an imminent communist revolution, former soldiers formed a right-wing movement and demanded the right to run the country they had defended. The movement's black-shirted militia won widespread approval by attacking strikers. In 1922 Fascist violence against the left intensified. While the traditional elites failed to form a stable parliamentary bloc that excluded the Socialists and Fascists, Mussolini jockeyed for office. In October, the king invited Mussolini to form a cabinet. At first he tried to pursue his goals without alarming the establishment or infuriating Fascist zealots, but the balancing act failed. In May 1924 the assassination of the Socialist politician Giacomo Matteotti by a Fascist hit squad shocked Mussolini's conservative fellow travelers and caused a storm of protests. In January 1925, he publicly accepted responsibility for the murder and then proceeded to suppress his left-wing foes. Over the next three years the Parliament, increasingly Fascist-dominated, passed laws that erected a one-party dictatorship.[6]

Once the dictatorship was in place, however, Mussolini never ruled absolutely. Not only did he have serious rivals within the Fascist Party but the traditional elites—the military, the Catholic Church and the king—also exercised extensive independent powers. The army had already passed up two opportunities to depose him. On the first occasion, when the Blackshirts appeared ready to storm Rome and seize power in 1922, General Armando Diaz, then head of the army, told the king that if he declared a state of emergency the army would obey, but it would be "good not to put it to the test." Two years later, when Mussolini was implicated in Matteotti's murder and the scandal might have ended his premiership, the army preferred to cut a deal with him rather than side with his political opponents.

The relationship between the Fascists and the military was always uneasy. Officers and men swore loyalty to the House of Savoy. According to the Italian constitution, the king was commander in chief during wartime. Senior officers regarded the armed forces as the only rightful bearers of arms for national defense. To them, the thugs who made up the Blackshirts did good work in administering castor oil and truncheons to Socialists—the sort of internal policing that they had no desire to do themselves. But if the Fascists took power, would they rewrite Italy's constitution, abolish the monarchy and replace the professional army with a black-shirted people's militia? It was a real concern. Still, top-ranking soldiers accepted Mussolini, albeit at arm's length, first as prime minister and then as dictator. What drew the armed forces and the Fascists together in the first place was a powerful set of ideas about future war and what needed to be done to wage it successfully.[7]

When it came to military theory, Italian soldiers did not differ from their peers the world over. They too tried to understand the experiences of 1914–18 and impose order and meaning on wars to come. Naturally, individual war planners disputed just how radically the lessons of the war could be applied to resource-poor and industrially backward Italy. Yet all of them agreed that war was no longer a contest between rival armies, but a life-and-death struggle between whole peoples and economies. A future war would, according to one high-level defense paper, "absorb all the political, intellectual, economic, and social energies of the nation." Nations that were prepared to mobilize all of their strength would win. States that possessed the means to wage total war were great powers; those that did not were all potential victims in the pitiless world of international competition.[8]

In the early 1920s Italy struggled with a huge public deficit, which consumed about a third of state expenditure. Finance officials pursued deflation and balanced budgets. That required spending cuts. As a result military budgets fell below what war planners believed to be their necessary minimum. Worse still in the eyes of the senior officers, for the first time in Italy's history civilian politicians took an active peacetime interest in military affairs. This intrusion was bad enough, but something even more overtly political alienated the officer corps from parliamentary democracy. Put simply, Italy's postwar politicians seemed incapable of imposing the type of regimented national unity, social discipline and economic controls that all theorists of total war believed to be indispensable to victory. The Fascists, however, openly aspired to do so.

Fascists practiced the politics of mass mobilization. Not everything about theories of total war was fascist, nor was everything about Italian Fascism reducible to the glorification of total war; but mobilization in 1914–18 had made fascism imaginable, and fascists everywhere returned the favor by elevating total war to a form of art.[9]

Italian Fascism was not Mussolini's individual creation. The swashbuckling Futurist poet Gabriele D'Annunzio had the best claim as the intellectual father of the doctrine. Mussolini was not even the most dogmatic Fascist. Other party bosses such as Italo Balbo, the dashing Blackshirt leader and champion aviator, came out higher on that score. But to Mussolini fell the job of making Fascism into a reality. And deep in the foundations of his Fascism lay thoughts of 1917–18.

In his speeches and writings the Duce spoke of arms, autarky and empire. History was an inescapable struggle for domination. Peace was a truce during which empires readied for war. The Fascists cultivated the myths and symbols of the Roman Empire and sought to take Italy's national unification of 1859–70 to its logical conclusion. Italy had once been a world superpower; it was now a great power; it would soon be greater by conquest. Italy's imperialism in East Africa (1889–90) and in Libya (1911–12) was an unfinished project. In 1919 Rome had obtained some of what Italy had fought for, but further gains in the eastern Adriatic, the Danubian basin and the eastern Mediterranean awaited. One day a new Fascist Rome would seize Gibraltar and the Suez Canal and once again command the Mediterranean.

Often pictured in military garb, Mussolini promoted the cult of the warrior-chieftain destined to lead Italians into the future. That meant making Italy fit for a future of warring autarkic empires (the "epoch of nations behind walls," as he would later call it) that he had first glimpsed in 1917–18.

When he was a Socialist, he had craved war to make a revolution. Wars made revolutions, revolutions made wars. Now, as a Fascist, as Duce, Mussolini wanted to complete Italy's national revolution. Italians would set aside their fierce regional loyalties and hostility to the state and unite under Fascism. Critics accused the Fascists of trying to fuse the public and private, the military and civilian, into one crushing "totalitarian" state. The Fascists eagerly adopted the new term, totalitariansim, to describe their ideal of a militarized society.[10]

Mussolini's goals of empire and autarky should be understood in terms of the same siege mentality that inspired Japan's conquest of Manchuria, the Soviet Union's first Five Year Plan and Hitler's demand for living space. Before Mussolini, the makers of modern Italy knew that the unified state of 1861 had to compete with the advanced nation-states by building up steel, engineering and arms industries and by binding the national economy with roads and rails. Italy's lack of such mineral resources as coal and iron inspired among the ruling elites dreams of external expansion. The growing population of Italy also needed living space. Well before coming into office, Mussolini voiced concern about finding an outlet for Italy's surplus people and described imperialism as the "foundation of the life of every nation that aspires to economic and spiritual growth." As dictator, he refused to accept that Italy's dependence on foreign imports of fuel and other raw materials rendered it incapable of waging total war. "To live," he said, "means not submitting to fate, not even to what has now become a commonplace, our so-called deficiency in raw materials. It is certainly possible to defeat even this deficiency with other raw materials."[11]

Once in office, the Duce began to prepare Italy for total war. France, Britain and Italy had quickly set up the type of civil-military committees to plan the all-embracing mobilization that military experts the world over advocated. In January 1923 a Supreme Defense Commission and a Subcommittee for the Preparation of National Mobilization were established to, in Mussolini's words, "apply the discipline of the frontline" to the whole Italian population and economy.[12]

Thoughts of total war shaped broader economic policies as well. In the early years Mussolini practiced economic liberalism to reassure foreign investors and his conservative backers. But the ex-Socialist had little faith in free markets. His ideal—and that of a rising cohort of visionary public and private technocrats for whom wartime industrial mobilization and planning epitomized modernity—was a managed economy. This ideal first took root with the creation of the "corporate state." In 1926 the Ministry of Corporations was set up to supervise employers, professionals and workers federations. To regulate economic life, the Fascist regime also instituted a hydra-like network of new state agencies and local party committees.[13]

Corporatism in practice favored employers, especially the big ones. The war had accelerated the rise of vast industrial conglomerates, in metals, chemicals and engineering, which were uncompetitive in a world of open international trade and which ran into trouble once wartime munitions contracts and government subsidies ceased. The postwar slump, the Red scare and the unwillingness of politicians to discipline the workforce convinced industrialists to offer Fascism their qualified support. Boardrooms remained for the most part free of direct state intervention, but industry and government agreed that Fascist trade unions had a monopoly right to speak for workers.[14]

Fascist monetary policy similarly favored the industrial tycoons. In 1926 Mussolini made pegging the lira at an inflated rate of exchange to the gold standard a matter of national prestige. The overvalued lira hit Italy's small entrepreneurial exporting firms hard by making their goods less competitive on world markets. The industrial conglomerates, however, needed maximum purchasing power to import raw materials to produce items for the home market. Naturally, it was the big corporations, which had first formed under Italy's wartime arms czar, General Alfredo Dallolio, that would be needed to mass-produce the munitions for a future total war.[15]

The lingua franca of total war infused other sectors of the economy and public policy as well. The Fascists encouraged the production of synthetic rubber, fibers and resins and invested in large hydroelectric plants. The Duce fought a "battle for wheat" to make Italy self-sufficient in food by raising yields, land reclamation and high duties on imported grains. Along with the battle for wheat came the "battle for births." The dictator, who taxed bachelors and rewarded mothers, subscribed to the geopolitical logic of the day: there was strength in numbers. "To count for something in the world," Mussolini said, "Italy must have a population of at least 60 million by the 1950s. . . . what are 40 million Italians when compared with 90 million Germans and 200 million Slavs?"[16]

On top of investing in autarky and population growth, Mussolini devoted more resources to the military. Although the two older services, the army and navy, received the most, the Fascists embraced air power as a symbol of the regime's modernity and dynamism. As Giulio Douhet, the theorist of future war, and others urged, Mussolini founded in 1923 an independent Italian Air Force. By 1926 Italy's air strength of 800 machines was second only to that of France.[17]

Unfortunately for Mussolini, Italy never armed as fast as he would have liked. Deep down he was an all-outer, but he was also pragmatic enough to realize that he could not push the conservative establishment or the economy too far too fast.

For their part, the generals preferred Mussolini to the men who had governed Italy just after the war. He spoke of national mobilization and asserted the nationalist agenda abroad. In the summer of 1923, when a quarrel with Athens erupted over Albania, Mussolini ordered the armed forces to seize the island of Corfu to force the Greeks to back down. To military men embittered at Italy's treatment in 1919, the Corfu crisis was a salutary display of Italian independence. The army could do business with the Duce. At the height of the Matteotti crisis, when he needed the army's support most, Mussolini curbed Fascist zealots who wanted to "fascistize" the army and made the Blackshirts subordinate to the armed forces.

Mussolini's unwillingness to transform the army into a popular Fascist militia was not simply a concession to the generals. It represented a convergence of ideas. In the early 1920s, when budgets were tight, General Antonino Di Giorgio, the pro-Fascist war minister, proposed economizing on fully trained manpower to invest in modern weapons. The military establishment balked at the idea. Di Giorgio's proposal for a small elite force would demote Italy from the rank of nations capable of waging prolonged all-out wars.[18]

In April 1925 during a Senate debate, when the time for a decision arrived, Mussolini poured cold water on Di Giorgio's reforms. Mussolini wanted a fully modernized strike force, but he wanted a big army too. After Di Giorgio resigned, the Duce placed himself at the head of the armed forces. Sadly for him, Mussolini could never fully impose his will or order on the armed forces. Most of all, his dealings with the army were a never-ending source of frustration, which often came in the person of General Pietro Badoglio.[19]

Born in 1871, Badoglio was the embodiment of the haughty Piedmontese elite that dominated the officer caste. Before 1914 he saw action as an artillery officer in Italy's colonial wars. During 1915–18 he swiftly climbed the ranks. As a strategist, Badoglio was neither brilliant nor bold. He was more the careful and cunning type who preferred to overwhelm an enemy at the right moment with all his guns on the right spot. His ability to walk away from a crisis smelling like roses was uncanny. Under Mussolini he enjoyed wealth, titles and influence. Yet his only loyalties were to the Crown, the service and his own glory. In the summer of 1943, not only did he help to engineer the Duce's downfall, he became Italy's first post-Fascist head of government just in time to switch to the Allied side. In 1925, to placate the king and the army, Mussolini had made Badoglio a marshal and appointed him chief of the armed forces general staff. Thereafter, the Duce did his best to sideline him by trimming his powers and surrounding him with rival officers, but the crafty old marshal remained the Duce's top military adviser until 1940.[20]

Had Badoglio been a romantic systematizer of future war like Blomberg, Ishiwara or Tukhachevsky, his dealings with the Duce might have been less fraught. But in military outlook Badoglio was more akin to Araki, the Japanese war minister who recognized that resource-poor Japan would lose an all-out arms race against the Soviet Union. Badoglio was similarly well aware of Italy's manifold shortcomings as a garrison economy, and he did not see war looming. Mussolini, however, always toyed with ways to use force. To him Yugoslavia emerged as the most likely target for his next military venture. After the Austro-Hungarian Empire collapsed in 1918, the new state of Yugoslavia stood in the way of Italian ambitions in the Danubian basin. During the 1920s Rome and Belgrade bickered over their frontier. A budding Italian protectorate over Albania also strained relations. In July 1925, when Badoglio took over as head of the supreme general staff, he humored the dictator by telling him that a plan to "deal a robust blow" to Yugoslavia was in the works.[21]

In October 1926, eager to fight Yugoslavia, Mussolini took Badoglio up on his boast. Yet planning against Yugoslavia had scarcely started. Badoglio had not called a single meeting of the service chiefs in 1926. What was the urgency anyway? Badoglio for one did not believe—as wishful thinkers, including Mussolini, did—that Yugoslavia was on the verge of internal disintegration. He was not against a war per se. He just hated to lose. Finding reasons why Italy might lose was not difficult. For one thing, Yugoslavia had received large shipments of modern arms from France, Belgium and Czechoslovakia. Italy might win a war against Yugoslavia alone, Badoglio calculated, so long as the war was brief. The trouble was that France courted Yugoslavia as an ally against Germany. The French government would not allow Italy to dismember a French ally. And if France—at that time Europe's mightiest air and land power—intervened, then the war would be very brief and calamitous for Italy.[22]

So, throughout 1927, Badoglio dragged his feet. If the Duce wanted to fight Yugoslavia, then he had to isolate it first diplomatically. In the meantime the armed forces demanded more money. Mussolini promised to deliver. In July 1927 he went to the service chiefs and ordered a "systematic preparation for war" to be completed in five years. The Duce said that war against Yugoslavia was not imminent, but war would come. Never one to pass up an opportunity to push Mussolini's deadlines far into the future, Badoglio affirmed that Italy could not be ready for war before 1932 at the earliest. Months later Paris and Belgrade signed a mutual assistance pact. And Badoglio, with all the purposeful sluggishness he could muster, got on with what he made sure was a painstakingly detailed exercise in drawing up war plans.[23]

As the 1920s closed, the Duce's war against Yugoslavia was ever more remote. Despite large hikes in arms spending, the military demanded more money than Italy could afford to spend. Intelligence about the military balance was gloomy. In 1928 the army staff estimated that within weeks of mobilization France could deploy twenty-five and Yugoslavia twelve divisions on their frontiers with Italy, while Italy, the attacker, would have only sixteen. Since 1926 the air force had lagged behind that of France. French bombers could climb higher than Italian fighters. Italy's aircraft makers would not be able to replace combat losses fast enough to maintain frontline strength. The war would have to be brief anyway. As the Duce learned from the Supreme Defense Commission in 1929, Italy could not fight a long war. Stocks of raw materials were too low; industry could not make all the finished goods that would be needed for a long haul; the demand for costly and unreliable imports would therefore soar. Balbo, Mussolini's air force minister, described Italy's predicament best. "We are moving among giants," he said, "giants in wealth, in finance, in raw materials, in technical and mechanical plant and equipment."[24]

DURING THE 1930s the world changed so fast that Italy could not keep pace. Ideas about how states should be armed and economies organized that had been pioneered by the Italians were applied elsewhere with more resources and better results.

Economic nationalism was one of them. Early during the Great Depression, some foreign observers thought that Fascism had shielded Italy against the world slump, a myth that Rome played up. But the reality was different. Italian exports, especially foodstuffs, declined sharply. Stock markets fell. Industrial production shrank by a third. Unemployment, already high, jumped to a million.

Having made the lira's value a matter of prestige, Mussolini stubbornly held onto the gold standard until 1936. Defending the overvalued lira called for greater austerity, including national wage cuts ordered by decree. As the crisis deepened, Fascist Italy took further measures to manage the economy, including by 1934 full control over foreign-exchange movements. One of the masterminds behind this economic armament was a jolly-faced statistician named Alberto Beneduce. During the early 1930s this gifted bureaucrat and acolyte of autarkic economic development reshaped Italy's whole system of industrial finance and management.[25]

The process started in 1930–31, when the Italian banks that funded the country's steel, shipping and engineering industries began to go bust. If these banks collapsed, then so too would Mussolini's arms makers. Beneduce—who had first opposed Fascism but was seduced by the chance to realize his dreams of gigantic cartels and buzzing assembly lines—organized a bailout. In 1933 he set up a state-owned, profit-motivated umbrella company called the Institute for Industrial Reconstruction, which took over the imperiled manufacturers. He also set up government-run credit institutions to invest in industrial growth and job-creation projects through the sale of state-guaranteed bonds. In 1936, to crown Beneduce's work, the Bank of Italy was nationalized, thus shifting responsibility for corporate governance further to the state.[26]

Like Takahashi Korekiyo, the elderly finance wizard who engineered Japan's recovery from the worldwide slump through state intervention and arms spending, Beneduce erected economic controls in response to the emergency. However, unlike in Japan or Germany, Italy's military, thanks to Mussolini's policy of adherence to the gold standard, did not enjoy a sharp rise in the arms budgets. Italian armaments expenditure climbed slowly until 1935. Thus, Italy's top military men, whom Mussolini had ordered to get ready for war against Yugoslavia, adopted a surprising attitude to the World Disarmament Conference: they wanted them to succeed. Even before the conference convened, Dino Grandi, Italy's foreign minister, proposed a truce in arms spending to freeze world armaments in anticipation of cuts. In September 1931 the League of Nations adopted the idea. Self-interest naturally lay behind Italy's disarmament policy. If disarmament succeeded, it would act as a brake on the arms growth of Italy's foes. While they disarmed, or at least armed more slowly, Italy could race forward. But the disarmament that would buy Italy time to close the arms gap with France and Yugoslavia—like all interwar disarmament—was doomed.[27]

For some of the Duce's top men the issue was not how to make disarmament work but what would happen after it failed and Germany rearmed. General Pietro Gazzera, the Duce's war minister, had dismissed the "German danger as a second order problem, to be left to the distant future." Others were not so sure. "I do not trust the Germans," Badoglio told Grandi, "and I do not think they will ever move for our interests." When the world financial crisis halted intergovernmental payments in 1931, Grandi worried that German rearmament would ultimately overawe France and Italy. "Arming a Germany free from the burden of reparations is a very different thing from arming a Germany burdened by them," he warned the Duce.[28]

Mussolini had made up his mind long before the disarmament conference met. "Either everyone disarms or Germany arms. We must support her. We must be extreme in this respect. . . . France will not want to disarm and the blame will be hers." For years, several possible future wars darted about in his mind. As Badoglio and other advisers had told him often, in the Yugoslav case, the stumbling block was France. France feared Germany most of all. A rearmed Germany, the Duce thought, would be more of a benefit than a loss for Italy. With France and Germany locked in a struggle, Italy would be free to smash Yugoslavia. "But we must give unto Germany," the Duce told General Gazzera in June 1930, "and not be given. We must be . . . towing, not be towed. . . . We'll be at war between 1935 and 1936. . . . Within four or five years Germany will be ready to wage war on France."[29]

The crucial question was how quickly Germany would rearm. During the first eighteen months of Hitler's chancellorship, Mussolini was prepared to believe that Germany would rearm in a measured way. Some of his officials said that Germany would be militarily deficient for a decade. The Germans, they added, would not want to provoke everyone else in Europe to rearm by rearming "excessively."[30]

But there was no way of telling what the Germans might do. Hitler stressed to every influential Italian he met that he admired the Duce and wanted to ally with Fascist Italy against the French. But he was not typical of the men around him or pan-German conservatives more generally, who saw Austria falling within the greater Germanic empire, including those parts of Austria taken by Italy in 1919.[31]

In Rome many officials, Badoglio and Grandi among them, simply did not trust the Germans. They saw Austria as a useful buffer zone between Italy and its potentially powerful neighbor to the north. Mussolini shared some of their misgivings. In the early 1930s he courted Austria's proto-fascist Chancellor Engelbert Dollfuss as an Italian client. Army and air force planners, meanwhile, began to prepare for operations in Austria should the Germans try anything.

Ultimately, if a rearmed Germany was going to be more of a benefit than a threat, then, as the Duce had said years before Hitler took office, Italy would have to do the "towing" and not be "towed." That meant containing German rearmament. To do this, Mussolini put forward his Four Power Pact of March

1933. He proposed that Paris, London, Berlin and Rome form a directorate to revise the peace treaties; Germany would rearm in stages; and the four would discuss colonial issues. Mussolini told his ambassador in Berlin to deliver the draft text with a message for Hitler. According to Italian intelligence, the message read, French arms factories were working "at high pressure." The French high command thought that "France would have to wage a preventive war as soon as possible, both against Italy and against Germany as long as France and her allies still had a military supremacy. The Italian armaments were not yet completed. Germany could not be prevented from rearming. France therefore had to utilize the present favourable moment to render both powers harmless for years to come." In July 1933, envoys from the four countries signed on to the pact's principles of peace and cooperation. But, like all the other diplomatic efforts to slow the arms race, Mussolini's Four Power Pact flopped. The Italian attempt to raise the specter of a preventive war by France to curb German arms growth failed, too. Whenever Italian diplomats suggested rearming in stages, German diplomats wearing patronizing smiles replied that Hitler would think about it.[32]

While the diplomatic wrangling continued, reports piled up that the Germans were arming at breakneck speed. What made this news doubly troubling for the Duce was evidence that Italian armaments had fallen further behind those of France.[33]

Much to Italo Balbo's disappointment, the biggest gap was in the air force. While in public Balbo extolled the air force as a war winner, in private his staff told him that the French were spending much more than Italy on men and machines. Rivalry with Germany would soon crank up French outlays even higher. In a last gambit to make the air force Italy's chief instrument of war, Balbo tried to take Badoglio's job as chief of the armed forces general staff. Mussolini would gladly have replaced Badoglio if he could, but not with a political rival and a fanatic for one branch of the services to boot. At the end of 1933 Mussolini made Balbo governor of Libya instead.[34]

Sending Balbo into semi-exile did nothing to solve the problem of an arms race that had come too early for Italy. In March 1934 Berlin published a large arms budget. Big hikes in French arms spending were bound to follow.

In mid-June, in a bid to "tow" instead of being "towed," the Duce met Hitler at Venice. The two men talked past each other. Hitler said that a German-Austrian union was off the agenda for now. All he wanted from Dollfuss was a few concessions to Austria's Nazis. The Duce said that he did not want his man in Vienna bullied. Mussolini later asked Hitler to scale down German rearmament and rejoin the disarmament talks. Hitler's reply to this was a tedious sermon about Germany's equality of rights. "A fresh Italian initiative on the disarmament question," the German report of the meeting predicted with confidence, "is not to be expected."[35]

On July 25, weeks after the Venice summit, while his family was enjoying Italy as guests of the Duce, Dollfuss was shot dead during a botched Nazi coup in Vienna. As a show of force, the Duce rushed troops to the frontier. Although Hitler knew that the Austrian Nazis had prepared to engage in terrorist acts, he was most likely ignorant of their exact plans. He would not have approved of a full-blown coup because of the harm it would do to relations with Italy. Although the crisis soon subsided, this sudden dose of the German menace alarmed Mussolini. "Today," the Fascist dictator told his chiefs of staff on September 3, 1934, "our political orientation is against Germany."[36]

During 1934, Mussolini was concerned not just with Europe. War plans for the conquest of Ethiopia had been in the works since 1932. The year before, the French premier, Pierre Laval, had told Grandi that East Africa offered fertile ground for Italian imperialism. The idea appealed. Ethiopia lay between the Italian colonies of Eritrea and Somaliland. In 1896, Italy's first attempt to capture Ethiopia had ended at a place called Adowa, where Ethiopian warriors wiped out an Italian colonial army. If the situation permitted, erasing this humiliation from Italy's military record alone was reason enough to attack Ethiopia. But at the time Mussolini wanted a showdown with Yugoslavia first. So the Ethiopian project was shelved for later.

In December 1934 Mussolini reversed his priorities. He issued a top-secret directive to the service chiefs. "The problem of relations with Ethiopia," it began, "has recently moved onto a different plane: from diplomacy to a trial of strength." This "historic" problem had to be solved for all time through the "use of force." Mussolini's directive then took on a very distinctive form. In the years to come, the same melodramatic language and now-or-never logic he used would turn up at other critical times and places, when—under the pressure of a spiraling arms race—hopes and fears would merge into a decision, and a decision into action.

"Time is working against us," Mussolini warned. Soon Ethiopia would transform from a feudal kingdom into a centralized state capable of mobilizing all its strength. Purchases of advanced military hardware and training from Europe had raised the quality of Ethiopia's armament. "In my view," the Duce declared, "Ethiopia's military preparations are a serious potential threat to our colonies, especially if we become engaged in a European war.... The longer we wait to liquidate the Ethiopian threat, the more difficult and costly the war will be."

According to the Duce, the international situation also favored a preventive war in East Africa. Europe would be at peace for about two or three years. France wanted Italy's help against Germany, so relations between the two countries were on the mend. Yugoslavia was eager to follow the French example. These new alignments had temporarily removed "the danger of another German attack on Austria."[37]

Confirmation of Mussolini's reading of the diplomatic scene came in January 1935 when French premier Laval traveled to Rome to confer with the Duce. Mussolini, who liked to convince others that his secret agents had told him things that no one else knew, played on French fears. "Germany is actually arming itself very rapidly," he said. "The air force that causes so much preoccupation in England is quite real." There was no way to "turn the clock back" except war. Laval replied that the French would not fight to "punish" Germany for rearming. Then the only option, Mussolini said, was a new treaty that legalized German rearmament and that also secured for France and Italy a "margin of superiority." Laval agreed, and, although he later denied it, he rashly offered the Duce a free hand in Ethiopia, so long as French commercial interests were not harmed, in exchange for Italy's help with the containment of Germany.[38]

In the months that followed, the crisis over German rearmament heated up. In March Germany expanded its army and air force. France replied by increasing the size of its army. Negotiations between France, Czechoslovakia and the Soviet Union for mutual assistance pacts against German aggression progressed. So did talks between Italy and France on the exchange of air and ground units in the event of a war against Germany. Italy also tried to bind Austria, Hungary and Yugoslavia into a Danubian bloc. Italian rifles, ammunition and other equipment covertly found their way to Austria. In April Mussolini met Laval and Britain's prime minister, Ramsay MacDonald, to discuss German rearmament. Mussolini also made a big show of committing himself to the defense of the League of Nations and of the status quo in Europe, while his plans for a war with Ethiopia matured.

To Badoglio, Italy's alignment with France made sense. He enjoyed talking to the French General Maurice Gamelin about making war on Germany. What puzzled him was the Duce's directive to attack Ethiopia. Badoglio did not object to colonialism. He had fought during the Adowa campaign. In the late 1920s he had ruthlessly suppressed a rebellion in Libya. Badoglio did not accept Mussolini's argument that it would be easier sooner rather than later to crush Ethiopia, and that Europe was tranquil enough for Italy to risk sending a huge army to East Africa. He advised waiting until 1936. The heads of the three services expressed doubts as well. General Alfredo Baistrocchi, the army's new pro-Fascist chief of staff, however, became more eager as plans unfolded. So long as the British did not oppose it, Admiral Domenico Cavagnari, the head of the navy, embraced the war as a practical demonstration of why Italy needed a very big fleet.[39]

During the summer of 1935, while Italian soldiers landed in East Africa, and Italian propagandists hurled abuse at Ethiopia, the British appeared to be getting ready to stop Italy. The developing crisis depressed the French. However unreliable the Italians might be, they at least talked about joint military operations against Germany. Yet Italy was only a useful ally against Germany; Britain was an indispensable one. If an Anglo-Italian war came, France would join Britain.

In London no one cared very much about Ethiopia. A top-level committee of officials concluded that no vital British interest would be harmed if Ethiopia fell to Rome. Some worried that Italy might suffer another Adowa. The victory of a "black country against a European nation" might stir things up in the British Empire. The snag in allowing Italy simply to go ahead was Ethiopia's membership in the League of Nations. If Italy attacked, then all members would be obliged to penalize the aggressor. According to Britain's top admiral, economic sanctions administered by the League of Nations and enforced by the Royal Navy, especially an oil embargo, would provoke Italy into a desperate "mad dog" act of retaliation that would lead to full-scale war.[40]

For months now in London, officials had debated whether Germany or Japan represented the more urgent threat and how to divide up limited resources to arm against the two of them. The sudden arrival of Italy into the mix was thus most unwelcome. Diplomats suggested the time-honored solution of buying the Italians off with a transfer of territory in East Africa between the two empires. Mussolini was not interested. He decided to push the British as far as he could without forcing them to fight. He had a good idea of how far he could push. The Duce had read top-secret British documents stolen by his spies that made London's lack of concern for the fate of Ethiopia all too clear.

Predicting the outcome of an Anglo-Italian war required no great flights of strategic imagination. In Rome Badoglio warned the Duce that "I believe the situation in which we shall find ourselves [in the event of war with Britain] is by a very long way the gravest that our country has ever faced in its fortunate history of national construction and consolidation." Admiral Cavagnari was equally glum. In London the head of the Royal Navy, Admiral Ernle Chatfield, thought it might be worth crushing Italy to "reassert our dominance over an inferior race." By the time the Italians invaded Ethiopia on October 3, the British warships were assembled at Gibraltar and Alexandria for war. Mussolini's army in East Africa would be isolated and then starved into submission. Yet the victory would come at a price. And it was potential losses at sea, especially in major surface ships, which gave British officials reason to pause. Preventing Italy from making Ethiopia a colony would be little solace if doing so deprived Britain of the strength it needed to win a war against Japan and Germany.[41]

So, while Italy's soldiers marched, Britain enforced a limited embargo and sought a compromise that would leave the League of Nations undamaged. That was of course impossible. Mussolini refused to be coerced into talks. In his directive of December 1934 he had stressed that the Italian attack had to be swift and decisive in order to limit the time for sanctions and diplomacy to work. But General Emilio De Bono, the Fascist colonial minister to whom Mussolini had given the job of planning and executing the war to circumvent Badoglio's delaying tactics, bungled the invasion. In November Mussolini replaced him with Badoglio. In the months that followed, through the patient application of overwhelming firepower, Badoglio destroyed the Ethiopian Army and thereby strengthened his position as Italy's top soldier.[42]

By May 5, 1936, the war was over. "Italy at last has her Empire," Mussolini roared in front of a cheering crowd on Rome's Piazza Venezia. A unifying surge of patriotism swept the peninsula. The economy picked up, too, thanks to the sudden boom in munitions work. All in all, Mussolini had won an amazing victory. But, like so many successful men in the history of international affairs, he did not fully understand the reasons for his success. In Berlin someone else was making the very same mistake.[43]

CHAPTER 5

"SHOULD WE ACCEPT THE REARMAMENT OF GERMANY?"

In December 1933, almost a year after Hitler took office, and only six months after German arms spending began to climb markedly, a senior staff officer in the French Air Force Ministry asked a straightforward question: "Should we accept the rearmament of Germany?" Germany's withdrawal from the League of Nations and the disarmament conference, the officer wrote, showed the impracticality of trying to conclude an agreement that would hold Germany to the arms levels prescribed by the Treaty of Versailles. Policies to stop Germany from rearming had been proposed, but none stood any chance of success. The great powers could, for instance, first agree among themselves on a disarmament convention, and then impose it on the Germans. But the fact that all the great powers were hostile to a coercive solution "condemned it beyond hope." Alternatively, they could agree to disarm to Germany's level. But would the British, the Italians, the Soviets or for that matter the Germans, who had already armed well above what the Treaty of Versailles permitted, accept this? No, was the officer's answer. Anyway, both Britain and France wanted a "margin of superiority" over Germany. France might try to force a unilateral solution on Germany, but this option would almost certainly draw it into a war against Germany without the support of Britain, Italy or the United States.

Only two viable possibilities existed. First, France could let Germany rearm but refuse to recognize its legality. Inevitable excesses in Germany's military build-up would invite replies from the other powers, and the blame for starting an arms race would fall on Berlin. Under these circumstances, France might just be able to organize concerted international action to contain Germany. However, "this policy is damned by its own fatal outcome," the officer concluded, "namely the unlimited armament of Germany and, as a by-product, the inevitable over-armament of France."

Second, France could accept German rearmament within the framework of an international convention on limits and controls. Britain and Italy wanted such a convention, and Hitler claimed he wanted one too. The problem was that France would lose its freedom to arm as it pleased. Even if this was the correct policy, it was unlikely that any French government would risk the anger of French voters by signing an agreement that would legalize a fully armed Germany. Then again, if Germany armed without such limits and controls, would a future government be able to persuade the French people to make the severe sacrifices necessary to keep pace with the Germans in an open-ended arms race?

Setting the imponderables aside, the officer put forward two certainties. Time to make a deal on German armaments was running out. Each passing day made it more difficult to negotiate. And, if no agreement emerged, then "a new arms race following on from all-out German rearmament would be extremely risky and should give pause for reflection. It is something to be avoided at all costs."[1]

THE FRENCH STAFF OFFICER was wrong about time slipping away: the chance to make a deal on disarmament had run out at least twelve months before, in 1932. During 1934–35, therefore, when officials in Paris and London accepted what had long been foreseen as the outcome of failed disarmament negotiations—uncontrolled German rearmament—Europe entered the first stage of a grueling arms race that would peak in 1940.

The story of how Europe arrived at this juncture begins with decisions made at the Paris Peace Conference of 1919, when Germany was forced to disarm. In the Treaty of Versailles, the victorious powers described German disarmament as a first step toward "the initiation of a general limitation of armaments by all nations."[2]

During the 1920s expert committees under the authority of the League of Nations began to work out ways to regulate, limit and, one day, reduce world armaments. The work of the technical experts, however, bogged down. Superficially, the problem seemed to be one of definition. The assembly-line logic of industrial-age warfare had erased the dividing lines between workers and soldiers, iron ore and armor plate, machine tool and machine gun. In this new situation, how do you define war material or armament? No answer narrow enough for real disarmament could be found. The step from great industrial potential to great armaments appeared to be only a matter of peacetime planning. So, for instance, in the 1920s, when Soviet war planners surveyed the large automotive industries of the United States, France and Britain, they saw the potential for thousands of tanks and airplanes rolling out of the factories. When Japan's total-war officers looked out on the huge war potential of the continent-sized great powers and the great European empires, their hearts filled with fear and envy. And in the sinister half-light of the early 1930s, when general rearmament began, the whole exercise of disarming became more and more divorced from the way in which soldiers imagined future wars. While the disarmers searched for the magic minimum numbers of tanks, guns and planes to insert into the blank tables on draft disarmament treaties, the armers dreamed of organizing entire economies to churn out tanks, guns and planes in vast quantities.[3]

Radical disarmers argued that banning armaments altogether would make war impossible. In February 1928, using this logic, the Soviet Union sent to the League of Nations a draft convention proposing the "general and complete abolition of all armed forces." The proposal was greeted with the same tongue-in-cheek cynicism that had inspired it. While extolling the ideal of eternal peace, delegates to the Preparatory Commission for Disarmament explained that in practice total abolition was impossible unless security was organized first. "The planet upon which these Russian proposals could be put into practical operation," sighed the world-weary delegate from London, "would be a better and a happier world than that which we at present inhabit." For their part, Stalin and his men saw disarmament as camouflage for rearmament in preparation for a war to extinguish communism.[4]

The Soviet call for the total abolition of armaments was calculated to mobilize the American and European peace movements to oppose arming in their countries. The propaganda tactic had limited impact, however, because absolute pacifists and radicals were a small, if vocal, minority. Peace-minded internationalists, who wished to put diplomacy before force in the affairs of states, made up the majority. To them, force was a last resort to deal with lawbreakers: a necessary evil in an imperfect world. What really angered peace campaigners were the profits made by private arms makers in the global arms trade, not the arming of the nation for self-defense. Another 1914–18 had to be avoided, most agreed, but not at all costs. For them, a genuine desire for an end to war sat comfortably alongside a powerful sense of patriotism and a conviction that the nation and its defining values had to be defended against naked aggression.[5]

The founders of the League of Nations in fact never imagined a world without armed forces but instead envisioned one in which states armed just enough to enforce a collective peace and ensure their own safety. The problem was that armaments were nothing if not competitive, and one state's safety was another's vulnerability. One escape from this dilemma was to place overwhelming strength in the hands of the League of Nations. Although the French had often proposed the creation of a force available to the League, ultimately all states were too jealous of their national sovereignty to establish a heavily armed international police force.

And so, in a fragmented world of states all too conscious of the competition between them instead of their interdependence, disarmament became a game of convincing others to disarm in the way that was most helpful to one's own defense. Across the English Channel this game was played with ferocious self-righteousness. The British insisted that the continentals (namely the French) should slash their land and air forces so that the Germans would feel content with a modest increase to their own forces. This reasoning flabbergasted Frenchmen. Surely disbanding regiments and squadrons alone would not safeguard the peace? The French insisted that a treaty on automatic assistance in the event of German attack must come before anyone could begin to speak about reducing French arms, let alone increasing German ones.[6]

In February 1932, when fifty-nine national delegations assembled in Geneva for the opening session of the long-awaited World Disarmament Conference, everyone knew that the standoff in Europe had to be resolved first before any progress could be made. The conference, alas, only made things worse. The British argued that the French had to accept changes to the Treaty of Versailles; the French asked for security guarantees in exchange. British and U.S. officials attempted to classify weapons into offensive and defensive types and to ban or reduce the killing power of the former. French officials worked out ways to phase in and verify limited German rearmament. The Germans, who stood somewhat aloof from the fray, told everyone that now was the time to make good on the promise that German disarmament had only been the prelude to universal disarmament. The game of persuading everyone else to disarm to one's own benefit became one of avoiding the blame for the failure of the talks. With the eerie clarity that often comes at critical moments in world affairs, many could see what was happening and felt helpless to stop it. "The only recourse [to a disarmament convention] is a kind of armaments race," warned the French prime minister, Édouard Herriot. "Imagine what this arms race would become." At the end of 1932, while their colleagues back in Berlin set their minds to the practicalities of arming, the German delegates walked out of the Geneva talks. Only the formal recognition of Germany's equality of status in armaments brought them back to the negotiations. In January 1933, the government in Germany changed. In July 1934, the conference adjourned for good.[7]

Was an opportunity squandered? Hitler would not have entered into disarmament by choice. A government headed by one of his predecessors might have signed a disarmament convention, but only one that would have closed the military gap between France and Germany. For the French to accept a change in the arms balance, the British would have had to offer them a defensive alliance. Even if one could reasonably imagine these conditions falling into place, the resulting deal would have been not about cutting armaments but about regulating a German arms build-up. And, even if that had been worked out, other destabilizing pressures would have come into play. Japan and the Soviet Union, for instance, would not have cut back their armaments programs for the sake of stability in western and central Europe. Technological change driven by a rearming Germany, especially in military aviation, would have prompted a race in the quality of weapons. And, even if instead of the Nazis an army-dominated regime had taken power in Berlin, that regime would almost certainly have given in to the temptation of racing ahead to achieve military supremacy in Europe once the boundaries of a disarmament agreement had been reached. If an opportunity was squandered in 1932, it was only the chance to cut a short-lived deal on European armies and air forces.

In the final years of the Weimar Republic, disunity between London and Paris was a prime cause of the disarmament deadlock; once Hitler took office, disunity between the powers with the greatest stake in upholding international order was a precondition for runaway German rearmament. As the arms race spiraled, the great powers became ever more reluctant to commit to allies. This general unwillingness of states to combine their military strength was both a cause and a consequence of the arms race. The underlying reasoning for dodging alliances was almost always the same: while statesmen wanted the benefit of allies who would fight alongside them if war came, no one wanted to pay the price of committing themselves in advance to fight what military experts everywhere predicted would be another total war.

Historically, states formed alliances to acquire influence over an ally, or to combine forces to deter or launch wars. The First World War transformed attitudes toward allies and alliances. In the summer of 1914 the soldiers of two heavily armed alliance blocs marched to a war that was supposed to be over by Christmas. Four ghastly years of seemingly purposeless killing led to the widespread (though mistaken) belief that the prewar alliances had themselves been responsible for engulfing Europe in total war. For the victors, this way of thinking found concrete form in the foundation of the League of Nations. The League's charter called on members to act together to stop aggression. The "new" diplomacy of collective security—in effect a universal obligation to punish aggressors—replaced the "old" one of military pacts.

Enthusiasm among the victors for collective security quickly melted away. U.S. legislators rejected membership in the League because collective security implied an unqualified obligation to fight in faraway wars. Although there were advocates of the League in Britain, some in high office, collective security proved more useful to the British as an excuse to evade French pleas for an alliance than as a genuine policy. During the 1920s the Americans flexed their financial muscles to promote a liberal-capitalist peace in Europe, but rejected security entanglements; the British sought to act on the continent as a middleman; and the French searched for ways to check German ambitions and draw Britain into an alliance.[8]

The preference for living without alliances rather than trying to find safety in them was encouraged by the collapse of the liberal economic order of the 1920s. As we have seen, the Depression enabled soldiers and civil servants in Japan and Germany to apply certain ideas about how states should be armed and how economies should be organized. Arms, autarky and empire left no room for lasting partnerships. However, the urge to erect walls and form closed economic blocs was not confined to those states that embraced dictatorship. The political shockwaves caused by the slump played out differently in the democracies, but the urge to put one's own safety and prosperity first was no less strong.

Economic nationalism intensified trans-Atlantic disputes over reparations and war debts. Washington raised tariffs, and U.S. dollars flew out of Europe. The French raised tariffs and set import quotas on foodstuffs to protect their farmers. In 1931–32, Britain, the birthplace of free trade, shocked the world by abandoning the gold standard and organizing its empire into a trading bloc. The French, who stuck with the gold standard and who at first seemed strangely immune to the global downturn, dragged their feet over a one-year standstill on intergovernmental payments of war debts and reparations to relieve the German banking crisis. By doing so, Paris infuriated London and Washington. In the summer of 1932 Britain and France agreed to cancel future German reparation payments in exchange for war debt cancellation. Washington choked on this proposition. As the financial crisis deepened, Britain and France defaulted on their war debts. In April 1933 the devaluation of the U.S. dollar set off aggressive devaluations elsewhere. A last opportunity for London, Paris and Washington to work together backfired when in July the World Economic Conference broke up amid accusations of bad faith.

Only a few months later, urged on by General Blomberg and others, Hitler abandoned his initial caution over rearmament. In the deeply divided world of the early 1930s, even someone lacking Hitler's vast fund of low cunning would have had little difficulty blocking the formation of a coalition to stop Germany rearming.

IN BERLIN, SOME WONDERED whether France might act alone against Germany. There was not much chance of this happening, however. While Hitler waited, the French searched for ways to put international controls over what secret intelligence told them was a fast-growing German Army. "If Germany continues to rearm," Prime Minister Édouard Daladier told British and American diplomats in June 1933, then "France will increase its armaments so as to maintain its current superiority. . . . France would greatly prefer an effective system of controlled and supervised disarmament. The question remains to find out if effective controls can be instituted."[9]

General Maxime Weygand saw things differently. For years now the French Army chief had fought a bitter campaign with successive left-wing prime ministers to spend more on defense and prevent deep cuts in French armaments for the sake of disarmament. In doing so, the sixty-six-year-old general exercised all the subtlety of a sledgehammer. An ultraconservative by instinct, Weygand had earned a reputation as a gifted staff officer while serving under General Ferdinand Foch, the celebrated soldier who had halted the German onslaught in 1914. As Foch's right-hand man, Weygand quickly climbed the ranks and received a first-hand education in civil-military relations under the stresses of total war. When the First World War broke out, the French Army exercised something close to a dictatorship, but as the war years wore on and the bloodletting increased, the politicians began to assert their authority over the war's conduct. In 1917 this process climaxed with the appointment as prime minister of the left-wing firebrand Georges Clemenceau. France's war became Clemenceau's war, and "War," as he famously said, "is too serious a business to be left to soldiers." He rallied the French under the banner of a republican victory and kept a firm hand on Foch, who had become supreme allied commander in the last stage of the war.[10]

When the war ended, the right-wing generalissimo and the left-wing prime minister clashed bitterly over the peacemaking. Foch wanted Germany dismembered: the Rhineland should be detached and turned into a buffer

zone friendly to France. As Clemenceau soon discovered, the American president, Woodrow Wilson, and the British prime minister, David Lloyd
George, rejected this idea for a number of reasons, not the least of which was
that taking territory away from Germany would preclude a Franco-German
reconciliation. Foch was determined to push France's frontier to the River
Rhine. He attacked Clemenceau for failing to convert his fellow peacemakers to the French Army's idea of peace. Unable to fire the popular supreme allied commander, Clemenceau simply had to put up with Foch's political
heckling and intrigues. For his part Foch broke the primary rule governing
civil-military politics in the Third Republic—the supremacy of civilian authority. Foch approached President Raymond Poincaré, who shared his views
on the peace terms and loathed Clemenceau, to have the prime minister replaced. Clemenceau, who was not nicknamed the Tiger for nothing, was too
cunning to be outflanked by a political novice. Clemenceau's cabinet backed
him. Instead of an independent Rhineland, he obtained from Wilson and
Lloyd George promises of security treaties and a fifteen-year occupation by
the victors of the west bank of the Rhine.[11]

Foch, Weygand and other hardliners complained about what they saw as
a soft peace. While Germany was disarmed, the French Army was superior.
While French troops stood on the Rhine crossings, Germany was vulnerable.
But the nagging question for French soldiers was how long would this situation last? "Weakness in your enemy," Marshal Foch warned, "does not create strength in you."[12]

In the 1920s French strategists became obsessed with French national
weakness. The war had taught them the same lesson that it had taught their
counterparts across the Rhine. Industrial-age warfare was a life-and-death
struggle between societies and economies. Winning meant harnessing the
totality of national resources. Against this measure, France suffered from two
key shortcomings when compared with Germany: fewer people and a smaller
industrial economy.[13]

At the time of Napoleon's coronation as emperor in 1804, France had been
the most populous country in Europe. By 1861, with a faster growth rate, Germany had overtaken France, while France's birth rate stagnated. From the
1870s, fear that the demographic trend pointed to relentless depopulation had
gripped France. With 1.3 million dead and 3.5 million wounded, France had
suffered in 1914–18 the highest casualty rate relative to the size of population
than any other combatant except Serbia. This loss of young lives tormented
a national psyche long plagued by fears of decline. By the early 1930s French
armaments planners faced the uncomfortable fact that forty million French

might soon be pitted against seventy million Germans. Well before the arms race began, France had lost the population race.[14]

Economically, late-1920s France witnessed an industrial boom. Between 1924 and 1929 French industrial production grew faster than that of anywhere else in Europe. The chemical, petroleum, electrical and automotive industries led the way. Despite this stunning spurt of growth, French war planners still had plenty to fret about. Although France was per capita a wealthier nation, on the eve of the Depression the industrial potential of Germany was twice that of France's. For the essentials of arms production, France was reliant on imports of coal, copper, nickel, lead and zinc, oil, rubber and cotton. French arms planners knew that in another total war against Germany, allies would be vital to supply the men, money and raw materials necessary to win. But which states would in future ally themselves to France? In the 1920s, France signed military agreements with the "successor" states that had benefited territorially from Germany's defeat and the breakup of the Austro-Hungarian Empire: Poland (1921), Czechoslovakia (1924), Romania (1926) and Yugoslavia (1927). Yet, as useful as these small states might be in a war against Germany, they could not replace the formidable manpower and economic strength of Russia, the United States and the British Empire, all of which had retreated into their own forms of isolation.[15]

All in all, France lacked the *depth* of armament to win a single-handed conflict against Germany. France needed armaments and allies. French officers and their right-wing parliamentary allies had no faith in disarmament and collective security as alternatives. At first, France tried to enforce the Treaty of Versailles alone. Its inability to do so was exposed in 1923–24, when the conservative former president Raymond Poincaré, now prime minister, sent troops into the Ruhr Valley to punish Germany for overdue reparations and to try to detach the Rhineland from Germany. In response, the German government paid the Ruhr miners to strike; occupation troops forced them to work. Months of industrial unrest and violence took a heavy toll on the French. The occupation deepened France's alienation from Britain and the United States; the value of the franc fell; the Reichsmark sped into hyperinflation. London and Washington stepped in to negotiate a settlement. The occupation backfired financially and diplomatically, and Poincaré's efforts to promote separatism among the Rhenish people failed.[16]

The Ruhr crisis was a turning point. After the western European powers guaranteed the Franco-German border in the Treaty of Locarno of 1925, Paris took a more conciliatory line toward Berlin. In the late 1920s French strategy also shifted from treaty enforcement to the security of its frontiers. In 1927–28 compulsory military service was shortened from eighteen to twelve months, and the total number of active divisions was reduced from thirty-two to twenty-five, or about 500,000 men stationed at home and in the empire. Another expression of this change was the start of one of the most notorious military projects of all time—the Maginot Line. Survey work for fixed defenses along the Franco-German frontier began in 1922. Five years later a detailed blueprint for the eighty-seven-mile line of fortresses was approved. In January 1930 the first tranche of the total 5.5 billion franc price tag was allocated. Work began that year, when the pugnacious war hero André Maginot was war minister. By 1937 the installations along the German border were finished.[17]

The French Army's case for the construction of the Maginot Line was logical and consistent with the military thinking of the day. It was as logical and consistent as Stalin's first Five Year Plan, the Japanese Army's conquest of Manchuria and Colonel Thomas's concept of arming Germany in depth. The purpose of the high-tech frontier defenses was to offset France's demographic inferiority. At the start of a future war only a relatively small number of French fortress troops would be needed to hold off many more numerous German attackers, while the mobile elements of the French Army assembled to counter German breakthroughs. The Maginot Line would prevent the Germans from winning a quick victory and from seizing (as they had done in 1914) France's industrial and resource-rich northeastern provinces. A prolonged defense would buy French planners time to mobilize France's economy and overseas empire. With time, France's allies would do the same. With resolve, France and its allies would win by turning the arms balance against Germany. And, best of all, if the Maginot Line convinced the Germans that they could not win quickly, then perhaps the risk of losing a long war would deter them from ever attacking at all.[18]

For the French Army, the government's decision to build the Maginot Line was a major political victory. However, Weygand and most other senior officers were far less happy about the army reforms of 1927–28. The problem with a one-year period of compulsory military service was that it turned the army into a training cadre instead of a ready fighting force. Conscripts passed through the army at a faster rate, and much of the trained army was absorbed in training fresh entrants. Looming over the horizon too was what the French called the "lean years," caused by the low birth rate during the war when so many men were at the front. From 1934 to 1938 the number of young men available for conscription would drop from 240,000 to fewer than 150,000. If the one-year service law remained, then the size of the standing army would shrink. In January 1930, when Weygand was appointed chief of staff, he made his priority a restoration of two years of compulsory military service.

For a right-wing militarist like Weygand, extending French military service to two years had a deeper attraction than just raising the strength of the army. Weygand, and others like him, idealized France as a national community ordered according to conservative values. With its integrity and patriotic zeal, the army was the essence of this ideal. Postwar demobilization, liberalization and a deepening of the left-right divide in French politics alarmed conservatives, who worried whether France could once again stand the test of total war. Fear of communism at home and abroad made social change appear all the more threatening to the right. Weygand and his staff worried that only one year of military service gave the army too little time to instill sufficient patriotism in the annual cohorts of raw recruits and inoculate them against left-wing ideas. Much to his great alarm, in the first two years of Weygand's tenure as army chief of staff, working-class activism and popular pacifism appeared to be growing stronger day by day. The Great Depression radicalized the jobless, and the start of the disarmament conference at the League of Nations in February 1932 created an opportunity for the left to achieve deep cuts in French armaments and to block a lengthening of the period of conscription.[19]

Weygand and his advisers would have accepted disarmament if it had meant the creation of an international force poised ready to punish Germany automatically for any treaty violations. What they were against was the scheme devised by Prime Minister Édouard Herriot, the leader of a center-left coalition government. Herriot, who took office in June 1932, and his war minister, Joseph Paul-Boncour, proposed a "constructive" plan that included the creation of a heavily armed international force, in which Britain and the United States would participate, but which also reduced national armies (including the French Army) to citizen militias. Weygand was furious. France's professional army was already emaciated: now Herriot wanted to replace it altogether with a motley horde. During meetings of the Supreme War Council in October 1932, France's military and civilian leadership met to debate the plan. Herriot emphasized that France had to take the initiative in proposing a workable scheme of disarmament: if disarmament failed, the blame had to be Germany's. Herriot had no illusions. "I am convinced," he said, "that Germany wishes to rearm." He saw disarmament as a way to prevent France's isolation and a ruinous arms race that France was bound to lose. Disarmament offered a chance to fasten some international controls on German arms and to win security guarantees from London and Washington. Weygand behaved as though Herriot's plan was a huge prank concocted deliberately to annoy him.[20]

For Weygand disarmament was bad enough. What really angered him were cuts to France's defense budget before the Geneva negotiations had ended. One of the cruel ironies of the 1930s was that the Depression was slow to take hold in France and that the French economy was one of the last to recover from its debilitating effects. In 1930–31, while other countries suffered, the French economy remained strong and the Bank of France held one quarter of the world's gold reserves. From 1932 onward, however, France began to feel the slump. Industrial activity slowed and unemployment soared. In response, French governments clung to the gold standard. To defend the franc's value, French officials tried to balance the state budget. This left them no choice but to slash public spending and raise taxes. Public works and social spending took the deepest cuts, but defense too suffered under austerity. From 1931 to 1934 French defense spending declined by twenty-two percent.[21]

The defense cuts came at an inopportune moment, but they were not an ill-conceived bid to disarm single-handedly. Although popular support for disarmament had made defense cuts politically expedient, the overriding reasons why the French turned to deflation in the early 1930s lay in the economic experience of the 1920s.

From 1924 to 1926, because of astronomical wartime state spending and borrowing, the value of the franc plummeted and inflation soared. At the end of 1926 the franc stabilized. Two years later, when it was fixed to the gold standard, it was pegged at one-fifth of its 1913 value. The French understood this valuation to mean that four-fifths of their wealth had vanished. Yet pegging the franc to gold also kicked off a remarkable recovery. French politicians and economists developed an almost mystical attachment to the gold standard. In 1930–31, when their economy appeared untouched by the effects of the Wall Street crash, the French, with smug satisfaction, accepted their good fortune as the just reward for fiscal discipline. From 1932 to 1936 deflation won cross-party backing, despite strong evidence that the policy was failing. Successive governments of the center-left and then of the right found that the state budget could not be balanced. No relief appeared in sight, yet they persevered. To float their currency, as the British and the Americans had done, would start a wage-price spiral that would generate inflation and, most perilous of all, social upheaval and political chaos. With growing ranks of unemployed and a deepening ideological divide, the preservation of domestic peace weighed heavily on the minds of French politicians. Small wonder that in February 1933, only weeks after he became prime minister and Hitler took office, Daladier refused to boost military spending. "Financial considerations must take precedence over military policy," he said. "A balanced budget is the best guarantee of national security."[22]

During 1933 Weygand tried to shift Daladier's priorities. He sent the prime minister intelligence about what the Germans were up to. It was bone-chilling stuff, dauntingly explicit in its depiction of the direction and magnitude of the German threat. Nazism, Weygand wrote, had excited the German "warrior spirit." Hitler's offer to rearm on an equal par with France was a cunning trap. "In reality, there will be no equality," he wrote, "but a very pronounced superiority for Germany given the military culture of this nation and the intensive efforts already undertaken to prepare the German arms industry for rearmament." France must therefore hold on to its military superiority. Daladier and his advisers did not dispute the content or reliability of this intelligence. There was no reason to do so. The French military, which controlled the collection, analysis and distribution of intelligence, had well-placed spies in Berlin. An agent code-named "L," for instance, whose identity remains a mystery, but who must have been a senior German official, supplied dossier after dossier of top-secret papers. Yet intelligence had a limited impact on French policy making in the first phase of German rearmament. Why? Because politicians like Daladier, who had also been a war minister, had heard it all before.[23]

Throughout the 1920s and early 1930s, the French military drew up absurdly inflated estimates of German strength. According to these, and despite the restrictions of the Treaty of Versailles, Germany commanded forces capable of launching a successful surprise attack on France. Within weeks of a national call-up, the German Army could grow from 150,000 full-time soldiers and policemen to four million men—mobilized from veterans' organizations, covert and public paramilitary units and sports clubs. By converting airliners into bombers and putting prototypes of combat aircraft into rapid production, Germany could bomb Paris with 700 aircraft immediately and with over 3,000 within a couple of months. To sustain the attack, civilian factories stood ready to switch effortlessly to munitions production.[24]

In Berlin, French intelligence would have made enjoyable reading: Blomberg, Thomas and Knauss would have laughed uncontrollably at the outlandish claims the French made about German capabilities. In part, these exaggerated French estimates were the result of a tendency of intelligence everywhere to overrate foreign military strength. But the scary image of a covertly armed Germany was also a useful political device. In budget battles fear of a German attack helped pry resources for defense out of the government. French politicians, who saw through the crude scare tactics, had grown accustomed to reading intelligence reports with some skepticism.[25]

Nobody in Paris thought that a fully armed Germany under the Nazis was a good idea. Yet genuine questions remained. How imminent was the German menace? What should France's response be? In the summer of 1933 Daladier, a shrewd politician with a sharp mind, saw things in this way: he did not take Hitler's protestations of peace seriously; nor did he accept Weygand's lurid warnings. "France must above all get through [the] financial crisis," he said. "Once [the crisis] is overcome, in 1936, we will be able to view things differently." Daladier knew that "Germany's industrial capacity was such that she could build up armaments far more rapidly than could France"; France could try to out-arm Germany, but this would be the "worst" outcome. What he wanted was a verifiable and enforceable disarmament. Weygand saw no special benefit to verification except as a tripwire for military sanctions. What he wanted was France to be well armed and backed by brawny allies. In private conversations, he admitted that France was "safe for a considerable time without any great effort." What France needed to do was put an end to the disarmament talks, which he liked to call a big "joke," and put its trust in its own army.[26]

French soldiers and politicians disagreed about what should be France's immediate response to German rearmament, but on one thing they could agree: France could not launch a preventive war. In late 1933–34 Weygand liked to hint that French troops, perhaps in cooperation with the Poles, might act against Germany. Some right-wing politicians publicly demanded it. Rumors of a potential French action spread across Europe. Yet few in authority seriously considered it. According to one well-informed Soviet source, the French high command believed that a preventive war would lead to a protracted war. "If the war dragged on, and Germany had the chance over the course of the war to arm itself, and present a sustained resistance, then the war would lose its preventive character: it would simply be war. Today, France cannot count on a quick decisive victory over Germany because Germany has already achieved a significant level of armament." Memories of how quickly France had been worn down and isolated during the Ruhr Valley occupation of 1923–24 were too fresh for anyone to contemplate unilateralism lightly. Most had learned to distrust simple military solutions to complex political problems.[27]

In early 1934, politicians more to Weygand's liking came into office. The events that brought this change began with the suspicious death of a con artist named Serge Alexandre Stavisky. Police inquiries into his crimes implicated top politicians in bribery. Conservatives and the far left accused the government of a cover-up. On February 6, 1934, far-right paramilitary leagues, long frustrated by parliamentary politics, marched in Paris to protest against corruption. Rioting began. To prevent what seemed to be a fascist coup in the making, the police opened fire. Fourteen fell dead, hundreds more were wounded. Although Daladier held his nerve and restored public order, he felt compelled to resign.

In Daladier's place, Gaston Doumergue, a conservative grandee, formed a right-leaning parliamentary coalition and a "national unity" cabinet, in which the war hero Marshal Philippe Pétain became war minister. Foreign policy appeared to change. In public, Doumergue talked tough on disarmament. His foreign minister, Louis Barthou, opened negotiations with Moscow and Rome that would lead in 1935 to a mutual assistance pact with the Soviet Union and a military accord with Italy.

In March 1934 Doumergue's ministers took a fresh look at French policy. Weygand's interventions were strident. He objected to any deal short of rock-solid international (that is, British and American) guarantees of security and intrusive controls on German arms spending, arms manufacture and military training. If these could not be achieved, he wanted France to retain its freedom to arm: "Anything is better than disarming when Germany is rearming." His willingness to see Germany rearm rather than to pursue disarmament troubled some. Barthou—no dove by anyone's measure—worried about France's ability to compete with Germany in an all-out arms race.[28]

Tensions rose on March 22 when Germany made public its military budget. A major increase in German armaments spending caused an uproar in the French press. French intelligence estimated that the published budget revealed only a third of the true value of German defense spending. The debate now split between those who wanted to make a break with disarmament and those who wanted some sort of deal that would slow down and put into place international monitoring of German arms growth. Barthou and the diplomatic corps cautioned against abandoning arms control altogether; Weygand pressed for troop increases. Doumergue, who read the German military budget as a sign that Hitler would not accept an arms deal, backed the hardliners. On April 17, the French government issued a diplomatic note blaming Germany for sabotaging the disarmament talks; now France would "place its own safety in the forefront of its considerations."[29]

Abroad, the April 17 note received mixed reactions. The Germans condemned it. One American official—and some French ones, too—thought it might force Germany back to the Geneva talks. The British saw it as a blunder, for France now appeared to be guilty of starting an arms race. In Paris no one view of what should follow the April 17 note won out. Some thought that France had embarked on a huge arms build-up, while others hoped for a diplomatic solution. Weygand was unfazed. He had got what he had wanted: the disarmers had been silenced. So long as French arms grew in good time, there was no immediate danger. "The French Army staff believes that it has a considerable margin of superiority over Germany," explained General Maurice Gamelin, Weygand's deputy. "We will see how long it will take for the Germans to catch up with the 20 billion we have spent on armaments!"[30]

With retirement approaching in January 1935, Weygand spent his last months in command lobbying for more men and money. To expand the size of the standing army and compensate for the "hollow years," he called for an extension of compulsory military service to two years; he also wanted earlier cuts to the army's budget restored. Some opposition to lengthening military service came from the left, but on March 14, 1935—thanks to Hitler's conscription proclamation days before—the two-year conscription law passed with a big parliamentary majority.[31]

After the April 17 note, and more so after Hitler's faits accomplis of March 1935, French arms spending began to increase. French intelligence intensified the sense of urgency by circulating hair-raising warnings of what would happen if France remained idle while Germany armed at top speed. Well before Hitler unveiled the Luftwaffe, the head of the French Air Force had argued that the speed of German air expansion had made air disarmament futile. The French Air Force therefore won the biggest share in the rise in defense spending in 1934–35. The French Navy gained approval for a battle cruiser and planned to build two 35,000-ton battleships. The extra money allocated to the army's weapons budget in July 1934 and March 1935 (once Germany enacted conscription) was by comparison modest, and even that modest rise was cut in the summer of 1935. Somewhat perversely, despite Weygand's role in bringing about the April 17 note, the army benefited the least of the three services from the spending increases.[32]

Fitfully then, France joined the arms race. Once Hitler began to rearm openly, there still seemed to be enough time to take steps to ensure that France was formidably defended and more closely aligned to Britain before Germany caught up with and outstripped France in armaments. Weygand's successor, his deputy, General Gamelin, took some comfort in France's deep reserves of trained men. And, in spite of the policy of deflation, French politicians did not scrimp on the Maginot Line. Now that the Franco-German frontier would soon be fortified, General Gamelin knew that his job would be to convince the politicians to modernize the army.[33]

IN LONDON THE SHIFT in government thinking from disarmament to rearmament ran more smoothly than it did in Paris. It was not that the British found disarmament any less intractable than the French, nor was the policy debate in Whitehall that much less heated. Instead, a much calmer domestic situation made things easier for the British to reconcile themselves to the turn of events. In 1934–35 Britain began to enjoy an economic recovery when France started to feel the worst of the Depression, and British cabinets changed with far less frequency than those of the French.

When Britain began to rearm, the fighting services, the Foreign Office and the Treasury had their own view of how much to spend and on what kind of armaments, and jockeyed to make their view policy. To help define defense priorities and balance defense plans with anticipated resources, the British government had developed since 1919 an elaborate machinery of interdepartmental subcommittees. The supreme objective of this bureaucratic mechanism was to impose rationality and purpose on the making of defense and foreign policy, and in the 1930s the man who most enthusiastically sought to impose a rational design on British rearmament was the hawk-featured chancellor of the exchequer, Neville Chamberlain.

Born in 1869, Neville Chamberlain was the second son of Joseph Chamberlain, industrialist, social reformer, parliamentarian and champion of imperial unity. Of his two sons, Joseph favored Neville's older half-brother, Austen, as his successor in politics. So, while Austen (a future foreign secretary) read history at Cambridge University, the young Neville studied metallurgy at the local college in the family's native city of Birmingham to make a career in industry. Doggedly tenacious, Neville possessed a Herculean capacity for work and an unshakable confidence in his ability to solve any problem. In 1911 he joined the Birmingham town council. Four years later he was mayor. Health, housing, curbing the liquor trade, municipal savings schemes: all fell target to his coldly rational logic. Mayor Chamberlain's approach was essentially technocratic: any social problem would yield to rational solutions methodically arrived at and properly administered, managed and resourced.[34]

In December 1916 the new prime minister, David Lloyd George, appointed Neville Chamberlain director general of national service to tackle the growing problem of manpower shortages in the army and industry. Foolishly, he accepted the post without demanding a seat in parliament, a place in the cabinet and defined powers. Jealous of their own claims on manpower policy, the War Office and the Ministry of Labour combined forces to frustrate him. Days after taking office, Lloyd George pressed Chamberlain to think up a way to free young men working in the war industries for combat by replacing them with older, less fit men in non–war-related jobs. In doing so, Chamberlain took the concept of total war to its logical conclusion: if the state could conscript soldiers, he asked himself, why could it not conscript workers, deploy them as need be and pay them army salaries? Better yet, why not turn "the whole war industry of the country into State-owned concerns in which everyone should be only an officer or a private and all the surplus should go to the State"? Lloyd George, like his French counterpart, Clemenceau, had come into office in 1916 committed to waging all-out war at all costs. But he had also promised the trade unions for the sake of industrial peace that labor conscription would come only if a patriotic call for volunteers failed. Chamberlain scrapped his "industrial army" plan and made little headway with a voluntary scheme of enlistment. Not long after, he resigned.[35]

This tough lesson in the limits of total mobilization might have cost him his future in national politics, but Chamberlain entered Parliament in 1918. Throughout the 1920s he served ably in successive Conservative cabinets. Under Prime Minister Stanley Baldwin, Chamberlain spearheaded the Tory answer to the enfranchisement of more working-class voters and the rise of Labour as the chief party of opposition—a reforming brand of popular conservatism that cleared slums, controlled rents, built low-cost housing and broadened access to health insurance and pensions.

Then came the Wall Street crash of 1929. Britain could not escape the plunge in world trade: industrial output fell and unemployment topped two million. Champion of free trade and the gold standard, Britain responded with deflation. From the opposition benches, Chamberlain watched as Ramsay MacDonald's second Labour government wrestled with an enormous deficit and spiraling unemployment benefit costs. The Bank of England depleted its reserves to defend sterling's gold value. The financial crunch came in the summer of 1931. French and American loans were needed to top up the Bank of England's reserves. To reassure the market, MacDonald raised taxes and slashed the budget, including relief for the jobless. His Labour cabinet broke apart. In August he formed a new National Government dominated by the Conservatives. Still, the flight from sterling continued. On September 17, the Bank of England, which rejected exchange controls as a solution, stopped defending the pound.

Britain's unilateral devaluation angered officials in Washington and Paris and caused a stampede as others followed London's lead. But coming off the gold standard also made for an early homegrown industrial recovery under Chamberlain, who, after MacDonald's National Government won the October 1931 elections, took the toughest job in the cabinet, the Treasury. His first act was to raise import duties on finished goods and raw materials. In the summer of 1932, with a ruthless eye out for Britain's own needs, he worked out with the Dominion governments a regime of preferential tariffs within the empire. Apart from his "scientific" tariffs to shelter the home market and form an imperial economic bloc, Chamberlain was not going to do anything "flashy." He would manage the value of the floating pound, not control currency flows like Japan or Germany. Nor did he go in for all that "Mumbo Jumbo" about creating jobs with loan-financed public works, not because he abhorred state intervention into the economy but because that much intervention was overkill.[36]

In April 1934, when Chamberlain stood up in the House of Commons to give his budget speech, he reported a large surplus. A year later came another surplus. Now he cut taxes for the "small" man. "There is no magic in it," Chamberlain told radio listeners on the night of his 1935 budget speech. "The application of the principles of sound finance have established confidence in industry." He told the jobless masses that work would come. Behind tariff walls, Britain would prosper. In coming years, he promised that he would take for the state less of the national income in taxes. What he did not talk about that night, but knew full well, was that a big slice of Britain's future wealth would have to go on armaments. The question was how much? Sadly, as things turned out, the 1935 tax cuts would be his last.[37]

Thanks to his handling of the economy, Chamberlain's authority in cabinet was even greater than that usually bestowed upon the head of the Treasury. With the elderly Prime Minister Ramsay MacDonald fading, and his designated successor Stanley Baldwin struggling against an almost overpowering lassitude, Neville Chamberlain found himself with each passing month taking on the leadership of the government. He reveled in his growing influence, for the chancellor surveyed the problems of confronting government and thought he saw workable solutions for them all, including the foreign policy predicament of the day—disarmament.

Chamberlain scoffed at dreamers who expected the world to disarm instantly, or worse, those who insisted that Britain should disarm before anyone else. As he told the cabinet in November 1932, negotiations had stalled because France and its allies were "afraid of reducing their armaments without some security that Germany was not rearming while they disarmed. Consequently all proposals based on immediate disarmament within a very short time appeared to those nations to be a gamble of their security on German good faith." The way ahead was for Europe to disarm in five-year stages, he proposed, with progress from one stage to the next tied to German good behavior. Not only would staged disarmament promote a sense of confidence and security, but it would also give armaments manufacturers ample notice to stop investing in new weapons and to shut down their factories.[38]

As Chamberlain soon discovered, the flaw in his plan (and that of other plans too) was that the Germans were not content to remain "unarmed" while everyone else "disarmed." Recognition of Germany's equality of status in armaments in December 1932 had conceded as much. The arrival of the Nazis a month later to the sound of goose-stepping paramilitaries bellowing blood-and-iron anthems left little room for doubt. In March 1933 Chamberlain wrote to his sister that "the best opinion seems now convinced that the Germans are only looking for an opportunity to declare that the Disarmament Conference has failed in order to rearm and defy the world."[39]

In the second half of 1933 the view that German rearmament was inevitable, and that the French had been chiefly responsible for blocking disarmament, persuaded the British cabinet that France had to be made to see the "actual facts": the Germans would soon openly rearm without limits or controls, and that would be the worst possible outcome. The only way to reverse the deteriorating situation was to convince both Paris and Berlin to accept some measure of controlled German rearmament.[40]

In January 1934, failing anything else, the British issued another disarmament scheme. Two months later Chamberlain suggested buttressing disarmament with a security pact. All the European powers, including Germany, would guarantee each other's security and promise to place forces at the disposal of a victim of aggression. He called this his "limited liability" plan. It was wholly typical of British attitudes toward France and alliances generally. Chamberlain's plan seemed in one stroke to crack the dilemma of French security without Britain jeopardizing anything very concrete. It was a clever compromise. The only sticking point was that the French had heard this sort of thing too often before to like it.[41]

THAT GERMANY PREPARED secret mobilization plans, experimented with prototypes of forbidden weapons and would arm at full throttle if given half a chance—these were all conclusions the British had reached long before Hitler became chancellor.

No master spy was needed to learn that the Germans wanted to rearm. German diplomats said so often enough. The question was how geared up was Germany for the day when it would rebuild its forces. British intelligence usually answered this question by first describing how German officials had prevented the Allied Control Commission, which had been assigned the job of disarming Germany after 1919, from doing its job thoroughly. When the commission was withdrawn in 1927, the German Army took "steps to re-create a powerful armaments industry." Proof of this sort of preparatory work turned up in April 1929, when the Secret Intelligence Service (MI6) produced a stolen copy of the German Army's mobilization plan. The plan described how a field army of sixty-three divisions would be assembled in four weeks. While there was no doubt that the document was authentic, the War Office (correctly) doubted that German industry was able to arm that many divisions.[42]

With each passing year, officials could no longer be sure. Evidence that the Germans were getting ready to rearm piled up. British spies scarcely needed to work hard to keep tabs on the Germans. The French eagerly volunteered secret reports thoroughly documenting German violations of the Treaty of Versailles. What the British learned on their own was not as alarming as the French would have them believe, but no one could question that during the Geneva talks Germany was doing everything it could to rearm short of expanding its army, navy and air force.[43]

Evaluating prototypes of forbidden weapons was one thing, but mass-producing tanks, guns and bombers quite another. In 1931–32 allied intelligence reported that German industry was about ready to do just that, and that Hitler, upon taking office, sped up industrial preparations for rearmament. By the end of 1933, the British cabinet saw that Germany was set to make a crash build-up of its forces a fait accompli.[44]

This growing sense that Europe would soon be a much more dangerous place shifted the British cabinet's priorities. Talk of disarmament gave way to rearmament. Chamberlain's thinking changed, too. In October 1933, when Germany left the League of Nations, the chancellor of the exchequer concluded in characteristically sober terms that "common prudence would seem to indicate some strengthening of our defences."[45]

The prospect of a bigger defense budget came as a relief to the chiefs of staff. In the early 1920s they had asked for large arms programs, especially the navy and air force, and made some headway in getting what they wanted. In 1925, Winston Churchill, the chancellor of the exchequer at the time, cut public spending, including defense, in order to peg sterling on the gold standard at its

pre-1914 parity with the U.S. dollar. The service chiefs grumbled about Treasury tightfistedness, but the situation was never as bad as their arguments at the
time (or historians since) suggested. In the late 1920s defense funding was generous enough for the army to conduct the world's most advanced trials in mechanized warfare, the air force to create sixteen new squadrons and the navy to
launch as much new warship tonnage as any of its rivals. Even in 1932, at the
height of the financial crisis, British defense spending remained competitive
with that of the other great powers.[46]

What really caused the chiefs of staff sleepless nights was the double wallop of the Depression and disarmament. As in France, these two converging
threats to the defense budget demanded great ingenuity from the service
staffs. It was not easy to defend their share of national wealth during the
greatest economic calamity in history. Arguably, in terms of spending, the
British chiefs came out of the crisis much better off than their French colleagues. Where the British staffs truly excelled themselves, however, was in
shaping Britain's disarmament policy to suit their needs.

The Royal Navy elevated into an art form the stratagem of persuading
everyone else to disarm to one's own benefit. The air force proved equally
skilled in quashing the idea that the abolition of military aviation should be
British policy, and it succeeded in persuading ministers that bombing, though
it should be outlawed in Europe, be permitted for "police" purposes in remote
places inside the empire. British diplomats even found themselves ready to
argue that, whereas all the other powers should reduce their air forces to 500
front-line machines, the British Empire should be allowed to raise its total to
about 1,400 aircraft.[47]

Now this was exactly the sort of disarmament diplomacy that Maurice
Hankey liked. Ever since 1897 when Hankey joined the Royal Marines, working his way up from the Mediterranean fleet to naval intelligence in London,
and then to the heights of cabinet government during the war, what drove
him was an unwavering faith in Britain's imperial mission. One British Empire, he used to say, was worth a thousand Leagues of Nations. For him, disarmament was a useful device to protect a strategic advantage, but no
guarantor of peace. As secretary to the cabinet and head of its secretariat,
Hankey was the high priest of bureaucratic order at the top of British defense, the man of secrets who made the whole administrative machine tick.[48]

The bane of Hankey's life was the so-called ten-year rule. Back in 1919,
the cabinet decided that defense expenditure should be calculated on the basis
that Britain would not be engaged in a major war for ten years. As every

budget battle since 1925 had shown, Treasury officials had used this rule as a very effective bureaucratic cap on defense expenditure. For British war planners during the first years of the Great Depression, when arms and training budgets were squeezed tight, the phrase "ten-year rule" came to symbolize—all out of proportion with reality—everything that they saw as muddle-headed about defense.

During the 1920s the Royal Navy had trumpeted Japan as a mortal threat to the empire to justify the construction of new warships, and the Royal Air Force had used the French "menace" similarly for aircraft purchases. Although most officials accepted these two enemies as notional ones for planning purposes, the idea that Britain would go to war with either Japan or France seemed far-fetched. Then in September 1931, thanks to Colonel Ishiwara and his fellow Kwantung army conspirators in Manchuria, who had just taken offensive military action to turn Manchuria into a great bastion from which to wage total war against the Soviet Union, Hankey and the chiefs of staff suddenly had a clear and present danger with which to demolish the ten-year rule. During 1932 Hankey used his influence to lobby ministers, to set the agenda as well as the pace of the policy debate—all toward beginning a fresh growth in Britain's armaments.

Hankey's efforts paid off in November 1933, when the cabinet created the Defence Requirements Committee. Made up of the chiefs of staff and top civil servants from the Treasury and the Foreign Office, with Hankey as chairman, the committee's task was to suggest ways to repair the worst gaps in Britain's defenses in the five years to 1939. (Mobilization experts picked 1939 as the target date for the completion of rearmament, which was something of a lucky guess, because they projected that it would take that long to prepare British industry for war.) Unlike in France, where questions of defense spending were tangled up in disarmament politics, the Defence Requirements Committee began to separate talk of rearming from that of disarming. And so, a golden opportunity to shape Britain's defense had arrived, and everyone in Whitehall knew it.

For the Royal Navy the timing seemed promising. The new man at the top and chairman of the chiefs of staff, Admiral Ernle Chatfield, had impressive credentials that included wartime service on the staff of the legendary Admiral David Beatty, and during the 1920s a string of higher-ranking commands and senior Admiralty postings. A skilled political operator, he had the social graces and intellect to get what he wanted, and what he wanted was what every First Sea Lord had wanted since 1919:

an ironclad government commitment to do whatever it took to make certain that Britannia ruled the waves.[49]

Backed by Hankey, Chatfield went to the Defence Requirements Committee to win the argument for the navy. What he and his planners hoped for was an expensive ten-year program of warship building to replace old ships, as well as a much larger fleet. To achieve this, he needed to keep Japan in the forefront of the discussion. To clobber the Japanese, after all, you needed a huge fleet, a global network of naval bases and stocks of fuel and ammunition. Chatfield also needed to make sure that the three chiefs did not fall out among themselves. During Churchill's time at the Treasury, he had exploited the bitter rivalry between the navy and air force to curb naval spending. As chairman of the chiefs of staff, Chatfield did not want to repeat that bureaucratic blunder. He persuaded his colleagues to temper their mutual rivalry and to arrive at the committee with a roughly balanced wish list.

Unluckily for the navy, during the four months that the Defence Requirements Committee deliberated, Germany became a far more frightening threat than faraway Japan. Although the Japanese might strike at British bases in the Far East, run the British out of China and cause panic in Australia and New Zealand, Germany, with its growing air force, might soon be able to deliver a "knockout blow." Months before Hitler took office, Stanley Baldwin grimly told Parliament that "no power on earth" could protect the man on the street from being bombed. The bomber, which would "always get through," robbed Britons of an invulnerability that they had enjoyed since Nelson triumphed at Trafalgar. As German rearmament loomed, the British tabloids shocked their readers with lurid images of German bombers blotting the skies over sprawling London. No government could ignore this public anxiety.[50]

No one in Whitehall disputed that *both* Japan and Germany were first-class threats. Assigning priority, however, to one or the other would have long-term consequences about which of the three armed services would have first call on the nation's resources. So, when the Defence Requirements Committee got down to work during the winter of 1933–34, the debate revolved around priorities. Chatfield and Hankey tried to steer the discussion toward the chiefs of staff's order of priorities: the defense of the Far East (Japan), Europe (Germany) and India (Russia).

About Germany, the chiefs of staff predicted that in five years Berlin would command a sizable army, air force and navy. By then the Germans might try to bully the Poles or Czechs, but they would not be ready to run the risk of a total war. The service chiefs predicted that, over the next five to eight years Britain and France would possess a "clear advantage" over Germany in offensive armaments.[51]

This estimate puzzled the two civilians on the committee, Robert Vansittart of the Foreign Office and Warren Fisher of the Treasury. Why were the chiefs of staff so relaxed about German rearmament? Vansittart, who believed that Germans carried the human race's most dangerous strain of militarism, used his skill for forceful debate to label Germany potential enemy number one. Fisher, who shared Vansittart's low opinion of the Germans and accepted his priorities, suggested that the best way to safeguard the Far East was to rekindle the pre-1914 Anglo-Japanese alliance, even at the cost (or, to Fisher's mind, benefit) of infuriating the Americans. For Vansittart, however, an alliance with Tokyo was not practical politics. Instead, he argued more realistically that Japan would only dare to attack the empire if Britain had suffered defeat in Europe first, and so it made sense to protect Britain from German air attack before anything else.

These were powerful arguments. Chatfield and Hankey did all they could to depict Japan as the more lethal potential threat in the five to eight years it would take Germany to rearm, but to no avail. To make matters much worse, the head of the air force failed to hold up his end of the debate. Air Chief Marshal Edward Ellington was the type of staff officer who stored up ideas, once learned, in a sort of mental kit bag. While this approach worked for some, Ellington had an unfortunate habit of pulling the wrong idea out at the wrong moment, and this made the chiefs of staff appear even less sound on the German threat than Vansittart and Fisher had supposed.

Eventually, Hankey salvaged what he could from this bureaucratic setback with a carefully balanced report. The Defence Requirements Committee identified Germany as Britain's "ultimate potential enemy," but the committee's spending proposals were more or less distributed the way that the three service chiefs had originally laid them out, including measures to strengthen Britain's defenses in the Far East. On the big question of future fleet strength, the Admiralty would have to bide its time.[52]

The navy in fact had no choice. From March to July 1934, as the conclusions of the Defence Requirements Committee worked their way through the cabinet, the rising strength of the Luftwaffe and the "knockout blow" loomed ever larger. On March 8, during a debate in Parliament about the Royal Air Force budget, Baldwin gave voice to these growing anxieties by pledging that if disarmament failed, the government would "see to it that in air strength and air power this country shall no longer be in a position inferior to any country within striking distance of our shores."[53]

Only a few (cynical navy officers mostly) questioned whether the mission of the Luftwaffe would in fact be a knockout blow, or that such a masterstroke was even feasible (which, given the technology of the era, it was not). One reason why the theory stuck was that the British had good intelligence on the expansion of German aircraft factories. The unanswered question was how fast would the Luftwaffe grow? Estimating the future output of a whole industry was a tall order: analysts racked their brains over many factors, including the number of available workers, the number and efficiency of various machine tools, available factory floor space, raw material inputs, finance and the rate of engine production. Estimates varied according to expectations. Inside the British Air Ministry, Ellington and his staff saw no reason to be alarmed just because German workers were busy. You cannot build an air force overnight: so ran the air staff's mantra. The Germans would build their Luftwaffe methodically, training pilots and ground crews, constructing airfields and hangars and stockpiling reserves. "A nation so admittedly thorough as Germany," one air force officer explained, "will not be content with a mere window-dressing collection of aircraft and pilots."[54]

At the Foreign Office, Vansittart was fuming. Why would Germans arm at a leisurely pace? His own forecast that the Luftwaffe would grow at breakneck speed collided with that of the Air Ministry in the summer of 1934, when the French shared reliable intelligence about the German Air Force. According to the French, air minister Hermann Göring aimed to have 500 first-line aircraft in service by October 1935. The French said that the Luftwaffe ultimately intended to triple or even quadruple that number, although they did not know by what date. Ellington told the cabinet that the Luftwaffe would not reach that size before 1945. Vansittart fired off a blistering critique disputing the air staff's prediction and accused them of complacency.[55]

While Vansittart quarreled with the air force staff and the British government struggled with what to do once Germany began to rearm openly, Chamberlain stepped up to impose order on the chaos. To him the cost of modernizing and expanding the navy against Japan, equipping a small expeditionary force for a war in Europe and building an air force against Germany, all in five to eight years, was staggering and might endanger Britain's economic recovery. Choices had to be made between various contingencies; in his mind, Germany was threat number one.

Focusing on Germany simply made good sense. At home, spending large sums on aircraft and air defense could be sold to the British taxpayers. Raising a formidable air force also offered a potent way to send a clear message to Berlin. "Our best defence would be the existence of a deterrent force so powerful as to render success in attack too doubtful to be worthwhile. I submit," Chamberlain wrote, "that this is most likely to be attained by the establishment of an air force based in this country of a size and efficiency calculated to inspire respect in the mind of a possible enemy."

Deterrence based on a home-based air force offered a logical alternative to disarmament; and it entailed no obligation on the French. Here, Chamberlain picked up on the ideas popularized by Basil Liddell Hart, the defense journalist. Liddell Hart and other defense intellectuals saw Britain's break in 1914 with its historic maritime strategy to wage total war on land as a huge blunder. For centuries Britain had relied on blockade, finance, small expeditionary forces and the mass armies of European allies to bring its continental enemies to heel. By sticking to this British Way of War, so ran the argument, the British had only ever waged as much war as was needed to obtain their political and commercial goals, instead of being dragged into costly and futile wars to destroy their foes. By relying on air and sea forces, Chamberlain argued, Britain could deter Germany without entering an all-out arms build-up, and without promising the French to come to their assistance with another mass army.

Turning to the navy, Chamberlain understood why the Admiralty was so eager to turn Japan into adversary number one. He knew that the navy's ultimate goal was more money for more battleships. Everyone could play that game. In his critique of the Defence Requirements Committee's findings, he slightly overstated his case for effect. He had no intention of losing control of arms spending by yielding too much too early. Chamberlain told his cabinet colleagues that they had to face the facts "courageously": a decision about the future size of the navy would have to wait until naval disarmament talks with Washington and Tokyo had concluded.[56]

Now this was exactly the sort of Treasury meddling that the service chiefs hated. In disgust Hankey confided to his diary that Chamberlain was "over-obsessed with the threat from Germany." In the cabinet Chamberlain set out his revisions to the Defence Requirements Committee report. The £76.8 million of extra money to repair deficiencies was reduced to £50.3 million, with a greater share going to the air force. The service ministers protested. Even the air minister complained that the chancellor's funding proposals did not allow for the stockpiling of reserves. Chamberlain, who relished a good debate, made his case and won. The army's share was cut in half; the air force's budget was raised; the navy's share of the deficiency fund was also reduced; and decisions about shipbuilding were postponed.[57]

With the cabinet's approval of the revised proposals of the Defence Requirements Committee, British rearmament began. The first outward sign of change came on July 18, 1934, when a huge majority in Parliament voted for Scheme A, the air force's expansion plan, which would raise its front-line strength up to 836 planes by 1939.

However, in a pattern that was to recur time and again, as soon as the British had decided on a rearmament program, the assumptions and expectations upon which the program was based began to slip. Another secret report from Paris set things in motion. Convincing and largely accurate, this French intelligence placed a huge question mark beside the Royal Air Force's belief that the Germans would be methodical in the build-up of the Luftwaffe. According to French spies, the output of German aviation factories would rise to about 140 planes per month in 1935. And, at that rate, by the end of 1936, the Luftwaffe would have a front-line strength of roughly 1,300 aircraft. At the first favorable moment, the French predicted, Hitler would present his powerful new air arm as an accomplished fact.[58]

On November 28, 1934, the question of what to do about illegal German rearmament was raised in Parliament. Winston Churchill, the Tory rebel who had initiated the debate, gave voice to public fear about a knockout blow and called for a British bomber deterrent force. In reply Baldwin revealed that the German Army had already grown to 300,000 men, and that estimates about the number of military aircraft in Germany varied from 600 to 1,000 machines. There was no need for "panic," he reassured the House of Commons. Certainly, the German Air Force was growing fast, but Scheme A, which had been accelerated a few months earlier, would preserve a margin of nearly fifty percent over Germany until the end of 1936.[59]

Over the next three months more diplomatic and military measures followed. In February 1935 London and Paris issued a joint statement condemning unilateral violations of the Treaty of Versailles. Both the Czechs and the French announced that they would lengthen compulsory military service. Then came the British Defence White Paper of March 4, 1935. It had been issued to educate the public about the need for greater arms spending, which would jump from £113 million in 1934 to £136.9 million in 1935. While Britain had worked tirelessly for peace since 1919, the paper explained, it had run down its armed forces. Now that disarmament was at a "standstill," the time to repair "serious deficiencies" in defense had come.[60]

During the debate in Parliament on the rise in arms spending, some argued that Britain had now contributed to a new arms race. Chamberlain scoffed at this allegation. "If we were not to abandon all idea of defence we were bound to show a big increase in [arms spending] and bound to publish our justification."[61]

When British ministers arrived in Berlin for talks on March 25 and 26, Hitler told them that Germany had reached air force parity with Britain. This lie was frightening enough to be believed—at least for a time. The Führer's bluff set off a storm of accusations and counter-accusations in Whitehall. Vansittart, who renewed his attack on the air force staff, urged a doubling of the size of Scheme A. To embarrass the government into rearming faster, he leaked to the press news of Hitler's claim of parity. In Parliament, Baldwin back-pedaled on his assurances of the previous November. Officials, he shrugged, had misled him. Once the dust settled, Hitler's claim to have reached air force parity with Britain was shown by air force intelligence to be false, but the upward pressure on British rearmament continued to mount.[62]

The chiefs of staff knew a good thing when they saw it. Anxiety about the speed of German rearmament, above all intelligence that Hitler was borrowing immense sums to fund it, gave them a stick with which to beat Chamberlain. During the summer of 1935 the Defence Requirements Committee called for a creative approach to national expenditure to rearm more quickly. Chamberlain had wanted to rearm within the bounds of government revenue, but he too saw that Britain must "hurry" if the Germans were to be deterred. Once Hitler and his generals realized that they could not win an arms race, he calculated, equilibrium would follow. In this way deterrence would act as a safety valve, relieving the pressure to rearm across Europe and making everyone a bit more reasonable. For reason to prevail, Chamberlain would tolerate a deficit. So long as borrowing stayed within sensible limits, the economy would not suffer unduly. And that was exactly the point. Rearmament was a rational act intended to deal with a calculating enemy, not a way of life.[63]

CHAPTER 6

THE MILITARY-INDUSTRIAL COMPLEX

T he United States fascinated the total-war systematizers. No other nation had been furnished with so many of the prerequisites of overwhelming military potential. The minds of Japanese total-war officers like Ishiwara Kanji boggled at the sheer scale of the United States. Over 120 million people, twice the number of Japanese, distributed over a landmass of three million square miles, twenty times that of Japan's. And, unlike Japan and its puny colonial empire, the United States and Central and South America, over which the United States exercised economic and political predominance, enjoyed superabundance in foodstuffs and raw materials.[1]

The Soviet Union was also a continent-spanning great power rich in people and natural resources, but as Red Army war planners like Mikhail Tukhachevsky knew, nothing could compare with the gargantuan size and potential armaments output of the U.S. economy. By the end of the First World War, with the growth of giant U.S. corporations such as U.S. Steel, Ford, General Motors, Firestone, Westinghouse and DuPont, Americans made half of the world's manufactured goods. During the 1920s, as greater numbers of American farmers cultivated their fields with motorized tractors and American workers operated electric machine tools inside the world's most disciplined factories, U.S. productivity continued to climb.[2]

When General Werner von Blomberg was a guest of the U.S. Army in the autumn of 1930, he marveled at America's supercharged machine-driven economy, with its abundance of cars, radios, refrigerators and other affordable consumer appliances. What if this energy was applied to arms manufacture? he wondered. The U.S. Army was small, not much larger than his own disarmed service, but its capacity for growth struck Hitler's future war minister as tremendous. Military experts agreed that the United States did not need a large conscript army, and they approvingly quoted what President Calvin Coolidge had said in November 1928: "The present size of our army is fully adequate . . . but we must continue to complete it through the National Guard and the reserves and especially through the organization of our industries to supply them with arms." In armaments, as Georg Thomas would have put it, the United States possessed vast potential depth and did not need much breadth to be safe. With Canada to the north and Mexico to the south, and bounded by huge, ocean-sized moats east and west, Americans lived under no immediate armed threat from any direction. The U.S. Navy was formidable enough to repulse a transoceanic invasion—just in case anyone suddenly went mad enough to try to improvise one—and U.S. airmen boasted that their bombers could destroy any attackers without the heavy guns of the navy's battleships. And even if a foreign power tried to amass the titanic air-sea armadas that would be needed to invade North America, the Americans would have ample warning and time to build up the defenses of their supremely autarkic and enviably secure continental fortress.[3]

The question that soldiers abroad every so often pondered was how long it would take the United States to mobilize and to project large military forces into Europe or Asia. Back in 1917–18, U.S. arms growth had been brief but spectacular. In nineteen months four million men put on uniforms and nearly half of them set foot in France. With remarkable speed U.S. industry equipped them with most of their stores except, crucially, artillery, tanks and aircraft. British and French arms factories made up for this shortfall. Still, the Americans geared up fast. In July 1917 President Woodrow Wilson set up the War Industries Board to organize arms production. When the overloaded U.S. economy fell into disarray in the winter of 1917–18, he appointed the financial wizard Bernard Baruch as "arms czar" to impose order on the industrial effort. With time U.S. arms output would have dwarfed that of any other nation.[4]

In the decade that followed, military experts the world over assumed that the Americans had learned the lessons of 1914–18. As evidence they pointed to the National Defense Act of June 1920, which gave the assistant secretary of war the task of overseeing the preparation of industrial mobilization plans. A stream of War Department publications, congressional reports, war memoirs and academic studies impressed foreign observers with the significance of this work. In admiration, Soviet war planners dubbed the rational practice of setting up dual-purpose civilian-military factories the American style of industrial mobilization preparation.[5]

When the 1930 industrial mobilization plan was issued, most foreign experts approved. It proposed four super-agencies to oversee industry, conscription, labor and propaganda, all under the president's control. American war planners clearly did understand that victory in total war required the greatest possible concentration of all political, military and economic forces in the hands of one ultimate agent.[6]

THE AMERICAN MILITARY had clearly learned from the First World War. "A modern war is a war of nations rather than of armies," declared the army chief of staff, "because it involves a mobilization of the entire resources of these nations." In 1919 it seemed unlikely that there would be another total war anytime soon in Europe much less on American soil, where Bolshevism and subversion allegedly appeared a more immediate threat, but army planners still tried to imagine wars to come. Like their colleagues the world over, they saw international affairs as an eternal Darwinian struggle for survival. To prepare for another total war, the army staff asked for a standing force of half a million men and conscription to build up a deep reserve of disciplined men. Not surprising for a nation that had always distrusted a standing army as a possible tool of authoritarian repression, Congress rejected peacetime compulsory military service. It was too reminiscent of the sort of Prussian militarism the nation had just expended blood and treasure to destroy. Instead, the National Defense Act of 1920 capped the peacetime strength of the army at 280,000 and the National Guard at 500,000, both of which would form the basis of a wartime army of three million men. Much to the relief of the top brass, the act gave the regular army authority to organize and train the National Guard, which until then had come under the slapdash supervision of state officials.[7]

Although foreigners envied the security that Americans enjoyed and considered a skeletal army as a logical result of that blessing, over time, U.S. Army officers found much to gripe about. For one thing, the size of the army never reached its authorized levels. The strength of the regular army hovered at 120,000 men, while the National Guard and other reserves added up to only about 200,000. American attitudes toward the wider world discouraged lavish investment in the army. Like every other great power touched by the world war, Americans wanted "maximum security with a minimum commitment," said Secretary of State Charles Evans Hughes. Though fervently against U.S. membership in the League of Nations, presidents Warren Harding and Calvin Coolidge championed disarmament and legal norms against war. By promoting a peaceful world community, so ran their reasoning, the United States could keep the federal budget and taxes low and enrich the world through free trade rather than police it with armed forces.[8]

Republican foreign policy matched the nation's mood. Most Americans saw their entry into the First World War as a cosmic catastrophe. Some thought that crooked Europeans had hoodwinked them into it. Others believed that greedy financiers and industrialists had arranged it in order to earn obscene profits from the orgy of arms spending. The groundswell of regret over the war and the aversion to anything that smacked of militarism reinforced a sense of isolation in the army.[9]

During the early postwar years, the fear of communist insurrection and current training and procurement needs took priority over grand plans for industrial mobilization. This forlorn planning chore fell to a group of officers assigned to the assistant secretary of war. Much of this work was purely mechanical. The planners calculated wartime requirements, mapped the nation's industrial plant and then contacted potential suppliers to draw up realistic production timetables. Yet, taken as a whole, this Industrial Mobilization (or M-Day) Plan was nothing less than a blueprint for converting the United States into a gigantic war machine governed by mushrooming bureaucracies armed with extra-legal powers over life and property. Astonishingly, the wider apparatus of the federal government took little notice of this politically explosive activity. That suited the army chief of staff, General Charles Summerall, who utterly opposed civilian officials meddling in procurement plans. But the soldiers could not do the job alone. They needed the know-how and above all the cooperation of industrialists.[10]

Like most Americans, the captains of industry saw 1917–18 as a mistake. War had pushed up taxes, stoked inflation, distorted markets and created a new vocabulary and rationale for the "regimentation" of industry. Businessmen who had served as army procurement officers recalled the war in a patriotic haze, but most did not want to relive the harrowing experience of watching "big government" armed with special powers improvise a war economy. Memories of what President Wilson's conservative foes condemned as his "war socialism" remained vivid. The government had commandeered private plants, nationalized the railways and, most notoriously of all, seized a telegraph firm when its president refused to allow his employees to unionize. "This is a crisis," a War Industries Board official told the steel magnates, in language that had and would become common in other places and other times, "and commercialism, gentlemen, must be absolutely sidetracked." After the war, the attack on business continued. The American Legion, trade unions and polit-

ical campaigners ranging across the left-right divide demanded a law grant-
ing the president the power to enact a universal service or total conscription
of men and wealth. Why should some fight and die abroad, they argued on
Capitol Hill, while others sat at home and turned a profit or earned more for
their labor? The burden of waging total war had to be spread evenly by the
state. Not surprisingly then, when the army approached business for help with
planning, the corporate chiefs snapped to attention.[11]

Always leery about what the soldiers might do in a real crisis, business leaders sought to shape a future mobilization to their way of thinking by working
with the army. Thousands of executives and trade association leaders signed up
as reserve officers to offer their expertise. After the army founded the Army
Industrial College in 1924 to train its own economic mobilizers, businessmen,
especially the heads of the big corporations, eagerly lectured to the army's
bright-eyed planners about running a successful enterprise. The upshot of all
this military-industrial collegiality was a convergence of views about how—
with the minimum of government interference—to make a war economy work
with market forces and, above all, managerial autonomy. Most total-war
theorists agreed that the control of the market was essential to victory, but
American soldiers embraced a decidedly profit-driven model of industrial mobilization that owed more to Adam Smith, the eighteenth-century founding
father of free-market economics, than to General Ludendorff. The soldiers
also rejected expanding existing branches of the federal government to administer a war economy. Businessmen feared that any wartime expansion of
the government would become irreversible once peace returned, and that this
leviathan of coercive economic management might fall into the hands of radicals. Better to erect temporary, civilian-led super-agencies staffed by patriotic
businessmen and army planners than run that horrific risk.[12]

Of course, not all the soldiers and industrial tycoons agreed. Some dissenters
made their views well known. Among the most vocal was Bernard Baruch, a
regular speaker at the elite Army War College and the Army Industrial College. The son of an émigré Jewish doctor, during the 1890s he had climbed his
way up from being office boy in a brokerage firm to wealthy Wall Street investor.
President Wilson propelled him to national fame when he made him head of the
War Industries Board. After his brief and successful stint as arms czar, during the
1920s he became a unique sort of American total mobilization evangelist.

For Baruch war was an unavoidable evil rooted in economic progress. Since
the nineteenth century, individual enterprises had grown into large corporations to exploit new production technologies and economies of scale. Now
the corporations were growing into even larger national cartels. Government

needed to grow in size and power, to control this potentially tyrannical concentration of economic power, otherwise the living standards and freedoms
of ordinary Americans would suffer. To ensure prosperity at home the leaders of nearly every industrial nation, Baruch argued, would also have to vie and
at times fight over the world's resources. The United States needed to be
ready. In 1919 Baruch had pleaded to retain an embryonic, peacetime War Industries Board. Leaving mobilization plans to the army, he feared, would result in military dictatorship. A civilian-led body dedicated to war plans would
ensure democracy. In a future war, this "super-agency" would manage industry, control wages and prices, and conscript men and wealth. Ultimately,
Baruch saw this radical application of state power in wartime as essential to
save free-market capitalism from socialism. What made socialism attractive
was its promise to end great booms and busts. Even the mighty U.S. economy
had suffered a severe slump in 1920–21 caused by wartime overproduction,
trade dislocation and pent-up inflation. Washington thus needed a control
mechanism to gear up the economy for total war and then to gear it down to
free-market conditions once peace returned.[13]

Baruch's teaching made few full converts in the army and industry, and it
ran contrary to the thinking of the president-elect of 1929, Herbert Hoover.
Like Baruch, Hoover became famous during the war, first as head of the relief commission for Belgium and then as food administrator in Wilson's administration. Born in 1874 into a humble Quaker family, Hoover, again like
Baruch, was a modern self-made man of considerable wealth. Trained at Stanford University as a geologist, he developed new techniques to mine gold in
Australia and coal in China. During the 1920s he served both Harding and
Coolidge in the powerful post of commerce secretary.

Unlike Harding and Coolidge, Hoover was not a dogmatic free marketeer. Although an anti-statist by instinct, he believed in government as expe-
diter rather than in no state at all. In his vision of a modern America, the
federal government had a duty to shield working people from the excesses of
laissez-faire capitalism, but not by meddling in the economy with coercive
laws and intrusive bureaucracies. Instead, the government's role was to spur
business into self-regulation through private trade associations. Out of enlightened self-interest, chummy chief executives voluntarily clubbing together
would stabilize the free market by rationalizing production. They would also
create mass demand for their mass output by paying good wages and promote social peace by offering their employees humane work conditions.[14]

As commerce secretary, Hoover took some interest in the War Department's mobilization planning. He found all the divisive talk in the press and

on Capitol Hill about wartime dictatorship and socialism repugnant. Once in the White House, the new president sent his loyal minion Patrick Jay Hurley to the War Department to dispel such talk by completing a full-fledged M-Day Plan. Under Hurley, the army deputy chief of staff, General George Van Horn Moseley, an arch-centralizer, and his eager assistant, Major Dwight D. Eisenhower, tackled the problem of how to turn a peacetime democracy with a free-market economy into a gigantic centrally controlled war machine geared up to make the most efficient use of the nation's resources.

Moseley's first-draft scheme caused a stir because it ceded too much power to the military. Through successive refinements, Eisenhower struck a more acceptable balance couched in the reassuring tones of President Hoover's voluntaristic managerialism that seemed—*on paper* anyway—to work.[15]

In private, Eisenhower took a stiffer line. His friend Bernard Baruch believed that he had completely grasped his case for an all-powerful super-agency to run a war economy, though they differed about the suspension of the free market in war. While he worked on the 1930 M-Day Plan, Eisenhower's fellow officers, some of whom opposed wartime super-agencies, nicknamed him Dictator Ike because he suggested that Hoover should exercise a "virtual dictatorship" to combat the Depression. When Congress set up a commission in 1931 to study ways of equalizing the burdens of war, critics of military economic planning argued that military men and industrialists were creating Frankenstein's monster. On paper the M-Day Plan looked prudent enough, but when energized in the high-voltage hysteria of a national emergency, the aroused military-industrial behemoth could wreak havoc with the nation's liberties.[16]

Three decades later, after he had led victorious armies into Nazi Germany and served in the White House as the Cold War mounted, Eisenhower reflected on his career, often at the nexus of the state, the economy and the army. Now he realized that back in the 1930s he had eyed the sleeping monster up close. In January 1961, in his last presidential address, the great soldier-statesman warned that the East-West arms race had given rise in America to a "permanent arms industry of vast proportions" and "an immense military establishment" that now worked in "conjunction" with "grave implications." "We must guard against the acquisition of unwarranted influence," he said, "whether sought or unsought, by the military-industrial complex. The potential for the disastrous rise of misplaced power exists and will persist."[17]

IN 1932, THE CONTROVERSY over the M-Day Plan briefly hit the headlines, but with the U.S. economy falling into unprecedented depths and free-market

capitalism itself in danger of global extinction, few devoted much attention
to industrial war planning. At first, the slump heralded by the Wall Street
crash looked like an economic glitch, but the magnitude of the devastation
soon became clear. As markets and prices collapsed and business investment
dried up, factories cut back their output or closed down. By 1933 unemployment reached nearly twelve million, a quarter of the workforce. Half the
workers in chemicals, steel and machine industries, for example, lost their
livelihoods. With bank failures accelerating, the entire financial system
teetered on the brink. Hunger and fear swept a dispirited nation. Shanty-
towns sprung up in empty urban spaces as the homeless sought refuge. Farm
foreclosures blighted the countryside. Some wondered whether the United
States was ripe for revolution.

Against the downward spiral, Hoover exercised his doctrine of the cheerleader state. But his idea of enlightened corporate managers working in unison
to safeguard economic growth flopped. As the crisis took hold, he met with
employers to urge them not to cut wages but to maintain demand; he asked
state and municipal authorities to contract building work to stimulate the economy. But employers cut wages, hours and jobs; with tax revenues shrinking,
local officials found they had little for job creation. To make matters worse,
Congress voted to raise tariff barriers against imports. As many predicted,
American exports suffered when trading partners retaliated. In a futile effort to
shore up the financial system and raise business confidence, Hoover slashed
federal spending, raised taxes and clung doggedly to the gold standard.

During 1932, an election year, no relief was in sight. Dour and stiff-
collared, Hoover appeared indifferent to the misery. Much too late to help him
politically, he took direct action to stimulate a recovery and help the needy. In
1924 Congress mandated that each World War I veteran should receive a war
service bonus redeemable in 1945. During the summer of 1932, thousands of
jobless veterans and their families came to Washington to demand payment
now, but the Senate refused. Several thousand of the disappointed veterans
settled in makeshift shelters in sight of the Capitol. Smelling a communist-
pacifist coup in the making, the army's new chief of staff, General Douglas
MacArthur, exceeded his order to disperse the so-called Bonus Army with enthusiasm and bloody results. He ordered the gassing of the demonstrators and
burning of their shelters. Several veterans died in the attack. The politically
tone-deaf Hoover got the blame and lost the election in a landslide to the
Democratic governor of New York, Franklin Delano Roosevelt.[18]

In March 1933 Roosevelt took the oath of office. In his inaugural address,
he told his fellow citizens they had "nothing to fear but fear itself." Then he

began to transform the presidency. Roosevelt was a New York blue blood with an Ivy League education and an abiding sense of Christian duty that in someone less charismatic and manically optimistic might have seemed condescending. His goal had always been the White House. He had served during the war as assistant secretary of the navy, and in 1920 the Democrats selected him as their vice presidential candidate. During the next twelve years of Republican ascendancy, and despite a devastating bout of poliomyelitis that paralyzed his legs for life, he fought hard in New York State politics to keep his career going. The steel braces that held up his legs in fact had a metaphorical quality to them: he faced every trial with the utmost confidence, calm and a metallic will.

Roosevelt did not enter the White House with a master plan, only with the vague notion that there needed to be one. The New Deal, he called it. Like Baruch, he feared that if left unchecked, corporate America would in time regiment everyone to serve capitalism. Through the democratic process, the federal government was the only legitimate embodiment of the nation as a whole. The government could not wait and hope that market forces would create a stable and fair society. It had to safeguard individuals, communities and democracy itself from the potentially tyrannical accretion of economic power by boardroom plutocrats.[19]

For Roosevelt the slump was not only a crisis to be met but also a chance to effect sweeping political change. His greatest obstacle, however, was the political system itself. The original thirteen colonies that had formed the United States did so in a rebellion against a tyrannical English monarch. So the leaders of the rebellion rigged their 1790 Constitution to prevent the presidency from becoming an oppressive central authority. State and municipal authorities were responsible for public services, and the president was locked into an unending struggle with legislators, who controlled the purse strings, and an independent judiciary. The only eventuality the founders foresaw that would legitimately require the president, as commander in chief, to tilt the balance of political power in his favor was war.

That war strengthened the president's power was not lost on anyone. Even the knee-jerk anti-statist Hoover had likened the ravages of the Depression to that of a war. Roosevelt did the same thing with far greater dynamism to pave the way for a huge expansion of the federal government and a lengthening of its reach into national life. "I shall ask the Congress for the one remaining instrument to meet the crisis," he said in his inaugural address, "broad Executive power to wage a war against the emergency, as great as the power that would be given to me if we were in fact invaded by a foreign foe."

Indeed, the First World War was the New Deal's intellectual inspiration. After President Wilson's administration had built a big bureaucratic apparatus to manage the war economy, a whole generation of liberal American planomaniacs wondered why the experiment in central planning could not be replicated to impose "super-management" on the nation's "industrial anarchy" in peacetime. Forward thinkers of this type gravitated into Roosevelt's inner circle, his brain trust of Columbia University advisers. What these tweedy apostles of big government shared with him was a conviction that the Depression had shown that the free market was not self-correcting and that the moment had come for government action.[20]

As events unfolded, however, the New Deal was not as coherent as the brain trusters imagined. Much to their annoyance, Roosevelt absorbed their advice but shared little of his thinking with them. All high ideas one minute, the next he could be ruthlessly pragmatic—even adopting some of Hoover's initiatives as his own. Always open to advice from differing perspectives, Roosevelt preferred to improvise a program by taking a good idea from one source and then slapping it together with a suggestion from someone else. In London the chancellor of the exchequer, Neville Chamberlain, dismissed Roosevelt as a snake-oil salesman, while France's Socialist leader, Léon Blum, studied the New Deal to discover the elixir of economic life. When asked what his political philosophy was, Roosevelt replied that what worked, worked. He might have added, what worked, worked, so long as he ran the show.

To exploit his firm Democratic majorities in the House of Representatives and the Senate, and the mobilizing sense of urgency that he and others encouraged with a metaphorical state of war, the White House unleashed a torrent of legislation and bold initiatives. In his first hundred days, Roosevelt rescued the banking system by invoking the wartime Trading with the Enemy Act to declare a bank holiday and allow the government to control currency and gold flows. The Emergency Banking Act that followed allowed the banks to reopen under state supervision.

In quick time followed federal spending cuts to balance the budget, an end to bans on alcohol sales and legislation to control the market for agricultural goods. A Federal Emergency Relief Administration sprang up to administer unemployment assistance. The Civilian Conservation Corps mobilized millions of idle youths to work in the nation's parks. The new Public Works Administration with a $3.3 billion budget created jobs through state spending. After that came the Tennessee Valley Authority: a huge regional development plan across seven southern states. The National Industrial Recovery Act set maximum work hours and minimum pay rates and crucially guaranteed the right of labor to unionize. The administration introduced the National Recovery Administration to plan, regulate and rationalize industrial output by setting prices and sponsoring industrial compacts to prevent overproduction. Over the next three years the flood of legislation and spending continued, with laws to regulate bankers and stock traders, to offer mortgage relief and to establish a groundbreaking new system of social security.[21]

Most of the New Deal super-agencies had 1917–18 precedents. The Tennessee Valley Authority, for example, revived a wartime investment in a new state-owned nitrate factory and hydroelectric project. The National Recovery Administration was a descendent of the War Industries Board, an ancestry that was not lost on corporate executives. As its head, Roosevelt appointed a fifty-one-year-old soldier turned entrepreneur, General Hugh S. Johnson. During the war he had served as one of Baruch's industrial mobilizers and ever after revered the speculator as the fount of all economic truth. As head of the National Recovery Administration, Johnson set out to tame the free market, end the cycle of boom and bust, raise living standards and improve labor practices. His super-agency offered business leaders a deal: to ride out the slump, they would be allowed to set prices and form cartels; in exchange they would have to agree to draft and adhere to national codes of fair practice on minimum wages and employment conditions. Businesses compliant with a code would be allowed to display a Blue Eagle insignia to let consumers know that they were doing their bit for the emergency economic effort and so deserved their dollars. To supervise the drafting of the codes, a huge bureaucratic hydra of thousands sprang up, which became the prime target for conservative vilification.[22]

The explosion of federal government services astounded ordinary Americans. Until the New Deal they had only ever come into contact with the federal government when they visited the post office or joined the army or navy. Social scientists tried to classify Roosevelt's revolution. Was it a corporatist experiment akin to Mussolini's Fascism? The Civilian Conservation Corps of 1933 bore an uncanny resemblance to Hitler's Labor Service of 1934. Roosevelt's innovative use of the radio to beam his message into living rooms and Johnson's ubiquitous Blue Eagles smacked of the totalitarian regimes in Europe. Hoover accused the New Dealers of harboring aspirations similar to those of "Socialism, Communism, Fascism, Nazism and National Regimentation. . . . All have in common the idea of the servitude of the individual to the state, and the denial of liberties unassailable by the state."[23]

Most businessmen took Hoover's line. Although the National Recovery Administration permitted cartelization, something that industry badly needed, and business interests prevailed in the writing of the codes of practice, what bothered industrialists was the pro-labor legislation enacted under the New Deal. During 1917–18 the labor movement had made great strides, but during the 1920s union membership sank and employers reasserted their domination of the workplace: that meant grueling forty-eight-hour weeks, no job security and few benefits. Some progressive chief executives accepted that they had to bargain with a fast-expanding labor union movement and accepted joint state-industry economic management as the central fact of modern life; but arch-reactionaries such as the Du Pont family railed against such state intervention. The Du Ponts and others funded the American Liberty League, a right-wing, pro-business lobby that denounced the New Deal as a communist plot. Roosevelt was no closet socialist bent on state ownership of industry; he just wanted a fair deal for workers. Yet he and his advisers raised the specter of state coercion if industrial leaders failed to yield to social reform, and business leaders resisted him in the courts and funded his political opponents. Neither side could afford an all-out fight: Roosevelt knew that a forced entry into the boardrooms might cause a collapse of the fragile economy; the corporations knew that the federal government could barge into the boardrooms, especially under an even more radical administration.

Eventually, as the decade wore on, the New Dealers and businessmen settled into a tense routine of give and take. But certain implacable foes like the Du Ponts always remained in Roosevelt's sights. The giant chemical producer was a major munitions maker and exporter. When in 1934 the progressive Republican Senator Gerald Nye wanted a special inquiry into the activities of the arms manufacturers, Roosevelt encouraged him because such an investigation was a shot across the bow of his foes in banking and industry. Nye held that arms exporters sparked wars to yield profits, and he grilled witnesses to confirm it. However, the Senate inquiry, which had independent investigative powers, took on a life of its own in isolationist America. When the president needed New Deal money to buy warships and spend it on the army air corps to create jobs, he did not want Nye interfering. So he set up a new inquiry under Baruch and Johnson to study the profits of arms making, with no intention of hearing from them. He politely ignored Nye's findings when they were presented to him in June 1935.[24]

The arms inquiry made Roosevelt no friends in the army, especially once Nye began to probe industry's role in the making of the industrial mobilization plan. The deep cuts Roosevelt had imposed on federal spending to balance the budget had also aggravated the army's manpower problems. In 1933 the infuriated chief of the army staff, General Douglas MacArthur, told the president that when America lost the next war he wanted "an American boy, lying in the mud with an enemy bayonet through his belly and an enemy foot on his dying throat" to curse the name "Roosevelt." Apoplectic, the president reprimanded his most senior soldier, whom a year before, he had called one of the most dangerous men in America. MacArthur apologized, but relations remained uneasy.[25]

Roosevelt would later regret that the lurid headlines generated by Nye's inquiry into the "merchants of death" bolstered isolationism. An admirer of Woodrow Wilson, Roosevelt always believed that Americans had a special reforming mission in world affairs. Yet, unlike his mentor, who never grasped the value of the tactical compromise, Roosevelt trimmed his sails to the prevailing wind. When he ran for the Democratic nomination in 1932, he denied that he aspired to take the United States into the League of Nations. When he became president, he appointed the sixty-two-year-old Tennessee Senator Cordell Hull as his secretary of state. Hull believed that trade was the greatest civilizing force in world history and the trend toward autarky—what he called "economic armament"—the supreme threat to world peace. Roosevelt knew that a man who spoke of world trade and good neighbors was unlikely to provoke an isolationist backlash against his administration.[26]

Such a backlash had the potential to wreck Roosevelt's presidency. To sustain the momentum behind the New Deal and create a bipartisan reforming coalition, he needed the backing of liberal Democrats and progressive Republicans. Among the progressive Republican senators stood many arch-isolationists, including Nye and William Borah, the influential former chair of the Senate Foreign Relations Committee. Unlike the president's foes in industry, these men could block the New Deal altogether if he openly challenged them. This left him little room for action abroad. So Roosevelt donned the mantle of global cheerleader for peace and disarmament. In 1933–34 he pushed forward formal American recognition of the Soviet Union in order to bring Moscow into play on the side of peace and economic stability. Also during those years, with a naïveté that made State Department officials cringe, the president implored Europeans to scrap all their offensive weapons as a solution to the Franco-German crisis. In early 1935, as a trial balloon, Roosevelt proposed that the United States join the World Court, but the isolationists shot that down. In August that year, the president acquiesced to the first of Congress's Neutrality Acts, a series of laws that prohibited U.S. banks from lending to war-debt defaulters and belligerents, banned U.S. industry from selling and shipping belligerents arms and forbade U.S. citizens from sailing in the ships of warring nations—all the alleged entanglements that had dragged the United States into the First World War.[27]

At any rate, with the nation paralyzed by the Depression, Roosevelt had no choice but to put a domestic recovery before anything else. Convinced that the origins of the Depression lay in the inner workings of the U.S. economy, not the global one, he decided that the only way out was through inflation. That was the underlying logic of the New Deal. Inflation would shrink debts, boost asset and commodity values (especially for farm goods) and liquefy the credit system. While the dollar remained fixed to the gold standard, though, inflation was impossible, and so, in June 1933 Roosevelt floated the dollar. A month later he sent his notorious "bombshell" message to the World Economic Conference in London, flatly rejecting currency stabilization.[28]

And so international cooperation to fight the Depression came to an unhappy end. The other great international project, disarmament, would soon follow. Roosevelt regarded "an insane rush to further armaments in Continental Europe . . . infinitely more dangerous than any number of squabbles over gold or stabilization of tariffs." When a reporter asked him about the French demand for continuous inspection of German disarmament before agreeing to disarm too, Roosevelt said that it made good sense: "I would not disarm unless I had assurance that the other fellow is going to disarm."[29]

He would soon discover the terrible truth of that logic.

CHAPTER 7

THE NAVAL ARMS
RACES BEGIN

S ir John Simon's face flushed with anger. Britain's foreign secretary had just listened to the opening statement of Hitler's envoy, Joachim von Ribbentrop, translated by the German interpreter. Weeks earlier Britain had invited a German delegation to London for naval disarmament talks. This first meeting on June 4, 1935, was meant to be only a businesslike exchange of views. But Ribbentrop arrived at the Foreign Office with a demand. Either Britain recognize as a precondition to further talks Germany's right to build a fleet thirty-five percent the size of the Royal Navy or he would fly home to Berlin. Simon, a skilled lawyer and negotiator, was furious. "It is not usual to make such conditions at the very beginning of negotiations," he said.

While translating Ribbentrop's words, Paul Schmidt, the interpreter from the German Foreign Ministry and a veteran of many international meetings, wondered what the weather would be like on the flight home. How could this Nazi buffoon be so crass? Schmidt asked himself. Ribbentrop's take-it-or-leave-it tactic would surely backfire. Yet Schmidt and his colleagues did not leave immediately. For two days Robert Craigie, the Foreign Office's expert on naval armaments limitation, asked the Germans for clarifications. Then, in the paneled Board Room of the Admiralty building, where many momentous decisions in the history of the Royal Navy had been made, diplomats and naval officers from the two nations assembled. To Schmidt's amazement, Simon agreed to Ribbentrop's precondition. So long as agreement could be reached on all the issues surrounding naval disarmament, the foreign secretary stipulated, Britain would accept the thirty-five percent tonnage ratio between the two fleets.

Over the next two weeks, the two sides concluded a naval agreement. While working out what thirty-five percent would mean in practice, the Germans agreed to divide up their total tonnage proportionally into each category of warship. So Germany would build up to thirty-five percent of Britain's tonnage in battleships, aircraft carriers, cruisers and so on. The only exemption was submarines. The Germans could in principle build a submarine fleet as large as Britain's, but in practice they agreed to launch less than half that number. The Germans also agreed to limit the weight and gun caliber of their future ships according to whatever standards were set at the upcoming naval disarmament conference. Throughout the talks, Ribbentrop emphasized that Hitler attached great political significance to the thirty-five percent ratio. Even the warship building of third parties, France and the Soviet Union, would not disturb the balance between London and Berlin, except by mutual consent. When asked how long Germany would observe the ratio, Ribbentrop replied with absurd solemnity, "Forever." Craigie, who had seven years in mind, shrugged his shoulders in acknowledgment.[1]

Ribbentrop's success in London surprised everyone, most of all Germany's foreign minister, Konstantin von Neurath, who had hoped that a botched job would discredit Hitler's roving ambassador. The French were furious: the naval agreement endorsed a violation of the Treaty of Versailles. Vansittart and other British diplomats thought so, too, but they also thought that the naval deal was worth making.

Admiral Chatfield did not care what the French (or anyone else) thought. Like so many other officials in London, he held France responsible for wrecking the Geneva disarmament conference. Naval disarmament would not be their next victim. Not that Chatfield put very much store in disarmament as the secret to everlasting peace. For him, naval arms control served only one practical purpose: persuading foreigners to build their fleets, if build a fleet they must, in a way that the Royal Navy found convenient.

Before he became First Sea Lord, Chatfield's schooling in the possibilities and pitfalls of arms races and naval diplomacy had been thorough. At age thirteen, in 1886, he followed his father's career by serving on the cadet training ship *Britannia*. By 1900 he qualified as gunnery expert, just when the pace of technical change was about to increase with the arrival of powerful steam turbines, face-hardened alloy steel armor plate and all-big-gun weapons and long-range fire-control systems. In the decade before 1914, Chatfield witnessed the great naval race between Britain and Germany, when Admiral "Jackie" Fisher and his successors blunted the challenge from Admiral Alfred von Tirpitz with a burst of battleship building and technical innovation. This contest between the shipbuilding industries and treasuries of Britain and Germany pushed the boundaries of industrial and scientific achievement. Battleships grew from 16,000-ton vessels bristling with a mix of guns to 30,000-ton ships carrying uniform main batteries of fifteen-inch guns. Under Fisher, the Royal Navy also pioneered the battlecruiser, which carried battleship-size guns but sacrificed armor protection for greater speed. During the war Chatfield took part in the major engagements against the German fleet in the North Sea as flag captain of the battlecruiser squadron.[2]

After Germany's defeat, Chatfield was appointed to the Board of Admiralty. At that time a naval arms race against the United States loomed. In 1916 the United States had begun a warship-building program that would give its admirals a fleet "second to none." The British were not in a hurry to surrender their hard-won naval ascendancy to an upstart. At the Paris Peace Conference, efforts to work out the postwar balance between the two English-speaking navies got nowhere. The Americans insisted on continuing with the 1916 program. Admiralty planners discussed ways to stop it. Some fantasized about a preventive war; others spoke about incorporating the captured German fleet into the Royal Navy. Yet no one really wanted a trans-Atlantic war, or even an Anglo-American naval arms race. After all, with its vast industrial economy and enormous wealth, the Americans could outstrip all comers.

By the spring of 1921 the British faced a tough choice. If the United States finished the 1916 program and Britain did not respond, the naval war planners feared, it would be "practically impossible to catch up" with the Americans. So the Royal Navy began work on four super-battlecruisers. Displacing 50,000 tons and carrying sixteen-inch guns, they would outclass everything afloat or being built. It looked like an all-out naval race was on. Yet the U.S. Congress and American voters were in no mood to spend millions of dollars on battleships—unless of course they were provoked. And so to halt the naval spiral, the United States invited the naval powers to Washington for a conference in November 1921. In his welcoming address, much to the dismay of American admirals, the new secretary of state, Charles Evans Hughes, proposed to scrap much of the world's navies and most of the newly laid-down ships too. British admirals did not want to give up their monster battlecruisers or concede equality in battleship tonnage to the Americans (something Hughes asked for later), but they did not want their American counterparts to build a fleet "second to none" either. A choice had to be made. They made a sensible one. The British delegation cooperated with the American political leadership enough to ensure that the American politicians could ignore the howls of protest from the U.S. Navy.[3]

On Hughes's suggestion the United States, Britain and Japan agreed on a ratio in battleship and aircraft-carrier tonnage of 5:5:3, respectively. With a few exceptions permitted to even out the quality of battleships between the fleets, they imposed a ten-year halt on battleship building. The naval delegations also agreed to standard features for each category of ship: the uppermost size for battleships was 35,000 tons, and armed with guns of no greater caliber than sixteen inches; the maximum size for cruisers was 10,000 tons, armed with guns no larger than eight inches; the maximum size for aircraft carriers was 27,000 tons; and so on down to small ships such as destroyers and submarines.

Chatfield's presence at the Washington conference as Britain's top technical adviser was fitting. So much of what was enshrined in the 1922 Washington Naval Treaty would shape the rest of his career. The treaty in fact made the future fairly predictable. After 1931, battleship building would begin again, to replace all the world's obsolete vessels in line with the Washington ratios. In the meantime rivalry switched to other classes of ship. In the four years after the treaty, the Royal Navy did very well, building nearly as much new warship tonnage as the Japanese and the U.S. navies combined. In 1925, at the peak of this burst of modernization, Chatfield took charge of shipbuilding and industrial planning. In his mind one task stood out above the rest of his managerial work: husbanding enough industrial capacity to rebuild Britain's battleships in the coming decade. Before 1914 Britain's private warship industry had grown fat on a glut of Admiralty orders for big ships carrying complex gun systems. In the 1920s, apart from the building of two 35,000-ton/sixteen-inch-gun ships permitted to Britain to compensate for similar ships in the American and Japanese fleets, Britain's private warship makers would have to survive (and maintain surplus plant) on a lean diet of orders for small vessels and state subsidies. Since no one anticipated that the worst economic slump in world history was just around the corner, this exercise in industrial management seemed like a challenge but by no means impossible.

What worried Chatfield was a trend that he became aware of in 1926. The price per ton of warships was skyrocketing. With many competing demands on the public purse, he asked his colleagues, would future governments spend taxpayers' money on battleships? There were good reasons to think they would not. The cost aside, the battleship had an image problem. During the First World War, while thousands of men perished each week in the trenches, the big ships had done seemingly little. Some of these expensive titans fell victim to mines, torpedoes and submarines. Why not instead just buy lots of these small, cheap weapons? After the American General Billy Mitchell sank a captured German battleship in 1921 with bombers, big-ship admirals the world over performed intellectual acrobatics to explain how the next generation of high-tech battleships could withstand attacks by air-dropped bombs and torpedoes.

In 1929 Chatfield left the Admiralty to take up a fleet command just as the Depression began to wreak havoc on Britain's shipbuilders. Because of deflation and the lack of a plausible foe to arm against, orders for warships had tailed off after 1926. With the onset of the slump, orders for merchant ships fell off sharply too. Ship makers went bust or gave up the arms trade altogether. By doling out a few contracts and scarce cash, the Admiralty salvaged what it could. Surviving firms rationalized the entire industry by buying up stricken rivals, absorbing their assets and closing down some surplus plant. Because much of the overcapacity in the private sector—including specialist labor, large slipways and gun, gun-mounting and armor-plate factories—had been maintained in expectation of better times, the reduction was dramatic. By 1935 Britain's naval building capacity had shrunk by about half.[4]

The start of this industrial calamity coincided with a fresh round of naval diplomacy. Paradoxically, the Royal Navy was the victim of its own success. During the early 1920s the Admiralty had built up a large stock of cruisers that annoyed the Americans, who demanded parity in that class of ship too. The United States would settle for fifty cruisers each; the British claimed they needed seventy to patrol the empire. In 1927 the powers met during the stultifying heat of a Geneva summer to compromise, but the talks ended in a blistering row instead. Three years later the naval powers met again in London. Prime Minister Ramsay MacDonald sought to jump-start general disarmament by settling the cruiser dispute first. Against Admiralty advice, British ministers agreed to scrap a lot of old and some not very old cruisers, whittling the total down to fifty vessels. Between them, London, Tokyo and Washington also scrapped nine more old battleships. None of this disarmament crippled the Royal Navy. What hurt most about the 1930 London Naval Treaty was a five-year extension to the building holiday on battleships. Yet no one could have foreseen this at the time. For had the slump not come, the delay would not have mattered. But just when Britain's warship makers needed a surge of big contracts to keep them healthy, a famine set in.

In January 1933, when Chatfield returned to head the Admiralty as First Sea Lord, the situation was bad but not irreversible. A good chunk of the warship industry was closed or closing down, but Britain's building capacity was still the largest in the world. There were enough dockyards, steel foundries and engine shops to upgrade the old battleships that would be in service for a few more years while the rest of the warship industry began to assemble a new fleet of battleships.[5]

In the meantime the danger was a naval arms race: if there was ever a moment in the nearly 130 years since Admiral Lord Nelson defeated the French fleet at Trafalgar for the world's navies to arm at full speed, and thereby consign Britain's long naval mastery to history, this was it. Until the early 1940s all of Britain's shipyards, gun, gun-mounting and armor-plate factories would simply be too busy modernizing or replacing old ships to out-build the entire world.

In Europe a naval arms race was already gathering force. In 1931 the Germans launched the first of what would be three pocket-battleships. These novel 10,000-ton vessels employed diesel motors that gave them large cruising ranges. Armed with eleven-inch guns, they carried larger guns than faster vessels, such as big cruisers, and were faster than ships armed with bigger guns. In 1932 and 1934 the French responded with two fast pocket-battleship hunters of 26,500 tons armed with thirteen-inch guns. The Italians then replied to the French with two 35,000-ton battleships carrying fifteen-inch guns. The French, in their turn, planned to do the same in 1935.

Something had to be done to stop the spiral, and that something was disarmament. With the Washington treaty due to expire in 1936, the British prepared to host a naval conference to replace it. During 1934–35 Chatfield worked out with the Foreign Office and his staff a new system of naval limitation that would reduce the danger of an all-out naval race starting too early for the Royal Navy to win.

Chatfield's most important aim was to abolish the Washington tonnage ratios. Britain's quarrel with the Americans over parity as well as other disputes seemed to confirm a theory subscribed to by many British diplomats and naval officers: namely, that the underlying cause of competition in warships was national pride. Who, after all, wanted to have the world's second, third or fourth navy? If everyone stopped fussing about their place in the global pecking order, so the British believed, then the worldwide naval arms balance would in a decade or so come to reflect real differences in national needs and resources: the Royal Navy would come out on top, followed by the U.S. Navy, the Japanese Navy and then all the rest.

The British also sought to discourage one-upmanship in warship building. One driver behind the pre-1914 naval arms race had been an action-reaction cycle of bigger and better ships. Britain's four super-battlecruisers of 1921 threatened to start the cycle all over again. The Washington Naval Treaty stopped this escalation by setting maximum tonnages and gun sizes for all types of combat vessels. As Chatfield told his staff, the most important legacy of the Washington treaty was "stopping the principle of going one better." If each naval power conformed to fixed standards and published their building plans in advance, then no one need fear being trumped by an entirely new and revolutionary class of warship. The Admiralty in fact wanted everyone to build smaller battleships. Its preferred size was 25,000 tons carrying twelve-inch guns, because smaller battleships were cheaper to build and easier to maintain.[6]

And cost was no small matter. Admiral Chatfield did not just want to replace old ships with new, he wanted to persuade the cabinet to expand the fleet. In this respect Japan's aggression in Manchuria in 1931 was a godsend. During the 1920s the Admiralty had painted the threat from Japan in lurid colors to justify requests for more ships and for work on fortified docking and repair facilities in Singapore. But war with Japan was unlikely (Japanese naval planners did not consider Britain a potential enemy until 1936). Even pro-navy ministers asked why the admirals got so worked up about such a remote eventuality. After Manchuria, however, war with Japan no longer looked so far-fetched. With Germany rearming too, Chatfield wanted the government to build a two-power standard fleet; in other words, a navy big enough to beat the Japanese and at the same time defend Britain against the largest fleet in Europe.[7]

Taken together, what Admiral Chatfield hoped to achieve at home and abroad was mind-boggling in its sheer audacity. He planned to win the debate in the cabinet for the money to build a big fleet, greater than that of any other nation. And, to make sure that this could be done in an affordable way, without any potentially lethal naval arms races breaking out before Britain could win them, he intended to persuade all major sea powers to sign up to a new British-inspired system of naval disarmament.

While Japan's aggression in China helped the Royal Navy make its case in the cabinet, German rearmament was more problematic. As Chatfield learned in 1934, the Foreign Office and the Treasury saw the rise of the German Air Force as the greater peril to Britain's national survival. Not only did they want to divert money away from the navy to the air force, the Treasury suggested negotiating a deal with Tokyo that would make fleet expansion unnecessary. Why not deter Tokyo by stationing bombers and submarines in Singapore? The panic that gripped London in March 1935 after Hitler unveiled the Luftwaffe was a bad omen for anyone who wanted to argue that Britain must spend the lion's share of the defense budget on battleships.

After Hitler openly broke the army and air force clauses of the Treaty of Versailles in March 1935, the future of the German Navy hung in the air.

During talks with British diplomats in 1934–35, though, Hitler mentioned that he would be willing to sign a bilateral treaty with Britain to limit the size of the German fleet.

During the 1920s Hitler had absorbed some of the ideas of Captain Lothar Persius, the naval journalist of the Berlin *Tageblatt*, who claimed that Tirpitz's battleship spree had needlessly added Britain to Germany's wartime foes. Germany could not win a naval arms race, Persius argued, so why provoke the British by trying? To isolate France and clear the way for his wars of expansion and racial purification, the Nazi leader believed that Germany should align itself with Britain and Italy. When he took power in 1933, Hitler decided to offer the British a bargain: he would cap Germany's fleet at thirty-five percent the size of the Royal Navy, if Britain did not interfere with Germany's program of domination on the Eurasian landmass.

Admiral Erich Raeder, the head of the German Navy since 1928, did not know what to make of Chancellor Hitler. He knew that the Nazi leader had parroted the ideas of Captain Persius. That was a worrying sign. The journalist, after all, was known as "an enemy of the navy." The admiral, on the other hand, was a short, bookish workaholic who lived for little else but the German Navy. He had joined it in 1894 at eighteen and rose quickly up the ranks. He became a protégé of Tirpitz, the relentless mastermind behind the pre-1914 Anglo-German naval arms race. Raeder learned from Tirpitz that international politics was reducible to one simple formula: the worth of any nation was measured solely by the strength of its navy and its overseas empire.[8]

So for Raeder the naval mutinies of 1918 followed a year later by the scuttling of Tirpitz's great fleet were tragedies beyond endurance. But endure he did. During the 1920s, while the peace treaty limited the navy to six old battleships, a few small cruisers and not much more, Raeder stayed in uniform. He was custodian of Tirpitz's legacy, and patience was the virtue he cultivated most. He needed it. Navies could not be built overnight. From start to finish, modern battleships took four or five years to make, and Germany was not permitted to build any. Under the Weimar Republic, survival was the priority. Before Raeder became head of the navy, reports that it had secretly funded illegal rearmament had caused a terrific scandal. It handed the navy's foes in Parliament grounds to cut naval spending of every kind. Raeder, whose hatred of parliamentary politics was second only to his hatred of communism, ingratiated himself with leading politicians to lobby for more money for the fleet. His efforts paid off in 1928 with the pocket-battleship building program. They were not the full-sized battleships that Raeder craved, but at least they rescued his navy from sinking to the status of a coast guard. Once Germany's equality of status in armaments was recognized in 1932, Raeder laid out a much more ambitious five-year schedule of warship construction, one that included enlarged pocket-battleships, U-boats and an aircraft carrier.[9]

During his first meetings with the new chancellor, Raeder stressed the value of a strong navy. Hitler, it turned out, needed little convincing. He may have absorbed the heresies of Captain Persius, but Hitler was also a man who drew battleships and thumbed through warship annuals to relax. In 1933, not wanting to do anything too conspicuous that would antagonize London, Hitler authorized secret work on U-boats and two enlarged pocket-battleships. During meetings in 1934 Hitler and Raeder discussed the key questions: How big should the navy be? And what would be its purpose? The navy wanted a fleet as big as that of the French, which was about half the size of the Royal Navy. For Raeder and his senior advisers this seemed like a realistic goal for the next ten years, and probably the most that the shipbuilders could handle. Someday, if the German Navy were ever going to break out of the North Sea and steam onto the world's oceans, then the "British problem"—as German naval men liked to describe it—would have to be solved. But that was for the distant future. For now, a conventional fleet half the size of Britain's would give Germany command of the Baltic Sea (and in wartime, security for vital shipments of Swedish iron ore) and enough striking power to occupy the French. Yet Hitler, who sought to appease the British with an act of seeming generosity, wanted to cap the navy at about thirty-five percent the size of Britain's. Much to the bafflement of Admiral Raeder and his top staff, he failed to make the Führer see the huge difference between the thirty-five and fifty percent ratios.[10]

In London, Chatfield's staff agreed that a German claim for naval equality with France would be hard to resist by "logic." During 1934 naval intelligence detected intense activity in German shipyards, including work on U-boats. But, they assumed, the competing demands for raw materials, industrial plant and skilled labor among the army, navy and air force would curtail the growth of all three services. Since Hitler was likely to give the army and air force priority, the British naval planners predicted that the German Navy would grow to one-third the size of the British fleet by 1942. If Raeder received all the money and steel he wanted, then the German fleet might reach parity with France by then, but with France and its allies arming on land and in the air, why would Hitler prioritize the navy? There could only be one answer to that question: Hitler wanted a war with Britain. Yet, if that were true, Chatfield's staff reasoned, Raeder would not build an inferior-sized fleet of battleships. In a fleet-to-fleet battle, the smaller fleet would be sunk.

If the Germans were in a hurry to confront Britain, then Raeder would not build a small version of the Royal Navy but a so-called "freak" navy, that is, of light hunter-killer vessels built to break out of the North Sea and scatter into the Atlantic to destroy British mercantile convoys. What worried the naval planners in London were signs that this was what Admiral Raeder intended: the pocket-battleships were perfectly suited to waging this kind of cruiser warfare.[11]

Admiral Raeder was an authority on cruiser warfare. He had written scholarly studies of the topic. And, despite his intolerance of any criticism of Tirpitz, he knew that the old admiral's battleship-building spree had doomed the German fleet to near irrelevance during the war. Hitler said that war against Britain was unlikely for years to come. Hence all naval plans against France, Poland and Russia would be premised on British neutrality. Germany could build a regular fleet against those foes and inch toward one day renewing the contest with Britain perhaps in a less orthodox way. What about submarines? In 1917 the U-boats had nearly done what the battleships could not: brought Britain to its knees by sinking supply ships. Captain Karl Dönitz, the fanatical submariner who ran the new U-boat arm, argued that with enough boats and ace skippers organized into hunting packs he could starve the British. Raeder was unimpressed. Like virtually all of his contemporaries the world over, he believed that the U-boats had scored only a temporary success because the British had been caught off guard: once Britain had adopted countermeasures, such as organizing merchant ships into escorted convoys, the U-boat had been reduced to the status of a nuisance. Besides, since 1917 the Royal Navy had perfected an amazing device for locating submerged submarines, namely, sonar. Dönitz cursed the British Admiralty because he knew that they publicly exaggerated the efficiency of sonar to deceive everyone into believing that the submarine had been beaten. He was right, they did. And no one listened to Dönitz, least of all Adolf Hitler, until 1940. By then it was too late.[12]

Before Ribbentrop and the other German delegates arrived in London in June 1935 for naval talks, the British had discouraged them through diplomatic channels from talking about a thirty-five percent ratio. What the Admiralty wanted from the Germans was to agree to build their new ships in conformity with international standards. If the Germans built conventional battleships, cruisers and destroyers, that would prevent them from building a "freak" navy to wage deadly cruiser warfare against Britain. When Ribbentrop insisted on acceptance of the thirty-five percent ratio, Admiral Chatfield and his staff advised the cabinet to say yes provided that the Germans agreed in turn to build a conventional battlefleet.

Hitler believed that the signing of the naval agreement was the first step in his grand diplomatic design. He assumed that the British understood that the deal was about more than warships. Throughout the naval talks, the British in fact scrupulously discouraged Ribbentrop from drawing any wider implications from the deal. It was a technical deal about navies, nothing more. And Chatfield believed that he had bamboozled Raeder. Germany could have reasonably claimed tonnage parity with France at the upcoming naval conference, but now Raeder had to settle for much less. "The basis of the Führer's decision," one German naval command memo explained, "is the intention to exclude any possibility of antagonism between Germany and Britain for the future and thus also finally rule out any naval rivalry between the two countries. . . . The agreement is entirely satisfactory for the navy."[13]

Entirely satisfactory "for now," the memo might have added, because that was what Admiral Raeder had in mind. He would oversee the rise of the largest fleet he could and use the thirty-five percent naval agreement to lull the Admiralty into a false sense of security. By 1949 the German Navy wanted eight battleships, three aircraft carriers, eight heavy cruisers and seventy U-boats. At that stage, perhaps, the naval race with Britain would be on again. For the moment, work on twelve U-boats began and the two enlarged pocket-battleships were restarted as 30,000-ton/eleven-inch-gun battlecruisers. Work on two bigger battleships based on the naval agreement also began. But the navy's ship designers soon found that designing a well-protected battleship carrying eight fifteen-inch guns on a ship of 35,000 tons was nearly impossible. Tellingly, Raeder solved the problem by allowing them to cheat by building a 45,000-ton ship instead.[14]

In London, Chatfield too was satisfied—for now. A German naval build-up made it easier to persuade the politicians to pay for a two-power fleet. The deal with Germany was a good start to getting the world to accept a new naval treaty. During 1936–37 the Admiralty would present their rivals with a great burst of building. Work on five battleships, four aircraft carriers and fourteen cruisers would start. Chatfield took special interest in the specifications for the battleships. At the battle of Jutland in 1916, he had watched in horror as three under-armored British battlecruisers suddenly exploded under a hail of German shells. The psychological shock cut deep. Never again, he swore, would British sailors fight in such vulnerable ships. Britain's first five modern 35,000-ton ships would be heavily protected against bombs, shells and torpedoes, but armed with only fourteen-inch guns instead of the maximum fifteen-inch guns allowed for under the new naval treaty. That did not matter. Superior British seamanship and ship design would give the Royal Navy a winning edge—even if other navies cheated on the size of their big ships.[15]

In December 1935 Chatfield and his staff were in good spirits. Challenges lay ahead, but things might just go their way. "Other nations may shortly be in a favourable position to challenge us at sea," Chatfield warned ministers:

> Germany is in the process of building a brand-new fleet and has started a lap ahead. On the other hand, we still have something to rely on in our naval experience and the fact that we have turned our national engineering skill into naval channels, also our shipbuilding capacity, our great dockyards and bases, and the naval instinct of the nation which enables the fleet to be manned with superior seaman. If, therefore, we take up the task wholeheartedly, and accept whatever sacrifices are necessary, the position can, we are certain, be retrieved gradually. The world knows we can do it and seeing us make a determined start may realise the futility of challenging us.[16]

ONE THING THAT COULD (and eventually did) help wreck the prospects of Britain holding onto its naval supremacy was an arms race across the Pacific. Providing the Japanese did not go on a warship-building spree, there was little danger of the U.S. fleet growing. The Admiralty no longer cared much whether the Americans claimed parity or superiority—a decade of naval rivalry had proved that the U.S. Congress would never spend the dollars necessary to build the fleet up to full strength anyway.

The top echelons of the U.S. Navy saw things in a similar way. During the 1920s the Republican presidents Warren Harding and Calvin Coolidge had sought to reduce the fiscal burden of a large fleet through diplomacy without jeopardizing the relative strength of the navy. Disarmament reflected the Republican attitude toward taxes, the size and power of the state and America's place in the world. Harding and Coolidge were not against the navy as such, only excessive peacetime armaments. They understood that it was not just the vast waters of the Pacific and Atlantic that isolated America from the barbarities of Asia and Europe, but also the navy.

In 1929 the Republican Herbert Hoover entered the White House. Like Prime Minister MacDonald, Hoover too hoped to jump-start world disarmament with a naval treaty. At the 1930 London conference Hoover overrode the advice of the U.S. Navy's General Board (that is, the general staff) and concluded a naval treaty. U.S. naval officers believed that the British, always ready to invoke the ideas of peace and disarmament for their own selfish ends, had "hoodwinked and bamboozled" "Uncle Sam" first in 1922 and, thanks to Hoover, again in 1930. Each time Americans came away with parity on paper, but in practice U.S. officials had given away more than they got in return. After the Washington treaty, the British battleship fleet was larger in gross tonnage than the American; the Royal Navy's inventory of cruisers, destroyers and submarines was larger and more up to date than that of the U.S. Navy; and the British Empire afforded British naval war planners a worldwide network of bases to project force globally. In 1930 the Americans compelled the British to scrap a lot of serviceable cruiser tonnage, but the U.S. Navy's General Board was forced to accept an inferior number of the big 10,000-ton/eight-inch-gun cruisers they preferred. Britain, moreover, had the world's biggest merchant navy, and large trade ships could in wartime be converted into light cruisers by mounting a gun on them.[17]

As the U.S. Navy quickly learned, what made the 1930 treaty damaging was the Depression. Like their counterparts in the Admiralty, the U.S. Navy's General Board feared that the slump, if it continued, might shut down most of America's private shipyards before battleship building could begin again. In 1931 Hoover slashed funding for new ships and pressed on at Geneva for greater disarmament. Only in his final year in the White House, 1932, did he approve naval orders to help keep the shipyards working. Luckily for the navy, the shipbuilders had entered the 1930s with order books full for civilian vessels. Most big firms would not go bust before 1933.[18]

In September 1930 Hoover appointed Admiral William Pratt as chief of naval operations. Unlike almost every other naval officer, Pratt saw the logic of Hoover's drive for economy and disarmament. His heresy ran very deep. Whether or not the British had a margin of superiority did not bother him much: Pratt did not accept the thesis held by most of his colleagues that a clash of commercial interests had locked the two major English-speaking nations into naval competition. What worried Pratt, who had spent much of his early navy days in China with the Asiatic Fleet, was Japan.[19]

When Colonel Ishiwara Kanji and his co-conspirators sparked the conquest of Manchuria in September 1931, and the fighting spread to Shanghai in January 1932, Washington condemned these acts as flagrant violations of the international agreements safeguarding the territorial integrity of China. Henry L. Stimson, Hoover's secretary of state, announced that the United States would refuse to recognize any territorial changes in China undertaken by force. As a precaution, the United States moved warships from the Atlantic to the Pacific.

In the late 1920s the U.S. Navy assumed that, given the mammoth inequality in industrial resources between the two countries, only in an alliance
with Britain would Japan dare make war on the United States. That changed
in 1931–32. Suddenly, executing "Orange," the code name for the navy's war
plan against Japan alone, seemed all too imminent. Orange envisaged the U.S.
fleet crossing 7,000 miles of Pacific waters to rescue the Philippines and force
the Japanese fleet to offer battle. Once the U.S. Navy had sunk the Japanese
fleet, it would strangle Japan with an economic blockade.

For more than a decade the details of Orange had obsessed the navy's best
minds. Since London and Washington had agreed in 1922 not to erect fortified bases in the western Pacific, just keeping the fleet supplied and in good
repair was going to be amazingly complex. U.S. planners knew that their adversary would try to even the odds by ambushing the larger U.S. fleet along
the way to Manila with bombers and submarines. They calculated the scale
of these attacks and how many aircraft carriers, cruisers, destroyers and submarines would be needed to protect the battleships. When they counted how
many ships were available in 1932 and would be in years to come, the total
was not enough to make plan Orange work.[20]

By the end of 1932, Pratt, no doomsayer by any measure, was worried. Unless the navy started to grow and place orders with the private shipbuilders
soon, the United States would fall into naval armaments decline for years to
come. But things began to shift in November 1932 when Hoover lost the election to the Democrat, Franklin Roosevelt. The navy had always fascinated
Roosevelt. In 1897, at age fifteen, his Christmas gift was the navalist's bible,
A. T. Mahan's *The Influence of Sea Power Upon History*. In his twenties, he
dreamed of a career modeled on that of his flamboyant cousin, President
Theodore Roosevelt, who was building up the Great White Fleet as a symbol of America's fast-growing strength. From 1913 to 1920, during the largest
naval boom in U.S. history up to then, Franklin served President Woodrow
Wilson as assistant secretary of the navy. By the time he entered the White
House, Roosevelt identified so closely with the service that he annoyed the
soldiers by habitually referring to the navy as "us" and the army as "them."[21]

Even so, Roosevelt was not going to do anything rash about the fleet. He
had been elected in the midst of the worst economic slump anyone had ever
seen. In his inaugural speech he promised to "wage war" on poverty and in
world affairs to be a "good neighbor." He was not about to crank up the defense
budget and prompt a naval arms race. Roosevelt's biggest problem was getting
congressional approval for a massive plan of public works to put millions of
the unemployed back into jobs. He knew that he could mobilize his support-

ers and the Congress behind the New Deal but not warship building. In June 1933, though, he used his executive powers to allocate a modest sum earmarked for job creation to be spent on thirty new ships: eighty-five percent of the cost of a vessel, White House officials told reporters, went to labor, and many private and government shipyards happened to be in Democratic constituencies.

Roosevelt decided to let someone else take the risk of championing a cause that might otherwise rebound on him. He had the willing surrogate for greater naval rearmament in the chairman of the House Committee on Naval Affairs, Carl Vinson of Georgia. In September 1914 Vinson had thought that battleships were a waste of money that only profited the steel barons, but the conflict in Europe convinced him that a navy "second to none" was the only guarantee against total war reaching American soil. Well before Roosevelt took office, Vinson had lobbied hard for new ships to be built in private dockyards to keep the industry alive. In January 1932, weeks before U.S. diplomats joined others from fifty-eight other states at Geneva for the World Disarmament Conference, he introduced a bill that called for what the navy wanted most: authorization for a ten-year plan to replace the fleet's obsolete vessels and to expand the navy up to treaty strength. Despite Vinson's clever string-pulling in Congress, without Hoover's backing, the bill failed. In January 1934 Vinson tried again, and this time succeeded. Congress agreed to authorize the White House to replace obsolete ships and build up the navy to full strength, according to the terms of the naval arms control treaties, by 1942. Roosevelt explained to the newspapers that Vinson's bill merely allowed him to replace old vessels with new ones, and that the upcoming naval conference in London would surely result in "further reductions" to world naval armaments.[22]

Admiral William Standley, who succeeded Pratt as chief of naval operations in July 1933, was relieved. Warship building as job creation rescued the shipbuilding industry from certain decay. Yet he was uneasy. Standley could not figure Roosevelt out: all high ideas one minute, ruthless pragmatism the next. Did the president want to disarm or build a big navy? Unlike Pratt, Standley had no time for disarmament, except in one respect. At least the Washington tonnage ratio set a maximum size for the U.S. Navy. Without that benchmark, who knew by how much the politicians would have cut the navy since 1922? What worried Standley was the upcoming naval conference in London. Japan demanded equality with Britain and the United States. The British proposed doing away with the Washington tonnage ratios altogether. And Roosevelt spoke in public and in the cabinet about substantial naval reductions.[23]

During meetings in 1934 to discuss America's position on a new naval treaty, Standley asked Roosevelt if he would allow "a slight increase of [overall] tonnage" if that made a deal with London and Tokyo possible. The president said no. He had just called on Europe to cut land and air armaments; he could not just turn around and accept bigger navies. Furthermore, if the naval talks were going to fail, Japan had to take the blame; that would make convincing Congress to spend the money for more warships less tricky. Roosevelt did not care about parity with Britain; he wanted to isolate Japan, even if that meant an end to naval disarmament and an arms race.[24]

Just about everyone agreed that a naval arms race was unlikely anyway. With its army committed in China and nearly half of the national budget going to defense already, the Japanese would be crazy to provoke a warship-building competition with an industrial colossus like the United States. One of Admiral Standley's top staff officers, however, raised a concern. "In the event of a naval race with Japan," he argued, "it is better to race her in orthodox types in which we would start the race with a head start, than to race in a new type, in which case we would start from scratch." But what if the Japanese Navy launched some revolutionary type of warship? In that case even new American warships might be "entirely outclassed."[25]

In fact, building a revolutionary type of super-battleship that would outclass anything for years to come was exactly what the Japanese Navy had decided to do, and planning started in late 1934. The Japanese naval staff originally imagined ships of 50,000 tons carrying twenty-inch guns, but by July 1936 the designers came up with a better-balanced yet even more gargantuan design of 70,000 tons armed with eighteen-inch guns. Work began in November 1937 and March 1938 on the first two of what were meant to be four Yamato-class ships, and they were finished in December 1941 and August 1942. With these ships, Japanese armaments planners intended to leapfrog the navy's strength in a single "bound" from inferiority against the U.S. Navy to "absolute superiority."[26]

Formally, the Japanese Navy had begun to measure itself against the U.S. fleet in 1907. Two years earlier at the battle of Tsushima, Admiral Tōgō Heihachirō's combined fleet had annihilated the Russian Baltic fleet, so the U.S. Navy, at least for budgetary purposes, was the only plausible maritime opponent. Japanese naval officers really began to worry about the Americans after 1916. The scale and speed of the U.S. battleship construction boom prompted by the European war shocked them. If Washington continued to build up its fleet at that rate, the Japanese fleet would be dwarfed and the whole Pacific Ocean reduced to an American-dominated lake.[27]

In 1918 Japanese planners drafted a construction program for eight modern battleships and eight battlecruisers, a force they regarded as adequate to deter the Americans from attacking Japan. Right from the start, though, there was little prospect of the navy getting the resources it needed to complete the entire eight-eight plan. In 1921 the navy budget ate up an unsustainable 31.6 percent of national spending, and the Japanese economy was falling into a recession.

The invitation to the Washington conference thus came as something of a relief to the Japanese cabinet and navy brass. Navy Minister Admiral Katō Tomosaburō, who had been chief of staff to Tōgō in the war with Russia, had been the driving force behind the eight-eight fleet. The sixty-year-old admiral and cabinet minister understood that the time had come to stop the naval arms race.

For Katō the situation was clear-cut. Germany's recent defeat had proved that "national defense is no longer the monopoly of the military." In future wars the side with the most powerful industrial economy would win. Japan could not risk war with the Americans, let alone an all-out arms race. "Even if we should try to compete with the United States," he told legislators in 1919, "it is a foregone conclusion that we are simply not up to it. . . . Whether the US, with its unlimited wealth and resources, would continue its naval expansion is up to that country. My policy is to build up an adequate defensive force within the limits of Japan's national power."[28]

When he arrived in Washington in November 1921 as Japan's chief delegate, Katō knew that the conference was a chance to halt a ruinous arms race. When he heard Secretary of State Hughes proposing to cap levels of naval strength at roughly where they stood and to scrap much of the 1916 naval program, it did not take him long to see a bargain in the making. Japan's naval armaments would be frozen at the point of its maximum national financial and industrial effort, while the U.S. Navy would be frozen at a point well below its maximum potential strength. His job, as Katō saw it, was to compromise just enough to make sure that no one in the U.S. administration, Congress or newspapers paid the slightest attention to the howls of protest from American admirals to make the navy "second to none."[29]

With the approval of the cabinet and his unrivaled authority, Katō Tomosaburō quelled hostility toward the naval treaty from inside the service. Even Tōgō, the semi-retired hero of Tsushima, blessed the 5:5:3 tonnage ratios as good enough. Katō stepped off the boat from the United States with his standing as a senior statesman enhanced. In 1922 he became prime minister, but he died the next year.

Katō Tomosaburō's premature death helped to clear the way for enemies of the naval ratio to assert themselves. The most important of these was the navy's chief of staff, Admiral Katō Kanji (no relation). Katō Kanji had accompanied Katō Tomosaburō to Washington as a technical adviser. During the negotiations, a dispute between the two men broke out over the naval ratio. Katō Tomosaburō considered a sixty percent ratio in battleships and aircraft carriers sufficient for defense, especially as the Americans had agreed to leave their bases in the western Pacific unfortified, while Katō Kanji considered that force level as too little and, worse, a humiliation.[30]

The quarrel between these two men and their admirers, who filled the ranks of the Naval Ministry and the naval staff in the 1920s, revolved around the way in which staff officers in all navies predicted the outcome of sea battles. According to accepted mathematical calculations, Japan needed a seventy percent ratio in ships to secure slightly better than even odds of defeating an American trans-Pacific attack along the lines of the U.S. war plan Orange. For Katō Tomosaburō, ten percent was not a significant shortfall. In real war lots of factors, including dumb luck, came into play that made nonsense of peacetime rules of thumb. Even so, making this hypothetical sacrifice to avoid the very real danger of an arms race was simply worth it.

Katō Kanji and most of his supporters knew that the seventy percent ratio was only a war-game computation. Still, they waged a relentless bureaucratic guerrilla war against Katō Tomosaburō's followers in the Naval Ministry, the so-called "treaty faction." During the 1927 Geneva naval talks, Katō Kanji and other like-minded officers made dire public pronouncements about Japan's vulnerability to naval attack. Japan must stand up to Anglo-American bullying and demand a seventy percent ratio in naval auxiliaries, they ranted, even if that set off a naval arms race.

Behind what seemed like "samurai" fanaticism to many U.S. naval officers, who followed the infighting in Tokyo closely, lay genuine strategic concerns as well as something fundamentally political. During the 1920s, as the U.S. Navy modernized its older battleships, their cruising ranges doubled, so that any advantage Japan gained from the non-fortification of U.S. bases in the western Pacific was eroded. Katō Kanji and his "fleet faction" sought a better balance in heavy cruisers and submarines to compensate. After all, they did not need a spy in Washington to tell them the broad outlines of plan Orange, and they knew that their best chance of winning was by damaging or sinking as many U.S. battleships as they could before the two fleets came within gun range of each other, and the fleet's auxiliaries would be doing a lot of the fighting during the attrition phase of a trans-Pacific campaign.[31]

That apart, what really irked Katō Kanji and many others was that they knew that the U.S. planners calculated the odds in a future war in the same way as they did. Both navies spoke a common language in which victory and defeat were spelled out in warship tonnages. So for Katō Kanji the American insistence that Japan accept sixty percent of U.S. tonnage was a message that read: "We want a military veto over your rising national strength and influence in China." For Katō, obtaining a seventy percent ratio in cruisers at the next naval disarmament talks was meant to be a reply: "We will not be intimidated from exercising our sovereign rights." The inclination to see the most sinister motives at work behind each other's disarmament goals warped perceptions. Likewise, while U.S. naval officers saw commercial competition as the engine that drove their naval rivalry with Britain, Japanese naval officers saw competition for China's markets as the driver behind their dispute with the Americans.

For the fleet faction the final straw came in 1930. At the London naval conference, the Japanese delegation, despite every effort at sabotage from the naval staff, arrived at a deal with the Americans. Although the U.S. Navy had swallowed a bitter pill in agreeing to build only eighteen heavy cruisers to Britain's twenty-five, the Japanese naval staff considered that many large cruisers in the U.S. arsenal—six more than Japan—an intolerable threat. Still, to avert a naval arms race, Prime Minister Hamaguchi Osachi's cabinet and the navy's pro-treaty faction for the last time imposed their authority.

In June 1930 Katō Kanji resigned. His "right" as naval chief of staff to exercise "supreme command," he said, had been ignored. Katō knew that Japan could not win an all-out war against the United States because of the inequality in the two economies. But that was exactly the point. Unlike total-war systematizers such as Tukhachevsky, Ishiwara or Blomberg, Katō believed that with technical, tactical and operational supremacy he could contravene the one unbreakable rule that nearly everyone had learned from the last war—that the most powerful economies would always win in the end. The naval treaties prevented Japan from making the most of its inferior resources because they imposed conformity in warship design and openness in building plans. Outside of the treaty system, Japan could build in secret revolutionary types of new warships. With a superbly equipped fleet, Japan could win a swift victory before the United States could mobilize and project its crushing strength across the Pacific. Ultimately, even if the United States tried to win an all-out naval arms race, Katō wrote, "the effect will be that Britain and Japan will be drawn together and the United States will become another Germany."[32]

While Katō Kanji in semi-retirement lobbied against the treaty, the forces unleashed by the Depression and the military conspiracy in Manchuria rocked the government in Tokyo to near collapse. A wave of ultranationalist violence peaked in May 1932 when naval cadets murdered Prime Minister Inukai Tsuyoshi during a botched military coup. Against this background of economic and political upheaval, power shifted within the state away from the civilian party politicians to the military-bureaucratic elite.

A shift occurred inside the navy too. During 1933–34, the navy minister, Admiral Ōsumi Mineo, purged the service of pro-treaty officers. Responsibility for determining the size and shape of the fleet was handed over to the naval staff. "If the United States should take a strong stand in opposition to our fundamental policy" on parity of naval armaments, Ōsumi told his fellow cabinet ministers, then "we must resolutely repel it, and with this in view we must proceed to complete [naval] preparedness."[33]

Admiral Ōsumi, a fifty-four-year-old bull-necked amateur wrestler with good political antennae, knew that there was no way Washington or London was going to offer Japan naval equality at the upcoming naval conference in 1935. That was a given. Tension with the United States, however, would help solve two other urgent problems. The first one was the Japanese Army. The fighting in northern China and the growth of Soviet armaments in Asia threatened the navy's claim to a huge slice of national resources. With Finance Minister Takahashi Korekiyo spending his way out of the economic slump, this was no time for the navy to take second place in national priorities.

The second problem was industrial. Until the 1920s Japan's shipbuilders had enjoyed amazing expansion. But the slowdown in naval building after 1922 and the postwar economic slump generally cut profits and growth. The industry had only just started to recover when the Great Depression hit. In November 1931 the navy rescued firms with contracts for light cruisers, destroyers and submarines. Keeping the private shipyards in business solved only part of the problem. Although making warships was extremely profitable, private shipbuilders preferred the steady business of civilian customers to the boom or bust of naval work. With U.S. shipbuilding capacity estimated at five to ten times bigger than Japan's, the naval planners knew that they had to bring the whole sector under their control to maximize Japan's output. Conquest by procurement was the answer. The navy swamped the private shipbuilders with lucrative orders, boosting their profits, crowding out most civilian business and, in effect, taking control of the whole industry.[34]

The first sign of American rearming came in March 1934 with the Vinson Act to raise the U.S. fleet strength to treaty limits. The Japanese Navy did the same with orders for forty-eight ships. "A race with the United States would become unmanageable," General Araki Sadao protested, "and I think it would eventually lead to war." Admiral Ōsumi Mineo waved away gloomy prognostications. The money and resources would be found. The navy's super-battleships were in fact a cost-effective way to spend the defense budget. Besides, as one Naval Ministry pamphlet put it, "in the course of history there have been countries which were ruined by defeat in war, but there has never been a single country that was ruined by excessive expenditure on armaments."[35]

In December 1935, two years of preliminary negotiations and arming came to a head when delegates from ten nations packed the Locarno room in the Foreign Office for the second London naval conference. Nearly everybody expected it to fail. Admiral Nagano Osami arrived with orders to return with a recognition of Japan's equality in tonnage with Britain and the United States or to withdraw. President Roosevelt's emissary, Norman Davis, a born optimist, told everyone that there was "no chance" of success unless Japan dropped its demand for naval parity. Only the British, for whom a new treaty was so important to uphold their naval supremacy, looked for success.[36]

"What our peoples will be particularly anxious to ensure is that, when the present naval treaties expire," Prime Minister Stanley Baldwin told the delegates, "we shall not each feel that our main duty is to 'go one better' than our neighbours in the evolution of new types and increased sizes of ships. This we believe to be the most expensive and dangerous of all types of naval competition."[37]

Determined to go *two* better in battleship size and hitting power, the Japanese delegation dodged every ingenious compromise the British could concoct and instead proposed cuts in offensive arms for Japan, the United States and Britain down to a "common upper limit" that they knew would be rejected. Top officials in Washington and London believed that Japan would sooner or later cave in if threatened with a naval arms race by both the United States and Britain. So, when the Japanese withdrew from the talks on January 15, 1936, the way was clear for a multilateral naval arms treaty, above all one rigged to regulate global warship building to the Royal Navy's benefit.

Admiral Chatfield certainly got most of what he wanted in the final text of the London Naval Treaty of March 1936: the duty to publish building plans in advance; upper limits on the size of all ships; a ban on "freaks" like Germany's pocket-battleships and even a ban on new 10,000-ton/eight-inch-gun cruisers. The Americans did not get an extension of the Washington tonnage ratios, but Admiral Standley stopped the British from reducing the size of future battleships. The U.S. Navy, he explained, needed big robust ships that could bear up against attacks on a trans-Pacific voyage, and so the maximum size was set at 35,000 tons armed with fifteen-inch guns.

Roosevelt worried that the naval treaty might prevent the United States from catching up in light cruisers if the British went on a sudden building spree. Nothing in the new treaty, the State Department reassured him, would stop the United States from building as many light cruisers as Congress would pay for. The British offered reassurance too in the form of an exchange of diplomatic notes. "We are in full agreement that there must be no competitive building between our two countries," the British note read, "and that neither country should question the right of the other to maintain parity in any category of ship." Admiral Standley may have doubted that Roosevelt or Congress would spend millions of dollars to keep up parity if the British gradually started to race ahead in battleships and cruisers. Admiral Chatfield was counting on it.[38]

CHAPTER 8

"WE HAVE REACHED
A PLATEAU"

At the beginning of the 1930s the world plunged into unparalleled economic disorder and misery. As the industrialized countries scrambled to protect their contracting economies from the Depression, in February 1932, a long-delayed World Disarmament Conference met in Geneva to establish a global equilibrium on armaments. In all but one of the great powers, war planners faced an unwelcome future of large cuts in forces through disarmament and the liquidation of nearly entire arms industries as a result of the world slump.

By 1936, everything had changed. From the low point of 1933, worldwide arms spending had nearly tripled. In part because of the soaring demand for armaments, industrial activity everywhere heated up. The output and price of raw materials shot up too. Shipyards sprang to life with new warships rising on the stocks. Once idle, factories for the manufacture of munitions of every type began to consume raw materials, expand plant capacity and employ engineers and skilled workers again. The production of combat aircraft accounted for the largest expansion. In all the major nations, workshops turned out propellers, motors, airframes, undercarriages and instruments in ever-increasing volume and technical sophistication. The armaments boom extended beyond the assembly of tanks, guns and planes to the construction of roads, bridges, railways, airfields, frontier fortifications and storage, repair and training facilities.[1]

The mounting arms race encompassed more than outlays on munitions and infrastructure. Governments, first under the pressure of the slump and then of the arms race, had to intervene more vigorously and continually into industry, trade and society. Military staffs, at times allied to civilian technocrats, called for more thorough peacetime readiness for wartime production, the diversion of national resources to heavy industry and armaments, the control of private business and market forces and the disciplining of whole societies to work and fight. Everywhere the buzzwords of the total-war systematizers entered the vocabulary of everyday politics. The call to arms rationalized and legitimized certain policies. Because future war would be "totalitarian," the prevailing political impulse was to make state power "total," societies "regimented," economies "planned" and "autarkic." Planning, whether military or economic—with the distinction between them becoming more blurred all the time—was invoked as the way to make the future certain.

To international observers, 1936 thus marked the moment when global armaments competition began to resemble a giant vortex fast gathering momentum and drawing the great powers with unequal intensity into a relentless totalitarian future. While some resisted, others gave way.

ON MARCH 7, 1936, Adolf Hitler won another easy foreign-policy victory. German troops occupied the Rhineland in breach of the treaties of Versailles and Locarno. Afterward, he beguiled London and Paris with talk of détente and legal limits on the wartime use of bombers and gas. With most of the Treaty of Versailles undone, some officials in London and Paris believed that Berlin could now be coaxed into a new European settlement. Germany could not arm at full speed forever without inviting economic collapse. A slowdown was due sometime soon.

Hjalmar Schacht thought so too. Hitler's economic wizard had overseen Germany's break with the liberal economic order and its rapid rearmament. But now that Germany had asserted its independence and armed, the time had come to improve the trade position and acquire colonies. Schacht did not object to rearming, he just wanted it to be capped to what the economy could handle. That limit was approaching. Since 1934 a huge deficit in the balance of payments had developed. To import food and raw materials to keep the workforce fed and factories humming, Germany had to earn foreign exchange by selling abroad. And, with the global economy on the upswing, and German manufacturers eager to regain their share of world markets, the time had come to divert resources from arms to exports. Raising exports, Schacht and other top economic officials knew, would require a devaluation of the Reichsmark in cooperation with the United States and Britain; otherwise those countries would simply retaliate with competitive devaluations of their own or raise barriers to German goods. What in effect Schacht and other economic officials suggested was a commercial peace with

Washington and London that would invariably lead at least to a temporary lull in European armaments competition.[2]

This was exactly the sort of economic strain that foreign observers expected would sooner or later curb German arms growth. Schacht, however, had little impact because his influence was nearly at an end, and because the Nazi leadership and the military ignored the self-defeating consequences of an ever-spiraling arms race.

Back on October 18, 1935, the day that Hitler told the generals to "rearm and get ready" as fast as they could, General Blomberg had instructed the three service heads to spend beyond Schacht's earlier financial estimates. Predictably, the services went on a spree. Arms spending almost doubled. The demand for oil, rubber and metals to rearm rose. The navy had already placed so many orders that the shipyards could not accept any more, but they did what they could to work faster. In December, the army's chief of staff, General Ludwig Beck, who only a year before had worried that army expansion should not be so rapid as to provoke too great a reply from Germany's neighbors, argued that the army needed more mobility and offensive punch to counter the arming of those neighbors. He now planned for a rise in the number of expensive tank and motorized formations in the thirty-six-division army, regardless of cost. General Erhard Milch's expansive ambitions for the Luftwaffe matched those of Beck's for the army. In October 1935, Milch added to the air force's successful Rhineland Program of 4,021 aircraft an extra 1,305 machines, including the first batch of advanced Heinkel He III medium bombers.[3]

By the time German troops crossed the Rhine, then, Blomberg and Schacht were at loggerheads over armaments spending, raw material imports and large-scale investment in autarkic projects such as synthetic fuel. The war minister was already fighting a bureaucratic battle with the service chiefs about the unity of the armed forces under him. He was not about to let the esteemed central banker regulate the breadth or depth of arming. In theory Blomberg, like his co-visionary of future total war, Colonel Thomas, wanted an economic dictator to unify civilian and military war preparations. What he did not want was someone who would question all-out arming and autarky on the grounds that Germany should ultimately function normally in a world of trading nations. Blomberg's faith in the authoritarian state to command the economy was almost mystical. Where there was a will, he believed, there was a way.[4]

The dispute between Schacht and Blomberg worked its way up to Hitler. Typically, in the dog-eat-dog internal politics of the Nazi regime, Hitler did not wade into the details or make overt choices himself but instead entrusted a loyal follower to work out what he wanted. The job fell to Göring. Steam-rolling over Schacht and other conservative technocrats not only suited his bullying personality and military outlook but gave him a foothold in the running of the economy. It also allowed the forty-three-year-old Nazi pal-adin the chance to realize two goals he had long championed: all-out rear-mament and autarky. For Göring, the idea that private business or market forces should shift resources and obstruct the interests of the "national com-munity" was ludicrous.[5]

At first Schacht welcomed Göring's appointment in April 1936 as com-missioner for foreign exchange and raw materials. Here was an opportunity to divert blame away from himself for unpopular decisions. He soon saw his mistake. Göring assembled his own staff to push through Hitler's policy, which amounted to maintaining "the same tempo of rearmament" no matter what. For this chore, at first anyway, Göring proved himself adept at overrid-ing expert technical advice. "Measures which in a state with a parliamentary government would probably bring about inflation," he explained with the air of a man in touch with some higher truth, "do not have the same results in a totalitarian system." General Blomberg was unhappy that the head of the Luftwaffe had now taken a leading position in the running of the economy, but he did not balk at the substance of Göring's policy choices of autarky and accelerated rearmament. Thanks to the air chief, in June 1936 both the army and air force again sped up their expansion plans.[6]

As Schacht had foreseen, though, the economy had reached its limits that summer. In six to eight weeks stocks of raw materials would be exhausted. Ammunition factories worked at only seventy percent capacity. Other firms worked fewer hours too. Reichsbank officials pressed for a managed devalu-ation of the Reichsmark and a rise in exports, including arms sales to foreign countries. Göring rejected this course. He would not decelerate rearmament. Instead, to avert a foreign-exchange crunch for another year or so, he launched a coercive drive to seize all the pounds, dollars and francs in private hands for the state and boosted exports through state subsidies.[7]

Still, shortages of iron, steel and non-ferrous metals held things up. The navy's plans already lagged behind. The air force needed 20,000 more tons of steel a month to meet its targets. Shortfalls in steel also delayed the army's procurement timetable for barracks, vehicles, ammunition, guns and railway building. The army's equipment program, originally scheduled for completion in 1942, now stretched to 1948. General Friedrich Fromm, the head of the army's administrative branch, wondered whether even trying to achieve the new goal of a wartime army of 3.6 million men organized into 102 divisions by 1940 was reckless. The burly, forty-eight-year-old, conservative-thinking Fromm felt uneasy in the new Reich. To him the coming of the Nazis seemed as though a barbarian horde had descended on Berlin. Yet, he had to admit, Hitler had delivered on his promises to the generals. Germany was arming, but why at breakneck speed? From a professional standpoint, what troubled Fromm was the tendency of the staff's expansion plans to zoom past training, financial and industrial limits.

In August 1936 Fromm laid out in detail the financial and material costs of the future army. The price tag was a colossal nine billion Reichsmarks, double what had been projected two years before. In theory, he wrote, if the foreign exchange could be found to buy the raw materials on time and industry acquired the skilled labor and plant to make weapons, ammunition and stores, the project was feasible, but it entailed serious consequences. The most important followed from the speed of the build-up. To deliver the needed volume of equipment, the arms producers would have to expand their plant capacity and workforce. After 1940 the arms makers would be left with a huge overcapacity that would be surplus in peacetime but needed in war. To maintain the plant, the army would have to feed industry a diet of follow-on orders absurdly beyond peacetime needs. By 1942 the cost of doing so would be greater than the budget of the peacetime army. Of course, much of the excess plant could be retooled to make consumer goods, but this would be a painful and costly readjustment that would reduce industry's readiness for war. Unless there was already a plan to use the army in 1940, Fromm wrote, it made good sense to avoid this boom-and-bust cycle and arm over a longer stretch of time.

A man who perpetually hedged his bets, Fromm did not offer his superiors firm advice but instead asked probing questions: Could the foreign exchange and raw materials problems be solved? Could export earnings cover the follow-on costs of the overcapacity in the armaments industry after 1940? And, most of all, was "there already a firm intention to use the armed forces by a fixed date?" Fromm did not get a reply to his last question. General Werner von Fritsch, the head of the army, thought that most of the training and supply difficulties could be solved. "It is the will of the Führer," he wrote, "that a powerful army is to be created in the shortest possible time."[8]

So rather than prompting a slackening of the pace, the industrial bottlenecks of 1936 only added more urgency to the belief of the Nazi elite and the military men that the arms race must be continued and intensified at all costs. External pressures had been building up all year. France and Britain began major arms programs. The growth of Soviet heavy industry under the first two Five Year Plans amazed onlookers. And, for the Soviets, the year 1936 was the most spectacular so far in terms of large rises in the output of arms.[9]

Hitler described Soviet arms, autarky and ideology in shrill tones. He complained to foreign statesmen and journalists about the Franco-Soviet and Czech-Soviet mutual assistance pacts of May 1935. Czechoslovakia, he liked to say, was the Soviet air base in the center of Europe. Anti-Bolshevism reached fever pitch with the outbreak of civil war in Spain. After the Spanish Army botched a coup against the left-wing government in Madrid in early July 1936, Hitler and Mussolini backed General Francisco Franco while Stalin sent assistance to the Spanish Republic.[10]

In August another escalation in German armaments took place. In one of those very rare instances, Hitler took pen to paper to write a memorandum outlining the Four Year Plan. Germany would arm like Russia in a deliberate act of military-economic emulation and convergence. For all his bemoaning the Soviet menace, Hitler and his military men—like their colleagues in London and Paris—did not rate the Red Army very highly. But admiration in Berlin for Soviet multi-year plans to arm and industrialize ran deep, especially among the total-war systematizers like Blomberg and Thomas. Hitler hated communism, but he admired Stalin's totalitarian ways.[11]

In the Four Year Plan memorandum, the full text of which first went to Göring and Blomberg, Hitler set out his thoughts on rearmament. The preamble, echoing *Mein Kampf*, described history as a struggle for survival, with Bolshevism as the most hideous weapon yet wielded against the Germans by "worldwide Jewry." No people, above all the Germans, could give up the struggle because defeat would mean "annihilation." The only answer to the "unified aggressive will" of the Soviet Union lay in the build-up of a colossal German war machine. Here the do-or-die language and logic so typical of the spiraling arms race crept into the memo. "The military resources of this aggressive will are," Hitler wrote, "rapidly increasing from year to year. One has only to compare the Red Army as it actually exists today with the assumptions of military men of ten or fifteen years ago to realise the menacing extent of this development. Only consider the results of a further ten, fifteen or twenty years and think what conditions will be like then." In National Socialism the Germans had found the "ideological solidarity" to conquer "living space." "*The extent of the military development of our resources cannot be too large, nor its pace too swift,*" Hitler wrote, underscoring for emphasis. Where possible, Germany must achieve 100 percent autarky in raw materials, especially fuels, rubber and iron ore. The job of economic officials was to set targets. The failure of industry to cooperate in meeting these targets was sabotage and so punishable by death. "Either German industry will grasp the new economic tasks or else it will show itself incapable of surviving any longer in this modern age in which a Soviet state is setting up a gigantic plan." Germany too needed a plan to carry out two tasks: "I. The German armed forces must be operational within four years. II. The German economy must be fit for war within four years."[12]

To the outside world the first sign of this step-up in German rearmament came on August 24 with the extension of military service in Germany from one to two years. On September 9 Hitler delivered the official announcement of the Four Year Plan at the Nuremberg rally. Five days earlier, in Berlin, Göring read out Hitler's memorandum to a meeting of ministers, including a delighted Blomberg and an annoyed Schacht. Hitler had handed Göring the responsibility of "safeguarding rearmament." A showdown with Russia was inevitable, Göring emphasized. And "anything the Russians have achieved in building up [their armaments and industry], we can also do."[13]

Hitler believed that only three countries had the internal cohesion and rearmament to withstand the rising Soviet peril: Germany, Italy and Japan. At about the time Hitler intervened in Spain, he also decided to sign a pact with Japan. In Tokyo the cabinet agreed that breaking Japan's diplomatic isolation outweighed the drawbacks of associating with Berlin. In the resulting Anti-Comintern Pact of October 25, 1936, Germany and Japan agreed to oppose the Communist International and (in a secret protocol) to do nothing to assist Russia if it attacked either signatory. Typical of alignments in the rush to build garrison states and autarkic economies, the Anti-Comintern Pact proclaimed ideological affinity but did not commit either signatory to go to war for a common cause.[14]

Mussolini's turn toward Berlin began with the Ethiopian war of 1935–36. British and French resistance to the colonial conquest convinced the Duce that he had more to gain by aligning with Germany than joining in its containment. As the crisis escalated, Hitler offered Mussolini supplies of fuel and other goods to circumvent the League of Nations' embargo in return for a settlement on Austria. After an Anglo-French bid to find a peaceful end to the war fell apart in December 1935, Mussolini replied warmly to Hitler's overtures. In January 1936 Mussolini told the German ambassador in Berlin that he had no objection to Austria falling into Germany's orbit. Weeks later he added that Italy would not oppose a remilitarization of the Rhineland.[15]

During 1936 Mussolini spoke often and vividly about the ideological affinity between the Fascist and Nazi regimes. That year, with defense budgets across Europe rising, ideas about how states should be armed, economies organized and the masses mobilized—ideas that for him had come together in 1917–18 and his brand of fascism had espoused ever since—were now also in the ascendant. By arming and challenging the old world order, Italy and Germany were speeding down a "congruent" totalitarian path, the Duce thought, and in that sense shared a "common fate."[16]

The widening divide between the totalitarian states and the democracies, and the economic "siege" of Italy by the League of Nations, prompted Mussolini to accelerate preparations for total war. He told the Supreme Defense Commission in February 1936 that "the economy had not only to be directed but truly dominated by the prospect of war." On March 23, as the Ethiopian war climaxed and Mussolini felt a sense of "growing military strength," he delivered one of his blood-and-thunder speeches to the National Assembly of the Corporations. He announced a vast "planning scheme" to develop the economy for the "inevitability that the nation will be called to the trial of war." "When and how," he said, "nobody can say, but the wheel of destiny runs swiftly. Otherwise how can one explain the policy of colossal armaments inaugurated by all nations? This dramatic eventuality must guide all our activity. In the present historical period the fact, war, is, together with the doctrine of Fascism, a determining element in the position of the State towards the economy." Mussolini's March 23 speech on autarky prefigured (and certainly helped to inspire) Hitler's Four Year Plan memorandum. Italy had to achieve "the maximum economic self-sufficiency within the shortest possible time," the Fascist dictator exclaimed. Italy had to cut fuel imports by half, and vital raw materials had to be stockpiled. The armaments industries, because of their scale and significance in war, had to be concentrated and directed by the state. "It is perfectly logical," Mussolini reasoned, "within the Fascist state that these industries should cease to have even the façade of private enterprise, which they had lost in practice in 1930–31. The state is their only customer. They will not have time or opportunity to produce for private consumption, but instead they will have to work almost exclusively for the armed forces."[17]

With industry booming and unemployment falling thanks to state spending on war materials, no wonder Mussolini brimmed with confidence that he could pick up the tempo. To "regulate and discipline" the arms makers, he put Italy's wartime arms czar, General Alfredo Dallolio, at the helm of a new Commissariat for War Production, while Alberto Beneduce, the Duce's financial wizard, tightened his grip on the economy overall. A new dirigiste banking law in 1936 made the state the regulator of credit. Beneduce issued commercial loans with an eye to promoting industrial growth in sectors vital to armaments. Industrialists soon found themselves organized into cartels that allocated output quotas to minimize competition and overcapacity. Like some unstoppable bureaucratic hydra, Beneduce's apparatus of control, the Institute for Industrial Reconstruction, soon dominated the producers of iron, steel, engineering, shipbuilding, chemicals, coal, oil and synthetics, while other new state agencies regulated trade, currency flows and wages and prices.[18]

Still, no amount of economic reorganization planned in Rome was going to make up for Italy's relative poverty in iron, coal and oil. With time, Italy could have reduced its reliance on foreign machinery, certain raw materials and foodstuffs; but, as Mussolini would soon discover, time was not on his side. The drive to self-sufficiency and the escalation in arming in fact made Italy more dependent on foreign fuels and other imports. The empire proved much more of a drain on the Italian economy than a fund of potential strength. At least Japan's conquest, Manchuria, had the mineral deposits and other natural resources to be turned into a mighty bastion of total war through multi-year plans; apart from gold, Ethiopia was largely barren.[19]

In July 1936, Mussolini decided to assist the Spanish rebels against the Republic. No doubt he was roused by the anti-Bolshevik frenzy sweeping Europe that year and regarded the whole venture as a quick blow against the communists in Madrid, Paris and Moscow. Backing fascism in Spain made strategic sense too. An ally on France's southern frontier would be valuable, as would the opportunities for commercial and naval cooperation. But what started as a limited operation, within months escalated into a major deployment of Italian ground, air and naval forces. Italy did not have the resources to fight another expeditionary war and prepare for total war all at once. General Mario Roatta, the intelligence chief who organized aid to the Spanish junta, cautioned Mussolini against intervention in a style strikingly similar to Colonel Ishiwara's warnings about war in China. "Spain is like quicksand," Roatta said. "If you stick in a hand, everything will follow."[20]

The vast expense of arms, autarky and war also sent public spending sky high. The deficit tripled from 1934 to 1936. To balance state revenue with spending, taxes rose, with the middle and upper classes taking the biggest hit. In addition to orthodox measures to raise money such as issuing state bonds, Mussolini's finance wizards turned to draconian means, such as nationalizing foreign investments. They made patriotic appeals too. In 1936 Italian women turned their gold wedding rings over to the state and raised 400 million lire for the nation's coffers. Printing more money covered about thirty percent of the deficit for 1935–36, but this put upward pressure on prices. With inflation looming, the balance of payments out of kilter, gold and foreign-exchange reserves shrinking and the appetite for fuel and metals growing, Italy arrived at a crossroads in July 1936, when the League of Nations lifted sanctions. Italy could devalue the lira, stop subsidizing exports and return to the world economy, or pursue self-sufficiency. Italy lacked the resources to practice autarky on the scale of the Soviet Union or Germany. Mussolini thus took a middle course: devaluation and tighter state controls on consumption and trade. In October 1936 the lira was devalued forty percent in line with the dollar and the pound. Exports recovered, yet half of the trade went to the empire and Germany, and in the form of barter. Some journalists, recalling Fascism's liberal trade practices of the 1920s, wrote that the lira's devaluation was a sign that the Duce had not yet fully taken the totalitarian turn. They were mistaken. Mussolini's mind had been made up more than a decade before.[21]

DURING THE FIRST STAGE of German expansion, Hitler hoped to reach an understanding with both Britain and Italy. He tried to reassure the British that he had no wish to challenge them at sea or demand parts of their empire, provided they left him alone on the continent. To his utter bewilderment the British ignored him.

After the remilitarization of the Rhineland in March 1936, Hitler assumed in relation to Britain the attitude of a humble petitioner of whose good nature unfair advantage had been taken. Had he not been "magnanimous" over the naval treaty in 1935? What concern did the meddling English have about the fate of eastern Europe? Was not Germany the continent's bulwark against Bolshevism? Instead of gratitude, all he got from the British was a barrage of diplomatic notes and questionnaires.

In contrast to the British, Mussolini, whom Hitler considered a heroic visionary like himself, knew how to make a deal. Long an admirer of the Duce, Hitler was impressed by his victory in the Ethiopian crisis. Nearly everyone in Berlin expected Rome to have given in. German staff officers credited Italy with a first-rate arms industry, a good air force and fleet, but nowhere near the economic strength to risk an all-out war against Britain, never mind France too. Yet Mussolini had held his nerve and won Ethiopia. To Hitler, a man too quick to reduce the complex anatomy of cause and effect in world affairs down to the mere exercise of will, this could only mean that Britain had been exposed as a declining power while Italy had proven itself a rising one.[22]

After Germany and Austria signed a treaty in July 1936, which eased tensions between Berlin and Vienna for a time, and after Germany and Italy aided the Spanish Army rebels and the Four Year Plan was launched, Hitler wanted Italy to unite with Germany and Japan in an anticommunist, totalitarian bloc. In September he sent the Nazi Party's top jurist, Hans Frank, to Rome. He saw the Duce at the splendid Palazzo Venezia and invited him to Berlin the following year. "The Führer is anxious," Frank emphasized, "that you should know that he regards the Mediterranean as a purely Italian sea"—despite Germany's intervention in Spain. Although he had little hope of success, he went on seamlessly: Hitler also wanted Mussolini to know that he was sending Ribbentrop as ambassador to London in a last-ditch effort to negotiate a rapprochement.

Mussolini swiftly ran through the items raised by Frank. Yes, he was delighted that Austria was no longer a source of friction between Rome and Berlin; that they were giving battle to Bolshevism in Spain; and yes, France was doomed to decay from a "terrifying" demographic "decadence." Yet he dwelt on what Frank had said about Britain. "Hitler was right to make an attempt with Ribbentrop," Mussolini conceded. "But it will not succeed. Ribbentrop will accomplish nothing." The dictator then used one of his favorite tricks. He confessed that he had come by a certain secret British document. "England only intends to live with Germany," he said that Italian espionage had revealed, "in so far as it will give her time to achieve rearmament."[23]

Mussolini wanted that message relayed to Hitler. While force of circumstances as well as common values and practices had helped to push the two dictatorships closer together, Mussolini was still alive to the danger of being "towed" by Germany rather than doing the "towing." Intelligence depicted Germany as arming with daunting speed. In June 1936 the air force chief, General Giuseppe Valle, toured Germany as a guest of the Luftwaffe and returned convinced that "by the beginning of 1938 Germany will possess the strongest air force in Europe." Better to be a friend than a foe of Germany, he advised. The Italian military attaché in Berlin reported that the German Army already had 800,000 trained and well-equipped troops. By the end of 1937 it would be a "formidable" war machine. Britain too, in response to Germany, had begun air and naval rearmament in 1935–36 that would yield "satisfactory" results by 1938. The British ambassador bragged to Italy's foreign minister, "Rearmament is proceeding actively and rapidly, and, as far as the Navy and Air Force are concerned, no difficulties are being met either in materials or in manpower. There are difficulties," he said with a hint of modesty, "with recruitment for the land forces, where there are shortages; but the British Government is determined to overcome all possible obstacles in this field too."[24]

For Italy the danger was being squeezed between fast-growing German air and land forces on the continent and fast-growing British air and naval forces in the Mediterranean. An Anglo-German détente, something Hitler seemed to be pursuing through Ribbentrop's mission to London, would be a disaster for Rome. Whatever mutual affinity Fascists and Nazis voiced or structural features the two dictatorships shared, regimes that espoused great armaments and self-contained national economies engendered a competitive and predatory form of expansionism that could not be counted on to observe a handshake between dictators. Germany might double-cross Italy if it could get a great advantage by doing so.

To help prevent this unhappy occurrence and take advantage of the seismic shifts in European politics brought about by German rearmament, Mussolini had to keep London and Berlin at daggers drawn. They did not need much help. Still, the Duce liked to play things safe. He intended to convince Hitler that any British effort to come to terms with Germany was nothing but a sham to buy time for Britain to rearm. That was a message Hitler was more than prepared to believe.

On October 24, 1936, Mussolini's son-in-law, Italy's new foreign minister, Count Galeazzo Ciano, met Hitler in his private study at Berchtesgaden. After a long-winded exchange of flattery, Hitler described how he had rejected British bribes to turn against the Duce during the Ethiopian war. The democracies, he said, had formed a bloc hostile to Fascism and Nazism. The Führer inquired after the state of Anglo-Italian relations. While Mussolini harbored no sinister anti-British designs, Ciano explained, it would be "stupid" to ignore Britain's anti-Italianism. Britain was no less anti-German. "If there are no positive and direct indications of this," he warned, "it is because England is trying to gain the time necessary to complete her rearmament."

Then came the big moment. Ciano handed Hitler the fruits of Italian skullduggery: a dossier of thirty-two top-secret British Foreign Office papers headed "The German Peril." One paper advised that "it was vital for Britain to speed up and complete her rearmament in order to be ready to face any eventuality." Hitler flew into a rage when he read himself called a "dangerous adventurer." "England, too, was led by adventurers when she built her Empire. Today," he sneered like some honest broker unjustly maligned, "it is governed merely by incompetents."

After a violent outburst about Spain, Russia and Bolshevism, Hitler turned to the subject of British encirclement: "there is no doubt that England will attack Italy or Germany, or both, if she feels that she can do so with impunity and with ease." Italy and Germany must form an anti-British bloc under the banner of anti-Bolshevism:

If then England were to continue to form offensive plans and merely sought to gain time to rearm, we would defeat her on her own ground, since German and Italian rearmament is proceeding much more rapidly than rearmament can in England, where it is not only a case of producing ships, guns and aeroplanes, but also of undertaking psychological rearmament, which is much longer and more difficult. In three years Germany will be ready, in four years more than ready; if five years are given, better still. But the military power achieved by our two countries will, even in the latter case, be such as to make England desist from any aggressive attempt.

In response Ciano "deeply impressed" Hitler by outlining Italy's arms build-up. During Ciano's visit, the two governments concluded a pact that affirmed their cooperation in Spain and their resolve to fight communism. On November 1, 1936, during a speech in the cathedral square in Milan, Mussolini proclaimed the new Rome-Berlin agreement as "an Axis around which all European states who want peace can revolve."[25]

Europe of course did not suddenly start to turn on a new axis. Instead, the arms races just continued to gather speed much faster than Italy could go. Yet Mussolini thought he had won himself time and space while Britain, France and Germany locked themselves in rivalry. As Ciano told him, Hitler intended to "remain cautious and to buy time to complete a level of rearmament that would give him the certainty of success." So too would Italy. Before Ciano left for Berlin, Mussolini made a big show of stepping up rearmament. The Commissariat for War Production controlled 1,200 factories devoted to arms output, he told the newspapers. Aircraft producers were authorized to extend the workweek to sixty hours, twenty above the norm. More men and equipment had been authorized for the army and navy too.[26]

The situation was not quite what the headlines suggested. True, the Italian Air Force was ordered to build 3,000 aircraft to "command" the Mediterranean by the spring of 1938. And, after the Ethiopian crisis, Admiral Domenico Cavagnari played on the British threat to promote the naval staff's six-year expansion plans. "Britain has revealed itself," he explained in lurid terms to the Duce, "to be opposed to all our imperial aspirations in principle. . . . If we accept that our destiny will take us into confrontation with Britain, then there is the inescapable need to strengthen our navy." But Spain and colonial pacification had already consumed huge sums. In August 1936, on the advice of finance officials, Mussolini ordered service spending capped. Arms growth had to be curtailed if the public finances were going to benefit from the lira's devaluation.[27]

And so the three service chiefs were unhappy. With Italy marching alongside Germany, the driver of the arms spiral, and the Duce boasting about
great armaments and autarky, it seemed to them perverse that they should
want for cash. At a meeting on November 5, 1936, Marshal Badoglio asked the
chiefs of staff, "What conclusions can therefore be drawn from Mussolini's
[Axis] speech? There is a tendency to unify our efforts with those of the
Rome-Berlin Axis," he answered for himself, "and there is a message of peace
for all other countries. Moreover, Mussolini has told me privately that he intends to adopt a benevolent attitude towards France, but this intention does
not mean that the 1935 military accords with Paris are valid. Another important thing emerges from the speech, namely that the Mediterranean is vital
for Italy." Badoglio then reminded the service heads about the spending caps
they had agreed to in August. Each took a turn to complain. Cavagnari demanded, How was the navy supposed to upgrade the fleet? Valle asked, How
was the air force supposed to reach the 3,000-plane target and build new
bases in the colonies? General Alberto Pariani grumbled, How was the War
Ministry going to replace the munitions and equipment expended in Ethiopia
and modernize the army all at the same time? Badoglio, a skilled bureaucratic
manipulator, had a clear goal in mind when he provoked this outburst. Unconvinced about the value of the Axis with Germany and the potential for
further expansion in the Mediterranean, he made his own defense priority
plain. "We should not delude ourselves," he told the chiefs. "If we do not provide for the defence of the homeland, then we cannot wage war beyond our
own frontiers." In any European war, he added, they would not be shooting
at poorly equipped Africans. Unless the Duce could find a lot more money,
it was pointless to discuss the problem of any service arm in isolation. "I will
ask to meet Mussolini again," he reassured them, "because it is not possible
to remain in the dark about these problems which are vital for our security in
the Mediterranean." Badoglio summed up with deliberate irony: "Military
preparations should always be in line with government policy."[28]

What troubled Badoglio was Mussolini's pursuit of two conflicting goals.
On the one hand, the Duce seemed to understand that preparing for total
war required a huge investment over the long haul and that Italy suffered
from certain disadvantages. Lagging behind was one thing, but dropping out
of the arms race quite another. "In a world armed to the teeth," Mussolini
later explained, "to lay down the arms of self-sufficiency would mean putting
oneself tomorrow, in the case of war, at the mercy of those who had unlimited resources for war. Self-sufficiency was therefore a guarantee of peace and
an impediment to the eventual aggressive designs of the richer countries." On

the other hand, with Britain and Germany locked in rivalry, and relations with France and Yugoslavia improving, Mussolini became convinced he could win another quick war if the opportunity arose. Victory over Ethiopia no doubt inspired him. And so did the military theories of General Pariani.[29]

Born in 1876, Pariani was a forward-thinking soldier obsessed with the speed and firepower that modern technology could bring to the battlefield. During the war he was decorated for valor in combat and served as a military adviser to Italy's delegation to the Paris Peace Conference. In the 1920s he held a series of army staff positions, including chief of operations. By the time preparations for war against Ethiopia began, Pariani was deputy army chief of staff under General Alfredo Baistrocchi. Both men agreed that the army needed to be modernized—more tanks, new guns and lots of trucks—and that the officer corps needed to be imbued with youthful dynamism. Where the two officers departed was over the character of future war, and what sort of war Italy could get ready for. Baistrocchi, like Badoglio and others, expected the next European conflict to be a total war. To wage it, the army needed advanced weapons, and also maximum numbers to withstand the long, grinding attrition of machine-age warfare. That was, after all, precisely the kind of war all the great powers expected to fight. Settling for a small well-equipped force would therefore amount to an abdication of Italy's claim to great-power status.

Pariani, a man given to shock-and-awe fantasies, believed that with superior agility and ferocity the army could dominate future battlefields. If Italy deployed an elite corps of fast-moving tanks and motorized infantry, supported by aircraft hurling tons of high explosive and gas bombs ahead to paralyze foes, he argued, rapid results could be achieved, especially against the British in Egypt or the Sudan. Baistrocchi too liked the idea of "wars of rapid decision." Like Pariani, he thought Italians had an innate flair for such audacity. But the danger was that "lightning" raids in Spain or North Africa might quickly escalate into a very big war. "The war that you foresee will be long, very long," Baistrocchi cautioned Mussolini in September 1936, "the lightning war to which the hack strategists, who are utopians, allude is a pleasing aspiration for [us] all, [but] realizable only when there is an enormous discrepancy in strength between the belligerents—look at Italy with more than 400,000 men, 1,200 guns and 400 airplanes against Ethiopia without guns or aircraft."[30]

A few weeks later the Duce fired Baistrocchi and replaced him with Pariani. Mussolini knew that to wait until Baistrocchi or Badoglio thought the army was ready meant nonstop inaction. Yes, he would strive for autarky and

great armaments, but in the meantime he wanted to exploit Italy's geo-
graphical position and the European situation to score quick results. A man
of action, the Duce was eager to test himself in war again. In October 1936 one
confidant recorded Mussolini's ruminations:

> "The next war will be a war of seven weeks." A pause. "We can do it. We
> do not need to consult anyone. Think of the surprise of the Italians on the
> day that they would wake up and find in the newspapers this item: an Ital-
> ian air squadron has bombarded the British naval squadron at Malta. It is
> believed that X number of ships have been sent to the bottom." Another
> pause. "I liked the definition of Pariani. He said to me the other day—'we
> must be prepared to fight a war of brigandage'—quite right!"[31]

As THE NEW YEAR of 1937 began, Hitler saw the international situation un-
folding his way. Russia was arming, but the fear of Soviet communism was
driving Poland, Romania and Yugoslavia into Germany's political sphere.
Stalin threatened Spain, but the terror of his purges had plunged the Soviet
Union into chaos. As soon as Germany was fully armed, France would seek
terms. The British people were tough, he thought, but their leaders were inept.
With Britain arming against Italy, he would forge stronger ties to Fascist Italy.
Above all else German rearmament proceeded apace. When the first of the
big wars arrived in five or six years, Germany would be ready for it.[32]

Ever since Hitler assigned Göring the authority to execute the Four Year
Plan in October 1936, the head of the air force had in fact done everything
possible to push arming forward. Drawing on military men, party loyalists
and business technocrats eager to experiment with autarky, he set up a new
organization to take control of the raw materials, labor, agriculture, wages,
prices and foreign-exchange movements. He began a huge scheme of investment in the manufacture of iron, steel, fuels and synthetic substitutes. To
manage the economy, Göring's bureaucracy tightened its grip on business.
On December 17, he assembled Germany's top industrialists in a large hall in
Berlin. The old laws of economics no longer applied, he declared. It was his
job to knock down the obstacles to rearmament. Germany would not again
be defeated by a blockade. Business must expand the industrial base now
without the fear of being burdened later by overcapacity. "Whatever happens," Göring bellowed, "our capacity will be far too small. The struggle that
we are approaching demands a colossal measure of productive ability. No end
of the rearmament is in sight. The only deciding point in this case is victory

or destruction. If we win, then business will be sufficiently compensated. . . . We are now playing for the highest stakes. . . . All selfish interests must be put aside. Our whole nation is at stake. We live in a time when the final battles are in sight. We are already on the threshold of mobilization and are at war, only the guns are not yet firing." A few days later Göring ordered the whole of the aircraft industry to operate on a mobilization footing.[33]

To raise Germany's relative strength against Britain, especially in naval armaments, Göring also championed Hitler's policy of good relations with Italy. In January 1937 he visited Rome to discuss with Ciano and Mussolini operations in Spain and Austria and (something Hitler wanted to encourage) Italy's departure from the League of Nations. Time and again, Göring underscored Germany's value as an ally in another Anglo-Italian showdown in the Mediterranean. While discussing the bomber versus the battleship debate with the Duce, the head of the Luftwaffe emphasized the importance of Italian naval expansion in the competition against Britain. Evidence from air attacks on Spanish ships, he said, confirmed what he had always believed: air forces cannot destroy a fleet in a "truly decisive" way. "It is necessary to keep naval armaments in view at all costs, in consideration of the fact that England is building five battleships over and above her normal programme." Mussolini, eager to make exactly the same point, replied that Italy would soon have two refurbished and two new battleships, twenty-four cruisers and 100 submarines. Taken together, Göring observed, the Italian, German and Japanese fleets "constitute a very considerable naval force compared with other countries."[34]

Nonetheless, probably before his Rome visit, doubts started to creep into Göring's mind about Germany's ability to pull ahead in the arms race. Despite all the fanfare and burst of activity that surrounded the Four Year Plan, it was going to take years before results would begin to show. Shortages of raw material and skilled labor constrained rearmament. As soon as Göring put the aircraft industry on a war footing, raw-material shortages forced him to revise the order and set new priorities. Germany's steel mills could not keep up with military orders, many of which had to be canceled. A system of steel rationing was introduced. Blomberg and Thomas complained bitterly about all the metal going to imposing government buildings. And, so desperate was the need for foreign exchange, Germany was exporting as much steel as it was devoting to armaments and the Four Year Plan combined.[35]

And now Germany was not the only nation arming. "The global politico-military situation is characterised by the fact that at an accelerated speed all states are building up their military strength," one member of the Reich's Defense Council observed in November 1936. That month France, after a sluggish start, picked up the pace of arms spending. The most immediate worry was British rearmament. Göring's deputy, General Milch, was impressed by the strides being made by the British aircraft industry. In two years, he estimated, it would be ready for war. Göring was not at all confident that the Four Year Plan would make Germany invincible.[36]

On February 25, 1937, Göring spoke to the Italian ambassador in Berlin about the arms race. No one was "surprised" by British rearmament, least of all Germany, he said. Although the British lagged behind in certain aspects of aviation technology, that did "not diminish the 'gigantic effort' that [British rearming] represents, which is the more to be feared in that it is carried out by a country that has sufficient economic resources to bring it to full completion and perhaps even extend it." British military expansion, in fact, was driving up world commodity prices, making it more difficult for other states such as Germany to rearm. At great length, Göring emphasized that British armaments were aimed at not just Germany but Italy, too. He urged Mussolini to build more battleships. "The common [British] threat," he said, "requires Italy and Germany to remain more than ever united, consolidating the Rome-Berlin Axis." When Göring began to ramble on about his visit to Rome, the Italian ambassador interrupted him and asked pointedly about what Germany was going to do in reply to the British arms build-up. Even accounting for a certain amount of exaggeration to press home his point, Göring's candor was still amazing. "We have reached a plateau," he confessed. "All that was humanly possible to launch and organise in advance we have already done. Any more is absolutely impossible. . . . The consequence for us will be psychological more than anything: any of us who still had some hope in possible 'arrangements' with Britain now must lose it. I first of all must accustom my airmen to consider the British as their potential enemies and therefore to prepare to fight the British too. We can perfect organization, accelerate the pace within the limits of possibility, but . . . nothing more."[37]

CHAPTER 9

GUNS AND BUTTER

I t was January 18, 1936, a Saturday. In the study of 11 Downing Street, London, the official residence of the chancellor of the exchequer, Neville Chamberlain opened his copy of *The Times* and scanned the news. Italian troops had pushed deep into Ethiopia. The Scandinavian states had reaffirmed their loyalty to the principle of collective security. France was troubled by another cabinet crisis: Pierre Laval's administration was teetering toward collapse. French ratification of the Franco-Soviet mutual assistance treaty would go ahead soon. And the night before, the British foreign secretary, Anthony Eden, had made a "dignified" speech setting out Britain's desire to negotiate European peace and disarmament.

Joseph Goebbels also made a speech the same night as Eden. Hitler's propaganda minister claimed that his country was a poor one in need of raw materials and guns. "We can do without butter," Chamberlain read with growing exasperation, "but not without guns, because butter could not help us if we were to be attacked one day. Some people say there is a world conscience which is the League of Nations, whose part it is to preserve the peace of the world, but I prefer to rely on guns."[1]

For a year now, Chamberlain, the supreme problem solver, had been weighing up guns and butter. Pressure steadily grew from the chiefs of staff and inside the Treasury to arm faster. Warren Fisher, the permanent undersecretary, had intelligence that Germany was "increasing her internal floating debt secretly as a means of finding money for accelerated rearmament." Originally, Chamberlain had been against borrowing to arm. Yet, by the summer of 1935, the growing menace of Germany's armaments had changed his mind. "Germany is said to have borrowed over £1,000 millions a year to get herself rearmed and she has perfected a wonderful industrial organisation capable of rapid expansion for the production of the materials of war. With Mussolini hopelessly tied up in Ethiopia and Great Britain disarmed," Chamberlain reasoned, "the temptation in a few years time to demand territory etc. might be too great for Göring, Goebbels and their like to resist. Therefore we must hurry our own rearmament and in the course of the next four or five years." The Ethiopian crisis, too, impressed him with the need to arm. What annoyed him was not that Mussolini had "flouted" the League of Nations but that he had "flouted" Britain. "What I shall work for," he promised, "is a Britain strong enough to make it impossible for her wishes to be flouted again." With a general election approaching in November 1935, Chamberlain wanted the Conservative-dominated National Government to campaign on a defense program.[2]

Stanley Baldwin, who had become prime minister in June, was opposed to campaigning on defense. He feared a backlash at the polls because of the deadlock at the world disarmament talks and the government's wavering support for the League of Nations in the crisis over Ethiopia. "A vote for the Tories is a vote for war," ran one Labour Party slogan. Baldwin claimed that higher defense spending was essential to fulfill Britain's obligation to collective security. "There has not been, there is not, and there will be no question of big armaments or materially increased forces," he promised. "What we do want, and what we must have," Baldwin explained, taking a leaf out of Franklin Roosevelt's book of political tricks, "is to replace our pre-war construction of ships in the Navy with modern ships. It does not mean increasing the Navy." Whether the government's victory at the polls on November 13 would have been altered markedly had Baldwin been more candid about rearmament, no one will ever know. Afterward, though, Chamberlain wondered about what would happen once voters discovered that they had been deceived. "When the country learns what we have spent this year on armaments over & above estimates," he wrote, "it is going to get a great shock. And it will be a very good thing because it may help to prepare them for worse—much worse—to come."[3]

He was right. By the end of 1935 it was clear that there would be no letup to the arms race anytime soon. For over two years industrial intelligence had told ministers what they had always assumed: Germany was arming at the utmost of its industrial might. Long before the Four Year Plan, officials took it for granted that Germany had a master "plan" for autarky. After March 1935 British observers noticed that the language of all-out economic mobilization became more pronounced in German public life. Even the central banker Schacht, a defender of private capital and the free market, uttered the same phrases as the Nazi autarkists. The military wanted to usurp private enterprise too. The dictum of the nineteenth-century Prussian military philosopher, Carl von Clausewitz, that war is the pursuit of policy by other means, no longer applied. Modern systematizers like the failed ex-warlord Erich Ludendorff proclaimed that in an age where "totalitarian warfare" prevailed, war was waged between entire nations for survival, not for limited goals. "The totalitarian State is to be one of military State socialism," ran the Nazi line, "so far as economic policy is concerned. Peacetime economic organisation must be adapted to wartime needs."[4]

In weighing up how much of the nation's wealth would be devoted to defense, Chamberlain was not going to put guns before butter. He would increase the speed and magnitude of rearmament, but not excessively so under the impulse of fear. To do so would damage long-term economic growth. Peacetime economic organization was distinct from that of wartime. Britain could not turn its entire industry over to arms at the expense of exports. A healthy balance of trade had to be maintained to earn foreign exchange to make purchases abroad. To stockpile more and more arms without a time scale and goal in mind would lead to the sort of reckless open-ended arming that General Fromm would soon worry about in Berlin. Industrialists would divert ever more factory-floor space and employ ever more labor in munitions work. The state would be drawn in to subordinate business and labor interests and to enforce the fulfillment of national production targets. In time the arms boom would have to end in a bust, or the weapons would have to be used. Turning Britain into a garrison state made sense in wartime—that was how the last war was won—but in peacetime that had profound political implications. To arm like Germany, Japan, Italy or the Soviet Union would mean adopting the sort of physical controls on production, consumption, trade and capital movements that the totalitarian states employed.

That there were limits in peacetime as to how far a democracy could arm without resorting to wartime-like controls was not Chamberlain's view alone. Back in 1933–34 war planners estimated that the fastest the country could stockpile essential raw materials and prepare industry for a smooth conversion to war production was by 1939. To try to arm much faster, or to "organise . . . our industries in peacetime so completely" that they were ready for war at once, was "unthinkable in a democratic country like ours." Experts the world over in fact agreed that ever greater state control was the inevitable outcome of high-pressure arming.[5]

The thought that Britain might be driven step-by-step into practicing a form of military communism or totalitarianism by the arms race and then, in all likelihood, into total war, appalled Chamberlain. The answer to this problem was deterrence. That elegant concept captivated him. Deterrence was the safety valve that would prevent arming from becoming a way of life. Let other nations amass colossal armies and regiment their factories and young men; Britain would concentrate its resources in the air and on the sea. "I am pretty satisfied now," Chamberlain wrote in February 1936, "that if we can keep out of war for a few years we shall have an air force of such striking power that no one will care to run risks with it." Relying chiefly on air power to deter war would keep the economy from collapsing under the weight of colossal land armaments, compel Hitler into diplomacy and arms limitation, free Britain from any entangling alliances with France and its allies and, so he thought, be ideal for preserving the peace of Europe and Britain's liberal political economy.[6]

Chamberlain understood that the danger of initiating a spiral into totalitarianism lay in the relationship between the state and the economy. During the worst years of the Depression, he had been bombarded by calls for national "planning." Radicals and progressives on the right and the left looked to Soviet-style multi-year plans as the only salvation from unbridled capitalist competition and overproduction. Planomaniacs—whether proto-fascist ones such as Oswald Mosley, socialist planners in the labor movement or Liberals such as Lloyd George—disagreed about who should control the plan. Would it be elected politicians, a new class of state technocrats or an authoritarian corporate state similar to Fascist Italy's? In the Conservative Party, the young Harold Macmillan, who labeled "planned capitalism" as the "middle way" between unrestricted individualism and socialism, proposed a "parliament for industry." In 1934–35, while chairing a party committee studying industrial planning, Chamberlain evinced no enthusiasm for new parliaments or hydra-like state bureaucracies. The committee agreed that the government must "put before the people a reasoned up-to-date defence of non-intervention; otherwise the positive appeal of Socialism or Fascism will carry the day." Chamberlain was not opposed to organized capitalism, but he did not want to use the power of the state to push too hard too fast. That might disrupt the recovery and send big business into a panic. What he wanted instead was to nudge industry into "self-regulation."[7]

The representatives of British industry too wanted self-regulation. But the political forces unleashed by the industrial downturn and fear of war moved in a much more interventionist direction. In 1934 the regulation of the arms trade came under the spotlight. Across the Atlantic, the U.S. Senate opened hearings into the activities of the private munitions companies. U.S. legislators wanted to know whether the world's top munitions companies, Dupont, Vickers, Schneider, Krupps, Skoda and so forth, conspired to trigger wars in

Asia and South America to boost sales. In October 1934 the British government responded to sensational newspaper coverage of the U.S. hearings by setting up a royal commission of its own. The true aim of its inquiry, however, was to shield the private arms makers and existing system of state contracting from too much public attention. Both the right and the left kept the issue alive, however. Both advocated nationalization. Peace groups argued that arms making was too dangerous to be left to profit-hungry conglomerates; on the right came calls for nationalization and state planning because arms production was too important to national safety to be left to the free play of market forces.[8]

The upshot of all this debate was that big business felt increasingly threatened as arming sped up by government-imposed plans and controls, with threats to the arms firms being only the thin edge of an impending interventionist onslaught. A future Labour government, so employers feared, might use state controls to subordinate private enterprise in order to tackle unemployment. At a meeting in October 1935 industry representatives complained to Baldwin and Chamberlain about a recent Conservative Party conference resolution that backed "organizing" industry for defense. "The Government had no idea of nationalising or socialising industry or of imposing an organisation on industry from without," the chancellor replied: "The [government] contemplated, however, that the [arms] programme would be one of considerable magnitude and considerable organisation would be required to prevent overlapping and competition in demands for skilled labour, and to reach an understanding about priorities." Chamberlain explained that he wanted industrialists to self-organize and that public anger over profiteering on armaments had to be avoided.[9]

Industry was not reassured. The aircraft firms, above all, feared nationalization as a consequence of the arms race because the state was their chief customer. Ever since March 1935, when Hitler claimed that the Luftwaffe was as big as the Royal Air Force, and Baldwin pledged again to parity in the air with Germany, the demand for more aircraft in Britain had grown. Although Air Chief Marshal Sir Edward Ellington had been reluctant to expand too quickly with aircraft that would soon be obsolete, he too now saw the need to press ahead with an impressive "shop window" force to deter Berlin. By the summer of 1935 the air force asserted itself with renewed energy under a new air minister, Lord Swinton, a confidant of Baldwin, and a new deputy director of air plans, Group Captain Arthur ("Bomber") Harris, the man who in a few years time would preside over the firebombing of German cities with the heavy four-engine bombers that he now only dreamed about. Harris and

his staff thought in terms no longer of numerical parity but of qualitative supremacy in flying range and bomb loads. With bigger, heavy machines, so the
air planners thought, in a future war Britain could deliver more bombs to
more German (or Russian) targets.[10]

In the meantime fresh intelligence indicated that the current air program,
Scheme C, was inadequate. In 1937 Germany would pull ahead in the air arms
race. The air staff feared that Britain would lack the front-line strength and reserve aircraft to cover losses in the opening of a war, as well as the pre-prepared
factories to start making aircraft once the shooting and bombing started. In
February 1936 the cabinet therefore authorized Scheme F, a new plan, com-
prising 2,204 front-line aircraft and reserves. The air force had won another big
budget victory. Yet the air planners did not feel content. In their view, future
war was fundamentally a slugging match between rival aircraft industries. The
side that could build the mightiest bomber fleet would win. Would Britain,
even with four-engine machines, outbuild and outbomb Germany?[11]

On March 3, 1936, the new Defence White Paper justified the rise in
Britain's air strength as a deterrent to European war. The government acknowledged that building the extra aircraft would create "an exceptionally
heavy demand" on industry and skilled labor but it could be done without
impeding normal trade. The air staff disagreed. The aircraft industry was already months behind on old orders; how could Scheme F be completed without a change in industrial and labor practices? "Our potential enemies," read
one especially bleak air staff memorandum, "are dragooned under forms of
government wherein the normal economic essentials and social decencies
which apply in our own democracy are ignored or perverted. . . . In Russia the
Soviet system provides an inexhaustible mass of slave labour and permits a
disregard of the interests and welfare of the individual, which would not be
tolerated in the British Empire. The regimes in Germany and Italy produce
in effect the same results, and in particular the same mass discipline and industrial organisation towards war output, as in Russia." How could a liberal
democracy like Britain compete with the fast-arming totalitarian states without undergoing some sort of deep political and economic change?[12]

The Royal Air Force was not alone in pondering this question. In France,
General Maurice Gamelin was asking himself the same thing about his country. After succeeding Weygand as commander of the army in January 1935, he
feared that there was little time to waste in arming. Born in 1872, Gamelin was
an unflappable intellectual who spent his spare time with the tranquil pursuits
of art and philosophy. A man of tact and patience, he hoped to break the debilitating stalemate between the soldiers and civilians that had marred the

Weygand years. With the Maginot Line nearly complete and the tide seeming to turn toward more money for defense, Gamelin made his priority the upgrading of the army and air force with better tanks, guns and air support. A dedicated student of total war, he wanted not just these advanced munitions for the opening battles of the next war but also the industrial capacity to crank them out in vast quantities.[13]

That was one reason why he opposed the heresy of Colonel Charles de Gaulle. According to de Gaulle, France's national cohesion and social discipline did not match that of the fascists. The only recourse, therefore, was to train a hard-core elite force of six tank divisions manned by long-service professionals. To Gamelin, such ideas, which found favor with right-wing defense critics who hoped to embarrass the government, were not only bad from the strategic perspective, because France needed the capacity to fight a long war, but politically damaging too. Left-wing politicians accused de Gaulle and his backers of trying to form a praetorian guard and subverting the democratic ideal of the nation in arms. Thanks to de Gaulle, tanks acquired an aura of fascism. But Gamelin wanted elite tank units, as well as a mass conscript army and the capacity to equip them: that meant convincing politicians of all stripes to take an interest in organizing a powerful munitions industry.[14]

Gamelin's desire for civil-military coordination was of course nothing new. After 1919 the army had wanted to set up a military-dominated bureaucracy for that purpose. But in 1921 the task went to a joint civil-military body, the Supreme Defense Council, run by General Bernard Serrigny, who was France's counterpart to Germany's apostle of centralization, Georg Thomas. Serrigny wanted to create a super-planning cell with the legal authority to reach into all "corners of government" to ensure "that it is better prepared to fulfill . . . its wartime tasks." Sure enough, however, every corner of government opposed him. The army and the navy did not want to become subordinates to a new supreme command, nor did they wish to loosen their grip on weapons design and purchasing. Finance and industrial civil servants rejected Serrigny's long-debated draft national mobilization law because it risked "the complete nationalisation of commerce, industry and agriculture." Even in total war, they argued, "a more flexible and liberal organisation was desirable" than the one Serrigny envisaged. Serrigny, who found himself marginalized by the ministries, never discovered a workable compromise between drafting mobilization plans in relative isolation and keeping the whole economy on a permanent war footing.[15]

General Gamelin, like most of his fellow officers, rejected Serrigny's "exaggerated centralization." France's top soldier wanted the government to get things done in the industrial sphere of war preparations—the way the generals wanted naturally—and to leave the army to its own devices. The problem was that during the second half of 1935 there was no sign that the government would act soon.

Pierre Laval, the ex-socialist lawyer turned ultra-conservative who became prime minister in June 1935, remained, like all his predecessors, wedded to the gold standard. In the weeks before he took office, the Bank of France hemorrhaged gold and industrial activity and national revenue fell, but Laval was determined to defend the franc and impose deflation as a form of social discipline, which meant, among other things, slashing state spending. Defense outlays, which had started to grow, were capped. The army's equipment budget was cut. To Gamelin and his staff, this was bad enough. But with the economic outlook uncertain, it was impossible to convince the arms makers to deliver on existing contracts or to invest in plant for future mass production, because they feared being stuck with excess capacity.[16]

Deflation of course did not stop France arming, but it was not at the speed and scale that Gamelin reckoned necessary to keep up with Germany. What made this lethargy all the worse was the state of France's alliances. The talks begun the year before by the then foreign minister, Louis Barthou, with Czechoslovakia, the Soviet Union and Italy had resulted in mutual assistance treaties with Prague and Moscow. In the spring of 1935 the Italians too signed agreements for joint military action against the Germans. In October, however, the onset of the Ethiopian war placed a question mark beside future Franco-Italian cooperation. Forced to choose between two potential allies, Gamelin was never in any doubt. Britain, even with its small army and overbearing diplomacy, would be the decisive source of strength against Germany.

By late November 1935, after nearly a year as France's top soldier, with not much to show for all his lobbying, General Gamelin's superhuman patience snapped. At a meeting of the high command, Laval said that France could not break with Britain, but he had reassured Mussolini of his good will over Ethiopia. Voicing his conviction that Europe could not be at peace unless France and Germany made peace, he affirmed his readiness to make concessions to achieve disarmament. "In any case," he declared, "we can never compete with Germany in an arms race." Trying "would lead to war." Laval wanted a tête-à-tête with Hitler. Although the French pact with Moscow was almost ratified—something that would sour a friendly overture to Berlin—he had deftly sidestepped Stalin's wish for military cooperation. Afterward, Gamelin went home dejected. He wept for the destiny of his country.[17]

EARLY IN 1936, Laval was in deep trouble. He had managed to annoy nearly everyone in France. Few in the political elite now believed that the budget could be balanced or that deflation would stimulate a business revival. Many conservatives suspected Laval of being a closet authoritarian and were leery of his use of decrees to manipulate the market. Socialists despised him for his wheeler-dealings with Mussolini over Ethiopia and the misery the working class endured under his economic policies. With a general election approaching in April-May and the left-wing parties coming together to offer voters a single progressive program, the center-left Radicals, which had propped up Laval's administration in Parliament in successive votes of no confidence, finally dumped him. On January 22, he resigned. Albert Sarraut, a Radical former premier, formed a caretaker administration to govern until the spring elections.

Gamelin was glad to see Laval go, but until a new government took office, new defense initiatives were unlikely. In the meantime he devoted himself to reversing Laval's budget cuts and stopping the politicians from doing anything rash. The danger spot was the Rhineland. For some time now, it was evident that Germany was covertly preparing to occupy the demilitarized zone. French generals had long written off the Rhineland as little more than a diplomatic bargaining chip. The British made it abundantly clear that they valued the zone in the same way. Without British backing, a war over the Rhineland was a losing proposition. What worried Gamelin was that another German outrage might just be enough to prompt the politicians into some sort of "madcap solution."

So, well before Hitler gave the order to occupy the Rhineland, Gamelin warned Sarraut that there was no quick and painless way to knock the Germans back. Any foray into the Rhineland would spark an all-out war. France must not isolate itself, as it had done in 1923, in a reckless go-it-alone war (and war it would have been because Hitler would have fought, though he counted on not having to do so). Germany had "a war potential that is far superior to ours," Gamelin told Sarraut, and Germany's industry was entirely mobilized. In the weeks following the German coup, he pressed ministers to increase defense spending and exact "compensation" from the British, specifically staff talks, for the loss of the demilitarized zone and the blow to French prestige. The result was disappointing. In April defense spending rose. The British reaffirmed their pledge to defend France and Belgium from an unprovoked German attack but did not offer firm plans for military assistance. And Belgium, a key French ally, declared itself neutral.[18]

During the spring of 1936, Gamelin's problem remained arms deliveries. Orders for new heavy tanks were months behind. The German Army did not have a "marked superiority" yet, he said, but would soon. The next government would have to do something fast. One solution was to imitate the "totalitarians": allow private industry to function under the tight control of the state. Gamelin thought too much state control would stifle the innovation that flows from competition. He preferred a "mixed" sector, one that included thriving private companies working alongside state-owned ones. In his view the state should manage private arms makers with incentives to acquire modern machine tools and build reserve plant for war, while government factories undertook commercially unattractive work. But what if the next government, as some foresaw, was Socialist? Just like the left in the United States and Britain, the French left had clamored for nationalization of private arms firms to thwart the "merchants of death." Gamelin worried that nationalization might cripple output. Others thought it was exactly what was needed to shift French arming into high gear.[19]

When the elections came, the Popular Front of the Radicals, the Socialists and the Communists won. This coalition of the lower middle classes, workers and peasants was born of a longing for relief from the Depression and a fear that the republic was in peril. To many on the left, the toppling of Daladier in February 1934 by the ultra-right leagues looked like a rehearsal for a full-blown fascist coup. Laval, with his severe deflation and dictatorial decrees, appeared to be playing a French Chancellor Brüning to some shadowy French Hitler. In 1934–35, the Communists, urged on by the Comintern to unite with other anti-fascist parties, played handmaiden by cajoling the Radicals into the coalition. By the time Laval fell, all three parties had worked out a common manifesto offering social justice, a strengthening of democratic institutions and a restoration of prosperity. Many conservatives feared that a Moscow-inspired coup was underway, a misperception reinforced by the unprecedented wave of strikes that accompanied the Popular Front's victory. By early June, in what was part spontaneous celebration, part industrial action, two million workers had gone on strike. Léon Blum, France's first Socialist premier, negotiated an end to the strikes. At the Hôtel Matignon, his official residence, the employers agreed to pay hikes, paid holidays, a forty-hour workweek and collective bargaining rights.[20]

The Popular Front was resolved to transform French society, but Blum was no power-crazed Bolshevik. With his characteristic bushy mustache and pince-nez, the dapper sixty-four-year-old Socialist drew his sense of moral mission from his Jewish heritage and an abiding faith in rationalism. A brilliant dancer, fencer and student, he had read law and literature at the Sorbonne. When war came in 1914, like most Socialists, he joined the "sacred union" of national defense and accepted a wartime post as a civil servant in public works. Toward the end of the war, when young radicals in his party looked to Lenin for inspiration, Blum preached reform and legality over revolutionary conspiracies. In the early 1930s he rose to the top of his party as a tireless campaigner for the League of Nations and disarmament.

When he became prime minister, Blum rejected calls from within his party and from the trade unions to control and plan the economy. In France, as elsewhere, planomania had taken hold of progressives of all stripes, but not Blum. For one thing, most Radicals, his center-left coalition partners, would never approve. That aside, deeper reasons lay behind Blum's moderation. He distinguished between "exercising power" within a parliamentary capitalist system and "conquering power" when the time was ripe for socialism. To try to "conquer power" prematurely would only pave the way for the dictatorial terror that gripped Russia, Italy and Germany. Since in France the conditions for true socialism were a long way off, the task of the Popular Front was to work slowly toward it. So Roosevelt's New Deal appealed to Blum as a model more than Soviet-style plans. He wanted to revive the economy by raising the purchasing power of the masses with a modest scheme of public works and limited state intervention. The Popular Front's election manifesto only called for more government control over the financial system, a new ministry for the economy and the nationalization of the arms industries. For Blum nationalization was an important step to a "disarmed" peace. If all governments owned their national arms industries, so ran his logic, then disarming everywhere would be all the more practicable.[21]

Blum had given the political economy of war a lot of systematic thought. He saw a ratchet-like relationship at work between the nature of a regime, its economy and the scale of its armaments. Fascist states embraced war, mobilized the masses and closed their economies. For democratic states to arm in this way was a "solution . . . almost as dangerous as the threat." As he said in 1933, "One does not fight fascism by adopting its methods and developing a fascist spirit, no more than one fights against the danger of war by developing a spirit of war."[22]

On June 10, 1936, two days after the mass strikes had ended, Gamelin marched into the Hôtel Matignon to discover what Blum, the famous disarmer, would do about arming. Most officers felt shock at the election result. Weygand, for one, feared that the army would be poisoned with communism. When Gamelin entered the premier's spacious sunlit study, his host greeted him with a broad smile. After brief pleasantries, Gamelin—in an exchange eerily reminiscent of the first ones between Hitler and his top soldiers— placed his cards on the table. He told Blum that he "did not consider himself at all a Marxist but felt that he had a social spirit." Anyway, he expected to keep the army out of politics and hoped that the government would take care to do the same. Blum warmly agreed and expressed his concern for national defense. "You mustn't, in this regard, fear the socialists. I assure you that they understand the gravity of the circumstances currently unfolding in Europe." Gamelin now sealed the bargain. He observed that the army was not "troubled" by the effort to bring justice to the "world of the worker." Indeed, the general added, as though reciting some philosophical imperative, the army was "above class struggles."[23]

DURING 1936, the intensifying arms race, Mussolini's victory in Ethiopia, Hitler's march into the Rhineland and the Spanish Civil War convinced critics of the British government in Parliament and officialdom that the Baldwin-Chamberlain team was bungling the whole job of arming and was putting the nation in peril.

The attack began in December 1935, when Britain's prophet of air power, the founder and former chief of the Royal Air Force, Hugh Trenchard, complained to *The Times* that the machinery of defense was dysfunctional. Trenchard, like most of the air force zealots, believed that Hankey, the cabinet secretary, had rigged the defense decision-making machinery to favor the navy. Hankey saw the criticism as an attack upon his influence and the elaborate machinery of defense-planning committees he had carefully built up. As cabinet secretary he had learned that the armed services and other ministries always fought tooth and nail against centralization. His credo was interdepartmental cooperation and coordination rather than centralized control. Appointing some new arms czar, as the critics urged, just when huge resources were being diverted to armaments, would upset the "psychology" of his "machine." Worse still, this new man would come between Hankey and the prime minister.

Sadly for Hankey, in February 1936 his critics won support in Parliament to appoint an arms supremo. If there must be a new minister for the coordination of defense, Hankey thought, that man should be plugged into the apparatus without altering the established lines of authority. Baldwin loved the idea. The new man would have to be someone with no axe to grind for any one service (specifically the air force) and who would accept being a coordinator rather than a decider. The only question was who? On March 8, Thomas

Inskip, the self-effacing attorney general, was appointed. The news was greeted with muffled approval.[24]

Winston Churchill, who had wanted the post and whose name had flashed in everyone's mind as a front-runner, was disappointed. From the day he had walked out of Sandhurst in 1895 as a dashing young officer, he had fought in wars, wrote about war and sought high office in wartime. Churchill first came to national prominence in 1899 during the South African war. As a war correspondent, he valiantly took command of the defense of an armored train that had been ambushed by the Boers. Taken prisoner, Churchill made a daring escape back to London. In 1900 he was elected to Parliament as a Conservative. Four years later as a staunch free-trader he crossed over to the Liberals from the increasingly protectionist Tories. Most Tories never forgot this defection or his partnership with the much-despised Lloyd George. In the years before 1914 Churchill rose to the cabinet. War found him in the Admiralty. Leading the navy in an epic struggle was a calling he believed he had been born for. He engrossed himself in the details of strategy and operations, including the ill-fated Dardanelles landings. Though hardly his fault alone, the disaster at Gallipoli wrecked Churchill's reputation. In 1915, as a condition of joining the new coalition, the Tories insisted that he be shuffled out of the cabinet. Churchill joined the army in France. Two years later, Prime Minister Lloyd George recalled him to serve first as minister of munitions, then minister of war and finally as colonial secretary.[25]

When the Conservative Party broke with the Lloyd George coalition in 1922, Churchill's prospects sank. After he won his parliamentary seat as an independent anti-socialist candidate in 1924, the Tories took him back. Many of them, Baldwin and Neville Chamberlain included, admired his dynamism, yet distrusted his judgment and found his compulsion for shameless grandstanding unbearable. During the early 1930s, while the Tories occupied the opposition benches and then helped form the National Government, Churchill's political capital plummeted. He fought bitterly with Baldwin to prevent greater self-rule for India in what may have been an ill-judged attempt to succeed him as party leader. In any event, Churchill found himself isolated on the right wing of the party.[26]

To work his way again back to the top, Churchill had two choices. He could curry favor with Tory bigwigs in the hope of promotion, or he could rally a broad base of support in the parliamentary party on some question of vital national importance and thereby establish himself as the clear successor to Baldwin. As the 1930s wore on, Churchill tried both strategies with an equal lack of success.

The issue of vital national importance he latched onto was defense. While MacDonald was prime minister first as Labour Party leader and then after 1931 at the head of the National Government, Churchill opposed disarmament as an extravagant sham—and when it involved scrapping warships, a dangerous one. A fierce nationalist utterly devoted to Britain's imperial mission, he had little regard for the League of Nations except as a means for France to dominate Europe and, after 1936, as a cloak for an anti-German alliance. Churchill did not fret about Japan's drive into Manchuria—that was Stalin's problem—or Italy's into Ethiopia. His admiration for Mussolini led some to wonder whether he harbored dictatorial ambitions himself. Germany, though, was different. For Churchill the Nazis were a new and more vulgar form of Prussian militarism with a violent strain of anti-Semitism. Like everyone else in official circles, he saw that Germany had the capacity to dominate Europe and menace Britain.[27]

Before Hitler began to arm openly, Churchill argued that it was madness to allow Germany military equality with France. "Thank God for the French Army," he liked to say. France would be the sentinel of peace on the continent while Britain stood apart to devote itself to the air, the sea and the empire. From 1934 Churchill focused his speeches in Parliament on the escalating air arms race. Officials in the British and French governments who wanted Britain to arm much faster fed him information that he used to compile his own, often inflated, figures on German arms. In May 1935, using such numbers he embarrassed Baldwin into admitting he had been wrong about the growth of the Luftwaffe. That summer, as the Government of India Act passed, Churchill was riding high on the arms race. Baldwin offered him a seat on a committee studying air defenses, which he accepted on condition that he could continue to speak out in Parliament on defense. Having found the government's weak spot, Churchill intended to exploit it for all the political capital it was worth.

IN EARLY 1936, while the defense coordination job was still in the offing, Churchill dampened his criticisms. On March 8, as Germans troops fanned out into the Rhineland, he visited Chamberlain to discover his chances: if he was still in the running, then he would continue to restrain himself; if not, he would attack the latest Defence White Paper. Chamberlain knew that Churchill had been struck off the list weeks before but replied that he had no idea what Baldwin intended to do.[28]

Years later the makers of the Churchillian myth would depict their hero at this time as a lone visionary, toiling against the folly of lesser men who had failed to grasp the peril facing the nation. Strange as it may seem now, back then Baldwin, Chamberlain and others saw Churchill not only as a risk to the smooth running of the rearmament plans but also as an overzealous though well-intentioned militarist who might, if given half a chance, inadvertently bring the entire economy crashing down and send the country sliding into a political crisis of untold consequences.

Everyone who knew Churchill understood that he would never be content to "coordinate" defense and that he would seek to expand his mandate. That ruled him out of the defense coordinator job. Everything he said in Parliament made clear that his quarrel with Baldwin was not over the ultimate enemy (Germany) or the deterrent (air forces) but on the speed and scale of arming. Like Napoleon, whose bust he liked to keep nearby, Churchill was no abstract systematizer of war, but a nuts-and-bolts devil-may-care practitioner. For him history was the unending story of great captains, such as his famous eighteenth-century ancestor, the Duke of Marlborough, who led the English-Dutch grand alliance to victory against the despotic French. But as reviewers of Churchill's *Marlborough: His Life and Times* noted in the 1930s, large-scale political, social and economic forces and structures were distinctly absent from the book. The same was true of Churchill's grasp of the dilemmas of his own life and times. The answer to the German problem, or any problem, was inspired leadership. Churchill saw no danger of forcing the nation into irreversible economic and political change if arming ratcheted up.[29]

Once he learned of Inskip's appointment to the job of defense coordinator, Churchill made a series of blistering speeches against the policy of arming within the bounds of a normally functioning economy. In April he sparred with Chamberlain in the House of Commons, arguing that interference with trade and industry would "not necessarily [entail] war conditions, but conditions which would impinge upon the ordinary daily life and business life of this country." Three months later, while Blomberg, in Berlin, wrestled with Schacht behind closed doors over the financing of raw material imports for German armaments, Churchill raised the temperature of his rhetoric in Parliament:

> All I ask is that the intermediate stage between ordinary peacetime and actual war should be recognised; that a state of emergency preparations should be proclaimed, and that the whole spirit and atmosphere of our rearmament should be raised to a high pitch, and that we should lay aside a good deal of the comfort and smoothness of our ordinary life, that we should not hesitate

to make an inroad into our industry, and that we should endeavour to make the most strenuous efforts in our power to execute the programme that the government have in mind at such a pace as would make them relevant to the ever-growing dangers that gather around us.[30]

In early May 1936 Churchill tried to persuade Lord Weir, a tough Glaswegian industrialist with a well-earned reputation for knowing as much about mass-producing weaponry as any man alive, to join his campaign. The two men knew each other from 1917–18, when Weir ran aircraft production and Churchill was minister of munitions. In the 1920s Weir was an advocate of an independent air force and an expert adviser on defense coordination and industrial war plans. In 1935 he became an adviser to the cabinet and the air force. Turning Lord Weir against the government would cause a headline-grabbing scandal.

"Everywhere use is being made of your name," Churchill wrote to Weir. "Ministers quote it in public and in private. Are you quite sure you are right in lending all your reputation to keeping this country in a state of comfortable peace routine? All I hear makes me believe that the whole life and industry of Germany is organised for war preparation. . . . I can only hope and pray that your judgement has not been deflected by detail and good nature from the true proportion of affairs."

"'The true proportion of affairs'—that is the real problem," Weir shot back. "Are we to take 'the whole life and industry of this nation and organise it for war preparations'? If I was completely confident that this was essential, I would not only advise it but push hard in spite of its grave effects and dislocations."[31]

That was no idle boast. As a mass-production pioneer, Weir was as ruthless a rationalizer as Italy's Alberto Beneduce. In the 1920s Weir brought central planning to the electricity industry with such gusto that Gosplan officials in Moscow would have applauded. Yet in all but dire emergencies he embraced laissez-faire. Like Hankey, he preached coordination in arms procurement rather than top-down control. As the arms race accelerated, he feared that the politics of high-pressure arming might crush Britain's free-market economy. Excessive profits for aircraft firms, for instance, might force the government to nationalize the industry. "To blackmail the state in emergency is a present to Socialism, Communism and all evil movements," he wrote, and "no sector of Private Enterprise can do this by itself, [without] risking all Private Enterprise." In the cabinet he spoke against emulating "countries such as Germany and Russia, i.e. peace production with a war type of control." "I was averse," he later explained, "to doing anything which would turn industry upside down by creating a war spirit and practice, but I felt that we must quietly but very rapidly find an effective British compromise solution as opposed to merely copying the dictatorial system."[32]

On the question of preparing for war, Weir differentiated between two broad tasks. One was building up enough forces to deter rivals; the other was building up enough latent munitions-making capacity to out-arm enemies once a war started—what Germany's Colonel Thomas called arming in *breadth* and *depth*. As an adviser to the industrial war planners, he was the driving force behind the successful "shadow" industries that helped Britain out-produce the Germans in combat aircraft from 1939 until 1943. The shadow system worked by identifying civilian factories that could be converted swiftly to munitions work and training them in weapons production through small "educational" orders. When the air force's Scheme F was authorized in February 1936, for instance, Weir extended the shadow air industry program to encompass the automobile manufacturers and other light-engineering firms.[33]

Weir was puzzled by Churchill's apparent inability to grasp the difference between building up forces to deter war in peacetime and ramping up the economy to wage total war. Churchill seemed to be saying that Britain should "copy" the dictators by moving the economy onto a war footing whatever the risks. What troubled him after he rebuffed Churchill's letter was a nagging sense that without "dictatorial" powers, assembling an air fleet big enough to impress Hitler might be impossible.

The problem, so he thought, was organized labor. Like so many self-made men, Weir was a fanatical individualist who regarded collective bargaining with trade unions as an abomination. In January 1936 he warned ministers that the availability of skilled men would set the pace of arming. Engineering, shipping and metallurgical firms would need 150,000 extra skilled workers to finish the arms plans on time. Overcoming this bottleneck might mean confronting the resistance of the labor unions to, among other things, the "dilution" of skilled jobs; in other words, hiring unskilled men at lower wages to do basically the same work.

The whole issue was political dynamite. Ministers could not be seen permitting arms makers to reap enormous profits while attacking protective work practices and pushing down wages for skilled workingmen. That could lead to crippling strikes and a smoldering sense of grievance. Most economic war planners understood that the trade unions would only yield to war "controls" if the workers received "fair treatment" in peace and war. Industrial peace, put simply, was the linchpin of national cohesion in war. And Neville Chamberlain, as pro-business a chancellor as there ever was, considered that labor leaders, with the experience of the Depression on everyone's mind, had good reason to fear that an armaments boom followed by an arms bust would leave many of their members unemployed or on reduced pay.[34]

Weir in fact overestimated the problem. Over the next three years in the aviation plants, managers and union representatives would make local deals to dilute skilled jobs. Although the shortage of skilled men was always a headache, employers learned how to utilize men more efficiently as the industry expanded and modernized. Employment in the sector jumped in 1935–39 from 27,000 to 161,000.[35]

But, in the summer of 1936, all this lay ahead. And, while in France workers were out on mass strike when the Popular Front swept into office with a pledge to nationalize the French arms industries, ministers in London assembled on June 11 to discuss the danger of war breaking out before 1939 and the need to speed up arming. Speaking for the Foreign Office, Vansittart said that war involving Germany and France, perhaps over Czechoslovakia, seemed imminent and might come as early as 1937. Others, including Chamberlain, were not so certain. "The disturbance of industry produced by the acceleration might result in grave consequences," he said, "and any alteration could only be justified by overpowering conditions." If the cabinet wanted to go faster, especially in aircraft production, Weir said, they would have to use statutory powers to move men from the automobile to the aviation industry. Yet this kind of "interference in peacetime would produce entirely novel difficulties and dangers gravely affecting the financial and economic stability of the country." "If we interfered and took full powers to obtain acceleration of production," he asked, "would not the economic consequences make war certain?" Weir added that setting up a Ministry of Supply, as Churchill had urged, would only result in delays.[36]

The following month Churchill led a delegation of Tories to confront Baldwin on defense. He told the prime minister that a Ministry of Supply was needed in order to arm faster. "I do not at all ask that we should proceed to turn ourselves into a country under war conditions, but," he went on seamlessly, "I believe that to carry forward our progress of munitions we ought not to hesitate to impinge to a certain percentage—25 percent, 30 percent—upon the ordinary industries of the country, and force them and ourselves to that sacrifice at this time." Baldwin confessed that he and his chancellor had considered a "halfway house" between a peace and war economy. He did not think it would work; trying it might ruin the economy. If he thought that war powers were needed, he would seek them. Did the delegation believe that war with Germany was inevitable? asked Baldwin. "I certainly do not consider war with Germany inevitable," Churchill answered, "but I am sure that the way to make it less likely is to afford concrete evidence of our determination in setting about our rearmament."[37]

Thomas Inskip was thinking the same thing. Since he got the post of defense coordinator, he had tried to find the optimum trade-off between arming with enough determination to impress Berlin, yet not so fast as to turn the British nation into a garrison state. Fresh to the job, he told the service chiefs that if "Germany re-armed with dangerous speed, it might be necessary for us to accelerate our own programmes, modify or reverse the Cabinet decision [about the size of the army], and pass from a peace system of production into some form of war system." Later, when industrialists asked him whether they should now give munitions work priority over exports, he "reserved his position." But by November 1936 he was no longer sure. Arming within a "business as usual" economy was already generating uncontrollable pressures and pushing up wages and prices. "If we were to interrupt and break down the process of the industry of peacetime, we would run the risk of destroying the financial fabric of the nation," he told Parliament. "It would be difficult to stop when once you had begun to turn this country into one vast munitions-producing camp."[38]

Meanwhile in France, in the second half of 1936, Léon Blum, the country's first Socialist premier, who came into office promising "bread, peace and freedom" and who had argued for a year that Europe needed to shift from an "armed" to a "disarmed" peace, launched the biggest arms program ever attempted by a French government in peacetime.

That summer the external pressures on France mounted. In July rebellious soldiers tried to overthrow the newly elected Popular Front government in Spain. With the help of Mussolini and Hitler, the putsch escalated into a savage civil war. The parallel between Spain and France—each a politically divided society with a right-wing officer caste and a new left-wing government—did not pass unnoticed. The next month, the German government ordered that compulsory military service be lengthened from one to two years. Then came in rapid succession Hitler's Four Year Plan, the Anti-Comintern Pact and Mussolini's declaration of the Rome-Berlin Axis.

With Germany and Italy on the march, Blum knew that France needed to raise the military stakes or risk war through the appearance of weakness. "One appears almost ridiculous proposing new ideas on disarmament," Blum confessed to the League of Nations assembly on July 1, "when all of Europe is resounding to the clash of arms." Yet he had not given up on reversing the arms spiral. When Schacht arrived in Paris a month later speaking of a deal on trade and a return of some of Germany's pre-1914 African colonies as a step to a Franco-German détente, Blum explored the idea, but was wary of sending the wrong message. "We believe our position stronger than a few months ago," he told Schacht. "France does not tremble in the face of war, but she does not want war."[39]

As part of the Popular Front's defense reforms, Daladier became both army minister and minister for national defense. In the latter role he took the chairmanship of a new Supreme Defense Committee, which brought together the service chiefs and ministers. At the inaugural meeting on June 26, Daladier explained that in Berlin, Blomberg coordinated tri-service planning; in Rome, the Duce did that job; in Moscow, Voroshilov did it; and London had just appointed Inskip. For France the job of ensuring a unity of purpose in arming now fell to him. The first order of business, indeed the most "agonizing" problem in the sphere of national defense, was industrial mobilization. Industry was neither geared up to make the arms the services needed in peace or in an all-out war. Fortunately, Daladier continued, the necessary legislation for the nationalization of the most important weapons firms was already working its way through Parliament: the state would soon take direct action.[40]

Three years before, Daladier had been unmoved by Weygand's dire warning about what was happening across the Rhine. Now he devoured every clue of secret intelligence about German rearmament. Of course much in Europe had changed since his cabinet fell in 1934, but he also trusted Gamelin in a way that was impossible with his pig-headed predecessor. And the message from Gamelin and the secret services was emphatic: Hitler's Germany was preparing for total war. On the strength of this intelligence, Daladier became a compelling spokesman for accelerated arming. In early July he appeared in front of parliamentary defense commissions, arguing that the German Army would soon grow to 650,000 men. It was equipping new formations with tanks and other vehicles to wage a "war of movement." For now, as Gamelin had told him, the French Army could repulse a German attack. But unless France, too, acquired the modern tanks and guns to form a mechanized reserve behind the Maginot Line, it would become more vulnerable each year. Although Germany lacked adequate stocks of certain raw materials, the big arms firms, Krupp, Rheinmetall and Borsig, worked at full blast. Nationalization of France's arms plants would grant the state the control it needed to stay in the arms race with minimum cost and maximum centralization of production and preparations for all-out war.[41]

At last, things were moving, but Gamelin was worried. Nationalization seemed much more like a left-wing gimmick than a practicable industrial policy. Robert Jacomet, the top civil servant at the new Ministry of Defense, told Gamelin that Daladier was all for it. "Time is short," he stressed. Arms production was stagnant. To erect a "powerful parallel state industry" alongside the private one would take too long. "Our interest is therefore to get our hands on existing factories and to modernise them fast." The way forward was to buy up shares in the most important firms and thus create a mixed state-private sector managed by the government. "The political wave is for nationalisations," Jacomet said enthusiastically. "To carry them out, the new government will give us all the money we need without any complaint. They will not pay for any alternative solution." This logic was irresistible.[42]

On August 11, at about the time Blomberg and Göring read Hitler's Four Year Plan memo, the French Parliament passed the nationalization bill. To the left, the bill was sold as a way to put warmongering arms dealers out of business; to the right, the law was a limited measure to shore up defense. In Britain news of the law sent shockwaves through the boardrooms. Industrial moguls such as Weir watched what they feared most unfolding across the Channel. Would this massive state intervention end in disaster in France as he and others predicted it would in Britain?[43]

Now that French Army planners would have leverage over industry, Daladier wanted a multi-year plan of arms growth. Germany's two-year conscription decree of August 24 spurred things on. With France in demographic stagnation and the "lean years" of scarcity in young men approaching, Gamelin saw no point in forty million French entering into a manpower race with seventy million Germans by stretching French conscription to three years. Staff analysis showed that Germany would soon outnumber France in trained men by at least two to one, anyway. Instead of more men, what Gamelin wanted was modern tanks, guns and trucks to blunt a German attack. Daladier agreed and asked the generals to come up with an army modernization program.[44]

What happened next was a complete reversal of roles in French civil-military relations. Gamelin and his staff submitted a four-year plan costing nine billion francs, a figure that dwarfed all earlier plans. Daladier raised an eyebrow when he read it. "It is too low," he said, "and certainly lower than the urgency of the situation demands." The defense minister added another five billion francs to Gamelin's budget, with a large portion for tanks, guns, ammunition and preparations for the mobilization of industry. The generals "accepted my proposal," Daladier later recalled, "smiling with scepticism at the prospects of the government approving it." He showed them up. During an "emotional" interview with Blum and his finance minister, Daladier explained that the French Army would fall perilously behind unless something was done now. On September 7, 1936, the cabinet authorized the fourteen-billion-franc army program.[45]

The air force came up with a fresh plan, too. Back in the summer of 1935, the air staff believed that they had a technical, organizational and, for a while, numerical edge against the Luftwaffe. In April 1936, the air force was confident that France still had "a temporary superiority," but that the output rate of German aviation plants was growing swiftly. In June, though, air intelligence officers predicted that by 1938 Germany would reach a front-line strength of 3,000 aircraft. All the more alarming, the new types of German bombers would be faster than current French fighters. With Paris only an hour's flying time from airstrips in the Rhineland, this impending crossover in air strength might be enough to trigger Berlin into launching a calamitously destructive war that France would almost certainly lose.[46]

To make such comparative estimates and apocalyptic predictions, French Air Force planners, like their counterparts in London, filled the gaps in their knowledge about the German industry with fantasies about the super-efficiency of totalitarian organization and social control. These presumptions sharply contrasted with what they knew best, the poor state of their own suppliers. Ever since the birth of an independent air force in 1928, the Air Ministry had tried to rationalize the aircraft industry and failed. Although the state was their chief buyer, the private companies frustrated every government effort to induce them into adopting mass-production techniques. Some technocratic visionaries looked to a public-private partnership to stimulate growth through industrial concentration and scientific management, but the investment and the demand were lacking until June 1933, when air rearmament Plan I was authorized. Despite this sudden burst of orders—and a doubling of the workforce to 32,600 in two years—the aircraft producers remained stuck in their artisanal ways and hopelessly behind on the production target of 1,010 aircraft by the start of 1936. Just when the Luftwaffe was pulling ahead in production and quality, French air planners found themselves unable to step up their own effort. The only solution, as they saw it, was a massive state-driven intervention into the aircraft industry.

Pierre Cot, Blum's new air minister, was just the man to get that job done. This charismatic forty-year-old Radical was a rising star in French politics. A lawyer by training who had seen action in the First World War, Cot had made a name for himself as air minister in 1933. Politically, he was a peculiar member of his party. The Radicals straddled the center-left of the spectrum, but in many ways Cot swung well over to the left. State planning as a means of combatting the inequities of free-market capitalism appealed to him. During a visit to Moscow as air minister, he was wonderstruck by Soviet central planning and production, which seemed perfectly suited to the mass assembly of huge fleets of bombing planes. And it was bombers he wanted to build. Like so many forward-looking men of his era, Cot was awed and appalled by the horror of air warfare. As air minister, he rationalized the passenger airlines and tried to do the same with the aircraft producers, but his time in office was cut short when the Daladier government fell in February 1934.

Back at the Air Ministry in June 1936, Cot was shocked by intelligence projections of German air strength. Over the next six months the air minister and his staff of aspiring production technocrats used the nationalization law to take hold of the aircraft industry. By creating a mixed sector of state and private firms, they hoped to rationalize the whole industry through investments in plant, equipment and training. At the same time Cot proposed Plan II, a stopgap four-year scheme for 2,400 fighters and bombers. Once industry was ramped up for mass production, a bigger plan could be put through. Yet Cot believed he was playing a losing game. As he told the Supreme Defense Committee, what counted in air warfare was industrial potential, and the truth was that Germany's was "incomparably higher" than that of France. France's hope lay in the added industrial potential of allies: Britain, France's east European allies, Czechoslovakia, Poland and, above all, the Soviet Union.[47]

THE ESCALATION OF THE ARMS RACE in the summer of 1936 raised the financial pressure on France. For over a year three governments had fought doggedly to adhere to the gold standard while investors hedged against a devaluation of the franc by buying foreign currency. French gold reserves and bank deposits dwindled. The only way to uphold confidence in the franc was through fiscal discipline. But with the economy stagnant, exports priced out of foreign markets and tax income in sharp decline, no administration was able to make expenditure balance with revenue.

By early 1936, politicians, treasury officials and financiers now saw salvation in devaluation as the way to boost exports, stimulate economic growth and cut the deficit. The economies of countries such as Britain that had come off the gold standard early, after all, had recovered early. During the election Blum denounced deflation and endorsed state-funded public works to create work and revive demand, but not a break with the gold standard. It was still taboo with voters, who feared an inflationary spiral if the franc fell. Blum had other reasons to be cautious. Announcing devaluation in advance would spark a renewed flight from the franc. And doing so unilaterally would prompt France's trade partners to devalue too or raise tariff barriers to protect their own exports, thus nullifying all the benefits of coming off the gold standard in the first place.

When Germany doubled its standing army in August 1936 and France replied with a plan for the army, navy and air force of twenty-one billion francs, the exodus of capital accelerated. France's gold reserve fell close to fifty billion francs—the figure that war planners considered the minimum war chest. Everyone knew that the Popular Front could not cut the deficit and fund work-creation projects, nationalize the arms firms and buy arms without borrowing. By hoarding their capital abroad, private speculators in effect vetoed the policies of the Popular Front. Many Frenchmen, including Blum and his economic advisers, wondered whether a liberal financial system was compatible with the gigantic armaments effort that they had just set into motion.[48]

Autarky was one way to go. France could copy the totalitarians by imposing exchange controls. With the arms race gathering force and France lagging behind, adopting a variant of military socialism appeared rather attractive, modern even. As Pierre Cot admitted, no matter how "odious" the Nazi regime was, it "permits Germany to concentrate more funds and more resources on its air force than any other state." Daladier, too, admired German efficiency: now and again he muttered "if only I was served like Hitler." Even Blum felt the totalitarian tug: "by attempting to oppose fascism's bid for power . . . one is too often tempted to follow in its footsteps."[49]

Yet resist he did. A totalitarian turn was not only morally distasteful but dangerous too. "Germany is on the verge of an economic and financial catastrophe because of rearmament," Blum's economic experts told him. France could not be that reckless. The Popular Front would face fierce opposition to closing the economy. Many on the right, including Radicals in Blum's own cabinet, and the financial community, would regard the imposition of currency controls as the start of an irreversible slide into full-blown communism. The ensuing political crisis would certainly shake confidence at home and overseas in the French economy and further set back France's efforts at climbing out of the Depression anytime soon.

Exchange controls would also have isolated France. Without the prospect of British and American support, Blum knew, France did not stand a chance against Germany. Going autarkic would be as good as choosing sides. "The logical inclination of our internal policy," he told Parliament, "would lead us to adopt coercive measures against the export of capital and currency speculation. But that would be to create a contradiction between our policy which seeks a community of action with the great Anglo-Saxon nations and the signing of a monetary agreement aimed at restoring activity and liberty to international trade." In June, after the election, the Americans had approached the Blum government about currency stabilization. Secret talks got underway, and the British joined them. But Blum was in no hurry to conclude an agreement. He hoped to restore calm at home first before taking the franc off the gold standard, but the depletion of the gold reserve made any further delay impossible. On September 26, the Tripartite Agreement on monetary stabilization was announced, and France devalued the franc. The United States and Britain did not retaliate. As officials in Washington, London and Paris intended, the deal affirmed the shared liberal-capitalist values of the great democracies. It was a conspicuous act of political solidarity in the game of feints and gestures that passed for alliances in these years, indeed one comparable to the forthcoming Anti-Comintern Pact and the Rome-Berlin Axis.[50]

Devaluation of the franc was supposed to attract capital back into France, but only a trickle of gold returned. Investors and savers had no faith in the fiscal discipline of the Popular Front. Given Blum's defense and social welfare plans, they expected another fall in the franc or exchange controls. Over the winter of 1936–37, French officials negotiated with Britain for a loan to prop up the franc, but the British wanted to know what the French government was going to do about its deficit.

So once more Blum faced the dilemma that would torment him his whole time in office: he needed to spend to stimulate the economy and stay in the arms race, but he could not spend enough without scaring private capital into flight. No wonder to his dying day he believed that the power of private finance to shape the destinies of nations had to be curbed. Yet he remained resolute against exchange controls. Aside from cutting France's ties with Britain and the United States, he feared that if he resorted to totalitarian methods of work creation and arms production, France would not only succumb to autarky but eventually to totalitarianism too. While the financial situation frustrated him no end, the arms race closed in too. In November 1936, the Foreign Ministry sent Blum a study of "Rearmament in Europe." "During 1936, the manufacture of arms has reached a scale never equalled since 1918," the paper began. Germany was becoming one huge armed camp. Britain was arming fast too. Swift progress had been made in aircraft production. Industrial preparations for all-out war were in full swing. Italy was making guns and bombers at a feverish rate. "As Europe stands," the paper grimly declared, "France could not remain indifferent in the face of the quickening pace of German and Italian armaments."[51]

Blum needed little convincing. No "disarmed" peace appeared in sight. The talks with Schacht had made little headway, and no one was really sure that the sly banker had any sway over Hitler anyway. On January 30, 1937, in a speech to the Reichstag, Hitler rejected British and French diplomatic overtures. Blum now understood that he too had to make a choice of ghastly simplicity: guns or butter? He chose guns.

On February 13, 1937, the Popular Front government declared a "pause" to social reform. A plan to spend twenty billion francs on public works to create jobs was dropped. Blum explained to his disappointed working-class supporters that defense had to come before his "new deal." The government raised through a public appeal a defense loan of ten billion francs. Over the next two years the government budget for social welfare fell in real terms to below that of Blum's right-wing predecessors, while defense leaped from one-quarter to one-third of all state spending.[52]

The Popular Front was now thoroughly trapped in the vise-like grip of internal and external contradictions, with the arms race tightening the screw. A government elected to rescue French workers from the slump with social reform diverted ever greater resources to arms. A government committed to arming against two totalitarian states—which had nationalized munitions factories and launched four-year arms plans—rejected exchange controls and a full-blown planned economy to secure ties with Britain and the United States, two allies indispensable in a struggle against Germany. And a government dedicated to the defense of democracy against fascism at home and abroad declared nonintervention when civil war broke out in Spain.

At first Blum wanted to send arms to the Spanish Republic. Yet it soon became clear that to do so would bring down his government. Intervention might also set off a European war or, as many feared, a civil war in France. The British, too, urged a policy of nonintervention to contain the conflict. As the war dragged on, men and arms secretly crossed the frontier with official knowledge. Even so, nonintervention opened a deep wound that sapped Blum's government of moral purpose.[53]

The ideological struggle across the Pyrenees also deepened fissures in France. French fascists mobilized support by portraying the Popular Front leaders as Soviet stooges and subjected Blum to anti-Semitic abuse. However, the fascists had limited impact because French conservatives, unlike in Italy and Germany, did not bring them into or even close to government. Of far greater significance were the big employers. The election result and the mass strikes of 1936 had sent them reeling. The concessions they made on holidays, union rights and the workweek stuck in their craws. While trade union ranks swelled, employers began a guerrilla war to retake lost ground. They made the forty-hour week the focus of their attack. Partly out of a fear that the state might nationalize their factories and partly out of sheer malice, the industrial magnates did not invest in modern machinery to raise productivity. Underinvestment, chronic work stoppages and skilled-labor shortages made worse by the restricted workweek held back France's industrial recovery for almost two years.[54]

OBSERVERS OF THE INTERNATIONAL SCENE over the winter of 1936–37 could not help but notice the way in which France was slipping in strategic estimates everywhere. Hitler told Goebbels that internal disorder would force the French into accommodating Germany. The French military attaché in Berlin reported with alarm that the Germans scorned French strength. In London, officials decried the evil times that had befallen France; most blamed the Popular Front. Hankey vented his spleen to Vansittart at the Foreign Office: France "is inoculated with the virus of communism, which is at present rattling the body politic, delaying much needed rearmament and causing acute internal dissension. . . . In her present state she is not a very desirable ally." Vansittart considered Blum a naïve and weak premier who spouted a lot of "flapdoodle" about disarmament, and who "has evidently not the faintest idea of what he is up against in Hitler." The British ambassador in Paris complained that the industrial chaos "reduced France to the status of 'quantité négligeable' in the councils of nations."[55]

What all these observers overlooked was the paradox of France's predicament: by trying to build a gigantic war machine, the Popular Front sent France spinning out of control, while the centripetal forces of the arms race nearly tore it apart.

CHAPTER 10

"NEXT TIME WE'LL URGE ON
THE OTHER SIDE"

After Adolf Hitler had proclaimed German rearmament in March 1935, Mikhail Tukhachevsky composed an article for *Pravda,* the official organ of the Central Committee of the Communist Party. "When Hitler came to power in January 1933," wrote the Soviet Union's foremost total-war planner, "he claimed that he needed four years to overcome the economic crisis and unemployment in Germany. This was empty demagoguery. Now we can see that what lay behind this demagoguery was a more realistic four-year plan to raise gigantic armaments." To expose "Hitler's anti-Soviet and revanchist plans," Tukhachevsky quoted passages from *Mein Kampf* about the German "problem" of "living space" and the need to find it in the east.

As the article dealt with the most sensitive area of state policy, the draft went to Stalin, who approvingly underscored Tukhachevsky's prediction that "in coming years the National Socialists will intensively develop their offensive forces, especially bombers, motorised divisions and submarines." Yet he struck out sentences that described Hitler's designs against the Soviet Union and revised the draft to stress the German threat to Britain and France. Stalin believed that Germany, in fact the whole capitalist-imperialist world, wished to extinguish the Revolution, but there was no point, he thought, in reminding the ruling circles in London and Paris that Hitler's urge for military conquest might be channeled eastward.[1]

VIEWED FROM MOSCOW, the coming of the Nazi regime in January 1933 was just one more nasty feature of a capitalist system spinning out of control. Lenin had predicted more than a decade before in his theory of imperialism that the monopolistic and overproductive tendencies of capitalism would inevitably lead to crisis and war. The onset of the Great Depression and the rise in militarism and fascism heralded by Japan's conquest of Manchuria appeared to confirm the truth of Lenin's forecast. As the struggle between the major imperialist countries to protect their markets and sources of raw materials intensified with alarming speed, every good Bolshevist knew that what also increased was the danger of the capitalist world joining together to satisfy its destructive internal impulses by colonizing the Soviet Union.

During the early 1930s, Stalin and his inner circle adopted policies to forestall the capitalist world forming an anti-Soviet coalition. The most conspicuous was breakneck industrialization to turn the Soviet Union into an unassailable economic and military bastion. A foreign policy that seemingly promoted universal peace and complete disarmament was another way to stave off the approaching showdown with the forces of imperialism. Appeals for disarmament mobilized peace activists abroad to oppose military build-ups and to agitate against aggression. Nonaggression pacts with Romania, Poland, Italy, France, Finland and the Baltic states also promised to make it much more difficult for the ruling classes in these countries to "seduce" their people into an anti-Soviet adventure.[2]

Still, nothing could prevent the capitalist countries seeking relief from the economic downturn by expanding their armaments. As Stalin told the party's Central Committee in June 1932, the only branch of industry in the crisis-ridden capitalist world that did not appear to be suffering from the effects of the Great Depression was arms manufacture:

> The bourgeois states are furiously arming and rearming. What for? Not for friendly chats, of course, but for war. And the imperialists need war, for it is the only means by which to redivide the world, to redivide markets, sources of raw materials and spheres for the investment of capital. It is quite understandable that in this situation so-called pacifism is living its last days, that the League of Nations is rotting alive, that "disarmament schemes" come to nothing, while conferences for the reduction of naval armaments become transformed into conferences for renewing and enlarging navies.[3]

In armaments Stalin planned for self-sufficiency. During 1932, the Five Year Plan delivered vast quantities of modern equipment to the armed forces. Although the results did not reach overly ambitious target levels raised by the fear of war with Japan, at the start of 1933 the deeply insecure men inside the Kremlin were for the first (and last) time confident about the rising stockpile of Soviet armaments, especially air forces. At the Party Congress of January 1933, Kliment Voroshilov, the defense commissar and one of Stalin's stalwarts, presented comparative tables of arms spending and the output of bombers, tanks and other weapons showing that the Soviet Union was outstripping its rivals. The time had come for the Soviet leadership to relax the pace of development. A poor harvest the previous summer and the policy of collectivization of agriculture resulted in 1933 in widespread famine. That year investment in industry slowed down to a more realistic rate of expansion. Investment in munitions production plants declined. The projected rate of growth in military spending was curtailed. Arms output would remain steady, but the slowdown annoyed Tukhachevsky. For over a year he had been complaining about the shortfalls in output of tanks, guns and combat aircraft, as well as the lack of preparations for mobilization of the whole economy. What was the point of targets and multi-year plans, he grumbled, if they were not fulfilled? The headstrong total-war systematizer singled out industrial managers for the brunt of his criticism because, as preparation began for the second Five Year Plan, they often put the demands of the economy as a whole before the demands of defense.[4]

Over the next two years Tukhachevsky laid down plans for the modernization of the army and air force on an ever greater scale and waited for external events to create the internal conditions to accelerate arming. Not that the delivery schedule for weapons was modest by global standards: the Red Army would receive annually 2,000–3,000 aircraft, 2,000–3,000 tanks, 6,000–8,000 guns and about 10,000 trucks. With more aircraft, tanks, artillery and trucks coming into service, the army tried to implement (with mixed results) Tukhachevsky's revolutionary doctrine of deep battle. Ingenious, furiously driven and utterly captivated by technology, Tukhachevsky's mind latched onto dozens of new experimental projects, including flying tanks, chemical and biological weapons and airborne and glider-borne assaults. What worried him most was the developing air arms race. Along with a few like-minded officers on the service staffs and in the field commands, he composed an apocalyptic study of how the European and Japanese air forces could launch devastating preemptive attacks on the Soviet Union's industrial infrastructure to clear the way for invading armies.[5]

Tukhachevsky knew that the image of a capitalist bolt from the blue was a great bureaucratic device for advancing the interests of the armed forces. In February 1934, he warned Voroshilov that "the extreme tension in the Far East and the suspicious behaviour of Poland and Hitler's Germany make the first years of the second Five Year Plan particularly intensive in the development of the power of the Red Army." Two months later he sent Stalin intelligence on the growing air menace, in which he complained that British aircraft companies refused to sell the Soviet Union the most advanced designs though they warmly welcomed German buyers. The secret survey and its multiple tables projected the fast-growing air strength of all the major powers over the next two years. It noted that in Britain the press baron Lord Rothermere had called for an air force of 8,000 machines; in France the press agitated for a huge bomber force on the scale of 1918; in Germany the first civilian recreational flying clubs had formed, and civil aviation was convertible to military purposes; and in Japan the aviation factories had grown 240 percent in just four years. By 1936 the major powers would have first-line air strengths of 2,000–3,500 aircraft each, with the escalation in Japanese and German airpower driving the various "arms races." "In the next two to three years," so the intelligence report concluded, "the focus will continue to be on the further improvement of aircraft speed and ceiling." Flying higher and faster would demand far greater engine performance and vastly improved aerodynamic designs.[6]

The message was clear. The Soviet Union could not relax the pace in the air arms race against the capitalists. Soviet aviation needed to push further and harder. Since the Red air forces would have to deal with enemies in Europe and the Far East at once, Tukhachevsky argued that the Soviet Union needed a twofold or threefold numerical superiority, in other words "a minimum of 15,000 planes in operation." With such an air force, Tukhachevsky and his co-planners dreamed, they could command the skies. When the planning figures were put to Sergo Ordzhonikidze, the commissar for heavy industry and a man who was used to getting what he wanted from his factory managers by knocking heads together, he did not blink. Of course the aviation plants and the ancillary factories could build such a force. Voroshilov, however, was doubtful. He had had enough experience with his egotistical subordinate's "abstract" projects about tanks and aircraft, especially his habit of making unrealistic production projections based on crude linear computations. But if Ordzhonikidze said he could deliver the machines, then the commissar for defense was not going to challenge him. As it was, he had enough headaches with Gosplan in raising the number of mechanized brigades to fifty over the next two years, as Stalin had ordered. Tukhachevsky, naturally, supported this fresh initiative with barely contained excitement. "Such a development," he wrote, "will create a Soviet military power that none of our enemies can withstand."[7]

In 1934 German rearmament did not dominate the defense debate in Moscow. After years of collaboration, German and Soviet intelligence analysts had an idea of what weapons the other could produce in quantity. Tukha-

chevsky, who visited Germany in 1932, did not credit his German counterparts with a grasp of the awe-inspiring possibilities of machine-age warfare.
In terms of tanks and aircraft, projections by the Red Army staff showed Germany lagging behind France, Britain and the United States for years to come.
The problem posed by German rearmament, at least at first, was what impact
it would have on Britain and France, and France's east European allies. While
they devoted their energies to enforcing the Treaty of Versailles, Europe was
in deadlock. If the deadlock broke and Germany armed, then Europe would
be free to regroup and launch an anti-Soviet crusade.[8]

Things apparently began to shift in January 1934, when Warsaw and
Berlin signed a nonaggression pact. Reports from Paris disclosed that the
French would not forcibly prevent Germany from rearming and that the
French preferred to legitimize German armaments to justify an escalation in
French rearmament. Efforts to establish good relations with Berlin, meanwhile, came to nothing. Berlin seemed intent on one thing only. "The foreign policy of Germany is directed at rearmament," ran one bulletin.
"Everything is being done secretly to expand the army, to provide it with armaments, from cannons to airplanes. But to do this Hitler needs time and
money. In order to win time and gain foreign credits Hitler had resorted to
his well known pacifist manoeuvres."[9]

Stalin agreed. For the time being there was no need to ratchet up arming
as a direct and immediate response to Germany's covert rearmament. Not
that he believed the Soviet Union was invincible. As Voroshilov and Tukhachevsky often complained, industry as a whole lacked mobilization plans; the
output of ammunition and explosives lagged behind wartime requirements.
Yet in most categories, except warships, Russia could hold its own against the
largest military nations, specifically France and Japan. Soviet tank production, in fact, was "not inferior to the armies of the most important capitalist
states." Even though the capitalist world was sinking deeper into economic
crisis, Stalin had good reason to think that the Soviet Union had just passed
from inferiority to real strength, in the breadth and depth of its armaments.
In December 1933 he boasted that the Japanese militarists who threatened
Russia with war did not grasp the relationship between economic and military power. In any case, after the excesses of the first Five Year Plan, Stalin understood that the economy needed a steadier rate of modernization, autarky
and technological self-sufficiency. The central planners loosened their grip
on individual enterprises, and incentives to individual workers were introduced. The new Five Year Plan placed a priority on consumer goods. Bread
rationing ceased.[10]

Instead of cranking up rearmament, Stalin turned to diplomacy to deal with the mounting danger in Europe. A master at outwitting his enemies at home, he reveled in the idea that he could manipulate ruling circles abroad with trade deals and security pacts. For Stalin, peace-diplomacy was simply a tool to slow down the forces of historical change, not an end in itself. What good was lasting peace if it held back the cause of global socialism? What good was violent change if it came too quickly for the Soviet Union to exploit the situation? To fend off threats, the country would champion "collective security" and the "indivisibility of peace."

The front man for Stalin's pacific diplomacy was the fifty-eight-year-old Maxim Litvinov. More professorial than revolutionary in appearance and manner, the commissar for foreign affairs was a shrewd diplomatic operator and a skilled charmer. In September 1934 Litvinov took the Soviet Union into the League of Nations, after a decade of Soviet diplomats decrying the organization as a capitalist conspiracy. He also negotiated a marked improvement in relations with France, Britain and the United States. At Geneva, though, Litvinov struggled against the widespread impression that Moscow's newfound love of the League of Nations and collective security was opportunistic and shallow. In Moscow he fought to have his voice heard in the inner sanctum of the Kremlin. In the Soviet pecking order, the Foreign Ministry did not rank alongside those of Defense, Trade or Industry. As a category, diplomats (who often met in private with double-talking foreigners) were suspect. Although Litvinov was an old Bolshevik, Stalin kept him at arm's length and frequently expressed contempt for his profession and advice. For counsel on world affairs, Stalin relied much more on Molotov, the Soviet premier and an arch-isolationist, the defense chief Voroshilov and other men from the Politburo.[11]

To Stalin, entering the League of Nations made good sense. After Japan and Germany withdrew, the assembly in Geneva offered him a platform from which to frustrate an anti-Soviet alliance. At the end of 1934, according to rumors picked up by Soviet agents, that threat would likely come in the form of a German-French-Polish-Japanese front. The way for such a coalition would be cleared if Hitler could convince the French to allow him to rearm as a preliminary to eastward expansion. The key to the situation lay in Paris. While the French opposed German rearmament, and talks between Litvinov and French diplomats about some sort of new security system in eastern Europe made progress, the danger could be forestalled.[12]

Events moved swiftly in 1935. In February, London and Paris issued a joint warning against unilateral German rearmament. The French ambassador in

London told his Soviet counterpart that Britain and France had agreed that "German arms are already formidable enough that any further acceleration in the tempo of German rearmament would bring nothing good." Britain, France and Czechoslovakia increased defense spending. On March 10, Göring unveiled the Luftwaffe. A few days later Hitler announced conscription in Germany. The Soviet Union supported efforts at Geneva to condemn German rearmament. Negotiations between Paris, Prague and Moscow resulted in mutual security pacts in May 1935. Later that summer the Communist International spurred on communists in the capitalist democracies to ally with socialists against fascism under the banner of the Popular Front.[13]

As the arming of nations gathered momentum, Tukhachevsky also swung into action. In papers critical of the current staff plans, he urged Voroshilov and Stalin to reinforce the western frontier against a German-Polish attack. On March 22, the Politburo agreed to strengthen the forces deployed along the western and eastern borders. A few days later the Politburo also decided to be more forthcoming to the League of Nations about the true size of the defense budget. Stalin wanted the world to know that the Soviet Union had not neglected its defenses. Other measures swiftly followed. On April 14, Ordzhonikidze, the commissar for heavy industry, told senior defense officials—including Voroshilov and Tukhachevsky, both by now promoted by Stalin to Marshals of the Soviet Union—that the aviation industry in 1935–36 could step up production of airframes and aircraft engines to achieve a total output of 17,000 aircraft. Eight days later the Politburo decided to double the size of the air force over the next two years to a front-line strength of 10,000 machines, including 1,138 naval aircraft, and to expand the aviation industry. At the end of May it decided to raise the peacetime strength of the armed forces to over a million by July 1936, to 1.37 million by January 1937 and then to 1.5 million by January 1938.[14]

At first, though, speeding up arming turned out to be a lot tougher than anyone expected. In 1934–36 the Soviet economy underwent terrific growth as the production plants and infrastructure projects started under the first Five Year Plan came into operation. The productivity of factories and farms climbed fast. The national income doubled. Consumer goods became more plentiful. Yet, while the rest of the economy prospered, in 1935 armaments production slumped. Aircraft output alone fell by almost forty percent. The holdup stemmed from the daunting industrial, organizational and technological problems of manufacturing advanced weapons in quantity. Arms designs became more complex, and industrial managers tried at the same time to adopt the latest mass-production techniques. This experience was not unique to the

Soviet arms industries. All the fast-arming great powers in varying degrees suffered similar mid-1930s production slumps, especially in aircraft production, as all-metal monoplanes replaced wood-and-fabric biplanes.[15]

The production slump of 1935 was a temporary hiccup. In July, when asked about the economic planning targets for 1936, Stalin ordered that above all else defense spending must not be cut. The Soviet arms slowdown of 1933 had come to an end. The arms acceleration prompted by Germany had begun.[16]

DURING 1936, THE STATE of international relations became grimmer. The global arms race boomed. Italy conquered Ethiopia. The League of Nations suffered one blow after another. Soviet relations with Britain and France, which had improved markedly in the previous year, sputtered out. French officials dragged their feet over staff talks to implement the Franco-Soviet-Czech mutual-assistance pacts. German troops marched into the Rhineland, and Hitler claimed the ratification of the Franco-Soviet security pact as a pretext for the coup. Despite persistent Soviet attempts to improve relations with Berlin through trade talks, German officials remained stone-faced.[17]

To counter the rising peril, Molotov, Tukhachevsky and Stalin repeated time and again in speeches and interviews with foreign reporters that the Soviet Union was ready to fight in the east and west. In January 1936, Tukhachevsky announced that the Red Army would soon reach a peacetime strength of 1.3 million men.[18]

By the summer of 1936 there could be no mistaking the ideological divide in Europe. With the outbreak of the Spanish Civil War and the election of Blum's Popular Front government in France, Nazi propaganda raised the specter of communism on the march across the continent. By October Soviet guns, planes, tanks and advisers started to arrive in Spain. The Soviet Union would wage a proxy war against Germany and Italy on the Spanish peninsula, maintaining a balance between shoring up Republican resistance enough to keep the war ticking over as a distraction without alienating Britain or undermining the left in France.[19]

In September 1936, weeks before Mussolini declared the Rome-Berlin Axis and Berlin and Tokyo concluded the Anti-Comintern Pact, Litvinov pleaded with Stalin, Molotov and Voroshilov to back his alliance-building diplomacy, which they saw as a dead-end: "The belligerent German foreign policy and the colossal growth of German armaments frighten many governments from signing defensive unions or pacts of mutual assistance, and raise doubts about the effectiveness of such pacts, and many doubt that they can contain Germany from taking military action," he correctly diagnosed:

> Has not the time come to raise the issue of a single large defensive bloc? I have in mind, if I may put it this way, the consolidation of various small scale pacts and unions existing in Europe directed against Germany, and all revisionist countries. A mutual pact of assistance against any aggressor, which would include the USSR, France, Czechoslovakia, Rumania, Yugoslavia and Turkey, 275 million people, would make Germany think twice and change its policy. Such an overwhelming bloc would no doubt gather around it other small countries. Poland would be unlikely to object to such a bloc, and Germany would only be able to depend on Hungary. Such a bloc would have the respect of England and Italy as well, even if they did not join it, the bloc would have their sympathy in the goal of containing Germany. I know from conversations with [the French foreign minister] that he agrees. On the other hand we should not doubt for a moment that the efforts of Hitler are directed at the creation of an opposing bloc directed against the USSR, or at least its isolation. And its chances for realising such a bloc have considerably improved recently.[20]

Stalin rejected the idea. Supporting French efforts to contain Germany was one thing; taking the lead in an anti-German bloc was another. Such a bold step might stampede the whole capitalist world into an anti-Soviet bloc. At the same time, efforts to come to terms with the Nazi regime through the Soviet trade delegation in Berlin were making no progress either. Soviet diplomacy had reached an impasse.

Ominously, intelligence disclosed that the Nazis intended to establish a good working relationship with Britain and that the regime felt an abiding hatred of the Bolsheviks. Was a rapprochement with Britain a precursor to a German drive into the Ukraine? Although other sources indicated that there was no secret war plan against Russia as part of the Anti-Comintern Pact, the Soviet leadership believed that such a plan must have been in the making. A former German diplomat revealed to Soviet agents that the German Army did not believe that it would be ready to wage war on Russia before 1938. For now, so ran the unpleasant news from Berlin, Germany would instead foment dissent inside the Soviet Union through sabotage and subversion.[21]

Marshal Tukhachevsky also sounded the alarm about the rapidly expanding Nazi war machine. The Red Army needed more divisions, motorized artillery and better railways to defeat the German-Polish invaders. Germany had taken the lead in tank production, he told Voroshilov and Stalin, and its aircraft output surpassed earlier estimates. By 1938, the Luftwaffe would have 7,000 front-line aircraft. Despite the "gigantic" arms capacity of the Third Reich, the Red Army staff calculated that a German-Polish attack could be defeated so long as the Soviet Union had a twofold or threefold superiority in the air. Tukhachevsky, always the doomsayer, predicted that Germany would soon be able to mobilize overwhelming armed strength.[22]

Still, secret intelligence and the estimates of the military men fed the Kremlin's obsession with the peril of "capitalist encirclement." It reinforced the determination of Stalin and his inner circle to pursue the arms race with ever greater intensity and resources. Official rhetoric reflected this resolve. On November 28, 1936, just after the signature of the Anti-Comintern Pact, Litvinov told the assembly of the League of Nations that "the Soviet Union is strong enough to take care of itself." In an *Izvestiia* editorial that day, Molotov took up the same theme. "In order best to defend peace and the peaceful enterprise of the peoples of the USSR," he wrote, "we must believe exclusively in our own strength." Ten days later Litvinov warned the Japanese foreign minister, Arita Hachirō, that in response to the Anti-Comintern Pact, the Soviet Union would be "forced against our will and at great expense to place large military forces in the Far East for defense. . . . No one is so naïve as to think that Japan or Germany need each other's help to deal with communism at home!"[23]

The intensification of the arms race from 1936 onward, and the prospect of all-out war against a German-Polish combination in the west and Japan in the east, had an enormous impact on Stalin and thus the Soviet Union as a whole. The mounting external threats accelerated the extreme centralization of power in the hands of the Soviet leader. Always ruthless and relentless in the pursuit of political power, Stalin increasingly identified the triumph of socialism with consolidation of his personal dictatorship. When he emerged in the 1930s as the winner in the fierce struggle for power within the party after Lenin's death, he used a combination of persuasion and cunning to impose his policies on the Politburo and the wider party-state apparatus. Slowly, as the last of his remaining rivals fell, Stalin shed the pretense of collective decision making at the top. During 1935–36, the Politburo became much less an executive body than a rubber stamp for the execution of Stalin's will.[24]

As nearly all foreign military analysts assumed, the concentration of power in the Soviet economic and political system made it amazingly responsive to Stalin's perceptions of external and internal threats. The volume of state spending allocated to arms shot up from sixteen to thirty-three percent in the danger years 1936–40. Unhappy with the poor performance of the arms makers in 1935, Stalin oversaw a massive shake-up of the sector at the end of 1936. While in Germany the Nazis, with the support of the military, launched the Four Year Plan in self-conscious emulation of the Soviet command economy, in Russia officials removed the defense industries from control of the Ministry of Heavy Industry and set up a new ministry for them. It comprised eleven departments (each specializing in everything from aviation to radios) and assumed responsibility for 274 arms factories, workshops, laboratories and schools. Like some hydra-headed monster, the burgeoning military-industrial complex expanded and grew more elaborate with amazing speed. By 1939 one ministry had multiplied into four—aircraft, armaments, ammunition and shipbuilding—each with its own labyrinth of subdivisions manned by growing ranks of administrators, most of whom came of age under Stalin and devoted themselves to Stalinism.[25]

Foreign military experts assumed that under the Soviet totalitarian system, the "unpatriotic" forces of the market and the profit-seeking behavior of soulless businessmen must have been quashed. But the system was more complex than that. Each year Stalin worked out how much he wanted to spend on armaments (usually after an argument with Voroshilov, who always wanted more rubles), but then the armed forces ordered what they needed from the arms industries in a "market-like" form of exchange. Even though there was a bureaucratic mechanism in place to enforce the "plan," decentralized arms contracting in this internal market created great scope for friction between the military and their suppliers.[26]

Generally, the military wanted the largest volume of arms it could get from industry, while industry wanted arms orders that it could fill without jeopardizing the steady growth and smooth running of the economy overall. Despite the ever-spiraling demand for more guns than butter, which sucked ever more plant and workers into the defense sector, the soldiers complained that they could not force industrial planners to accept all their orders. To frustrate the military, plant managers resorted to every bureaucratic trick in the book to refuse or delay contracts, including using secrecy regulations to deny them cost and production data. "The plan is compiled and assignments are handed out to the factories," one officer protested. "The factories set the plan in motion but in a short period of time the whole thing goes to nothing and begins again from the beginning." Worse, sheltered from free-market competition and the danger of going bust, factory heads economized on time, effort and rubles by making equipment that fell below the quality and performance standards set

by the purchasing authorities, and colluded with the officers responsible for enforcing standards into certifying inferior, though not necessarily defective,
goods.[27]

The bitterest dispute between the army and industry involved the mobilization plan. In theory, since everyone worked for the same boss, planning
how the civilian economy would switch over to armaments should have been
relatively easy. But industrial planners, who were preoccupied with fulfilling
current demands, lagged behind in preparing the mobilization plan.
Tukhachevsky could scarcely contain his anger at the delays. "If the present
situation drags on," he grumbled, "in the event of war the army will eventually meet with very serious disruptions."[28]

On the age-old principle of divide and rule, Stalin kept his military men
and industrial managers at loggerheads. The last thing he wanted was the rise
of a strong center of rival power in either the army or industry. In the Soviet
system there could only be one supreme economic-military chief. Stalin in
fact took a deep interest in the organization of the armed forces and weapons
design and production. During the summer of 1935, on the eve of the massive
expansion of the army, he offered Voroshilov opinions on everything from
the size and distribution of units to the composition of corps and divisional
level staffs. As arms production heated up after 1936, he studied the daily
summaries of aircraft and aero-engine production. If shortfalls developed,
Stalin demanded explanations and suggested corrective measures. He took
an equal interest in the production of tanks and warships.[29]

In fact, Stalin made his weight most felt in naval armaments in the years
before the war. Tukhachevsky and others thought that building anything more
than a small coast guard was a waste of resources, but Stalin wanted to build
a splendid fleet of battleships. The only obstacle was the backwardness of his
warship industry. After the Revolution the Tsar's warship yards were dissolved,
and Russia's leading naval engineers fled abroad. As with most advanced technology, Soviet officials tried to leapfrog ahead in naval construction by im-
porting foreign expertise and equipment. Italy built some ships for the Soviet
Union, but France, Britain and the United States were unwilling to help Stalin
construct a big navy or sell their most advanced warship technology. When in
the summer of 1936 the British Foreign Office inquired whether the Soviet
Union would adhere to the new naval arms control treaty, Stalin seized the opportunity to exchange his signature on the London Naval Treaty for British
help in raising a Red fleet.

While the diplomats discussed the naval treaty, Soviet purchasing agents
approached top British naval arms firms to place orders. The Admiralty

kicked up a storm. Not only did they not want to take the risk of top-secret technology going to the Soviet Union through trade deals but they also balked at helping Stalin build a navy in the first place. "It is fairly certain that the USSR only want outside help for the moment," one British naval officer protested; "as soon as they have sucked the brains of [our] armaments experts they will revert to home production." In 1937 a compromise emerged. The Admiralty would allow British firms to sell the Soviets second-rate designs, provided Russia joined the British-inspired system of naval arms control. After all, the British admirals joked, the Russians were too backward to mount a serious naval challenge for decades. At the same time, in Moscow, Stalin's admirals drew up plans for a grand fleet of twenty battleships and ten battlecruisers all in gross excess of treaty limits. With Japan about to wreck naval arms control anyway, Stalin reckoned, why cap his own naval ambitions?[30]

THE ACCELERATING ARMS RIVALRY placed ever more pressure on the leaders of the great powers to exercise control over their economies and to pay much closer attention to the internal cohesion of their populations. The Soviet state owned and controlled the means of production, and like the right-wing totalitarian regimes, it enforced the loyalty of the masses by mobilizing popular support and repressing dissent. The hunt for internal enemies, "wreckers" and spies was a regular feature of life under Stalin, yet the intensity of each wave of terror varied. Terror could of course gather its own momentum through the local initiative of over-zealous security officials, but as a tool of dictatorship Stalin could raise, lower and direct terror with a remarkable degree of control.[31]

In August 1936 Stalin set in motion a fresh wave of repression against those considered counter-revolutionaries. Together with his awesome executioner, the commissar for internal affairs Nikolai Yezhov, and other trusted men, he directed the arrests and executions of members of the secret police (NKVD) and then of party members who had opposed regime in one way or another. The Soviet leaders asked for lists and quotas of other economic and military administrators due for "liquidation." Relentlessly, the Great Terror of 1937–38 swallowed 1.6 million people (out of a population of 100 million). The NKVD executed about 700,000, with most of the rest sentenced to imprisonment in the expanding network of gulags. Then, at the start of 1938 a signal went out from the Kremlin, and the terror slowed.

The overlap of the terror with the acceleration of the arms race was no mere coincidence. Stalin had lived through the great upheavals of the first two decades

of the twentieth century and had often reflected on the nature of war and revolution. Japan's victories over the Tsar's armed forces in 1904–5 had almost top-
pled the old regime; three years of total war did knock it over in 1917; and the
next year Germany fell to the Allies due to an internal collapse. Stalin had
learned the lesson. The hammer blows of a future all-out war would render the
Soviet state vulnerable to the enemy within. As he explained to a private gathering of top officials, defending the internal cohesion of the socialist state was
everything. "We will mercilessly destroy anyone who, by his deeds or his
thoughts—yes, his thoughts—threatens the unity of the socialist state," Stalin
said. Molotov later recalled that "1937 was necessary. If you take into account
that after the revolution we chopped right and left, achieved victory, but the
survivals of enemies of various tendencies remained and [because] of the growing threat of fascist aggression they might unite. We were driven in 1937 by the
consideration that in the time of war we would not have a fifth column."[32]

Stalin regarded the Great Terror as a logical extension of arming. Remov-
ing older party cadres who might prove unreliable in a crisis and replacing them
with younger and better-educated elites was a way to harden the Soviet state
for the trials of total war. To move preemptively against "double dealers"—
those who professed loyalty but who either knowingly or unconsciously undermined the regime—made sense to Stalin. The dictator was tortured by the
thought that many of his subordinates in the party and state colluded to deceive him about the fulfillment of orders and instead promoted narrow bureaucratic interests. The army and industry, two vital components of state
power, worried him most. He hounded his old comrade Sergo Ordzhonikidze,
the commissar for heavy industry, into suicide for the crime of sheltering his
factory managers from Stalin's wrath. With Marshal Voroshilov's wholehearted
approval and support, the Soviet dictator also purged the upper echelons of
the armed forces—and among the victims was Tukhachevsky.[33]

Stalin's abrasive, outspoken and dynamic deputy commissar for defense
was a marked man. Not because he singled out Germany as the ultimate
enemy (Stalin saw the threat) or disagreed with Stalin about the scale of rearmament or military doctrine (they agreed on most things except battleship
building) but because Tukhachevsky, the consummate total-war systematizer,
had displayed an unhealthy habit of elevating military necessity to the point
of demanding the subordination of the whole economy to the army. It was
only one more logical step to assert that the soldiers should run the state.
Stalin did not want a budding Napoleon around in a crisis.

And so in May 1937 the secret police came for Tukhachevsky. Like so many
others, he confessed under torture to spying for Germany. "Comrades, the

fact that a military-political conspiracy existed against Soviet power I now hope that no one doubts," the Soviet dictator told the surviving senior commanders of the Red Army in June. "He [Tukhachevsky] gave our operational plan—our holy of holies—to the German [Army]." That month the NKVD shot Tukhachevsky. Hundreds of other top-ranking officers suffered his fate, and 34,501 other officers were dismissed.[34]

While the terror unfolded, the Soviet Union moved onto a war footing. The army grew quickly from 1.5 million men in 1937 to over four million by 1940, and arms production in the same period more than doubled. Although the purges removed tens of thousands of officers from the armed forces, the training schools poured out many more. The growing demand for weapons of increasing technical sophistication and complexity caused a rapid inflation of procurement costs. Although Stalin was generous with the annual defense outlays, the soldiers found that their extra millions of rubles bought fewer and fewer goods. The chief of the Red Army staff, Marshal Alexander Egorov, complained that "there is no military item for which we have not had a price increase by 10, 20, 30 or more percent." In naval armaments, the forced pace of technical development outstripped the skills of the engineers and constructors. The sea trials of the *Kirov*, the Red fleet's newest heavy cruiser, were a fiasco. Underperforming turbines and 800 tons of excess weight made the cruiser slower than planned. During the test firing of the 7.1-inch guns, the decks buckled. A test-fired torpedo knocked off the cruiser's propeller. Not surprisingly, the debacle ended in the arrest of the head of the navy's acceptance commission.[35]

How much the purges hindered Soviet arms growth is unclear. The decimation of managers, technicians and workers certainly set back output and technical progress. The terror also raised tensions between the armed forces and their suppliers. Accusations of "wrecking" flew fast and furious as output targets went unmet or weapons underperformed. Industry's failure to draft a realistic mobilization plan sealed the fate of some planners. "The present mobilisation plan is in an extremely bad state and threatens the danger of the disruption of industrial mobilisation," reported one of Molotov's officials. "In most People's Commissariats, although mobilisation-plans exist on paper, they are unrealistic, contain *wrecking* proposals, are out of date, and not backed up by resources." Unrealistic wartime production targets based on inflated intelligence only made matters worse. The army staff estimated that Soviet factories had to be able to outproduce a Nazi war machine that could churn out 42,000 aircraft and 48,000 tanks a year—which turned out to be double and quadruple the average annual production the

Third Reich actually achieved in 1942–44. In July 1938, more resources went into drafting the mobilization plan, but, as Voroshilov told Stalin, the sticking point was the lack of coordination between the army and industry. In October 1938, Molotov, chair of the highest defense committee and Stalin's confidant, read a long technical survey, the depressing subtext of which was that industry could not produce the munitions that would be needed to triumph over a German-Polish-Japanese bloc.[36]

The news that Soviet industry was not yet ready to win an all-out macroeconomic slugging match against its fascist enemies was bad enough, but Stalin and his inner circle also learned that they had lost the lead they had once enjoyed in the air. From 1936 aircraft output had risen, but not quickly enough for Stalin and the air force planners. The aviation industry was caught between two clashing demands: higher quality and quantity. As experience everywhere would show, aircraft firms first needed to learn how to manufacture the new high-performance all-metal monoplane fighters and bombers efficiently before they could be turned out in mass quantities. All the great powers had some trouble leaping over this technical-industrial hurdle. As the new head of the Soviet aviation sector, Mikhail Kaganovich, pointed out, the biggest headache was expanding the workforce fast enough to keep pace with rising production. Recruiting, training and motivating a huge army of workers for the aircraft industry, which leaped from 39,000 to 200,000 personnel in 1936–38, confounded plant managers—even in the land of workers and peasants. And the rapid rate of industrial expansion meant that they had to rely on people who lacked the skills, experience and work discipline to make high-quality combat aircraft. In time, managers figured out how to organize, reward and discipline workers to increase productivity. Meanwhile, in the hunt for culprits generated by the terror, the aircraft designers and technicians took the blame for their industry's shortcomings.[37]

Among them was chief engineer Andrei Tupolev. During the early 1930s, Tupolev had pioneered all-metal monoplanes and multi-engine bombers. Obsessed with flying higher, faster and farther, Tupolev was fanatical about quality standards and labor discipline. The sight of workers smoking and chatting drove him crazy. His hard-driven management style won him few friends, and he became the target of backbiting by his rival engineers and senior industry administrators. "Analysis of the causes of unsatisfactory rates of introduction and production of new aircraft shows," ran one slanderous report, "that one of the main causes is the completely intolerably hostile attitude of chief engineer Tupolev of the aircraft industry chief administration to the introduction of machines not of his design." In October 1937 the secret police arrested him for sabotage and espionage, but he was not executed. Gifted aircraft designers were in short supply. Instead, the NKVD employed a tried and tested solution of regimenting the aviation experts. Tupolev, along with hundreds of other engineers, found himself a captive in a prison design bureau.[38]

Three months after Tupolev's incarceration, Voroshilov received an alarming study written by his air staff of the Red Air Force's relative standing: "The year 1937 was marked in all leading capitalist states by a significant development of quality indicators in military aviation (speed, bomb load, armament, acceleration, increased sustainability to enemy fire, distance, altitude limit). The fascist states of Germany and Italy have achieved the most success in comparison to 1936–37. The quality increase is present in both experimental and mass production." Analyzing combat between German, Italian and Soviet aircraft in the skies over Spain, the air force's top brass judged that the Axis powers had overtaken the Soviet Union in air armaments owing to wreckers and complacency in the aviation industry. "If at the beginning of the war in Spain we had an obvious advantage in military aircraft, by now the Germans and Italians have reached us even with a small advantage for themselves. Of course, in the experimental sphere they have even better models in development. We did very little during 1937 in terms of modifying the existing aircraft and in constructing new models," the reported concluded.

Voroshilov resolved to do everything he could to rush the latest prototypes into mass production in the next two to three years. Until then, Stalin and his top officials had to face an unnerving fact. Germany had pulled ahead in the air arms race and the German lead would widen for some time to come.[39]

STALIN KNEW THAT to deter attackers he needed not only to prepare the economy and the armed forces for all-out war but to do so in such a way that likely aggressors would see that the costs of making war on the Soviet Union outweighed potential rewards. But projecting the image of Soviet strength was not an easy matter. Failing to do so enough might tip the decision in foreign capitals toward embarking on an anti-Soviet crusade. Yet trumpeting the size and fighting power of the Red Army and the output of the Five Year Plans too much offered anticommunists everywhere what they needed most to vilify Bolshevism. Hitler, for one, would often rattle off an inventory of Red Army hardware to impress foreign visitors with the Soviet menace.

As it was, the faster Germany rearmed, the faster the Soviet propaganda machine spewed out pamphlets, books and newsreels in multiple languages extolling the virtues of the Red Army. Where Moscow's emissaries could influence a free press, they encouraged and if necessary even bribed journalists to pen affirmative articles about the Soviet Union's war-making capabilities and peaceful diplomacy.[40]

Despite the propaganda effort, in the capitals of the great powers few leaders, intelligence analysts and senior soldiers took the prospect of offensive Soviet military action seriously. Some differed of course. In Paris, Pierre Cot insisted that France needed to harness the might of Soviet military aviation to threaten Hitler. But Cot and others like him were isolated. Geography complicated matters. Russia did not share a border with Germany or Czechoslovakia. To wage war on the Third Reich, the Red Army needed passage rights through Poland and Romania, two states that had serious territorial and ideological differences with their vast neighbor. On top of the problem of geography, the Soviet obsession with secrecy left foreign analysts wondering about the reality behind the smoke screen. When assessing the military capabilities and organizational aptitude of the Germans, European war planners tended to fill in the gaps in their intelligence with their worst fears, but with the Soviets they were a lot less generous. The "Teutons" did everything with diabolical cunning, the "Bolshies" with mind-boggling ineptitude. Memories of Russia's poor showing in earlier wars and a widespread sense of technological-organizational supremacy over the Slavs all fed the habitual belittling of the Red Army. British and French military guests at Red Army maneuvers in 1935–36 reported that the Russians could field modern tanks and planes and stage spectacular parachute drops, but that they lacked the leaders and tactical skills to employ advanced weapons aggressively beyond the borders of the Soviet Union.[41]

Stalin executed his senior commanders and many of his officials to harden the Soviet state for total war, but the purges only reinforced the belief abroad that the Russians were too incompetent to become a first-rate military power. Senior British and French officers noted that the Red Army purge removed the leading tank enthusiasts. French Army intelligence graphically described the Red Army as a "decapitated corpse." During 1937–38 the chief of the German Army staff did not consider Soviet intervention a significant contingency in his war plans against Czechoslovakia. And, while the generals disputed Hitler's claim that Britain and France would do nothing if Germany attacked the Czechs, no one questioned the Führer's judgment that Russia was not "geared up" for aggressive war.[42]

It was no secret that foreigners judged that the purge had hobbled the Red Army, but in December 1937 Stalin learned first-hand what senior officers in the Japanese Army thought. Intelligence had sent him a transcript of a Japan-

Marshal Mikhail Tukhachevsky: Stalin denounced him as a "Red militarist"

Colonel Ishiwara Kanji dreamed of turning Manchuria into a vast military-industrial complex

In 1941 Major (later General) Albert C. Wedemeyer wrote President Roosevelt's grand plan to win the arms race against Germany

General Georg Thomas, Germany's champion of total-war economics

The foot soldier Benito Mussolini in 1916: total war reshaped the man and made his totalitarian politics

On parade together but out of step: Mussolini and Italy's top soldier, Marshal Pietro Badoglio

Joseph Goebbels flanked by Adolf Hitler and Hermann Göring, 1943: the Goebbels diaries are an invaluable source for Hitler's thoughts on the arms race

Stalin and his military deputy Kliment Voroshilov: it was no coincidence that as the arms race accelerated in 1936–7 Stalin decided to purge the Red Army

Three men who helped make the German war machine: General Werner von Fritsch, General Werner von Blomberg and Admiral Erich Raeder

Diplomatic fantasists: Italian Foreign Minister Count Galeazzo Ciano shakes hands with German Foreign Minister Joachim von Ribbentrop in August 1939

In June 1936, Léon Blum became prime minister of France: the spiralling arms race soon presented him with a stark choice—guns or butter?

Édouard Daladier became France's prime minister in 1938: was his swing from a man of the left to one of the right driven by the arms race?

British Prime Minister Neville Chamberlain on his return from Munich in September 1938: he believed that he could halt the arms race through deterrence

The arms race accelerates: light tanks roll through Red Square on 9 May 1938

The arms race accelerates: British bombers on the assembly line in 1939

Left: A man with a plan: in May 1940 General Maurice Gamelin threw the dice in an all-or-nothing gamble and lost

Below: A man with a plan: in May 1940 Adolf Hitler threw the dice in an all-or-nothing gamble and won

The young Dwight D. Eisenhower: in 1930 he would write the War Department's first industrial mobilization plan. Thirty-one years later President Eisenhower coined the phrase "military-industrial complex"

President Franklin Delano Roosevelt aboard a battleship: he feared that an open-ended arms race against a totalitarian-dominated world would crush a progressive way of life

Left: The two prime ministers who led Japan into total war in 1940–1: Prince Konoe Fumimaro and General Tōjō Hideki

Below: President Roosevelt's great arsenal of democracy in action: seemingly endless B-24 Liberator bombers on the assembly line at the Ford Willow Run plant in Detroit, Michigan

ese report on the arms balance. In men and machines Japan was inferior compared with the Soviet Union, so ran the secret report, but the terror had severely weakened the Red Army and created a heaven-sent opportunity for the Japanese to exploit. This was alarming news at a time of rising tensions in the Far East. Despite ongoing talks between Moscow and Tokyo to keep the peace, the thousands of miles of poorly marked Manchurian-Mongolian-Siberian frontier was a constant source of friction. As both sides piled up arms in the region, firefights, abduction raids, espionage and violations of airspace by reconnaissance aircraft increased. In June 1937 on the Amur River, along the northern end of the Siberian-Manchurian border, a fierce battle between Soviet gunboats and Japanese shore guns took place. Neither side came out ahead, and Moscow and Tokyo ordered their forces to withdraw, but the Japanese Army in Manchuria—the Kwantung army—interpreted the episode as a Soviet provocation followed by a swift climb-down in the face of stiff Japanese resistance. As Soviet intelligence discovered, unruly Kwantung staff officers, including General Tōjō, were spoiling for a fight against Stalin's "paper tiger" and resented the "spineless" attitude of the army's top brass and the timid politicians back home in Tokyo.[43]

In July 1937, minor clashes between Chinese and Japanese troops erupted into full-scale war. To draw Japanese forces away from the Siberian-Mongolian frontier, the Soviet Union signed a nonaggression pact with Nationalist China and supplied Chiang Kai-shek's forces with arms. Meanwhile, Stalin resolved that the next time the Kwantung army picked a fight he was going to teach them a lesson. The moment came a year later. In July 1938 Russian and Japanese troops began to concentrate at Changkufeng, close to where the borders of Manchuria, Korea and the Soviet Union joined. Emboldened by what it saw as the Amur victory, the Kwantung army was determined to push back a Soviet probe onto some disputed high ground. The fighting became a test of wills, and Stalin had the edge. His intelligence services confirmed that Tokyo did not want its field commanders to start another war. Stalin knew he could take the calculated risk of inflicting heavy losses on the Japanese without the crisis spiraling out of control. However, he found it difficult to convince his own field commander that he wanted to give the Japanese a bloody nose. General Vasily Blyukher, who had sat on the tribunal that passed the death sentence on Tukhachevsky and who had seen many of his own staff arrested, wondered whether the order to attack was an NKVD trap. Impatient for action, Stalin picked up the telephone: "Tell me honestly, comrade Blyukher: do you truly want to fight the Japanese?" He got the message. After ten days of bloodletting involving thousands of soldiers and hundreds of tanks and

combat aircraft, the Japanese realized the Red Army had no intention of re-
treating. The Japanese negotiated an armistice.[44]

In the Far East, Stalin won the battle of nerves. Through good intelligence
and the prudent application of limited force, he knocked the Japanese Army
back for a time. In Europe, though, Stalin could not and did not want to
stick his neck out. In March 1938, after Germany invaded Austria, the ever-
optimistic Litvinov pleaded with Stalin, Molotov and Voroshilov to make an
unambiguous statement in support of collective security and the Franco-
Soviet-Czechoslovak security pacts. They remained silent. With the mobilization plans in disarray and the Soviet Union lagging behind Germany in
the air arms race, the risk of getting dragged into an all-out war was enormous. The lack of confidence in their ability to win an air war probably explains why the Russians were so cagey with the Czech Air Force about joint
action against Germany.

From the vantage point of the Kremlin, the crisis of 1938—Hitler's threats
against Czechoslovakia and Chamberlain's persistent attempts to appease him
through face-to-face negotiations—must have looked ominously like the
diplomatic prelude to either the formation of a pan-capitalist coalition or an
Anglo-French bid to turn the German war machine toward the Ukraine. At
any rate, the field belonged to Chamberlain and Hitler, and neither one of
them wanted to bring Stalin into play. The same was true of the French, who
would have fought alongside the British, but not in combination with the
Soviets. The French foreign minister, Georges Bonnet, made this clear to
Litvinov. Some feared that Bolshevik agents would act as a malign force trying to trigger a great war to spread communism across Europe, but Russian
officials told the Czechs that they could not count on the unilateral support
of the Soviet Union if they went to war; as the Czechs had insisted in 1935,
for the Franco-Soviet-Czechoslovak pacts to operate, the French had to take
action first. At the height of the crisis, Litvinov urged Stalin to mobilize the
Red Army and to publicize the fact loudly to deter Hitler. Stalin as usual ignored Litvinov. Instead, the Red Army's western districts quietly undertook
precautionary measures, probably as discreet pressure on the Poles.[45]

At the Munich conference of September 1938, Chamberlain, Daladier and
Mussolini turned over to Hitler the German-speaking parts of Czechoslovakia, leaving the Czechs with a much-reduced rump state. To Stalin, a tyrant
well versed in Russia's proud past as a European great power and Eurasian
empire, the most galling fact about Munich must have been the absence of
Soviet representation. As everyone knew, a true great power—a mighty nation with the capacity to wage great wars—would not have been ignored.[46]

DIPLOMACY CAN CHANGE RAPIDLY, but arming has its own inexorable logic. Over the winter of 1938–39, as Europe buzzed with rumors of surprise German attacks on Britain, Poland and Romania, the arms race sped toward its inevitable climax. *Pravda* declared that the long-anticipated "second imperialist war" had already begun. The "aggressor states" would soon attack the "so-called democratic" ones to carve up the globe for their own economic benefit. As the capitalist apocalypse neared, the all-important question for Stalin was whether it would consume the Soviet Union too.[47]

On March 10, 1939, Stalin spoke to the Eighteenth Congress of the Communist Party: "It is a distinguishing feature of the new imperialist war that it has not yet become universal, a world war." Why, he asked? "Combined, the non-aggressive, democratic states are unquestionably stronger than the fascist states, both economically and in the military sense." They could resist with force, but instead they appeased. "To what then are we to attribute the systematic concessions made by these states to the aggressors? The bourgeois politicians know that the first imperialist world war led to the victory of revolution in one of the largest countries." Another world war would ignite more revolutions. So instead of resisting the aggressors, British, French and American politicians egg on the Germans and the Japanese to attack the Soviet Union. But Berlin cruelly disappointed them, "for instead of marching further east, against the Soviet Union, they have turned, you see, to the west and are demanding colonies." And so now "everybody is arming, small states and big states, including primarily those which practice the policy of [appeasement]. Nobody believes any longer in the unctuous speeches which claim that the Munich concessions to the aggressors and the Munich agreement opened a new era of 'appeasement.' They are disbelieved even by the signatories to the Munich agreement, Britain and France, who are increasing their armaments no less than other countries."[48]

Five days later, on March 15, 1939, Hitler set off a chain of events that completely transformed the diplomatic situation for the Soviet Union. In a blatant violation of the Munich agreement, German troops invaded what remained of the Czech state. At the end of the month, fearing that Germany might attack Poland next, Britain and France guaranteed Poland's independence.

Now that they were faced with impending total war against Germany, the support of the Soviet Union was no longer a factor that British and French statesmen and soldiers could ignore, and Stalin knew it. Yet right from the start, incompatible aims doomed the negotiations for a grand British-French-Soviet military alliance. All Britain wanted was a limited arrangement that would shore up the east Europeans and with luck deter Hitler from attacking

Poland, but that would not bind London to Moscow. Yet Soviet officials feared that anything but the most ironclad military alliance would leave them alone to fight a life-and-death struggle against Germany cunningly masterminded for them in London and Paris.[49]

In May Stalin purged the diplomatic corps and replaced Litvinov with the hard-nosed Molotov. While Molotov rejected British attempts to limit the scope of any triple alliance, on the other side of the Soviet Union, firefights broke out at a desolate place on the Mongolian-Manchurian frontier called Nomonhan. Molotov believed that the Japanese were acting at the behest of Berlin and Rome to disrupt the triple-alliance talks. In no time the fighting escalated into another full-scale test of wills between Stalin and the hawkish officers of the Kwantung army. Over the next three months, this little war followed the same pattern as the earlier encounter at Changkufeng, except this time on a much bigger scale: the Japanese attacked with terrible ferocity, the Red Army stubbornly poured in men, tanks and aircraft, and both sides endured huge numbers of casualties, yet this time the Japanese suffered an unambiguous and crushing defeat.[50]

In August 1939 Britain and France sent low-level military missions to speak face to face with Voroshilov and his staff. In sheer frustration, Stalin and Molotov had probably given up at this point on a triple alliance. A year earlier Russia had stood isolated and powerless; now everyone knocked at the Kremlin's door. Hoping to dissuade London and Paris from fulfilling their guarantees to Poland, Hitler decided to cut his own deal with Stalin. On August 23, Ribbentrop arrived in Moscow with a no-nonsense offer: Stalin could share in the spoils of Hitler's war on Poland, and there would be no obligation for Russia to plunge into any resulting European war. Stalin accepted. As though by some special means he knew what had troubled the Führer for some years now, he coaxed Ribbentrop into ridiculing Britain as a potential foe. "The British Army was weak," Stalin said, "the British Navy no longer deserved its previous reputation. England's air arm was being increased, to be sure, but there was a lack of pilots. If England dominates the world in spite of this, this was due to the stupidity of the other countries that always let themselves be bluffed. It was ridiculous, for example, that a few hundred British should dominate India."[51]

On September 7, four days into the "second imperialist war," Stalin met in the Kremlin with Molotov and other Politburo men. Basking in the historic moment, he was in a gregarious mood. Of course, he said, he had wanted an alignment with the "so-called democratic countries," but they wanted something for nothing. So instead he made a pact with Hitler. "We see nothing wrong in their having a good hard fight and weakening each other," Stalin explained. "It would be fine if at the hands of Germany the position of the richest capitalist countries (especially England) were shaken. Hitler, without understanding it or desiring it, is shaking and undermining the capitalist system. *The position of Communists in power is different from the position of Communists in the opposition.* We are the masters of our own house. Communists in the capitalist countries are in the opposition; there the bourgeoisie is master. We can manoeuvre, pit one side against the other to set them fighting with each other as fiercely as possible. *The nonaggression pact is to a certain degree helping Germany."* After this admission Stalin mused: "*Next time we'll urge on the other side."*[52]

CHAPTER 11

"THEY ARE SERIOUS, THE ENGLISHMEN"

Joseph Goebbels, the German propaganda minister, was reading about the new British Defence White Paper. It was February 18, 1937. According to the London press, the chancellor of the exchequer, Neville Chamberlain, would spend £1.5 billion on the armed forces over the next five years. That would "triple" British armaments. "They are serious, the Englishmen," Goebbels confided to his diary. "It is a good thing that we don't have to catch up, . . . we are already ahead. We are the pacesetters of the new age."

Over the next two days Goebbels followed the defense debate in the British Parliament. Baldwin gave a "good" speech justifying higher military expenditures, he noted. To win support the prime minister had used the same rallying cry that Hitler often employed ("we are lagging behind"). No wonder Chamberlain's spending plan passed with an "impressive" majority of 184 votes. Still, wrote Goebbels, the British had been "very stupid." Now everyone had a pretext to arm faster. And the scale of the British defense program revealed just how weak the British were "at the moment." When the propaganda minister quizzed Hitler about the fresh spurt of British arming, the Führer was not at all concerned. "We will arm even more," he replied.[1]

To make sure that he could "arm even more," Hitler had put Hermann Göring at the helm of the Four Year Plan in 1936. Over the winter of 1936–37, Göring had started to assemble a huge administrative apparatus to control the economy. The Reich diverted half of all industrial investment to achieving the Four Year Plan's output targets, in particular for the iron and steel, chemical and engineering industries, all at the expense of consumer goods and living standards. To produce synthetic fuel and rubber, Göring found a cadre of bright young technocrats at the chemical giant IG Farben. They were eager to spend the enormous sums of money he gave them to realize hitherto unprofitable manufacturing processes on a colossal scale. Some of these wide-eyed industrial managers found their way into Göring's hydra-like bureaucracy, while others acted as willing agents of autarky working on the inside of Farben and other top companies. Over the next three years production of synthetic fuel rose swiftly, and an entire ersatz-rubber industry sprang up from nowhere. Yet, although the initial results were impressive, even amazing in some cases, production perpetually fell short of targets and the ever-growing demand for more raw resources, especially fuel.[2]

Above all, the Four Year Plan did nothing to relieve the immediate bottleneck to accelerated rearmament, the steel shortage. By the end of 1936 iron ore and scrap metal had shrunk to one month's supply, while the price of these and other key commodities on the world markets had shot up because of the global economic recovery and arms boom. So that they could keep their blast furnaces and rolling mills working without disruption for want of raw materials, the Ruhr steel barons pleaded with government officials for a fifteen percent cut in output, which was granted in November 1936. Domestic consumption, including arming and self-sufficiency projects, absorbed the whole cut. During the first half of 1937, to take the pressure off the balance of payments, exports received the highest priority. In January of that year, rationing was introduced for nonferrous metals (aluminum, copper, lead, zinc and tin). Steel was rationed a month later.[3]

The immense and uncoordinated expansion plans of the armed forces now ran up against the realities of Germany's economic predicament. As metal rationing was imposed, General Blomberg tried to set priorities: equipment for new army divisions, warship construction and the procurement of advanced aircraft all had first call on resources. In October 1936 the army estimated it needed 270,500 tons of steel per month; from February 1937 its monthly quota was 195,000 tons. The building of barracks, training schools and other military establishments was curtailed. The schedule for construction of frontier fortifications was stretched to the end of the 1940s. The army's equipment program slipped too. Ammunition depots, General Friedrich Fromm, the head of the army's administrative branch, calculated, would not be fully stocked until March 1942, or later. "It must be pointed out with all clarity," the army staff complained in May 1937, "that without the necessary increase [in the steel allocation] there must be a slowdown in the growth of the army and an impairment of our striking power in war for years to come."[4]

The steel shortage hit the Luftwaffe just as aviation technology underwent a revolution driven by the arms race. By the mid-1930s ponderous wood-and-fabric biplanes gave way to sleek all-metal monoplanes powered by high-performance motors and equipped with closed canopies, variable-pitch propellers, retractable landing gear and wing flaps. The first variants of the Messerschmitt Bf 109 fighter, the Dornier 17 light bomber, Heinkel 111 medium bomber and Junkers 87 dive bomber—Germany's principal combat aircraft of the early war years—all entered production in 1936–37. Air force planners and aviation industry managers expected that putting these complex and expensive models onto the assembly lines would slow down output and send production costs soaring. Göring did not lose any sleep about the size of the aircraft procurement budget. In planning sessions he liked to tell General Erhard Milch and other officials that "it was stupid to rack one's brains" to save a couple million marks. Milch needed no convincing. Unlike his fellow planner in the army, General Fromm, he did not worry about building up a bloated military aviation industry that would not be needed in peacetime. The moment had arrived for the Luftwaffe to make the next big technical-industrial breakthrough and assume mastery of the skies.

In January 1937 Göring approved a huge production plan of 7,943 aircraft over eighteen months, running from April 1, 1937 to October 1938. Despite his efforts to shield the air force from metal rationing, however, a scarcity of raw materials began to hit the aircraft industry hard. From May to September 1937 the aircraft factories received only 300,000 tons of the 750,000 tons they needed. The number of workers employed in aviation, which was supposed to mushroom, shrank from 109,750 to 98,250, with an estimated 2,800 laid off in ancillary firms. In June 1937 Milch trimmed 429 aircraft from the plan and postponed delivery for others. Four months later he briefed Göring about the full implications of the shortage in raw materials: aircraft output would have to be slashed by twenty-five percent, the expansion of the aviation industry by sixty-six percent, anti-aircraft gun production by seventy-five percent, and the provision of civilian air-raid shelters by 100 percent. Even though Göring and his staff had seen this coming, the realization that the growth of the Luftwaffe had flattened out must have come as a jolt.[5]

While the shortage of raw materials became more acute, Minister of Economics Schacht made a last attempt to slow down arming and to restore Germany's severed commercial links with the outside world. He argued successfully for a huge proportion of steel output to exports to earn much-needed hard currency, but domestic demand, thanks to the drive for arms and autarky, was insatiable. Factories making arms had no incentive to export; factories that were not making arms could not purchase the raw materials they needed. In the summer of 1936 and early 1937, Schacht spoke to French and British officials about a return of Germany's pre-1914 African colonies and favorable trade and financial terms to strengthen his hand against Göring. With the global economy on the upswing and many German manufacturers eager to grab a big share of foreign markets, Schacht judged that the time was right for a change of direction.[6]

Meanwhile Colonel Thomas, the head of the military-economic planning staff, was frustrated. The struggle for authority over the economy between Schacht and Göring was causing chaos. Although he had welcomed the Four Year Plan as the solution to the shortage in raw materials, Thomas now feared that the overzealous Göring, whose grasp of economic planning was slight, might send the gigantic war machine they were assembling careering out of control. The time had come to rein in the head of the Luftwaffe, whose partisanship for his own service was all too plain. In February 1937 General Blomberg, armed with a memorandum drafted by Thomas, appealed to Hitler to clarify the distribution of responsibilities: according to Thomas, Schacht should have final authority over the peacetime economy; the high command (that is, Blomberg and Thomas) should be in charge of arming in peacetime and the economy overall at the start of a war; and Göring's administration of the Four Year Plan (and his influence) should wither away as soon as its job was done.[7]

Blomberg, Thomas and Schacht all believed that the steady shift of economic authority to Göring was somehow contrary to Hitler's wishes. What they failed to understand was that the faster Germany's arming was ratcheted up, the less control they had over the economy and the rate of expansion and use of the armed forces. Göring saw what was happening. Relentlessly, he fought to tighten the regime's control over the economy. The steel industry was his battleground.

Since the advent of the Nazi regime, industry, which had benefited from the smashing of the trade unions and the end of collective bargaining, had come under the organization and regulation of the state in an interventionist onslaught led first by Schacht and now Göring. Although big business resented state interference, corporate managers, even in the aircraft industry where they were the most reliant on military orders, enjoyed a large degree of autonomy in the running of their firms. The Nazis lauded the idea that entrepreneurial competition spurred on creativity and efficiency. The profit motive also acted as an inducement to private business to work for the state. It was rarely necessary to resort to terror or nationalization. "Economic life may be free only so long as it is able to solve the problems of the nation," Hitler said in April 1937. However, even under the Nazis, private businessmen resisted making investment decisions that ran counter to their expectations about the long-term profitability of their companies. In particular, the Ruhr steel barons did not want to invest in the costly process of smelting Germany's deposits of low-grade iron ores. They preferred high-quality Swedish ores and calculated that, once the arms boom was over, they would no longer need the unprofitable spare production capacity. Göring demanded that the steel makers reduce Germany's dependence on imports and raise domestic production. Schacht urged them to oppose the idea. On July 23, 1937, weeks after he cut aircraft production targets, Göring organized a meeting with the steel tycoons. The "saboteurs of rearmament" would be defeated, he shouted. Hitler had empowered him to build three state-owned steelworks to smelt low-grade ores and to nationalize the mines. In September, recognizing defeat, Schacht, though he retained the presidency of the Reichsbank, offered Hitler his resignation as minister of economics. Göring replaced him temporarily. Not one to waste a chance to gloat, Göring telephoned Schacht from his old office to tell him, "I am now sitting in your chair!"[8]

ON SEPTEMBER 25, 1937, not long after Göring's battle with the steel industry reached a climax, Mussolini arrived for a four-day state visit. The Duce's hosts spared no effort in regaling him with the dynamism of National Socialism. On September 26, Mussolini watched the German Army and Air Force on field maneuvers in Mecklenburg, where the latest dive-bombers, artillery and tanks were displayed. The next day the Duce was taken to the Krupp works at Essen and a chemical plant at Hanover. The message was clear: Hitler's army was a formidable machine of war backed up by the tremendous capacity of German industry.

Back in Rome, Mussolini told Victor Emmanuel III that "Germany's military preparation continues at a very fast pace, but at the moment we have nothing, or very little, to learn." Although he drew no particular lessons from Germany on how Italy should arm, the visit did confirm Mussolini in his belief that Italy must align with Hitler's Reich to exploit the pivotal changes in Europe brought about by German rearmament. Britain, a "satiated" nation, was Italy's number-one foe. France was doomed to internal chaos, socialism and demographic decline. So long as London and Berlin remained locked in mutual military hostility, so he thought, Italy would be free, if the opportunity arose, to act in the Mediterranean, North Africa or the Middle East, and to exercise influence in Europe by leading the Axis politically. "When [the war in] Spain is over with," the Duce mused, "I will invent something else, the character of the Italians must be forged in combat."[9]

Count Galeazzo Ciano also wanted to be close to Berlin, but not too close. At Berchtesgaden in October 1936, he had roused Hitler with the idea, supported by secret papers, that the British were stringing him along with diplomacy to buy time to arm. Hitler angrily replied that if the British continued to spurn him, then Italy and Germany would arm against them. In three, four or—better still—five years, they would be ready for a showdown. Ciano considered this time frame realistic based on what he knew of Italy's armaments. Many dismissed him as little more than a playboy, the handsome yes man who married the boss's daughter in 1930 out of the ambition to succeed him. Ciano was in fact a shrewd political operator with a sharp wit and a maniacal streak. In June 1936, at age thirty-three, he became foreign minister. He championed the Axis and Italy's entry into the Spanish Civil War as the hallmark of Fascist dynamism. Ciano, himself a man of no small ego, agreed that Italy could exercise power in Europe by dominating the Axis and, in November 1937, by signing the Anti-Comintern Pact. "The alliance of three military empires such as Italy, Germany, and Japan tips the scale," he wrote, "with an unprecedented armed force." Even so, as the arms race accelerated and the peril of European war grew, Ciano worried that his father-in-law's realism ended where his vanity began. And what concerned him most was the way in which Hitler's men and some Italian officers inflamed Mussolini's desire for swift victories.[10]

General Alberto Pariani was chief among those who dazzled the Duce with the idea of fighting "wars of rapid decision." After his promotion to army chief of staff in October 1936, he challenged Marshal Badoglio's authority over war planning and began to transform the army to fit his shock-and-awe doctrine. Like many operational theorists before and after, Pariani was obsessed with the idea that speed and mobility enhanced by new technologies could revolutionize military affairs. In February 1937 he ordered the transformation of the army's three-regiment divisions into "binary" two-regiment divisions. These leaner, meaner formations, Pariani imagined, would be well suited to his revolutionary doctrine. After a ten-year modernization scheme, the peacetime army would consist of twenty-four binary, twenty-four standard, twelve mountain, three motorized and three armored divisions. Many senior officers protested that the binary divisions lacked the firepower and reserve strength necessary to deliver or withstand a sustained attack. The war of 1940–43 proved them right.[11]

Pariani's ideas would have made some sense had the Fascist state possessed the finance and industry to deliver the tanks, guns, trucks and aircraft they called for in double-quick time. During 1937–38, though, Italian military spending fell by twenty percent from the previous year. Although the Italian economy continued to recover in 1937, industrial capacity did not grow enough to increase arming. A shortage of skilled labor for the manufacturing industries impeded a rise in productivity. To pick up the pace, the engineering firms, which produced weapons, could have invested in special-purpose machine tools to modernize production and reduce the skills that workers needed to run them. But this would have resulted in a big jump in the import of expensive foreign technology just when the regime was striving for self-sufficiency. Expanding armaments and building the infrastructure of an autarkic economy already placed a huge demand on Italy's shrinking hard-currency reserves. In October 1937 General Alfredo Dallolio, the Duce's arms czar, concluded that "more than ever the availability of financial resources will determine the upper limits of our rearmament effort."[12]

By June 1937, under the auspices of Alberto Beneduce's Institute for Industrial Reconstruction, the Italian state owned the biggest share of domestic industry of any nation in Europe except the Soviet Union. The state's holdings included about half of the iron and steel industry, almost all the shipbuilders, a quarter of the aircraft makers and about half of the weapons and ammunition factories. In theory, this gave the state control over industry, but in practice Italian corporate managers, just like their German counterparts, retained a lot of autonomy in the running of their firms. And, also like their colleagues to the north, Italian industrialists resisted investments that might jeopardize the long-term profitability of their companies, especially the build-up of excess productive capacity that would have the sole purpose of serving what they saw as a temporary armaments boom. Managers in state-owned factories wanted to earn large profits too, and often colluded with private entrepreneurs to keep prices high and to divide up the arms market between them. Moreover, low wages and short production runs for military orders made it financially attractive for the arms industry to stick with labor-intensive batch production.

In Italy, as in Germany, steel production was a bottleneck to rearmament. From 1921 to 1936 most Italian producers recycled scrap iron to make steel rather than using smelted iron ore. Making more steel from iron ore instead of scrap metal and raising the capacity of the blast furnaces and rolling mills overall, as the Duce wanted, would have required a huge outlay in new plant and in surplus capacity that could never have been recouped through expected domestic sales. Despite that, Beneduce's planners and the steel mill moguls agreed in 1938 to invest heavily in new plant to smelt ore. The decision was couched in the rhetoric of autarky, but the underlying motive was in fact commercial. Their chief goal was to cut the cost of making steel in Italy so that the producers could compete on the recovering world market.[13]

While Italian industry responded sluggishly to the arms race, the advance of Italian military technology also stalled. The quality of its small arms, mortars, guns and the specialized vehicles needed to move infantry, artillery, engineers and supplies fell steadily behind that of the other major European armies. The cause lay not simply with the small size of the engineering sector: the carmaker Fiat was, after all, a technically sophisticated and successful mass producer and exporter. The army in fact had made some very poor choices. In 1930, for instance, the arms maker Ansaldo had bought the right from British Vickers to build Carden Lloyd Mark VI tanks. Called the CV29, these flimsy machine-gun carriers and other similar models came into service from 1934 onwards. Operational experience with them in Ethiopia and Spain showed that they lacked the armor, horsepower and firepower to deliver crushing blows. Yet Pariani ordered hundreds more of these light tanks instead of developing a gun-armed medium-sized tank. As he told a gathering of officers in November 1937, light tanks would be the spearheads of his new model army. The light tank, he proclaimed without the slightest flicker of doubt, "acts more with its mass than with its machine gun, like a horse." Not only did this peculiar thinking stunt Italian tank development for several critical years to come, but by the time war came, industry did not have the capacity to correct the mistake quickly enough to make a difference.[14]

In 1937 Italian aviation technology also stalled. Partly because it had great success with biplanes, the air force remained fixed on them for too long. While test flights with new monoplanes disappointed pilots, Italians flying the Fiat CR32 biplanes shot down hundreds of Spanish Republican aircraft, including Soviet-built I-16 monoplane fighters. In close combat a skilled pilot could exploit the CR32's maneuverability to offset the superior speed of monoplanes. However, the main reason why the air force fell behind in the development of all-metal monoplanes was the inability of the aviation industry to build reliable motors above 1,000 horsepower. Engine makers did not have the design skills to manufacture high-performance, water-cooled motors because for years they had relied on imported technology. As a result, even aerodynamic monoplanes, such as the Breda 65, the Macchi C200 and the Fiat G50, were underpowered, undergunned and more difficult to handle than similar warplanes built abroad. In 1938 possibly corrupt and certainly mismanaged design competitions compounded this chronic backwardness. The Air Ministry selected the new Fiat CR42 biplane instead of the superior Caproni-Reggiane Re2000 monoplane fighter (based on the American

Seversky P-35). Eventually, by 1943, after reluctantly adopting an excellent Daimler-Benz motor, Fiat began to produce a good high-performance monoplane fighter, the G55 Centauro, but by then it was too late.

The bomber fleet also suffered from the lack of a good high-performance motor, as well as reliable radios, navigational aids and bombsights. Aircraft designers compensated for the low-powered engines by producing tri-motor bombers, including the distinctive Savoia-Marchetti 79, which flew faster, further and delivered more bombs than either the twin-engine Heinkel 111 or Dornier 17 but which lacked the rugged all-metal construction and defensive weapons of the German warplanes. In 1937 several Italian firms began work on long-range four-engine bombers. A year later General Valle, the chief of the air force staff, considered purchasing the rights to build the American Boeing B-17 flying fortress. But in 1940 his successor, General Francesco Pricolo, a man who blithely ignored the advice of technical experts, selected the four-engine Piaggio P108 bomber instead, which he regarded as "very similar" and in some ways even "superior" to the B-17. Unfortunately for those who eventually flew the P108, too few of them were manufactured for Piaggio's engineers to work out all of the bomber's many design defects, which made the huge machine prone to sudden mechanical failure. Mussolini's youngest son, for one, the thrill-seeker Bruno, died at the controls of a P108 when it crashed during a test flight in August 1941.[15]

The one thing upon which military men as varied in their views as Badoglio, Pariani and Valle could agree was that Italy's war in Spain wasted scarce resources that could have otherwise been spent arming. In Berlin Blomberg and Thomas opposed aiding the Spanish insurgents on the same grounds. Mussolini and Hitler expected Franco to win quickly, but as the Spanish Civil War dragged on, the unofficial intervention forces of the Axis grew, with Italy's expanding out of all proportion to any immediate reward. While the Luftwaffe's Condor Legion never exceeded 5,000 men, by February 1937 Italian land and air forces on the Iberian Peninsula rose to nearly 50,000 "volunteers." Hitler realized that the deepening Italian involvement in the war helped to isolate Italy from Britain and France and make Mussolini more reliant on the Axis for clout in Europe.

Meanwhile, Göring took charge of Germany's effort in Spain. He offered the rebels arms in exchange for large shipments of Spanish iron ore, tungsten and bauxite. Italian officials complained about the way in which Göring tried to turn Nationalist Spain into a virtual satellite of the German economy. Italy's patchy battlefield performance did little to redress the imbalance in influence over the Nationalists. Most humiliating of all, in March 1937, during the battle of Guadalajara, Republican forces sent Italian troops attempting to encircle Madrid into headlong retreat. Only a few weeks later, in sharp contrast, the bombers of the Condor Legion shocked the world by destroying the Basque town of Guernica.[16]

As the Duce's Spanish venture trundled on, relations with Britain remained cool. London wanted the Italians out of Spain; Rome wanted Britain to formally recognize the conquest of Ethiopia. In January 1937 the two nations agreed to respect the territorial status quo in the Mediterranean, but afterward diplomacy made little headway. In London the service chiefs formally labeled Italy a potential enemy and drew up war plans; at the same time Ciano strung the British along with emollient words of peace. Although war was remote, an incident in Spanish waters might have propelled things to the brink. In September 1937 Italian submarines began a covert pirate war against vessels carrying Russian arms to the Spanish Republic. British flagged cargo ships were hit. In one encounter an Italian submarine mistakenly fired a torpedo that just missed a British destroyer. Through intercepted radio traffic the Admiralty confirmed the identity of the attacker. Yet neither London nor Rome wanted an open confrontation at that point. To avert a crisis, France and Britain convened an international conference to organize naval patrols to protect neutral shipping en route to Spain. The Italians, who had ordered their boats home before the delegates met, agreed to join the patrols.[17]

Meanwhile, during 1937, British diplomats reported Rome's increasing alarm at the growth of British armaments, especially the navy's. In May that year Mussolini surprised U.S. officials with his enthusiasm for President Roosevelt's call for a halt to the frenzied stockpiling of armaments. "Italy would back such an arms limitation move," the Duce explained to the press. Then he revealed his true motives. "And all the other powers would come in too. They would have to. None of them can long keep up the pace they are going now and they know it. . . . And Italy wants peace. She needs peace for a long time in which to develop the resources now at her command."[18]

Predictably, Mussolini's self-serving plea for a general slowdown in the arms race to uphold Italy's relative position flopped. Arming across Europe proceeded apace. With each passing month, time became more and more a real player in international politics. If war preparations could not be trimmed to Italy's level of speed, then everything would depend on how well the Duce and his officials could master the arms race, with all its tricky tidal currents. As 1937 came to a close, time appeared to be on Italy's side. Franco advanced steadily. Although Britain was arming fast, Prime Minister Chamberlain wanted talks. Everything now turned on the Axis. German strength could be put to Italian purposes. "It is not true that Italy is second in the Axis," Mussolini said to Ciano. "The opposite is true." In Berlin, Mussolini had told Hitler that Germany would run "war preparations" while he himself ran the "foreign policy" of the Axis. In the next three to five years the Axis would be ready for total war. A joint Axis committee to secure autarky was established. The Italian Navy was eager to coordinate war plans with the Germans. Shipbuilding had suffered from the same raw material and labor shortages that slowed down arming overall, while the British were making "exceptional" progress. Alone, Italy could never beat Britain at sea, but with Germany and Japan on its side the navy's prospects would be much brighter. On December 4, Ciano sent Göring a message: Italy would lay down two more 35,000-ton battleships that would be ready for war by 1941. A week later the Duce announced that Italy would leave the League of Nations. The day before Christmas 1937, Ciano recorded Mussolini's thoughts. "The Duce is calm," he wrote. "This morning he explained to me the new air force armaments program. . . . We must tighten our belts and arm ourselves. Everything leads us to believe that the conflict is inevitable. In which case we must not lose our greatest advantage: that of the initiative."[19]

It was a comforting illusion, but an illusion just the same, for the initiative lay elsewhere.

In July 1937 Colonel Thomas sent Hitler a report on the state of German rearmament. The steel shortage and the inefficient way in which that vital military resource was being distributed was the target of his blistering criticism. "The battle for steel is even being fought with underhanded means," he complained. "This disorder undermines the smooth running of the economy and endangers the authority of the state."[20]

The report was the frustrated cry of a soldier who had devoted his whole career to putting the theory of total war into practice. Like his boss, Blomberg—or for that matter any of the total-war systematizers—Thomas had complete faith in the power of the authoritarian state to mobilize everyone and everything for "totalitarian" war. "The battle for steel," as Thomas called it, ran contrary to what preparing for total war should be: ruthlessly ordered, rational and managed centrally by technocrats such as himself. Instead, confusion reigned. The responsibilities of the state and the Nazi Party were becoming entangled. Arms programs—including fortifications, bomb shelters and strategic railways—were behind schedule. The whole point of drawing up arms plans and setting production targets, after all, was to fulfill them.

Once Göring's new steelworks were up and running in a few years, the steel bottleneck would be, in part at least, relieved, but not the political issue of control. After Schacht resigned in September 1937 as minister of economics, Walther Funk, a former financial journalist and devoted Nazi, became his permanent replacement. He was little more than Göring's front man.

Through the summer of 1937, Blomberg continued to appeal to Hitler to raise the steel allocation to the armed forces and to set priorities among the competing arms plans. Admiral Erich Raeder also asked Blomberg to do so several times. All three services suffered from steel and labor shortages, but warship building had already fallen a year and half behind. While the Royal Navy was expanding fast, the German Navy would not even achieve the level of a thirty-five percent fleet that the naval treaty allowed before 1944. On October 25, Raeder wrote to Blomberg, demanding that the war minister obtain from Hitler an immediate decision about the future of the naval program.[21]

Hitler never dedicated himself to hands-on administration. Like the bohemian artist he thought he was, Hitler liked to paint the broad brushstrokes of policy and then leave the implementation to his warring subordinates. Ever since the rearmament of Germany began in earnest, he entrusted the details of finance and industry first to Schacht and Blomberg, and then, under the pressure of the arms race, increasingly to Göring. For four years Hitler's military policy had been to devote ever more resources to armaments. The stagnation of German arms growth in 1937 owing to the steel and skilled-labor shortages, however, forced him to adopt a more direct role.

Like so many bent on military supremacy before and after, Hitler assumed that the armed strength of his enemies would remain fairly constant or grow at a modest rate, while his own sped ahead. What he did not expect, but should have guessed, was that all the nations around him—France, Czechoslovakia, Poland, the Soviet Union, Britain and soon enough the United States—perceiving the menace, would arm quickly. So far he had dismantled the Treaty of Versailles without cost. Mistakenly, he attributed his success to the folly of his opponents, but the truth was that France and Britain wanted to co-opt Germany back into the equilibrium among the armed European states. Yet there were boundaries to their forbearance, and Hitler was starting to sense them. And, as the arms race intensified, time had become a real player, and with each passing month was starting to work against him.

As 1937 drew to an end, Hitler became convinced that Britain's effort to negotiate détente was nothing more than a ruse to buy time to arm. Ciano had planted the idea in his mind back in October 1936 and had even produced stolen British documents to prove it. Yet that did not deflect Hitler from his chosen path. He would promise to leave Britain's global maritime empire alone so long as the British did not oppose his bid to overawe France and dominate the Eurasian landmass by force. To make such a deal Hitler turned to his diplomatic genius, Ribbentrop. In June 1935 the ex–wine merchant and roving envoy, to the amazement of the career diplomats, had returned from London with a naval treaty in hand. In October 1936 Hitler demanded a repeat performance. He appointed Ribbentrop the German ambassador to London with orders to persuade his hosts to join the Anti-Comintern Pact. Alas, even if Otto von Bismarck, Germany's greatest statesmen, could have been brought back from the dead and dispatched to London, this would still have been a diplomatic mission impossible. For his part, the hapless Ribbentrop kicked off eighteen long months of ineptitude and farce in London when he arrived at Buckingham Palace to present his credentials and greeted King George VI with the Nazi salute.

As it dawned on him that Ribbentrop would fail, Hitler also learned through Göring, Blomberg, Thomas and others that the steel squeeze was slowing down rearmament, especially the Luftwaffe. Göring told Hitler that he was doing everything he could to raise steel production, but in the interim Germany's foes, above all Britain, were arming fast. What Hitler knew of British rearmament came from two chief sources: the European newspapers, which he had read to him each day, and reports of his military advisers. The press in general presented the picture that London wanted to project of a well-supplied industrial economy that would soon produce air and sea armaments of adequate strength to deter attack. What Hitler's military men told him remains difficult to piece together. Yet the reports of the German military attaché in London were clear enough. General Geyr von Schweppenburg described the scale of rearmament begun in 1936 as "unprecedented in British peacetime history." In September 1937 he warned that Germany might extract some concessions from the British before the end of 1938, but after that British armaments would be strong enough to counter any blows. If war broke out against France and Britain, Germany might score some early successes, but in time the overwhelming economic strength of Germany's two likely foes would come into play. "Germany cannot win a war against the British Empire," Schweppenburg concluded. All of Hitler's top military men, Generals Blomberg,

Fritsch and Beck, Colonel Thomas and above all Admiral Raeder, with varying degrees of apprehension, saw things in a similar way.[22]

For most professional soldiers, as well as many civilians who thought about
the implications of the last total war systematically, preparing for the next
one was a practical exercise in large-scale military and economic planning.
Victory would go to the nation whose industry could field the greatest forces
and whose society could endure relentless privation without cracking first.
Winning was thus not simply an exercise in the scientific management of
material resources, most would have agreed, but a political act, one that tapped
the deep passions and "spiritual" strength of entire peoples. But, when push
came to shove, and the question of war or peace arose, most placed their bets
on the big battalions and the well-stocked factories.

General Blomberg and his colleagues did not expect a total war soon. "The
general political situation justifies the supposition that Germany need not
expect an attack from any side," he wrote in the summer of 1937. "In addition
to the lack of desire for war nearly everywhere, especially the Western powers, grounds for this judgement are the inadequate armaments of some states,
including Russia." Germany was rearmed, but not ready for an all-out war. In
May 1937 Blomberg went on an official visit to London. Upon his return he
spoke with Hitler. No record of what was said was made, but the war minister probably reported the eagerness of his British hosts for détente with
Berlin. Five or more years of peaceful coexistence with London, to intensify
rearmament, out-arm the French and surpass the Soviets would have suited
Blomberg and the three service staffs admirably.[23]

In London and Paris, officials trying to picture what was going on inside
Berlin expected that these sorts of pragmatic military calculations, Germany's
well-known shortages of raw materials and hard currency and the sort of economic analysis propounded by Schacht would act as moderating influences.
At some stage German rearmament would reach its limit, many argued,
which would compel the Third Reich to seek a military and economic accommodation with its neighbors. Others predicted that an economic crisis
might push the regime into violent action. As it happened, Hitler, replying to
Blomberg's request for a resolution of the steel crisis, called a meeting of his
top military men and foreign minister for the evening of November 5, 1937.
It was time for one of the Führer's melodramatic monologues.[24]

Hitler spoke from notes for several hours. According to the notes taken by
Colonel Hoßbach, he said that he wished to explain his ideas about Ger-
many's external relations in light of the previous four and a half years of rule.
In the event of his death, he added, to underline the importance of the occa-

sion, that his words should be regarded as his "last will and testament." The sweeping survey of the shifting international scene that he delivered that evening combined the pseudoscientific biological racism of *Mein Kampf* with the apparently hard numbers, calculations, comparisons of forces and geopolitical analysis that usually filled the pages of the elaborate estimates drafted by the army, navy and air force planners. Each offered intellectual justification, direction and legitimacy to the other.

Hitler began with an attack on Schacht. The German people could never be free, prosperous and safe in a world of fluctuating markets and trade, he said. Within the frontiers of 1919, autarky, especially in food, was impossible. Austria and Czechoslovakia would have to be absorbed within the Reich to arrest the "decline of Germanism." To do so, "German policy had to reckon with two hate-inspired antagonists, Britain and France, to whom a German colossus in the center of Europe was a thorn in the flesh, and both countries were opposed to any further strengthening of Germany's position either in Europe or overseas." Britain would only ever offer concessions in the form of overseas colonies once Germany was fully armed and the British Empire was in trouble. He did not share the view, held by the military men he addressed that night, "that the Empire was unshakeable."

"Germany's problem could only be solved by means of force and this was never without attendant risk." The questions were "when" and "how" to risk using force. In Hitler's view there were three scenarios to consider. The first was a continuation of the arms race to 1943–45. After that, Germany's position in terms of advanced weapons and training would decline: "Our relative strength would decrease in relation to the rearmament which would by then have been carried out by the rest of the world. If we did not act by 1943–45," he continued, picking up the seemingly irresistible do-or-die logic that usually attended moments like this, "any year could, in consequence of a lack of reserves, produce the food crisis, to cope with which the necessary foreign exchange was not available, and this must be regarded as a 'waning point of the regime.' Besides, the world was expecting our attack and was increasing its counter-measures from year to year. It was while the rest of the world was still preparing its defenses that we were obliged to take the offensive."

The next two scenarios offered opportunities well before 1943 for action against Vienna and Prague. If France was crippled by civil war or if war broke out between Italy against France and Britain over Spain, Hitler suggested, then Germany might exploit a favorable opportunity to seize Austria and Czechoslovakia.

Once Hitler finished, Blomberg and Fritsch spoke up. They were staggered by the implications of what the Führer had said. They were not opposed to intensifying the arms race into the 1940s (that was their policy too); they did not take issue with the Nazi leader's exposition on race and the need to conquer living space in central and eastern Europe; they were not (after four years of collaboration) hostile to Hitler or the Nazi regime; what prompted them to speak out vigorously was the large risk in scenarios two and three of a premature war against France and Britain combined. To run such a risk invited a ruinous conflict that Germany could not win. Even if France was already at war with Italy, the two generals argued, the French Army could still for years to come field "forces superior to our own on our western Frontier." Hitler, however, reassured them that Britain, and thus France too, was not eager for a fight.

Göring then suggested that the time had come to wrap up the intervention in Spain. No one objected. Admiral Raeder said nothing. The anti-British theme that ran through everything Hitler said probably pleased him. Anyway, he was eager to get on with the steel allocation. He was in luck. In a pattern that would recur over the next two years, Hitler expressed his growing anger toward Britain with orders for more warships: the navy's steel ration jumped by 29,000 tons per month.[25]

In the following weeks, Blomberg and Fritsch tried to persuade Hitler that provoking France and Britain was reckless, that much of what he wanted could be achieved without the risk of a big war and that the arms race would eventually turn Germany's way. Others took up a different line of argument. "For a long time to come," wrote the deputy head of the Foreign Ministry, Ernst von Weizsäcker, "we cannot consider engaging in a war with England as our opponent. What we want from England we cannot obtain by force, but must obtain by negotiation." He emphasized that "time is in England's favour and not ours in the matter of armament. Therefore we do not have an unlimited period for negotiations." Never failing to tell his master what he wanted to hear most, Ribbentrop waded into the debate: "England is behind in her armaments; therefore, what she is playing for is to gain time. England believes that in a race with Germany time is on England's side—exploitation of her greater economic resources for armament—time for extending her alliances (e.g. the United States)."

Hitler saw the great trend. The more he pushed, the more resistance he would meet, and the more the internal armaments politics of his foes would be transformed too. Arming for total war had a logic all its own. "I bet you," he told Ribbentrop, "that in five years Churchill will be Prime Minister and then we will be in a fine mess! I can assure you that I won't wait until I have been cornered. I will strike before then and tear up the web that the English spider wants to weave around me."[26]

Of course, Hitler was right. The trajectory of British armaments politics was clear. Winston Churchill spoke compellingly about cranking up the British economy to produce armaments. With more time and more pressure to arm, especially the pressure of the expanding German war machine, the fear that arming too fast would turn Britain into a totalitarian war machine would be displaced by the fear of defeat. And, while this inexorable process gathered force, the man driving the Führer into a corner with his twin-track policy of armaments and diplomacy was Neville Chamberlain.

Ever since the Defence Requirements Committee had fixed 1939 as the year when Britain should be ready for war, a dispute between Treasury men, diplomats and Defence officials had raged about how to master the arms race. Could Britain, within the boundaries of a liberal economy, arm enough to deter war? If 1939 was the year of maximum danger and Germany the "ultimate" enemy, did it make sense to devote vast resources to building a huge battle fleet to win global naval supremacy, when those ships would not be finished before the mid-1940s? Might not war in Europe come before 1939? And if it might arrive early, then should not every effort be made to raise a big army and air force to fight Germany? Should Britain move closer to France, its most important potential ally in a war against Germany?

Chamberlain, the supreme problem solver, had his own plan. Britain alone, he thought, could buck the great trend of an ever-spiraling arms race and ever more thoroughgoing state controls over national life. Building formidable air defenses, a big (though not the world's biggest) navy and a small modern army would deter Germany from attacking Britain, and by extension France. Britain did not need to take the political risks of creating a state-run militarized economy in peacetime to prevent war. Time was to play for.

In Chamberlain's view the £1.5 billion of defense spending (including a £400 million defense loan) spread over five years that he had announced in February 1937, which so impressed Göring, Goebbels and others, represented the fastest that Britain could arm without throwing the balance of payments out of kilter. Yet, by April, there were already signs that costs would continue to soar. "No one is more convinced than I am of the necessity for rearmament & for speed in making ourselves safe," Chamberlain huffed. "But the services, very naturally, seeing how good the going is now and reflecting that the reason is sure to follow, want to be 100% or 200% safe on everything." The cost of planes, ships and tanks was rising fast, and he considered tax rises to compensate. "All the elements of danger are here," he observed, "increasing cost of living, jealousy of others' profits, a genuine feeling that things are not fairly shared out & I can see that we might easily run, in no time, into a series of crippling strikes, ruining our [arms] programme, a sharp steepening of cost due to wage increases, leading to a disastrous slump and finally the defeat of the government and the advent of an ignorant and unprepared & heavily pledged [left-wing] Opposition to handle a crisis as severe as that of 1931."[27]

Pressure to arm much faster than the chancellor and his officials thought safe came from within the Foreign Office and from the armed forces. Opinion among the diplomats was split between optimists who thought that Germany would eventually make a deal on arms control, frontiers and trade, and pessimists who, after the militarization of the Rhineland in 1936, had lost hope in an agreement.

Robert Vansittart, the permanent under-secretary for foreign affairs and Britain's most senior professional diplomat, was a diehard pessimist. In December 1936 he circulated a long, dense and foreboding paper, "The World Situation and British Rearmament." In it Germany was portrayed as the storm center of the arms race, drawing Japan, Italy and Spain into the "vortex." The Nazi regime was bent on a war of expansion and saw Britain as the chief obstacle to victory. Radicals demanded that Hitler lash out at Britain, but the top echelons of the army acted as a brake on "irresponsible party-elements." "Germany," he wrote, "is admittedly not yet ready for war on a considerable scale, militarily, economically or politically. The army wants time, must have time, to create a better balance between the purely military preparations and the essential economic preparations—raw materials, food-supplies for the nation. These are facts of great import and comfort. But on any showing Germany will be ready for big mischief at least a year—and probably more—before we are ready to look after ourselves." The only real answer to the Nazi menace lay in intensifying the arms race by arming much faster, even at the cost of trade and finance, to reduce the time lag between when Germany and Britain would be ready for war. "Time is vital," Vansittart warned, "and we have started late."[28]

Nearly everyone who read the paper found it too gloomy, including the cabinet secretary, Maurice Hankey, and the chairman of the chiefs of staff, Admiral Chatfield. Both men questioned whether Germany, when its economic situation was so dire, would risk war with Britain before 1939. Hankey and Chatfield recognized the device that Vansittart so skillfully employed of putting forward an inflated threat assessment to advance a particular policy, because they had used the same trick themselves. Vansittart wanted to concentrate most of the nation's resources on arming against Germany. What made his paper particularly troublesome to Chatfield was that it fed into the inclination of the politicians to spend ever more on the air force just when he hoped to convince them to build the navy's planned world-commanding fleet.

Only a few months earlier, Hankey and Chatfield had dealt with an equally grim forecast similar to Vansittart's, drafted by the air, army and navy planners. In October 1936 the Joint Planning Committee had put together a projected study of war in 1939 against Germany. It was a shocker, vivid in depicting a rapid shift of military power away from the victors of 1919. Surveying Britain's potential allies in a future European war, the planners dismissed Russia as unreliable and France as hopelessly lagging in the arms race. Indeed, by adopting "totalitarian" methods of war preparation, Germany had given itself a decisive edge in initial striking power at the outset of a war against democratic Britain and France. By 1939 the Luftwaffe would be powerful enough to knock Britain out of a war with concentrated air attacks on London and other key targets, or do the same to France with a combined bomber and tank offensive. By winning quickly, so ran the argument, Germany would nullify the superior economic resources that France and Britain could bring to bear with time in a long war.

In error, a copy of the draft study made its way to the prime minister's office before Hankey and the deputy service chiefs could hedge its conclusions with a lot of ifs and buts. Baldwin became "extremely cross" when he read the unedited study. Conservative backbench defense critics were attacking the government over the scale and pace of rearmament, and the press was whipped up into near hysteria over the German air threat. The last thing he needed was an official paper circulating around Whitehall declaring that in 1939 Germany would be able to pulverize London with a few weeks of intensive bombing and, worse still, that a democratic state was doomed by its very nature to lose an arms race against a totalitarian one.[29]

But in fact the joint planners, among them Group Captain Harris, had crafted the study to shock the politicians. With the lessons of the last war in mind, the planners dismissed limited rearmament against totalitarian Germany as potentially fatal nonsense. Every ounce of national strength had to be made ready for total war. Many senior staffers attributed the reluctance for all-out rearmament to the "moral disarmament" championed by the "pacifist" left and espoused a conservative brand of nationalism and imperialism, often with a lacing of technocratic authoritarianism behind it. "Too many of our leading officers," complained Captain Liddell Hart, the defense journalist, "are sympathetically inclined towards Fascist, and therefore un-British ideas." It was no quirk of fate that one of the army's leading tank theorists and a systematizer of future war, General John Fuller, joined the British Union of Fascists after he retired in 1933. As the arms race sped up and the planners studied the problem of survival in a world that might soon be dominated by totalitarian competitors, it was also no wonder that they drew unflattering comparisons with the social discipline, organization and hence military might of their own nation. Few of them really wanted to re-create something akin to fascism in Britain, but they could not help but admire the way in which the totalitarian regimes armed.[30]

Hankey, too, wanted to give the politicians a good jolt to scare them into spending more on arms, but not quite in the way the draft study did. The planners, Hankey explained to the prime minister, had taken "worst-case" analysis too far. He felt that they had underrated the difficulties Germany would face in launching a bolt from the blue. Britain's air defenses would improve dramatically in the next few years. "There is no magic in the year 1939," he assured Baldwin.[31]

This assessment was not just a bureaucratic move to mollify a peeved prime minister; it also expressed Hankey and Chatfield's expectations of how the arms race should unfold. Britain did not need to make a choice between arming to deflect a German knockout blow and winning the race for global naval supremacy. It could afford to do both. While Vansittart criticized the service chiefs for not pressing harder for greater air armament, Chatfield and Hankey blamed the diplomats for failing to reduce the number of Britain's potential foes. Relations with Japan and Italy might be repaired. A showdown with Berlin might be staved off for years. Time worked for Britain. By playing the long game, they argued, Britain would master the arms race. Chatfield, who put the navy and the empire first, even thought Germany should be diverted into self-defeating wars. "If we were convinced that if Germany succeeds in Czechoslovakia, Poland or Rumania she would eventually dominate Europe or threaten us in the near East," he told Vansittart, "it would be perhaps conceivably better to fight her at once. For she cannot remain as she is, that is the one clear thing in the world. But I conceive she will run more risks of disaster than dominance by such action, as she will always have behind her armies the growing military strength of England and France with their undisturbed financial strength."[32]

Admiral Chatfield considered that a premature war with Germany would be a disaster. Resources would be diverted away from the navy to the army and air force, and from the big ships to small ones to protect cargo ships from U-boats and bombers, while the U.S. and Japanese battleship fleets, locked in their own mutual antagonism, expanded. The navy's grand plan to uphold Britain's naval mastery needed a decade of peace to succeed. In 1937 the Royal Navy had made a good start at out-building everyone. That year work began on five 35,000-ton battleships, two aircraft carriers and seven cruisers. This huge program, on top of what had already been ordered, was the most that the slipways, armor and ordnance factories could handle for two years. Chatfield's problem was what would happen from then on. The cabinet had yet to make a decision about the ultimate size of the fleet. According to the approved plan, construction would slow down after 1938, but he wanted to keep the ship-yards working at full blast up to 1942, building at least three more battleships and four more aircraft carriers than the cabinet had already agreed to pay for. To push his building program forward, Chatfield ideally wanted the govern-ment to make a public pledge to maintain a fleet equal to the strength of the German and Japanese navies combined, one similar to Baldwin's 1934 prom-ise to maintain air parity with Germany. Once such an open-ended promise to voters had been made, it would be unthinkable for a future government to retract it. Thereafter, the Admiralty would hold a trump card to play in the annual budget rounds with the Treasury.[33]

By 1937 the air force planners found Baldwin's air parity pledge more of a burden than a blessing. They no longer thought in terms of numerical parity but instead hoped to win a technological edge with four-engine bombers. With fewer crews flying bigger long-range aircraft, the Royal Air Force would be able to drop more bombs on Germany than the Luftwaffe could drop on Britain. In 1937, though, the heavy bomber was only on the drawing board. Until the 1940s the air force would have to keep pace with the Luftwaffe in light and medium aircraft. In February 1936 the cabinet had approved Scheme F to provide Britain with a strike force that would match Germany's in 1939. As happened time and again, not long after work on the new program started, intelligence showed that the Luftwaffe intended to rearm faster than ex-pected. Schemes G and H were drawn up to boost the numbers, but the air planners doubted that the aircraft industry could deliver the aircraft.[34]

In 1936–37, the aviation industry was in the complicated transition between batch and mass production. To crank up output, the air planners had intended to organize the industry centrally by placing orders for a few preferred designs with groups of firms. But industry representatives rejected anything that smacked of state planning and control. Lord Weir advised the air minister, Lord Swinton, against such a "war regime." State coordination rather than control proved to be correct. The aircraft companies, afraid that they might be nationalized unless they delivered the goods, steadily organized themselves for mass output. They modernized the factories and shared efficient production techniques. The introduction of increased technical standardization made subcontracting and the preparation of shadow plants in the automotive sector easier. As a result, after 1938, the British output curve surged and outstripped Germany's two years later. Luckily, the air force sacrificed *quantity* for *quality* in the first two years of high-pressure growth. Indeed, had air planners focused resources on mass-producing the best-performing models of 1936, the Supermarine Spitfire fighter and the four-engine Avro Lancaster bomber, the two mainstays of the wartime Royal Air Force might never have been built.[35]

In the meantime no one could be sure that the British aircraft industry would improve. The pace of technological change and thus the unit cost of aircraft might continue to climb. Intelligence forecasts of German Air Force expansion alarmed the air staff. In October 1937 the air planners concluded that the Luftwaffe would possess in 1939 about 400 more bombers than they had originally thought. The Air Ministry quickly drew up a new plan, Scheme J, which would give Britain a bomber force of 1,400 aircraft capable of hitting Germany from English bases. The race for bomber parity was still on, but for how long? What if Göring stepped up bomber production again? "It is difficult to see (even assuming the most drastic degree of state intervention and control) how a standard of air strength . . . which would be necessary to provide any adequate military deterrent against the risk of attack by Germany," Lord Swinton told the cabinet, "could be attained as early as 1939."[36]

In fact, any British official who wanted to imagine what breakneck rearmament might do to Britain's economy, social stability and politics only needed to look across the Channel to France under the Popular Front. Many French people feared that their country was on the brink of either a fascist or a communist revolution. The Popular Front coalition was formed to forestall a revolution of the radical right; many conservatives saw its victory at the polls as the advent of communism. The civil war in Spain augured ill for France.

As a Marxist, Léon Blum believed that peace and social justice would come through revolution. When he became France's first Socialist premier in June 1936, however, he judged that the country was not ready for a socialist "conquest of power"; instead he set out to "exercise power" within the parliamentary capitalist system and to prepare the ground for radical social progress later. To do otherwise risked plunging France into a crisis that would lead to totalitarianism of the left or right. As he so often said, in the fight against fascism lay the danger of paving the way for it.[37]

By June 1937, after months of struggle to keep France in the arms race while preserving its liberal financial system, Blum ran out of options. Even after the devaluation of the franc in cooperation with London and Washington and the "pause" in social spending to favor armaments, the Bank of France still hemorrhaged gold. "We patch up the French situation every so often," the U.S. treasury secretary, Henry Morgenthau, lamented, "but with the constantly increasing proportion of their budget going for war purposes we really cannot help them." While the speculators tormented Blum, conservatives attacked the forty-hour workweek and his budget. To reverse the flight of capital, Blum's financial advisers drew up various deflationary budgets, all of which included tax hikes, a freeze on arms spending and cuts to social welfare. These measures would have robbed the Popular Front of its purpose.

Another way to bring the speculators to heel was exchange controls. Blum had always rejected them as the slippery slope to totalitarianism. Yet, against his instincts and propelled by circumstances and logic not of his own making, Blum groped for a solution "between exchange controls and absolute, total, unregulated [financial] freedom." To do so he asked Parliament for special powers to regulate financial flows by executive decree. On June 20, the lower chamber agreed, but the more conservative Senate voted 198 to 82 against. Several ministers called for mass action on the streets, but Blum shrank from a popular show of force against the upper chamber. Outraged protesters would be easier to mobilize than to disband. The last thing France needed was a constitutional crisis that might trigger a revolution. On June 21, much to the anger of his most passionate supporters, Blum resigned. "I have had enough," he told the American ambassador. "Everything that I have attempted to do has been blocked."[38]

To save the Popular Front coalition, Blum served as deputy premier under Camille Chautemps of the center-right wing of the Radical Party. The reshuffled cabinet shifted politically to the right. Georges Bonnet, the new finance minister, devalued the franc again. A brief recovery followed, but the jobless rate remained high. Industrial activity languished. Inflation rose and fueled labor unrest. To attract capital back into the economy, Bonnet imposed austerity. What little remained of Blum's public works' scheme was axed. The rate of growth in arms spending was curbed. "If one wants at the same time butter and guns," Bonnet said, reversing Blum's priorities, "then it is necessary to give up these great arms programs." Bonnet accepted that France, with its liberal system of finance, could not equal the military effort of totalitarian Germany. Trying might bankrupt France and tempt Hitler to attack. In July the cabinet shaved 2.3 billion from the 13.4 billion francs the armed services had asked for in the 1938 defense budget. Naval building took the most draconian cut, while the army and air force received slight increases above their 1937 budgets.[39]

The service chiefs railed against the slowdown. With Berlin and Rome arming fast and London an uncertain partner without much of an army, France needed to arm at full tilt. Admiral François Darlan complained that the French fleet would fall below the combined might of the Axis navies by 1939–40. General Gamelin warned that the standing German Army would soon be twice the size of the French. Like their colleagues in London, French staff officers praised the discipline and good order of Germany's regimented economy so as to cast an unfavorable light on France's strike-ridden factories and left-wing economic policies. "National Socialism," the army staff wrote, "has aimed to achieve in the time of peace the economic mobilisation of the nation for war." Once again the service chiefs tried to frighten cabinet ministers into spending more money on armaments with hair-raising intelligence about armor-plated Teutons storming their way toward Paris. This time politicians did not budge. Even Daladier, the defense minister, was forced to accept Bonnet's economies. In any case the arms industry already had more orders than the factories could possibly handle. While the economy as a whole was depressed and big business was reluctant to invest, French armaments output remained flat.[40]

Of the Popular Front's ministers, Pierre Cot was the most affected by Blum's resignation. In the Chautemps cabinet he was isolated. Cot hated the arch-reactionary Bonnet even before he trimmed the air force budget. Known as an admirer of the Soviet Union, the air minister was vilified by right-wing legislators and newspapers. The nationalization of the aircraft industry in 1936 infuriated big business. The fear of seeing the Luftwaffe over Paris stirred public anxieties most. All in all, Cot was in a tough spot. He knew that much could be done to modernize the air force, but he was also aware that Germany ultimately possessed far greater industrial potential than France. In a one-to-one air arms race (and air war), France was bound to lose.

As Cot told the Supreme Defense Committee, the only real answer to the German peril was to build an international coalition of overwhelming strength to deter Berlin with the threat of devastating aerial attack. That France needed strong allies was undisputed. Gamelin saw a British alliance as the key to victory over the Reich. Most senior officers thought that Poland, Romania, Czechoslovakia and Yugoslavia would be useful allies early on in a big war. Many held out the hope that Fascist Italy might be persuaded to rekindle the nascent military talks of 1935. What made Cot's ideas political dynamite was that he placed absolute faith in an alliance with the Soviet Union as France's only hope. Although Paris and Moscow had signed a mutual assistance pact in May 1935, the French high command showed little enthusiasm for staff talks with their Soviet counterparts. Most of the military establishment rated the Red Army's offensive capacity as low, doubted that effective air cooperation was technically feasible and deeply distrusted the Kremlin. Cot brushed aside these objections. After Blum authorized exploratory staff talks with the Soviet Union in November 1936, the air minister eagerly dispatched an air force mission to Moscow to discuss war plans and technical-industrial collaboration. Meanwhile, the army high command, the Defense Ministry, including Daladier, and even some top-ranking air force officers did everything they could to stymie the talks.[41]

Cot could have ignored his detractors had air force growth sped up. In 1937, though, Germany built 5,606 aircraft, the Soviet Union 6,033, Britain 2,218, Italy 1,794 and France just 370. This dismal output was inevitable while the aircraft sector was restructured as a nationalized industry. Of the three armed services, the Air Ministry's nationalization plan was the most far-reaching and disruptive, encompassing eighty percent of the airframe makers. Despite the accusations of his critics, Cot was not hostile to free enterprise. The Air Ministry did not buy up whole firms but instead set up mixed private-state companies organized regionally. Cot recruited dynamic young managers to run the new firms for profit. Aviation research and development stayed in the hands of private investors. The workforce grew from 34,235 in 1936 to 81,289 in 1939. Morale in the nationalized plants rose sharply along with productivity. Sadly for Cot, the massive injection of cash that his sweeping technocratic drive for industrial efficiency needed to jump-start production was lacking in 1937. So too were good prototypes. The air force staff had dreamed for too long of the unrealizable high-performance hybrid, a multi-purpose combat plane that could perform equally well as a bomber, a dogfighter and a spotter.[42]

During the second half of 1937, Cot's political foes hauled him in front of Parliament's aviation committee and grilled him about the state of aircraft production and aviation technology. Long before Blum resigned, Cot was in the habit of putting a rosy gloss on everything to keep his political foes at bay. But the worse things got, the wider the gap became between industrial reality and the industrial fantasy that the air minister spun for his colleagues and legislators.

The drop in French aircraft production was an open secret. In London industrial intelligence analysts pieced together what they could from public and

commercial sources. The news was bad. At the start of the 1930s British officials blamed most of Europe's troubles on rampant French militarism; now
France's lack of militaristic drive alarmed them. Worse still, what British intelligence analysts could discover, German and Italian ones could also find
out. And nothing could tempt Berlin and Rome to act recklessly more than
French vulnerability. When Chautemps visited London in November 1937,
Neville Chamberlain offered him technical assistance in aviation and suggested, very politely, that perhaps the French prime minister was not fully informed about the current performance of the French aircraft industry.

Chautemps was furious, and when he got back to Paris he telephoned Cot
to demand answers. The embattled air minister assumed the self-righteous attitude of a principled man unjustly persecuted for his principles. No one took
the air threat from Germany more seriously than he did. How was he supposed to compete with Göring, who received all the money, raw materials
and industrial plant he needed to build up the Luftwaffe? A democracy such
as France simply could not out-arm a totalitarian state. France's only hope
was an alliance with the Soviet Union, the "greatest air power in the world."
On December 8, Cot told the Supreme Defense Committee that he needed
a sixty percent increase in his budget to crank up the production of aircraft.
Budgetary constraints, he said, had prevented him from executing his plans
effectively.[43]

Chautemps responded with a cabinet reshuffle in January 1938 that removed Cot. The left-wing radical was a political liability at the head of such
a sensitive ministry. His relationship with top-ranking officers, moreover, was
strained. In public, officials put a brave face on the strength of the air force.
But in private a sense of apocalyptic gloom fell over politicians and top-
ranking officers. "The situation is extremely grave," wrote General Joseph
Vuillemin, the new air force chief. "We do not know what the future holds but
I am quite convinced that if a conflict erupts this year, the French Air Force
would be annihilated in a few days."[44]

In LONDON, the prime minister, Stanley Baldwin, was ailing, and on May 28,
1937, Neville Chamberlain replaced him. Upon moving into 10 Downing
Street, Chamberlain felt liberated. He sought to dominate his cabinet and
relished the chance to put the business of government in order. He understood that the most pressing issue confronting the nation was the arms race.

Chamberlain always saw arming as a rational act, one that could be fine-
tuned to have positive political effects. Building up an air force, upgrading

the fleet and the regular army would be enough to convince Hitler and his generals that it was better to talk than to compete in arms. However, so far no one in Berlin seemed to get the message. Instead, with Germany setting the pace, the arms race went on. Why Berlin was not getting the message seemed clear to Chamberlain. The arms programs of 1936 needed time to complete. Once Britain was unassailable, Berlin would be responsive. And to show that London could be reasonable, someone needed to speak to Hitler. "I believe the double policy of rearmament & better relations with Germany & Italy will carry us safely though the danger period," he wrote, "if only the Foreign Office will play up." After March 1936, when Germany remilitarized the Rhineland, the diplomats had shown very little interest in improving relations with Germany. Vansittart foretold doom. Foreign Secretary Anthony Eden wanted to cozy up to the French and trade insults with Mussolini. On the prime purpose of diplomacy, Chamberlain sided with Hankey and Chatfield. "Without overlooking the assistance which we should hope to obtain from France, and possibly other allies," the service chiefs argued, "we cannot foresee a time when our defence forces will be strong enough to safeguard our territory, trade and vital interests against Germany, Italy and Japan simultaneously. We cannot, therefore, exaggerate the importance . . . of any political or international action that can be taken to reduce the numbers of our potential enemies and to gain the support of potential allies."

Diplomatically, everything hinged on Germany. "If only we could get on terms with the Germans," Chamberlain wrote, "I would not care a rap for the Musso." An agreement with Germany would leave Italy out on a limb and free up strength for the Far East. To negotiate a European settlement with Germany, he intended to bypass the Foreign Office as well as the small circle of Nazi radicals and conservatives that vied for Hitler's ear—and negotiate with the Führer himself. Hitler had said he wanted the frontiers of central Europe altered to bring into the Reich the ten million Germans living in Czechoslovakia into Austria. If this could be achieved peacefully, then the steam would go out of the arms race. Arms control would follow. Trade deals would break down German autarky. A new political equilibrium would be founded on Anglo-German cooperation.[45]

Meanwhile, in the second half of 1937, as the arms budget continued to expand, the British economy stopped growing. Exports declined and imports rose. Wages and prices also climbed. A recession loomed. "What a frightful bill we owe to Mister Hitler," Chamberlain wrote, "damn him!" Luckily, skilled labor was "doing well" from the arms boom and trade union leaders had pledged to back rearmament until the international scene became less menacing. Still, Chamberlain wanted to show that all classes would pay a fair share of the defense bill. In April, in his last budget as chancellor, Chamberlain raised income taxes and established a new sliding-scale tax on business profits called the National Defence Contribution, which was meant to shore up the legitimacy of the fiscal system and promote industrial peace by preempting accusations that workers were being soaked by fat-cat employers who profiteered on military contracts. In reaction to this peculiarly socialistic redistribution of wealth from a stalwart Tory, the Conservative Party and business lobbyists raised an uproar. Shocked by the backlash, Chamberlain dropped the National Defence Contribution. A flat-rate levy on business profits was introduced in June 1937 instead.[46]

The stalling economy and the setback over the National Defence Contribution showed just how potentially explosive the rising burden of arms was becoming. The trend of ever greater arms spending and production threatened to turn labor against the bosses and the masses against the state. To extract more from the economy for defense, greater discipline over society would be needed. But without mass consent, that could be achieved only by recasting the British state.

Even if the arms race soon achieved equilibrium, the strain of maintaining enormous armaments in an indefinite cold war against the Axis powers would involve levels of taxation, budget deficits, social privation and the regimentation of workers and factories so crushing that only a different kind of state could bear it. In October 1937, John Simon, Chamberlain's successor at the Treasury, made this grim forecast while presenting a review of spiraling defense costs. He argued that arms spending had to be correlated with resources. He proposed that the service staffs determine how much money they needed up to 1941 and the Treasury project just how much would be available. Thomas Inskip, the minister for the coordination of defense, should then put the two together into a single, coherent grand strategy.[47]

The report that Inskip drafted in late 1937 was the supreme statement of how the government might impose rationality on rearmament and thereby check those forces at home and abroad threatening to destroy the nation's liberal way of life. Inskip declared the economy the "fourth arm" of defense. Britain could never defeat Germany with a knockout blow. Victory could be achieved only in a titanic war of attrition between vast arms-producing economies. German war planners made the same calculations. They knew that Britain with its superior resources would in the end win a protracted war, so long as it entered the conflict with "sufficient economic strength . . . to make the fullest uses of resources overseas, and to withstand the strain." In peacetime, Britain's defenses only needed to be strong enough to show Berlin that it could not win a quick war, because the Germans knew that they would lose a long one. A balance had to be struck, therefore, between arming enough to repel a first strike and safeguarding economic and political stability to prevail in a long, all-out war. "Nothing operates more strongly to deter a potential aggressor from attacking this country than our stability," Inskip warned, perhaps thinking of France, "but if other countries were to detect in us serious signs of strain, this deterrence would at once be lost."

In 1938 and 1939, the period of maximum danger, Inskip recommended that the government should "press forward resolutely" with spending much more than in any previous year. After that, unless there was some slackening of the pace, the government would have to take the plunge and institute controls over labor and industry to stay in the arms race. During this two-year spurt, he added, priority should be given to the forces needed to repel a knock-out blow, in other words improving fighter and anti-aircraft artillery defenses against the Luftwaffe, replacing old warships with new ones and equipping the small regular army with modern equipment.[48]

To Chamberlain, Inskip's report embodied the measured, focused and rational approach to the arms race that he had always advocated. Inskip's recommendations became policy in February 1938. That year Chamberlain hoped to halt the arms race through diplomacy. Alas, the prime minister's diplomacy was doomed to fail, for the great competition was neither in his nor in anyone else's power to stop.

CHAPTER 12

" . . . A DIFFERENT
KIND OF NATION"?

In the closing months of 1937, to escape the pressure and loneliness of his top job in the Nazi regime, Field Marshal Werner von Blomberg found solace in the company of a twenty-five-year-old blonde. Early in December the love-struck sexagenarian decided to marry her and spoke to Hitler about it. Blomberg explained that his fiancée was a lowly Berlin typist, a "girl from the people," and added that the strict code of the officer corps precluded marriage across the class divide. Eager to endorse this union between the upper-crust soldier and the working-class typist as an example of his new racial order, Hitler offered to act as a witness to the ceremony.

The nuptials took place on January 12, 1938, and Hitler and Göring signed the marriage certificate. Days after, rumors began to fly. Apparently a Berlin call girl had married a senior army officer, the war minister no less. The chief of the Berlin police visited the War Ministry to discover whether the Fräulein Luise Margarethe Gruhn recorded in his files as a prostitute was in fact the same woman now registered as residing in the private apartment of Field Marshal von Blomberg. She was. The police chief was redirected to Göring, who gingerly raised the matter with the Führer.

By all accounts, the news of the scandalous aspects of Blomberg's marriage came as a shock to Hitler, who felt betrayed by his war minister. Few things mattered to him more than his prestige. If the news broke that he had blessed the marriage, he would be made a laughingstock. Confronted with the facts, Blomberg at first refused to have the marriage annulled and step down. On January 27, though, after a long talk with Hitler, he resigned and departed with his bride to Capri for a year of self-imposed exile.

Who would be the new war minister? Werner von Fritsch, the chief of the army, was a front-runner. Back in 1936, however, Hitler had received a secret police file on the bachelor general, who was accused of procuring the services of a male prostitute. At that time Hitler had ordered the file destroyed; now he wanted a fresh copy. As it happened, Heinrich Himmler, the head of the SS (the Nazi Party's special police), still had the original. Fritsch learned of the impending charge from Hitler's army adjutant, Colonel Friedrich Hoßbach. Distraught, baffled but defiant, Fritsch demanded to defend himself in front of a military court of honor. Eventually, he was cleared, but in the interim he was out of the running as war minister.

On February 4, Hitler announced Blomberg's and Fritsch's resignations. He took Blomberg's post of commander in chief for himself. Blomberg had suggested Göring, but Hitler rejected him. As a sop to his ego, Hitler promoted Göring to field marshal. Replacing Fritsch as army chief was General Walter von Brauchitsch, an ardent Nazi who owed Hitler a personal debt of loyalty for having financed his divorce to marry his mistress. General Wilhelm Keitel, a compliant and capable administrator, became Hitler's chief of staff in the new armed forces high command. To obscure the facts behind the war minister's departure, other changes were announced on the same day. Besides Blomberg and Fritsch, over sixty other top-ranking officers were retired or transferred in favor of ambitious younger men. Hitler also replaced several key ambassadors and promoted Ribbentrop to the post of foreign minister.[1]

In terms that future-war systematizers like Blomberg would instantly recognize as the logical implication of readying Germany for total war, the press communiqué of February 4 heralded the reshuffle as the "strongest concentration of all political, military and economic forces in the hands of the supreme leader."[2]

NOT LONG AFTER the Blomberg-Fritsch affair, events once again favored Hitler. By 1938 Austria had become a German satellite. Hitler was in no rush to achieve *Anschluss*, the political union of the two German-speaking nations that had been outlawed by the peacemakers in 1919. Instead, he planned to erode Austria's sovereignty year by year as Germany's armaments grew.

On February 12, during a meeting at Berchtesgaden, Hitler bullied Austria's chancellor, Kurt von Schuschnigg, into taking two Austrian Nazis into his cabinet as well as making economic concessions to Germany. Back in Vienna, Schuschnigg did the only thing he could to stem the tide of German political-economic penetration. On March 9, he announced he would hold a referendum in four days on Austria's independence, one he was certain to win. A vote in favor of sovereignty would not only assert Austria's independence but would also publicly snub Hitler. The news stunned Berlin. Spurred on by Göring, Hitler improvised the forced annexation of Austria. While staff officers threw together the invasion plan, Operation Otto, Hitler sent Schuschnigg an ultimatum demanding he resign. Facing certain military defeat, Schuschnigg yielded. On March 12–13 German forces invaded Austria.[3]

The *Anschluss* was a complete triumph. Hitler experienced a tremendous boost in his personal prestige. As he said in the autumn of 1937, he had planned to wait for some upheaval in France or the outbreak of war in the Mediterranean to distract Europe before moving against Austria, but thanks to Schuschnigg's rash defiance and the speed of the operation, everyone had been caught off guard. Austria was digested whole: Nazi thugs rounded up Austrian Jews and communists, while Göring added Austria's economic resources and armed forces to Germany's war machine.

After the *Anschluss*, Hitler studied the map of Europe, meditated on the arms race and asked himself what game Britain was playing. Back in November 1937, Lord Halifax, the leader of the House of Lords and a close associate of Chamberlain, had visited Germany as Göring's private guest. In a meeting with Hitler, Halifax explained that Britain did not oppose changes to the frontiers of central and eastern Europe so long as change came about through peaceful diplomacy. Halifax then asked about disarmament. "Today," Hitler replied, "England herself was arming to a degree which had no parallel in English History. Was England ready to abandon her rearmament?" He "knew that the English answer to this question was to describe English rearmament as making up lost ground. Germany found herself in the same situation." Halifax thus confirmed what Hitler already knew. Britain would never accept *his* proposed division of spheres of influence whereby Germany would have free rein to expand eastwards, while Britain would be left unchallenged by Germany on the high seas. The British offer to negotiate was only a ruse to buy time to arm. Hitler did not want to tinker with frontiers; he wanted to transform Europe through wars of racial conquest. The English "spider," as Hitler had put it, was weaving its web.[4]

No one did more to confirm to Hitler this reading of British diplomacy than his ambassador to Britain, Joachim von Ribbentrop. When he had turned up in London at the end of 1936, he tried to worm his way into the inner sanctum of power by ingratiating himself with the English aristocracy. Once he realized he was getting nowhere, he began to spend much more of his time exercising his cunning in Berlin—close to the Führer—than in London.

During the winter of 1937–38, Ribbentrop explained to Hitler why he had failed to sell the British Hitler's deal on maritime-continental spheres of influence. "England does not desire in close proximity a paramount Germany," he wrote, "which would be a constant menace to the British Isles." The only answers to the English menace lay in the assembly of a gigantic war machine and aligning with Italy and Japan a global coalition of authoritarian states to threaten the British Empire. "England is behind in her armaments—therefore, what she is playing for is to gain time." In the meantime, threatening the British Empire would deter London—and by extension Paris—from interfering if Germany fought a quick war in central Europe. But the time for a small war in Europe was running out. Two opposing coalitions were forming, one led by London, the other by Berlin. Once these two alliances had become "rigid," any sort of far-reaching accord would be out of the question. And once the enemy coalition was strong enough, Britain would "sooner or later" fight. Chamberlain and Halifax "see no possible basis for an agreement with Germany (they consider National Socialist Germany capable of anything, just as we consider the British capable of anything); therefore, they fear that someday they might be forced by a strong Germany to accept solutions that are not agreeable to them. In order to meet this contingency England is at all events preparing by military and political measures for a conflict with Germany." Ribbentrop concluded in stark terms: "Henceforth, regardless of what tactical interludes of conciliation may be attempted with regard to us, every day that our political calculations are not actuated by the fundamental idea that England is our most dangerous enemy would be a gain for our enemies."[5]

Ribbentrop's exposition of the arms race as accelerating toward the stage at which the military advantage would cross over from Germany to its enemies, principally Britain, reflected and reinforced Hitler's thoughts. When would the crossover begin? And how much more could Germany achieve before then? "One often hears and reads of 1939 as the year in which England will be able to act with greater strength," Ribbentrop reported to Hitler. "In my view," he continued, "it is likely to be later, particularly in terms of the English naval program."[6]

On April 21, 1938, five weeks after Austria had been annexed, the Nazi leader met with General Keitel to discuss the war plan against Czechoslovakia. Hitler said that the "tempo" of German arms expansion was "too slow," especially artillery production and work on frontier fortifications, but the "relative" balance was still in "our favour": Germany mined over three times more minerals than France; Britain had only started arming nine months before; its new battleships would not be launched for another two years and most of its air force was "obsolete." There was still time to deal with Czechoslovakia.

Hitler told Keitel that he planned a masterstroke on the model of the *Anschluss*. War against the Czechs, however, could not "come out of the blue." That would provoke "hostile world opinion" that might lead to a "serious situation." Events would instead have to escalate rapidly into war from some staged incident. The army and air force would have only four days to defeat the Czechs. "Faits accomplis," Hitler emphasized, "must convince foreign powers of the hopelessness of military intervention."

The success and timing of the attack would also depend on Italy. Germany needed Italy to deter Britain and France. If Mussolini had a new venture planned in Africa or the Mediterranean, Hitler explained to General Keitel, then the timing of their masterstrokes could be synchronized. It would be Ethiopia and the Rhineland all over again. If not, then he would push the Czech war into the "distant future," fortify the western frontier and "wait and see" what happened next.[7]

In the spring of 1938 Hitler had every confidence in Mussolini, a man he described as a strategic realist, "fully able to estimate military possibilities." As Operation Otto unfolded, Hitler contacted the Duce to seek his acquiescence to the *Anschluss* and got it.[8]

Mussolini had accepted the *Anschluss* as the inevitable outcome of Germany's growing strength, yet he had hoped to stave off the event for a time. At the beginning of 1938 what weighed upon his mind was the need for economic consolidation and rearmament. The huge cost of the Spanish intervention and rearmament had almost bankrupted Italy. During the briefings in February at the Supreme Defense Commission, Mussolini endured a withering barrage of facts and figures showing just how remote autarky was. The two new battleships laid down at the beginning of the year could not progress according to schedule because of a lack of money, armor plate and other materials. Italy would soon fall ever further behind other expanding navies. To help prevent an escalation in the size and firepower of battleships that would render the navy's new battleships obsolete, Italy agreed to sign the London Naval Treaty of 1936.

Mussolini wanted to march with Germany into an all-out war against the western democracies, but he was in no hurry. He wanted to play a long game and a short game. Intelligence about German rearmament pointed to 1940 as the earliest year when Hitler would be ready for the big showdown. Until then, while the Italian people, made uneasy by the *Anschluss*, learned to love the Axis, Mussolini intended to exploit the standoff between Paris, London and Berlin to squeeze everything he could out of Britain. Hitler guessed right: Mussolini dreamed of a fresh coup to follow up his victory in Ethiopia. The Duce imagined that he held the initiative, an unwarranted optimism that General Pariani and others helped nourish by feeding him plans for a surprise attack on Egypt. The spring of 1939, the general predicted, was the "most favourable moment" for such a bold stroke against Britain.[9]

For now, thanks to the Axis, Rome enjoyed being courted by London. Everyone knew that Chamberlain only wanted to cut a deal with the Duce to smooth the way for one with the Führer. The danger lay in his succeeding. What room would there be for Italy in a Europe run by Britain and Germany? For the moment, anyway, fortune smiled on Rome. In February 1938 Anthony Eden resigned as foreign secretary. The exit of that notorious anti-Italian hawk from high office in London, as well as the rise of the Anglophobe Ribbentrop in Berlin, reassured Mussolini and Ciano. The Easter Agreement of April 16 supplied yet more comfort. Britain agreed to recognize the conquest of Ethiopia if Italy withdrew its "volunteers" from Spain and ended its subversive activities against the British Empire in the Middle East. With General Franco's victory just around the corner, the deal was good for Italy. Mussolini had snubbed the French, lulled Britain into a false sense of security and gently reminded Germany, just before Hitler's state visit, that Italy was still a free agent.[10]

Hitler arrived in Rome on May 3. The Italians did everything they could to outdo the warlike spectacle the Germans had put on for Mussolini the previous September. Hitler's packed schedule culminated at Naples on May 5 with a review of the fleet and air force exercises, which impressed him. Hitler hoped to discover what use the Duce had in mind for these forces. If Mussolini had some new venture up his sleeve, then Hitler's attack on Czechoslovakia could be timed to coincide with it. In readiness, Ribbentrop arrived with various draft treaties for a full-blown military alliance for his hosts to sign. But Mussolini and Ciano dodged serious political discussions. Signing a public or even secret military alliance would jeopardize British cooperation in legitimizing Ethiopia's status as an Italian colony. Not only that, but an alliance would bind Italy to Germany, just when a crisis over Czechoslovakia loomed. Exploiting Germany's rising strength for Italian purposes made sense; getting sucked into a total war too early, and more for Germany's benefit, did not. Ribbentrop's glib talk of global war did nothing to inspire confidence among his hosts. During the fleet review, he handed Ciano another draft treaty for an Axis military alliance. Ciano handed over his own alternative draft, which, as one German diplomat put it, resembled more "a peace treaty with an enemy than a pact of loyalty to a friend." Ribbentrop fumed in protest. "The solidarity which exists between our two regimes has become so clearly apparent," Ciano replied with a faintly sarcastic grin, "that it makes a formal treaty of alliance unnecessary."[11]

Hitler journeyed home knowing that Mussolini had no immediate plans for a blow against either the British or French empires. "Italian policy for the time being is directed towards consolidation and rest," read one foreign ministry report. All the same, Hitler now contemplated war against Czechoslovakia within the year. The "constellation" of forces, he told one of his officials, "could get worse."[12]

GERMANY'S SUDDEN ANNEXATION of Austria prompted a series of military and political reactions abroad that intensified the arms race. As Hitler knew, the faster his potential enemies armed, the faster Germany's relative military strength declined.

Before the *Anschluss*, Chamberlain had carefully hatched his plan for a European settlement founded on Anglo-German cooperation. Changes at the Foreign Office made his task easier. In January 1938 he made Vansittart chief diplomatic adviser to the cabinet, a "promotion" that removed him from the everyday running of the Foreign Office. The next month the relationship between the prime minister and his foreign secretary, Eden, broke down. That a last effort should be made with Berlin was about the only thing upon which the headstrong elder statesman and the volatile rising star agreed. Chamberlain hoped to split Mussolini from Hitler with talks, while Eden (rightly) wished to cold-shoulder the diabolical Duce. Once widely regarded as the most vocal champion in the cabinet of the League of Nations, Eden considered Europe's only salvation to lie in closer British diplomatic and military ties with Washington and Paris. Now free to steer his own course in European politics, Chamberlain did not want to get bogged down in President Roosevelt's bizarrely complex proposal for one big conference on world peace or endless debates with unreliable and disagreeable Frenchmen.[13]

On February 16, four days before Eden resigned and Halifax succeeded him, the cabinet approved Inskip's recommendations for a £1.65 billion ceiling on arms spending and a shift in air rearmament away from bomber parity to fighter and anti-aircraft gun defenses. A sound economy and ever more powerful air defenses—so went the strategic logic—would prevent war by deterring Hitler. Apart from anything else, Chamberlain calculated, this go-it-alone strategy would in a year or so give him the big stick he needed to back up a tough line in Europe *without* formal alliances.

Admiral Chatfield approved of Chamberlain's foreign policy but found his defense policy maddening. Inskip's cap on arms spending ruled out the big push in warship building from 1939 onward that the Admiralty had hoped the cabinet would underwrite. So Chatfield hit back in two ways. As chairman of the chiefs of staff, he led his army and air force colleagues, who had their own axes to grind, to demand that the politicians take the plunge and institute controls over industry and labor to arm faster. "We are attempting to carry out an armament programme, on a scale never yet attempted except in war, in peace conditions, and subject to a policy of non-interference with normal trade which cannot fail to be a serious handicap," they argued (making the habitual critical comparison of British rearmament with that of the totalitarians without acknowledging the potentially explosive consequences of imitating them), "when we are competing with potential enemies whose whole financial, social and industrial system has, in effect, been mobilised on a war footing for at least three years. . . . What we desire to do," the chiefs wrote, hoping to scotch Inskip's report, "is to call the attention of the [cabinet] to the fact that our approved rearmament programme is falling behind and that in our opinion it will fail to give us security in time."[14]

The Admiralty also tried to capitalize on Japan's refusal to sign the London Naval Treaty of 1936 by lobbying for a bigger fleet. In February 1938 Washington, Paris and London warned Tokyo that unless it was prepared to abide by naval arms control, the nations that had signed the treaty would raise the standard size and gun power of battleships. Almost everyone assumed that the threat of a naval arms race against the United States and Britain combined would be enough to force Tokyo to comply. But the Japanese Navy, now dominated by the anti-treaty "fleet faction," forced the government to ignore the threat and accuse the British and Americans of starting a naval arms race. For months now, naval intelligence in London and Washington had assumed that Japanese warship planners were probably building vessels in excess of treaty regulations but had no idea that they had started feverish work on the first two of four gargantuan 70,000-ton battleships carrying eighteen-inch guns, which in a gunnery duel would destroy anything afloat or rising on the stocks. In reply to Japan, the signatories to the London treaty decided to raise the maximum battleship tonnage and gunnage to only 45,000 tons and sixteen-inch guns. British naval constructors put the finishing touches on the design of a new 40,000-ton/sixteen-inch-gun battleship while the Admiralty lobbied ministers hard to endorse its master plan for world naval supremacy. Unhappily for Chatfield, the one thing that was guaranteed to top the navy in the cabinet's list of competing priorities occurred: Hitler had gone on the rampage again by annexing Austria.[15]

Hitler's triumphant entry into Vienna angered Chamberlain. Everyone expected that one day Germany would absorb Austria, but British officials had hoped it would be the result of talks rather than a brutal coup. "For the moment," Chamberlain railed in a letter to his sister on March 13, "we must abandon conversations with Germany [and] we must show our determination not to be bullied by announcing some increase or acceleration in rearmament." The next day he chaired the cabinet. Britain needed to show its resolve, but how? Lord Swinton, the air minister, had plenty of ideas. When Hitler annexed Austria, the air staff knew that the time had come to present the cabinet with an expansion scheme that would give them what they had wanted for nearly twenty years—the biggest slice of the defense budget for a huge, war-winning fleet of bombers. Swinton, therefore, presented the largest plan for air expansion that the air staff could hope for, Scheme K. Inskip told colleagues that not only would it blow the cap off arms spending agreed on by the cabinet only weeks before and leave less money for the navy and army, but even more workers—beyond the 93,000 already in the arms factories—would have to be found. Mobilizing the aircraft industry and diverting even more finance, skilled labor and industry to making armaments had inescapable political implications.[16]

Under the pressure of the arms race and two years earlier than expected, the cabinet had arrived at the treacherous boundary between what could be done to prepare for total war within the limits of Britain's free-running liberal economy and the first momentous step toward totalitarianism. "There was a fundamental difference in our position from that of other nations," John Simon, the chancellor of the exchequer, remarked. "If we became involved in war, we could adopt unorthodox measures such as excessive borrowing, inflation of currency and so forth. At the present moment, however, we were in the position of a runner in a race who wanted to reserve his spurt for the right time but did not know where the finishing tape was. The danger was that we might knock our finances to pieces prematurely." The cabinet put off a decision for now. Chamberlain needed to compose his public statement on the *Anschluss*. He left the cabinet meeting to tell the House of Commons that Hitler had undermined the "confidence" of Europe and had increased the "efforts of the various nations to make further provision for their safety in an unsafe world."[17]

In Parliament all sides condemned Hitler: the left reaffirmed the principles of the League of Nations; the right called for armaments, alliances and imperial unity. Chamberlain announced a defense review. Over the next few weeks the government was in a tight spot. Critics demanded to know whether Britain suffered from a bomber gap in relation to Germany. Churchill, fed with a lot of erroneous numbers from various sources, including the French, criticized air rearmament and advocated in a terrific speech a Grand Alliance to deter Hitler. In reply Chamberlain could not reveal the U-turn from bomber parity to air defense without committing political suicide. To reassure the right-wing dissenters and the newspapers, the prime minister appointed Lord Winterton, a one-time Tory rebel close to Churchill, as deputy air minister. On May 12, to Chamberlain's horror, Winterton's first speech was a confidence-destroying ramble, the highlight of which was a silly rebuke of the man he was meant to win over. "If the Archangel Gabriel stood at the dispatch box and produced an air expansion scheme," Winterton joked, Churchill would still not accept it. Emboldened, Churchill and his admirers demanded a full inquiry into aircraft production. Some government backbenchers now wanted one too. Winterton resigned. Days later, Lord Swinton, exhausted from overwork, followed him.[18]

While the government took a drubbing in Parliament, behind the scenes the defense debate raged on. On March 22, the cabinet discussed air force expansion. Ministers assumed that Hitler acted recklessly because Britain was for the moment weak. Perhaps 1939 was the year of supreme peril after all? If so, then the air force, especially fighter defenses, needed to grow faster. What the cabinet did not discuss was what impact Britain's rising strength in armaments and the growing political consensus behind intensifying the arms race would have on the Führer. Hitler had predicted at the end of 1937 that Churchill might be prime minister in five years; the way things were going, that charismatic champion of all-out rearmament and encircling alliances would move into 10 Downing Street much sooner than that. In any case, Chamberlain saw the logic of ratcheting up air rearmament much higher than he was willing to go only a few months before. The Air Ministry wanted 70,000 more workers for the aircraft industry to assemble airframes and motors. More would also be needed to make ancillary parts. A study of the raw-material supply found that 800 aircraft per month was a feasible target. But to raise output the government would now have to take a firmer hand in shifting the nation's productive resources away from civilian commercial use if the scheme was going to succeed.[19]

The next day Chamberlain met with the leaders of trade unions to seek their cooperation and that of employers in an acceleration of arms production.

The meeting made a big splash in the press. Later that day Chamberlain walked into the House of Commons to make a dramatic statement. From now on, arms, not trade, would have first call on industrial resources. "In order to bring about the progress which we feel to be necessary," the prime minister announced, "men and materials will be required, and rearmament work must have first priority in the nation's effort."[20]

Chamberlain had begun to institute a quasi-war economy in peacetime. The *Anschluss* had prompted him to create a sense of national emergency. Organized labor began to accept hitherto unacceptable work practices like the dilution of skilled jobs to help crank up military output. In April income taxes went up. Defense as a share of total state spending climbed to thirty-eight percent. The Royal Air Force took the biggest slice. The cabinet adopted Scheme L, which included more fighters than the air staff had wanted, but which ministers insisted upon. Under the Air Ministry's much-improved procurement organization, aviation plants geared up to mass-produce the advanced monoplanes, including Hurricanes and Spitfires, along with the amazing Rolls-Royce Merlin engines needed to power them. In 1938 the navy's budget also rose above Inskip's budget cap. The shipyards worked at capacity. The Treasury approved the import of over 10,000 tons of armor plate for warships, to cover a temporary shortage in the domestic supply. Work on two new 40,000-ton battleships and on additional smaller ships began. The Admiralty took some consolation in the fact that naval intelligence had discovered that in Germany shortages of skilled workers and raw materials had caused severe delays to Admiral Raeder's construction schedule.[21]

Air force planners cheered when they heard that armaments would now take priority over trade, but this was still not enough. "Short of national mobilisation on German lines," they wrote, "there is little we can do to improve our standard of war production within the next few dangerous months." In the cabinet Simon made the same point: "Germany had got rid of her war debt; had not such good social services as we; controlled wages and could enforce loans. Their standard of living was also lower than ours. We could not do those things." Britain could not compete with Germany "unless we turned ourselves into a different kind of nation."[22]

IN JANUARY 1938 Prime Minister Chautemps formed a new government. He had decided to govern France from the right. His new right-of-center cabinet consisted of ministers drawn exclusively from his own Radical Party. Only weeks later, however, the government was in crisis. Without the support of the Socialists and the Communists in Parliament, Chautemps could not command a large enough majority to approve his controversial finance bill and renew the decree powers he had demanded to tackle France's chronic financial instability and bitter industrial disputes. One day before the German Army invaded Austria, Chautemps resigned in a fit of petulance.

So, while Hitler made his triumphant entry into Vienna and the French people looked on in stunned silence, France was without a government. The unenviable job of forming a new one fell to the Socialist leader Léon Blum, who took up the task with all the tragic determination of an idealist who had too often compromised his principles and feared that his compromises would go unrewarded.

Blum now believed that France could only be successfully governed by a coalition that spanned the whole political spectrum. Once he had the backing of his Socialist Party and the trade unions to assemble an administration of national unity, Blum made an impassioned plea to the center-right opposition parties to join a new "sacred union" to defend the nation. They replied with a fusillade of questions: Would he intervene in Spain? What was his policy toward Rome? Would he impose exchange controls? Would Communists be appointed to the cabinet? Would he repeal the forty-hour workweek? Blum dodged these questions. He wanted a consensus on the principle of self-defense in a time of grave peril; the particulars of state policy would be the first business of the cabinet of unity. With hollow civility, Blum's opponents applauded his patriotism but rejected his leadership. Pierre-Étienne Flandin, the leader of the conservatives, wrote, "Mr. Léon Blum has not furnished any precise clarifications on the questions of foreign and domestic policy" that concerned the opposition.

Undaunted, Blum formed a Popular Front cabinet. "We shall increase France's armaments," he declared, "and endeavour to strengthen our friendships and alliances." One of his first acts was to allow more arms to reach the embattled Spanish Republic. On March 15, at a meeting of the Supreme Defense Committee, Blum proposed answering Hitler's invasion of Austria with a French intervention in Spain. Why, he said, not send General Franco an ultimatum: "If, within twenty-four hours, you do not renounce the assistance of foreign troops France will resume its liberty of action and the right to intervene." The image of French soldiers exchanging shots with Germans and Italians on the Iberian Peninsula horrified most of the committee. Daladier, the defense minister, expressed what most of them thought: "One would have to be blind not to see that intervention in Spain would unleash general war."[23]

Disappointed but not discouraged, Blum turned to national defense. No longer content with half measures, he decided to take the plunge. To compete with the totalitarian states, France would emulate their methods. He drew up a far-reaching military-economic program that was, as he later explained, "analogous to the Russian Five Year Plans or Göring [Four Year] Plan." To pay for it he was going to raise taxes on income and profits, borrow heavily and adopt something like Schacht's Mefo bills; in other words, he was going to inflate the economy by printing money in the form of credit notes to buy munitions. Arms production would be the flywheel of a high-speed, state-led industrial revival. The only difficulty was that investors were likely to export a lot of the additional credit generated in this way unless the loop of credit creation and reinvestment was closed. To do that, the Bank of France would introduce a system of controls over the exchange market.[24]

A year earlier Blum had opposed exchange controls as the slippery slope to totalitarianism; now the risk of defeat in total war overshadowed everything else. The only obstacle was London and Washington. In September 1936, Britain, the United States and France had agreed to stabilize the exchange rates between their currencies in the Tripartite Agreement, which, among other things, was an act of political solidarity. Going autarkic now was as good as forsaking the democratic camp. The U.S. treasury secretary, Henry Morgenthau, saw Blum's predicament and sent word to Paris that he would not oppose a temporary imposition of exchange controls. As the French prime minister pushed deeper into the arms race, Morgenthau's news encouraged Blum, even if it was not clear how the White House or Downing Street would react. "Certainly it is a kind of tragic irony," he remarked, "that a nation devoted to peace and human progress is compelled to strain and concentrate all its resources for a gigantic military effort."[25]

On April 5, the French Senate rejected Blum's finance bill and refused to grant him decree powers in economic affairs. The Socialist leader faced the same choice he had in June 1937. Should he challenge the Senate by calling the workers out onto the streets, or bow to the authority of the upper house? Some Popular Front activists had staged a violent protest near the Senate while it debated Blum's legislation, but the enthusiasm on the left for mass action that had been palpable a year before had dissipated. At any rate, Blum refused to take that last precarious step and instead resigned. A showdown with the Senate, he sighed, "would have meant launching France on an adventure which we would not have been able to master, manage, or lead."[26]

Unable to arm faster from the left, France lurched over to the right. This final change in the political character of French arming was presided over by

Édouard Daladier. Some said the fifty-four-year-old Daladier, short, stout
and balding, resembled Napoleon. On April 10, he formed a cabinet dominated by the Radical Party and moderate conservatives. Much to Blum's irritation Parliament at once granted his successor the temporary decree powers
in economic matters that the Senate had just refused him. Daladier further
strengthened his executive authority by retaining the Defense Ministry. Although the former history teacher and war hero had entered politics in 1919
as a modernizer on the left wing of the Radicals, no one was quite certain
where he stood in 1938. Daladier's appeal as a "strong man" of Napoleonic de-
cisiveness ready to take command in a time of crisis stretched across the political divide.[27]

On defense, however, Daladier's position was clear enough. He wanted to
pick up the pace of arming. The only question was how fast? Under
Chautemps, Bonnet as finance minister had reduced military spending and
resisted modest hikes in defense expenditure at the start of the year. "If France
should have to continue to arm at the present rate," Bonnet later warned, "it
would be necessary to regiment the entire population, placing the civilian
population on soldiers' wages and soldiers' rations." Faced with that prospect,
Bonnet preferred to give up the arms race (which he thought France could
never win anyway) and let Hitler dominate eastern Europe rather than accept
the type of Bolshevik government he feared most, which would "regiment"
France.[28]

Daladier refused to see things in such stark terms. In March 1938 a strategic assessment had landed on his desk. This brief but compelling paper argued
that time worked against Germany. The faster France and Britain armed, the
sooner they would outstrip Germany in armaments. In the interim, Hitler
might exploit their temporary weakness and that of Russia to coerce concessions out of the Czechs or even to crush them in a quick war. Like his top adviser General Gamelin, Daladier was frustrated that France had ambled along
for two years in the arms race while Germany sprinted ahead. Some combination of policies and domestic political alliances that would stabilize the
economy and speed up arms production had to be found.[29]

By the start of 1938 Daladier had realized it was "no longer possible to remain within [the bounds] of liberal formulas, to attach oneself to monetary orthodoxy, to the liberty of exchange, to the liberty of foreign commerce."
France, so ran his logic, "must resolutely embark on the path taken earlier by
Germany and Italy." He saw little risk of France falling to totalitarianism by
arming like the fascists. "Ours are methods of freedom," he proclaimed. "The
hour has come to prove that France can face the dangers which threaten her

while remaining faithful to her genius." But he still needed to tread very carefully. Blum had been prepared to impose exchange controls to discipline investors. Daladier could not do so without alienating free-market conservatives, not to mention Washington and London. On May 4, 1938, he devalued the franc rather than expend gold to shore it up or impose exchange controls. To solve France's financial woes, Daladier decided to roll back the labor rights that Blum had codified in the Matignon agreement, above all the forty-hour week, strengthen the hand of employers and thereby attract investment capital back into the economy.

Initially, Daladier tried to strike a bargain between the union leaders and the employers, promising to use the power of the state to protect the interests of workers. Union leaders wanted to compromise on the forty-hour week so long as the prized law remained intact and workers earned overtime; employers saw their chance to kill the law, squeeze more hours out of their workers at ordinary rates of pay and maximize profits. In May Daladier issued a decree that allowed the forty-hour workweek law to be suspended in munitions plants, while talks between the trade unions and employers remained deadlocked. At the same time he read a stream of intelligence that painted a different (sometimes exaggerated) picture of social discipline across the Rhine: "All of the resources of the nation are now mobilised," ran one secret bulletin. "Germany is essentially a vast factory where the worker labours more than nine hours per day. In certain industries factories operate nonstop." In August 1938, his patience eroded by grim images of totalitarian industrial regimentation in Germany, Daladier declared that he was willing to revoke the forty-hour week and put France "back to work."[30]

Daladier briefly appeared to solve the problem of how to arm at high speed within a liberal financial system. When he took office, gold flowed back into the French central bank. After the franc devalued, investors, encouraged with favorable terms, repatriated as many as twenty-two billion francs. But speculators remained jittery and reacted anxiously to war scares. They kept a close eye on the soaring defense burden. In March 1938, twelve billion francs were added to earlier programs, with total arms expenditure rising to thirty-three percent of state spending. The projected defense budget for 1939 climbed from twenty-five to thirty-seven billion francs. Finance officials calmed the money markets by setting up a new currency stabilization fund and an autonomous national defense fund fed with revenue from higher taxes, duties and loans in the form of short-term national savings bonds, but many expected that Daladier would sooner or later be forced to devalue the franc again or control the foreign exchange market.[31]

All three French armed services benefited from the spending hikes that followed the *Anschluss,* but the air force received a massive sixty percent increase on its 1937 budget. Spending this sudden injection of cash was the job of the new air minister, Guy La Chambre. A protégé of Daladier, La Chambre emerged from the same modernizing cohort of young Radicals as Pierre Cot, but he was more a political fixer than a grand visionary. La Chambre reorganized the Air Ministry and established exactly the sort of working relationship that the generals wanted with their civilian boss. La Chambre restricted his role to supplying the men, money and machines the air staff wanted; he left war plans and technical matters to the air force top brass.

La Chambre's priority was to mass-produce the high-performance monoplanes that would give the air force a chance against the Luftwaffe. In the previous two years, the aircraft industry had been concentrated under nationalization for mass output, but it lacked the investment to do little more than assemble obsolete planes in batches. La Chambre now had the money and the political backing to rationalize, retool and enlarge the state-owned plants, to expand the workforce, standardize production techniques and revive the private-sector manufacturers. In March 1938 he presented Plan V, a two-year program to build 2,617 front-line combat aircraft and another 2,122 in reserve. That would demand a sixfold rise in production, from the best current rate of fifty airplanes per month to well over 300. Even at this pace, the air planners had no illusions about overtaking the Luftwaffe. Secret sources told of German airfields with rows upon rows of modern bombers lined up within striking range of Paris and factories spitting out more at rates above 400 per month. A lot of this intelligence was exaggerated, more the product of the habit of threat inflation and sheer panic than cool analysis. As a result, the French, like the British, switched air strategies. Instead of competing against Germany in bombers or forming an air alliance with the Soviet Union to contain Hitler as Cot had ardently advocated, the French air planners decided to devote forty percent of Plan V to fighters in defense of their airspace.[32]

Unhappily for French officials, the upshot of Plan V was that the nation would be dangerously vulnerable to German air attack for a year. The first twenty-five advanced fighters did not join the air force until September 1938. They would not start coming off the assembly lines at full speed until 1939. And France would not have a truly modern air force until late 1940. Much the same could be said of tank and artillery production. France needed time, but Hitler might not wait.[33]

AFTER THE *ANSCHLUSS,* no one needed a crystal ball or a master spy in Hitler's chancellery to predict that Czechoslovakia was now the danger spot to European peace. The union of the German peoples of Austria and Czechoslovakia into greater Germany had been a constant feature of Hitler's pannationalist rhetoric. With the Austrians now part of the Reich, the three million Sudetendeutsche who lived on the other side of the German-Austrian border with Czechoslovakia would be next.

The Soviet-Franco-Czech defense pacts of May 1935 made a Sudeten crisis potentially explosive. Everyone expected Hitler to browbeat the Czech government the way he had the Austrians. Would the Czechs offer concessions that would satisfy Hitler's stated aim of unifying all ethnic Germans, or would Prague defy him and trigger an attack? If a German-Czech war erupted in this way, would France and then the Soviet Union declare war? And if Germany struck France, would Britain fight?

In Paris and London, war planners agreed on one thing: there was little that could be done to prevent a "decisive defeat" of Czechoslovakia if Germany attacked. The Czechs had a small, well-equipped army with a mobilized strength of 500,000 men. They also had strong fortifications facing Germany, but a tiny air force. Worse, Czechoslovakia was now open to attack southward from Germany and northward from Austria. No doubt they would put up a brave fight for a month, French Army staffers predicted in March 1938, and exact a heavy toll on the attackers in men and equipment, but the outcome would still be a "crushing" German victory.

Certainly the French Army could assist the Czechs by attacking Germany. In Paris war planners studied the feasibility of a quick strike into western Germany. Evidence collected by spies posing as workmen disclosed that Hitler's new defenses along the border would not be finished before 1939. But to mount such an attack with a good chance of success, they concluded, would demand "a complete reorganisation of our army and the restructuring of our military policy." For French soldiers the whole point of having small east European allies was to pin down German forces on several fronts when France found itself in a life-and-death struggle with Germany: France's small allies were not supposed to drag France into a fight for its life at the wrong moment over a regional issue. French strategists had hinged everything on the German war machine hammering itself to pieces trying to smash open fortress France first, while France and its major allies, above all Britain, mobilized their superior military and industrial strength. "We can do nothing to prevent the dog getting the bone," wrote British war planners, who drew conclusions identical to those of their French counterparts, "and we have no means of making him give it up, except by killing him by a slow process of attrition and starvation."[34]

General Gamelin and Admiral Chatfield, the top military advisers in Paris and London, both had their own reasons to oppose total war over the issue of Czechoslovakia in 1938. Gamelin considered France unready. Strikes, turmoil on the money markets and the merry-go-round of ministers disrupted arms production and weakened national cohesion. When he became chief of staff of national defense in January 1938, with authority over all three services, Gamelin told Daladier that he wanted to intensify arming. As everyone could see, in the emerging age of totalitarian warfare, nothing showed up France's lack of fitness to compete more than the forty-hour workweek. Gamelin said it had to go. "Our armaments production," the defense staff urged, "must be taken with all urgency whatever the financial and industrial repercussions." "I am in complete accordance with your views," Daladier replied.

Once Daladier became prime minister, Gamelin saw his best chance to push ahead with higher levels of arms spending and national discipline under a government led by a man who shared his goals. Germany had made major strides in armaments, but it was not too late for France to stay in the race. The danger lay in a premature war. France needed time to arm and to strengthen its alliances with the other great powers. "France alone," the general said, "if she can still hope to defend its metropolitan territory effectively and her African empire, can only engage in a victorious war through alliances." For Gamelin the ideal outcome of the brewing crisis over the Sudetenland, like that over the Rhineland two years earlier, would be a definite and automatic British undertaking to defend France. France's weakness in the air—apart from being a compelling argument to avoid war—provided the means to draw out this commitment from the British. "Aerial cooperation with Britain," Gamelin told Daladier just before he left for talks in London, "is indispensable."[35]

Chatfield also played for time. He told the cabinet that the worsening crisis in Europe warranted intense rearmament and controls over industry, but the last thing he wanted was an alliance with France. Long before the *Anschluss*, the service chiefs had opposed staff talks with the French because they thought they would block détente with Berlin. "I cannot help believing," Eden complained before he resigned, "that what the Chief of Staff would really like is to re-orientate our whole foreign policy and to clamber on the band wagon with the dictators, even though that process meant parting company with France and estranging our relations with the United States." After the *An-*

schluss, Chatfield and the other service chiefs, supported by Hankey, warned the cabinet against a pledge of support for either Paris or Prague that might spark a great war. The navy conjured up bogus figures to makes its case. Knowing full well that German shipyards already had about as much work as they could handle, the Admiralty told the cabinet that if Hitler denounced the naval treaty in a fit of anger over an alliance with France, then colossal sums of money would be needed to outbuild the German fleet. With the global naval arms race escalating and the Royal Navy preparing for another burst of shipbuilding to stay ahead of the rest, the last thing Chatfield wanted was a war in Europe that would suck resources away from the fleet and leave the way open for Japan and the United States to gain an incontestable lead.[36]

Chamberlain did not need any convincing. He opposed alliances to deter war over the Sudetenland, especially one with France. "We cannot help Czechoslovakia," he wrote, echoing the words of the service chiefs; "she would simply be a pretext for going to war with Germany. That we could not think of unless we had a reasonable prospect of being able to beat her to her knees in a reasonable time and of that I see no sign." Still, Chamberlain had to do something to stop a crisis over the Sudetenland plunging Europe deeper into the maelstrom of armaments, opposing alliance blocs and total war. If tightening alliances would accelerate the spiral, perhaps the reverse approach would have the reverse effect? "Whether we liked it or not we had to admit the plain fact that we could not in our own interests afford to see France overrun," Chamberlain told his foreign-policy cabinet. "At the same time there was this great advantage under the existing scheme of things, we had entered into no kind of definite and automatic commitment. We still, in theory at least, retained full liberty of action. . . . This had the great advantage that we were able to keep both France and Germany guessing as to what our attitude in any particular crisis would be and no doubt this in itself had a restraining effect both upon France and upon Germany." Lord Halifax wondered "what the French General Staff thought of the prospects of successful offensive operations to relieve Czechoslovakia. . . . France was admittedly helpless in the air. Germany was in a strong position to hold up any advance by land. No doubt the French authorities would face up to the facts."[37]

Indeed, Daladier had faced the facts. The most important was that France needed Britain. But in London the foreign and defense policy establishment was opposed, as it had been since 1919, to offering France a military alliance. Until British policy changed, Daladier played for time. The French premier's choice of foreign minister reflected this dilemma. Joseph Paul-Boncour, Blum's foreign minister, told Daladier he would like to continue in his job.

France, he said, needed to honor its commitment to Prague even if that meant going to war alone. "The policy you propose is a good one," Daladier replied, "the honourable course for France to follow. Sadly, I do not believe that we have the capacity to follow such a policy. I will take Bonnet."[38]

A short, natty, right-wing Radical, Bonnet was determined to avoid war—any war. In public France would affirm its military pact of May 1935. But through diplomatic channels the foreign minister would warn Czechoslovakia's president, Edvard Beneš, that France could not fight without the British and that Chamberlain wanted a deal over the Sudetenland. So did Daladier, but he did not share Bonnet's optimism for France's future in a German Europe. He had long ago abandoned hope that Germany would be content within a new equilibrium. Daladier had not found an index to the secrets of Hitler's soul, no window into his mind. The man at the center of the regime was a mystery to him as he was to everyone else who puzzled over the Nazis. But his service intelligence chiefs' description of the Nazi regime as one intoxicated with the drive for conquest and domination had a powerful ring of historical truth. And the former history teacher Daladier saw the historical parallels. For centuries the great nations had perpetually struggled for mastery of the continent. Under Napoleon, France had sought to rule all of Europe. Now Hitler wanted this and more.

On April 27, Daladier traveled to London for a summit with Chamberlain, whom he found tiresome and unsympathetic. The French premier said that the French service chiefs wanted staff talks with their British colleagues; his host offered technical cooperation between air forces. As a way to pin the British down, Daladier proposed a strong joint statement affirming the rights of small nations to check German ambitions. It was Daladier's view that "the ambitions of Napoleon were far inferior to the present aims of the German Reich." Chamberlain replied that his "blood boiled" at the way the Germans ran roughshod over the liberties of the small nations. But, when war or peace was at stake, Chamberlain the great hawk-faced problem solver had no time for Chamberlain the outraged man of emotion. Hitler, he said, might temporarily accept a Czechoslovakia transformed into another Switzerland, a "neutral state on a federal basis." And the tensions in Europe might possibly be relaxed in that way. In reply Daladier again tried to pin Chamberlain down on some sort of joint action. If Germany dominated eastern Europe, Hitler would have the resources he needed to fight a long war in the west against France and Britain. Again the prime minister dodged his efforts. Britain would find a peaceful way out of the coming crisis and flush Hitler out about his true goals. "German claims were rather like mushrooms," Halifax observed, "in that they grew in the dark, and if we could succeed in bringing them into the open, though there might be dangers and disadvantages in doing so, we should at least know where we were; and we should know what claims were really being made, and be on firmer ground on which to decide what action should be taken."

Before leaving, Daladier gave Chamberlain something to chew on. He knew the British could not stand idly by if Germany overran France. If Germany attacked Czechoslovakia, he said, "France would scrupulously respect her obligations, which were contained in the 1935 treaty. France must respect her signature and Great Britain, whose school-children were taught the importance of honouring their promises, would readily understand the attitude of France." After Daladier returned to Paris, the U.S. ambassador, William Bullitt, a close confidant, asked him whether France would indeed fight for Czechoslovakia. "With what?" he snapped, referring to the state of the French Air Force. All he could do was arm and wait for Chamberlain's diplomacy to play out. The game now belonged to London and Berlin. And, as French intelligence warned, "Germany's present superiority [in armaments] is without doubt the principal reason it desires to precipitate a war sooner rather than later."[39]

On Saturday May 21, 1938, three weeks after the stormy Anglo-French summit in London, and only a little over a week since Hitler and Ribbentrop returned from their state visit to Italy without the military alliance they had sought, the Czech Army began to mobilize. A mysterious secret source had spooked it into defensive measures by sending a false warning of an impending German attack.[40]

As Czech reservists joined their regiments, Chamberlain rushed down to London from a fishing holiday in Scotland. Halifax told the ambassador in Berlin to warn Ribbentrop, together with his French colleague, that if Germany attacked Czechoslovakia, France would be obliged to act and Britain might intervene too. French and British intelligence, though, found little evidence of German preparations for an attack. Was it a false alarm? Prime Minister Chamberlain did not think so: "I cannot doubt in my own mind (1) that the German Government made all preparations for a coup (2) that in the end they decided after getting our warnings that the risks were too great (3) that the general view that this was just what had happened made them conscious that they had lost prestige and (4) that they are venting their spite on us because they feel that we have got credit for having given them a check."[41]

On Monday, May 23, the crisis was over. Journalists used their imaginations to fill in the blanks about what had just happened. Faced with Anglo-French resistance, the papers contended excitedly, Hitler had climbed down. The Führer, who avidly followed the headlines as a barometer of his standing, was furious. There was after all nothing more damaging to his self-esteem than the thought that others judged him weak. Germany had suffered a loss in "prestige," he told General Keitel. Days before the crisis the general had sent Hitler a revised version of the war plan against Czechoslovakia, with no date of execution set. Afterward, Hitler furiously rewrote the political preamble of the plan to read, "it is my unalterable decision to smash Czechoslovakia by military action in the near future." The deadline was October 1, 1938.[42]

In the context of the shifting arms balance, Hitler's anger crystallized his resolve to act sooner rather than later. The Führer had always been supremely confident in his ability to shape the world according to his own design. The *Anschluss,* so he thought, proved him to be a better judge than the military experts of the motives and forces that moved other nations. While Ribbentrop warned again that Britain was playing for time to arm and form alliances, Hitler pondered the ebb and flow of time and how to master it. Then suddenly in May the Czechs mobilized; London and Paris issued warnings; the German attack everyone expected did not happen. For Hitler the crisis was a prelude of unpleasant things to come. If Germany's foes believed that he had just yielded to verbal warnings when Germany was running ahead in armaments, then what would they do in 1939 or 1940 when they felt much stronger?

Hitler, who saw the great trend in European armaments and diplomacy, had no intention of waiting to discover the answer. On May 28, he spoke to his senior officials: "It is my unshakable decision that Czechoslovakia should be wiped off the map." He looked directly at his top-ranking soldiers, Keitel, Brauchitsch and Ludwig Beck, and said, "we will deal with the situation in the East [Czechoslovakia] first. Then I will give you three or four years [to plan and arm] and then we will deal with the West [France and Britain]."

There were good reasons to delay the attack. The army needed to perfect tactics to break through the Czech fortifications; and Germany's defenses along the frontier with France also needed strengthening. But Hitler, employing the inevitable now-or-never logic of fast-escalating arms races, offered his analysis of why he had to act quickly: in two or three years Czech defenses would be stronger; British "rearmament will not be completed until 1941/42"; "French rearmament will likewise take many years"; Russia was "not geared up for aggressive war." Furthermore, relations between London, Paris and Rome remained very tense. Italy, which was determined to make gains in the Mediterranean and to exploit "French weakness," should not be "underestimated." Ultimately, the Führer emphasized, the decision to "seize the favourable moment" for a small war belonged to him alone. To get ready for that day, Hitler ordered an "extreme acceleration" of rearmament.[43]

During the summer of 1938, German rearmament reflected Hitler's plan for a swift war against the Czechs and then a big war with France and Britain sooner than he had previously anticipated. The navy again benefited from Hitler's growing antagonism toward Britain. He ordered the completion dates for the two 42,000-ton battleships, the future *Bismarck* and *Tirpitz,* to be brought forward. The tempo of U-boat assembly also picked up. Despite the fact that the shipyards had limited capacity for a sudden spurt, and that a naval arms race against Britain—never mind France and Russia too—would be futile, Admiral Raeder blithely accepted the benefits and implications of Hitler's turn to the west. In June 1938 he ordered war planning against Britain to begin.[44]

Hitler also ordered the army to expand faster and an increase in the production of small arms, mortars, artillery, tanks and ammunition. To deter a French offensive in the west while the army invaded Czechoslovakia, he demanded that the Westwall, Germany's answer to the Maginot Line, be completed. Ex-corporal Hitler took great personal interest in the planned 375-mile line of fortifications: he wrote thirty-two pages of suggestions on every aspect of their design, right down to the latrines. When he learned that the army did not expect to finish the Westwall until 1948, he "exploded" with rage and appointed Fritz Todt, the autobahn builder, to start a crash building program. Todt, a brilliant engineer and manager, redeployed 250,000 workers and army sappers from other tasks and diverted huge quantities of scarce steel, cement and transport to finish the frontier barrier by the summer of 1939. The "heroic" feat of Todt's workers was trumpeted by a propaganda campaign to reassure the German people and to intimidate the French.[45]

Much more potential for the intimidation of the French and the rest of Europe lay with the Luftwaffe. Although British and French aviation was catching up fast, the Germans had a widely acknowledged lead in 1938. Indeed, in August 1938, the French Air Force chief, General Joseph Vuillemin, paid an official visit to Germany as Göring's guest, and although he saw nothing that his intelligence staff had not already confided in him, he was still severely shaken by the impressive show of Luftwaffe strength. When Göring asked whether his government would fight for the Czechs, he replied defiantly: "France will keep her word." But in private the general was less confident. "If war does break out at the end of September," he told the

French ambassador in Berlin, "there won't be a single French plane left in a fortnight."[46]

Ironically, while the Luftwaffe dominated Europe psychologically, the leaders of the air force made a decision that would hobble its technical progress into the war. In reaction to Hitler's speech of May 28, Göring placed a huge order for 7,000 Ju-88 twin-engine bombers (out of a total two-year plan for 16,000 aircraft of all types) and turned over half the aircraft industry to make them. The champion of the Ju-88 was Dr. Heinrich Koppenberg, the director of Junkers. One of the go-getting entrepreneurs of the Nazi arms boom, he promised Göring he could build airplanes in Germany "exactly the way Ford builds cars in Detroit." To achieve "economies of scale" and of "scope," Koppenberg organized the bomber industry into a series of feeder factories. Each one specialized in making a standard part—wings, fins, tails, instruments, cockpits, landing gear and engines—to be fixed to the fuselage on assembly lines. By churning out bombers like Model Ts, Koppenberg planned to make 250 Ju-88s a month by 1939.[47]

In many ways investing in the Ju-88 as the standard bomber made sense. It was a fast, versatile aircraft, ideal for close support of the army as a dive-bomber and capable of hitting targets in England or sinking ships with torpedoes. But the launch of this giant industrial undertaking helped to stunt German bomber development at the twin-engine medium bomber stage, just when British and U.S. air planners looked to the four-engine bomber as a war winner. In the mid-1930s German aircraft makers had designed a prototype four-engine Uralbomber to strike targets in European Russia, but the Luftwaffe shut down the project in 1937. The fixation of Göring and other officers with the medium bomber compounded this initial error. The Spanish Civil War had shown them that dive-bombing was an accurate way to strike battlefield targets in support of ground forces, a mission that four-engine aircraft could not perform well. When Koppenberg unveiled the Ju-88, it seemed like the perfect all-around solution to the Luftwaffe's need for a standard bomber that could offer the army tactical support or act independently as a strategic force to terrorize city dwellers into surrender. After the London Blitz of 1940–41 proved this assumption wrong and Göring saw the need for a heavy *Amerikabomber*, the aircraft industry was too deeply committed to the Ju-88 to mass-produce one of the new prototypes quickly.[48]

As foreign intelligence analysts had detected in 1938, the intensification of the arms race pushed Germany's economy to a perilous state. During 1937 and early 1938, work on industrial projects such as explosives, synthetic fuel and rubber plants lagged behind schedule because of a lack of raw materials and labor. The manufacture of aircraft, guns and ammunition had stagnated. Steel remained a key bottleneck. In the summer of 1938 Hitler doubled the steel quota for the armed forces to 658,000 tons. By August, armaments and an accelerated version of the Four Year Plan claimed over forty percent of Germany's rising steel output. In 1938 military spending climbed to nineteen percent of national income. That year the Reichsbank had hoped to end the unorthodox funding of rearmament. The issue of Mefo bills ceased, but short-term state bonds to fund rearmament and autarky took their place. Up to 1938, within the limit set by the availability of foreign currency, both the military and the civilian sides of the economy had grown, even if civilian consumption had lagged. Now the only way for Germany to speed up arming was to divert even more resources to the military at the expense of civilian demand and living standards. "The armed forces should not concern themselves with the fate of the economy," Göring told army planners. "The collapse of parts of the economy was irrelevant." But many officers, General Thomas among them, and other state officials did worry. The civilian economy could not just be allowed to collapse, and with it public morale. With the demand for arms booming, various state agencies and industries competing for scare resources and commodity prices rising, a slide into inflation threatened.[49]

Apart from worries over the economy, a number of top men in the army and the diplomatic corps felt uneasy about Hitler's imminent rush to a war against the Czechs. The most outspoken was General Ludwig Beck. Like so many conservative German staff officers of the old school, he had welcomed Hitler's rise to power and the nation's resurgence under the Nazis. As army chief of staff, he had been one of the masterminds behind rearmament, pushing for faster and larger army expansion.

On November 5, 1937, Hitler briefed his senior commanders about his intentions toward Austria and Czechoslovakia and his view of the shifting arms balance in Europe. Shortly after, Beck learned the details. To a man dedicated to the rational application of force for attainable political ends, nearly everything the Führer had said annoyed the dour army chief of staff. Not that he opposed Hitler's immediate goals, or even the use of force. Austria should join the Reich, the army chief of staff agreed; the sooner that Czechoslovakia was neutralized, the better. What irked Beck was Hitler's survey of the international scene and the opportunities it presented. The whole idea that somehow Germany had attained a lead in the arms race, and that this head start had to be exploited soon, struck him as dangerous nonsense.

To Beck the bloodless *Anschluss* had been a stroke of luck that had not altered the fundamentals of the forces arrayed around Germany and the nation's capacity to cope with them. In early May, while Hitler admired Mussolini's battleships and bombers in Naples, Beck described in a memo to his boss, General von Brauchitsch, the Reich's military and political balance.

Attacking Czechoslovakia, Beck warned, would trigger total war against an overwhelming coalition that Germany could not possibly defeat. Since the *Anschluss*, he pointed out, Britain and France had begun to arm much faster. Daladier had turned France away from Bolshevism and revived French national unity. Beck saw deep-rooted hostility in all directions. The British would exploit a German-Czech war to prevent the Reich's resurgence as a power factor in Europe. The French, who considered the *Anschluss* a humiliation, and who still had the strongest army in Europe, would not allow the Czechs to be crushed, especially with Britain behind them. And behind Britain and France stood the industrial colossus of the United States. The Soviet Union too would fight, with air and naval attacks first and then later with its armies. Germany might count on Italy's help, but what use would its inferior strength be? Beck repeatedly emphasized that there was no way to localize a war with Czechoslovakia, or to defeat it quickly enough and then to turn around and overwhelm the French. After Germany had occupied Bohemia, Britain and France would wage a war of grinding attrition. Germany was bound to lose. "The military-economic situation of Germany is bad," he wrote, "worse than in 1917–18. With its current allies, armaments and economy, Germany cannot expose itself to the danger of a long war."[50]

After Hitler restated his intention on May 30 to attack Czechoslovakia, Beck began a one-man bureaucratic guerrilla war to stop what he saw as a reckless rush into total war. Over the next two months he tried to enlist the support of Brauchitsch and other senior officials. Through coercive diplomacy, he told them, London and Paris might agree to the secession of the Sudetenland. But fighting a big war now risked Germany's existence.

Meanwhile, in June and August, Hitler addressed the officer corps. As head of state, he appealed to their loyalty and reassured them that France and Britain would not fight. Some agreed, others remained uncertain, most simply obeyed. Beck, having failed to organize a collective protest, did the only thing he could do: he resigned. Slowly, the chief of staff's efforts to avert war chiefly for technocratic reasons evolved into resistance to the Nazi regime. During the war he became a central figure in the conspiracy among the old ruling elite to kill Hitler. After a July 1944 bomb plot failed, Beck shot himself.

That was a fateful end for a dedicated soldier who had done so much to raise the German Army—unilaterally, outside any arms limitation framework—to become one of Europe's premier fighting forces. In 1938 Beck would have been satisfied to perfect the army for years. "How can I prevent war?" he found himself asking over and over that summer. Regrettably, Beck could not stop the vast arms spiral that he had helped to set in motion only a few years before, nor its political consequences.[51]

DURING 1938, ONLOOKERS everywhere noted that the arms race had entered a new intense phase. "The law of ever increasing public expenditure is now transformed into the law of ever increasing armaments expenditure," declared one German war planner. "Thus armaments have a new consequence, one which deeply distorts social and economic development." Global arms spending would climb by another ten or fifteen percent in 1938 above the previous year, and probably total more than triple of that spent in 1913, the year before the last total war. The upshot of all this arms growth was a scramble on world markets for scarce raw materials and a rush into autarky. And, "in spite of the most strenuous efforts of all countries to achieve self-sufficiency in the supply of war materials," the war planner concluded, no doubt obliquely commenting on Germany's predicament, that many of them were "not in a position to meet their demand for advanced weapons and munitions from their own production."[52]

Intelligence analysts in London and Paris made the same observations. Studies of Germany noted a step-up in regimentation and a dangerous build-up of pressures generated by all-out preparations for war. In 1938 the Nazi state imposed bureaucratic controls on German workers, raised taxes on wages and profits, controlled prices, sacrificed consumer goods and rationed resources. Major Desmond Morton of British economic intelligence, an authority on total war who bemoaned his country's laissez-faire approach to the arms race, circulated a study of British and German rearmament. He wrote, "Germany, Italy, the USSR and the USA and a number of other countries appear to have learned the great lesson of the last war, which we have not, until recently, viz., that you must plan economic mobilisation . . . before you put it into action. . . . I think that we must be wasting a great deal of money as a result of our lack of planning, lack of method, lack of words, that Industry and Economics must be regarded in modern war as a fourth arm of defence and must therefore be allowed to play a larger part in defence councils." Most who read the report thought that there was much to learn from the Third Reich about arming but knew that Britain could not go very far down the totalitarian path without undergoing fundamental social and political upheavals. As Sir John Simon, the chancellor of the exchequer and perpetual voice of restraint, put it, Britain could match German rearmament "if we had a 'Hitler' and a population prepared to accept a 'Hitler.'"[53]

That, of course, assumed that governments could always make a choice. The pressure of the arms race might be greater than the wills of men. Looking across the English Channel, some wondered whether the pressure on France might become irresistible. In July 1938, after more than a decade of debate, the French Parliament finally passed the Law for the Organization of the Country in Time of War. According to the British intelligence analysis of its contents, "It is suggested ... that this law is remarkable in that, if fully enforced, it would turn the Government of France into something closely resembling a Dictatorship and would confer on the Minister for National Defence, or in certain circumstances the Chief of Staff, the powers of a Dictator, so long as the country was content to abide by the law. In fact it suggests that the only remedy democratic France has been able to apply to Authoritarianism—at least in time of war—is suspiciously like the disease."[54]

CHAPTER 13

THE GREAT ACCELERATION, 1938–39

On September 6, 1938, the National Socialists gathered for their annual party rally at Nuremberg. For days paramilitaries strutted on the Zeppelin Field while loudspeakers proclaimed the beauty of war. In bellicose speeches, leading Nazis vilified the Czechs as the fiendish oppressors of the Sudetenlanders, the three million Germans who lived in Czechoslovakia concentrated in a horseshoe-shaped region on the other side of the German and Austrian frontiers. Göring decried the Czechs as "a miserable pygmy race" in cahoots with Moscow and the "Jew Devil." Hitler's speech in front of massed ranks of soldiers took place on September 12. Some expected him to issue an ultimatum, but instead he recited the alleged wrongs done to the Sudetenlanders first by the peacemakers of 1919 and then by the Czechs. "An end must be made of depriving these people of their rights," he shouted to thunderous applause.[1]

After Hitler spoke, thousands of Sudetenlanders rioted. For months he had carefully orchestrated the crisis, instructing Konrad Henlein, the Sudeten German leader, who took part in British-brokered talks with the government in Prague, to turn up the heat on the negotiations while the army prepared for the invasion. Now Hitler waited for the right moment to give the order.[2]

Then, unexpectedly, Chamberlain offered to fly to Germany to confer with Hitler. The airplane, the icon of Europe's preoccupation with self-destruction, became—or so it seemed—the means of its salvation. The German leader, who portrayed himself as merely the defender of the Sudetenlanders, could not reject Chamberlain's offer without hardening world opinion against himself. At their first meeting in Berchtesgaden on September 15, the Führer said he would attack Czechoslovakia. Chamberlain, who studied Hitler's eyes for any trace of madness and found none, then demanded to know why the Führer had wasted his time and motioned to leave. To the scowling Nazi warlord's later regret, he decided to play along for a while. If the prime minister could guarantee the Sudetenlanders the right of self-determination, then he was prepared to discuss how to implement it. Chamberlain said he could do no such thing without first consulting his cabinet. In the interim Hitler agreed to refrain from military action.[3]

Back in London, Chamberlain convinced his cabinet to endorse a deal to cede the Sudetenland to Germany, and then squared it with the governments of France and Czechoslovakia. In Prague, President Edvard Beneš faced an ugly choice. If he opposed Chamberlain's effort to settle the dispute, he might find himself alone in a fight against Germany with only a vague assurance of support from Moscow. Or he could trade the Sudetenland for international guarantees of what remained of his state. On September 21, Beneš and his advisers agreed to the second option. The next day Chamberlain flew to the German spa town of Godesberg to deliver the news to Hitler. Everyone agreed that the Sudetenlanders should exercise the right to self-determination, Chamberlain said smugly; now all that had to be done was decide on a means of peaceful transfer.

Hitler had not expected the Czech government to yield to his demands. Working himself up into a rage, he threw obstacles in the way of a peaceful solution: surely the claims of Poland and Hungary to Czech territory had to be satisfied too, he shouted, and in any case he could not possibly stand aside another day while the Sudetenlanders suffered brutal Czech repression. Upping the stakes, the Führer demanded that the German Army must be allowed to occupy the Sudetenland immediately. Annoyed and deflated, Chamberlain flew home to determine what his divided cabinet, Beneš and Daladier would accept from what amounted to a German ultimatum. In the meantime the Czech and the French armies began to mobilize.

Hitler, of course, had never wanted to acquire the Sudetenland peacefully. He wanted war and all of Czechoslovakia. But Chamberlain's relentless diplomacy had cornered him. If he rejected a deal that granted him everything he had demanded in public, then he could not attack without revealing that his true goal had been war all along. On September 26, he received word from London. The Czechs had rejected his Godesberg ultimatum. Chamberlain was still willing to act as a go-between, but he warned Hitler that if he attacked Czechoslovakia, Britain would support France and its ally. In reply Hitler delivered a venomous speech in front of a capacity audience at the

Berlin Sportpalast. Over and over he had reassured his generals that France and Britain would not fight; they had warned him that Germany could not win a large-scale clash against the western powers. Should he run the risk of an all-out war now? Visibly strained, he began to waver. On the evening of September 27, he presided over a military parade. Berliners watched in grim silence. That day he also learned that the Royal Navy had mobilized. Instead of ordering the attack, Hitler accepted Mussolini's offer to mediate a resolution to the crisis.[4]

On September 29, Chamberlain, Daladier, Hitler and Mussolini met at Munich to cede the Sudetenland to Germany and to guarantee the borders of what was left of the Czech state. They also discussed the territorial claims of Poland and Hungary. At their last meeting the next morning Chamberlain handed Hitler a document that he had drafted the night before. Would the Führer agree in future to settle all European disputes through the peaceful method of "consultation"? The Nazi dictator signed the statement. Overjoyed, Britain's supreme problem solver flew home with the Anglo-German declaration in his breast pocket. Later that day he addressed newsmen and a crowd of jubilant admirers. "I believe it is peace in our time," he told them.[5]

The stalemate, so it appeared, had been broken. If everything unfolded the way Chamberlain now expected, the Anglo-German declaration would soon be followed by negotiations on trade, colonies, arms control and a lasting European peace. In no time the arms race would fizzle out. Yet, as those in the midst of the maelstrom soon discovered, after Munich the arms race continued apace. The determination of all parties to frustrate others through the piling up of arms had achieved its inevitable consummation. While the high drama of the crisis gripped the world, the vicious system of military competition locked everyone into place.

A chance ironic remark scribbled by a high-ranking Treasury man in the margin of the air force budget captured something of the general predicament: "It seems a strange result of the Prime Minister's policy of appeasement that we should be devoting so enormous a sum to the slaughter of civilians in other countries."[6]

NEARLY EVERYONE REGARDED the events in Munich as a masterstroke of coercive diplomacy. Even Hitler's critics in the diplomatic corps and the upper echelons of the army reconsidered their doubts about his judgment. The embryonic conservative resistance, some of whom had that September made makeshift plans to storm the Reich Chancellery if a general war broke out, shelved their plot. Why would anyone challenge the leader who in the short space of five years had reversed the terrible humiliation of 1919?

Yet the Führer was angry: Chamberlain had thwarted his war plan. Shortly after leaving Munich, Hitler told Göring that the British decision to mobilize their fleet had tipped the balance in his mind against war. But the months of insistent warnings from his generals against a long war and the tepid response of Berliners to the military parade on September 27 also weighed heavily in his decision to pull back from the brink of war. Frustrated, angry yet coldly calculating, Hitler knew that the arms race was steadily turning against him and that his enemies, principally Britain, sought to contain him with the threat of a total war that Germany could not win.[7]

He now had two choices. One was to forsake the arms race and accept the political deal that Chamberlain had set out at Munich. With the economy under the mounting pressure, this option had its attractions. Hjalmar Schacht and his officials thought so. Then again, Hitler could intensify the arms race and slowly undermine the Anglo-German declaration. He never seriously considered the first possibility. Within hours of signing Chamberlain's scrap of paper, orders for greater war preparations went out. The Führer's ultimate goal of race war and the conquest of "living space" in the east could not be achieved within a political equilibrium regulated by the diplomacy of the great powers. In any event he could not escape the vast arms spiral that he had done so much to set into motion. Meanwhile, he followed the political debate in London. Chamberlain's foremost Conservative Party critics, Eden and most of all Churchill, would soon get the upper hand. Only one way appeared open and Hitler took it. He plunged deeper into the arms race with all the vigor that Germany could muster.[8]

On October 14, Göring gathered top-ranking state officials in the Air Ministry to reveal Hitler's latest instructions. "Everybody knows from the press what the world situation looks like," he began, "and therefore the Führer has issued an order to carry out a gigantic arms programme which will make all previous ones pale into insignificance. . . . The strength of the air force must increase five-fold; the navy must build warships at a faster rate and the army must procure at top speed large quantities of weapons, in particular large-calibre guns and heavy tanks." Göring then came to the big question: How could all these ambitious targets, which raised "unimaginable difficulties," be fulfilled? "The treasury is empty and the factories are backlogged with orders for years to come." Despite these difficulties, he intended to change the situation no matter what. "Paper studies are of no use," he declared in this triumph-of-the-will fugue; he wanted only "positive proposals."[9]

Much to the relief of General Georg Thomas, the recently promoted chief of the war economy staff in Hitler's new armed forces high command, this fresh upsurge in rearming was going to be properly planned, coordinated and controlled; the administration of rearmament had so far been chaotic, wasteful and beset by turf wars. Now, though, in order to regiment the whole economy with ruthless coherence, Göring revived the long-defunct Reich Defense Council. Under the pressure of the arms race, he used the total-war buzzwords of industrial rationalization, state control and planning with a born-again vigor. The Nazi regime would register every German in a central card index and allocate workers according to state priorities; the tax system would be streamlined to yield more revenue for the state; most civilian building work would cease; wage and price controls would keep inflation in check; and again the allocation of steel and other raw materials for the armed forces would increase. Central planning extended to the armed forces. Hitler wanted priorities to be set among the competing needs of the army, navy and air force, and a multi-year expansion plan drawn up to achieve them. He set 1942 as the target date for completion of most major armaments programs.[10]

Hitler understood that he had to win a great war in the west before he could seize territory for living space in the east. Rearmament would be directed against France and most of all Britain, whose influence he wanted driven from the continent. "War by Germany and Italy against France and Britain," ran the briefing notes the Führer had dictated to General Keitel, "with the object of first knocking out France. That would also hit Britain, as she would lose her bases for carrying on the war on the continent and would then find the whole power of Germany and Italy directed against herself alone." To get ready for the big war in the west, Hitler instructed Ribbentrop to confer with Rome to turn the Axis into a military alliance and to strengthen Germany's ties with Japan. Poland had to be drawn into the Anti-Comintern Pact. And what remained of Czechoslovakia, with its factories, armaments and gold and foreign-currency reserves, had to be absorbed into the Reich.[11]

Hitler's post-Munich armaments boom presented the German Navy with a threat and an opportunity. Germany did not have the capacity to build both a big navy and a big air force. And evangelists of air warfare had for years now boasted that air forces could sink ships more cheaply than could other ships. With good reason, Admiral Raeder feared that Hitler might transfer the primary responsibility for fighting Britain, along with a bigger share of resources at the navy's expense, to Göring's Luftwaffe. Yet the admiral had already seen how Hitler vented his anger at the British government after the May crisis by speeding up shipbuilding. With Japan toppling the whole British-inspired system of naval arms control and the naval arms race picking up speed, the time was now ripe for Germany to break free of the naval agreement with Britain and challenge its sea supremacy. Over the summer of 1938 the navy's planners studied how to defeat their arch-enemy. Most agreed that their best chance for success lay in using Germany's small fleet to disrupt Britain's overseas trade. Ideally, then, over the next few years Germany should build as many oceangoing U-boats, heavy-gun cruisers and pocket-battleships to attack oceanic commerce as the shipyards could handle.

When in late November Raeder met Hitler to discuss this strategy, the Führer lost his temper. Perhaps now regretting that he had cramped warship building with the naval agreement of June 1935, Hitler complained about the weakness of the German fleet and the inferior quality of its ships. Raeder leaped up and offered his resignation, but the dictator calmed him down. Over the next few weeks the naval staff drew up the ten-year Z Plan of warship building. It included six 60,000-ton super-battleships to fight a fleet battle with the Royal Navy, as well as a dozen pocket-battleships, twenty-four cruisers and over two hundred U-boats, all ideal for hunting British merchant vessels. Raeder asked Hitler to prioritize the smaller vessels that could be built more quickly than the six gargantuan dreadnoughts. "If I could build the Third Reich in six years," he reportedly replied, "then the navy should be able to build six battleships in six years." Raeder knew his moment had come. If the Führer wanted the big ships built, then the navy needed more resources. On January 27, 1939, much to the admiral's pleasure, Hitler ordered that the navy's plan for a great battle fleet to challenge Britain should be given absolute priority in the rearmament process.[12]

IN THE MONTHS FOLLOWING the Munich agreement, Chamberlain learned that Britain could not escape the arms race. Despite his extraordinary attempts to buck the great trend of ever larger armaments and ever tighter state control over social and economic life, the pressure to ratchet up British military and economic efforts became overwhelming.

When Chamberlain had first flown to confer with Hitler, most of his cabinet, a majority of parliamentarians and the public supported him. But once Hitler rejected the prime minister's proposals for an orderly transfer of the Sudetenland and then issued an ultimatum, opinion slowly turned against Chamberlain. Although almost everyone wanted peace, there was something unseemly about a British prime minister flying to and fro doing what looked like the bidding of a militaristic madman. A groundswell of moral outrage against "appeasement" and above all the Nazi regime steadily gathered force over the winter of 1938. In Parliament, Eden, Duff Cooper (who had resigned as First Sea Lord over Munich) and Churchill rode high on this anti-appeasement wave. They demanded a tougher line against Berlin together with a steep rise in British armaments, including some form of national service.[13]

Chamberlain did not want to slacken the pace of British rearmament, nor did he want to plunge deeper into the arms race. He was trapped in the dilemma of intense military rivalry as well as the inner logic of his own foreign policy. To force Germany to negotiate rather than risk war, Hitler had to be deterred. And the only way to deter him was to arm, especially in the air. On October 3, the prime minister met with cabinet and explained (according to the official minutes) that "he had been oppressed [during the crisis] with the sense that the burden of armaments might break our backs. This had been one of the factors which had led him to the view that it was necessary to try and resolve the causes which were responsible for the armaments race. . . . It was clear, however, that it would be madness for the country to stop rearming until we were convinced that other countries would act in the same way. For the time being," he summed up, "we should relax no particle of effort until our deficiencies had been made good. That, however, was not the same thing as to say that as a thanks offering for the *détente*, we should at once embark on a great increase in our armaments programme."[14]

A great increase in armaments, Chamberlain complained, was exactly what his critics in the newspapers and Parliament demanded. While his supporters still outnumbered his detractors, he could keep the anti-Munich hardliners at bay, but pressure to intensify arming from inside the foreign policy and defense establishment posed a bigger problem. Over at the Air Ministry, the new secretary of state, Sir Kingsley Wood, a savvy political operator with an owlish appearance and a Methodist faith, told the air staff that while the terror of the Czechoslovakian crisis was still fresh in everyone's memory, now was the time to push through a big aircraft procurement plan. Air Marshal Cyril Newall and the other bomber zealots on his planning staff needed no encouragement. The navy could not win a war against Germany. The army was too small to do any good. Only the air force could make Britain's voice heard. "In these days of power politics the race is to the strong and the strong are not those who can merely defend themselves but those who have the will

and the means to give, in the last resort, the backing of force to their influence in the world," the air staff wrote, expounding their bare-knuckle view of
international politics. "This we cannot do if we are inferior in air power, which
means striking power, any more than in the last century we could have done
if we had been content to accept an inferior fleet." According to the latest intelligence, Göring and his high-ranking advisers wanted a large force of
medium bombers with smaller payloads than the heavy prototypes. The air
staff realized that they might now take the lead in heavy bombers and over-
turn the priority that the government had given to the air defense of Britain.
To do so, they submitted air-rearmament Scheme M to build 12,000 new aircraft by April 1942, with much of the money and industrial resources allocated to expanding the bomber force. The air staff calculated that the
enormous scale of Scheme M would force ministers to enact legal powers to
organize and control factories and workers.[15]

In an October 31 cabinet meeting, Wood argued that Britain had to catch
up in air armaments or risk war erupting through "weakness." To speed up and
expand air rearmament, he was prepared to turn over responsibility for aircraft
production to a new Ministry of Supply led by an "outstanding person" who
had compulsory powers to issue orders to industry and labor. Pressure for a
step-up in the mobilization of the economy came from the army minister
too. Inskip, the minister for the coordination of defense, who had studied the
problem of how to accelerate arms production on a voluntary basis, concluded
that there was no point in setting up a Ministry of Supply unless it had legal
authority to direct the economy. Chamberlain said that there had been "a
good deal of talk in the country and in the press about the need for rearmament by this country. In Germany and Italy it was suspected that this rearmament was directed against them, and it was important that we should not
encourage these suspicions. . . . Acceleration of existing programmes was one
thing"—the prime minister fretted over his impossibly subtle distinction—
"but increases in the scope of our programmes which would lead to a new
arms race was a different proposition."[16]

The cabinet had again run up against the perennial problem: How could
Britain gear up its economy for an all-out arms race without succumbing to
totalitarianism? After the *Anschluss*, the cabinet had tilted industrial priorities
from trade to arming and had raised the ceiling on defense spending to new
heights within the boundaries of a liberal economy. Signs of serious strain
followed. Gold reserves shrank, exports declined and the value of the pound
sank. The sort of capital flight that had plagued the French Popular Front

governments now loomed large. So did inflation. Indeed the air force's Scheme M pointed to the inexorable trend of ever-expanding armaments. Treasury men worried that a continental-size standing army was next. And they knew that these massive arms programs could only be sustained in peacetime by adopting the wealth-consuming apparatus of wartime finance. One enterprising junior economist in the Treasury came up with a cunning plan. Britain, he suggested with amazing political naïveté, should impose exchange controls, employ the jobless in munitions factories, divert the bulk of state investment from civil to military purposes and accept an adverse balance of payments for years to come. Senior officials gasped. "It is true that Germany, with a controlled economy," admitted another Treasury economist, "has succeeded in rearming, and that France, with a free economy, has not." But, bemoaning the "dangerous" tendency to "believe that all the things which Germany and Japan are forced to do are the best things for us," he rejected the totalitarian model of autarky to boost armaments.[17]

On November 7, the cabinet met once again to discuss air rearmament. John Simon, the chancellor of the exchequer, warned that Scheme M was "so costly" that he doubted "it could be financed beyond 1939/40 without the gravest danger to the country's stability." Wood emphasized that Britain had the chance to push ahead of Germany in heavy bombers. "If our air strength could be increased, it would give strength to the Prime Minister in his further efforts for peace. It would also assist us in the efforts which we hoped to make to obtain limitation of armaments." But Chamberlain doubted that Britain "could beat Germany in an armaments race. Such a race was not merely a question of money, but also of industrial capacity and the labour force; in that respect Germany had the advantage over us." The prime minister again sought to impose order and purpose on the arms race with deterrence: "In our foreign policy we [are] doing our best to drive two horses abreast, conciliation and rearmament." It was, he said, "a very nice art to keep these two steeds in step." Building up the fighter defenses rather than starting a race in heavy bombers that Britain might lose made sense to him. Hitler only had to be convinced that he could not win a quick war in the air. That could be achieved by investing in air-raid shelters, anti-aircraft guns and advanced monoplane fighters, along with that chain of early-warning radars that the air force was erecting around the island. The cabinet thus approved a modified version of Scheme M, which prioritized the production of fighters over bombers, and increased the air force's fighter squadrons from thirty-eight to fifty and the number of bomber squadrons from seventy-three to eighty-five.[18]

A week later the whole atmosphere of the armaments debate began to change markedly. So far, British attempts to follow up on the Munich agreement with Germany were met only with stone-cold silence. What was happening in Berlin? One diplomatic source disclosed that Hitler toyed with the idea of canceling the Anglo-German Naval Treaty when his fleet reached thirty-five percent of the British fleet, but nothing more concrete than that. Then on November 10, on what came to be called *Kristallnacht,* the Nazi regime launched vicious attacks against German Jews. Göring organized the looting of their shops and the burning of synagogues; Nazi storm troopers and secret police rounded up tens of thousands of Jews and sent them to concentration camps; state officials confiscated Jewish wealth; and Hitler decreed further measures to segregate and stigmatize all German Jews.

In Britain, *Kristallnacht* hardened attitudes. Lord Halifax for one was horrified. A sense of aristocratic obligation had inspired the fifty-seven-year-old former viceroy of India to dedicate his life to enlightened governance and the perfection of human civilization in the shape of the British Empire. He wanted to avoid a colossally devastating war, but, like so many after Munich, Halifax felt that things had gone one ignominious step too far. "No more Munichs for me," he remarked. *Kristallnacht* largely confirmed that the threat from the Nazi regime was not just a mind-bending problem of statecraft but a new episode in the eternal struggle between the forces of civilization and the swamp. Halifax knew that Chamberlain saw things in a similar way but found it frustrating that he remained so wedded to the Munich agreement.

At a meeting of the prime minister's foreign policy advisers on November 14, Halifax circulated a top-secret report from well-placed sources inside the Nazi regime. "The Munich settlement has left Herr Hitler in a dissatisfied and spiteful frame of mind," it read. "He was to some extent balked; he has realised that his country was against war and that he has not been given chief credit for preventing it; he has been unpleasantly surprised by the readiness of the Western Powers to learn their lesson." The report disclosed in unnerving and engrossing detail that Hitler intended to expand eastward through force of arms if necessary, but in the first instance through the internal subversion or "atomisation" of small nations like Poland and Romania. "If I were Chamberlain," another unnamed insider quoted Hitler as having remarked, "I would not delay for a minute to prepare my country in the most drastic way for a 'total' war and I would thoroughly organise it. If the English have not got universal [military service] by the spring of 1939 they may consider their world Empire lost."[19]

Based on this intelligence, Halifax argued that nothing could be gained by resuming talks with Germany. The report painted a stark picture of decision making in Berlin. Radical anti-British hawks of the Ribbentrop-Goebbels sort were advising Hitler to take up arms against Britain, while "moderate" elements (the army, Göring and Schacht) voiced caution. At the moment the radicals had the upper hand. To correct "the false impression [among the hawks] that we were decadent, spineless and could with impunity be kicked about," Halifax offered two suggestions. Having picked up on the press campaign supported by many leading Tories for some sort of national service, he wanted to institute a compulsory national register of men fit for the defense forces or munitions work. He also wanted another sharp rise in aircraft production. Chamberlain was skeptical. He did not think that Hitler planned to attack just out of the blue. Now that the German people had come to realize "that what was facing them was not a mere joy ride into Czechoslovakia but a first-class European war," he wanted to restrain Hitler by manipulating public opinion in Germany through covert radio propaganda and other methods. Everything that could be done to speed up arming was already being done. He did not think there was much point in registering names now unless the government was prepared to conscript men into uniform.[20]

Over the next two months pressure to intensify the arms race mounted. Chamberlain, arguing that dramatic military measures would weaken the moderates inside Hitler's court and fortify the hawks, barely withstood the pressure. The campaign in the press and Parliament for an escalation in the arms race centered on the national service register—a step toward peacetime conscription—and the creation of a Ministry of Supply. During a summit meeting in Paris at the end of November, the French urged an expansion of the British Army. "More [British] divisions were needed," Daladier told Chamberlain, "and as far as possible they should be motorised." In December, as a sop to Tories in Parliament demanding a national service register, the government unveiled a scheme of voluntary registration. Meanwhile, more alarming evidence emerged that disarmament would be out of the question for years to come: in December 1938 the German government announced it would exercise its legal right under the naval treaty to build up its U-boat fleet to equality with the British submarine force. It also declared—contrary to earlier assurances but as Raeder had always planned—that the German Navy would install heavy guns on the last two of its five large cruisers.[21]

The start of 1939, therefore, found Chamberlain dispirited. The idea that he could manipulate Hitler by discrediting the radicals around him and shoring up the moderates appealed to his every-problem-has-a-solution mind. But nothing seemed to be going his way. On January 11–14, he visited Rome to meet with Mussolini. He hoped to get through to Hitler via his Axis partner, but nothing came of it. Worse, intelligence from Germany revealed that the economic chaos caused by breakneck rearmament might soon prompt Hitler into a "mad dog" act. That Hitler fired Reichsbank President Schacht on January 20 seemed like an ominous sign that the hawks in the Führer's inner circle now held sway.[22]

Three days later, Halifax delivered the chilling news that Hitler would soon gamble everything on a desperate all-out preemptive strike against London. The Luftwaffe would pummel the city from bases in Germany as well as airfields captured by the German Army in Belgium and Holland. It was not known by British officials at the time, but this war scare originated from false rumors spread by German intelligence officers worried about the reckless course of Hitler's foreign policy. They had hoped that a sudden show of force by Britain might encourage their Führer to be more cautious. What they did was reinforce the hand of Lord Halifax and other ministers who argued for an expansion of the British Army to reassure France of their support. Chamberlain now authorized full staff talks with the French. And, in words that provoked shouts of joy in Paris, he announced in Parliament that any "threat to the vital interests of France from whatever quarter it came must invoke immediate British cooperation."[23]

In February, after he had made a few good speeches about the formidable scale of British rearmament and his government's willingness to reopen talks with Berlin, Chamberlain's mood picked up. Hitler "missed the bus last September," he wrote, "and once you have done that in international affairs it is very difficult to reproduce the situation. We have seen where our weak points were and have strengthened them, so that they could not make nearly such a mess of us now as they could have done then, while we could make much more of a mess of them."[24]

The period of maximum danger had passed—or so it seemed.

ÉDOUARD DALADIER FOUND the Munich summit humiliating. Grim-faced and taciturn throughout, he endured the experience out of necessity rather than conviction. So ashamed was he of the abandonment of a French ally that he briefly mistook for a lynch mob the throng of grateful Parisians who had gathered at the airport to welcome him home. Unlike his cheering admirers, Daladier held out very little hope for peace. "The Munich agreement is really only a short respite," he told a confidant. "Hitler will find a pretext for an armed conflict before he loses his military superiority."[25]

General Gamelin and the other service chiefs thought much the same. In mid-October they assessed France's strategic predicament now that Czechoslovakia was no longer a military factor and the *Anschluss* had added to German strength. The Third Reich now dominated eastern Europe, Gamelin wrote in despair, and might soon issue demands for a share of colonies in Africa. "Whatever the future orientation of Germany's drive for expansion, France must remain closely allied to Britain, and that would certainly mean resisting German demands for colonial concessions as well as opposing a German advance into Eastern Europe." Britain and France would be able to exert influence over the course of events and block German and Italian ambitions only with "increased military power." For France, Gamelin continued, "this military power will stem above all from our efforts to re-establish our internal stability, augment our armaments and with all speed increase our birth-rate."

General Vuillemin, the head of the air force, was even more emphatic and gloomy in calling for a redoubling of air rearmament: "We are perhaps owing to our fortifications and natural frontiers sufficiently armed to resist an attack by land; we could certainly not say the same thing about our air defences. . . . In the case of a conflict breaking out during 1939 with the Axis coalition, the forces at France's disposal, especially in the air, will be insufficient, even if reinforced by the British Royal Air Force. From 1940 onwards, it is hoped that the planned expansion of French as well as British air power will be well on the way to completion."[26]

All this confirmed what Daladier already knew. The Munich agreement signaled the start of a new, more intense phase of the arms race and France had to adapt to this unforgiving world of emulation or capitulation. Given a free choice, Daladier would have used the power of the state to command the economy to crank up arming. Some top trade union leaders also saw the need for a multi-year plan to arm. Senior defense planners on the service staffs needed no persuading. Some legislators called for a new Ministry of Munitions to direct defense production. And the Ministry of Commerce and Industry saw the need for the state to organize manufacturing into regional groups and draw up mobilization plans. Anxious to help France achieve monetary stability, U.S. Treasury Secretary Morgenthau again indicated he would not object to France introducing exchange controls. But Daladier's difficulty lay not in finding officials who agreed with him, but in building a national consensus. To rearm on a vast scale for total war, Léon Blum had tried to take control of the economy with a coalition of the left. Not only did he fail, but the attempt had sent the nation into a tailspin. Daladier learned from Blum's failure. What could not be done from the left would have to be done from the right. But conservatives in Parliament and the business associations opposed anything that smacked of a government-directed and controlled economy as a step toward the Sovietization of France. If Daladier could not regiment both labor and capital, and to attempt to discipline big business to the advantage of organized labor had destabilized the economy, then the only remaining option was to discipline workers to the advantage of employers. At least that way France could make its maximum effort with a brand of authoritarian capitalism.[27]

At the beginning of November, therefore, Daladier made this final break with the ideals of the Popular Front by appointing as his finance minister Paul Reynaud, the wealthy sixty-year-old conservative politician and dogmatic free marketeer. A short, terrier-like man with a sharp intellect and a gift for snappy presentation, Reynaud loved contentious causes. He had been an early convert to the abandonment of the gold standard and had championed Colonel Charles de Gaulle's tauntingly provocative idea of establishing a mechanized praetorian guard to defend the republic. Advised by a small team of bright, young financial wizards, Reynaud threw together his ideas in a matter of days. His program to jump-start industrial production over three years was simple: drastic economies in public spending except for defense; a dramatic hike in taxation to balance the budget; a severe reduction of labor rights, including an end to the forty-hour workweek, and investment in new plant to revitalize industry. In an unabashed exercise of executive power that Reynaud described as falling just short of the "totalitarianism" of the right or the left, Daladier enacted thirty-two decree laws to implement the finance minister's sweeping new program. "We live in a capitalist system," Reynaud declared in a radio address on November 12. "For it to function we must obey its laws. These laws are those of profits, individual risk, free markets and growth by competition. . . . A country which next year is going to spend 25 billions of francs for national defence cannot afford the luxury of great public works. Machine guns are more necessary today—alas—than stone fountains for villages. . . . To the foreign nations who are listening to us we announce that the France of the two-day weekend is no more."[28]

French industrialists and capital holders cheered. Finally, the day of reckoning for which they had waited since June 1936 had come. In the French Parliament, Blum's Socialists and the Communist Party condemned Reynaud's demolition of the Popular Front's labor reforms. In response to Reynaud's radio address, violent wildcat strikes broke out in the automotive industry. The police used force to end them. The trade unions called for a general strike on November 30. Daladier deployed troops to maintain order and threatened to dismiss any civil servant who took part in the mass walkout. The police, meanwhile, arrested the shop-floor militants, and factory owners sacked them. As a result, the general strike fizzled out. Afterward, managers in the chemical, electrical, motor and aircraft industries introduced stringent work routines to regiment their workers. While trade union membership fell by a quarter, Reynaud's pro-business tactics reaped quick results. French investors repatriated capital in record amounts, and for the first time in years industrial production shot up.[29]

The disciplining of the workforce paved the way for a fresh burst of arming, but had the breakthrough come too late? After Munich, many prominent members of the French foreign policy and defense community thought so. The severe blow to French prestige brought out the gloomy side of nearly everyone. Inside Daladier's cabinet, the foreign minister, Georges Bonnet, spoke for those who took the Munich agreement seriously and thought that France had to adjust to a continent dominated by the Third Reich. Since Hitler would seek to consolidate his hegemony in central and eastern Europe, France had to cut its ties with Poland and most of all the Soviet Union. French influence in eastern Europe and the Balkans could take the form of trade but not entangling security alliances. While Germany expanded eastward, France would build up its frontier defenses and develop its colonies in Africa and the Far East. The navy, which had the most to gain from a national policy of empire and sea power, backed Bonnet. Even Gamelin, in his darkest post-Munich mood, agreed. But the army's top planners and some diplomats voiced fierce opposition. If Hitler secured the wheat, oil and other raw resources of the Danubian basin all the way down to the Black Sea, then the German war machine would be unstoppable even against the mobilized military-economic strength of the British and French empires combined.[30]

While Bonnet negotiated with Ribbentrop a Franco-German declaration along the lines of the Anglo-German one, Daladier pondered the debate between his top men. He knew that Bonnet's policy of retreat would place France on course to second-class status, yet he could not dump his foreign minister, a man of influence among the conservatives who propped up his cabinet and who preached détente with Berlin. At the end of November, as his battle with the trade unions peaked, Daladier hoped that the British might offer support for a firmer policy toward Germany. When he welcomed Chamberlain and Halifax to Paris, he apologized for raising the question of armaments so soon after Munich. "It was essential that France should not slacken her efforts in the matter of defense," he told them. French defense spending, Daladier emphasized, had risen to twenty billion francs in the last two years; by 1940 France would have 4,000 tanks; his government planned to purchase 1,000 combat planes from the United States and he expected the mass production of combat aircraft in France to increase fivefold in the next six months. With the military forces of the Axis working in close collaboration, Daladier pressed his guests for a similar partnership. "France must make greater effort with regard to aviation," he added, "whereas Great Britain . . . should make more rapid effort with regard to land armaments." Chamberlain wanted France to recover its strength to deter Germany, but he was not yet ready to plunge deeper into the arms race by expanding the British Army; he also questioned the claim that French aircraft output would soon multiply fivefold. He approved of talks between French and British war planners, and he reassured his host that the Royal Air Force too would grow at a very rapid rate, but for now all Britain could offer the French was two army divisions.

The encounter with his British counterpart left Daladier fuming. Chamberlain, that "desiccated stick" as he called him, had offered him little support and had had the gall to question his claim about dramatic increases in French aircraft output. Yet as the din of policemen battling angry picketers on the streets of Paris had been almost audible in the conference room, Daladier conceded that Chamberlain had a point. Despite rumors in the European press that the two countries had agreed to a military alliance, the relationship was at a low ebb. Chamberlain and Halifax were off to Rome just when the Italians began an anti-French propaganda campaign intended to extract concessions. Worse still, all incoming intelligence from Berlin warned that Germany's shortage of raw materials and the foreign-exchange crunch might force Hitler to act soon.[31]

Remarkably, almost as though the new year itself had somehow closed a door on the last six years, Daladier's outlook brightened during the first eight weeks of 1939. An economic crisis might prompt Hitler to act within the year, he thought, but if not, then German arms growth would reach its natural limits while France's prospects would dramatically improve. Now that the unions had been cowed and investors won over, the economy would gear up; air rearmament Plan V would deliver a modern air force; and Britain would grow stronger. Gamelin, who snapped out of his doldrums, nourished Daladier's rekindled spirit. "We can envisage with confidence the possibility of an approaching conflict that would pit France and Britain against the totalitarian states of the Berlin-Rome axis without reckoning eastern Europe in the calculation," he wrote in a study of the arms balance. "We must not forget that time is more on our side than that of our enemies and that, with the help of American industry, we can wage a war of materiel against them fairly rapidly, which they would not be able to endure for long." Grave, level-headed and resolute, Daladier began to speak of blocking Hitler's march eastward. "Once assured of the resources of wheat and petrol it requires [by dominating eastern Europe]", he warned the French Senate's Defense Commission, "there is every reason to believe that the Reich will turn definitively on France which would constitute the sole remaining element of resistance on the continent."[32]

The change of attitude in London toward a French alliance probably did more than anything else to hearten Daladier. In a devious way the French had helped make that change happen. French intelligence officers had also picked up on the rumors of a German preemptive air strike on London. Although they dismissed them as bogus, it was decided to send the rumors across the Channel as genuine intelligence just the same. Why not give the British a jolt? As an indirect result of the ploy, the British cabinet voted to hold high-level staff talks with France to plan for war against the Axis.[33]

As THE CRISIS over Czechoslovakia heated up, Mussolini contemplated war. On September 17, 1938, two days after Chamberlain first met Hitler, Mussolini told Ciano he had made up his mind. If the coming war remained limited to Germany, France and the Soviet Union, he would remain "neutral." "If Great Britain intervenes, generalizing the war, giving it an ideological character," said the self-styled man of destiny, "then we will throw ourselves into the furnace. Italy and Fascism could not stay neutral." But, with the exception of General Pariani, who relished the idea of fighting his way to the Suez Canal, the Duce's top-ranking military men—Marshal Badoglio most of all—advised against war. As it turned out, the Duce did not have to make a real decision. On September 28, 1938, Mussolini acted on Chamberlain's last-ditch appeal to restrain Hitler.[34]

At Munich, Mussolini played the peacemaker. That he did so helped to mislead Chamberlain and many others about the Duce's true motives. They thought he might seek a closer relationship with Britain and France to counter the Führer's ascendancy in central and southeastern Europe. Mussolini was not interested in playing that game. In a few years the big war he craved would come. Italy needed to keep up the pace in the arms race. But the competition had become too burdensome for "a country richer in men, intelligence, and bearing than in iron, coal and petrol." Voicing the Duce's frustration at this mismatch between ambitions and staying power, his official press spokesman, Virginio Gayda, accused Britain and France of double-dealing. Why had arming in Britain, France and the United States been given a "fresh impulse" since the Munich conference, he asked? The Duce's mouth-piece accepted that Chamberlain meant what he said about desiring peace, but he found the "renewed" energy behind British rearmament and the drive toward some form of peacetime national service in Britain difficult to recon-cile with the prime minister's good intentions.[35]

One way to strengthen Italy's relative position was to move closer to Ger-many, the storm center of the arms race. The chance to do so came in the last week of October. With such colossal conceit that he made Ciano's blood boil, Ribbentrop telephoned to declare that he would come to Italy bearing a mes-sage from the Führer for Mussolini. When he arrived in Rome, the German foreign minister proposed a defensive alliance between Berlin, Tokyo and Rome. Up until now, he told Mussolini, Hitler had hesitated to suggest a tri-partite alliance because "he considered that the great democracies would have intensified their rearmament and that those people in France and England who represent the trends towards conciliation with the totalitarian states would have had their positions weakened. Hitler has now come to the con-clusion that, independently of any new political event, France and Britain have made and will continue to make the maximum effort as far as arma-ments are concerned. Nevertheless," Ribbentrop continued, as though stating some irrefutable physical fact, "the advantage gained by Germany and Italy is so great that we can no longer be overtaken."

Mussolini deflected the offer of an alliance. For now he did not want to squander his chance to squeeze concessions out of London and Paris in the colonial sphere by making his allegiance to Germany crystal clear. "When the alliance between Germany and ourselves seems to be ripe," he told Ribbentrop, "it will be necessary to lay down its objectives. We must not make a purely defensive alliance. There would be no need of one, since no one is thinking of attacking the totalitarian states. Instead we wish to make an al-liance in order to change the map of the world."[36]

Over the winter of 1938–39, the Italians pressured the British government into ratifying the Easter Agreement of April 1938, which had pledged Britain's support for international recognition of Italy's conquest of Ethiopia in return for the removal of Italian "volunteers" from Spain and a halt to Ital-ian subversion in British-mandated Palestine. Afterward, Ciano turned up the screws on the French. Emulating Germany's war of nerves against the Czechs, he orchestrated a shrill propaganda campaign that demanded the French possessions of Tunisia, Corsica, Nice and Savoy. Instead of a shock-

and-awe land offensive into Egypt, Mussolini now dreamed of a rapid air-naval war against France.[37]

However, only weeks after Ribbentrop's trip to Italy, false rumors that Britain and France had concluded a military alliance at the summit meeting in November prompted a re-evaluation of the immediate worth of a tripartite alliance. That Mussolini might soon challenge France was one thing, but taking on France and Britain went beyond even his capacity for warlike fantasies. On January 1, 1939, in a decision born of weakness, he ordered Ciano to turn the ongoing technical cooperation between the Axis armed forces into a military alliance.[38]

Confirmation, if any was needed, of Germany's value to Italy as a makeweight against Britain came ten days later. "The rearmament which Germany is feverishly carrying out," Chamberlain said to Mussolini during his visit to Rome, "led the world to think that the Führer has in mind some new coup which might be dangerous for the general peace." "Germany has rearmed and is rearming on an imposing scale," Mussolini replied, "but this rearmament must be considered in relation to the rearming of all other nations and particularly in relation to Russian rearmament on which there is no precise information but which must be considered to be on a large scale." Chamberlain said, "Germany's scale of armament is too imposing to have only a defensive aim." The next day, Ciano confided to his diary with evident glee that "German rearmament weighs down upon [the British] like lead. They would be ready for any sacrifice if they could see the future clearly. This dark preoccupation of theirs has me more and more convinced of the need for the Triple Alliance. With such an instrument in our hands we could get whatever we want."[39]

The dark preoccupation of Italy, on the other hand, was British rearmament. During the winter of 1938–39 the full measure of Britain's naval expansion was making itself felt in Rome. Britain had already begun work on over 200,000 tons more of new ships than any other great power. Even with four new battleships being built, Italy *alone* could never hope to hold onto even its current level of inferiority against the Royal Navy, never mind the British and French fleets combined. In alliance with Germany, the Italian planners calculated—with tables projecting competitive fleet building into the 1940s—that it might be possible to achieve a combined strength of about half that of the French and British navies. Expansion of the air force and the re-equipment of the army, meanwhile, suffered from chronic shortages of skilled labor, modern industrial plant and raw materials, the price of which had risen sharply on world commodity markets thanks to the arms boom. As

Mussolini himself acknowledged in December 1938, when he allocated two billion lire to the replacement of artillery, the army experienced the greatest difficulties modernizing.[40]

After Germany suddenly occupied what remained of the Czech state on March 15, 1939, and Britain and France reacted by solidifying their alliance and extending security guarantees to eastern European states threatened by the Axis, Mussolini persisted with alliance talks despite having been kept in the dark about his ally's coup. In a Europe divided between two armed camps, what choice did Italy have? he asked the Fascist Grand Council. Italy could not perpetually "waltz" among the great powers, never committing itself to one or the other. "The problem for us is a different one. It is the relationship of forces within the Axis," he continued, taking refuge in his favorite illusion. "The demographic relationship has moved in favour of the Germans. . . . Militarily the relationships are these. Germany has twice the number of divisions; our navy is twice the size of Germany's; our air force in relation to the German is one to five; industry one to twelve. So the annexation of Czechoslovakia has altered the internal relationships of the Axis in Germany's favor. But we have a political advantage: we are the arbiters of the situation in Europe."[41]

On April 7, in answer to Hitler's annexation of the Czech state, Mussolini ordered that Albania, a de facto Italian protectorate, be annexed. Having restored the political balance in the Axis, so he thought, the Duce now played for time. In his speeches and correspondence with Chamberlain, he declared with sincerity that Europe needed a long period of peace. What he did not add was that, so long as the cold war in Europe did not turn hot until 1942–43, Italy could face the big showdown fully armed according to its plans. For years now intelligence out of Germany and everything that Ribbentrop, Göring and Hitler had said in private indicated that they did not foresee a big war until the 1940s. When Göring visited Rome on April 16, Mussolini asked him what he thought would be the most favorable time to seek a trial of strength. The field marshal said that "the Axis Powers ought to wait a little longer until their rearmament had reached a more favourable stage in relation to those of the democracies." The Duce invited him to be "more precise." Göring answered "that in the years 1942–43 the ratio of armaments between Germany and Britain would be appreciably more favourable, especially in the naval sphere." Mussolini then asked, "What ought we to do until the time is favourable for a general conflict?" Göring replied, "The Axis powers must rearm to the teeth and should even now place themselves in a state of mobilisation."[42]

Mussolini needed no encouragement. "We need to arm ourselves," he had proclaimed at the end of March. "The watchword is the following: more guns, more ships, more planes. At any cost, with any means, even though we will have to do away with everything called civilian life." But the ratcheting up of rearmament was more rhetorical than real. Even if they had been organized, managed and resourced better, Italy's munitions industries faltered in the arms race. In the spring of 1939 Ciano began to worry about the confrontation between Germany and Poland and the "disastrous" state of the Italian armed forces. He fretted, too, about his father-in-law's growing preoccupation with "form" rather substance in military matters.[43]

Still, during the negotiations leading to the Pact of Steel of May 22, 1939, which bound the Axis in a future war, Ciano and Mussolini emphasized that the big conflict must not come for at least three years. "Germany, too," Ribbentrop blithely reassured them, "is convinced of the necessity for a long period of peace [to complete its rearmament], which should not be less than four or five years."[44]

No keen observer of international political, military and economic developments over the winter of 1938–39 could overlook the way in which the division of Europe into two opposing blocs solidified. Viewed from Berlin, these developments appeared ominous. Since the Munich agreement, the tempo of British and French arming had not slackened. Under Daladier, France had made great strides in reviving its economy, too.

Most experts reckoned that Germany had a lead over France and Britain in air and land armaments, but France and Britain were closing the aviation gap. The United States was now arming, too, though, according to Germany's military attaché in Washington, General Friedrich von Boetticher, not on the "boundless" scale that President Roosevelt and his "Jewish friends" would have liked. German war planners always assumed that the Americans would use their vast industrial economy and raw resources against Germany; and, as London and Washington had intended, the Anglo-American trade treaty of November 1938 was seen in Berlin as confirmation of this basic fact. General Thomas, who in the first months of 1939 delivered a number of lectures to high officials about the state of German armaments, grasped the message. "In the past," he told his audiences, "the Clausewitzian view that he who destroys the enemy army will win the war was true. Today the Anglo-Saxon view holds the same validity: destroy the economy, then you also destroy the armed forces and with this also the people in question."[45]

In his lectures General Thomas struck a note of pride. "We can say that the whole German rearmament with regard to men and materiel can be described as an achievement of the German people that is unsurpassed in the world and a testimony to the focused direction of the state leadership and also testimony to the dynamism and creativity of the German people." For the next couple of years, Germany and its Italian ally possessed a "superiority" in initial "striking power." However, he cautioned his listeners, this lead could not be maintained. At the moment Germany might have an impressive breadth of armament, but it lacked the depth to win an all-out war against Britain and France assisted by the United States. The same was true of the arms race: "The western powers have learned a lot from the events of September 1938 and they have the intention to catch up with the clearly visible German lead in rearming." While Germany and Italy were already arming "at full speed," Britain, France and the United States had yet to mobilize their "full economic potential" to produce "considerably greater armament than the states of the Rome-Berlin Axis." Thomas continued:

> If the political situation led to a prolonged arms race we must of course be clear that the western powers are because of their economic capability to rearm in a position to catch up with Germany in about twelve to eighteen months. The vast economic power of Britain, the US and France is in the long run greater than that of the Axis, and the western powers will not be faced with the same difficulties that Germany and Italy always have in terms of raw materials and manpower. If there was such an arms race and a subsequent war the outcome of the war will among other things depend on whether the Axis could decide the war through a rapid decisive strike. If this doesn't work, and if there is a war of attrition then the depth of the war economy i.e. staying power will prevail.[46]

Hitler, too, saw the way the arms race was turning. Though he did not want to read negative military analyses of the type that General Beck had circulated before the Czech crisis, the assessments of the service staffs reached him in one form or another. He did not need briefings from the military experts to grasp what was happening. After Munich the European newspapers, which he avidly followed, reported the upsurge of British and French rearmament, especially of air forces, and speculated on the political significance of low-level Anglo-French staff talks. By spring 1939, at any rate, the trend was unmistakable. "It is becoming more and more evident," as one German diplomat described it, "that England and France are following a tactical procedure, involving a highly accelerated rearmament programme combined with simultaneous pronouncements of solidarity by means of which they seek to exert 'peace pressure' on the 'totalitarians.'" Hitler later explained: "The time gained by postponing a general conflict with the western powers would have worked out definitely to Germany's advantage, only if England had not meanwhile introduced general conscription and embarked on large-scale rearmament. If the conflict had been delayed, these measures would, however, have ensured that Germany's purely military superiority would be [overtaken] by her enemies even on land."[47]

With each passing month, the failure of Hitler's post-Munich arms acceleration became all too clear. In January 1939 Hitler dealt with Schacht's claim that a further hike in military spending would trigger an inflationary slide by firing him. In a speech shortly after, in which he dismissed the "supposed superiority" of the western powers in defense and finance, he urged the German people to "export or die!" Once again spending on the armed forces and the Four Year Plan rose, but the titanic expansion plans of the three services never had a chance of success. Accumulating the reserve fuels and building the fuel-storage depots for a Luftwaffe of 24,000 planes and the giant anti-British Z Plan fleet alone would have taken years and a huge slice of the men, money and materiel needed to make the bombers and battleships. In March the air planners concluded that a fivefold rise in aircraft output was impossible, anyway. A month later they issued a reduced expansion plan, but that too was slashed because of a scarcity of raw materials. Anti-aircraft gun production lagged behind schedule. So did Göring's beloved Ju-88 program. A forty percent cut in the steel ration for the armed forces did not help. During the summer of 1939, aircraft and ammunition output slumped. Though the army benefited from the looting of Czech and Austrian armories, and the addition of the Czech munitions industry to German capacity, the targets for small arms, machine guns, artillery and tanks all had to be cut. At the moment when Britain began to conscript and equip a large army to fight alongside the French, General Brauchitsch made dire predictions about the stagnation in the German Army's growth. The reduced raw-material rations, he warned Hitler, amounted to "the liquidation of the army's rearmament effort." Still basking in the priority status that Hitler had conferred on the Z Plan, only the navy entered 1939 with optimism. In February 1939 the Italian naval attaché in Berlin found the usually lugubrious Admiral Raeder in jolly spirits. He looked forward to collaboration between the two Axis navies and to a long period of "relative peace" to build up their fleets.[48]

Much to Hitler's annoyance, while the arms race spiraled beyond Germany's capacity to win it, Ribbentrop's efforts to form a totalitarian coalition stalled. Despite the enthusiastic support of the Japanese military attaché in Berlin, his government in Tokyo decided not to join a military alliance that might drag them into a war against Britain just when tension with the Soviet Union along the Manchurian-Siberian frontier was heating up. Italy agreed to a bilateral alliance. But talks with Poland failed. In 1934 the Poles had signed a nonaggression treaty with Berlin and had also joined in the evisceration of Czechoslovakia. Ribbentrop sought to resolve the territorial disputes between Berlin and Warsaw arising from the Treaty of Versailles, specifically the return of the coastal city of Danzig (Gdansk) to Germany, and rail and road links through the so-called Polish Corridor that separated East Prussia from the Reich, as a preliminary to Poland adhering to the Anti-Comintern Pact against Russia. That would preclude Poland from joining an anti-German alliance. If the Poles submitted, then Germany's eastern frontier would be secure for the coming showdown with Britain and France. The Poles, however, refused to turn themselves into German vassals. On March 31, 1939, to deter Hitler from further expansion, Britain announced that it guaranteed Poland's sovereignty. France did the same.[49]

When Hitler heard the news of Britain's guarantee to Poland, he yelled, "I shall brew them a devilish potion!" On April 1, in a launching ceremony brimming with loaded references to the pre-1914 naval arms rivalry, Hitler named Germany's new battleship *Tirpitz*, denounced Britain's "policy of encirclement" and promoted Raeder to grand admiral. "I have made Germany strong again and built up its [armed forces] on land, at sea and in the air," he said. "Now that other countries openly declare their intent to arm, and to constantly rearm, there is only one thing I can say to these statesmen: they will not wear me out!" That day he also ordered plans for war against Poland. The significance of the occasion was not lost on the Admiralty or on Chamberlain, who had "little doubt that the Germans would denounce the [naval agreement] as and when it suited them, irrespective of any excuse." When Hitler addressed the Reichstag three weeks later, he fulfilled the prime minister's expectation. After listing all the military hardware that Germany had taken from the Czechs—enough to equip forty divisions, he claimed—Hitler denounced both the Polish nonaggression pact and the Anglo-German Naval Agreement of June 1935.[50]

On May 22, when Hitler presided over the signing ceremony for the Pact of Steel with Italy, he still believed that the coming conflict with Poland would not escalate into a European war. Certainly he would move against the western powers before Germany started to fall behind in the arms race, but, as Göring had told Mussolini, that would not occur for two or three years. The German Navy needed time to expand. Italy, too, needed time. The next day Hitler met his senior military men in the Reich Chancellery. As always, he surveyed the international scene and spoke of living space in the east, Poland's demise and British antagonism. "Fundamentally," he explained with tortured logic, a "conflict with Poland beginning with an attack on Poland will only be successful if the western powers keep out of it. If this is impossible, then it will be better to attack in the West and to settle Poland at the same time." Although in the past statesmen always strove to win short wars, he explained, Germany must plan for a long one of ten or fifteen years against Britain and France. In answer to questions from Göring, who was skeptical about the possibility of attacking Poland without provoking a general war, Hitler emphasized that he did not want the naval building scheme modified in any way and that all the target dates for the various arms programs should be "modelled on the years 1943 and 1944."[51]

Driven by a powerful sense of destiny, regret over having lost his nerve back in September 1938 and sheer rage against Britain, Hitler calculated the likelihood of waging a limited war against Poland. During the summer of 1939 he kept his top soldiers, diplomats and other senior officials in the dark. Was the crisis with Poland supposed to end in another Munich? Would Britain and France go to war? Hitler tried to persuade London and Paris that the true target of his eastward aggression was the Soviet Union; he also sought to wreck their efforts to strike a deal with Moscow to deter Germany by trying to make one of his own with Stalin. In July serious trade and political negotiations began between Berlin and Moscow. A bargain with Russia over Poland would not only deprive the western powers of an eastern ally but also give Germany access to the Soviet Union's vast supply of raw materials and so bypass the maritime blockade that Britain and France would impose if war came.[52]

As ever, air power played an important role in Hitler's decision making. On July 3, at the Luftwaffe's Rechlin testing ground, he enjoyed a display of advanced prototypes. He saw the maiden flight of the world's first rocket-propelled aircraft, test flights of the Ju-88 and other new models and a mock-up of the first turbo-jet fighter. Göring and his top-ranking officials intended to demonstrate to the Führer a German lead in the air arms race. General Milch told Hitler that the most advanced technologies he saw were only in the experimental stage. Yet, despite the efforts of his air force adjutant to correct the misimpression, Hitler thought that some of them would enter service shortly.

At any rate, the Führer reassured the air force top brass that war against the western powers would not come before 1943.[53]

Not everyone thought so. Alarmed at the visible resolve of Britain and France to fight if Germany attacked Poland, Mussolini sent Ciano to warn Hitler that Italy was not prepared for war. On August 12, the Italian foreign minister arrived at Berchtesgaden, where Hitler had closeted himself away from anyone who might try to persuade him that a big war in Europe would ultimately end in Germany's ruin. "France and England cannot intervene because they are insufficiently prepared militarily, and because they have no means of injuring Germany," Ribbentrop explained to Ciano, "while [Germany]—particularly by virtue of its air force, which is very much stronger than the other two air forces put together—is in a position to strike at all the Anglo-French centres." "France and England will certainly make extremely theatrical anti-German gestures but will not go to war," Hitler too reassured Mussolini's emissary, "because their military and moral preparations are not such as to allow them to begin the conflict." Ciano returned to Rome depressed and unconvinced.[54]

Over the next three weeks Hitler adhered to his plan to attack Poland regardless of the risk of prematurely starting the big war he planned for in two or three years' time. As Ribbentrop's diplomacy with the Soviet Union and military preparations for the attack on Poland converged, on August 22, four days before the attack in the east was first scheduled to commence, the Führer, in very high spirits, addressed his top military men. If war against Britain and France should come—so ran his theme—then better now than later. His reasons varied. Now was the right moment; he was in his prime; Mussolini stood solidly with Germany; men of little worth led Britain and France; Franco had just won the civil war and would assist the Axis; and the nonaggression pact with Russia, which Ribbentrop had just negotiated with Stalin in Moscow, would blow a huge hole in the encirclement strategy of the western powers.

The underlying rationale, however, was the arms race. "It is easy for us to make decisions," Hitler explained:

We have nothing to lose; we have everything to gain. Because of our restrictions our economic situation is such that we can only hold out for a few more years. Göring can confirm this. We have no other choice, we must act. . . . A permanent state of tension is intolerable. The power of initiative cannot be allowed to pass to others. The present moment is more favourable than in two or three years' time. . . . England and France have undertaken obligations which neither is in a position to fulfil. There is no real rearmament in England, but only propaganda. A great deal of harm was done by many Germans, who were not in agreement with me, saying and writing to English people after the solution of the Czech question: The Führer succeeded because you lost your nerve, because you capitulated too soon. This explains the present propaganda war [so Hitler glibly described the accelerated arms competition against Britain]. The English speak of a war of nerves. One factor in this war of nerves is to boost the increase in armaments. But what are the real facts about British rearmament? . . . No substantial strengthening of the navy before 1941 or 1942. Little has been done on land. . . . A little has been done for the air force, but it is only a beginning. . . . England does not want a conflict to break out for two or three years. . . . France is short of men (decline in the birth rate). Little has been done for rearmament. . . . It is nonsense to say that England wants to wage a long war.[55]

Some of the officers present had misgivings about what Britain and France would do and of Germany's staying power in a long war, but the staggering news of the Nazi-Soviet Pact helped silence them. Briefly now, however, Hitler wavered. The revelation of the pact with Moscow had not blunted the resolve of London and Paris to stand by their guarantees. Then a discouraging message from Mussolini arrived: Italy could not wage war unless Germany made impossibly huge deliveries of war materials. Hitler delayed the attack on Poland until September 1 to try one more time to divide his adversaries. He failed. Unable to erase the self-defeating consequences of his diplomatic provocations or halt to his benefit the self-perpetuating dynamism of the arms race, Hitler decided to risk a great war by attacking Poland.[56]

WHILE GERMANY'S diminishing lead in the arms race encouraged Hitler to go for broke in the summer of 1939, it also encouraged Britain and France to stem the tide of Germany's eastward expansion and to accept war when it came. Hitler's demolition of the Munich agreement on March 15 by ordering the German occupation of what was left of Czechoslovakia had flabbergasted Chamberlain. Warning signs had appeared, but he believed that London had only narrowly escaped a "mad dog" German air attack that winter and that the forces of moderation in Berlin had gained ground. Now the Munich agreement was discredited. Chamberlain's critics in Parliament and the press had the upper hand. During the spring he slowly adjusted to an outright policy of containment against Germany in partnership with France. For him the adjustment was agonizing, but adjust he did.[57]

On March 17 in his home city of Birmingham, the day before his seventieth birthday, Chamberlain condemned the Prague coup and committed Britain to oppose a German bid to dominate Europe. "In our country we must review what has been done to ensure national safety. Nothing must be excluded. Every aspect of national life must be looked at from a new angle," he added, with deliberate emphasis. That day an alarming (but erroneous) warning that Hitler would present the Romanians with an ultimatum prompted Chamberlain and Halifax into shoring up resistance in eastern Europe to Germany's bullying tactics. The cabinet endorsed the policy of containment and another acceleration of the arms programs. "We are not strong enough ourselves & we cannot command sufficient strength elsewhere to present Germany with an overwhelming force," the prime minister wrote. "Our ultimatum would therefore mean war and I would never be responsible for presenting it. We should just have to go on rearming & collecting what help we could from outside in the hope that something would happen to break the spell, either Hitler's death or a realisation that the defence was too strong to make attack feasible."[58]

In the interim Chamberlain planned to build a bloc of states, including France, Poland and the Soviet Union, that would declare their mutual hostility to German aggression. Events, however, swiftly overtook him. Intelligence now warned that Hitler would soon "swoop" down on Poland. Alarmed, Halifax and his top advisers pressed for a public initiative to assist Warsaw. Though skeptical of the intelligence, Chamberlain accepted that something had to be done to support the Poles while Britain gathered together some sort of eastern front. On March 31, to cheers from his backbenchers, he told the House of Commons that Britain would back Poland if Germany threatened its independence. Daladier seconded the British guarantee of Polish independence with a French one. A week later Mussolini annexed Albania. In reaction, Britain and France guaranteed the independence of Romania and Greece, too.[59]

The guarantees set in motion a revolution in Britain's approach to the arms race. Ever since Britain had started to rearm, Chamberlain tried to buck the trend of regimenting whole economies and societies. Air and naval forces offered a limited means of deterring Hitler without a continental-size army (and the arms industries to support it) or committing to continental allies. After the Munich agreement the limited liability became untenable. By February 1939, with Halifax's support inside the cabinet and pressure from Parliament, the army had won its case that it needed more men, equipment and reserves to bolster French morale and to help prevent Belgium and Holland from falling into German hands. A limited strategy of deterrence in peacetime made sense, but "it was a mockery," Chamberlain told his cabinet, "to call the present conditions 'peace.'" As though yielding to a force of logic not of his liking, the prime minister accepted first a doubling of the army reserve and then on April 24 the introduction of conscription of all men aged twenty and twenty-one for military service. The army's top planner cheered the first decision—"a continental commitment with a vengeance!"—and then gasped at the staggering implications of the second.[60]

He was not alone. Taking its cue from Chamberlain's Birmingham speech, the impeccably liberal magazine *The Economist* advocated emulating the totalitarians as Britain plunged deeper into the arms race: "The one great lesson that can be drawn from German economic experience in recent years is that well-organised control can secure the maximum utilisation of a country's resources for the piling up of armaments without resort to inflation." Chamberlain understood that providing tens of thousands of conscripts with uniforms, stores, weapons, vehicles and barracks, while the economy was straining to expand the air force and the fleet, required government intervention. To ensure that a massive expansion of the army did not interfere with the air force and naval arms plans, the cabinet announced on April 20 its decision to set up a Ministry of Supply, with powers to impose priorities on industry, enforce binding arbitration on prices for military contracts and stockpile essential raw materials. Chamberlain, who had till now resisted the creation of hydra-like state bureaucracies, gave life to "a vast organ of central planning and control." With the unions and the opposition parties now clamoring for an adequate national defense, and public opinion in favor of a firm line against Germany, Chamberlain was no longer worried about sparking a social and political crisis by gearing up armaments production. With the expansion of the army, defense spending soared. Borrowing for defense doubled. In private, Treasury officials now thought the previously unthinkable: introducing price controls to keep inflation in check as well as other "abnormal" methods of regulating economic life. John Simon, the chancellor of the exchequer, warned that Britain could only run a quasi-war economy for six to nine months without suffering financial exhaustion. The unspoken implication of the chancellor's warning was that war, with all the powers that it would confer upon the state to control finance and industry, would be better than the arms race.[61]

While British ministers absorbed the dire consequences of another escalation in arming, General Gamelin and his staff evaluated the turn of events.
They knew it would take time for the British to raise the thirty-two-division
field force they now promised to send to France, but Britain's historic decision to conscript a mass army in peacetime broke the gloom that hung over
French planning. The news out of London fed into a general recovery in the
French outlook. As in Britain, after the Munich agreement of September 1938
and especially after the Prague coup of March 15, 1939, public opinion in
France became more militantly anti-German. Italy's anti-French propaganda
also helped to unify the nation behind a policy of resistance. The divide between left and right remained deep, but Daladier portrayed himself with success as the champion of French liberty. Despite their bitterness over Reynaud's
union-busting policies, organized labor and the moderate left-wing parties
supported the strengthening of France's defenses.[62]

Daladier authorized a tripling of defense expenditure without fearing that
he might trigger social and political breakdown or another flight of capital.
During the spring of 1939 the French Army drew up a four-year plan costing
sixty-four billion francs, while the air force expanded Plan V to achieve a total
production target of 8,094 aircraft by 1941. The French economic recovery in
1939 reinforced the rising tide of confidence in foreign and defense circles.
Gold flowed into the Bank of France. Industrial activity rose sharply. For the
first time in years, tanks, guns and other modern equipment started to roll
off the assembly lines in quantities. Tank production more than doubled to
1,059 units. Benefiting from the reforms of air ministers Cot and La Chambre, aircraft output climbed, too, from 533 machines in 1938 to 2,277 in 1939.
With the Americans promising to sell France 1,500 combat planes a year as
well, the air staff no longer considered their situation irretrievable.[63]

During the spring of 1939, British and French war planners met regularly
to deliberate on how to defeat the Axis. For General Gamelin and the French
service chiefs, who always regarded a British alliance as the precondition for
victory over Germany and who had been frustrated for over a decade by their
colleagues across the Channel, the sense of relief was tremendous. Only a year
before, the British had refused to exchange anything more than rudimentary
technical data; now French and British staff officers met as equal partners to
make plans for mobilizing their two world empires to overwhelm their common foes. They saw the broad strategic scenario in the same terms. For two
or three years the Axis would have the initial advantage in striking power on
land and in the air, while Britain and France would have a crushing superiority at sea. "Germany and Italy," they agreed, "cannot hope to increase their

resources appreciably in the course of the war: they will therefore stake their chances of success on a short war. The United Kingdom and France, on the other hand, are in a position to increase their war potential from one month to another."[64]

The central theme of the British and French strategists—that time was on their side in the arms race or in war, if it broke out—not only encapsulated six years of thinking in both capitals about how to prevail over the Germans, but also shaped British and French deterrence policy in the last months of peace. So long as Hitler grasped that he could not win a short war, so ran the logic, he would shrink at the prospect of a long one over Poland. One way to drive the message home was to prevent Germany taking control of the resources of eastern Europe and the Balkans. All the economic intelligence out of Germany depicted a "hyper" armaments economy seizing up. French spies even reported the contents of General Thomas's lectures on Germany's military-economic impasse. "The economic situation in Germany is bad," Chamberlain remarked. "That's not a position in which to start a deathly struggle." No one, not even Chatfield, who replaced Inskip as minister for the coordination of defense, now spoke of allowing the Third Reich to gobble up its neighbors to the east and southeast. Forcing the Germans to fight in the west and east would buy time for the Allies to arm, French war planners concluded. Obstructing German imports of key commodities—iron ore, oil, pyrites and manganese—would also slow down the expansion of Hitler's war machine in peace or war.[65]

The calculation that Britain and France would outpace the Axis in armaments bred optimism in the summer of 1939. As the politicians became more determined to resist what they saw as another Hitlerian exercise in coercive diplomacy over Poland, their military advisers spoke about the superior staying power of the west, and the intelligence analysts reported the flaws in Germany's war preparations with greater clarity. Daladier told the U.S. ambassador in Paris that "he thought Hitler was now most hesitant to begin a war. The military position of France and Britain was much stronger than last September." "I have little doubt that Hitler knows quite well that we mean business," Chamberlain wrote. In a flash of foresight he wondered whether the rising tide of Allied strength might force Hitler to act before it was too late: "If he thought we [meant to attack him as soon as we are strong enough] he would naturally argue that he had better have the war when it suits him than wait till it suits us." At the end of July, though, the prime minister still believed that moderation would win out in Berlin. "You don't need offensive forces sufficient to win a smashing victory," he asserted. "What you need are defences sufficiently strong to make it impossible for the other side to win except at such a cost as to make it not worthwhile. That is what we are doing and though at present the German feeling is it is not worthwhile yet, they will presently come to realise that it never will be worthwhile. Then we can talk. But the time for talk hasn't come yet because the Germans haven't realised that they can't get what they want by force."[66]

Even the revelation of the Nazi-Soviet Pact did not blunt the resolve of Britain and France to go to war if Germany attacked Poland. Chamberlain had never put much store in Soviet assistance anyway. French war planners wanted an alliance with Moscow, but the setback did not knock them off course. On August 23, at an emergency meeting in Daladier's study, senior foreign policy and defense officials discussed France's next move. Bonnet tried to convince everyone that France had to wriggle out of its guarantee to Poland. He failed. Gamelin said that the army was ready to go to war. The Poles would fight briefly but "honorably." By the time Germany had crushed them, the British Army would have arrived in France to begin the long war. In sharp contrast to a year earlier, the air arms race encouraged a positive decision to oppose Germany. In a pugnacious mood, Guy La Chambre spoke for the air force. He explained that in aviation there had been great progress since September 1938. "In terms of fighters, we now have modern machines under mass production, and Franco-British strength now balances Italo-German strength. . . . Despite what we know of German air strength," he emphasized, "the state of our aviation must not weigh on the government's decision as it did in 1938."[67]

A week later the British Army's top planner recorded in his diary a similar sentiment. If war came, he wrote, then "we can't lose it. Last September we might have lost a short war. Now we shouldn't, nor a long one either."[68]

CIANO RETURNED FROM his meeting with Hitler on August 13 in sheer disgust. Had the Führer gone mad? Could he not see that by attacking Poland he would provoke Britain and France into war? As the cataclysm neared, Ciano frantically sought to convince his father-in-law to stay out of it. Several times he also proposed to London another four-power conference to defuse the crisis, but without any luck.[69]

On August 25 and 26, Mussolini wrote to Hitler. "At our meetings the war was envisaged for after 1942 and at such time I would have been ready on land, on sea, and in the air according to the plans that had been arranged. I leave you to imagine my state of mind in finding myself compelled by forces

beyond my control not to afford you real solidarity at the moment of action."
Six days later Ciano exploded in anger at the military men who had fed the
Duce's craving for bold stratagems. "We have no right to intervene," he told
a confidant:

> And I add—no interest either. We would have to take the biggest blows in
> a state of extreme vulnerability: the empire, Libya, the Aegean, the Mediter-
> ranean, the Western Alps. Are we in a state to do that? No, no, no. We have
> mind-boggling deficiencies. . . . [General] Valle, who has always been a big
> mouth, is shouting that he doesn't have any fighters and can only sustain
> fifty days of combat flying. And he is creating alibis for himself—saying
> that between Ethiopia, Spain and Albania—the air force has not been able
> to achieve a state of readiness. [Admiral] Cavagnari, who is satisfied with
> fuel supplies, says that the Italian navy is ready to get itself sunk: in com-
> parison with the English and the French, given that in the North Sea they
> will not have to take on an efficient German navy, the ratio will be six to
> one. Then [General] Pariani? Pariani is playing the boxing champion: an
> army thrust here, an army thrust there. The truth is, we are not ready.[70]

In the early hours of September 1, the German forces attacked Poland.
Later that day Chamberlain told his cabinet that the "events against which we
have fought so long and so earnestly have come upon us. But our consciences
[are] clear, and there should be no possible question now where our duty
[lies]." The issuing of ultimatums to Germany demanding a withdrawal from
Poland now had to be coordinated with the French. In Paris, Bonnet deceit-
fully tried to hold up the French ultimatum and in so doing caused a cabinet
revolt in London on the night of September 2. The delay, however, was just
that. On September 3, Britain and France declared war on Germany.[71]

Shunning the word "neutrality," Rome declared itself to be in a state of
"non-belligerency." And, with a gnawing envy, Mussolini looked on from the
sidelines as the "epoch of nations behind walls" that he had anticipated since
1918 arrived.[72]

CHAPTER 14

"THE ACID TEST . . . IS WHETHER ANYONE IS READY TO DISARM"

I n November 1936 Franklin D. Roosevelt won a second term by the largest margin of any U.S. president in living memory. The landslide looked like a mass endorsement of the president and his New Deal, but the victory was deceptive. The election had sharpened the divide in the fractious Democrats between southern rural conservatives and northern urban liberals. Conservative Democrats and Republicans feared that Roosevelt might promote "dictatorship" and "radicalism" on the back of his election triumph. And the president hurt himself by trying, with a notable lack of success, to increase the number of justices on a Supreme Court dominated by conservatives. The setbacks for a seemingly unstoppable president infused conservatives on Capitol Hill with the confidence to begin to push back on some New Deal reforms.

Roosevelt's troubles with Congress coincided with the first signs of a sharp downturn in the economy. Much of FDR's prestige hung on the belief that the New Deal had revived the economy. It had, but only modestly. In 1935–36 the jobless rate fell and productivity picked up. Enough so, in 1937 Roosevelt and his old friend at the Treasury, Henry Morgenthau, resolved to balance the budget. Critics on the left accused FDR of economic heresy, but in fact, the president was as fiscally orthodox as his predecessor, Herbert Hoover, in many ways. Tax revenues were rising, so it made sense to him to slash emergency spending to dampen inflation and raise investor confidence. The inflation was caused by, among other things, a huge influx of gold from crisis-ridden Europe. But cutting off the fiscal stimulus to the economy too early probably caused and surely did nothing to alleviate what his opponents called the Roosevelt recession of 1938. Factories shut and the ranks of the unemployed swelled again. By the end of the winter of 1937–38, more than two million workers had lost their jobs. In 1938 the unemployment rate climbed to nineteen percent, or over ten million workers. Discontent and social unrest slowly spread. During the midterm elections that year, the Democrats naturally took a beating at the polls. Roosevelt increasingly felt he was being squeezed between stubborn conservatives in Congress and left-wing radicals and crackpot demagogues offering economic quick fixes. "History proves," Roosevelt warned Americans during one of his radio fireside chats just weeks after the *Anschluss* "that dictatorships do not grow out of strong and successful governments, but out of weak and helpless ones."[1]

Roosevelt had long feared that economic failure would destroy democracy. In 1933, he spoke of mobilizing against the slump as though the country was under attack by a foreign army. A collective response like that of 1917–18 was vital to trigger a recovery. The nation had to act with a "unity of purpose." During his first term, it seemed to do so, but by 1938 the momentum was gone. One way forward was to impose discipline, but Roosevelt hated tyrants. Yet to try to impose a plan without coercive powers—as Léon Blum had struggled to do in France against growing countervailing and contradictory social, economic and political pressures—could send the United States spinning out of control. The president understood that he needed a popular cause to lubricate with a spirit of cooperation the millions upon millions of individual moving parts that made up the nation. Surely, he thought, the goals of general prosperity and social reform could inspire that kind of voluntary national unity. Yet, as the virulent spread of fascism seemed to show, perhaps only waging war had that kind of galvanizing effect. If so, then perhaps that ghastly prognosis explained the failure of liberal capitalism.[2]

In fact, to Roosevelt the military rivalry between the great powers of Europe and Asia seemed like a plague that afflicted its victims with a frenzy to buy arms that could only end in bankruptcy and war. "These are without doubt the most hair-trigger times the world has gone through in your lifetime or mine," he told his ambassador in Rome. "I do not even exclude June and July 1914, because at that time there was economic and social stability, with only the loom of a war. . . . Today there is not one element alone but three or more." The agony of Blum's Popular Front especially troubled him and Morgenthau because it revealed the stark trade-offs being made everywhere between guns and butter. "The British and the French are by their rearmament . . . incurring a serious danger of financial and economic collapse," diplomats informed him in April 1937: "France . . . will find it difficult to continue for more than a year at the present pace." Roosevelt recognized that the piling up of arms forced even liberal states to keep living standards low and to enforce social discipline. "Democracy cannot thrive in an atmosphere of international insecurity," he warned. "Such insecurity breeds militarism, regimentation and the denial of freedom."[3]

In armaments, Roosevelt's first instinct was to build up the navy. Apart from his lifelong affinity for the service, Japan's rejection of naval arms control justified upgrading the fleet, especially with job-creation money: the New Deal alone helped build two aircraft carriers, four cruisers, nineteen destroyers and four submarines. In July 1935 he ordered planning to start on new battleships. Cheered by Roosevelt's interest, naval planners let their imaginations rip. One bizarre study envisaged Europeans repaying their American war debts by building warships for the U.S. fleet. Another more sober study concluded that U.S. shipyards had the capacity to outbuild any foreign power, but history had shown that Congress would refuse to spend the money. "We will [thus] have a greatly reduced navy, falling behind other large naval powers and thereby losing prestige and influence in world affairs." Admiral William Standley, the chief of the navy, shared this gloom. He did not want to overload the shipyards, annoy Congress or provoke foreign navies by pushing through too large a program. He need not have worried. Roosevelt wanted to build battleships. In January 1937, arguing that the European arms race had forced his hand, Roosevelt announced that the navy would order two new battleships.[4]

Meanwhile, army air corps officers hoped to benefit from the arms race, too. After Göring unveiled the Luftwaffe in March 1935, U.S. air planners tabulated with envy the titanic sums spent on independent air forces in Europe. There was no independent air force yet—there would be none till 1947—and so aviators flew for either the navy or the army. In both services flyers were forbidden to speak of bombers rendering land and sea forces obsolete. But army pilots had read their Giulio Douhet and daydreamed of winning future wars by bombing alone, either by shattering a foe's national "will" by hitting cities or by daylight "precision" attacks on factories and railways. In 1933 Boeing designed a four-engine bomber, the B-17 Flying Fortress, that could deliver a 2,500-pound payload some 2,260 miles; after it made successful test flights in 1935, the airmen knew they had the machine of their Douhetian dreams.[5]

What the airmen now needed was political backing, a swelling budget and a high-tech aircraft industry to churn out bombers the way Ford churned out Model Ts. Luckily for the airmen, aviation fascinated Roosevelt. Some New Deal job-creation money was sent their way, and the president had them transport the mail during a dispute with the airlines. High-profile crashes of army flyers delivering mail, however, dramatically publicized the need for more investment in military aviation. From 1935 to 1938 the air corps budget nearly doubled.

The missing element was a large, harmoniously functioning aircraft industry ready to expand quickly for an all-out war. During the 1920s, U.S. aircraft companies relied on government orders to stay in business. Believing that the industry had reaped unwarranted profits in 1917–18 through collusion, Congress imposed a strict system of competitive bidding that minimized interaction between the military and industry, and between producers. But this system made selling aircraft a risky business venture. An aircraft firm might win the design competition but lose the production contract to a competitor.[6]

Still, driven by the urge to fly faster, further and higher, aviation pioneers such as William Boeing, Donald Douglas and Glenn Martin made the American aircraft industry the pacesetter in high-performance all-metal monoplanes. Foreign demand for U.S. aviation technology flourished. When in 1930 the Soviet Union's chief aircraft engineer, Andrei Nikolayevich Tupolev, toured U.S. firms, the labor discipline, ingenuity and efficiency amazed him. American airmen knew that their machines were the best, but they also knew that their highly price-competitive industry could assemble them only in batches. Total war demanded mass production. In September 1937 General Henry "Hap" Arnold, the assistant chief of the air corps, wrote, "At the present state of the industry, there is no such thing as a rapid and vast wartime expansion of an aircraft factory, it simply cannot be done."[7]

Organizing the aircraft industry into an integrated mega-machine would require a huge expansion of American air power on a European scale. But as long as Roosevelt hoped to lead the world to peace and disarmament by setting a good example, that kind of accelerated armaments expansion was out of the question. Washington's answer to the arms race was to promote peace through trade: through business not bullets, as Secretary of State Cordell Hull said. If the walls of autarky could be pulled down, so ran his thinking, then the arms race would grind to a halt as peoples and governments learned to enjoy the jobs and profits derived from trade. Assuming that a deal with London would set off a global stampede to free trade, Hull focused his commercial diplomacy on Britain. But the British proved especially averse to altering their preferential system of imperial trade. "Trade treaties are just too goddamned slow," yelled an exasperated Roosevelt. "The world is marching too fast."[8]

In October 1937 Roosevelt introduced a new idea, which might lead to concrete action. In a speech in Chicago, the stronghold of isolationism, he suggested that aggressor nations should be "quarantined." The isolationist press decried the speech. The State Department denied that sanctions against Tokyo, Berlin or Rome had been contemplated. Roosevelt explained that he had expressed an "attitude," not a program. Even a direct attack did little to alter the isolationist sentiment. In December, after Japanese bombers accidentally sank a U.S. Navy gunboat on the Yangtze River, some in Washington and London hoped for a show of joint naval strength in the Pacific. But Tokyo hurriedly made reparations, and the incident did not provoke a call for action from the American public.[9]

In January 1938 Roosevelt suggested to London a proposal that his closest foreign affairs adviser, the ethereal Sumner Welles, had been dreaming up for months: a step-by-step series of talks that would cascade through moral force into a global peace conference. The Welles plan struck Neville Chamberlain as a sanctimonious, harebrained scheme that would leave Britain in the lurch when it went wrong. The prime minister preferred his own plan. He would defuse the arms race by venturing to its very epicenter, Germany.[10]

NAZISM SICKENED ROOSEVELT. His political foes drew parallels between the New Deal and Hitler's socioeconomic projects, but Hitler's regime looked to Roosevelt much more like a grotesque parody of New Deal aims and values. Putting people to work with deficit-financed government spending on armaments destroyed economic growth and stamped out individual liberties under a boot of state regimentation.

At first Roosevelt thought the Nazis would run out of steam and moderates inside the regime would eventually prevail. Schacht's wizardry could not, after all, sustain deficits and trade imbalances and keep inflation in check forever. Germany could not achieve autarky, though it had a marginally better chance to do so than Japan or Italy. The president also distinguished between Germans and Nazis, hoping that the will of the masses would alter Hitler's course. Yet with each year the news got worse. Roosevelt's ambassadors in Europe vividly described Nazi brutality. American diplomats and soldiers catalogued the dizzying growth of German armaments and the responses of the other European powers. At the start of 1938, Roosevelt told his cabinet, "The economic situation in Germany has been getting very bad. Business is on the downgrade. Italy is in even worse shape economically . . . the same is true of Japan." He still had hope, which his cabinet shared, "that the type of government represented by these three countries is being severely tested from the inside, especially Germany, and that there may be a break in the log jam." But would such a "break" cause a change in German policy or a devastating war?[11]

While events unfolded, the cabinet backed Roosevelt's call for more warships, not to create jobs in the shipyards but to deter attack. On January 28,
1938, he asked Congress for funding to buy two more battleships, auxiliary vessels, anti-aircraft guns and investment in munitions plants for the army. The
surge in global armaments had forced him to do so, he explained. A few weeks
later six B-17 bombers made a headline-grabbing, 12,000-mile round-trip flight
to Buenos Aires, thus proving their reliability as long-range hemispheric defense weapons.[12]

In the run-up to Munich, Roosevelt and his advisers could only watch.
Like the bystanders in Moscow, the Americans attributed sinister motives to
Chamberlain's shuttle diplomacy. Some U.S. officials suspected he planned
to sacrifice the Czechs then negotiate a closed Anglo-German trade bloc.
Others, like William Bullitt, the U.S. ambassador in Paris, prayed that Chamberlain would succeed in saving Europe from the specter of Soviet communism. Most, like the president himself, swung between moral disgust at
"appeasement" and genuine hope that the prime minister's relentless pursuit
of the Führer would work.[13]

In Washington, the Munich agreement marked a turning point. As in
London and Paris, a sense of relief rapidly gave way to revulsion at what peace
had apparently cost. Roosevelt at first thought that the situation might have
changed for the better. "The acid test," he said, "is whether anyone is ready to
disarm." American diplomats put out feelers to discover whether any leaders
were willing to disarm. "They just smiled and said [disarmament] was a crazy
dream of those Americans," the president later recalled.[14]

And so Roosevelt stopped talking about disarmament. Now rearming per-
meated his thoughts. But the question was how to go about it. In the years before Munich, all the evidence coming out of Europe predicted that air forces
would be the decisive factor in any future diplomatic and military confrontation. The reason why Britain and especially France had surrendered to
Hitler's blackmail, so the Americans saw it, was the supremacy of the Luftwaffe. "The moral is," Bullitt wrote to the White House, "if you have enough
airplanes you don't have to go to Berchtesgaden."[15]

Roosevelt accepted that pithy lesson. Throughout October he and his advisers planned a spectacular rise in U.S. aircraft production. The Germans
had applied American methods of mass production to outstrip every other nation in air forces, so the Americans would now do the same thing. Henry
Morgenthau told his staff that the president "is thinking in terms of our producing 15,000 airplanes a year for this country. . . . give private industry 3,000
and we'll produce 12,000. He's thinking in terms of three shifts. . . . [and]

eight plants located around the United States." When the treasury secretary told the army chief of staff, General Malin Craig, about the plans, he was flabbergasted. Craig had been lobbying for more troops and investment in munitions factories for the army. "What are we going to do with fifteen thousand planes?" he demanded. "Who [are] you going to fight, what [are] you going to do with them, with three thousand miles of ocean?"[16]

On November 14, four days after *Kristallnacht*, Roosevelt called his top military and economic advisers to the White House. He described the state of the American aircraft industry and told them about intelligence (much of it erroneous) concerning the air race in Europe. Between them, Germany and Italy could put into the air about 10,000 aircraft, while France and Britain had 2,500 to go up against them. Aircraft production in France was "very low" and "not that much better" in Britain. "The recrudescence of German power at Munich," the president said, "had completely reoriented our own international relations . . . for the first time since the Holy Alliance in 1818 the United States now faced the possibility of an attack on the Atlantic side in both the Northern and Southern Hemispheres. . . . this demanded our providing immediately a huge air force so that we do not need to have a huge army to follow that air force." He considered sending a large army abroad undesirable and politically impossible. And then he confessed, "I am not sure now I am proud of what I wrote to Hitler in urging that he sit down around the table and make peace. That may have saved many, many lives now, but that may ultimately result in the loss of many times that number of lives later. When I write to foreign countries I must have something to back up my words. Had we had this summer 5,000 planes and the capacity to immediately produce 10,000 per year, even though I might have had to ask Congress for the authority to sell or lend them to the countries in Europe, Hitler would not have dared to take the stand he did."[17]

The president wanted a two-year production plan for 10,000 aircraft and the industrial capacity to produce 20,000 a year. While Roosevelt spoke, General Craig and his deputy General George Marshall, who had been working on expansion plans for the field army and industrial mobilization, silently stewed. When the president asked for opinions, Marshall said he disagreed with him. But General Arnold, the only aviator in the room, could barely contain his glee.[18]

Arnold was a disciple of General Billy Mitchell, the air force heretic who had been court-martialed in 1925 for saying that the invention of the bomber had rendered armies and navies obsolete; now events in Europe seemed to prove Mitchell had been right. Arnold later told his staff, "The President came straight out for air power. Airplanes—now—and lots of them! . . . A new regiment of field artillery, or even new barracks at an Army post in Wyoming, or new machine tools in an ordnance arsenal . . . would not scare Hitler one blankety-blank-blank bit!" The problem was how to make all those airplanes. Roosevelt spoke about seven new "government" aviation plants. But they could not be built overnight. Would the private factories make them? And why would they expand their capacity without a guarantee of long and profitable production runs?[19]

Meanwhile, at the German embassy, the military attaché was poring over press clippings, technical journals and official publications to piece together a report for Berlin on American rearmament. He looked over the latest version of the War Department's industrial mobilization plan and began to describe how the U.S. war machine would work once it really got going. "The president exercises dictatorial powers," he reported, "granted him to mobilise the economy totally."[20]

DURING THAT MEETING on November 14, 1938, Roosevelt set out much of his rationale for his air force rearmament program, but he stopped short of articulating his worst fears about what might happen if the United States succumbed to the arms maelstrom. He envisaged containment, as the strategy would later during the Cold War be called, which sprang from his concept of quarantine. The titanic rise of American air power would act as a deterrent against Germany. With the U.S. aviation industry backing them, France and Britain would have preponderance in potential air strength. That would give Hitler and his war planners pause for thought. If that failed, then Roosevelt would find a way around the neutrality acts to supply Britain and France with bombers to "pound" Germany into absolute submission. The president believed that "the morale of the German people would crack under aerial attacks much sooner than that of the French or the English." Relying chiefly on air forces to deter war in Europe, or to keep war away from the Americas if it broke out, would preclude any need for a multimillion-man army and a thoroughgoing regimentation of the U.S. economy.[21]

Sending a large army to Europe was both politically "out of the question" and "undesirable," Roosevelt had said. Something deeper lay here, however, than a reluctance to pick a fight with the isolationists in the press and on Capitol Hill. As 1939 wore on, he began to do that anyway, arguing with a measure of exaggeration that the Nazis posed a direct threat to the whole of the Americas. What really worried him, however, was the threat that militarization posed to the American way of life. A repeat of the 1917–18 mobilization might not only destroy the progressive social and labor legislation that had passed under his presidency, but it might, as many of the New Dealers expected, cede political power in America back to greedy chief executives and financiers.

Something even more frightening loomed. If Britain and France were defeated by Germany, Europe would come under an all-embracing totalitarian order, which would possess the raw materials, people and factories to build ships, bombers and armies to menace fortress America. Driven by fear of that threat, Americans would demand massive armaments of totalitarian proportions. The only way to equal the threat would be to emulate totalitarian forms of social and economic regimentation. Even if war never came, an intercontinental cold war would consume much of the nation's wealth and vitality. Roosevelt knew that democracy and reform would be trampled in the rush for armaments. He resolved to buck the great armaments trend.

In January 1939 during his annual address to Congress, Roosevelt asked for a jump in arms spending and spoke gravely about what was at stake.

> We, no more than other nations, can afford to be surrounded by the enemies of our faith and our humanity. . . . Our nation's program of social and economic reform is . . . a part of defense, as basic as armaments themselves. . . . The first duty of our statesmanship is to bring capital and manpower together. Dictatorships do this by main force. . . . Like it or not, they have solved, for a time at least, the problem of idle men and idle capital. Can we compete with them by boldly seeking methods of putting idle men and idle capital together, and at the same time, remain within our American way of life . . . within the bounds of what is, from our point of view, civilization itself?[22]

Roosevelt's question had a powerful resonance, for it echoed across time and space, back to the cataclysm of 1914–18, when the shells ran out and the factories could not make them fast enough to feed the storms of steel; to the postwar years, when people reveled in the loosening of state controls or longed for safety in multi-year state plans, collective crusades and colossal armaments. His question had been asked time and again after the Depression shattered the global economy and talk of disarmament yielded to an arms race. Where some prophesied a future of total war and longed for total victory, sacrificing freedom to planning was no price at all. Where others struggled against the logic of total war, paying that price was defeat.

Roosevelt's question resonated not just with New Deal liberals but also across the political divide. Respected defense pundits such as Hanson Baldwin of the *New York Times* assumed that the army's industrial mobilization plan would set up "dictatorial government in accordance with the totalitarian character of any future war." The business press predicted everlasting "war socialism." According to the steel-industry periodical *Iron Age*, "There is only one small group with a hope of profit in war, and that is the vociferous group that looks to war as the golden opportunity to do away with the profit system and the Constitution in one fell swoop." Fear of the New Dealers at war ran deep in corporate circles. When aircraft companies first learned of Roosevelt's plan for thousands of aircraft, they expected the nationalization of their factories. In 1939 *Business Week* found nearly every businessman an isolationist because "war would be a vehicle for the extension of government control over business." Leading anti-interventionists such as Herbert Hoover, the world-famous pilot Charles Lindbergh and the one-time New Dealer General Hugh Johnson also predicted that another total war would be fatal to democracy. As Senator Arthur Vandenberg, a man of that camp, wrote, "We cannot regiment America (and how!) through another war and ever get individual liberty and freedom of action back again. We shall be ourselves a totalitarian state, to all intents and purposes, within ten minutes after we enter this war as a protest against totalitarian states. And we shall remain one forever." Ultimately, these isolationists believed that, in a world dominated by totalitarian regimes, fortress America could remain democratic and safe. Roosevelt knew it could not.[23]

As arming got under way in 1939, Roosevelt also knew that the pressure point for initiating an American slide into totalitarianism lay in the relationship between the state and the economy. Pressure for a larger munitions industry came from the army. War planners such as General Marshall, who became army chief of staff in 1939, believed that formidable ground forces with the capacity for rapid expansion were essential to deter attack. Roosevelt resisted. He had discovered that buying the 10,000 aircraft he wanted and expanding plant capacity to build more was difficult enough without placing more burdens on industry. Still, the War Department kept up the heat. The assistant secretary of war, Louis Johnson, was an apostle of total mobilization and regarded U.S. entry into a European conflict as inevitable. At the War Department, he was locked in a vicious struggle over industrial preparations with his boss, Harry Woodring, an ardent isolationist. As a maneuver in his bureaucratic war, Johnson proposed that the White House establish a

War Resources Board in the summer of 1939 to explore various military-industrial munitions schemes.[24]

Roosevelt accepted the idea, as long as his old friend Bernard Baruch, who was a relentless advocate of "total mobilization," did not sit on the board. Back during the Czech crisis Baruch had started to lobby hard for the job of arms czar to pick up where he had left off in 1918. Johnson, however, appointed some of Baruch's acolytes to the committee. Roosevelt asked the thirty-nine-year-old chairman of U.S. Steel, Edward Stettinius, to preside, a sensible choice given his achievements in banking and industry. After that, if Roosevelt needed a lesson in how politically explosive mobilization and wartime controls were, the condemnation that the War Resources Board attracted gave it to him in spades. New Dealers attacked it as a cabal of business tycoons plotting to undo social progress. When the president closed it down in September 1939, businessmen shrieked in horror because they feared that the New Dealers would write their own grand plan for wartime industrial socialism.

The way Roosevelt reacted to the final report of the War Resources Board was especially revealing about his unease over escalating rearmament. Johnson and Stettinius had regarded their task as simply updating the army's industrial mobilization plan, a revised version of Dwight Eisenhower's original M-Day plan of 1930. The president, who was familiar with the plan, had made it clear that he thought it handed too much power to the army and business and infringed upon his authority as commander in chief. A man of little subtlety, Johnson had blithely shrugged off these objections. In its final report, the board recommended that the president should set up a super-agency headed by an "economic czar" selected from "the patriotic business leaders of the nation" to mobilize the country. When the report landed on his desk, the president condemned it as a "very comprehensive blueprint from which it would appear that this committee was prepared to take over all functions of the government." Acutely aware that in a high-voltage crisis the board's military-industrial Frankenstein's monster could go berserk and demolish American democracy, he refused to cede authority to an "arms czar." From now on he would improvise the apparatus of mobilization, pacifying and reconciling conflicting interests and pressures himself, exactly as he had improvised the New Deal, so that all the threads of political power stayed in his grasp. The War Resources Board report went into the White House trash can. "What do they think they are doing," Roosevelt shouted in exasperation, "setting up a second government?"[25]

After the fall of Poland in September 1939, Roosevelt began the tough battle against isolationists to bend neutrality in favor of London and Paris, and he pushed ahead with a gigantic expansion of American air power. The army also grew, and the navy laid out a ten-year construction plan that would furnish the United States with the fleet "second to none" that their forebears of 1916 had wanted. In January 1940 Roosevelt asked Congress for a whopping $1.8 billion for armaments. Though his critics accused him of trying to embroil the United States in the European war, his containment strategy of November 1938 remained unaltered.

Most observers expected a long war in Europe that would, barring something unforeseen, follow an inexorable cycle. The German Army would exhaust itself pounding French defenses, while the Allies mobilized their superior strength and began their own war-winning offensives. Voltaire once remarked, "God was always on the side of the big battalions." The total-war systematizers knew that industrialization had revised that rule. Now god was always on the side of the big economies. But then, in May–June 1940, the Germans had, it appeared, found a way to flout the new god of war. In a matter of weeks the French Army surrendered, and the British Army slipped back across the Channel.

CHAPTER 15

"MIRACLES CANNOT HAPPEN"

On January 21, 1940, the *New York Times* published an essay by Geoffrey Crowther, the editor of the influential London weekly *The Economist* and a keen observer of American politics. After gaining a first class degree in economics from Cambridge University, he had crossed the Atlantic to study at Yale and Columbia universities just as Wall Street crashed. Eight years later, on the recommendation of the famed economist John Maynard Keynes, Crowther became editor of *The Economist*. His January 1940 essay tackled a problem that had troubled Crowther and many others for several years. In it he asked, "Are the two great European democracies being driven, in an effort to defeat totalitarianism, to adopt all forms of totalitarianism itself? Will they ever be able to slough off their new martial uniforms and revert to the free-and-easy life of civilian countries? Is democracy in Europe committing suicide in self-defence?"

"By etymology," Crowther explained, "a totalitarian state is merely one in which the government runs everything. By popular usage, however, a totalitarian state is one in which the government not merely runs everything, but runs everything for the objectionable ends of aggression and conquest." On the surface, he admitted, it looked as though Britain and France were becoming totalitarian. "The outbreak of war in both of these normally democratic countries has been followed by a flood of decrees and edicts by government, subjecting the citizens to all manner of restrictions and obligations. The Englishman or the Frenchman is today almost as much under the thumb of discipline as the German [and] when they have fully mobilised for war they will control industry and commerce fully as completely as Germany."

Yet, Crowther assured his American readers, fundamental differences remained between Britain and France, on the one hand, and Germany, on the other. In a totalitarian state the citizens served the state; in the democracies the state served the citizens. Totalitarian states sought arms and autarky; democracies sought wealth and trade. In war a democracy had to arm itself and take precautions. "Arbitrary power in any form is a dangerous drug for any democracy to take; but," he continued, invoking the universal logic of national security, "the emergency requires drastic action." Still, the slide of Britain and France into wartime totalitarianism was by no means permanent. Safeguards such as parliamentary and judicial oversight would guarantee individual liberties. Moving on to a somewhat more mystical plane, he wrote: "The conclusion of the matter seems to be that it is not the outward forms of government that matter so much as the inward spirit that inspires them. What must at all costs be avoided is totalitarianism of the human spirit; and so long as the ordinary citizen retains his right to be informed, to question, to compare and to criticize, the State may assume all manner of arbitrary and extended powers and still not be the master. It will be merely a more powerful, perhaps a more effective, instrument of the people's will."[1]

OUTWARDLY, THE BRITISH and French mobilizations of 1939–40 certainly looked like a plunge into totalitarianism. As Crowther noted, the coming of war made it politically much easier than before for the two states to take greater control over their economies and societies for the purposes of arming and fighting.

In September 1939 both the British and French parliaments passed emergency legislation that granted the state sweeping wartime powers over people and property. Ministries of supply, armaments, shipping, information and economic warfare arose. These mushrooming state bureaucracies took control of foreign-exchange movements, trade and raw-material imports and allocations. An Anglo-French apparatus of joint committees also began to evolve to coordinate the blockade of Germany, war finance and foreign purchasing. In Britain the armed forces swelled to two million (or four percent of the total population) and in France to six million (or fourteen percent of the total population). Arms spending in both countries soared and arms production steadily climbed. From January 1939 to June 1940, French industry produced 1,913 tanks, more than in the previous three years combined. In 1939–40 French aircraft production sped up too, but not to the hoped-for rate of over a thousand machines a month. French Air Force planners looked to American aircraft factories to make up the deficit. In Britain the aviation industry switched into high gear, with deliveries rising from 748 machines in October 1939 to 1,081 in April 1940. British aircraft production overtook that of Germany by 1940. Production of tanks, artillery and small arms also expanded rapidly. Of course, all sorts of planning errors and bottlenecks bedeviled the British and French mobilizations. Soldiers on both sides of the Channel complained about shortages of equipment because of production bottlenecks. But with time, learning, better organization and more resources, such problems could be overcome.[2]

Time was central to Allied strategy. In time Britain and France would outgun Germany and strangle its economy. The initial German onslaught on France was to be prudently blunted, not recklessly preempted. Although disputes would crop up at the meetings of their Supreme War Council, especially over the size and rate of build-up of British troops and air forces in France, and though relations between Chamberlain and Daladier remained uneasy, on this point the two Allies saw eye to eye.[3]

After war broke out, Chamberlain thought about standing down in favor of another man more temperamentally suited to leadership in war, but the hawk-faced problem solver could never resist the allure of achieving the impossible. According to the textbooks, waging total war was straightforward. The way to win was to mobilize the nation to make the maximum "guns" and the minimum "butter" consistent with feeding, clothing and housing essential workers, and that required a highly centralized state apparatus that could apply an absolute top-down organizing pressure.[4]

Yet even a government armed with emergency powers could not simply crank up the intensity of mobilization to full throttle overnight. The bureaucratic machinery to control a war economy required months to evolve and much longer than that to perfect. (In Germany economic planners predicted that German munitions output would fall by twenty percent while making the transition from peace to war.) Applying too much top-down organizing pressure too fast risked provoking industrial unrest and resistance from business and labor. And, no matter how well the mobilization was managed, Britain would not emerge from the experience undamaged and unchanged. The question Chamberlain asked himself was how fast he should drive the nation toward an all-out effort. The answer that made sense to his coldly clinical mind was to calibrate the intensity of British mobilization to the overall strategic situation.[5]

On the continent two great armies were amassing behind fortifications. As Chamberlain's soldiers told him, "a complete and spectacular military victory . . . is unlikely under modern conditions." The French Army supported by the slowly expanding British Army was capable of defending France. For Germany, an attack on the west "whether successful or unsuccessful would entail such frightful losses as to endanger the whole Nazi system," Chamberlain wrote. Would Hitler take that risk? Month by month the Allies grew stronger and Germany relatively weaker. Allied victory depended on "convincing the Germans that they cannot win. Once they have arrived at that conclusion, I do not believe they can stand our relentless pressure, for they have not started this war with the enthusiasm or the confidence of 1914." Sooner or later Hitler would be faced with the perilous choice of an attack on France or the collapse of his regime under the growing weight of Allied arms and the blockade. Chamberlain predicted that Hitler would be swept from power even before he had made his decision.[6]

In the meantime Britain would arm in the air and on the sea, while building up its new army at a speed that would not overtax industry or require too great a centralization of economic controls. Although mobilization required the setting up of new wartime ministries and a labyrinthine structure of interdepartmental committees to coordinate the war effort, Chamberlain wanted to run his war through a small inner cabinet of ministers heading key departments and opposed the establishment of a separate "economic general staff." He preferred to assemble the bureaucratic apparatus to regulate supply and demand gradually, and to divide responsibility for the war economy among several ministries. He also wanted business and labor integrated into the machinery of economic management.[7]

Unlike their counterparts across the Atlantic, British businessmen did not regard wartime economic controls as the end of civilization. Still, they too feared that "war socialism" might become permanent unless they took a hand in running the war economy. And so once war broke out, businessmen flooded into government. The list of section heads at the new Ministry of Supply read like a who's who of corporate Britain. Some trade union leaders decried the flood of businessmen into the corridors of power, but most, just like the employers, wanted a hand in running the economy in the struggle against fascism. The unions demanded influence over employment practices and a cap on wartime profits; employers demanded greater dilution of skilled jobs and a cap on wages. To bring both sides together under the patriotic banner of industrial unity in time of war, the government pledged to involve both industrialists and organized labor in the planning of the postwar economy.[8]

In Chamberlain's halfway war economy—something a lot more intense than peacetime routine but not yet cranked up for an all-out effort—the Treasury remained a powerful influence over the rate of arming. As before the war, Treasury officials worried about declining foreign-currency reserves and bankruptcy before the war was brought to a victorious end. Roosevelt's policy of "cash and carry" of November 1939 came as a relief to hard-pressed Allied economic planners, but Britain and France still needed to slap down hard "cash" on the barrel before they could "carry" off the goods, which grew pricier all the time—and that meant maintaining a healthy export trade.[9]

Viewed from Paris, Neville Chamberlain's approach to total war looked like an extremely annoying variation on his approach to the prewar arms race, one that would leave the French Army with the brunt of the fighting. Daladier and his military supremo General Gamelin, were delighted to get the first divisions and aircraft of the British Expeditionary Force, but they wanted more of them and a lot faster.[10]

Despite all the authority that the Law for the Organization of the Country in Time of War granted him, total war for Daladier seemed more enfeebling than even his worst days as Blum's defense minister. At first he tried to form a national unity cabinet, but he failed to find a workable combination. As the premier who broke the Popular Front and crushed the national strike in November 1938, he lacked credibility with the left, and so in Parliament he had to rely on the right. Among conservatives, Daladier's punitive action of outlawing the French Communist Party and arresting its activists was more popular than his prosecution of the war. Many leading conservative political figures—like most French business leaders—feared that total war would inexorably generate totalitarian Bolshevism in France. After Poland fell, some of them hankered after a peace deal with Hitler brokered by Mussolini.[11]

Though tortured by the knowledge that France on its own lacked the staying power to prevail against the Third Reich, Daladier remained committed to the war. Winning meant playing for time—for Britain to raise an army and for France to draw on the industrial might of the United States. The 10,000 aircraft that London and Paris had ordered from American suppliers for delivery by the end of 1941 would make up for the crises in French aviation. In the meantime, Daladier knew, France had to achieve a great burst of high-intensity arming to get ready for Germany's first attack.

To boost production, Daladier pinned his hopes on France's new Armaments Ministry and its chief, Raoul Dautry. Called the Napoleon of the Railways, Dautry had a brilliant record as an industrial technocrat. When Daladier was defense minister in the Popular Front, he had been drawn to the idea of an organized economy to raise arms output. Now he may have thought that Dautry would slowly impose full-scale economic planning and central control through negotiations with industrialists and labor as the war went on. If so, he was right. Dautry was an admired entrepreneur who during 1914–18 had organized the laying down of strategic railways in record-breaking time. During the 1930s he turned the state railway from a strike-ridden white elephant into a superefficient transport network. The trade unions respected his genuine concern for the happiness of his workforce and his enlightened approach to labor relations.

Sadly for Dautry, the French economy was not a railway. He could not lay down new lines, order extra rolling stock, impose "rationalized" work routines, draw up a master timetable and then expect trains to run on time. Dismissive of men who differed with him, as France's arms czar he grew frustrated dealing with the army and other ministries. His direct control only reached as far as the state-owned arsenals and factories. In order to organize the wider industrial sector to feed the arms plants, he needed to work with other industrialists. Although arms production picked up, output was nearly always below what were in fact unrealistic targets propelled skywards by gross intelligence overestimations of German production. "To pass from a capitalist regime to a completely managed economy is not an easy thing," Dautry said. "To do so during a war is hopeless." Most would have disagreed with him: war was *precisely* the time to seize control of a free-running economy. But at heart Dautry was a true devotee of laissez-faire capitalism and wary of overpowering state controls, even if he would be the one wielding them.[12]

So too was the finance minister, the laissez-faire maverick Paul Reynaud. Back in 1938 Reynaud had led the charge against the French left, bashing the trade unions and reassuring parliamentary and boardroom conservatives that the Daladier cabinet had ended the social experiments and interventionism of Blum's Popular Front. Reynaud set out to lift investor confidence by balancing the budget, to boost arms output by abolishing the forty-hour week and to slash welfare spending. When the war came, the industrial magnates and labor unions signed a patriotic pledge to cooperate during the crisis, but no one in the government, least of all Reynaud, showed much inclination to meet the trade unions halfway on issues such as capping wartime profits on munitions making or on postwar economic planning.[13]

Reynaud plotted to replace Daladier. The relationship between the two pint-sized politicos was never friendly, and the finance minister did not bother to disguise his ambition, but when war broke out, an underlying political difference between them began to surface. Daladier pushed state expenditure to the maximum, running down France's gold and foreign-exchange holdings in the process. If France needed titanic shipments of American machine tools, aircraft and other goods, he was willing to run up the bill. The soaring costs troubled Reynaud. Like Chamberlain and the Treasury men in London, Reynaud hoped to use financial limits as a throttle on arming and on the inflation stoked by the arms boom. When he introduced his new budget in the Senate in December 1939, for instance, he spoke passionately about his dedication to free-market capitalism. Many Frenchmen wanted to know what France would be like after the war, he said. The state certainly needed to play a role in the postwar reconstruction, but "does that mean in France that an all-powerful totalitarian state will arbitrarily fix prices and salaries, that it alone will be entitled to conduct production, to control capital, to command profits, and to cover losses? That would be a despairing view if it were true." Frenchmen had had enough authoritarianism during the war already; if they were going to have it in peacetime too, he said, voicing the opinion of the right, "then why fight at all?" Reynaud's whole policy thus rested on running a moderated war economy to maintain business confidence and to continue to attract capital back into France.

At the current spending rates, however, France would be bankrupt by 1941. Reynaud had a solution: discipline workers by raising already high income taxes, cut back all non-military state spending even further and ration all household goods. Daladier, however, rejected shifting more of the burden onto ordinary citizens. He was probably hoping to provoke a financial crisis in a year's time, which would create the opening to alter the relationship between the state and private business and financial interests. After all, another model for organizing a war economy loomed large. Across the Rhine the Nazi regime had controlled money flows, dictated to the boardrooms, regulated supply and demand, allocated resources and planned exports and imports. Surely the French state could follow that example by seizing all French financial assets in foreign countries and taking an even tighter grip over the private sector. If Daladier was trying to push things to a head to impose an even more regimented economic regime, as Reynaud no doubt suspected, France's conservative finance minister was dead set against it.[14]

Daladier was locked in a struggle not just with his own finance minister and the conservative businessmen who controlled industry and finance but also with his top military commander. During the first month of the war, much to Dautry's amazement, the army pulled skilled men out of the factories and sent them to the front. As a result, output in some sectors dipped. When Daladier complained to Gamelin about the need for workers in factories and on farms, the generalissimo shrugged him off. War had appreciably tilted the relationship between them.

Since 1918 Gamelin had devoted his life to preparing for the time when he would lead the French Army in another all-out struggle against the Teutonic foe. In peacetime he had to mollycoddle the politicians; in war he preferred to keep them at arm's length and tell them as little as possible. In war they had only one important job, to supply him with what he needed to win. Gamelin's only real anxiety was whether the politicians, Daladier most of all, had the stomach for the fight.

Gamelin was sure of ultimate victory. Like nearly everyone in the Allied camp, he knew that France and Britain backed by America would in two or three years outgun Germany. Hitler's deal with Stalin, Gamelin knew, had blown a hole in the Allied blockade, but there was no telling how that connection would develop over the long haul. Germany was a deadly foe organized along totalitarian lines. The way in which it had used tanks and bombers to smash Poland offered Gamelin and his staff a glimpse into how Germany might operate from the north Belgium plain against France. The Germans knew that their best chance lay in the first clash. They would pack everything they had in one mighty wallop. Everything hinged on that first battle. Gamelin wanted to husband every man, machine and bullet he had to win it. A failed attack might be enough to cause the Nazi regime to implode. That was why he made only a token attack in support of the Poles. After Warsaw fell, he expected the Germans to strike in the west without much pause. When October passed and no invasion came, Gamelin began to think the German high command had wavered and thereby lost its best chance to strike. Their attack would now come in the spring or summer of 1940. By then everything had to be ready.[15]

During the intervening months Gamelin's biggest headache was calls for action against the German war machine along its periphery. At first, when he expected the Germans to strike France immediately after Poland fell, he too was in favor of some diversionary action in southeast Europe to draw the Germans away from the west. But once the war settled into a stalemate (the period often called the Phoney War), he saw such schemes as a potential drain on his forces facing the Reich.

The most persistent calls for a Balkan adventure came from General Maxime Weygand, Gamelin's predecessor, whom he had brought out of retirement to command French forces in the eastern Mediterranean. The archreactionary, like so many others, feared that total war would plunge France and possibly all of Europe into totalitarian communism. Weygand's solution was to seize the initiative by opening up a second front. Blithely ignoring all the political and logistical pitfalls to such an operation, not the least of which was convincing either the Greeks or the Turks to go along with it, he imagined landing Allied divisions either at Salonika or Istanbul as the galvanizing core around which a hundred Balkan divisions would coalesce to threaten Germany. Daladier, who began to wonder whether Hitler would attack France at all, latched on to the Balkan expedition with glee. With Poland fallen and the Soviet Union in league with Hitler's Reich, Weygand's ostensibly bold plan offered him a way to open a much-wanted second front. To Gamelin's way of thinking, the only thing that such a move would likely bring about was Italy's early entry into the war and a huge drain on the limited forces he had facing Germany. Luckily for the generalissimo, when the idea was presented in London, the British agreed with Gamelin.[16]

The debate about a Balkan front in France and Britain was indicative of a larger dynamic gaining momentum. War never was just the rational application of violence for some definable political goal; it was also the harnessing of the irrational passions, such as fear and hate, of the masses. The logic behind the Allied side of the Phoney War was too cool and too rational for nations on the brink of Armageddon, with memories of the last war still vivid. For Chamberlain and in some respects Daladier and even Gamelin, the Phoney War was a cold war, one where the aim was to out-arm the adversary rather than to fight and to signal the utter futility of a mass slaughter. The hope was eventually to watch the Nazi regime collapse under the mounting economic and political pressures of war. If an attack in the west came at all, it would be the final desperate and reckless act of a militaristic madman.

In 1939–40, years before nuclear weapons changed the game, that kind of cold war could not be waged for long. For many the nerve-racking tedium of being at war with little combat, whether experienced vicariously in newsprint or in person at the front, or any other form of emotional release, was demoralizing. For supporters of the war, the clamor for action expressed itself on the editorial pages and through political channels. Especially, though not exclusively, on the pro-war left, where the struggle against the Nazi regime was drawn in stark ideological terms, politicians wanted action. Some began to suspect that Chamberlain, Daladier and many of the men around them, who after all had "appeased" Hitler at Munich, did not want to wage war at all.

Over the winter of 1939–40, pressure against the seeming inaction of Daladier and Chamberlain built up. From inside government, it came from top officials and ministers who were eager to fight, brimming with war-winning stratagems and hoping to advance themselves on the tide of success. Their projects shared certain features. All promised to shorten the war by cutting off the supply to Germany of key commodities such as iron ore or oil. Their advocates attacked the rationale for inaction, namely that time worked for the Allies. With each year of the war, so ran one line of reasoning, German dominance of the Soviet economy would grow. With Russian factories and raw materials Hitler would have the means to win. Many officials apparently believed in this far-fetched scenario, but not coincidentally it also fed nicely into all the justifications for rushing ahead with a quick-win scheme.

Besides the Balkan expedition, two other seemingly more promising quick fixes began to captivate imaginations in London and Paris. The first centered on interrupting the flow of iron ore from neutral Sweden to the steel industry in the Ruhr area of Germany. For years before the outbreak of the war, French and British economic intelligence had pinpointed the Swedish shipments as a key German vulnerability. Some reckoned that if the iron-ore trade ceased, the German metallurgical industry would come to a halt within a year. The other critical German weakness was oil; much of their supply was coming from the Soviet Union's Baku oilfields in the Caucasus. In November 1939 French planners drew up plans to bomb Baku from French airfields in Syria.[17]

In Paris the navy touted operations in Scandinavia. Admiral François Darlan knew that if the war ended without the fleet engaging in some spectacularly useful operation, the politicians would not be willing to pay for its upkeep after the war. When the Soviet Union attacked Finland on November 30, 1939, the Allies suddenly had a pretext for intervention in northern Europe and, if that entailed picking a fight with Stalin and unleashing French bombers to hit the Baku oilfields, then to arch-reactionaries such as Darlan all the better. The navy's plan was to land a force at Petsamo, on the Arctic coast, which the Red Army had seized from the Finns. The landing would trigger a response from Germany, and then in reply the Allies would occupy the nearby town of Narvik in Norway, from which Swedish iron ore had to be shipped when the Baltic froze up in winter. For Daladier, who was feeling the heat in Parliament from those who wanted bold action, the Finnish war was a stroke of luck. Executing Darlan's plan would excite those who wanted something aggressive done to harm Germany, and those on the right who really wanted harm to come to the Soviet Union.[18]

Ignoring Gamelin's concerns about frittering away troops to peripheral theaters of war, Daladier took Darlan's strategy to London. For weeks now the British war cabinet had been contemplating using aid to the Finns as a pretext to interrupt the Swedish iron-ore trade too, but the British rejected the Petsamo project as a pointless provocation of the Soviet Union that could do little to help the Finns and only complicate matters with the neutral Scandinavians. The Allies instead agreed to send men and aircraft to Finland via Norway and Sweden, and to prepare for a large-scale expedition to cut off the Swedish iron-ore trade with the support of Oslo and Stockholm. But on March 13, 1940, before much could happen, the plucky Finns, who had beaten back the Red Army for weeks, signed an armistice. In Paris and London, Finland's capitulation provoked an angry political outburst. Daladier, who had needed a show of force in support of Finland to demonstrate his vitality as a war leader, faced a vote of confidence in Parliament. A majority of 300 parliamentarians abstained. Reynaud replaced Daladier, who stayed in the cabinet as defense minister.

Reynaud had achieved his ambition, but his support on the left and the right was shallow in a nation divided over the war. The new premier needed a quick military success to tighten his hold on office, one that struck a sharp blow at Moscow as well as Berlin. He wanted fast action to halt the flow of Swedish iron ore to Germany and air raids on Soviet oil wells in the Caucasus. Whether the Allies or Germany had time on their side, Reynaud could only guess. What he knew was that further inaction would lead to a swift end to his premiership and a radicalization of the war effort, which would extinguish the free-running economy forever. His top advisers drafted papers showing that Germany would win the long war and that something had to be done to reverse the situation. In London he demanded action to interdict German imports of Swedish iron ore and unveiled the French plan to bomb the Baku oilfields. Meanwhile he resolved to rid himself of Daladier, who brooded and sniped at him from the Defense Ministry, and General Gamelin, who greeted all of the new premier's gutsy boldness with mind-boggling military complications.[19]

Once again the British opposed a direct attack upon Russia. Chamberlain flew into a rage when he first heard of the Baku plan. To him the reckless French seemed bent on making certain Germany and Russia stayed allies of a kind. However, an expedition to Narvik or an even larger Scandinavian operation he found appealing. Some action on Europe's periphery that exploited Allied sea supremacy and which might have some fatal economic effect on Germany appeared attractive to him.[20]

Inside the war cabinet the biggest enthusiast for action in the north was the first lord of the Admiralty, Winston Churchill. Chamberlain's invitation to him to join the government had raised Churchill's political stock above other contenders, such as Anthony Eden, for the leadership of the Tory hardliners. It also turned him into a war-making dynamo. Jockeying to grab hold of the entire defense machinery for himself, Churchill drove the chiefs of staff, other ministers of state and the prime minister to distraction with a barrage of memos on all aspects of the war. Chamberlain, who found the boyish delight that his only real political rival derived from the war deeply troubling, took it all in his stride. After all, it was much better to have a politician as popular as Churchill in the cabinet, rather than outside criticizing it.[21]

Like Chamberlain, what attracted Churchill to a Scandinavian expedition was the prospect of turning the slow strangulation of the blockade into a quick thrust at a German jugular. Churchill delighted in clever stratagems, ruses and the whizz-bang of modern military technology. When he became political head of the navy, his first thought was how he could use it to disrupt the German war machine. Major Desmond Morton, Whitehall's head of economic intelligence and one of the fiercest proponents of economic warfare, had briefed him about the critical value of Swedish iron ore to German industry. Churchill's brain teemed with possibilities. The one that caused his naval war planners headaches was equipping a few old battleships with overhead armor shields to deflect Luftwaffe bombs so that the vessels could be safely sent into the Baltic to blockade German ports. More realistically, his mind steadily latched onto the idea of mining Norwegian waters as a precursor to a full-scale expedition. On March 28, the Allies agreed to begin the mining operation off Narvik on April 8.[22]

Before the Norwegian operation, Chamberlain felt optimistic about it, and of ultimate victory. To satisfy the fieriest critics, he reshuffled a few cabinet posts but made no substantive changes to his government or policy. Why should he do more when events would vindicate him? Hitler was "getting madder" all the time and nearly "off his head altogether," yet he had not attacked France. Chamberlain was sure that Hitler had let his moment to strike pass. The Führer "had missed the bus," he declared at a public rally. "To try the offensive [in the west] is to gamble all on a single throw," he wrote in a letter to his sister:

> If he succeeds, well & good: he has won the war. But if he doesn't succeed he has lost it, for he will never have another chance as good. On the other hand his weak points must be clear enough to him. Uncertain morale, insufficient stocks. The former he can maintain by his intensive propaganda & restrictions on information from without. The latter he is seeking to increase by putting every kind of pressure on the neutrals from whom he must draw his supplies and on Russia who has almost everything he wants most, if only he can get it. It is not difficult to hold the Allies on the west and he may well think he has a good chance of wearing out those impatient French, or perhaps stinging them into some rash & foolish adventure before he has to face another winter. That would be a policy with few risks & a fair chance of success, whereas the other is highly dangerous & might well be disastrous. I know which I should choose & therefore can't help believing that he will choose the same.[23]

On April 8, Allied mining off Narvik began. German forces, meanwhile, began an invasion of Denmark and Norway. Months earlier Germany had picked up intelligence about Allied intentions in the north. Urged on by Admiral Raeder, who was eager to secure Norwegian bases for a naval offensive against British shipping in the Atlantic, Hitler ordered a counterstroke to pre-empt the Allies. On April 9, the Germans achieved operational surprise, seiz-ing the initiative from the Anglo-French expeditionary forces with daring paratrooper drops on Norwegian airfields and well-executed seaborne assaults to take the major coastal towns. Allied troops fought hard in the face of Ger-man air superiority but soon retreated northward. Once the battle for France began on May 10, the Allies withdrew from the Norwegian campaign.[24]

In the same way that Finland's defeat had prompted Daladier's downfall, the Norwegian campaign caused Chamberlain's fall. In Parliament some spoke of putting Lloyd George, the all-outer of the last total war, into Downing Street, while others spoke of keeping Chamberlain but widening his cabinet. When Chamberlain defended his record in the House of Commons, Churchill's sup-porters pilloried him. "In the name of God go," one shouted. The opposition benches joined in. Although the prime minister won the confidence vote, too many Conservatives either voted against him or abstained for him to stay on. Chamberlain wanted Halifax to succeed him, but he declined, knowing that the job would fall to the one-man war machine, Churchill.[25]

Back in December 1937 Hitler had prophesied that the arms race would pro-pel Churchill into office by 1942. Germany would then be "in a fine mess!" he said. The Phoney War, like the arms race before it, had sped everything up.[26]

AFTER CONQUERING POLAND and partitioning it with Stalin, Hitler had hoped that the dazzling display of the might of his army and air force would persuade Paris and London to seek peace. On October 6, 1939, he publicly of-fered negotiations and put out diplomatic feelers. Nothing came of them. The Allies rebuffed him.[27]

In Paris, General Gamelin expected the German Army to attack without delay. This was precisely what Hitler had wanted, but the army was in no condition to strike at once. The Polish conquest had exposed flaws in train-ing and command that needed correction before an offensive in the west could start. Ammunition stores, already short before the war, had been de-pleted. Most of the army's divisions had lost up to half of their vehicles in the drive through Poland. Armored units only had light tanks. Newer medium and heavy models were still on order. Most senior commanders, who had warned against fighting a big war too soon, knew that a quick victory in Poland was one thing, but beating France and Britain quite another. "Paying due credit to our Panzer successes in Poland," one officer wrote, "we must nevertheless note that armour has little or no chance of success against the defences [in the west]."[28]

Yet for Hitler, as for the Allies, time was a player in the war as much as any other physical or psychological factor. What he quickly realized was that the Nazi-Soviet Pact and the Polish war had not altered the course of the arms race against Britain, France and increasingly the United States. And so the distinctive language and logic of a fast-receding chance to act filled Hitler's thoughts. On September 27, just back from Poland, Hitler told the army chief, General Brauchitsch, and his deputy, General Franz Halder, that he wanted to move against France fast. "'Time' will, in general," he said, "work against us when we do not use it effectively. The economic means of the other side are stronger. The enemy can purchase and transport [war materials from the United States]. Time does not work for us in the military sense either."[29]

On October 9, even before hearing the response to his peace overtures, Hitler wrote a directive on the strategic situation and set November 25 as the day for the attack on France to begin. In his memo the Nazi warlord described Britain as the historic foe, allied with France to block the rise of a great German Empire on the continent. Now the western armies were growing and their tank and bomber fleets swelling. "Time in this war, as in all historical processes," he noted, emphasizing once again the shifting arms balance, "is not a factor valuable in itself but must be weighed up. As things stand time is an ally of the western powers and not of ours." The victory over Poland offered a chance to fight the west without a threat from the east, he continued. These conditions were fleeting. No deal with Stalin, observed the world-renowned treaty breaker, could last indefinitely. Only military success could keep the Soviets neutral. Military failure would turn Moscow into an enemy. To keep Italy and Japan on board, too, a show of overwhelming military power was essential. The longer the war went on, the more serious the threat of American intervention would become. Hitler understood that France and Britain would wage a long siege. The Ruhr factories had to make war materials at full capacity for the whole of the siege, but Germany was vulnerable to the Allied blockade. The Allies could extend their front by moving into neutral Holland and Belgium and attack German industry from the air. "The longer this war lasts," Hitler predicted, "the more difficult it will become to maintain German air superiority." Losses to industrial capacity could not be replaced. "Surely," he argued, "the less Britain and France can hope to destroy the German army through a series of battles, the more they will strive to create the general conditions for an effective and long lasting war of attrition and annihilation."[30]

On November 23, before a large audience of admirals and generals, Hitler offered the same rationale for an immediate attack in the west: with time the Allies would stockpile armaments and broaden their alliances; Soviet neutrality could not be counted on; the economy was Germany's Achilles' heel; and Italy and Japan would not move until Germany scored a major success. As Chamberlain reckoned, Hitler was forced to choose between a long war that he could not win and a short and perilous one that had a slim chance of success. But he guessed wrong about what choice the dictator would make. Hitler continued on November 23: "It is a difficult decision for me. No one has ever achieved what I have achieved. My life is of no importance in all this. I have led the German people to a great height, even if the world does hate us now. I am staking my life's work on a gamble. I have to choose between victory or destruction. I choose victory." Hitler grasped the stakes. "Behind me stands the German people," he said, "whose morale can only grow worse." If the attack on France failed and the war turned into a long, all-out macroeconomic slugging match, he knew his regime would eventually crumble under the pressure of western armaments and economic strangulation.[31]

Hitler's top soldiers thought that attacking France at once was madness and bound to fail. A paper drafted by the army's deputy chief of staff argued that the army would not be ready to break the western defenses before 1942 (the year Allied war planners predicted they would be ready to attack Germany). The generals tried to persuade Hitler to retract his order to attack in the west, but he doggedly refused. What had begun before the war with Blomberg, Fritsch and Beck, as a political struggle between the generals and the Führer involving the authority over war planning, now evolved into a budding army opposition to Hitler. Officials in the Foreign Ministry, military intelligence and the army command, including Brauchitsch and Halder, began to talk about a coup if the Führer persisted with his "insane" order. Virtually all of these men had supported Hitler when he broke the Treaty of Versailles and turned German rearmament into a fast-accelerating armaments race. Now they faced daunting political consequences and the self-destructive forces they had a few years earlier helped to unleash.

Back on November 5, Brauchitsch and Halder had tried to change Hitler's mind. At the Reich Chancellery the Nazi leader had prepared for them. Brauchitsch told him the attack would end in disaster. The army was not yet equipped and the weather was bad. Hitler would not hear of it. Brauchitsch told him that the morale of the troops was poor in a way reminiscent of 1917–18. That was a loaded statement. In effect Brauchitsch told Hitler that his National Socialist revolution had failed to create a cohesive national-racial community ready for total war. The dictator flew into a rage, revealed that he knew about the conspiracy brewing among the generals, threatened to destroy it and then stormed out of the room. Brauchitsch was severely shaken. "Any sober discussion of these things is impossible with him," Halder concluded. When he got back to his office, Halder, who had been carrying a pistol in his pocket for weeks to shoot Hitler, now shrank from triggering a potentially uncontrollable chain of events that might not just end Hitler's rule but bring down the army as well. He ordered all the incriminating papers burned. The coup plotters, who did not represent a unified body of opponents to Hitler deep in the officer corps anyway, had lost the trial of nerves. At a later meeting, Hitler turned down Brauchitsch's resignation. Bad weather and the need to stockpile munitions postponed the western offensive. Hitler, as it turned out, had to wait until the spring of 1940 before he could take his all-or-nothing gamble.[32]

Germany's top generals did not have a war-winning plan. By stretching the war out until 1942, they probably hoped that a peace deal brokered by the Duce, the Pope or Roosevelt would rescue them. Three years was how long General Thomas, the head of the war economy branch in the armed forces high command, reckoned that Germany could hold out, so long as there were no big offensives and raw-material and foreign-exchange supplies were tightly rationed. Thomas was worried. He believed that Hitler's fixation on a swift battlefield result instead of the hard facts of economics and geopolitics was fatal. Thomas had dedicated his career to averting the sort of no-win situation akin to 1914–18 that the Third Reich now faced. In London and Paris those who interpreted the economic intelligence out of the Reich as disclosing a dire crisis were right. After September 1939 Germany's exports and imports shrank rapidly, the latter down by eighty percent. The Allied blockade was in fact working. Russian imports did not make up the whole shortfall and came at a political and military price. Contrary to the fanciful nightmare scenarios dreamed up in the west about the Germans taking over Soviet factories, oil wells and iron mines to outgun the Allies, Soviet purchasing officers used the leverage they had over resource-hungry Germany to buy up machine tools and blueprints for advanced weapons.[33]

Hitler understood the economic situation and knew what would happen if his gamble did not pay off, but a long war on a shoestring had no appeal. It would mean the slow death of his regime. "All historical successes come to nothing when they are not continued," he declared. Hitler wanted the economy geared up for a big burst of all-out arming, even at the cost of consuming in one shot all the resources to hold out for three years. When Thomas asked General Keitel to speak to Hitler about rationing raw materials and boosting exports to earn foreign exchange, he replied that "the Führer himself has recognised that we cannot last out a war of long duration. The war must be finished rapidly." Others told him the same thing. The "Führer has again emphasised energetically that everything is to be done so that the war can be ended in 1940 with a great military victory," the brilliant engineer Fritz Todt said. "From 1941 onwards, time works against us (USA-potential)."[34]

Years later, after 1945, when scholars picked over the statistics of the German economy during this phase of the war, they noticed a puzzling oddity. Although most foreign observers had assumed that totalitarian Germany was geared up for all-out arms production, arms output in 1939–41 had in fact been surprisingly low. It was not until Hitler made the agile moralist and able architect Albert Speer his arms czar in 1942 that the Reich was fully mobilized and an arms production "miracle" began. Predisposed to find diabolical cunning and Machiavellian genius in everything the Germans did in the military sphere, scholars assumed that something deliberate had taken place. Hitler did not want to deprive Germans of too much of their "butter" to make all the "guns" that he could—so ran the long-accepted explanation—because he feared domestic unrest. Since Hitler could not go for the utmost "guns" to wage all-out war, he had decided instead to seek a swift Blitzkrieg victory in the west.[35]

However, this story was the invention of clever scholars imposing coherence on what had in truth been the unintended consequence of a series of erratic decisions made by Hitler from 1936 onwards in feverish response to, among other things, the ever-spiraling arms race. Hitler had always wanted a total war economy, autarky and guns at the expense of butter, but the reckless turn in foreign policy he took in 1938–39 and the rapid shifts in rearmament priorities undermined that goal.

So did bureaucratic infighting. Thomas was forever complaining about the lack of central control and economic war planning. What had attracted him and his old boss Blomberg to Hitler in the first place was the promise of authoritarian rule over all aspects of German social and economic life for the purpose of arming. Instead of one supreme mobilization machine run by state technocrats (such as himself), various state and party bureaucracies proliferated hydra-like and vied against each other in wasteful turf wars. In Paris and London many top-ranking officials held up the German regime of total mobilization as a model of Teutonic efficiency, worthy of emulation, but the reality fell short of that image. When war came, an administrative dog-eat-dog struggle broke out for control of the German war economy between the Ministry of Economics under Walter Funk, the war economy branch of the armed forces under Thomas and the Four Year Plan apparatus under Göring. Back in the mid-1930s, in their battles with first Schacht and then Göring, Blomberg and Thomas had always wanted the high command of the armed forces to assume control of the economy in war. But Hitler had never agreed to cede that much power to his conservative generals.

Even so, administrative infighting was not the chief reason for the underperformance of German mobilization. For one thing, the untimely arrival of a big war against vastly superior economic forces had undercut the four-year arms plans Hitler had ordered in October 1938. Half-finished arms factories and chemical plants could not make weapons and explosives. Shifting industrial priorities and resources would take many months. Not all of the big industrial projects to achieve autarky could be dropped in favor of immediate munitions output. Even if the first battle in the west was won, no one knew how long the wider war would last. As Germany's foes in the west were also learning, though from different starting points, a highly organized and efficient war economy could not be so organized overnight. In Germany, not only was the chronic lack of raw materials an obstacle to increased production in 1939–40, but so was the shortage of skilled workers. As in France, many skilled men working outside the ring of protected arms firms found themselves in combat uniforms when they would have been better employed expanding the munitions sector. Another key problem was the much-neglected German railway network. In the first months of the war the railways could not cope with moving the army's men and materiel around and feeding the factories with coal and other raw materials to churn out munitions.[36]

After Warsaw fell, Hitler made aircraft (mainly Ju-88 bombers) and ammunition his two top production priorities. Tanks loitered at the bottom of the list. Together, medium bombers and ammunition consumed two-thirds of all the resources going into munitions in the first ten months of the war. Hitler did not want his big gamble to go wrong for want of shells, mortars and bullets. The shell shortages of 1915–16 haunted soldiers everywhere, but the Nazi leader demanded a gargantuan three-and-a-half-fold leap in output. Thomas, among others, including the army's supply officers, wondered where all the steel, copper, propellant and explosives needed to fulfill this impossible target were supposed to come from. The army and armed forces high command bickered over the target and scarce resources, but the supply officers still worked wonders in raising ammunition output from March 1940 on, in time to coincide with the battle for France. That burst of output, however, came too late to placate Hitler, who interpreted the disappointing production figures for February 1940 as the army dragging its feet in executing his offensive.

Thomas expected to be sidelined in the struggle over the war economy if things came to a head over shells. Hitler usually ruled against extending military authority over the economy. Thomas had also upset big business. Although before the war he had made reassuring speeches about business self-regulation and profit as an incentive to innovation, deep down Thomas saw industry as part of the military, chief executives as colonels who should snap to attention and market mechanisms as a nuisance. As in France and Britain, German industrialists defended their autonomy and capitalism from the centralizing impulses generated by total war. The Ruhr barons especially resented the army's heavy-handed intrusions into how they ran their firms and suspected that what the soldiers really wanted was a "military command economy," like the Soviet one. Thomas did nothing to allay these fears when he spoke of abolishing profits. In reaction to the shell crisis, Hitler formed a new Armaments Ministry in March 1940 under Todt. Although big business had not intrigued to get the ambitious engineer appointed, they had made their views well known. The chief artillery designer at Krupp, Erich Müller, had lobbied Hitler during a chance meeting to appoint a new civilian as ammunition czar. Once installed in the new post, Hitler's favorite engineer proved to be entirely amenable to the industrial tycoons. He endorsed the profit motive, backed industry self-regulation and altered the system for raw-material allocation to favor the big corporations.[37]

Although Hitler had decided to attack in the west without delay, he had only a vague notion of what form that offensive should take. In his October 9 directive, he spoke about improving Germany's strategic position by driving into Belgium and Holland, smashing as many Allied divisions as possible and then using newly acquired airfields in the Low Countries to begin a bombing campaign on Britain.

Ten months earlier he had also endorsed Admiral Raeder's huge Z Plan fleet of battleships, cruisers and U-boats as the "solution" to the British problem. But when the European war came, he scrapped all the newly laid-down big ships and canceled the Z Plan. Raeder despaired. He knew the surface fleet was too small to do more than prove its worth by going down fighting. U-boat attacks on Allied shipping, the counter-blockade against Britain, stood a chance of good results, but the sub-surface fleet was too small and the Atlantic too distant to mount a sustained campaign. That was one reason why Raeder was eager to invade Norway before the Allies got there. Hitler, too, turned to the U-boats. Admiral Dönitz, the top-ranking submariner, persuaded him that with a big ocean-going U-boat force he could bring the smug British to their knees.[38]

But before he could unleash bombers and submarines against his arch-enemy, Hitler had to do something about the Allied armies massing in the west. Brauchitsch and Halder cobbled together for him an uninspired plan. The two northernmost of three army groups in the west (A and B) would push into Belgium and engage the Allies. Since the two men hoped to put Hitler off the idea altogether, the last thing they wanted to do was give him a flashy operation that he could get excited about.

After General Erich von Manstein, the chief of staff of Army Group A, read this battle plan, he tossed it aside. Surely Brauchitsch and Halder knew that it would end in a stalemate. But Manstein had a flash of inspiration. Why not push forward with tank and motorized divisions under the command of Army Group A, which was positioned opposite Luxembourg, through the Ardennes forest and then head north toward the English Channel? That way, he thought, Allied armies rushing into Belgium would soon find themselves cut off and encircled by Germans. Punching through the hilly and dense Ardennes would be difficult, but the army's leading tank zealot, General Heinz Guderian, who had fought on that wooded terrain in the last war, assured Manstein that tracked and wheeled vehicles could cross it.

Over the winter of 1939–40 Manstein wrote to Halder about his bold insight. If he was expecting thanks from the chief of army staff, he did not get it. The two had long been professional rivals. Manstein had a reputation in the army as a whizz when it came to operational planning; Halder, who liked to solve math problems to relax, was a relentlessly logical strategic thinker. Before General Ludwig Beck had resigned in 1938 in protest against Hitler's reckless foreign policy, he had been grooming his favorite deputy, Manstein, to succeed him. But after Beck left, the stalwart Halder got his job. Apart from any antipathy toward Manstein, Halder opposed his maneuver for two reasons. First, Hitler, who had made a similar proposal, would jump at it and demand that the army adopt it. Second, even if the breakthrough plan worked, which was unlikely anyway, winning one battle would do little to check the effect of the vastly superior global forces steadily mobilizing against the Reich. General Halder, like Thomas and Beck before him, saw Germany's strategic prospects as bleak.

Halder had Manstein safely "promoted" out of the army group headquarters to command a corps, but word of his plan via some of his admirers reached Hitler. He wanted to hear more. Manstein, along with other new corps commanders, was invited to Berlin to breakfast with the Führer. Afterward, Hitler asked Manstein about his plan. Hitler, who could rarely sit through a military briefing for long without breaking into a tiresome monologue about what he had learned from the last war, sat in wide-eyed silence. The Nazi warlord marveled at Manstein's gutsy talk of speedy panzer thrusts, disorienting feints and deep encircling maneuvers behind the enemy lines to force them to surrender. Manstein's operational maneuver became Hitler's grand strategy, and much as Halder had predicted, the army was ordered to execute it.[39]

The army staff obeyed. Halder even warmed to his rival's idea, later claiming it was in part his own. Manstein's plan was refined, cross-checked with incoming intelligence about General Gamelin's likely opening move once the war in the west began and played out several times on tabletop war games to exhaust every stroke and counterstroke. Few senior army officers expected it to work. Still, everyone agreed, a bold plan with a slim chance of success was better than no plan at all.[40]

As WINTER TURNED to spring in 1940, General Gamelin expected the enemy to come at him via Belgium. Back in 1914, when they had executed their legendary Schlieffen plan, the German Army had attacked France that way. One purpose of the Maginot Line was to make sure that the Germans had little choice but to do the same again.

During the 1930s Gamelin had asked for tanks and trucks to build up a large mobile force to advance into Belgium. Until 1936, while Belgium was still formally a French ally, the two general staffs planned to form a defensive barrier on Belgian soil that linked up the Maginot Line to the North Sea. But that year Brussels declared itself neutral. Secretly, the two armies continued to liaise and exchange plans, but now the French Army was faced with the problem of waiting until Belgium was attacked and Brussels asked for help before it could ride to its rescue. Stage one of Gamelin's operational plan, therefore, became a dash into Belgium to form the most advantageous defensive front he could before the Germans arrived to offer him battle.

Gamelin and his staff considered three potential lines of defense in Belgium. The first, which ran along the Scheldt River through Ghent to Antwerp, was the least ambitious because it would secure only a thin strip of Belgium from the Germans. It was rejected. The second was a front running along the Albert Canal, Belgium's first line of defense. Gamelin did not believe Belgian troops could hold onto it long enough for the Allies to reinforce them, so it too was rejected. The third and prudent choice was the Dyle Line, which ran from Antwerp south along the Dyle River to the Belgian province of Namur, where it would join up with the Maginot Line. If that front could be held, it would leave much of Belgium's coast, its ports and Brussels in Allied hands and provide an excellent jumping-off ground for the Allied armies when they were ready to march into the Ruhr. Forming the Dyle Line became the goal of the Allies, with one crucial addition: Gamelin wanted to push the line much further north, toward the Dutch town of Breda. The Breda variant, as it became known, placed even greater urgency on the headlong rush into Belgium. To execute his Dyle-Breda plan, Gamelin committed thirty divisions, the bulk of his reserve forces, including the crack tank and motorized units of the French and British armies.

On May 10, German forces attacked Holland and Belgium. Gamelin beamed from a sense of relief and real joy. At last, the moment of truth had come. Brussels requested aid, and the Dyle-Breda plan swung into action. Allied divisions raced into Belgium to block what Gamelin expected to be the main thrust of the German Army. Over the next three days his mind remained fixed on the progress of his Dyle-Breda maneuver, while the German breakthrough at the Ardennes unfolded largely unnoticed. By the time the generalissimo and his staff grasped what was happening, like all classic military surprises, it was too late. On May 14–15 the Allies counterattacked and bombed the breakthrough point across the River Meuse at Sedan, but they failed to stop the flow of oncoming German tanks and trucks, which had begun their daring advance northwest in a "sickle cut" toward the sea. It was as though the two foes had each pushed on a revolving door, with the Allies charging northeast into the trap while the German spearhead swept into their rear, surrounding them.[41]

In Berlin the success of the breakthrough astonished everyone. "This is a miracle," Hitler shouted, "an absolute miracle!" Not that everything ran like clockwork, of course. There were plenty of hair-raising episodes. At one point Hitler, in a fit of nerves, actually ordered the armored breakthrough to halt. In Paris everyone was thunderstruck. On May 15 Reynaud called London. "We have been defeated," he told Churchill. The prime minister, long an admirer of the French Army, was for once at a loss for words. "We are beaten," Reynaud repeated tensely, "we have lost the battle." "Surely it can't have happened so soon," Churchill protested. He decided to see for himself. The next day he flew to Paris. At the meeting in the French Foreign Ministry, with the smell of smoke hanging in the air from the bonfires of secret files burning outside to prevent the enemy capturing them, Gamelin briefed the politicians on the state of the battle. A somber silence followed. Churchill asked the generalissimo about his reserves. Surely he could counterattack? All gone, Gamelin replied.[42]

Over the next few weeks French resistance fell apart. Britain evacuated its army and took as many French soldiers as the Royal Navy could from the beaches of Dunkirk, while the German Army closed the ring around them. Reynaud reshuffled his cabinet, bringing in the First World War hero Marshal Philippe Pétain to shore up morale. He also replaced Gamelin with Weygand, who formed a new defensive line along the Somme. The new generalissimo knew that the front would not hold indefinitely, and he feared that if the army collapsed a communist uprising would sweep France. He also expected the politicians to saddle the army with the blame for the catastrophe, when for him the fault belonged elsewhere. "What we are paying for is twenty years of blunders and neglect," he said. "It is out of the question to punish the generals and not the teachers who have refused to develop in the children a sense of patriotism and sacrifice."

On June 10, as the German Army advanced toward the capital and Italy entered the war, Reynaud's cabinet fled Paris. Two days after, Weygand asked for an armistice. Reynaud refused to seek one. He wanted to move the government to the overseas empire and fight from there. Weygand opposed him. The government could not flee, he insisted, without ceasing to be the government. Reynaud resigned. Pétain replaced him. On June 22, an armistice was declared. In July the French Parliament made Pétain dictator. He established his regime at Vichy. Pétain, like so many on the right, saw the defeat as an occasion to cleanse France of the left and begin anew in Nazi Europe. Vichy's leading personalities and backers believed that the defeat was a verdict on the nation's health. France lost because France was decadent. France, unlike totalitarian Germany, had failed the test of war because it was pluralistic, materialistic and soft.[43]

That sort of logic, the most insidious legacy of 1914–18, underlay the politics of the arms race, and not just in France but everywhere. It had been invoked over and over in the corridors of power, in countless intelligence reports and strategic analyses, most often when allegedly lax rearmament at home was compared with all-embracing military, social and industrial regimentation reputedly under way abroad. With the advent of Vichy, the French succumbed to this logic with a vengeance.

GAMELIN, WHO LIKE WEYGAND blamed the politicians of the Third Republic for the debacle to deflect from his own part in it, put the German victory down to the enemy's superiority in numbers, arms and methods. Many at the time and for decades after agreed, but in fact in 1940 Germany did not possess such advantages.

In terms of quantity, the German Army benefited from the delay between when Hitler first ordered his western offensive in October 1939 to May 1940, eight months that gave them the time to acquire more weapons and ammunition, but the Allies still had a broad and fast-growing lead in the numbers of men and equipment when the battle began. In 1940 Germany put 5.4 million into uniform, with three million of them available in the west. France mobilized 6.1 million men; the army had 5.5 million (including colonial units), with 2.24 million of them on the northwest front when Germany struck. By June 1940, Britain had put 1.65 million men into uniform and sent 500,000 of them to France. If the Dutch and Belgian armies are added, then three million Germans, or 135 divisions, faced four million Allies, or 151 divisions. In artillery the Allies had 14,000 guns while the Germans fielded 7,378. The four western Allies likewise outnumbered the Germans in tanks, 4,204 against 2,439. Most surprisingly of all, the Allied air strength was greater too: 4,469 Allied bombers and fighters against 3,578 German aircraft available for combat operations on May 10, 1940.

Turning to the comparative quality of arms, in tanks the Allies come out ahead. The firepower and armor of most Allied tanks were superior to those of Germany. Two-thirds of the German machines were light machine-gun/light-cannon carriers rather than medium and heavy tanks. The French heavy models, the SOMUA and Char Bs, outgunned anything that the Germans fielded. Much to the shock of German infantry, French and British heavy tanks could take multiple hits from anti-tank guns without stopping. German tanks had advantages too, including excellent radios, higher speeds and mileage and better turret designs, all suitable for the offensive—but in tank-on-tank fights the Germans often came off worse. The German Army fielded more modern anti-aircraft guns and had a bigger stock of up-to-date anti-tank artillery. French 47-mm anti-tank guns easily penetrated the thin-skinned German tanks, but in May 1940 they were in short supply. Still, the French proved adept at siting old and new guns together to form strongpoints. German tank crews at times had to dismount to dislodge them. No yawning qualitative gap existed in the air either. The Luftwaffe's ME 109 was better than the French Morane 406 and Potez 63 fighters, but not superior to the Dewoitine 520 or the American-made Curtiss Hawk. The German fighter had the edge on the British Hurricane, but not the Spitfire. Allied pilots proved to be able dogfighters and inflicted heavy casualties on their foes. The latest Allied bombers also compared well with German ones. Britain and France had nothing like the Stuka dive-bomber, but its tactical value has been overstated.[44]

As Gamelin suggested, the German Army may have employed better methods than the Allies. True, the Germans, following Manstein's basic idea, concentrated their tanks, men and planes at a potentially decisive spot with stunning results, but both sides had hoped to do the same. Like the German Army, the Allied Army consisted of a spearhead of elite tank and motorized infantry units with a long tail of second- and third-rate divisions. Gamelin wanted the two spearheads to slam into each other; Manstein planned using the German spearhead to throw the operational equivalent of a sucker punch. Some argue that the German Army had developed a vastly superior doctrine—a way of thinking about operations and organizing and training the army to execute them as one—that gave them an edge in maneuver warfare. The German doctrine emphasized teamwork between tanks and aircraft to break through enemy formations and offered wide scope for low-level initiative; French doctrine, called "methodical battle," emphasized teamwork between infantry and artillery, and when at hand tanks and planes, to fight carefully controlled engagements. Some suggest that the German doctrine reflected the youthful dynamism of the German Army, while methodical battle reflected the blinkered and hidebound mindsets (or organizational cultures) of the Allied generals. That sort of analysis, however, owes much more to the mythology of 1940 than to what in fact happened on the battlefield.[45]

Long before the battle of France, French and British military intelligence had monitored the elaboration of German doctrine. (Arguably, the British Army's tank experiments in the 1920s had inspired both the Germans and the Soviets.) Both armies raised tank units and debated how to use them effectively in cooperation with other arms. In the French Army, methodical battle became the doctrine because it offered the most promising way to blunt attacks from the more numerous Germans, and made the best use of short-term conscripts and France's huge advantage in artillery. When panzer units struck second- and third-rate Allied units (as they did at Sedan), the German doctrine worked brilliantly. When elite Allied formations clashed with the panzers, however, the infantry-artillery teams fought the tank-aircraft teams to a standstill. On May 14–15, when elite French and German units clashed near Gembloux in Belgium, the French doctrine won the day. Even Stuka attacks failed to silence the French artillery. What happened in June 1940—when the Germans regrouped to conquer the rest of France after their successful "sickle cut" and Weygand organized the remaining sixty-two Allied divisions into a fighting retreat—was even more revealing about the two rival doctrines. Rather than a lightning run into the Gallic hinterland, the Germans slammed into a resolute and well-executed defense. French guns took a heavy toll on the Germans, who had to pound away at the so-called Weygand "hedgehogs," dug-in defensive positions bristling with guns.[46]

Even if the panzer chiefs enjoyed a true blitzkrieg moment, it was very brief. During the Second World War the Anglo-American armies and the Red Army developed and perfected doctrines rooted in methodical battle. While brilliant panzer generals such as Manstein continued to do fancy footwork around the battlefields in 1944–45, the Anglo-American armies from the west and the Red Army from the east methodically ground him and his colleagues down to a final crushing defeat.[47]

If the first Brauchitsch-Halder battle plan, which envisaged the German Army storming into Belgium and Holland, had been executed in May 1940, and the two opposing armies had slammed into each other, there is every reason to believe that the battle would have ended in stalemate. If that had happened, there is also every reason to suppose that the Nazi regime would have soon imploded. Perhaps the generals would have deposed Hitler and sued for peace? After all, Hitler knew that he was wagering everything on a single shot. The German war effort might have staggered on for another year or longer, but eventually the long war of attrition would have turned overwhelmingly in favor of the Allies. The collective surge of adrenalin that the French would have enjoyed from blunting the first German onslaught would in all likelihood have strengthened their resolve. It would have also bought them time to organize their war economy with full access to the world's resources.[48]

Yet that was not what happened. Manstein's plan was executed and France fell in six weeks. Still, it could have all gone wrong for Germany. War planners tried to contain and even exorcise the imponderables, but chance as always played a big role in the contest of arms. If Allied intelligence had picked up clues about the German plan or even detected it early enough to foil it, things would have gone differently. The colossal traffic jam of tanks and trucks backed up waiting to punch through the Ardennes presented a superb target for Allied aircraft, for instance, one that they failed to detect. The outcome of the battle hinged on the German breakthrough coming as a surprise. Without knowing it, General Gamelin helped to make his defeat final. Despite warnings from several of his top war planners about the risk he was taking, the generalissimo sent the whole of his mobile reserves, the cream of the Allied divisions, into the Dyle-Breda plunge. Had he held a strong mobile reserve back in France, the outcome of the battle would have been different. In May 1940 Gamelin had also thrown the dice in an all-or-nothing gamble—and lost.[49]

IN LONDON, WHILE THE FRENCH government fled Paris, Churchill's cabinet discussed the future of the war. Should Britain fight on alone? For Churchill, who did not dwell on these sorts of decisions but instead trusted his gut, the reply was a resounding yes. Some members of his cabinet were not so sure. Lord Halifax did not want to take a diplomatic overture to Rome off the table without due thought, especially as Rome's intervention might help the French retrieve something out of their defeat. While discovering what sort of peace terms might be on offer made rational sense, Churchill, who had the support of his predecessor among others in the cabinet as well as cross-party backing in the House of Commons for a long fight against "Hitlerism," opposed even exploring the possibility of talks as the slippery slope into surrender. While the British Army evacuated Dunkirk, he steered the debate his way. The chiefs of staff proved very helpful, and in doing so once more demonstrated the elasticity of military advice. For years the chiefs had solemnly warned that Britain was utterly vulnerable to a German knock-out blow. Now, with Britain's chief European ally defeated, and the coasts of Norway, the Low Countries and France available to Germany for air and U-boat bases, they told ministers that Britain could definitely hold out.[50]

On May 22, 1940, the British government enacted a new emergency law, which gave it full control of "everybody and everything." Now arming went into high gear, the Treasury lost its sway and mobilization would soon become (thanks to a decade of planning and preparations) more successful than Germany's. The *New York Times* proclaimed the change: "Britain Goes Totalitarian—For the Duration." The writer of the article was much less gloomy than the headline. He wrote that the "question whether British democracy can adapt to these new dictatorial methods and survive as a democracy" was difficult to answer, "but the evidence is so far that it can."[51]

In Berlin, Hitler wondered whether the British would now cave in. The shock and awe of his *Blitzkrieg*, as the world's journalists were now calling his triumph, would surely persuade them to come to terms. In Washington, so the German military attaché informed the Nazi warlord, Roosevelt was warning Americans about the peril of a German attack. That was "laughable" talk intended to stir up support for the president's rearmament program. The attaché predicted that it would take at least another year and half before the United States could make any significant progress in building up its arms, and longer than that to pose a significant threat. "Miracles cannot happen," he concluded emphatically.[52]

CHAPTER 16

WARS OF RAPID DECISION?

The fall of France in May–June 1940 shocked the world. In nine months Hitler's armies had conquered Poland, Norway, Holland and Belgium, no small achievements, but defeating France was something else again. The German success must have sprung from some remarkable cause. Since the last war, the accepted wisdom had been that wars to come would be long and grinding macroeconomic slugging matches between thoroughly regimented nations. Now, journalists concluded that military affairs must have been revolutionized. The Nazis had discovered a new "strategy" called "*Blitzkrieg,*" ran the headlines, which combined the demoralizing effects of mass propaganda with the deadly hitting power of tanks and planes. Some well-informed defense pundits recalled what the Italian General Alberto Pariani had announced to the press a few years before: that Italy would wage "*guerre di rapido corso,*" or wars of rapid decision. Perhaps Mussolini had divulged the secret formula for quick battlefield victories to his Axis partner? Hitler later laughed at the idea. "The expression 'Blitzkrieg' is an Italian invention," he joked at a gathering of Nazi insiders. "We picked it up from the newspapers. I've just learned that I owe all my successes to an attentive study of Italian military theories."[1]

Yet the Führer, who always regarded his incredible guesswork and luck as masterful foresight and genius, relished the idea that he had transformed military affairs. Deep down he believed he was a master of war. In May 1940 his generals told him so. General Brauchitsch, the chief of the army, who only a few of months before had been contemplating toppling the dictator, now declared his Führer "the first soldier of the German Reich." Göring was even more gushing: "Adolf Hitler's genius as a warlord caused a revolution in warfare in that it breached strategic principles that had been held sacrosanct until now."[2]

IN THE MONTHS BEFORE Germany attacked Poland, General Pariani, the Italian army chief of staff, had energetically preached his doctrine of wars of rapid decision. With their vast economic strength, the Allies would plan long wars of attrition, he told Mussolini, and therefore the Axis must seek quick decisions on the battlefield through breakthrough and maneuver. Italy's annexation of Albania in April, he added, had opened the Balkans for a lightning war. "If we must go in for brigandage," Pariani told Marshal Badoglio, then "let us do it well!" Yet, as the big war neared and the dire implications of Italy's inferiority in armaments cast doubt on its fortunes as Germany's ally, even the shock-and-awe charlatan himself began to think again. "The theories of rapid war are to be followed technically," he equivocated with a little dexterity, "but we must not lose from view [the fact] that the life of the nation (and therefore of the army) must be assured in case the war might last longer."[3]

Once the war started, Marshal Badoglio, chief of staff of the armed forces and Italy's most famous soldier, lobbied hard for Pariani's removal. Many of his fellow generals found Pariani and all his bold talk of wars of rapid decision unbearable and utterly divorced from reality. With a great-power showdown fast approaching, the marshal considered the man and his ideas dangerous. Badoglio the cunning political operator with a highly developed sense of his own interests verged on the odious, but Badoglio the industrial-age soldier was prudent to a fault. If his long experience of ruthless colonial conquest and European total war had taught him anything, it was that numbers and economic endurance counted most. Italy had neither. No amount of militaristic zest or operational finesse was going to alter the fundamentals.

The marshal had in fact spent the last fifteen years applying the brakes to Mussolini's military adventures. In 1935–36 Badoglio had brought the Ethiopian war, which he opposed, to an end by using overwhelming firepower. Luckily for the Italian leaders, that war did not spark a conflict with France and Britain. In 1939 the Germans started a reckless war against Britain and France over Poland, and he saw no reason to court national disaster for Hitler's sake. He made no secret that he would prefer to fight alongside the Allies against the Germans. The war, Badoglio predicted, would grind on for a few years. Germany would expend tens of thousands of men trying to pound its way into France, if it tried at all. In the meantime, had Italy declared war, it would have been exposed to the full fury of the air and naval forces of the Allies. Fortunately, Mussolini had seen sense and declared Italy a "non-belligerent." As in 1914–15, Italy could join the war at an opportune moment. To convince Mussolini to do so, he made sure the Duce had for the first time in years a clear picture of Italy's armaments. Badoglio exposed Pariani's gross distortions of the operational readiness of the army and those of the air force chief of staff, General Valle. The army lacked everything from boots to anti-aircraft guns; only ten of sixty-six divisions were combat ready; the output of the latest warplanes had fallen behind. The fuel and ammunition stocks of all three services would last only a few months. Mussolini acknowledged the truth of the situation by firing Pariani and Valle. As his new chiefs of the army and air force staffs, he appointed Marshal Rodolfo Graziani, a diehard Fascist, and General Francesco Pricolo, an experienced flyer whose over-hasty procurement decisions would hobble his service. Mussolini hoped that these officers and other new men joining them at the top of the defense and finance ministries would bring a fresh dynamism to rearmament. Badoglio too wanted to arm at top speed, but he did not want the new service chiefs touting "operations not corresponding to reality" to the Duce. "It has always been my concern in [making] preparations," he told them, "to close the doors of the house [first] and then think about [taking] the offensive."[4]

Badoglio's statement captured the sentiment of most ordinary Italians, the elite, including King Victor Emmanuel III, financial and business circles, professional diplomats and the foreign minister, Ciano, who gave a sigh of relief at the declaration of non-belligerency. The Duce's son-in-law wanted to stop Italy falling any further into Germany's orbit. For him the speed with which Hitler and Ribbentrop concluded the Pact of Steel, which had supposedly launched the Axis allies on a four-year timetable of arming, and then plunged Europe into war by invading Poland, warned ominously of Italy's unhappy fate as Germany's junior partner. In the fall and winter of 1939, foreign diplomats and the American Sumner Welles, whom President Roosevelt had sent to Europe on a peace mission, found Ciano railing against the Nazi regime, especially the double-crossing Ribbentrop. He saw no reason to follow Berlin into an unwinnable war against the Franco-British alliance backed by the United States. In his full and vivid diaries, Ciano recorded (with poetic license) a one-man struggle to prevent his father-in-law's expansive ego and lust for war getting the better of his rational calculations.[5]

Observers everywhere expected the Italians to wait until the opening battles of the war indicated a likely winner before taking the plunge. Hitler, who, more than anyone else, praised Mussolini's far-sighted statesmanship, told his generals that Italy would not make a move until the German offensive in the west began. Intelligence about the struggle in Rome for and against prolonged neutrality persuaded officials in Paris and London, too, that Italy's choice would hinge on which way the war went. Some offensively minded naval war planners in the Allied high command had argued that Italy should be preemptively knocked out of the war; but instead the decision was made to exercise economic leverage to keep the Italians in check.[6]

Italy was extremely vulnerable to blockade. Most of its oil, coal, iron, copper, manganese, rubber and other raw materials had to be purchased abroad with scarce foreign exchange and transported by ship. As in Germany, the war caught industrial planners early in a four-year plan of investment in plant, infrastructure and domestic sources of raw materials. As the recently appointed head of war production, General Carlo Favagrossa, pointed out, raising aircraft output demanded large quantities of aluminum; to make 10,000 tons of aluminum consumed 300 million kilowatt hours of electricity; it was no use erecting aluminum factories without building new hydroelectric or coal-burning generators too. Italian industry was also dependent on imported manufacturing technology. Three-quarters of the machine tools that the aircraft makers needed would have to come from the United States or Germany. A modern machine tool industry could not be ordered into existence overnight. Italian autarky was a pipe dream anyway. "We are in the epoch of nations behind walls," Mussolini told his advisers. He was right, and much of what Italy needed to feed a war economy lay beyond the national ramparts.[7]

British officials hoped to curtail Italy's imports to ensure that it was not a back door for supplies into the Third Reich, but they also hoped to coax the Italians toward the Allies by weaning them off their dependence on Germany for coal. Over the winter of 1939-40 British diplomats proposed to the Italians a deal to trade huge shipments of British coal for £20 million worth of Italian arms. In Rome the political implications of a coal-for-arms pact escaped no one. Berlin had already protested about Allied purchases of Italian aircraft. How would Germany react if Italy started to ship more planes, anti-tank guns and ammunition to the Allies, and switched from Hitler to Chamberlain as chief coal dealer? Ciano, reveling in his anti-German mood, kept the British in play, but Mussolini opposed the deal.[8]

Hitler's war confronted Mussolini with a series of stark choices. Like Ciano, he was bitter at the way the Germans had treated them. "Our position is clear," he said, "and it was defined precisely with the Führer. We could not have been ready before the end of 42." He hoped that peace would be restored for a few years and that the arms race would continue as planned. But that illusion, like his belief that he could control the pace of events by dominating the Axis, was dispelled. The Allies refused Hitler's peace offer. At the beginning of October 1939, Hitler wrote to the Duce of his faith in victory. If the war continued, he would not allow the Allies to exploit time to arm. In bleak moments Mussolini was sure that Hitler, who had refused to be guided by the Italian's political wisdom, had squandered their chance to out-arm Britain and France. Germany was certain to lose what would be a long war.[9]

Still neutrality was not something Mussolini considered, at least not openly. As the war trade talks with London had underlined, once the war heated up, the Italian economy would be squeezed viselike between the twin pressures of the Allied blockade and the Third Reich's growing demand for raw materials. Given the choice of becoming an economic vassal of the Allies or of Germany, the Duce decided to stick with the Axis. In February 1940 he told Ciano that he refused to sell munitions to the Allies. In response, he knew, the Allies would cut off seaborne coal supplies from Germany. In March Ribbentrop arrived in Rome with a pledge from the Führer to supply Italy's coal needs via the railway link through neutral Switzerland.[10]

Like most contemporary military theorists, Mussolini believed that future wars would be prolonged conflicts waged by highly regimented or totalitarian economies and societies in control of autarkic blocs. Mussolini spent eighteen years trying to ready resource-poor Italy for the titanic struggles of the future. When the global arms race speeded up in the mid-1930s and left Italy behind, the Duce believed that teaming up with the Germans through the Axis partnership would close the gap with the two empires, the French and the British, that blocked his Mediterranean ambitions. In the meantime General Pariani enthralled him with his "wars of rapid decision." Not all wars would be won with the slow-gnawing action of mass and size, he said, but some with speed and mobility. Preparing to wage a total war after 1942 with Germany against France and Britain on the European continent made strategic sense to Mussolini because, in the interim, if the opportunity arose, he could use his nimble air, land and sea units to win a quick victory in the Mediterranean, North Africa, or the Balkans.

When war came in the summer of 1939, the Italian dictator discovered that his armed forces were not ready for war of any kind. At first he thought he would have a year or more to arm while the great powers slugged it out. "I am accelerating the tempo of military preparations," he reassured Hitler in January 1940. "Italy cannot and does not wish to become involved in a long war; her intervention should come at the most profitable and decisive moment."[11]

What became clear was that Italy could only gear up for one short burst of arming and fighting. In December 1939 General Favagrossa told Mussolini that, assuming the raw materials were available and the arms factories worked double shifts, the army—the least well-prepared of the three services—might be ready by October 1942. For Badoglio that meant being ready to defend

Italy's frontiers, but Graziani, Pariani's replacement, encouraged the Duce's ruminations over a "parallel war" in 1941 or 1942. Either way arming was costly. In 1939–40 arms spending doubled. The demand for raw materials skyrocketed, while foreign currency reserves shrank. And thanks to the scarcity of scrap metal and suitable ore on the world markets, iron and steel output fell. "One must admire the efforts made by the treasury," the dictator remarked. "The most worrying thing is the lack of raw materials." Italy's finance and trade officials had worked wonders sustaining imports through barter agreements, but the situation was not sustainable in a world at war. Raffaello Riccardi, the Duce's new minister of currency controls, worried about the mounting costs of the arms demanded by the service chiefs. Italy needed an export boom to earn foreign currency. A major export that the Allies wanted was arms, but the Duce refused to sell them any.[12]

The matter came to a head in mid-February 1940 at the Supreme Defense Commission. General Favagrossa and the chiefs of staffs presented the Duce with a long list of items in short supply: everything from howitzers and anti-aircraft guns for the army to sandbags for bomb shelters. The men in uniform wanted more money and materials. Italians could live without meat, and they could turn in a lot of their cooking pots for scrap, but soon arms output would stagnate unless more coal, iron and copper became available. Riccardi, as dedicated a Fascist theorist of corporate autarky as ever there was, told the soldiers—and by extension the Duce—that they were living in cloud cuckoo land. To meet the demand for 1940, he explained, Italy would need to import twenty-two million tons of goods costing twenty-two billion lire. Italy did not have the foreign currency, gold or projected trade income to cover anything like that volume of imports. Arming had to slow down. Riccardi and Graziani began to bicker. Badoglio broke in, thanked the currency minister for his candor, and then declared that he too would be candid: "We [the military] must say to the Duce, if this is what is wanted, this is what we need." Annoyed at Badoglio's dig and Riccardi's outburst, Mussolini shrugged off the looming economic crisis. Nations fell because of military defeats and revolutions, not bankruptcy. The Duce said he would spend the entire gold reserve to arm. For years he had been warned about budget excesses, but the state had always managed. He would sell trucks to the Allies, but never guns.

All of his bluff and bluster aside, the Fascist dictator was in no doubt about the implications of his decision to reject the British coal-for-arms deal and Riccardi's warning about the approaching trade crunch. Having spurned the British, he would now have to reckon with an acute shortage of raw materials once stockpiles had been consumed. After that, foreign-exchange availability and the tightening Allied blockade would severely restrict Italian arms growth. Output would probably peak in late 1940 or early 1941. Worse still, once Italy began to fight, stocks of lubricants, liquid fuels and ammunition would be consumed in three months. Joining the war on Germany's side would spell the end of petroleum supplies from Mexico and the United States, and Germany needed all the oil it could get from Russia and Romania.[13]

In January 1941 Hitler would speak to Mussolini (with his decision to attack the Soviet Union on his mind) and confess that he felt like a hunter with only one bullet left in his gun. The metaphor was equally fitting for the Duce's dilemma in early 1940. He would only have one shot. It had to hit the mark, hard and fast.[14]

Looming economic stagnation was the prompt but not the motive behind the Duce's urge to war. History, he declared, would wait for no nation. The revolution had to be speeded up if Italy was to take part in reshaping Europe and if Fascism was going to remake Italians. Without war Fascism would fizzle out. The epoch-making war the Duce craved could only be waged in "parallel" with the Nazi regime. Ciano's diaries record Mussolini's anger at Italians who wished for peace, neutrality and profit. "Have you ever seen a lamb become a wolf?" the Duce asked. "The Italian race is a race of sheep. Eighteen years is not enough to change them. It takes a hundred and eighty, or maybe a hundred and eighty centuries." By the spring of 1940 Mussolini also saw worrying signs that Hitler's revolution was under strain. A long war, he predicted, would ruin the Nazi regime. "I do not understand," he said, "why Hitler does not realize this. I myself can feel that Fascism is wearing out—a wear and tear which is not deep, but is nevertheless noticeable, and he does not feel it in Germany, where the crisis has already assumed rather alarming proportions."[15]

On March 17, a week after Ribbentrop had delivered Hitler's pledge to supply Italy with coal, the Axis leaders met at the Brenner Pass. Hitler did most of the talking. Smoothing over the disagreement between the two regimes about the timing of the war, Hitler explained that the arms race had forced him to act early against Poland. Now he would strike westward and bring the war to a rapid close, probably by the autumn. Mussolini interjected: Did Hitler "really" believe that? Yes, he said. The Führer went on to explain how the war might develop. If his offensive against France brought "the whole western system crashing down," then Italy should attack to deliver a "last blow." If a long war erupted, then Germany would wear the Allies down. Italy could then wait until the final moment to "supply the last ounce which would turn the scales definitely in favour of Germany and Italy." Mussolini asked for three more months to prepare before Hitler attacked France. If the offensive succeeded, he would "lose no time" in joining the fight. If the war became a long one, "then he would wait." Hitler approved. The Führer was prepared either way, though he had to admit "that in the long run the situation would be more favourable for our opponents." Mussolini knew that too. He also knew that Italy's military strength would decline the longer the war dragged on. His one chance to begin a parallel war in the Balkans or North Africa would pass. At the end of March, in a war-planning directive, the Duce confessed to his top commanders that he, like them, considered a "complete French collapse" under the weight of a German attack "very improbable."[16]

Then on April 9, Germany's invasion of Denmark and Norway electrified the atmosphere in Rome. Admiral Cavagnari, who feared that any rash action might put the fleet at risk, urged caution. Badoglio refused Graziani permission to plan for joint Axis operations. He did not want to limit the Duce's options, he said. As the war in Norway raged and Hitler's victory blossomed, attitudes in Rome changed. Mussolini was not the only one who saw fresh opportunities beckoning: the Court, the diplomats, including Ciano, and the military commanders, all now accepted the logic of going for broke. Ordinary Italians, too, favored war. On May 13, three days into the German offensive against France, the Duce told Ciano that he wanted to declare war soon. While Britain evacuated troops at Dunkirk, the Fascist warlord took command of the armed forces. On May 29, Mussolini met with his top-ranking military and diplomatic advisers. Italy could not afford to wait much longer and appear to be taking up arms when there was no risk. The Allies were finished. The United States could not rescue the democracies. The war would be over by September. Badoglio, cautious to the very end, delayed operations until June 10. That day he met with the service chiefs for final orders. "When the guns start to go off," Marshal Graziani told his colleagues with misplaced confidence, "everything will automatically fall into place."[17]

From the start Mussolini's parallel war misfired. The army's attack against the French on the northwest frontier, at great cost in lives, failed to make headway. British bombers struck Milan in the first of many raids against Italy's industrial heartland. As Cavagnari had feared, his battle fleet suffered damage and loss in every encounter with the Royal Navy. Graziani's much-delayed thrust into British Egypt in September 1940 became a rout by the end of the year. Italy's most stunning fiasco came in the Balkans. On October 15, two days after the arrival in Romania of a German military mission to secure the oil supplies, Mussolini ordered the invasion of Greece in order to "restore" the "equilibrium" within the Axis. Ciano was all for what was planned as a blitzkrieg. "With a hard blow at the beginning," the Duce's son-in-law predicted, "it is likely that [Greece] will collapse within a few hours."[18]

Within weeks of the Italian offensive the Greeks launched their own counterattacks that drove the invaders back into Albania. Mussolini's independent parallel war ended. With defeat on all fronts looming, the Duce accepted military assistance from the Germans, who treated their Italian allies as contemptible auxiliaries. As projected, the Italian war economy had geared up for one burst of production and then stagnated for the rest of the war. Still, Italian chief executives, like their counterparts elsewhere, proved very skillful in defending their long-term commercial interests, making weapons for a total war run from Berlin that could not be won.[19]

GERMANY'S DEFEAT OF FRANCE was a triumph for him, but Hitler realized its significance would shrink the longer the war wore on. Time remained a real player. Unable to calm the self-defeating political forces he had unleashed back in 1938 or halt to his benefit the self-perpetuating dynamism of the arms race, Hitler decided to expand the war.

Briefly, during the summer of 1940, Hitler expected the British to recognize his ascendancy in Europe and respond to his offer of peace, but the Churchill government refused to do so. To the extent that the Nazi leader had thought about what would happen after his offensive in the west, he imagined a prolonged campaign of strangulation against the British Isles using U-boats and bombers.

During 1940, Admiral Raeder lobbied Hitler to build up the U-boat fleet. The greater the navy's role in winning the war, he thought, the bigger the (surface and sub-surface) fleet would be after the war. Much to the annoyance of Admiral Dönitz, the U-boat chief, the big surface ships had taken priority when the navy began to rebuild in the 1930s. Most senior officers believed that at the end of the last war the Royal Navy had forever solved the U-boat problem by organizing shipping into convoys and by equipping escort vessels with an amazing new device (later dubbed sonar) that could locate submerged objects. U-boats would be a useful adjunct to the surface fleet, the admirals accepted, but not a war winner.

Dönitz, who refused to believe it, was obsessed with the killing power of his beloved submersibles. To evade sonar and the escorts, he proposed ambushing convoys at night on the surface with groups ("wolf packs") of U-boats to maximize their firepower. In 1939, however, the U-boat force was too small and the Atlantic too far away to make his tactics work. The situation began to change in 1940. With Norway and France under control, the navy had easy access to the ocean. Now what Dönitz needed was hundreds of U-boats and skilled crews to make his packs lethal. Hitler often spoke in favor of U-boats, but he never diverted enough resources to making them quickly enough to overpower the Anglo-Canadian, and later American, defenses. The Battle of the Atlantic evolved into one of the deadliest, most high-tech and dramatic campaigns of the war, but Dönitz (who would succeed Raeder in January 1943) was forever playing catch-up. His U-boat force did expand and become more deadly, but at the same time, thanks to the huge capacity of U.S. shipyards, the Allies expanded their ability to replace shipping losses. The Allies also learned how to use their shipping much more efficiently and how to destroy U-boats a lot faster than Dönitz could replace them and their crews.[20]

In the summer of 1940 Hitler felt that the Luftwaffe had a better chance than the navy of attaining swift results against Britain. Göring boasted that he could attain air supremacy over southern England, and his war planners felt confident about defeating the Royal Air Force. Through the summer and autumn the two air forces battled it out. German bombers first struck British air bases and then in August turned to the industrial cities. The Luftwaffe, however, was not equipped to bomb a nation into surrender with the ease that so many air force zealots had long imagined. From 1943 onward, vast Anglo-American air fleets of four-engine heavy bombers escorted by long-range fighters pounded Germany's cities and industry with 2.5 million tons of bombs—and even that colossal effort alone did not win the war. The Blitz of 1940 came nowhere near that scale of effort. Even the Luftwaffe's much-vaunted Ju-88 carried only about a fifth of the bomb load that the American Boeing B-17s or British Avro Lancasters would later release over Germany.

Even so, for the Luftwaffe the chief goal of the Battle of Britain was not to bomb its way to victory but to master the skies over southern England before a cross-Channel invasion. German bombers attacked to bait British fighters into the air so that German fighters could shoot them down. Both air staffs assumed that the Luftwaffe outnumbered the Royal Air Force, but in reality the two fighter fleets stood roughly equal in August 1940 with about 800 front-line aircraft each. As the air battle heated up, thanks to the greater output of the British aircraft industry and a steady supply of fresh pilots, the balance of attrition swung in Britain's favor. The Royal Air Force's chain of early-warning radars and its efficient command and control system also gave the Hurricanes and Spitfires a defensive edge. By the end of October the loss ratio between the attackers and the defenders was an unsustainable two to one.[21]

The Royal Air Force's stubborn defense deepened Hitler's misgivings about Operation Sea Lion, the plan for the invasion of Britain. German air supremacy over the English coast was essential to successful landings. Admiral Raeder's small surface fleet, which suffered heavy losses invading Norway, could not take on the Royal Navy. The Luftwaffe would have to beat back furious attacks on vulnerable troop transports from Royal Navy submarines, destroyers and battleships. Hitler had hoped that the preparations for invasion alone would persuade London to sue for peace. Briefly, in July 1940, it seemed like a peace party led by Lloyd George was coalescing in London, but Hitler underestimated Churchill's hold on his cabinet. Ultimately, nothing could so abruptly break his winning streak and restore Britain's international prestige than a botched German invasion. The Nazi warlord decided not to run that risk.[22]

If Britain could not be invaded or forced to come to terms, then the war would evolve into a long struggle between opposing economic blocs. In the west, that meant the Anglo-American bloc. The German invasion of Norway and the offensive in the west prompted Roosevelt to speed up his rearmament plans. On May 16, 1940, the president announced in Congress that he wanted to make 50,000 aircraft a year and to spend $1 billion on defense in the coming year alone. A plan to build a two-ocean navy soon followed. In September, Washington and London swapped British bases in the Caribbean and Newfoundland for fifty old U.S. Navy destroyers. The English-speaking nations were not yet allies, and there was still a vocal resistance to American military intervention in the European war, but in Berlin no one doubted that given time Washington and London would unite. The question was not whether but how long it would take for the United States fully to mobilize its potential might.[23]

In 1939, General Friedrich von Boetticher, the German military attaché in Washington, predicted that the United States would take at least eighteen months to two years to begin to rearm in earnest, with tanks and guns lagging far behind ships and planes. General Thomas and his staff predicted eighteen months at the most. One of his key officers, Major Walter Warlimont, who had in 1930 studied at the U.S. Army Industrial College, contributed to an estimate circulated in January 1940 on the potential speed and magnitude of U.S. rearmament. "After about a year or year and a half of industrial mobilisation," the report maintained, American "production capacity in nearly every category of armaments will climb to a level far in excess of all other nations."[24]

If the war dragged on, Hitler knew that any lag in American rearmament of six or twelve months would matter little. In speeches he ridiculed the United States as degenerate, but since the 1920s the capacity of American industry had at once fascinated and horrified him. He sought in his speeches decrying American decadence to allay public anxiety about America's entry into the war. Although Hitler preferred Boetticher's less flattering reports of American rearmament to those compiled by Thomas's war economy staff, there was no escaping the conclusion that the volume of American armaments would sooner or later become crushing. While engaged in trying to wear down the Royal Air Force over the autumn and winter of 1940–41, Luftwaffe planners and their suppliers in industry began to grasp the ominous implications of the nascent Anglo-American air alliance. The British had already taken over all the orders placed by the French with American aviation firms, raising the total earmarked for the Royal Air Force to 14,000 aircraft. What would the air menace in the west be like once American factories got into full swing? Roosevelt's pledge to build 50,000 aircraft a year stunned German Air Force officials working hard—but failing by fifty percent—to raise output to its planned target of 20,000 a year. Some questioned whether the United States could reach its gigantic target from a near standing start, but the American flair for mass production was legendary among European industrialists, especially aircraft makers. Back in the 1930s Dr. Heinrich Koppenberg, the director of Junkers, was not the only one proposing to crank out bombers the way Henry Ford made Model Ts. That lofty dream was the ambition of every air force planner from London to Moscow.[25]

In Berlin everyone agreed that the way to stem the rising tide of Anglo-American arms was to end the war with Britain. But how? Hitler was not the only one with doubts about Operation Sea Lion. The navy was not eager to improvise a major ambitious assault against the world's greatest sea power. The war had cut short construction work on Admiral Raeder's gargantuan Z Plan battleships, but that did not dampen his grandiose ambition for long. The naval staff now dreamed of a maritime empire stretching from northwest and central Africa to Iceland, which would pave the way for an epic struggle for naval mastery against the United States. The way to create that empire was to destroy the Royal Navy forever. "The realisation that America will be our next opponent must urge us on to achieve Britain's total defeat as quickly as possible," wrote one naval planner. Admiral Raeder thus discouraged Hitler from seeking a negotiated peace with Britain that would leave its navy intact. He wanted to use the French Navy to augment the two Axis fleets and unite Spain, Vichy and Italy in a Mediterranean campaign against Britain. The capture of Gibraltar and the Suez Canal, he figured, would knock out the "pivot" of Britain's global empire.[26]

Generals Brauchitsch and Halder warmed to a Mediterranean strategy. They briefly considered extending the war to Russia to preclude an Anglo-Soviet alliance, but they rejected opening a second front. "We can deliver the British a decisive blow in the Mediterranean, shoulder them away from Asia, help the Italians in building up their Mediterranean empire and, with the aid of Russia, consolidate the Reich which we have created in western and northern Europe. That much accomplished," they concluded, "we could confidently face war with Britain for years."[27]

While the army chiefs wanted to keep the eastern frontier with the Soviet Union quiet as the war in the west raged on, Foreign Minister Ribbentrop wanted to ally with Stalin against Churchill. Ever since Hitler made him his roving diplomat, Ribbentrop had dreamed of high-stakes diplomacy, himself the presiding genius decisively tilting the balance of power with the ghost of Bismarck in the background nodding in approval. In June 1935 he thought he had made that alliance in London, but he was wrong. In 1939 the Japanese had frustrated his grand design of a "world power triangle," but his trip to Moscow that summer had stunned the world. Now in the wake of France's fall, he was negotiating a tripartite alliance of Germany, Japan and Italy as a deterrent to Washington. The capper to that treaty (signed on September 27, 1940) would be the formation of an invincible anti–Anglo-American alliance with the Soviet Union.[28]

For Hitler, however, the only solution to his strategic dilemma was the destruction of the Soviet Union. In June and July 1940 he began to talk about it. His logic was simple. "*Britain's hope lies in Russia and the United States,*" he told his generals. "If Russia drops out of the picture, America, too, is lost for Britain, because elimination of Russia would tremendously increase *Japan's power* in the Far East. . . . *Russia's destruction must therefore be made a part of this struggle. Spring 1941.*" Over the next eight months, as the war raged over England, in the Atlantic and the Mediterranean, and the service staffs planned Operation Barbarossa, the invasion of the Soviet Union, Hitler mulled over the alternatives offered by his officials and rejected them. Some fragments of his thinking can be found on the pages of Halder's terse war diary. Air and sea warfare, Hitler told Halder, would take two years to choke Britain. At first he reckoned that American rearmament would not "peak" until 1945, but his estimate changed. Roosevelt's re-election in November made it clear that America would back Britain. American aid had made "the difference" in the air war and it would rise "significantly" in 1942 and after.

Russia was "the great problem of Europe." The sooner the Soviet Union was destroyed the better. The men in the Kremlin were cunning, but the Red Army was brittle and its commanders inept. Finally, in March 1941, in front of a large audience of generals and admirals, Hitler repeated that his goal in attacking Russia was to dash Britain's hope of American and Soviet alliances. "If England manages to hold out for 1–1.5 years," the Nazi warlord predicted, "then America's help would be effective. We would then need air force (anti-aircraft) and navy, battleships too."[29]

The upshot of what Halder and others scribbled in their notepads was that Hitler feared that if he sat tight and waged a siege in the west, Germany would in time be squeezed. Moreover, if the situation continued unbroken, the country would eventually be crushed between the west and the east. He had to take the initiative while there was time, as he had done against France, with the most hard-hitting weapon at hand—the army.

From that angle it mattered little whether Stalin intended to squeeze Germany, but that he could. That sort of analysis was logical and consistent with a whole grisly chain of thinking that stretched back to the trenches; it was logical and consistent with the ideas of future war that underlay the arms race; it was logical and consistent with increasingly raised states of military readiness and expanding total war that prompted aggression, inflamed world tension and, in an appalling degradation of civilization, rendered thoughts of preventive war logical and consistent.

In August 1939 Hitler and Ribbentrop had hastily concluded the Nazi-Soviet Pact to clear the way for the war on Poland. The initial pact was followed by a series of deals on the demarcation between the two respective spheres of influence, from the high north to the Balkans, and on trade. To Hitler and many of the men around him, Stalin's war with Finland, Soviet territorial demands on Romania and the tightening of the Soviet grip on the Baltic states looked like jockeying for an edge against Nazi-occupied Europe. "Every weakness in the position of the Axis brings a push by the Russians," Hitler said. "They cannot prescribe the rules for transactions, but they utilize every opportunity to weaken the Axis position." Stalin was in fact eager to supply Hitler with the raw materials he needed. Yet Hitler, who was remarkably unaware of his own duplicity, was quick to see it in others, even when it did not exist. Although Germany now dominated the western European economy and began to organize it to its benefit, the Nazi "new order" was not a blockade-proof bastion for waging trans-Atlantic total war. Food and fuel were its two critical weaknesses, and the Soviet Union, in the form of Ukrainian grain and Caucasian oil, was its principal supplier. Hitler resented the leverage that Stalin had over him. It irked him and his military and economic planners when Soviet officials requested in exchange for raw goods advanced German machine tools, weapons designs and the secret processes for making synthetic fuel and rubber. Ribbentrop's big idea of an autarkic Eurasian alliance with the Soviet Union had a geo-strategic allure, but Hitler was not going to swallow it. When Molotov arrived in Berlin in November 1940 for talks, Stalin's bullish deputy replied evasively about aligning with Germany against Britain. That ended talk of an alliance.[30]

Weeks after Molotov's visit, Hitler ordered preparations for Operation Barbarossa to begin, all dutifully recorded by Halder. What the army chief of staff's diary and other papers did not always fully document was the pseudo-scientific biological racism that laced Hitler's reasoning for the turn eastward. The soldiers always noted the more mechanical elements of strategy—force comparisons, statements of goals, means and troop dispositions and so on—that typically filled the pages of their war plans and strategic estimates. Everyone by now was familiar with the Nazi warlord's Manichean vision of world politics, the need for a pure race and vast space, how Germany was locked in a titanic fight against "Jewish-Bolshevism" and how Roosevelt and Churchill acted as the stooges of a diabolical "international Jewish conspiracy" against Germans. On paper the military side of strategy could be extracted from Hitler's wider vision and goals, the stuff of *Mein Kampf,* but in flesh and blood they were indivisible. Each offered intellectual justification, direction and legitimacy to the other. That was one reason why when Hitler ordered that Barbarossa should be conducted with extreme savagery toward Jews and commissars, the generals and admirals were not shocked or especially moved. Barbarity of that sort had started with the war in Poland. Hitler wanted it to continue with much greater dynamism, one that would in time culminate in the industrial-scale mass murder of millions of European Jews, Gypsies, communists, homosexuals and others.[31]

Brauchitsch, Halder and the other officers who carried out Barbarossa accepted it as a pitiless war of conquest. Unlike the attack on France, they also planned it from the start as a gigantic blitzkrieg. Opening a second front in the east troubled the army high command—Halder questioned whether London would give up just because Moscow fell—but if Russia could be smashed in weeks, then the division of resources between two fronts would be brief. "Now we have shown them what we can do," Hitler told his chief of staff after France fell. "Believe me, Keitel, a campaign against Russia would be child's play compared to that." The generals, who had once dismissed the Führer as a military crank, now believed him. Perhaps with the fast panzers and screaming dive-bombers, they wondered, warfare had indeed been revolutionized. God was not on the side of the big battalions, but on the side of the most maneuverable ones. Barbarossa reflected this hubris. The attack would be launched as a surprise, with the aim of smashing the Red Army in weeks. The enemy would not be allowed to withdraw and trade space for time, but instead would be encircled and crushed with three huge panzer thrusts. Everything hinged on speed. Everyone knew that they could not afford to let an eastern blitzkrieg become a long war of attrition.[32]

German estimates of the size of the Red Army and its arsenal of tanks and planes varied, but there was no doubt in Berlin that Russia had been arming at full tilt for a decade and that the Germans faced a massive foe, though much of its equipment would be dated. Systematizers of total war like Blomberg and Thomas had long admired the Soviet multi-year arms plans. Hitler's Four Year Plan of 1936, after all, was an emulation of the Soviet model. Yet the German attitude toward Russia was a jumble of admiration, loathing and contempt. Hitler watched with dread the newsreel footage of tanks, guns and planes during the victory parade in Moscow after the Finnish war, but the Red Army's poor showing in that war and the purge of the officer corps two years before had helped to convince him that the time was ripe to shatter the "clay" colossus. "The Russian is inferior," he said in December 1940. "The internal restructuring of the Russian army will not be better in the spring. [By then] we will have a perceptibly better position in leadership, materiel, troops, while the Russians will be at an unmistakably low point. Once the Russian army is beaten, then disaster cannot be forestalled." Hitler's dismissive views matched that of his top war planners. Like him they ignored the Red Army's superior performance against the Japanese in Manchuria and believed that inferior Slavs could never execute the sort of complex tank maneuvers that officers like Tukhachevsky had advocated. The Russian soldier would be tenacious in the defense of his homeland, army intelligence confidently reported, but the army as a whole would shatter after a few hard blows.[33]

General Thomas questioned the immediate payoff of conquering the Soviet Union, which would disrupt Soviet deliveries of raw materials. In early 1941 he wrote a stinging memo for Hitler on the topic, but he changed his mind months before the attack was due to begin. Ever since Todt's appointment as armaments minister, Thomas had lost ground in the economic turf war. The arms czar had rejected military control of industry and instead favored a sort of freewheeling, self-regulating and profit-seeking corporate imperialism that would run wild in western Europe. In February 1941 Thomas learned from Göring that the Führer planned to liquidate the Soviet elite and appropriate their factories, farms, iron ore mines and oil wells. As head of the Four Year Plan, Göring intended to take over the Soviet state-owned economy, and he wanted the general's help. In exchange, Göring offered Thomas and his economic planners a big role in running the Third Reich's new command economy of the east. The temptation for the guru of total war economy was too much. Thomas dropped his reservations and penned a fresh memo for Hitler. If the whole Soviet economy could be captured intact in the Blitzkrieg, he wrote, then Germany would have everything it needed (food, fuel, steel and arms plants) to win the coming world war.[34]

While General Thomas's heart raced at the thought of untold resources and centralized command in the new war economy of the east, the existing one in the west restructured itself to meet Hitler's latest set of production priorities: tanks, guns, half-tracks and U-boats. From July 1940 to June 1941, the month that Operation Barbarossa was to begin, the army doubled its panzer divisions to twenty. The output of medium tanks matched that jump in divisional strength. The rate of artillery and machine-gun output rose. U-boat assembly tripled. Ammunition production, the priority before France fell, was run down and the resources spent elsewhere. Existing stocks would be enough for a blitz into Russia. This burst of output was a real success for an economy that still needed to allocate scarce resources to exports to earn foreign exchange, which had to demobilize thousands of men from the army to work in factories, and which had already squeezed civilian consumption tight. And, at the same time, a big investment boom got under way to expand the capacity to make synthetic rubber, fuel, explosives and most of all aircraft. Once the Blitzkrieg was won, all resources would be shifted over to the war in the west against the Anglo-American bloc. A few days after Operation Barbarossa began, on June 26, 1941, General Milch, once again in charge of the Luftwaffe after a brief spell out of Göring's favor, told the armed forces high command that intelligence disclosed that Britain and the United States were already making more aircraft than the Axis by a large margin. At the current rates of expansion, he explained, the western Allies would be making twice as many aircraft as the Axis by the end of 1942. To counter this growing threat, German production needed to jump by 150 percent. "There is no time to lose," he emphasized.[35]

IN THE PERIOD BETWEEN the Nazi-Soviet Pact and the German attack on France, Stalin had every reason to believe that time would now be working for him. It appeared that the crisis of capitalism that had begun with the

Great Depression and erupted a decade later in the "second imperialist war" would engulf Europe for years, but would leave the Soviet Union untouched. Eventually, the dying capitalist world would lash out against the vanguard of socialism, but there was time enough to get ready for it.

Not only had the pact with Hitler bought time, it had also won Stalin territory. As Warsaw fell to the Germans, the Red Army moved into eastern Poland, up to the dividing line agreed with Ribbentrop weeks before. Lithuania, Latvia and Estonia came under Moscow's thumb. Further advances could be made to the northwest to shield Leningrad, a key military-industrial center, and to the southwest, toward the Bosporus Straits, the entry point for potential attackers into the Black Sea. The territorial and political gains made in Europe coincided fortuitously with a crushing victory over the Japanese Army on the Mongolian-Manchurian border.

Back in early May 1939 a detachment of the Kwantung army and Manchurian troops had crossed into Soviet-backed Outer Mongolia near a village called Nomonhan, east of the Khalkhin-Gol River. This border clash followed the usual pattern. Moscow issued a diplomatic warning; the Japanese cabinet and general staff in Tokyo urged caution, but the hotheads in the headquarters of the Kwantung army recklessly raised the stakes by committing more men, tanks, guns and aircraft; Stalin resolved to break them. In June, Georgy Zhukov, a forty-three-year-old son of a peasant, who had been swiftly promoted up the ranks because of his tough-minded and audacious style of leadership, took command of the Soviet forces in the region. After reinforcing his battalions with additional guns, aircraft and tanks, especially the first batches of the superb T-34 medium tank, the bullish Zhukov launched a massive surprise attack that integrated air and artillery bombardments with powerful tank and infantry thrusts along a wide front. By mid-September the beleaguered Japanese forces, stunned by the intensity of Soviet firepower, had suffered a crushing defeat, with casualties of about 18,000 men. The Kwantung army never challenged the Red Army again.[36]

Stalin's euphoria over this victory was brief. In an effort to strengthen the Soviet Union's northern borders, Soviet diplomats demanded territorial concessions from Finland. After weeks of talks, the Finns refused to budge and mobilized. At the end of November Stalin ordered an invasion. He expected a quick result, but the battle against the Finns turned into a David-versus-the-Red-Goliath headline-grabber that would have dragged Russia into the European war had certain French and British war planners got their way. The Red Army's offensive involving over a million of its soldiers bogged down immediately. The main attack in southern Finland ran into powerful fortifications protecting the narrow Finnish position across the Karelian Isthmus know as the Mannerheim Line. Attacks further north encountered stiff and spirited Finnish Army resistance in severe winter conditions. In February 1940 the Red Army concentrated more divisions in the south, including additional tanks, guns and bombers, and penetrated the Mannerheim Line. The Finns, who had inflicted over half a million dead, wounded and missing on the invaders, sued for peace.

In retrospect, what was amazing about the Red Army during the Finnish war was that, despite a savage casualty rate of sixty percent, it held together as a cohesive and resolute fighting force. That, and the Red Army's performance at Nomonhan, should have been a warning to any would-be attackers. But the Kremlin, the German Army staff and above all Hitler did not read the winter war that way. Everyone agreed, something was wrong with the Red Army. Stalin knew he needed to fix it immediately, but time was still on his side. The war in western Europe would trundle on for a couple of years yet.[37]

Kliment Voroshilov, the vainglorious defense commissar and one of Stalin's closest comrades, became the fall guy for the Finnish fiasco. At the Communist Party Central Committee of March 28 he read out a list of the army's failings, dripping with self-reproach. When Stalin spoke, he praised the fighting men but berated their leaders for shoddy equipment, poor training and inept planning. In April, days after Germany invaded Denmark and Norway, Stalin led an inquiry into the conduct of the Finnish war. For four days he grilled unit commanders about every aspect of the campaign. At the end, he summed up. The Red Army was not ready for a modern war of massed artillery, aircraft and tanks. Still, he concluded on an upbeat note, the war had been won and errors could be corrected. The Red Army did not just defeat the Finns, he said, "we have defeated their European teachers: we have defeated German defence equipment, we have defeated English defence equipment; we have also defeated French defence equipment. We have defeated not only the Finns but also the equipment of the advanced states of Europe. Not only the equipment of the advanced states of Europe: we have defeated their tactics, their strategy." Shortly afterward, Stalin demoted Voroshilov and replaced him with one of the few senior officers who had distinguished themselves during the invasion of Finland, Semen Timoshenko, a dedicated professional with a knack for offering the dictator useful military advice without challenging his absolute authority.[38]

In early May, while Timoshenko settled into his new post, events took a sharp and unexpected turn. German tanks broke through the French defenses in the Ardennes and executed a daring encircling maneuver. Within weeks the

British Army retreated across the Channel and France capitulated. Stalin was thunderstruck. What had happened to the French? They should have been able to hold out for at least a year or two. If the Germans could smash advanced armies such as those of France and Britain in weeks, what would they be able to do to the Red Army, which, as his own inquest into the Finnish campaign had amply shown, was not ready for modern war? All his fine words about having defeated the arms and strategy of the advanced states now seemed like a colossal conceit. As he absorbed the news of Hitler's Blitzkrieg, Stalin cursed. He yelled that Hitler would "beat our brains in." Time was now short. The Soviet defense machine geared up for an all-out effort. Industrial planners tore up their old industrial mobilization plan, which had not been fulfilled anyway, and drafted a new, more gargantuan one. Industry adopted an eight-hour workday, seven days a week. Output of the latest tanks and aircraft rose. In July–August overall munitions production shot up by an incredible thirty-eight percent. In September civilian factory managers received four weeks' notice to reorganize their production plants for "the delivery of arms [requirements] in full."[39]

The predilection of Soviet intelligence to inflate the German military threat became even more pronounced in the months after France fell. In August–September 1940 the Red Army estimated the strength of the German Army at 240 divisions, with about ninety-four of them near the Soviet Union. In fact, at that time the German Army only had about 140 divisions, with only sixty-six of them located in the east. Soviet officials, who like everyone else attributed the Blitzkrieg to a crushing superiority in the air, put the Luftwaffe's strength at 13,000–14,000 aircraft, or four times its actual size. That threat would only grow. Soviet officials who had toured German aircraft plants at the end of 1939 wrote gushingly of the Luftwaffe's advanced industrial processes and the quality of German aircraft. Now with all of Europe at the Germans' disposal, German aircraft production would go into high gear. According to a report by top-ranking Soviet air force officers, "The German aviation production industry has switched over to assembly line production, replacing the existing piece-by-piece production method. The quantity of output of aircraft by the beginning of 1941 will be approximately 20–24,000 aircraft a year, compared to 12–15,000 a year as observed during our first [tour of Germany] in 1939. Considering the exploitation of the aviation industries of Poland, Czechoslovakia, France and Holland, the output will constitute at least 30,000 aircraft a year or 100 aircraft a day." During the entire war German aircraft output only reached that level in 1944, and in all of 1941 total production amounted to only 10,000 machines. Significantly, Soviet aviation planners believed that Germany had the edge in the Battle of Britain. "We conclude," they wrote, "that British aircraft are inferior to German ones in combat quality and especially in the complexity of their construction and suitability for mass production."[40]

No one in Moscow could be certain about how long the air war over England would last, and whether it might end in an Anglo-German alliance aimed at the Soviet Union. Stalin hoped to manipulate international affairs much as he had always done, through diplomacy and deterrence. To deter attack, he needed to buy time to come out ahead in the intensifying arms race against Germany, and that meant making the Nazi-Soviet Pact work for as long as possible. While Hitler consolidated his hold in the west and Mussolini joined the war, Stalin shored up his sphere of influence in eastern Europe within the terms of the pact. In June 1940 the Soviet Union annexed the Baltic states. A month later Moscow bullied Romania into ceding the territory of Bessarabia and part of Bukovina. These moves rankled Berlin. Meanwhile, German military aid to Finland, the German Army mission to Romania, Italy's attack on Greece, German-Italian intrigues in Bulgaria, Hungary and Yugoslavia, German delays over the sale of advanced armaments technology to the Soviet Union and the Axis alliance between Berlin, Rome and Tokyo of September 1940, all raised eyebrows in Moscow.

In October 1940 Ribbentrop wrote to Stalin inviting Molotov to Berlin for negotiations. Hitler's top diplomat hoped the visit would be a first step toward his anti-British "world triangle," in which the Führer showed very little interest. Stalin saw the Berlin talks as a chance to discover the "real intentions" of Hitler and his allies by pinning him down on the specifics of their mutual relations, on everything from Bulgaria's fate to peace in China. Just before Molotov was due in Germany on November 10, Stalin scolded his advisers. One must be ready to learn constantly, he told them. "People are not studying the lessons of the war with Finland, the lessons of the war in Europe. We beat the Japanese at Khalkhin-Gol," he said. "But our aircraft proved inferior to the Japanese aircraft for speed and altitude. We are not prepared for the sort of air war being waged between Germany and England. . . . If in the future our armed forces, transport, and so forth, are not equal to the forces of our enemies (and those enemies are all the capitalist states, and those which deck themselves out to look like our friends!), then they will devour us." The negotiations in Berlin on November 12–14 ended in a chill. Ribbentrop tried to convince Molotov that Russia should join in carving up the defeated British Empire by pushing its frontiers into India and to the Persian Gulf. While the two diplomats took shelter from a night raid by Royal Air Force bombers, Stalin's right-hand man pressed his host for concrete answers about the boundary between the expanding German and Soviet empires in the Balkans, as well as the Soviet Union's wish to dominate the Bosphorus Straits. After Molotov returned home, Stalin gave his verdict on the Berlin talks. "It is incorrect to regard England as beaten," he said, refuting Ribbentrop's boasts. "Our relations with Germany are polite on the surface, but there is serious friction between us."[41]

While the preparations for Operation Barbarossa took shape in Berlin over the winter and spring of 1940–41, Stalin convinced himself that Germany could be kept at bay for another two years or longer, in other words long enough to repair the Red Army and expand Soviet armaments. Mobilization planners drew up a scheme to field a wartime Red Army of over eight million men organized into 300 divisions, sixty armored and thirty motorized, and an air force of 13,000–14,000 aircraft. Though the plan was totally unrealistic, at the time the planners thought that it could be achieved by 1942. In the meantime Stalin had no intention of being intimidated by or yielding to Germany in the Balkans. Much, he thought, would hinge on trade, which was the core of the Nazi-Soviet collaboration. In exchange for blueprints and machine tools for the Soviet arms industry, Stalin offered Hitler the raw materials he needed to wage war in the west. After May 1940 he cranked up shipments to appease Berlin, even though German deliveries of industrial goods had fallen behind. Once Britain's determination to fight on with American economic assistance became clear, Stalin believed that Hitler would never recklessly launch a two-front war, especially at the risk of disrupting reliable deliveries of raw materials from the Soviet Union.[42]

For that reason above all else, warnings from Soviet spies about the coming German attack and the build-up of German divisions in eastern Europe in the spring of 1941 did not rattle Stalin. He regarded warnings from spies, and overflights of Soviet territory by Luftwaffe reconnaissance planes, as provocations inspired by anti-Bolshevik hawks around Hitler, above all the German Army, or British secret agents attempting to sow tension between Berlin and Moscow. In March 1941 General Filip Golikov, Stalin's compliant head of army intelligence, dismissed a list of accurate intelligence about Operation Barbarossa that way: "I consider that the most likely date for the beginning of [German] actions against the USSR will be the moment of victory over England or the conclusion of an honourable peace for Germany. Rumours and documents speaking of the inevitability of war this spring against the USSR must be rated as disinformation coming from the English or possibly from German intelligence." Stalin only ever trusted his own judgment.

When Churchill wrote to him in April about Hitler's plan, he waved the letter away as a devious trap to drag Russia into the war. He may well have also reckoned, as the British Joint Intelligence Committee did until early June, that the transfer of German infantry, tanks and planes to within striking range of Russia was aggressive posturing intended to influence upcoming diplomatic and trade negotiations.[43]

By the start of May, Stalin's biggest worry was not the mounting reports of a German invasion but the thought that his soldiers would come to regard a blitzkrieg a year or two in the future as unstoppable no matter how well armed the Red Army was. At a Kremlin reception for 2,000 newly trained officer cadets, he decided to counter that kind of defeatism by giving them a "pep talk" before they joined their units. In an unforgettable performance, he told the young officers that in the last three years the Red Army had turned itself into a "modern" force armed with the best tanks, guns and aircraft. "Why was France defeated? Why is Britain suffering defeat, while Germany is victorious?" For Stalin the answer was simple. Since 1919 the French and the British had "rested on their laurels, . . . dizzy" with success. That overconfidence prevented them from modernizing as the Germans had done. "Is the German army really invincible? No. In the world there are not and have not been invincible armies. . . . From the military point of view there is nothing special about the German army in terms of tanks, artillery and aviation. . . . Besides, the German army has become boastful, self-satisfied and conceited. The military thought of Germany is not going forward; its military equipment is falling behind not only ours, but in terms of aviation Germany has even begun to be overtaken by America." A general proposed a toast to "Stalin's foreign policy of peace." The Soviet dictator corrected him. Peace was good because it bought time to rearm and reorganize the army: "We have up to now carried out a line [based on] defence—up until the time when we have reequipped our army, up until the time we have supplied the army with the modern means of battle. And now, when our army has been reconstructed, has been amply supplied with equipment for modern battle, when we have become strong, now it is necessary to go from defence to offence."[44]

Stalin's offensive-mindedness pleased his two top soldiers, Timoshenko and the rising star Zhukov, who had been promoted to army chief of staff five months before. When Timoshenko became defense commissar in May 1940, he was surprised to learn that there was no up-to-date operational plan for war in the west. The existing draft of 1938 envisaged a powerful offensive counterpunch against a German-Polish attack either north or south of the Pripiat' Marshes, a vast area of impassable wetlands straddling the Belarus-Ukrainian frontiers. This kind of offense-is-the-best-form-of-defense thinking reflected the kind of "deep battle" that Tukhachevsky and others had advocated. Staff officers now penned fresh drafts: one emphasized a prudent northern thrust into Poland, but that would come up against tough terrain and defenses; another envisaged a more daring southern thrust out of the Ukraine into Poland that would outflank and encircle the main body of German attackers.

In October 1940 Stalin endorsed the second option. "Defence is really useful only when it is a means for the organisation of an offence," he told Timoshenko, "and not as an end in itself." In January 1941 the high command held table-top war games attended by Stalin to test-run the northern and southern offensives in reply to a German invasion. At the games Zhukov gave a great performance as both the attacker and defender. He had already come to Stalin's attention for winning at Khalkhin-Gol (Nomonhan). Now he was the Soviet dictator's first candidate for the post of army chief of staff.[45]

Zhukov's promotion came as a surprise. As a combat leader, no one disputed his talents, but not many rated him as a military thinker. Aware of his limitations, he in fact tried to turn down the job, but Stalin insisted. Now, like soldiers the world over, the Red Army's new chief of staff struggled to grasp what had occurred in western Europe the summer before. Why had France imploded so quickly? Future war, as Red Army theorists had always envisaged it, would be a long drawn-out, macroeconomic slugging match. Vast tank and motorized armies supported by bomber fleets would operate with great speed and depth on future battlefields, but war would still be a grueling test of all-out economic mobilization and endurance. But perhaps the Germans had found a way to escape what for them was the death grip of a long war? Blitzkrieg, some argued, was invented by the fascist states of Germany, Italy and Japan because, unlike the Soviet Union, they lacked the raw resources to achieve autarky.

Because intelligence estimates inflated the size of Hitler's army and air force by three and even four times their actual strength, Timoshenko and Zhukov feared that the Germans might try to win a blitzkrieg against them sooner rather than later. "War," Zhukov told his fellow generals, "must be conducted in light of real possibilities. The German successes in the West, based on the massed use of tanks and motorised troops and aircraft, give much food for thought. Unfortunately, we do not yet have such large operational mechanised formations. Our mechanised corps are still at the embryonic stage. Yet the war could break out at any moment. We cannot make our operational plans on the basis of what we'll have in a year or two. We have to work with what our border units have at their disposal right now."[46]

Not surprisingly, Zhukov's first war plan, of March 1941, was a bold version of the sweep out of the Ukraine into southern Poland, as endorsed by Timoshenko and Stalin, a large-scale encirclement similar to what the Germans had performed against the Allies in 1940 in the Ardennes. According to his plan, "The most suitable is a deployment of our main forces to the south of the Pripiat' so that they can by means of powerful blows towards Lublin, Radom, and Krakow, set themselves one strategic objective: to defeat the main forces of the Germans and in the very first stage of the war to cut Germany off from the Balkan countries, to deprive it of its most important economic bases, and decisively influence in the Balkan states." Once the main body of the German Army had been crushed, the second stage of the war could develop with a deep thrust toward Berlin, Prague or Vienna. The Germans might gamble on an eastern blitzkrieg, but they would in fact fall victim to a Soviet one.[47]

On May 5, two months after Zhukhov wrote his first plan, he and Timoshenko had attended the Kremlin gala for the bright-eyed officer cadets at which Stalin made his rousing speech about offensive war. The planners took the supreme leader at his word. The Germans might try to impose a rapid decision upon Russia with a blitzkrieg: a rapid counteroffensive had the potential to do exactly the same to them. But until now every plan had assumed that the German attack would be under way before the Red Army launched its knockout southern thrust. Why wait, Zhukov wondered? The best time to hit the Germans with the utmost surprise, after all, was while they were marshaling for but not yet ready to begin an attack, not when they crossed the frontier. "Bearing in mind that Germany is holding its army in a state of mobilisation with fully deployed rear echelons, Germany has the ability to anticipate us in deployment and inflict a sudden blow," he wrote. "So in order to prevent that and to defeat the German army I consider it necessary that we should not under any circumstances surrender the initiative to the German high command." With Timoshenko's support, Zhukov drafted a fresh plan that envisaged a "concealed" mobilization in expectation of a German invasion and then a devastating pre-emptive blow to pave the way into Europe. Tukhachevsky, had he lived, would have stamped his seal of approval on what was quintessentially a bold "deep operation."

According to Zhukov, when on May 15 he and Timoshenko took the plan to Stalin, he flew into a rage. "Have you gone mad? Do you want to provoke the Germans?" Stalin growled. The two officers pointed to the ominous build-up of German forces near the frontier. Something had to be done to counter the threat. They referred to Stalin's speech ten days before. "I said that in order to encourage the [officer cadets] there," Stalin snapped back, "so that they would think about victory and not about the invincibility of the German army, which is what the world's press is blaring on about." Timoshenko recalled the unpleasant scene even more vividly. After Stalin called him a warmonger, Zhukov lost his composure and had to leave. As Stalin stormed out of the room he warned Timoshenko that "heads will roll" if the high command did anything to "provoke" Berlin or moved units without his permission.[48]

The preemptive strike was shelved. With the Red Army undergoing a massive overhaul, it was not ready to deliver such a blow anyway. As Zhukov later admitted, with three years of epic tank battles against the likes of General Manstein behind him, the May 15 plan was a fanciful piece of military thinking.

In the final weeks before Hitler ordered Operation Barbarossa to begin, Stalin remained convinced that time was once again on his side. In April he had negotiated a neutrality pact with the Japanese foreign minister, Matsuoka Yōsuke. Germany would not attack unless provoked or until a final settlement with Britain had been reached. Otherwise the war in the west would rage on for a year or two. He was not blindly trustful of the Führer but instead misjudged his capacity for recklessness. Still, in May–June 1941, Stalin approved the call-up of 800,000 reservists and took other precautions against a German invasion. Zhukov and Timoshenko warned him that the Red Army was dug in too close to the border for its own good, but Stalin opposed major redeployments for a defense in depth. Meanwhile, trainloads of grain and petroleum moved westward, and Soviet industrial planners requested eighty-five million rubles worth of foreign exchange to buy German machine tools for the arms industry.[49]

On June 14, a week before the storm broke, the Soviet news agency *TASS* released a statement denying friction between Berlin and Moscow: "The USSR, consistently with its policy of peace, has observed and intends to observe the provisions of the Soviet-German non-aggression pact, and therefore rumours that the USSR is preparing for war with Germany are lies and provocations."[50]

ON THE MORNING OF JUNE 22, 1941, over three and half million Axis troops, 3,600 tanks, 7,200 guns and 4,400 aircraft swept into the Soviet Union in what was meant to be a blitzkrieg. On the eve of Operation Barbarossa, in the west, the Red Army had deployed three (out of a total of five) million men, about 10,000 tanks, 19,000 guns and over 8,000 aircraft. The defenders should have been able to blunt the invasion. But the element of surprise and the operational skill of the German attackers turned Barbarossa into a catastrophe for the Red Army. The Luftwaffe did not have a numerical edge, but they had better-quality aircraft and destroyed more than half of the Red Army's planes by July. By September the Red Army had lost 3.3 million dead, wounded or captured, 15,000 tanks and 90,000 field guns and mortars. The leading panzers had advanced 400 miles into Russia. General Halder, not known for excessive excitability, marveled at the triumph. "It is thus probably no overstatement to say," the German Army chief of staff wrote on July 3, "that the Russian campaign has been won in a space of two weeks." The Führer needed a rapid decision in the east, and it looked like he had won.[51]

Yet, even after the horrific mauling, the Red Army fought on, called up reserves and counterattacked. In July the German advance was slowing down. By August Halder sensed failure. "The whole situation makes it increasingly plain," he wrote, "that we have underestimated the Russian colossus." As winter arrived, exhausted German units ran into fresh Soviet divisions from Siberia, some equipped with the new T-34, the best all-round medium tank of the war, and the gigantic 45-ton KV tank, against which the attackers had nothing to match. By December, with Moscow beyond German reach, the blitzkrieg had failed and the long savage war of attrition had begun.[52]

Despite the loss of territory, plant and workers, the centralized machinery of the Soviet war economy swiftly rebounded. With Herculean effort, key factories were moved to the safety of the Urals and beyond. Civilian output was ruthlessly cut and food strictly rationed. The central planners poured everything into arms manufacture. Incredibly, in 1941 and 1942 Soviet industry out-produced that of Germany in rifles, machine guns, artillery, tanks and aviation by huge margins. In fact, over the entire war more weapons came out of Soviet factories than German ones. Since the whole point of Barbarossa had been to seize Soviet resources and industry rapidly to stave off the coming surge of Anglo-American armaments, the illusion of blitzkrieg doomed the Nazi regime to ultimate defeat. The two-front total war, which Stalin had believed Hitler would never risk, was, as Stalin knew, beyond Germany's capacity to win.[53]

CHAPTER 17

"IS TOTAL WAR, THEN, THE PATH TO FREEDOM?"

A   s the 1930s came to an end, keen observers of world politics noted that nothing better illustrated the way in which expanding war and armaments compelled states to impose ever greater levels of national regimentation than Japan's war in China.

The fighting that began with a chance skirmish near Beijing at the Marco Polo Bridge in July 1937 swiftly escalated. In September 1937, to pay for the expanding China war, the Japanese Parliament approved a colossal 2.5 billion yen hike in military spending and enacted mobilization laws that gave the state direct control of the economy. To shift resources from "rice" to "guns," civil servants and military planners regulated trade and distributed commodities. They used wartime legal powers to steer capital investment into arms plants, override managerial autonomy and seize factories and cargo ships. While businessmen, especially cotton exporters, baulked at the central controls, in October the government established the Cabinet Planning Board, a super-agency to run the whole economy. The board fulfilled a fond ambition of the advancing cohort of reform bureaucrats and the total-war officers, who had long seen market mechanisms as an obstacle to organizing autarky. Inspired by the totalitarian economies of Germany and the Soviet Union, the modernizers of the Cabinet Planning Board worked out how to distribute the maximum food, fuel, iron ore and machine tools that Japan could import with its shrinking foreign-exchange stock to win the China war and to arm against the Red Army and the U.S. Navy.

In the spring of 1938, with no end to the war in sight, a new mobilization law strengthened the authority of the central planners. That year the quality of Japanese civilian life in Japan plummeted. Small businesses went bankrupt. Corporate tycoons decried "state socialism" and "bureaucratic fascism."

As exports flagged and foreign-exchange stocks dwindled, the central planners drafted a new four-year plan to raise arms output. Some officials acknowledged the fanciful nature of the plan. How could Japan defeat China and expand its industrial base when it lacked the foreign exchange to import the raw materials to do either? As one diplomat put it, Japan's economic predicament was like "an octopus eating its own tentacles."[1]

Ishiwara Kanji, now a general, had foreseen all this. He and other total-war officers had long argued that before fighting an all-out war, Japan had to expand its heavy industries and achieve autarky through gradual empire building. As the army's top planner in 1936–37, he had lobbied hard for a five-year plan of industrial growth. "Steel mills now," he bellowed, "guns later."

In June 1937 he got his wish. Prince Konoe Fumimaro, forty-five, a charismatic, widely respected modernizer, formed a new government. As prime minister, he endorsed the totalitarian "national defense state," the army's program for the growth of strategic industries in Japan and Manchuria and a profitable export-led economic revival.

Of course, all this depended on a long cycle of peace. Once the China war started, it became impossible to stop. Most army officers assumed that the Nationalist Chinese would surrender after the first severe blow. Yet Generalissimo Chiang Kai-shek's forces endured defeat after defeat. The Japanese Army poured more men into the fight and occupied Shanghai and Nanjing, but to no avail. The Nationalists signed a nonaggression pact with the Soviet Union, joined forces with Mao Tse-tung's communist guerrillas and began to receive aid from Moscow. Ishiwara, who had opposed the march into China, was removed from the general staff.[2]

Confident in its operational supremacy, the Japanese Army blamed its failure in China on outsiders. Russia, Britain and America encouraged Chiang Kai-shek and his allies, so ran the argument, into resisting Japan for their own malevolent ends. Thus the only way to win was to win over the Chinese and deter outside intervention. In November 1938 Prime Minister Konoe declared a New Order in East Asia and called for solidarity between the peoples of Japan, Manchuria and China. The appeal rang hollow and won few collaborators. Eventually, in April 1940, the Japanese burned their bridges with the Nationalists and set up a puppet Chinese government in Nanjing.[3]

Deterring outsiders was no less difficult. Clashes with the Red Army in 1938–39 had shown that a confrontation with Moscow could be extremely dangerous. Apart from harassing European territorial leases and concessions and commercial interests in China, there was little direct action that Japan could take against the Western nations. The only option, and the one that appealed most to the army, was an alliance with Berlin and Rome. A military alliance between the three Anti-Comintern allies would not only cow the Russians but also apply real pressure on the British. The Japanese Navy, however, did not want to be dragged into a war for German aims against Britain and in all likelihood the United States too, and it demanded an alliance that was limited to being anti-Soviet.[4]

When war broke out in Europe in September 1939, Japan's prospects worsened. Hitler linked arms with Stalin just as the Red Army defeated the Japanese Army at Nomonhan. The Chinese were no closer to caving in. Britain and France mobilized their economies. World commodity prices shot up. Japanese exports fell. The U.S. government started sending the Chinese economic aid. The United States threatened to nullify its commercial treaty with Japan. If that happened, irreplaceable American shipments of scrap metal, aircraft parts, machine tools and aviation fuel would cease. Meanwhile, the Americans were rearming. The U.S. Navy planned to expand beyond the 1922 Washington Naval Treaty limits. The U.S. Army placed large orders for bombers. All in all, unless something astonishing happened soon, Japan would be crushed vice-like between fast-growing Soviet and American armaments.[5]

Then, in May 1940, something astonishing did happen. Germany stormed into Holland and Belgium. France, too, fell. Britain would likely succumb. Now Europe's resource-rich colonies in Southeast Asia were vulnerable to pressure and exploitation. Perhaps a deal could be done with Moscow and the war in China ended? The chief obstacle remained Washington. Could some sort of deal be made with the Americans? Could they be deterred by a Japanese alliance with the Axis? Time, meanwhile, worked against Japan. After May 1940 it was clear that American armaments would sooner or later grow at a stupendous rate.

THE SPECTACLE OF the Phoney War at once fascinated and appalled Franklin Roosevelt. Behind formidable fortifications, vast economies mobilized in 1939–40 for an all-out contest of munitions manufacture. Seemingly, total war could arouse the galvanizing sense of popular common purpose that he had hoped his reforming New Deal would have inspired. Even the French and British democracies adopted state controls over economic and social life that to informed onlookers rendered them no less totalitarian than their Axis foes, Japan or the Soviet Union. That, after all, was the inescapable consequence of waging totalitarian war.

Roosevelt resolved to buck the great trend. The United States would supply the French and British with the bombers to defeat Germany, the totalitarian pacesetter. His critics, ardent isolationists of the left and the right, accused him of trying to embroil the nation in the faraway war. Many of them, including his predecessor Herbert Hoover, feared that a ratcheting-up of rearmament to enter the war would ultimately end in a totalitarian America. Roosevelt thought that his critics might be right. "We refuse the European solution of using the unemployed to build up excessive armaments which eventually result in dictatorship and war," he declared in January 1940. "We encourage an American way—through an increase of national income which is the only way we can be sure will take up the slack."[6]

But then in May–June 1940 disaster struck. Hitler's Blitzkrieg not only shattered the Allied armies racing into Belgium and swiftly forced the French to surrender but also threatened to wreck Roosevelt's strategy of containment. The president reacted by stepping up his arms program. On May 16, while German tanks surged through the Ardennes, he asked for an additional $1 billion in arms spending on top of the $1.5 billion he had already asked for that year. The navy wanted new ships, he said, and the army needed modern weapons. Above all, President Roosevelt wanted aircraft: the capacity to churn out 50,000 airplanes a year and a fleet that big for the services.[7]

A few days earlier General "Hap" Arnold, the chief of the army air force, had ordered his staff to calculate a maximum annual production target. They asked for a few hundred extra aircraft. "To hell with you," he shouted. "I'm going over to the White House now, and do you know what I'm going to tell the President? I am going to tell the President that we need 100,000 airplanes." Independently, Roosevelt arrived at what to him seemed like the feasible target of 50,000, but that was still five times more planes than any nation on earth had yet manufactured in a single year. The German military attaché estimated that a rise of American air strength on that scale would demand an incredible fivefold expansion of the U.S. aviation industry virtually overnight. General Arnold, too, questioned whether the aircraft makers really could find the workers and erect the extra plant to make 50,000 planes a year.[8]

So did Admiral Harold Stark and General George Marshall, the president's two top-ranking military advisers. The army and navy each had its own goals, and pumping out a lot of planes did not make sense unless growth in air power was balanced against other priorities. Ever since the war broke out, both the army and the navy had enjoyed extra money and lobbied for more. In August 1939, when Stark became chief of naval operations, the navy was already growing to its maximum tonnage allowance under the old Washington

Naval Treaty. Now that the naval treaties were defunct, Stark and his planners aspired to something gargantuan too. With threats looming in the Pacific and the Atlantic, they planned a two-ocean navy, a new formula for the very old ambition of a navy "second to none." Before France fell, Admiral Stark and the navy's most wily backer in Congress, Georgia Democratic Representative Carl Vinson, sought approval for a full seventy percent increase in the size of the fleet in politically palatable stages, eleven percent to start. After France fell and Britain looked vulnerable to the Blitzkrieg too, Congress loosened the purse strings. On July 19, 1940, to the wide-eyed envy of admirals the world over, especially in Tokyo, American legislators authorized a single vaulting seventy percent leap in U.S. naval armaments.[9]

General Marshall had bigger headaches. In Europe multi-million-man armies clashed with terrific speed and violence, but the U.S. Army numbered under 250,000 and fielded 1919-vintage weapons. Marshall did not aspire to muster the world's greatest army. His more modest aim was to raise the men and materiel to defend the Western hemisphere from any attacker. At the beginning of 1940 his goal was a "protective mobilization" force of 750,000 men and 250,000 in reserve armed with modern rifles, guns and tanks. During congressional hearings, Marshall said that the weapons for that force could be ready in two years, but he considered that forecast optimistic. In 1918, as a thirty-eight-year-old staffer in the army's headquarters, Marshall had seen first hand how a slow-blooming war economy had plagued the army's deployment to France. Twenty-two years later he worried that the mistake was being made again because the White House preferred to rearm on the hoof. Roosevelt had promoted Marshall because he unflinchingly spoke his mind, but the president's breezy decision-making style grated on Marshall's dour disposition.[10]

Time was oppressing both Stark and Marshall. Before May 1940 the army and navy had placed reams of competing contracts with arms firms already choked with priority orders. The fall of France and Roosevelt's mania for building aircraft made matters worse. Breakneck air and naval growth and the army's new goal of two million men in uniform by the start of 1942 would place even greater pressure on the munitions makers, and soon on the overall economy. The War Department's industrial mobilization plan had envisaged that conscription and the retooling of industry for an all-out military effort would follow the declaration of a national emergency. But in May–June 1940 Roosevelt did not send out a clarion call; he refused to appoint an "arms czar" to draft a grand production plan; and he did not set up a "super-agency" with wide-ranging powers to determine priorities and allocate resources in place of the free market. Marshall was not ready to draft millions of men because he lacked the training camps and equipment for a mass recruitment. What the service staffs wanted was government intervention to speed up arms output. On June 22, 1940, the day of the Franco-German armistice, Marshall and Stark asked Roosevelt to order round-the-clock shifts, seven days a week in the munitions plants and other key industries. Two days later they asked again. To defend the United States, they urged, "the concerted effort of our whole nation is required." Roosevelt turned them down flat. He insisted on "progressive" rather than "complete" national mobilization.[11]

One reason why Roosevelt and his military chiefs differed about mobilization was that they disagreed about how the war would and should unfold. Marshall and Stark had written off Britain and sought to defend a fully mobilized fortress America against attacks from a fully mobilized Axis-ruled Europe. Roosevelt still foresaw a limited air-naval war of containment fought through Britain and the French Empire. Events soon rewarded his optimism about Britain. In a stunning show of determination to fight on, the Royal Navy attacked the French fleet in July 1940 to prevent major units falling into Hitler's hands. Over the summer the Germans did not cross the Channel, and Britain held its own against the Luftwaffe. In August the president decided to send Churchill the fifty old destroyers he had asked for in May and, against Marshall's advice, sold him $362 million worth of old rifles and ammunition to help replace the British Army's equipment losses at Dunkirk. The Royal Air Force would benefit from the windfall of French orders that the Allies had placed with American aviation firms. In November 1940, as Hitler pondered a blitzkrieg against the Soviet Union—the vital step to fighting the budding Anglo-American air alliance—Roosevelt, once again overruling Marshall's advice, insisted that half of American aircraft output go to Britain.[12]

Always attuned to the electorate, Roosevelt pitched his support for Britain as vital to securing "fortress" America and played up the Nazi menace to the Americas. The German onslaught had persuaded Americans to arm, and yet isolationists on Capitol Hill and in the press decried aid to Britain as a reckless entanglement. Public opinion polls showed that most people agreed, saw Hitler's triumph over Britain as inevitable and wanted to "arm to the teeth" against Axis Europe. With its impregnable position, superior industrial power and abundant resources, the isolationists argued, the United States did not need Britain as an ally to remain safe. For Roosevelt, who respected the mobilizing power of fear, isolation was as good as giving in to the Axis. Out of fear of invasion, Americans would sacrifice their individual freedoms, prosperity and the pursuit of social justice to arm on a totalitarian scale. In his quarantine speech of November 1937, Roosevelt, alluding to that prospect, read out the passage in James Hilton's bestseller *Lost Horizon* in which the fictional High Lama of Shangri-La foretells a whirlwind of war. "There will be no safety by arms, no help from authority, no answer in science. The storm will rage until every flower of culture is trampled and all human beings are leveled in a vast chaos." With that eddying cyclone of destruction endangering everything that he had worked for since 1933, Roosevelt decided to break a taboo that every occupant of the White House since George Washington had observed and run for an unprecedented third term.[13]

To progressively increase arming ahead of the November election, Roosevelt had to reconcile a lot of contradictory pressures without provoking pitched battles (the sort that had tormented the Blum and Daladier governments in France) with powerful groups inside and outside Washington. On the one hand, the War Department and Bernard Baruch argued that the only way to manufacture vast quantities of arms was to set up a new agency run by soldiers and volunteer executives. On the other hand, leading New Dealers and organized labor opposed an extra-legal military-industrial bureaucracy from the fear that political power would permanently slip into the hands of corporate tycoons. In Congress allegations had already been made about shameless profiteering on defense work. To win a third term, Roosevelt could not afford to alienate his New Deal coalition by endorsing the War Department's plan. More importantly, he was loath to set up a separate center of power that could in an emergency expand out of his control. At the same time, the president did not possess his own administrative machine to run rearmament. Acquiring one would cause uproar in the boardrooms, where New Deal evangelists were routinely accused of plotting to exploit the escalating military threat as a pretext for executing their "totalitarian plan of nationalizing industry, conscripting the wealth and labor of all, and suppressing the normal incentives of management and industry in favor of the authority and control of government officials." Roosevelt briefly toyed with the idea of building state-owned and state-operated aviation factories, but events moved too fast to raise an entire arms industry from scratch. If the nation was going to arm smoothly and in good time, he needed the cooperation and expertise of the corporate establishment.[14]

So Roosevelt, the supreme improviser, decided to be his own arms czar and to deliver both guns and butter in spades. On May 26, in one of his fireside chats, he told radio listeners that in arming he would not sacrifice living standards or labor rights. "We have carried on an offensive on a broad front against social and economic inequalities and abuses," he said, employing a fitting military metaphor. "That offensive should not now be broken down by the pincers movement of those who would use the present needs of physical military defense to destroy it." In the same address he asked industrialists for their cooperation, emphasizing that he was not about to nationalize arms factories or go into competition with them.[15]

To reassure business still further, Roosevelt appointed conservatives to head the war and navy departments, the two purchasing agents for arms. Frank Knox, who had been the Republican vice-presidential nominee in 1936, now headed the navy, and Henry Stimson, Herbert Hoover's secretary of state, went to the army. In order to determine priorities, the president also set up the National Defense Advisory Commission—a blue-ribbon panel of chief executives, including William Knudsen of General Motors and Edward Stettinius of U.S. Steel—as well as representatives of labor and agriculture and cabinet officials. Soon volunteer businessmen gravitated to Washington to man the slowly sprawling bureaucracy of defense and economic subcommittees, but Roosevelt carefully circumscribed their authority. When Knudsen asked who the boss was, Roosevelt snapped, "I am." Although die-hard Roosevelt haters in the business world still accused him of implementing creeping socialism, the president in fact had no intention of controlling rearmament through a giant central-planning mechanism. Instead he wanted to stimulate the mass production of arms by creating a mass demand for them—hence his headline-grabbing 50,000-plane target—and by ensuring that business earned "reasonable" profits and received tax incentives and that the state accepted the financial risk of investing in new production plant. Roosevelt had turned off the pump-priming flow of deficit public spending for his New Deal back in 1938, but now he was steadily turning the spigot on again to gear up the economy for rearmament.[16]

In July 1940 Roosevelt orchestrated his nomination by the Democrats for a third term, prompting accusations of dictatorial aspirations from his critics. Much, he knew, would hang on the election, which was a means to start forging a consensus. Roosevelt's situation in 1940 was similar to that of 1938, when the New Deal stalled. Besides more pump priming of the economy through government spending, the missing element back then was a sense of common national purpose to invigorate the millions upon millions of individuals who made up the gigantic American work machine. Without that sort of unity, how could anyone impose on a capitalistic democracy a grand design toward a great purpose? Why, for instance, should industrialists embark on arms manufacture on the scale that the White House wanted when a new man might soon occupy it?[17]

In September 1940 the presidential campaign got into full swing against the backdrop of the introduction of the first peacetime draft in American history, as well as the deal to swap fifty U.S. Navy destroyers for British bases in the Caribbean islands. The election sparked a great debate between grassroots interventionist and isolationist organizations; the Committee to Defend America by Aiding the Allies battled the America First Committee. In language that would color politics for generations, the president slammed his isolationist foes as "appeasers" and crypto-fascists; they accused him of plotting to impose socialistic "totalitarianism." Thanks to Britain's stubborn resistance in the air war and the sensation caused in September by the anti-American Axis signed between Berlin, Rome and Tokyo, opinion turned Roosevelt's way. Having installed two prominent pro-interventionist Republicans to defense posts, the president touted himself as the candidate of national unity. His Republican rival, Wendell Willkie, a progressive Wall Street lawyer with plenty of backers in the boardrooms, also supported American aid for Britain. In October, with defeat looming, however, Willkie disavowed his interventionist leanings and denounced Roosevelt as a warmonger, but this tactic had little impact. With a big grain of salt, the president insisted he would not send American boys to fight in foreign wars. Whether or not they believed him, the electorate voted for the candidate most of them trusted to guide the nation through the escalating global cataclysm.[18]

In the autumn of 1940, Roosevelt's top brass and his new army and navy secretaries, all of whom agreed that the crisis would not pass without Americans fighting, pressed him to stop improvising and to start methodically answering the key planning questions for the service staffs: What kind of war did he expect to fight and how much armament would be needed to win it? One week after the election Admiral Stark sent Roosevelt twenty-six pages of sober strategic analysis that laid out the situation. Although the burden of defeating Japan would fall to the navy, the admiral concluded that the Far East was of secondary importance. "If Britain wins decisively against Germany," the admiral asserted, "we could win everywhere; but . . . if she loses the problem confronting us would be very great; and, while we might not *lose everywhere*, we might, possibly, not *win anywhere*." Not winning anywhere meant that the United States would be locked in endless hot and cold wars against a globe-spanning totalitarian bloc. To defeat Germany, America's ultimate enemy against which Stark proposed to concentrate the main military effort, Britain needed not only assistance but also the fully mobilized man-power of the United States.[19]

Then, on November 23, the British ambassador in Washington reported to the president that Britain would soon be broke. To fight on, the British Empire would need to be bailed out. The news came as no shock, only earlier than Roosevelt had expected. On December 9, while he relaxed in the Caribbean, Roosevelt ruminated over a letter from Churchill asking for money, shipping and munitions. Stark's warning that Britain's demise would plunge the United States into an open-ended war against an Axis-controlled world prompted Roosevelt to abandon any thoughts of a limited effort. If Britain fell, then America would be forced under the irresistible impulse of fear into all-out regimentation. The only real answer to the intensifying arms race and total war, he paradoxically concluded, was to turn the United States into a gigantic armaments machine—a "great arsenal of democracy"—capable of feeding the nation's forces and those of its Allies with the munitions they needed to crush totalitarian aggression everywhere and free the world from "fear."[20]

Over the next few weeks Roosevelt hammered home his message in speeches and press conferences. In a broadcast on December 29 he laid out the impelling logic for accelerated rearming:

> If Great Britain goes down, the Axis powers will control the continents of Europe, Asia, Africa, Australasia, and the high seas—and they will be in a position to bring enormous military and naval resources against this hemisphere. It is no exaggeration to say that all of us in the Americas would be living at the point of a gun—a gun loaded with explosive bullets, economic as well as military. We should enter upon a new and terrible era in which the whole world, our hemisphere included, would be run by threats of brute force. To survive in such a world, we would have to convert ourselves permanently into a militaristic power on the basis of war economy.

No lasting peace could be made with the Axis states, he added. "It would be only another armistice, leading to the most gigantic armament race and the most devastating trade wars in history."[21]

In January 1941 Roosevelt sent to Capitol Hill a bill to lend-lease America's allies an initial $7 billion worth of war materiel. That month too he authorized secret staff talks with Britain. To win the debate in Congress and the country, administration officials argued that control of Europe and Asia would give the Axis the capacity to outgun and blockade America. Isolationists pointed out that the bill was as good as a declaration of war on the Axis (and Berlin saw it that way). They also balked at the wide-ranging powers the bill granted the White House to dispose of American munitions without congressional approval. While supporters of the Lend-Lease Bill portrayed the war as another episode in the epic struggle between liberty and tyranny, good and evil, critics underscored the paradox of the president's policy. "Total war for total victory against totalitarian states can best be conducted by totalitarian states," argued Robert Hutchins, the president of the University of Chicago. "If the United States is to proceed through total war to total victory over totalitarian states, it will have to become totalitarian, too. Is total war, then, the path to freedom?" Roosevelt knew that serious-minded men like Hutchins had a point, but the isolationist alternative was even more threatening to liberty and progress. Whatever his private misgivings, Roosevelt won the public debate. On March 11, 1941, he signed the Lend-Lease Bill. Though only a few years earlier most Americans had adamantly opposed fighting in foreign wars, they now supported the "arsenal of democracy" policy. No doubt Roosevelt saw the irony that in his quest to rid the world of fear there was no better mass-mobilizer than fear itself.[22]

Back in July 1940 Roosevelt could promise Americans guns and butter because there was enough slack in the economy to make both. In 1941, however, with factories humming and employment rising, the civilian boom threatened to clash with arms growth. During the winter of 1940–41 Roosevelt reorganized the defense bureaucracy to deal with the problem. As usual, he rejected appointing a "'Czar' or 'Poobah' or 'Akhoond of Swats'" to take control, as the newspapers and military wanted. Instead, among other things, he set up an Office of Production Management, co-directed by William Knudsen of General Motors and Sidney Hillman of the Amalgamated Clothing Workers, to establish defense priorities. Later that year, as priorities inflated and shortages grew in key raw materials such as aluminum, the president added an Office of Price Administration and Civilian Supply and the Supply Priorities and Allocation Board to manage the problem. The growing ranks of volunteer businessmen and New Dealers in the defense machine probably helped to promote better coordination between state and industry, but the blurred lines of responsibility did not help. Nonetheless, the real drag on armaments production was neither administrative inefficiency nor even the lack of an economic dictator; the problem lay in the reluctance of big business to plunge too deeply into arms making.[23]

The Blitzkrieg of 1940 had persuaded businessmen, like most Americans, that the nation needed to rearm, but the burning question was how. During the election, Willkie had pledged to mass-produce tanks, guns and planes but also to curb big government. After Roosevelt won his third term, corporate leaders, especially savvy industrialists already acting as defense advisers, knew that the only way to protect boardroom autonomy was to come to terms with the New Dealers. As Roosevelt also recognized, an all-out state-versus-industry fight was a losing game for both sides.

What the industrialists feared most was being swamped by munitions orders. Anyone who had read the business press for the last decade knew that reliance on one supreme buyer—the towering, almighty state—was the perilous step toward de facto nationalization. In 1940–41, with civilian demand flourishing again, industrial barons shrank from losing market share and forgoing profits to mass-produce weapons for a left-wing administration that they did not trust. The car industry, for instance, the world's largest and (as the Red Army had long calculated) a vast reservoir of productive capacity for tanks and warplanes, refused to turn over even idle plants to defense work. For similar reasons industrial managers did not want to invest in new tools and floor space to feed the arms boom. Memories of being saddled with excess capacity in the crushing Depression years died hard.[24]

Roosevelt understood why business hesitated about rushing into arms work. Huge defense outlays alone would never spark the rearmament surge he wanted fast enough. After May 1940 he looked for concessions to the corporations that would stoke the arms boom without undoing his social reforms. For his most passionate admirers this was the beginning of Roosevelt's retreat from the original aspirations of the New Deal. Secretary of War Stimson best summed up the credo the White House adopted: "If you are going to . . . go to war . . . in a capitalist country, you have to let business make money out of the process or business won't work." Although new tax legislation in October 1940 at first glance lived up to Roosevelt's pledge to claw back excess profits on munitions orders, the law in fact had so many riders on it that in practice the big firms evaded windfall taxes. Cost-plus-fixed-fee contracts, especially with aircraft makers, encouraged gains in efficiency and innovation while ensuring healthy profits. Other tax incentives, such as the accelerated depreciation of new munitions plant, reduced the risk of acquiring excess capacity. Competitive bidding rules were relaxed. For the riskiest ventures, a new Defense Plant Corporation hired private contractors to build and operate them.[25]

Even so in 1941, the last year of nominal American peace and with high levels of consumer production (Detroit made nearly four million cars), the results of the arms drive were impressive. In the aircraft industry, floor space doubled and the workforce tripled. That year the United States produced over 26,000 aircraft, 6,000 more than Britain, the world's second-largest producer. The industrial basis had been laid for the combined Anglo-American bomber offensive of 1943–45 that would devastate German industry and cities. All that was needed now to put the American industrial war machine into full operation was the ultimate mobilizer—total war.[26]

During the spring of 1941, flummoxed by his refusal to plan systematically, Roosevelt's industrial and military chiefs again asked him for a grand plan. If war came, they all wanted to know what arms would be needed, how soon and for what goal. Hitler's attack on the Soviet Union on June 22 forced Roosevelt to tackle these questions methodically. Like their counterparts in Britain, U.S. intelligence had for months picked up clues about Operation Barbarossa. So informed, Roosevelt had framed Lend-Lease to permit U.S. arms shipments to Russia and any other potential ally. When Germany struck the Soviet Union, Roosevelt dispatched his trusted adviser Harry Hopkins to offer Stalin American aid. With a big slice of much-needed U.S. arms output now going to Britain and Russia, the calls from the military staffs for a plan became louder. On July 9, Roosevelt finally ordered the army and navy staffs to explore "the overall production requirements required to defeat our potential enemies." Later he added that he was not only asking about the scale of armaments needed by American forces but also those necessary to equip U.S. allies. While the world looked on as Hitler's first and last blitzkrieg surged toward Moscow, Roosevelt planned to win the global arms race for what Churchill would dub the Grand Alliance.[27]

In the U.S. War Department, the task fell to one of Marshall's new planners, Major Albert C. Wedemeyer. The major was one among a small number of American officers who had in the 1930s either studied at the German War College in Berlin or had served in that city as a military attaché. Like many men of this cohort, Wedemeyer was a gushing admirer of all things German and military, and politically an isolationist.[28]

Not that that mattered much in July–August 1941. An avid reader of military history and economics, and steeped in the literature of future war, Wedemeyer reveled in his work. Compiling and crunching the numbers for the future army and air force was a mind-boggling task. So keen was Wedemeyer to ensure that the U.S. Army had the tanks, guns and troop carriers to beat the panzer chiefs, he flooded his imagined battlefields with so many vehicles that his staff joked they would need to deploy battalions of traffic cops.

On the big canvas the work was fairly mechanical. What was the objective? Wedemeyer asked. To defeat the Axis. Where, how and when could the Axis forces be defeated? Where? In Europe. Asia was secondary. How? By first winning command of the Atlantic Ocean and the skies over Europe. Once those goals were achieved, Allied air forces would then shatter the German war economy through bombing while U.S. ground forces gathered in Europe. And finally the Nazi citadel would be stormed by American and Allied ground and air forces. How soon could the United States raise the men and materiel to achieve Roosevelt's objective? By July 1943, he figured, so long as "the industrial potential of the country is fully exploited. The urgency of speed and the desirability of employing our present great economic and industrial advantage over our potential enemies cannot be overemphasized."

Wedemeyer believed that the United States had to mobilize "urgently" because he appreciated the geo-strategic logic of Hitler's attack on the Soviet Union. It had been a preventive strike, he wrote, to knock Stalin out before he became too strong. Moreover, a successful blitzkrieg against the Bolshevik foe—something Wedemeyer like most senior staffers thought inevitable—would supply the Nazi regime with the space, food and raw resources it would need to convert Europe in a few years into an unassailable fortress against the swelling tide of Anglo-American armaments. To bring about Hitler's downfall before then, he concluded, the U.S. Army would need to send 215 divisions of 8.7 million men against 300 "fully equipped and splendidly trained" Axis divisions of twelve million men. Four decades later, when Wedemeyer was asked about how much his two years of study at the German War College had contributed to the drafting of his famous Victory Plan—as his war plan was called—he replied "not much."[29]

That was a telling remark, for indeed there was nothing especially German about the writing of the Victory Plan. It was logical and consistent with everything that had been written about 1914–18 and wars to come by soldiers as varied as Tukhachevsky, Ishiwara and Blomberg. The differences between these war planners was that in 1941 when Wedemeyer began to peer into the future, he asked the basic questions, had clear direction from the very top and had the most powerful, autarkic and secure industrial economy on earth on which to base his plan. This was a war-winning combination.

On September 11, a draft copy of the combined army and navy Victory Program landed on Roosevelt's desk. For months now he had mulled over the German advance and the fate of Britain and Russia. He was exasperating his advisers. Did the president want to declare war on the Axis? Always the improviser, Roosevelt probably had no definite idea himself. Strong opposition had formed in Congress to his moves to extend U.S. naval escorts for ships carrying aid to Britain and the Soviet Union. Though he could mobilize support for the Lend-Lease Bill, a declaration of war on Germany was altogether different. What he needed and spoke about was an "incident." The Battle of the Atlantic, as isolationists on Capitol Hill recognized, offered him the best chance of provoking such an incident. Only a week before the Victory Program arrived at the White House, the destroyer USS *Greer* was torpedoed by a U-boat off Iceland. The *Greer* incident was only the first of Roosevelt's cautious efforts to arouse among Americans another great mobilizing force—anger.[30]

While escalating his naval intervention in the Atlantic, Roosevelt resisted the transfer of ships from the U.S. naval base in the Pacific. Battleships at Pearl Harbor were meant to deter the Japanese, with whom relations had deteriorated since September 1940, when Tokyo signed a military pact with Berlin and Rome. In 1941 fresh talks between the new Japanese ambassador in Washington, Nomura Kishisaburō, and Secretary of State Cordell Hull on a modus vivendi made no headway. Influential men in Washington, above all the president, opposed any concessions to Japan that smacked of "appeasement" and refused, as Tokyo wanted, to abandon China. Selling out the Nationalist Chinese while trying to shore up Britain and Russia made no sense in the global war that Roosevelt planned to win. And so, while the ill-fated diplomacy went around in circles, and U.S. intelligence decoded the secret messages bouncing back and forth between Tokyo and Washington, offering them a partial insight into the tense debate among the Japanese, U.S. officials turned the screw on economic sanctions and built up forces in the Philippines, including long-range B-17 bombers. Some worried that squeezing the Japanese too tight might make them act before it was too late. Others wagered that the Japanese would not take the plunge into an unwinnable total war.[31]

WHEN IN JULY 1940 Prince Konoe became prime minister of Japan for the second time, the rising tide of Nazi victories appeared to open a brave new world of possibilities. He was the man on whom the flagging conservative elites and the rising reform bureaucrats and like-minded military officers had pegged their hopes. He promised to be the supreme reconciler, a popular politician who could pull off the impossible: save the essentials of the old system while ushering in a new one. Back in July 1937, when he had formed his first cabinet, Konoe had hoped to launch the empire on a five-year plan of industrial growth, financial recovery and institutional change, but the war with China wrecked everything. He had endorsed a swift reprisal against Nanjing, not the grisly quagmire that the war had become. In a naïve bid to undo his ghastly error, Konoe proclaimed in November 1938 a New Order in East Asia, a vast, harmonious Asian bloc of China, Manchuria and Japan, united against Anglo-American hegemony.

The Pan-Asian ideal fell flat. Even he, the widely esteemed peer with influential contacts in the Court, Parliament, civil service, military and business, could not stop the factional fighting that plagued Japanese politics, above all the overbearing influence of the army. And so he resigned in January 1939. Eighteen months later, however, with France trounced and Britain and the United States reeling, the chances of making sweeping changes looked bright. Konoe was enthralled by the global totalitarian trend. He was hardly a methodical thinker, and so, like Roosevelt early on in the New Deal, he drew on a brain trust of private advisers. To a man these scholars and retired officials aspired to remodel Japan along Nazi/Soviet lines. In the summer of 1940, with Hitler blazing the totalitarian trail, Konoe too saw that the old free-for-all Meiji political order had to be replaced by a highly centralized, Nazi-like, one-party state. Mobilization for the war with China had already propelled matters far in that direction anyway. All that was needed was someone with the political skill to finish the job.

For Konoe everything hinged on forming one all-embracing political party. As prime minister and the head of a popular mass movement, he would have the political clout to subdue factional rivalries. In his fuzzy totalitarian vision, he would have the power to set priorities and impose collective decisions on the fiercely independent army and navy ministries and the unruly service staffs. Konoe's new economic order would also extinguish once and for all economic liberalism. In Japan service to the state would replace private profit as the supreme motivator of business activity. Instead of market forces and entrepreneurial initiative, multi-year plans executed by government technocrats would govern every aspect of economic life.[32]

The army, of course, did not trigger the cabinet crisis that restored Konoe to office so that he could impose strategic direction on the military. The generals hoped that the appealing prince could sustain popular enthusiasm for the war with China and ever more intense social and economic mobilization to win it. Konoe knew this and so sought to stamp his personal authority on his new cabinet from the start. Before he agreed to lead a new administration, he held informal talks with his prospective army and navy ministers, General Tōjō Hideki and Admiral Yoshida Zengo. Unless they endorsed his agenda, so ran Konoe's unspoken threat, the military could find someone else to lead a new government of national unity. By the end of July the cabinet had endorsed broad goals: at home, political restructuring and a planned economy; abroad, a victorious end to the China war; closer ties with Berlin and Rome as a deterrent to U.S. meddling in East Asia; a temporary truce with Moscow; and, most significantly of all, a step-by-step advance southward into the rice, rubber and oil-rich colonies of French Indochina (now ruled by pro-Vichy colonial officials), the Dutch East Indies (run by colonial officials loyal to the Dutch government in exile in London) and British Malaya, Borneo and Burma. On August 1, 1940, Konoe's bellicose foreign minister, Matsuoka Yōsuke, declared that Tokyo would build a self-sufficient economic bloc, the Greater East Asia Co-Prosperity Sphere.[33]

However, as was so often the case with high-level strategy in Tokyo, the cabinet documents of July 1940 simply papered over chronic army-navy rivalry for national primacy. For the army, intense preparations for war against the Soviet Union would give it first call on scarce resources; for the navy, arming against the United States would do the same. Striking north against the Soviet Union was unthinkable, however, at least for now: Japan's troops were bogged down in China, while Berlin and Moscow were now bound by a nonaggression pact and the Kwantung army was licking its wounds after Nomonhan. In the heady weeks of June–July 1940, hawkish staff officers in both services lobbied for a southern advance by diplomatic pressure and if need be force, but for different reasons. For the navy, it was a sound step in a maritime grand strategy to secure the raw resources Japan needed to be free from Anglo-American economic strangulation. For army staffers, it was a means to isolate Chiang Kai-shek from foreign assistance and to acquire fuel supplies from the petroleum-rich Dutch East Indies. In drawing up operational plans, army staffers concluded that if force had to be used against the Dutch, it also made good sense to assault the nearby British naval-air fortress at Singapore, and that this could be done without much fear of retaliation from the United States.

Taking Singapore touched upon a crucial point of debate between the generals and the admirals. The navy's raison d'etre depended on war with the United States. It could suffer few defeats more damaging than allowing the army to establish the principle that Britain could be attacked without waging war against the United States too. After all, if the British, Dutch and French colonies could be rolled up without provoking U.S. intervention, why invest in more warships? And invest in warships was precisely what the navy wanted to do. Even with the four planned 70,000-ton super-battleships rising on the stocks, the naval planners gasped at the titanic increases in U.S. naval strength announced in 1939–40. How could they possibly cope with this escalating naval arms race? Cutbacks to the navy's steel quota to feed the army would doom the fleet to ever greater inferiority against the United States Navy.

Besides bureaucratic tactics, there were of course plenty of excellent reasons why the admirals saw London and Washington as "indivisible." The old guard in top posts in the navy—officers such as Admiral Yoshida, Konoe's navy minister, and Admiral Yamamoto Isoroku, the future mastermind of the Pearl Harbor attack—argued that Hitler's triumphs would force the English-speaking nations into a grand maritime alliance. Attacking Britain would therefore initiate an unwinnable all-out war against the world's mightiest industrial economy, the United States. The critics of the old guard—bellicose staffers who in the 1930s had backed the anti–arms control fleet faction against the treaty faction—rejected this sort of defeatist thinking. If you accepted that war against the United States was unwinnable, then you handed the army predominance in national policy making and Washington a veto over national policy. With the Americans set to build a gigantic two-ocean fleet and vast air armadas, and the alluring but deceptive exemplar of Hitler's Blitzkrieg burning in their brains, the navy's ultra-hawkish staffers began to speak of the logic of fighting the United States in a lightning action sooner rather than later.

But everyone at the ministerial level agreed that the war with China had to end to relieve the military-economic pressure. In July 1940, Konoe acted as a patient but not especially influential mediator between the two service ministers. Admiral Yoshida pressed for fresh talks with the Nationalists, and General Tōjō pushed for an Axis military alliance to isolate Chiang Kai-shek and intimidate Washington. Konoe's foreign minister, Matsuoka, whose self-gratifying fantasies of earth-shattering global alliances equaled those of Ribbentrop, backed the army.

Courting assassination from hotheads in his own service and pro-Axis soldiers, Yoshida stuck to the navy's old line. Irrevocably linking Japan's destiny to that of Germany would risk a war against the United States that the navy was bound to lose. Although he was a redoubtable sea dog only in his forties, the tremendous strain of holding out exhausted Yoshida, and in early September he suffered a nervous collapse. His successor, the more pliant Admiral Oikawa Koshirō, and his cunning deputy, Admiral Toyoda Teijiro, finessed the situation. Opposing the army was a losing game, so they decided to extract concessions in exchange for the navy's assent. First, the alliance had to include a secret clause making it clear that Japan alone would decide when it would fight alongside Germany and Italy. Second, the "cabinet and particularly the army would give special attention to naval preparedness." Everyone accepted the navy's conditions.[34]

And so the admirals scored a tactical victory in their effort to keep pace in the naval arms race. From October 1940 to March 1941, at the army's expense, the navy's steel quota would more than double. Still, in executing the southern advance, the admirals insisted that a clash with Washington had to be avoided. Above all, they opposed military operations against the Dutch East Indies. At a liaison conference between the service staffs on September 14, 1940, Admiral Kondō Nobutake of the naval staff summed up his service's awkward problem: "The navy has not yet completed its war preparations vis-à-vis the United States. They will be completed next April and Japan will stand a fair chance of winning on the basis of 'quick encounter, quick showdown.' But if the United States should turn the war into a protracted struggle, it will become very difficult for Japan. On the other hand, the United States is rapidly building ships and, in the future, discrepancies in the naval ratios will widen and Japan will not be able to catch up. In this sense, today is the most advantageous moment for starting a war."[35]

Although many naval officers and other officials warned that the Tripartite Pact between Germany, Italy and Japan would infuriate sooner than frighten Washington, supporters of the deal believed it could save Japan: the Germans would help compel the Dutch colonial authorities to agree to Japanese demands for more oil; Berlin would broker a pact between Moscow and Tokyo; Chiang Kai-shek would come to his senses and plead for peace terms: the Americans, always "level-headed," so Matsuoka said, would also see reason; if they did not, the Japanese Empire, allied with the Nazi regime and perhaps even supplied with Soviet raw materials, could face a long war against the United States anyway.[36]

On September 22, 1940, the Japanese began the occupation of northern Indochina with the coerced consent of the French colonial officials, but this move backfired badly. Roosevelt slapped a total ban on exports of scrap metal and aviation fuel to Japan, though, significantly, other oil exports would continue. Resistance hardened elsewhere too. For months Tōjō's staff had anticipated triumphant German landings on the English coast, but the British held out. They also reopened a vital supply route through Burma to the beleaguered Nationalist Chinese, a route that London only a few months earlier had ordered closed under Japanese pressure. Secret peace talks between Japan and Chiang Kai-shek stalled. And, in early 1941, talks over increased oil shipments between the Japanese and the authorities in the Dutch East Indies also got nowhere.

While the foreign policy of the second Konoe cabinet ran aground, the prime minister's domestic policy also floundered. The leaders of the big conservative political parties wanted to disband their organizations to merge with one led by him, but this was more from self-preservation than any enthusiasm for reconciling their genuine differences or surrendering their local power bases out in the prefectures. Back in February 1940, to the fury of the generals, one brave legislator had openly damned the army's handling of the war in China. He was expelled from Parliament and his speech erased from the record, but everyone knew that the army would not stop until all the political parties had been broken. So once Konoe formed a cabinet of national unity, the party bosses rushed to form a new Imperial Rule Assistance Association rather than wait for the army to dissolve their parties and, worse, employ reserve army officers instead of party functionaries to run local administrations for mobilization. And so, it was politics as usual under Konoe's umbrella association. If he really did believe he could found a one-party regime overnight, the prime minister must have been cruelly disappointed. In the effort to sway his unwieldy mass organization, Konoe soon found himself sidelining the reformers in favor of the old party bosses.[37]

The same was true for his new economic order. Once the corporate tycoons discovered that the technocratic zealots on the Cabinet Planning Board wanted to extinguish capitalism forever, they launched a public and behind-the-scenes campaign to stop them. Couching their criticism in wartime jingoism, corporate leaders argued that mobilization worked best when businessmen ran the economy through "self-governing central organs." Conservative politicians and right-wing radicals joined the furious chief executives in accusing the central planners of implementing a form of creeping communism. After all, did not the Meiji constitution guarantee private property rights? And in Germany and Italy industrialists still reaped profits. Inside Konoe's cabinet, which nearly collapsed over the issue, Kobayashi Ichizo, the economics minister and himself a businessman, led the attack against a "separation of ownership and management." Again Konoe ditched the most radical parts of his agenda.

As in Germany under the arms czar Fritz Todt, the economic policy adopted by Konoe in December 1940 recognized the need for centralized state management of production but put businessmen in prominent positions in the machinery of central control. Konoe's most ardent reformer, Kishi Nobusuke, who had turned Manchuria into one huge laboratory for a command economy, was dismissed. The corporate barons savored revenge. For years now, under the pressure of war in China and in the name of national security, they had witnessed the incredible growth of a military-bureaucratic behemoth that imperiled their autonomy and market mechanisms. The corporate barons decided to go after the despised technocrats. In their witch hunt they formed an uneasy alliance with the generals, who were incensed by plummeting production forecasts for steel, copper, chemicals and other essentials. In April 1941, the police arrested several senior officials of the Cabinet Planning Board for supposedly communist activities. In their place went top-ranking military men.[38]

For now big business and the military compromised. The centralizing trend would continue, but private ownership and profit would stay. Still, locking up a few of the most extreme apostles of the coming totalitarian age could do little to alter the dire economic facts. Japan did not have a spare automobile industry to convert into aircraft plants, or idle steel mills or much by way of untapped oil and mineral deposits. The economy depended on trade, and because of falling earnings from exports, the war with China and the economic embargo spearheaded by hard-liners in the re-elected Roosevelt administration, imports would soon nose-dive. In 1940 under the mobilization plan Japan's import capacity for iron, steel, non-ferrous metals, fuel and food had been 2.6 billion yen; in 1941 it was eight million yen.[39]

Against this backdrop of economic decline, the army's enthusiasm for going south cooled in April 1941. Matsuoka signed a neutrality pact with Stalin that month, which in theory released forces from the north for use in the south, but the army feared that Moscow might exploit a Pacific war to storm Manchuria. Japanese commanders in China pleaded for more men, and the army had few reserves to spare for operations in the south. Moreover, army staffers increasingly saw the push south for what, up to a point, it was, a maneuver in the inter-service rivalry for resources. Having accepted a steel cut, the army especially resented the navy's proposal to build three even more gargantuan super-battleships carrying unheard-of twenty-inch guns—to trump the Americans. Inside the navy, meanwhile, hawkish staffers strengthened their hand and became more bellicose about heading south even if that meant war with the United States. In part to apply the brakes to a southern thrust, and in part hoping that a deal could be reached with Washington, which was preoccupied with Europe, the army accepted the navy's premise that the United States and Britain were indivisible.[40]

Navy Minister Oikawa, too, hoped for a deal with the Americans. To hold the line against navy hawks while preserving his service's climbing raw-material quotas, he agreed with the army to limit the southward advance to diplomatic means. If, however, survival of the empire was threatened by economic strangulation, the navy would not hesitate to smash the U.S. fleet. Meanwhile, the admiral secretly worked with Admiral Nomura Kishisaburō, the new Japanese ambassador in Washington, to draft a deal that would ease tensions and restore trade. Had a deal been feasible, Oikawa would have scored a big success for his service and out-maneuvered the navy's hard-liners. But in the edgy circumstances of 1941, a deal was impossible. Negotiations between Nomura and Secretary of State Hull revolved in mind-numbing circles: the Americans wanted Japan to denounce the Axis, pull out of China and reverse the southward advance; for most Japanese officials that meant defeat. What they wanted was a truce that would allow a renewal of imports. Oikawa never admitted that the most favorable suggestions coming out of Washington were not *American* in origin but had been put forward first by the navy via Nomura.[41]

In early June word reached Tokyo of Hitler's impending attack on the Soviet Union. With army-navy collaboration at a low ebb, the north-south debate intensified. Matsuoka, who had only just returned from Moscow with a neutrality pact in hand, demanded that Japan join its Axis allies in the great crusade against the Bolshevik fiend. Once Hitler unleashed Operation Barbarossa on June 22, General Tōjō and his war planners, like most professional soldiers the world over, predicted a German victory in a matter of months. The Kwantung army prepared for a thrust into Siberia.

In the weeks before the German blitzkrieg, however, hawks on the naval staff had pushed ahead plans to occupy southern Indochina. Their aim was to build air and naval bases in the French colony in readiness for operations to seize the oil-rich Dutch colonies. Even cautious admirals recognized that two big land wars would divert the lion's share of shrinking resources to the army.

On July 2, the top-ranking military and political leaders assembled for an Imperial Conference in the presence of Emperor Hirohito. The purpose of these high-level gatherings was to ratify the decisions of the military leadership by airing them in front of the divine ruler, who by convention sat silently during the proceedings. At this meeting, however, no decision was reached about whether to go north or south. Instead, everyone agreed to get ready to push north and to occupy all of Indochina. Three weeks later, while army intelligence waited in vain for signs that Stalin was pulling troops out of the east to fight in the west, 40,000 Japanese troops marched into southern Indochina.[42]

In Washington code breakers intercepted the news from Japanese diplomatic traffic even before the first soldiers marched. Fearing that Japan might attack the Soviet Union or the British Empire, Roosevelt authorized a freeze on all Japanese assets in the United States. Britain followed suit. Whether he grasped the implications of his order remains unclear, but the freeze initiated actions by the U.S. State and Treasury Departments that resulted in a total oil embargo on Japan. The United States was Japan's largest supplier and the Dutch East Indies, following American's lead, also refused to sell oil to Japan. In August, while Roosevelt and Churchill met in Newfoundland to confer about the war and bulging boatloads of U.S. aid arrived at Russia's Pacific port of Vladivostok, Japan's military men now faced the slow threat of economic strangulation that they had resolved to break with force.[43]

From September to December 1941 the compelling language and do-or-die logic of fast-escalating arms races and total war gripped the top decision makers in Tokyo. Under the oppressive sense that time was running out, hope and fear merged into a decision reached by consensus, a decision that then flowed into fateful action.

At an Imperial Conference on September 6, the emperor heard the case for plunging into all-out war against the United States, Britain and the Dutch was officially aired before the emperor. General Suzuki Teiichi, the new director of the Cabinet Planning Board, gave the most important presentation. "At this stage our national power with respect to physical resources has come to depend entirely upon the productive capacity of the Empire itself . . . and upon vital material stockpiled thus far." He continued, describing a situation similar to Italy's the year before, and the sort of rationale for reckless action that had swayed even normally prudent Germans such as General Thomas to back Operation Barbarossa: "Therefore, as a result of the present overall economic blockade imposed by Great Britain and the United States, our Empire's national power is declining day by day. Our liquid fuel stockpile, which is most important, will reach bottom by June or July of next year. . . . I believe it is vitally important for the survival of our Empire that we make up our minds to establish and stabilise a firm economic base." Offered the choice between economic-military paralysis in less than a year or an admittedly risky southward thrust to seize the rich sources of oil, bauxite, nickel and rubber of Southeast Asia, the conference ratified a resolution to pursue talks with Washington and at the same time to get ready for war by mid-October. Near the end of the conference, Emperor Hirohito, Japan's thirty-nine-year-old divine ruler and commander in chief, read out a poem:

> *All the seas in every quarter are as brother to one another.*
> *Why, then, do the winds and waves of strife rage so turbulently*
>   *throughout the world?*

The unusual gesture had a poignant meaning for the military men at the table. Clearly the emperor wanted a diplomatic solution.[44]

For some time now Hirohito had quizzed his army and navy chiefs of staff about Japan's prospects in a war against the United States and did not like the answers. Each time the emperor pressed a point the service chiefs answered the same way: Japan was a dying patient in need of a drastic cure. That remedy was a blitzkrieg, an audacious maritime war of rapid decision that would gird Japan for total war before Washington could gear up to its full strength. The emperor asked General Sugiyama Hajime how long it would take to win. Three months came the reply. "You were army minister at the time the China Incident broke out," the emperor said, "and I remember you saying 'The Incident will be cleared up in about a month.' But it still hasn't been cleared up after four long years, has it?" China was vast, Sugiyama protested, and "military operations could not be conducted as planned." "If the hinterland of China is vast," fumed Emperor Hirohito, "isn't the Pacific Ocean even more vast? What convinces you to say three months?"

What troubled Japan's military chiefs was the emperor's clear resolve to put the brakes on the drive to war. Though under the Meiji constitution he exercised no actual decision-making authority, the emperor was the sacred symbol, the supreme ratifier and unifier without whom decisions about war and peace could not be legitimized before the people. To Japan's top-ranking soldiers and sailors, their loyal duty to the emperor was clear. As gold-braided technocrats, who truly grasped the underlying logic about the arms race and total war, their job was to persuade Hirohito that they were right. For his part the young ruler was not against diving into a great war if need be, but not an unwinnable one. For two decades now the senior sailors from his family and those who had served him as aides had often said that war against the U.S. military machine would almost certainly end in ruin. Before he accepted that terrible risk, he wanted all options explored and diplomacy exhausted. One power he had was to ask awkward questions. Another was to appoint prime ministers.[45]

As prime minister, Konoe had disappointed Hirohito. A year earlier Konoe had come back into office eager to catch the surging wave of change sweeping the globe, propelling imperial Japan into a new era, and to impose order on the endless infighting between the army and the navy. Now, he was drained of dynamism and nerve. Somewhat reluctantly, or so it seemed, Konoe was riding the same decade-long tide of war and arms racing that had propelled the most hawkish men into the upper ranks of the armed forces. Because Konoe could not control the political and economic forces he had helped to unleash, on October 16 he resigned before the final leap into war. Hirohito and his advisers had to appoint a successor, and their choice was a surprising one: the man upon whom the imperial court pinned its hopes for a last chance for diplomacy was General Tōjō.

Born in 1884, the son of a general, Tōjō had followed his father's path through sheer exertion and meticulous staff work rather than flair. Ishiwara had dismissed him as stupid "corporal" for his lack of theoretical vision, but that was unfair to a man whom admirers nicknamed The Razor. He may not have added anything very original to the corpus of military thought, but Tōjō knew it all by heart. And what he knew told him that unless Japan seized the material wherewithal to wage industrial total war, it would cease to be an independent great power. On the basis of that logic, he, more than anyone else in 1941, had been demanding an expanded war.

Still, for the emperor, selecting Tōjō to form a new cabinet was a clever gambit. His reputation for loyalty to the emperor was unequaled. Now Hirohito asked him to serve as head of government and war minister and to revisit one last time the logic of an inescapable war against the United States. If a deal with the Americans was possible, then the general had the grit to hold back the ultra-hawks. As the emperor wished, Tōjō took both the preparations for total war and a thorough review of a diplomatic truce seriously. As his new arms czar he appointed his old Manchurian colleague, the arch-centralizer Kishi Nobusuke. And between October 23 and November 1, he presided over dozens of meetings with top officials, reviewing every aspect of the military and diplomatic predicament.[46]

Not surprisingly, the compelling case for war went full circle. At an Imperial Conference on November 5, Tōjō reiterated in front of the emperor the rationale for an expanded Pacific war unless the Roosevelt administration accepted Japan's diplomatic solution. "If we enter into a protracted war, there will be difficulties," the prime minister asserted:

> The first stage of the war will not be difficult. We have some uneasiness about a protracted war. But how can we let the United States continue to do as she pleases, even though there is some uneasiness? Two years from now we will have no petroleum for military uses. Ships will stop moving. When I think about the strengthening American defenses in the Southwest Pacific, the expansion of the American fleet, the unfinished China Incident, and so on, I see no end to difficulties. . . . I fear that we would become a third-class nation after two or three years if we just sat tight.[47]

On November 26, the answer to the question of whether a diplomatic solution could be found came back from Washington: no dice. Between a Japan
struggling to hold together a crumbling military-economic situation allied
with Berlin and Rome and a United States arming at remarkable speed to
wage an all-out war with Britain and the Soviet Union against the Axis, there
was no room for a truce. Four days later Emperor Hirohito met with the leadership of the navy, the service that would bear the brunt of war against the
United States. He said that time was running out: "an arrow is about to leave
a bow. Once an arrow is fired, it will become a long-drawn-out war, but are
you ready to carry it out as planned?"

The admirals reassured Hirohito that they were "reasonably confident" of
success. Later one of them remarked that the emperor had "appeared to be
satisfied." At the Imperial Conference on December 1, 1941, Hirohito accepted
that war against the United States was not only inevitable but also perhaps
even winnable.[48]

CONCLUSION:
THE RACE GOES ON

As 1941 drew to a close, spiraling arms races and wars in Europe and Asia merged into one global war. For a decade Japan and Germany had provoked arms competitions. Now they hoped the conflict would usher in an Axis-ruled new world order. But the counter-vailing and self-reinforcing political, economic and military forces they had stirred up doomed their hopes from the start.[1]

As Japan's war planners had anticipated, their opening attacks yielded swift and stunning results. On December 7, 1941, Japanese carrier-based torpedo-bombers struck the U.S. fleet based at Pearl Harbor, sinking six battleships and damaging two others. On December 10, Japanese land-based torpedo bombers sank the *Repulse* and *Prince of Wales*, the two big-gun warships that Churchill had ordered to the South China Sea to intimidate Tokyo. During the months that followed, in a series of complex and daring lightning attacks, Hong Kong, Borneo, the Philippines, the Dutch East Indies and the British Empire's most formidable bastion in the Far East, Singapore, all fell to the Japanese.

In their southward advance, the Japanese sought to capture the resources they needed to feed their war economy—and occupy defensive rings of islands to wage, if necessary, a long war. "The chances are eight or nine out of ten that the war will become protracted," predicted the Japanese naval chief of staff, Admiral Nagano Osami. "In the event of a protracted war . . . we shall es-tablish during the first and second years the foundations for fighting such a war; during this period there is an assured chance of victory, but after the third year there is no predicting what the outcome will be."[2]

But the tide turned much sooner than he and his colleagues expected. Much like Germany's situation after the fall of France in 1940, Japan's blitzkrieg of 1941–42 did little to alter its strategic situation. Time did not work for Japan. The Japanese Empire had expanded its resource base, but most of its army was still bogged down in China, and it was now going up against the world's most powerful economy. Japanese admirals hailed the attack at Pearl Harbor as a triumph, but it was short-lived. At Hawaii Japanese aircraft had sunk battleships but failed to destroy the U.S. Navy's aircraft carriers, heavy cruisers, fuel stockpiles and repair facilities. And so the United States could mount a counterattack even before its arms production got into full swing.

The decisive check against Japan came in June 1942 at Midway Island. There U.S. carrier-based dive-bombers sank four Japanese aircraft carriers, and with them the cream of Japan's naval aviators and deck crews. Before the war, navies had measured their standing in the arms race in terms of battleships, none more so than the Japanese. They invested heavily in Yamato-class super-battleships to outgun the Americans, but the aircraft carrier proved to be the principal weapon of the Pacific War. After Midway, therefore, the sharp edge of the Japanese advance had been blunted. The war became a trail of attrition. The Japanese high command's foretaste of that war came at the battle for the island of Guadalcanal in the Solomon chain. From August 1942 to February 1943, the Americans and the Japanese fed more men, ships and planes into the frenzied slugging match, each hoping to overpower the other. In the end, the Japanese gave up.

Although the Japanese fielded highly disciplined fighting men and some first-class weapons—the famous Mitsubishi Zero fighter plane among them—Japan's war effort was as doomed as that of Mussolini's Italy. The Japanese fought longer and harder than their Italian allies, but by 1943 the eventual outcome was not in doubt. A tidal wave of U.S. armaments overwhelmed irreplaceable Japanese defenses. During the war, for instance, Japan built seven large fleet carriers, while U.S. shipyards launched thirty large fleet carriers and eighty-two smaller ones. In 1944 the Japanese aviation industry, at its peak, produced 28,000 warplanes, while the Americans assembled 96,000. Although "Germany first" was the official policy in Washington, in practice U.S. Pacific forces received strong reinforcements from the start. In fact, thanks to the steady flow of men and materiel, in the south and central Pacific the U.S. Army under General Douglas MacArthur and the U.S. Navy under Admiral Chester Nimitz could pursue their own separate strategies to pound Japan back. As MacArthur and Nimitz leapfrogged from island to island, American submarines and bombers decimated Japanese merchant shipping to deprive Japan's munitions plants of the supply of overseas raw materials that Tokyo had started the Pacific War to seize. And so, even before American B-29 super-fortresses began to firebomb Japan's cities in 1945, Japan's war economy was spluttering to a halt. The dropping of two American atomic bombs and the Red Army storming into Manchuria in early August 1945 only hammered home to Tokyo the enormity of its defeat.[3]

On December 11, 1941, four days after Pearl Harbor, Hitler declared war on the United States. His pretext was news of the U.S. Army's Victory Plan leaked to the isolationist *Chicago Daily Tribune* days before. "A plan prepared by President Roosevelt has been revealed," Hitler said with mock outrage, "according to which his intention is to attack us in 1943 with all the resources of the United States. Thus our patience has come to the breaking point." In fact, for months now, Admiral Raeder, whose U-boats were locked in an undeclared war with the U.S. Navy, had been urging Hitler to order attacks against unprotected U.S. shipping in the western Atlantic. Once the Japanese Navy attacked the U.S. fleet, Hitler rushed to fulfill Ribbentrop's Tripartite Pact by joining the war against the United States. His hope was that a successful Japanese blitzkrieg in the western Pacific would divert the Americans long enough for him to crush Russia.[4]

In 1942 that goal still seemed achievable. Although the Red Army had not crumpled as Hitler and his generals had smugly predicted, the German Army beat back Soviet attempts to relieve besieged Leningrad and Sevastopol and inflicted heavy losses on the attackers. In June 1942 the Germans launched an offensive in the southeast toward the Caucasus region to deny the Soviet war economy critical supplies of oil and other raw materials. Once again Hitler and his commanders hoped that a series of swift operational victories would turn the tide in the east, but the grim winter of 1942–43 shattered that illusion. The German drive to the Caucasus lost momentum and another German spearhead became bogged down in savage fighting at Stalingrad. While Hitler demanded that Stalingrad be taken, the Soviet high command concentrated fresh tank, infantry and artillery units that German Army intelligence had no idea even existed, north and south of the city.

Then, on November 19, 1942, Zhukov began a surprise encirclement that bagged the entire German Sixth Army. "The correlation of forces on the Soviet-German front has changed," Stalin boasted in February 1943, after the Germans at Stalingrad surrendered. "The fact is that fascist Germany is more and more exhausted and is becoming weaker, and the Soviet Union is deploying its reserves more and more and is becoming stronger." This was no idle boast. Soviet troops were being armed at an imposing rate. Thanks to a highly centralized system of planning, which out of wartime necessity left plenty of room for the delegation of authority and local initiative, the Soviet war economy would year on year out-produce the German one. On the battlefield, Stalingrad marked the turning point. From then on, the swelling Red Army would hold the initiative against the increasingly embattled Germans. In 1943–44, the Russians repelled powerful German panzer thrusts trying to encircle them in the Kursk salient southwest of Moscow and then, in one of the most spectacular operations of the entire war, drove the murderous German invaders out of the Ukraine.[5]

Well before Hitler declared war on the United States, some top officials in Berlin had concluded that Germany could not raise the armaments needed to defeat the constellation of powers arming against it. In November 1941, Fritz Todt, Hitler's arms czar, did not mince words. "This war can no longer be won by military means," he told Hitler. "How then shall I end the war?" asked the Führer. "It can only be ended politically," came the reply. But there was no way to turn back the clock, and Hitler knew it. Unable to erase the self-defeating consequences of the arms race or halt to Germany's benefit the self-perpetuating dynamism of total war, Hitler plunged deeper into the maelstrom.

Todt's death in an airplane accident three months later made sustaining the fantasy of a coming victory simpler. Albert Speer, Hitler's favorite architect, replaced Todt as arms czar and oversaw one final spurt of arms output that had a rationale in 1942 while victory in the east still seemed possible, but none at all other than prolonging the agony once that goal was clearly beyond reach. Speer, the quintessential ideological technocrat of the whole arms race, exaggerated his arms production "miracle" to hold up the illusion that the war could still be won; yet the rise in production in 1942–43 was real enough. With the voluntary support of the industrial barons, who were assured of profits and a role in running the central machinery of industrial mobilization, Speer and his counterpart in the Luftwaffe, General Erhard Milch, steered more and more labor, steel and other resources into making tanks, aircraft and shells. So long as this rationalization could evolve undisturbed, output boomed, above all in Milch's aviation industry, which benefited from a learning curve of rising productivity gains.

However, as the Anglo-American air offensive began to destroy Germany's industrial centers in 1943–44, the upward curve of Speer's arms miracle was cut short. And, caught in the vise-like grip of swelling Anglo-American armaments coming from the west and surging Soviet armaments approaching from the east, the collapse of Hitler's malfunctioning war machine was only a matter of time and effort on the part of Germany's enemies.[6]

The final assault began in the summer of 1944, when the western Allies landed at Normandy and in the south of France, and the Red Army smashed German defenses in Belorussia and pushed into Poland. In December, in a futile bid to replicate the lightning victory of 1940, German tanks attacked the Anglo-American armies through the Ardennes. This time the Americans halted Hitler's panzers. In the spring of 1945, while the Allies east and west moved in for the kill, Hitler reflected on why he had been defeated. He blamed "international Jewry," Roosevelt, Chamberlain, his Italian allies, his generals and the German people. The one cause that the Nazi warlord might have contemplated with some genuine insight was the arms race that had begun a decade before.[7]

Japan's surprise attack on December 7, 1941, and especially Hitler's ensuing declaration of war removed the political obstacles in the United States to the all-out arms effort that Roosevelt first spoke of in his "arsenal of democracy" speech. America had been attacked and the nation angered. Isolationism as a political force evaporated. Former President Herbert Hoover, consistent to a fault, argued that since America had joined in total war, Roosevelt needed "dictatorial" powers to run a "totalitarian" economy, though with safeguards to stop "fascist" methods from being frozen into the American way of life. Though in early 1942 a great clamor for an all-powerful military-industrial super-agency to mobilize the economy was raised, Roosevelt ignored it. His response as usual was measured. He added new committees to the machinery of central control and appointed as his arms czar the affable and politically vapid Sears Roebuck chief executive, Donald Nelson, a man unlikely to challenge White House authority or to become an American Albert Speer. Under Roosevelt the apparatus of industrial mobilization remained a hornets' nest of bureaucratic infighting between civilian and military armaments planners: New Dealers damned mushrooming mobilization bureaucracy as a corporate cabal and systematizers of total war like Bernard Baruch bemoaned its inefficiency.[8]

In fact, administrative inefficiency hardly mattered at all. The Japanese attack provoked the sort of supercharged thrust of national cohesion behind a great cause that President Roosevelt's New Deal and prewar rearmament had conspicuously lacked. The deluge of wartime military orders and spending in 1942–43 sparked an industrial Gold Rush to make weapons on an epic scale. Effective central control did not mature until after the arms boom was under way, and the result, despite some hiccups in the distribution of raw materials, was stupendous. An entire synthetic-rubber industry mushroomed almost overnight, steel production soared, shipyards assembled the new Liberty cargo ships at a rate that helped make nonsense of Admiral Dönitz's U-boat war and the entire automobile industry began to churn out tanks and aircraft in quantities that the era's consummate total-war systematizer, Mikhail Tukhachevsky, had once happily imagined. At Ford's gigantic Willow Run factory alone—which one awed-inspired visitor dubbed "the Grand Canyon of the mechanized world"—workers built 9,000 four-engine B-24 Liberator bombers at a peak rate of almost one per hour. By war's end, U.S. factories had produced nearly 300,000 warplanes, 1,556 warships, 5,777 cargo ships, 88,410 tanks and three million trucks and jeeps. [9]

Roosevelt won the arms race for the United States and its allies without making the choice between guns and butter faced everywhere else in varying degrees of severity. Some planners feared that runaway rearmament would impose material hardship on civilians, but the arms bonanza stoked a consumer boom, too. Workers spent their dollars in well-stocked supermarkets, bought clothes and shoes and enjoyed a film and a bite out. War hauled the U.S. economy out of the Great Depression. Liberals lamented the way it dampened the New Deal's reforming zeal, empowered the corporations and paved the way for what in 1961 President Eisenhower called the military-industrial complex.[10]

But the destructive pressure of armaments on the American way of life could have been much more severe. That possibility loomed in 1941–42, when the fate of the Soviet Union hung in the balance. No other state mobilized deeper, imposed more hardships on its people and did more to destroy the German Army than the Soviet Union. What scale of American effort would have been required had, as Major Wedemeyer predicted, the Soviet Union fallen? As it was, the United States did not raise the 215 divisions that the U.S. Army's Victory Plan had called for, but thanks to the Red Army, only ninety. Stalwart allies and an incredible, untapped reserve capacity for arms growth allowed Roosevelt to manage a deep plunge into totalitarian war without, as he and many others feared, triggering an irreversible slide into social, political and economic regimentation.[11]

That the arms race ended quite differently from the extreme projections by contemporaries of all political shades should not distract us from the grip that that imagined future of perpetual totalitarian rivalry held over them. The arms race had been a vast maelstrom, a tremendous torrent generated by unchecked competition, understood in terms of lessons drawn from 1914–18 and in all-embracing ideas about how to impose order and meaning on wars to come, and with the power to induce nations to mobilize their economies and societies with mounting intensity. As the arms race gathered force, it wrecked the master plans of those who embraced the totalitarian trend and those who tried to resist it. Those leaders who tried to master it found that they could not. Those leaders who tried to buck the great armaments trend found that they could not. For the United States, the only way to escape the vicious circle, as Roosevelt eventually recognized, was to take the plunge and hope to outgun the Axis.

Of course, we can see in retrospect that perhaps the atomic bombs churned out by the Manhattan Project would have offered the United States and its British ally a grisly way out of the accelerating armaments spiral had the Soviet Union collapsed. As it was, that ultimately irrational thermal nuclear perfection of total war arrived in time to mark the end of one phase of intense global military rivalry and to overshadow the next. The atomic bombing of Hiroshima and Nagasaki spurred on Stalin's budding bomb project to early success in August 1949. As the ideological confrontation between the United States and the Soviet Union intensified, the technological race accelerated. During the 1950s and 1960s, atomic bombs gave way to much more powerful hydrogen bombs, and long-range bombers to intercontinental ballistic missiles.[12]

Despite the arrival of the doomsday technology, though, the same processes and much of the same language and logic of the pre-1941 arms race fed into the Cold War. Conflict between the United States and the Soviet Union over Germany and Korea gave rise to two fast-growing, military-industrial hydras, and diverted the finite resources of both superpowers from butter to guns. The mounting cost of the U.S. nuclear and conventional force build-ups against its totalitarian foe revived real anxiety among some Americans of inadvertently erecting a "garrison state." Most prominent among them was President Eisenhower, who feared that the burden of an all-out armaments spree would crush a flourishing economy, and with it American liberties. This was the dilemma that Chamberlain, Blum, Daladier and Roosevelt had all confronted before.[13]

Eisenhower's way out of it was to rely chiefly on the threat of massive nuclear retaliation to deter Soviet nuclear *and* conventional attacks. But the ghastly logic of nuclear deterrence nearly came to a cataclysmic end in October 1962, when Nikita Khrushchev and John Kennedy clashed over Cuba. In the 1970s and 1980s, efforts to control the arms race through détente yielded to renewed belligerency and an arms boom. Yet, for all the terrifying hairpin turns and hair-raising crises of the nuclear arms race, something had changed this time around. For the United States and its European allies, bucking the totalitarian trend by establishing an uneasy equilibrium of mutually assured deterrence between the two heavily armed blocs was possible.

The strategy of containment that first Chamberlain and then Roosevelt attempted to employ against Hitler's Germany worked during the Cold War, but still at a cost.

The collapse of the Soviet Union in 1991 revealed just how burdensome the superpower arms race had been, not just for the Russians, but also for the triumphant United States. Overkill arsenals and bloated military-industrial complexes fatally crippled the Soviet economy and blighted America's national infrastructure, stunted its social progress and militarized its culture. Briefly, in the decade following the Cold War, the arms race had seemed a thing of the past. But terrorism, nuclear proliferation and a steady rise in global military rivalry have now re-energized that great backward force in world history and revived the danger that the price we must pay to feel secure will be too high.[14]

The rules can change, and so can the stakes, but the race goes on.

NOTES

For reasons of space, I have not provided an exhaustive bibliography of all the sources I consulted while researching this book. A bibliography of the sources cited here is available for download from the publications page of my Web site at King's College London. For a comprehensive list of contemporary literature in various languages, see E. M. Rosenbaum, "War Economics: A Bibliographical Approach," *Economica* (1942). In the notes below I cite sources in full in the first instance and thereafter in abbreviated form. References to private archives appear in full. Other printed primary sources are also cited in full. References to printed collections of documents include the series, volume, document or page numbers.

ABBREVIATIONS

ACS	Archivio Centrale dello Stato, Rome
ASMAE	Archivio Storico del Ministero degli Affari Esteri, Rome
AVPRF	Foreign Policy Archive of the Russian Federation, Moscow
Bottai D	G. Guerri (ed.), *Giuseppe Bottai Diario 1935–1944* (Milan, 1982)
BA-MA	Bundesarchiv-Militärarchiv, Freiburg
CDL	R. Self (ed.), *The Neville Chamberlain Diary Letters*, vols. iii and iv (London, 2002–5)
CDP	M. Muggeridge (ed.), *Ciano's Diplomatic Papers* (London, 1948)
Ciano	M. Muggeridge (ed.), *Ciano's Diary 1937–43* (London, 2002)
DBFP	*Documents on British Foreign Policy, 1919–39*, 2nd series and 3rd series (London, 1946–85)
DDF	*Documents Diplomatiques Français*, 1st series (1932–5) and 2nd series (1936–9), (Paris, 1963–)
DDI	*I Documenti Diplomatici Italiani*, 7th series (1922–35), 8th series (1935–9) and 9th series (1939–43) (Rome, 1953–)
DGFP	*Documents on German Foreign Policy, 1918–1945*, series C and D (London, 1949–83)
FA	E.B. Nixon (ed.), *Franklin D. Roosevelt and Foreign Affairs 1933–7*, 3 vols. (Cambridge, MA, 1969)
FDRL	Franklin D. Roosevelt Library, Hyde Park, New York
FRUS	Foreign Relations of the United States (Washington, DC, 1950–63)

HCDeb	House of Commons Debates, London
IMT	*Trial of the Major War Criminals before the International Military Tribunal,* 42 vols (Nuremberg, 1949)
LNDP	E.A. Reno (ed.), *League of Nations Documents and Publications, 1919–1946* (New Haven, 1973)
LSMG	A. Biagini and A. Gionfrida (eds.), *Lo Stato Maggiore Generale tra le due guerre: verbali delle riunioni presiedute da Badoglio dal 1925 al 1937* (Rome, 1997)
OO	*Opera Omnia di Benito Mussolini,* 36 vols. (Florence, 1951–62)
PPA	S.I. Rosenman (ed.), *The Public Papers and Addresses of Franklin D. Roosevelt,* 13 vols. (New York, 1941–50)
RGAE	Russian State Archive for the Economy, Moscow
RGASPI	Russian State Archive for Socio-Political History, Moscow
RGVA	Russian State Military Archives, Moscow
SHD-DAA	Service Historique de la Défense—Departement de l'Armée de l'Air, Vincennes
SHD-DAT	Service Historique de la Défense—Departement de l'Armée de Terre, Vincennes
TBJG	E. Fröhlich (ed.), *Die Tagebücher von Joseph Goebbels,* 1st series, 9 vols. (Munich, 1998–2006)
TNA	The National Archive, Kew, London
USMM	Ufficio Storico della Marina Militare, Rome
USSME	Ufficio Storico dello Stato Maggiore dell'Esercito, Rome

INTRODUCTION

1. Throughout this book I use the term "total war" the way contemporaries did to describe a great power conflict in which the whole of a nation's social and economic resources are called upon to win it. See, for instance, the essays in N. Angell et al. (eds.), *What Would Be the Character of a New War?* (London, 1933). For a discussion of the term, see R. Chickering, "Total War: The Use and Abuse of a Concept," in M.F. Boemeke, R. Chickering and S. Förster (eds.), *Anticipating Total War: The German and American Experiences, 1871–1914* (Cambridge, 1999), pp. 13–28; H. Strachan, "On Total War and Modern War," *International History* (2002), pp. 341–70; and Horne, "Introduction: Mobilizing for Total War," in J. Horne (ed.), *State, Society and Mobilization in Europe During the First World War* (Cambridge, 1997), pp. 1–17.

2. B. Eichengreen, *Golden Fetters: The Gold Standard and the Great Depression, 1919–1939* (Oxford, 1996).

3. In J. Maiolo, "Armaments," in R. Boyce and J. Maiolo (eds.), *The Origins of World War Two: The Debate Continues* (London, 2003), pp. 286–307, I discuss the various

definitions of the term "arms race" and examine the debate about its uses as an analytical tool.

4. B. Buzan and E. Herring, *The Arms Dynamic in World Politics* (New York, 1998), pp. 75–127; C. Glaser, "When Are Arms Races Dangerous?" *International Security* (2004), pp. 44–84; M. Geyer, "Militarism and Capitalism in the 20th Century," in N.P. Gleditsch and O. Njølstad, *Arms Races: Technological and Political Dynamics* (Oslo, 1990), pp. 247–75; D. Stevenson, *Armaments and the Coming of War: Europe, 1904–1914* (Oxford, 1982); R. Rhodes, *Arsenals of Folly: The Making of the Nuclear Arms Race* (New York, 2008).

5. See among the many examples: E.M.H. Lloyd, *Experiments in State Control at the War Office and the Ministry of Food* (Oxford, 1924), p. xi; É. Halévy, *Era of Tyrannies: Essays on Socialism and War* (London, 1967), pp. 204–19; J. Rueff, "Pourquoi, malgré tout, je suis resté libéral" (1934), reprinted in X-Crise, *De la recurrence des crises économiques* (Paris, 1982), pp. 63–71; A. Brockdorff, "Weltwirtschaft und Weltrüstung," *Wehrtechnische Monatshefte* (1935), pp. 492–6; L. Robbins, *Economic Planning and International Order* (London, 1937); W.H. Chamberlain, "War—Shortcut to Fascism," *American Mercury* (1940), pp. 391–400; J.F.C. Fuller, "The Development of Totalitarian Warfare," *Journal of the Royal Artillery* (1937), pp. 441–52; H. Butler, "Where Is Rearmament Leading Us?" *The Listener* (1939), pp. 1349–50, 1377; R. Riccardi, "Guerra economica," in his *La collaborazione economic europea* (Rome, 1943), pp. 1–37; G. Bottai, "Guerra e economia," *Critica Fascista* (1939), pp. 362–3; H.G. Wells's prewar fictional history *The Shape of Things to Come: The Ultimate Revolution* (London, 1933), F.A. Hayek's famous wartime anti-socialist polemic *The Road to Serfdom* (London, 1944) and G. Orwell's postwar dystopian novel *Nineteen Eighty-Four* (London, 1949) all echo these themes.

6. J.B. Condliffe, *Changing Structure of Economic Life* (Paris, 1939), p. 15.

7. D.C. Watt, *How War Came: The Immediate Origins of the Second World War 1938–1939* (London, 1989); A. Tooze, *The Wages of Destruction: The Making and Breaking of the Nazi Economy* (London, 2007), pp. xxii–v, 135–47; M. Harrison, "Why the Rich Won," pp. 1–28, paper presented to the conference "La mobilisation de la Nation à l'ère de la guerre totale, 1914–1945" organized by the French Ministry of Defence, Paris, October 26–28, 2004.

CHAPTER 1: DEEP WAR AND RED MILITARISM

1. L. Samuelson, *Plans for Stalin's War Machine: Tukhachevskii and Military-Economic Planning, 1925–1941* (Basingstoke, 2000), p. 142.

2. D. Stone, "Tukhachevskii in Leningrad: Military Politics and Exile, 1928–1931," *Europe-Asia Studies* (1996), pp. 1365–86. To put these numbers into perspective, during the whole of 1941–5, the Soviet Union manufactured 112,100 combat aircraft and

102,000 tanks and self-propelled guns. See M. Harrison (ed.), *The Economics of World War II* (Cambridge, 1998), p. 15.

3. Stone, "Tukhachevskii in Leningrad," p. 1379; Samuelson, *Stalin's War Machine*, pp. 92–112.

4. See, for instance, W.E. Chamberlain, *Russia's Iron Age* (London, 1935), p. 199, or O. Tanin and E. Yohan, *When Japan Goes to War* (London, 1937), p. 52.

5. K.E. Bailes, "The American Connection: Ideology and the Transfer of American Technology to the Soviet Union, 1917–1941," *Comparative Studies in Society and History* (1981), p. 426.

6. P.I. Holquist, "Violent Russia, Deadly Marxism: Russia in the Epoch of Violence," *Kritika* (2003), pp. 627–52.

7. O.V. Khlevniuk, *Master of the House: Stalin and His Inner Circle* (New Haven, 2009), pp. 1–38.

8. N.S. Simonov, "The 'War Scare' of 1927 and the Birth of the Soviet Defence-Industry Complex," in M. Harrison and J. Barber (eds.), *The Soviet Defence-Industry Complex from Stalin to Khrushchev* (London, 1999), pp. 33–46; P. Temin, "Soviet and Nazi Economic Planning in the 1930s," *Economic History Review* (1991), pp. 573–93.

9. R.W. Davies, M. Harrison and S.G. Wheatcroft, *The Economic Transformation of the Soviet Union, 1913–1945* (Cambridge, 2008), p. 113.

10. D. Stone, *Hammer and Rifle: The Militarization of the Soviet Union, 1926–1933* (Lawrence, KS, 2000), p. 102; R.W. Davies (ed.), *The Stalin-Kaganovich Correspondence, 1931–1936* (New Haven, 2003), pp. 219–20, 231.

11. S. Naveh, "Tukhachevsky," in H. Skukman (ed.), *Stalin's Generals* (London, 1993), pp. 255–73; Stone, "Tukhachevskii in Leningrad," pp. 1366–7.

12. S.W. Stoecker, *Forging Stalin's Army: Marshall Tukhachevsky and the Politics of Military Innovation* (Boulder, CO, 1998), pp. 135–80; Tukhachevsky, "New Questions of War," in R. Simpkin, *Deep Battle: The Brainchild of Marshal Tukhachevskii* (Dulles, VA, 1987), pp. 135–53.

13. A. Sokolov, "Before Stalinism: The Defense Industry of Soviet Russia in the 1920s," *Comparative Economic Studies* (2005), pp. 31–49; Stone, *Hammer and Rifle*, pp. 22–4; Stone, *Hammer and Rifle*, pp. 25, 31–2, 58–9.

14. A. Markevich, "Planning the Soviet Defense Industry: The Late 1920s and 1930s," *PERSA Paper* no. 37 (2004), pp. 1–38.

15. M. Chechinski, "The Economics of Defense in the USSR," *Survey* (1985), pp. 66.

16. Samuelson, *Stalin's War Machine*, pp. 45–7, 51–2, 59; Stone, "Tukhachevskii in Leningrad," pp. 1365–86.

17. Stone, *Hammer and Rifle*, pp. 87–93.

18. Simonov, "'War Scare' of 1927" and L. Samuelson, "The Red Army's Economic Objectives and Involvements in Economic Planning, 1925–40," both in Harrison and Barber, *Soviet Defence-Industry Complex*, pp. 41–44, 56–58; Stone, *Hammer and Rifle*, pp. 124–8.

19. I.F. Clarke, *Voices Prophesying War: Future Wars 1763–3749* (Oxford, 1992); RGVA, 33988/2/683-8; S. Main, "The Red Army and the Future War in Europe, 1925–40" and L. Samuelson, "Wartime Perspectives and Economic Planning: Tukhachevsky and the Military-Industrial Complex 1925–1937," both in S. Pons and A. Ramano (eds.), *Russia in the Age of Wars, 1914–1945* (Milan, 2000), pp. 171–85, 187–214; J.R. Harris, "Encircled by Enemies: Stalin's Perceptions of the Capitalist World, 1918–1941," *Journal of Strategic Studies* (2007), pp. 513–45.

20. RGVA, 33988/2/682/10-36; O.N. Ken, *Mobilizatsionnoe planirovanie i politicheskie resheniya konets 1920—seredina 1930-kh gg* (St. Petersburg, 2002), pp. 284, 306, 325–26; Samuelson, *Stalin's War Machine*, pp. 18–19.

21. L.T. Lih, O.V. Naumov and O.V. Khlevniuk (eds.), *Stalin's Letters to Molotov, 1925–36* (New Haven, 1995), pp. 208–9.

22. R.W. Davies, "Soviet Defence Industries During the First Five Year Plan," in L. Edmondson and P. Waldron (eds.), *Economy and Society in Russia and the Soviet Union, 1860–1939* (New York, 1996), p. 257; Samuelson, *Stalin's War Machine*, p. 124.

23. J. Haslam, *Soviet Foreign Policy, 1930–33* (Basingstoke, 1984), p. 73.

24. RGASPI, 74/2/38/52-3 (November 27, 1931); D. Watson, "The Politburo and Foreign Policy in the 1930s," in E.A. Rees (ed.), *The Nature of Stalin's Dictatorship* (Basingstoke, 2003), p. 142.

25. R.W. Davies, *The Industrialisation of Soviet Russia: Crisis and Progress in the Soviet Economy, 1931–33* (Basingstoke, 1996), pp. 457, 466; Davies, *Economic Transformation*, p. 149.

26. Stone, *Hammer and Rifle*, p. 140; Davies, "Soviet Defence Industries," pp. 250–6; Davies, *Industrialisation of Soviet Russia*, pp. 112–18.

27. Samuelson, *Stalin's War Machine*, pp. 29–34; M. Zeidler, *Reichswehr und Rote Armee 1920–1933: Wege und Stationen einer unge-wohnlichen Zusammenarbeit* (Munich, 1993); S.A. Gorlow, "Geheimsache Moskau-Berlin: Die militärpolitische Zusammenarbeit zwischen der Sowjetunion und dem Deutschen Reich 1920–1933," *Vierteljahrshefte für Zeitgeschichte* (1996), pp. 133–65.

28. Stone, *Hammer and Rifle*, p. 193; J. Milsom, *Russian Tanks 1900–1970* (London, 1970), pp. 21–38; Russia file K612, Vickers Archive, Cambridge University Library, UK; G.F. Hoffman, "Doctrine, Tank Technology, and Execution: I.A. Khalepskii and the Red Army's Fulfilment of Deep Offensive Operations," *Journal of Slavic Military Studies* (1996), pp. 294–96.

29. Stone, *Hammer and Rifle*, pp. 192–202; R.W. Davies, "Planning Mobilisation of the Soviet Economy in the 1930s," *PERSA Paper no. 28* (2004), p. 20.

30. M. Mukhin, "Employment in the Soviet Aircraft Industry, 1918–1940," *PERSA Paper no. 36* (2004), pp. 1–46; Stone, *Hammer and Rifle*, pp. 202–3.

31. Davies, *Stalin-Kaganovich*, p. 157; Samuelson, *Stalin's War Machine*, p. 137.

32. TNA, CAB 48/36, IFC/9, "Russia: Industrial Mobilisation for War," July 1931, and CAB 48/4, Industrial Intelligence Centre, FCI 45, December 14, 1933; DDF, 1, iv,

no. 308; Davies, *Industrialisation of Soviet Russia*; Samuelson, *Stalin's War Machine*, pp. 143–4.

33. Samuelson, *Stalin's War Machine*, pp. 139, 145.

34. Davies, *Industrialisation of Soviet Russia*, pp. 432–4; Harrison and Barber, *Soviet Defence-Industry Complex*, pp. 41, 70–95.

35. Davies, *Industrialisation of Soviet Russia*, pp. 317–25.

CHAPTER 2:
COLONEL ISHIWARA GOES TO MANCHURIA

1. J. R. Stewart, "Manchuria: The Land and its Economy," *Economic Geography* (1932), pp. 134–60.

2. F.R. Dickinson, *War and National Reinvention: Japan in the Great War, 1914–1919* (Cambridge, MA, 1999).

3. A.D. Coox, "The Kwantung Army Dimension," in P. Duus, R.H. Myers and M.R. Peattie (eds.), *Japan's Informal Empire in China, 1895–1937* (Princeton, 1989), pp. 395–428.

4. S. Hiroharu, "Manchurian Incident, 1931," in W.J. Morley (ed.), *The London Naval Conference and the Manchurian Incident, 1928–1932* (New York, 1984), pp. 119–230; S.N. Ogata, *Defiance in Manchuria: The Making of Japanese Foreign Policy, 1931–1932* (Berkeley, CA, 1964), pp. 48–9; L. Young, *Japan's Total Empire: Manchuria and the Culture of Wartime Imperialism* (Berkeley, CA, 1999), pp. 55–149.

5. M. Peattie, *Ishiwara Kanji and Japan's Confrontation with the West* (Princeton, 1975), pp. 21–5.

6. Ibid., pp. 27–83.

7. J. Weland, "Misguided Intelligence: Japanese Intelligence Officers in the Manchurian Incident, September 1931," *Journal of Military History* (1994), pp. 445–7.

8. R.J. Samuels, *Rich Nation, Strong Nation: National Security and the Technological Transformation of Japan* (New York, 1996), pp. 33–92.

9. M. Barnhart, *Japan Prepares for Total War: The Search for Economic Security, 1918–1941* (Ithaca, NY, 1987), pp. 22–34; C. Johnson, *MITI and the Japanese Miracle: The Growth of Industrial Policy, 1925–1975* (Stanford, CA, 1982), pp. 117–18.

10. L.A. Humphreys, *The Way of the Heavenly Sword: Japanese Army in the 1920s* (Stanford, CA, 1995), pp. 110–16; In *Japan Prepares for Total War,* Barnhart was the first to use the tag "total war" officers.

11. Peattie, *Ishiwara Kanji,* p. 187; H. Seki, "The Manchurian Incident, 1931," in J.W. Morley (ed.), *Japan Erupts: The London Naval Conference and the Manchurian Incident, 1928–1932* (New York, 1984), pp. 174, 211–13.

12. E. Pauer (ed.), *Japan's War Economy* (London, 1999), pp. 1–3; Humphreys, *Heavenly Sword,* pp. 42–59.

13. N. Takafusa, "The Japanese War Economy As a 'Planned Economy,'" and O. Kerde, "The Ideological Background of the Japanese War Economy: Visions of the 'Reformist Bureaucrats,'" both in Pauer, *Japan's War Economy*, pp. 9–22, 23–38; N. Takafusa, "Depression, Recovery, and War 1920–1945," in P. Duus (ed.), *The Cambridge History of Japan: The Twentieth Century* (Cambridge, 1988), pp. 451–93.

14. Johnson, *MITI and the Japanese Miracle*, pp. 83–115.

15. Takafusa, "Japanese War Economy," and Kerde, "Ideological Background," both in Pauer, *Japan's War Economy*, pp. 9–22, 23–38; R.J. Samuels, *Machiavelli's Children: Leaders and Their Legacies in Italy and Japan* (New York, 2004), pp. 140–50.

16. R.H. Myers, "Creating a Modern Enclave Economy: The Economic Integration of Japan, Manchuria, and North China, 1932–1945," in P. Duus, R.H. Myers and M.R. Peattie (eds.), *The Japanese Wartime Empire, 1931–1945* (Princeton, 1996), pp. 136–44; Young, *Total Empire*, pp. 183–221; Johnson, *MITI and the Japanese Miracle*, pp. 129–32; Samuels, *Machiavelli's Children*, pp. 144–5.

17. W.M. Fletcher, "Japanese Banks and National Economic Policy, 1920–1936," in H. James, H. Lindgren and A. Teichova (eds.), *The Role of Banks in the Interwar Economy* (Cambridge, 1991), pp. 251–72.

18. R.J. Smethurst, *From Foot Soldier to Finance Minister: Takahashi Korekijo, Japan's Keynes* (Cambridge, MA, 2007), pp. 189–267.

19. K. Ohkawa, M. Shinohara and M. Umemura (eds.), *Estimates of Long-Term Economic Statistics of Japan Since 1868* (Tokyo, 1965), p. 187; D.K. Nanto and S. Takagi, "Korekijo Takahashi and Japanese Recovery from the Great Depression," *American Economic Review* (1985), pp. 369–74; Johnson, *MITI and the Japanese Miracle*, pp. 119–20.

20. Humphreys, *Heavenly Sword*; J.B. Crowley, "Japanese Army Factionalism in the early 1930s," *Journal of Asia Studies* (1962), pp. 309–26.

21. Barnhart, *Japan Prepares for Total War*, pp. 34–6; A.D. Coox, *Nomonhan: Japan Against Russia, 1939* (Stanford, CA, 1990), p. 77.

22. Johnson, *MITI and the Japanese Miracle*, pp. 123–4.

23. B. Victoria, *Zen War Stories* (London, 2003), p. 30.

24. Coox, *Nomonhan*, pp. 75–84.

25. Stone, *Hammer and Rifle*, p. 188; Samuelson, *Stalin's War Machine*, pp. 128, 167–8.

26. *Manchester Guardian*, March 11, 1935; Coox, *Nomonhan*, p. 84; Peattie, *Ishiwara Kanji*, p. 198.

27. Smethurst, *From Foot Soldier to Finance Minister*, pp. 268–98; Johnson, *MITI and the Japanese Miracle*, pp. 120, 134.

28. Office of the Chief of Military History, US Department of the Army, Japanese Monograph no. 144, Appendix no. 1 (http://www.ibiblio.org/pha/monos/144/index.html).

29. Peattie, *Ishiwara Kanji*, pp. 191–222; Barnhart, *Japan Prepares for Total War*, pp. 42–49.

30. *The Times*, November 28, 1936. My emphasis.

31. G. Berger, "Politics and Mobilization in Japan, 1931–1945," in Duus, *Cambridge History of Japan*, pp. 118–37.

32. W.C. Kirby, "Chinese War Economy: Mobilization, Control, and Planning in Nationalist China," in J.C. Hsiung and S.I. Levine (eds.), *China's Bitter Victory* (New York, 1992), pp. 185–212.

33. M. Barnhart, "Japan's Economic Security and the Origins of the Pacific War," *Journal of Strategic Studies* (1981), p. 112.

CHAPTER 3: "REARM AND GET READY"

1. T. Vogelsang, "Neue Dokumente zur Geschichte der Reichswehr 1930–1933," *Vierteljahrshefte für Zeitgeschichte* (1954), pp. 454–5; A. Wirsching, "'Man kann nur Boden germanisieren': Eine neue Quelle zu Hitlers Rede vor den Spitzen der Reichswehr am 3 Februar 1933," *Vierteljahrshefte für Zeitgeschichte* (2001), pp. 517–50.

2. Wirsching, "'Man kann nur Boden germanisieren,'" p. 547.

3. M. Pöhlmann, "Von Versailles nach Armageddon: Totalisierungserfahrung und Kriegserwartung in deutschen Militarzeitschriften," in S. Förster (ed.), *An der Schwelle zum Totalen Krieg: Die Militärische Debatte über den Krieg der Zukunft 1919–1939* (Paderborn, 2002), pp. 323–58; R. Chickering, "Sore Loser: Ludendorff's Total War," in R. Chickering and S. Förster (eds.), *The Shadows of Total War: Europe, East Asia, and the United States, 1919–1939* (Cambridge, 2003), pp. 151–78; and more generally B. Barth, *Dolchstoßlegenden und politische Desintegration: Das Trauma der deutschen Niederlage im Ersten Weltkrieg 1914–1933* (Düsseldorf, 2003); D. Stevenson, *1914–1918: The History of the First World War* (London, 2004), pp. 371–500; R. Bessel, "Mobilization and Demobilization in Germany, 1916–19," in Horne, *State, Society and Mobilization*, pp. 212–22; T. Rohkrämer, "Strangelove, or How Ernst Jünger Learned to Love Total War," in Chickering and Förster, *The Shadows of Total War*, p. 187.

4. M. Geyer, "Professionals and Junkers: German Rearmament and Politics in the Weimar Republic," in R. Bessel and E.J. Feuchtwanger (eds.), *Social Change and Political Development in Weimar Germany* (London, 1981), p. 99; R.M. Muller, "Werner von Blomberg—Hitlers 'idealistischer' Kriegsminister," in R.M. Smelser and E. Syring, *Die Militärelite des Dritten Reiches* (Frankfurt, 1995), pp. 50–65.

5. M. Geyer, *Aufrüstung oder Sicherheit: Die Reichswehr in der Krise der Machtpolitik 1924–1936* (Wiesbaden, 1980), pp. 161–3; A. Gat, *Fascist and Liberal Visions of War: Fuller, Liddell Hart, Douhet, and other Modernists* (Oxford, 1998), pp. 80–103; K.A. Schäfer, *Werner von Blomberg: Hitlers erster Feldmarschall* (Paderborn, 2006), pp. 66–75.

6. Geyer, "Professionals and Junkers," pp. 102–18; W. Deist, "The Rearmament of the Wehrmacht," in W. Deist, M. Messerschmidt, H.-E. Volkmann and W. Wette

(eds.), *Germany and the Second World War: The Build-up of German Aggression,* vol. 1 (Oxford, 1990), pp. 375–92; D.K.J. Peukert, *The Weimar Republic: The Crisis of Classical Modernity* (London, 1993).

7. M. Geyer, "Das Zweite Rüstungsprogramm (1930–1934)," *Militärgeschichtliche Mitteilungen* (1975), pp. 125–72, and his "Etudes in Political History: Reichswehr, NSDAP, and the Seizure of Power," in P.D. Stachura (ed.), *The Nazi Machtergreifung* (London, 1983), pp. 101–19.

8. H.A. Turner, *Hitler's Thirty Days to Power* (London, 1996).

9. I. Kershaw, *Hitler,* 2 vols. (London, 1998–2000), vol. 1, pp. 29–375.

10. G.L. Weinberg, *Hitler's Second Book* (New York, 2004). Jünger vividly described the militarized "people's community" that Hitler—as well as the German officer corps—had in mind. In his *Total Mobilization* (1930), itself a vivid distillation of the logic of arming for total war, he envisaged a society in which "a person with the least apparent inclination for military conflict still finds himself incapable of refusing the rifle offered by the state, since the possibility of an alternative is not present to his consciousness." See E. Jünger, "Total Mobilization," in R. Wolin (ed.), *The Heidegger Controversy* (London, 1993), p. 134.

11. E. Syring, *Hitler: seine politische Utopie* (Frankfurt, 1994), pp. 170–80; H.-E. Volkmann, "The National Socialist Economy in Preparation for War," in *Germany and the Second World War,* i, pp. 173–8; A. Ringer, *Handel und Außenhandel: Neubau des Außenhandels im nationalsozialistischen Deutschland* (Berlin, 1933), p. 20; Tooze, *Wages of Destruction,* pp. xxiii, 8–12, 138–47; H.H. Herwig, "Geopolitik: Haushofer, Hitler and lebensraum," *Journal of Strategic Studies* (1999), pp. 218–41.

12. B. Simms, "Walter von Reichenau—Der politische General," in Smelser and Syring, *Die Militärelite des Dritten Reiches,* pp. 423–45; Kershaw, *Hitler,* i, p. 443.

13. K.-J. Müller, *Das Heer und Hitler: Armee und nationalsozialistisches Regime 1933–1940* (Stuttgart, 1969), pp. 88–150; Kershaw, *Hitler,* i, pp. 500–26.

14. DGFP, c, i, no. 16; Tooze, *Wages of Destruction,* p. 38.

15. R.J. Overy, *The Nazi Economic Recovery 1932–1938* (Cambridge, 1996), pp. 23–4; Tooze, *Wages of Destruction,* pp. 39–49, 53–4, 62–5; Volkmann, "The National Socialist Economy," in *Germany and the Second World War,* i, pp. 221–8.

16. R. Peter, "General der Infanterie Georg Thomas," in G.R. Ueberschär (ed.), *Hitlers militärische Elite* (Darmstad, 1998), pp. 248–57; G. Thomas, *Geschichte der deutschen Wehr-und Rüstungswirtschaft, 1918–1943/45* (Boppard, 1966), p. 489.

17. W. Stern, "Wehrwirtschaft: A German Contribution to Economics," *Economic History Review* (1960–1), pp. 273–74; BA-MA, RW 19/1261, "Die wehrwirtschaftlichen Leistungen Deutschlands im grossen Kriege' (no date); C. Fischer, "Scoundrels Without a Fatherland? Heavy Industry and Transnationalism in Post–First World War Germany," *Contemporary European History* (2005), pp. 441–64; E.W. Hansen, *Reichswehr und Industrie: Rüstungswirtschaftliche Zusammenarbeit und wirtschaftliche Mobilmachungsvorbereitungen 1923–1932* (Boppard am Rhein, 1978), pp. 154–205; A. Fischer,

"Die Lufthansa als Instrument der geheimen Rüstungspolitik? Ziviler Luftverkehr und Militärisierung in der Weimarer Republik," *Militärgeschichtliche Zeitschrift* (2005), pp. 465–86; Geyer, "Zweite Rüstungsprogramm," pp. 128, 132–4, 153–5.

18. B.A. Carroll, *Design for Total War: Arms and Economics in the Third Reich* (The Hague, 1968), p. 43; R-D. Müller, "The Mobilization of the German Economy for Hitler's War Aims," in B.R. Kroener, R-D. Müller and H. Umbreit (eds.), *Germany and the Second World War: Organization and Mobilization of the German Sphere of Power*, vol. 5/part 1 (Oxford, 2000), pp. 430–48; R. Barthel, "Rüstungswirtschafliche Forderungen der Reichswehrführung im Juni 1934," *Zeitschrift für Militärgeschichte* (1970), pp. 83–92.

19. BA-MA, RH 8, 975, General Liese, 16 May 1934; Deist, "The Rearmament of the Wehrmacht," in *Germany and the Second World War*, i, pp. 419–20.

20. Barthel, "Rüstungswirtschafliche Forderungen," pp. 83–92.

21. Tooze, *Wages of Destruction*, pp. 15–16, 28–29, 525; W. Abelshauser, "Germany: Guns, Butter and Economic Miracles," in Harrison, *Economics of World War II*, pp. 139–40; C. Kopper, *Hjalmar Schacht: Aufstieg und Fall von Hitlers mächtigstem Bankier* (Munich, 2006), pp. 59–273.

22. Tooze, *Wages of Destruction*, pp. 49–95, 99–114.

23. A. Barkai, *Nazi Economics: Ideology, Theory, and Policy* (Oxford, 1990), pp. 21–105; Tooze, *Wages of Destruction*, pp. 99–125.

24. DGFP, c, i, nos. 479, 499; M. Domarus (ed.), *Hitler: Speeches and Proclamations*, 4 vols. (London, 1990–8), i, pp. 322–34.

25. DGFP, c, iii, nos. 162, 281, 293, 373.

26. R. Wohl, *The Spectacle of Flight: Aviation and the Western Imagination, 1920–1950* (New Haven, 2007); Gat, *Fascist and Liberal Visions*, pp. 52–63.

27. P. Fritzsche, *A Nation of Fliers: German Aviation and the Popular Imagination* (Cambridge, MA, 1992), and his "Machine Dreams: Airmindedness and the Reinvention of Germany," *American Historical Review* (1993), pp. 685–709; R.J. Overy, *Goering: Iron Man* (London, 1987), pp. 32–3; E.L. Homze, *Arming the Luftwaffe* (Lincoln, NE, 1976), pp. 47–62.

28. B. Heimann and J. Schunke, "Eine geheime Denkschrift zur Luftkriegskonzeption Hitler-Deutschlands vom Mai 1933," *Zeitschrift für Militärgeschichte* (1964), pp. 72–86.

29. Homze, *Arming the Luftwaffe*, pp. 62–112, 192–5; L. Budraß, *Flugzeugindustrie und Luftrüstung in Deutschland 1918–1945* (Düsseldorf, 1998), pp. 293–470.

30. K.-J. Müller, *General Ludwig Beck: Studien und Dokumente zur politisch-militaerischen Vorstellungswelt und Taetigkeit des Generalstabchefs des deutschen Heeres 1933–1938* (Boppard, 1980), pp. 190, 415–24, and his *Generaloberst Ludwig Beck: Eine Biographie* (Paderborn, 2007), pp. 186–228.

31. H.-G. Seraphim, *Das politische Tagebuch Alfred Rosenbergs aus den Jahren 1934/35 und 1939/40* (Berlin, 1956), pp. 59–62.

32. F. Hoßbach, *Zwischen Wehrmacht und Hitler, 1934–35* (Göttingen, 1965), pp. 81–3.

33. Müller, *Das Heer und Hitler*, pp. 207–11; Schäfer, *Blomberg*, pp. 156–60; H. Höhne, *Die Zeit der Illusionen: Hitler und die Anfänge des Dritten Reiches 1933–1936* (Düsseldorf, 1981), pp. 287–300.

34. Domarus, *Hitler*, ii, pp. 651–80.

35. TBJG, I, 3/i, 279, pp. 313–14.

CHAPTER 4:
"WE ARE MOVING AMONG GIANTS"

1. M. Morselli, *Caporetto 1917: Victory or Defeat?* (London, 2001), p. 100; P. O'Brien, *Mussolini in the First World War: The Journalist, the Soldier, the Fascist* (Oxford, 2004), pp. 59–63.

2. OO, x, pp. 14–1, 36–8, 86–8, 140–2, 381–3.

3. R.J.B. Bosworth, *Mussolini* (London, 2002), pp. 37–99.

4. O'Brien, *Mussolini*, pp. 31–5; Bosworth, *Mussolini*, pp. 100–11.

5. P. Corner and G. Procacci, "The Italian Experience of 'Total' Mobilisation," in Horne, *State, Society and Mobilization*, pp. 223–40; O'Brien, *Mussolini*, pp. 95, 136.

6. Bosworth, *Mussolini*, pp. 123–216; A. Lyttelton, *The Seizure of Power: Fascism in Italy, 1919–1929* (London, 1973), pp. 42–201.

7. J. Gooch, *Mussolini and His Generals: The Armed Forces and Fascist Foreign Policy, 1922–1940* (Cambridge, 2008), pp. 13–22; G. Rochat, "Il Fascismo e la preparazione militare al conflitto mondiale," in A. Del Boca, M. Legnani and M.G. Rossi (eds.), *Il regime fascista* (Rome, 1995), pp. 151–65.

8. F. Minniti, "Aspetti organizzativi del controllo sulla produzione bellica in Italia, 1923–1943," *Clio* (1977), pp. 306–7; G.B. Künzi, "Die Herrschaft der Gedanken: Italienische Militärzeitschriften und das Bild des Krieges," in Förster, *An der Schwelle zum Totalen Krieg*, pp. 44–76.

9. R.O. Paxton, *The Anatomy of Fascism* (London, 2005), pp. 17, 28–32.

10. M. Knox, "Conquest, Foreign and Domestic, in Fascist Italy and Nazi Germany," *Journal of Modern History* (1984), pp. 1–57; O'Brien, *Mussolini*, p. 123.

11. C.A. Ristuccia, "The Italian Economy under Fascism" (DPhil Thesis, University of Oxford, 1999), pp. 5, 12–13; OO, xxii, pp. 29–38.

12 Minniti, "Aspetti organizzativi del controllo," pp. 305–15, and his "Alfredo Dallolio," in A. Mortara (ed.), *I protagonisti dell'intervento pubblico in Italia* (Milan, 1984), pp. 179–201; A. Curami and L. Ceva, "Industria bellica e Stato nell'imperialismo fascista degli anni Trenta," *Nuova Antologia* (1988), pp. 316–38.

13. Samuels, *Machiavelli's Children*, pp. 133–5; A. James Gregor, *Mussolini's Intellectuals* (Princeton, 2006), pp. 107–28; P. Morgan, "'The Party Is Everywhere': The Italian Fascist Party in Economic Life, 1926–40," *English Historical Review* (1999),

pp. 85–111; M. Salvati, "The Long History of Corporatism in Italy," *Contemporary European History* (2005), pp. 233–44.

14. F.H. Alder, *Italian Industrialists from Liberalism to Fascism* (Cambridge, 1995); R. Sarti, *Fascism and the Industrial Leadership in Italy, 1919–1940* (Berkeley, CA, 1971), pp. 1–78.

15. J. Cohen, "The 1927 Revaluation of the Lira," *English Historical Review* (1972), pp. 624–54; V. Zamagni, *The Economic History of Italy 1860–1990* (Oxford, 1997), pp. 247–52.

16. Zamagni, *Economic History,* pp. 274–85 and pp. 255–66; Ristuccia, *Italian Economy,* pp. 19–23; OO, xx, p. 364; C. Ipsen, *Dictating Demography: The Problem of Population in Fascist Italy* (Cambridge, 1996), pp. 50–68.

17. E. Gentile, "Impending Modernity: Fascism and the Ambivalent Image of the United States," *Journal of Contemporary History* (1993), pp. 7–29; Gooch, *Mussolini and His Generals,* pp. 52–60.

18. There was nothing special about the Italian predicament at this time. Senior officers in Japan and Russia also faced similar men-or-machines dilemmas and offered similar solutions. See Humphreys, *Heavenly Sword,* pp. 79, 92, 98–9, and N.S. Simonov, "'Strengthen the Defence of the Land of Soviets': The 1927 'War Alarm' and Its Consequences," *Europe-Asia Studies* (1996), p. 1356.

19. Gooch, *Mussolini and His Generals,* pp. 22–8, 72–81.

20. P. Pieri and G. Rochat, *Pietro Badoglio* (Turin, 1974).

21. LSMG, pp. 61–2; F. Minniti, *Fino alla guerra: strategie e conflitto nella politica di potenza di Mussolini 1923–1940* (Naples, 2000), pp. 39–43.

22. Gooch, *Mussolini and His Generals,* pp. 75–88, 111–20.

23. Minniti, *Fino alla guerra,* pp. 51–2; LSMG, pp. 93–101, 103–5.

24. Gooch, *Mussolini and His Generals,* pp. 82, 132–41, 174–87.

25. F. Mattesini and B. Quintieri, "Italy and the Great Depression," *Explorations in Economic History* (2006), pp. 265–94; F. Bonelli, "Alberto Beneduce, il credito industriale e l'origine dell'IRI," in P. Armani (ed.), *Alberto Beneduce e i problemi dell'economia italiana del suo tempo* (Rome, 1985), pp. 71–85.

26. M. De Cecco, "The Economy from Liberalism to Fascism," in A. Lyttelton (ed.), *Liberal and Fascist Italy* (Oxford, 2002), pp. 62–82; P. Ciocca and G. Toniolo, "Industry and Finance in Italy 1918–1940," *Journal of European Economic History* (1984), pp. 113–37.

27. See the annual tables in League of Nations, *Armaments Yearbook* (Geneva, 1929–36); A.G. Webster, "Anglo-French Relations and the Problems of Disarmament and Security, 1929–1933" (PhD Thesis, Cambridge University, 2001), pp. 187–8; Gooch, *Mussolini and His Generals,* pp. 123–9, 186–7.

28. DDI, 7, x, no. 174; Gooch, *Mussolini and His Generals,* pp. 127–28, 186–87.

29. Gooch, *Mussolini and His Generals,* p. 128; L. Ceva, "The Strategy of Fascist Italy: A Premise," *Totalitarian Movements and Political Religions* (2001), pp. 44–5.

30. Gooch, *Mussolini and His Generals,*pp. 189–202.

31. Bosworth, *Mussolini,* pp. 265–9.

32. DGFP, c, i, no. 83.

33. Gooch, *Mussolini and His Generals,* pp. 195–6.

34. C. Sergè, *Italo Balbo: A Fascist Life* (Berkeley, CA, 1987), pp. 145–288.

35. R. Mallett, *Mussolini and the Origins of the Second World War, 1933–40* (Basingstoke, 2003), pp. 23–4: DGFP, c, iii, nos. 5 & 10, 10–12, 18–19.

36. Gooch, *Mussolini and His Generals,* pp. 197–8; LSMG, pp. 311–16.

37. DDI, 7, xvi, no 358; LSMG, p. 341.

38. D.B. Strang, "Imperial Dreams: The Mussolini-Laval Accords of January 1935," *Historical Journal* (2001), pp. 803–4.

39. Gooch, *Mussolini and His Generals,* pp. 239–310.

40. S. Morewood, "The Chiefs of Staff, the 'Men on the Spot' and the Italo-Abyssinian Emergency, 1935–36," in G. Grün, D. Richardson and G. Stone (eds.), *Decisions and Diplomacy* (London, 1995), pp. 88–99; D.B. Strang, "'The Worst of All Worlds': Oil Sanctons and Italy's Invasion of Abyssinia, 1935–1936," *Diplomacy & Statecraft* (2008), pp. 210–35; C.A. Ristuccia, "The 1935 Sanctions Against Italy: Would Coal and Oil Have Made a Difference?" *European Review of Economic History* (2000), pp. 85–110.

41. G. Post, *Dilemmas of Appeasement: British Deterrence and Defense, 1934–37* (London, 1993), pp. 81–115; G. Rochat, "Badoglio e le operazioni contro l'Etiopia 1935–36," in his *Guerre italiane in Libia e in Etiopia* (Padua, 1991), pp. 99–120.

42. Gooch, *Mussolini and His Generals,* pp. 311–14.

43. OO, xxvii, pp. 268–9.

CHAPTER 5: "SHOULD WE ACCEPT THE REARMAMENT OF GERMANY?"

1. SHD-DAA, 1B 11, 11 December 1933.

2. D. Stevenson, "Britain, France and the Origins of German Disarmament, 1916–19," *Journal of Strategic Studies* (2006), pp. 195–224.

3. Communiqué au Conseil, no. 17, 17 May 1922, C308/1922/ix, Reel 2, LNDP.

4. Preparatory Commission, 5th Session, 4 April 1928, C165/M49/1928/ix, Reel 10, LNDP.

5. C. Lynch, *Beyond Appeasement: Interpreting Interwar Peace Movements* (New York, 1999); M. Siegel, *The Moral Disarmament of France: Education, Pacifism, and Patriotism, 1914–1940* (Cambridge, 2004); T.R. Davies, *The Possibilities of Transnational Activism: The Campaign for Disarmament between the Two World Wars* (Leiden, 2007).

6. Webster, *Anglo-French Relations,* pp. 70, 119–20, 241.

7. Z. Steiner, *Lights That Failed: European International History 1919–1933* (Oxford, 2005), pp. 755–96; D. Richardson, "The Geneva Disarmament Conference, 1932–34,"

in Grün, Richardson, and Stone, *Decisions and Diplomacy,* pp. 60–82; P.C.F. Bankwitz, *Maxime Weygand and Civil-Military Relations in Modern France* (Cambridge, MA, 1967), p. 53.

8. P.O. Cohrs, *The Unfinished Peace After World War I* (Cambridge, 2008).

9. DDF, I, iii, no. 376.

10. D.C. Watt, *Too Serious a Business: European Armed Forces and the Approach of the Second World War* (New York, 1975).

11. S. Schuker, "France and the Remilitarization of the Rhineland, 1936," *French Historical Studies* (1986), pp. 299–338.

12. P. Jackson, "France and the Problems of Security and International Disarmament After the First World War," *Journal of Strategic Studies* (2006), pp. 247–80.

13. B. Serrigny, "L'Organisation de la nation pour le temps de guerre," *Revue des Deux Mondes* (1923), pp. 583–601; D.M. Segesser, "Nur keine Dummheiten: Das französische Offizierskorps und das Konzept des Totalen Krieges," in Förster, *An der Schwelle zum Totalen Krieg,* pp. 113–74.

14. H. Dutailly, *Les problèmes de l'armée de terre française 1935–1939* (Paris, 1980), pp. 66–72; R. Tomlinson, "The 'Disappearance' of France, 1896–1940: French Politics and the Birth Rate," *Historical Journal* (1985), pp. 405–16.

15. J.-P. Dormois, *The French Economy in the Twentieth Century* (Cambridge, 2004), pp. 11–17; T. Imlay, *Facing the Second World War: Strategy, Politics, and Economics in Britain and France 1938–1940* (Oxford, 2003), pp. 237–8; P. Bairoch, "International Industrialization levels from 1750 to 1980," *Journal of European Economic History* (1982), pp. 294–304; R.J. Young, *In Command of France: French Foreign Policy and Military Planning, 1933–1940* (Cambridge, MA, 1978), pp. 13–32.

16. Jackson, "France and the Problems of Security," p. 254.

17. R. Frank[enstein], *Le prix du réarmement français, 1935–1939* (Paris, 1982), pp. 46–49; M. Alexander, "In Defence of the Maginot Line: Security Policy, Domestic Politics and the Economic Depression in France," in R. Boyce (ed.), *French Foreign and Defence Policy, 1918–1940* (London, 1998), pp. 163–94; M. Vaïsse and J. Doise, *Diplomatie et outil militaire* (Paris, 1993), pp. 345–57.

18. R.J. Young, "La guerre de longue durée: Some Reflections on French Strategy and Diplomacy in the 1930s," in A. Preston (ed.), *General Staffs and Diplomacy Before the Second World War* (London, 1978), pp. 41–64.

19. M. Alexander, *The Republic in Danger: General Maurice Gamelin and the Politics of French Defence, 1933–1940* (Cambridge, 1992), pp. 82, 83–4; Bankwitz, *Weygand,* pp. 208–89.

20. M. Vaïsse, *Sécurité d'abord: La politique française en matière de désarmement, 9 décembre 1930–17 avril 1934* (Paris, 1981), pp. 292–320; Bankwitz, *Weygand,* pp. 53–71; DDF, I, i, nos. 250, 268, 272, 273, 286.

21. J. Jackson, *The Politics of Depression in France 1932–1936* (Cambridge, 1985), pp. 23–34; Frank, *Le prix du réarmement,* pp. 26, 29–30.

22. K. Mouré, *The Gold Standard Illusion: France, the Bank of France, and the International Gold Standard, 1914–1939* (Oxford, 2002); L.D. Schwarz, "Searching for Recovery: Unbalanced Budgets, Deflation and Rearmament in France during the 1930s," in W.R. Garside (ed.), *Capitalism in Crisis: International Responses to the Great Depression* (London, 1993), pp. 96–104; P. Jackson, *France and the Nazi Menace: Intelligence and Policy-making, 1933–1939* (Oxford, 2000), pp. 66–7, 78; E. du Réau, *Édouard Daladier, 1884–1970* (Paris, 1993), pp. 103–5.

23. Jackson, *Nazi Menace*, p. 64.

24. Webster, *Anglo-French Relations*, pp. 85–6, 224–5; Jackson, *Nazi Menace*, pp. 49, 60, 55–6, 93, 123.

25. R.J. Young, "L'attaque brusquée and Its Use As a Myth in Inter-war France,' *Historical Reflections* (1981), pp. 92–113.

26. DBFP, 2, v, no. 207; Jackson, *Nazi Menace*, p. 78; du Réau, *Daladier*, pp. 99–112; Bankwitz, *Weygand*, pp. 54–5; G. Martel (ed.), *The Times and Appeasement: The Journals of A. L. Kennedy 1932–1939* (Cambridge, 2000), p. 135.

27. AVPRF, 05/14/97/29 (28 January 1934).

28. DDF, 1, v, no. 477; Vaïsse, *Sécurité d'abord*, p. 540.

29. Jackson, *Nazi Menace*, p. 103; Vaïsse, *Sécurité d'abord*, pp. 541–78.

30. Deist, "The Rearmament of the Wehrmacht," in *Germany and the Second World War*, i, pp. 417–18; Vaïsse, *Sécurité d'abord*, p. 593.

31. Alexander, *Republic in Danger*, pp. 42–4.

32. Frank, *Le prix du réarmement*, pp. 35–37; SHD-DAT, 7N 2638-2, 24 January 1935 and 2N19-3, 25 January 1935; P. Facon, *L'armée de l'air dans la tourmente: La bataille de France 1939–1940* (Paris, 1997), pp. 72–3; Frank, *Le prix du réarmement*, pp. 55–63.

33. SHD-DAT, 7N 2675, 8 April 1933.

34. D. Dutton, *Neville Chamberlain* (London, 2001); R. Self, *Neville Chamberlain* (London, 2006), pp. 1–50.

35. Self, *Chamberlain*, pp. 50–63.

36. Ibid., pp. 151–233; A. Booth, "The British Reaction to the Economic Crisis," in Garside, *Capitalism in Crisis*, pp. 30–55; Steiner, *Lights That Failed*, pp. 658–68.

37. Self, *Chamberlain*, p. 212; *The Times*, April 16, 1935.

38. TNA, CAB 23/72, Cabinet, 31 October 1932; CDL, iii, pp. 213, 309, 355.

39. CDL, iii, p. 379.

40. TNA, CAB 23/77, Cabinet, 30 September 1933 and CAB 24/245, CP 294 (33), 8 December 1933; HCDeb, 5, vol. 283, pp. 650–1; Martel, *The Times and Appeasement*, p. 151.

41. C.J. Kitching, *Britain and the Problem of International Disarmament, 1919–34* (London, 1999), pp. 166–9; CDL, iv, p. 65.

42. TNA, CAB 4/22, CID Paper No. 1134-B, March 1934; TNA, FO 1093/78, April 1929.

43. P. Jackson and J. Maiolo, "Strategic intelligence, Counter-Intelligence and Alliance Diplomacy in Anglo-French Relations Before the Second World War,"

Militärgeschichtliche Zeitschrift (2006), pp. 417–61; J.P. Harris, "British Military Intelligence and the Rise of German Mechanized Forces, 1929–40," *Intelligence and National Security* (1991), pp. 395–417; J. Maiolo, *The Royal Navy and Nazi Germany, 1933–1939* (Basingstoke, 1998), pp. 29–30.

44. TNA, CAB 60/12, PSO 317, 21 December 1931; CAB 48/1, ICF/450, 1 April 1933; Martel, *The Times and Appeasement,* pp. 57–8; S. Roskill, *Hankey: Man of Secrets,* 3 vols. (London, 1970–4), iii, pp. 54–62, 82.

45. Self, *Chamberlain,* p. 236.

46. D. Edgerton, *Warfare State: Britain, 1920–1970* (Cambridge, 2005), pp. 21–6; G.C. Peden, *Arms, Economics and British Strategy* (Cambridge, 2007), pp. 125–37; J.R. Ferris, *Men, Money and Diplomacy: The Evolution of British Strategic Policy, 1919–1926* (New York, 1989), p. 181.

47. D. Richardson and C.J. Kitching, "Britain and the World Disarmament Conference," in P. Catterall and C.J. Morris (eds.), *Britain and the Threat to Stability in Europe* (London, 1993), pp. 44–50; DBFP, 2, v, no. 179.

48. Roskill, *Hankey,* iii, p. 70; J.F. Naylor, *A Man and an Institution: Sir Maurice Hankey, the Cabinet Secretariat and the Custody of Cabinet Secrecy* (Cambridge, 1984), p. 58.

49. CHT/4/4, Chatfield papers, 3 November 1933 and 2 February 1934, National Maritime Museum, Greenwich, UK.

50. HCDeb, 5, vol. 270, p. 638; U. Bialer, *The Shadow of the Bomber: The Fear of Air Attack and British Politics, 1932–1939* (London, 1980), pp. 7–100.

51. B. Bond, *Chief of Staff: The Diaries of Lieutenant-General Sir Henry Pownall,* 2 vols. (London, 1972–4), i, pp. 24–38; P. Williamson, *Stanley Baldwin* (Cambridge, 1999), pp. 47–57, 305–10.

52. TNA, CAB 16/109, DRC 14, 28 February 1934.

53. N.H. Gibbs, *Grand Strategy: Rearmament Policy* (London, 1976), p. 543.

54. TNA, CAB 48/4, FCI 61, March 1934.

55. W.K. Wark, *The Ultimate Enemy: British Intelligence and Nazi Germany, 1933–39* (London, 1985), pp. 37–43.

56. Self, *Chamberlain,* p. 239; TNA, CAB 16/110, DC(M) 3 May 1934; CAB 16/111, DC(M)(32) 120, June 1934; Gibb, *Grand Strategy,* p. 115; Gat, *Fascist and Liberal Visions,* pp. 146–87.

57. Roskill, *Hankey,* iii, pp. 119–20.

58. Wark, *Ultimate Enemy,* p. 42; Jackson, *Nazi Menace,* p. 124.

59. HCDeb., 5, vol. 295, pp. 857–83; G. Stewart, *Burying Caesar: Churchill, Chamberlain and the Battle for the Tory Party* (London, 2000), pp. 204N18.

60. Peden, *Arms, Economics,* p.127; UK House of Commons, Command Paper 4827, March 1934.

61. CDL, iv, p. 119.

62. Wark, *Ultimate Enemy,* pp. 43–7.

63. Bond, *Chief of Staff,* i, pp. 76–7; Self, *Chamberlain,* pp. 252–3.

CHAPTER 6:
THE MILITARY-INDUSTRIAL COMPLEX

1. League of Nations, *Armaments Yearbook* (Geneva, 1930), pp. 595, 898; Peattie, *Ishiwara Kanji*, pp. 210–22; B. Emeny, *The Strategy of Raw Materials: A Study of America in Peace and War* (New York, 1934).

2. Bailes, "American Connection," pp. 430–1; D.M. Kennedy, *Freedom from Fear: The American People in the Depression and War, 1929–1945* (Oxford, 1999), pp. 13–27.

3. Schäfer, *Blomberg*, pp. 71–5; Angell, *Character of a New War*, p. 8; R.J. Art, "The United States, the Balance of Power, and World War II: Was Spykman Right?," *Security Studies* (2005), pp. 365–406.

4. R.D. Cuff, *War Industries Board: Business-Government Relations During World War I* (Baltimore,1972); H. Rockoff, "Until It's Over, Over There: The U.S. Economy in World War I," in M. Harrison and S. Broadberry (eds.), *The Economics of World War I* (Cambridge, 2005), pp. 310–43; R. Schaffer, *America in the Great War: The Rise of the War Welfare State* (Oxford, 1992), pp. 31–63.

5. Markevich, "Planning the Supply of Weapons," in M. Harrison, *Guns and Rubles: The Defense Industry in the Stalinist State* (New Haven, 2008), p. 80.

6. P.A.C. Koistinen, *Planning War, Pursuing Peace: Political Economy of American Warfare, 1920–1939* (Lawrence, KS, 1998), pp. 42–59.

7. P.M. Abramo, "The Economic and Military Potential of the United States: Industrial Mobilization Planning, 1919–1945" (PhD Thesis, Temple University, 1996), pp. 6–7; B. Greiner, "'Die Beschäftigung mit der fernen Vergangenheit ist nutzlos': Der "Totale Krieg" im Spiegel amerikanischer Militärzeitschriften," in Förster, *An der Schwelle zum Totalen Krieg*, pp. 443–65; J.W. Bendersky, *The "Jewish Threat": Anti-Semitic Politics of the U.S. Army* (New York, 2000), pp. 1–46; D.E. Johnson, *Fast Tanks and Heavy Bombers 1917–1945* (New York, 1999), pp. 27–9; J. Braeman, "Power and Diplomacy: The 1920s Reappraised," *Review of Politics* (1982), pp. 347–8.

8. G.C. Herring, *From Colony to Superpower: U.S. Foreign Relations Since 1776* (Oxford, 2009), pp. 436–83.

9. Bendersky, *"Jewish Threat,"* pp. 1–46; B. Greiner, "'The Study of the Distant Past Is Futile': American Reflections on New Military Frontiers," in Chickering and Förster, *Shadows of Total War*, pp. 239–51.

10. H.W. Thatcher, *Planning for Industrial Mobilization 1920–1940* (Washington, DC, 1943), pp. 15–96; T.J. Gough, "Soldiers, Businessmen and US Industrial Mobilisation Planning Between the World Wars," *War and Society* (1991), p. 69.

11. R.N. Stromberg, "American Business and the Approach of War, 1935–1941," *Journal of Economic History* (1953), pp. 58–78; W. Leuchtenburg, "The New Deal and the Analogue of War," in J. Braeman (ed.), *Change and Continuity in Twentieth Century America* (Columbus, 1964), pp. 81–8.

12. E. Trigg, "Industry and National Defence," *Army Ordnance* (1930), pp. 107–9; T.J. Gough, "Origins of the Army Industrial College-Military-Business Tensions After

World War I," *Armed Forces and Society* (1991), pp. 259–75, and his "Soldiers, Businessmen," pp. 63–98; Abramo, *Economic and Military Potential*, pp. 22–110; A.A. Blum, "Birth and Death of the M-Day Plan," in H. Stein (ed.), *American Civil-Military Decisions* (Tuscaloosa, 1963), pp. 63–7.

13. J. Schwarz, *The Speculator: Bernard M. Baruch in Washington, 1917–1965* (Chapel Hill, 1981), pp. 331–6; B.M. Baruch, *Taking the Profit Out of War: A Program for Industrial Mobilization* (privately printed, 1931).

14. R.D. Cuff, "Herbert Hoover: The Ideology of Voluntarism and War Organization During the Great War," *Journal of American History* (1977), pp. 358–72; E.W. Hawley, "Herbert Hoover, the Commerce Secretariat, and the Vision of an 'Associative State,' 1921–1928," *Journal of American History* (1974), pp. 116–40; Kennedy, *Freedom from Fear*, pp. 44–94; R.P. Adelstein, "'The Nation As an Economic Unit': Keynes, Roosevelt, and the Managerial Ideal," *Journal of American History* (1991), pp. 160–71.

15. K.E. Irish, "Apt Pupil: Dwight Eisenhower and the 1930 Industrial Mobilization Plan," *Journal of Military History* (2006), pp. 31–61; Koistinen, *Planning War, Pursuing Peace*, 42–63; D.D. Holt, *Eisenhower: The Prewar Diaries and Selected Papers, 1905–1941* (Baltimore, 1998), 138–42; United States Congress, *U.S. War Policies Commission: Hearings Before the Commission Appointed Under the Authority of Public Resolution No. 98* (Washington, DC, 1931).

16. Bendersky, "Jewish Threat," 311; Schwarz, *Speculator*, pp. 336–7; Thatcher, *Planning for Industrial Mobilization*, 97–186; Koistinen, *Planning War, Pursuing Peace*, pp. 227–52; S. Waldman, *Death and Profits: A Study of the War Policies Commission* (New York, 1932).

17. D.D. Eisenhower, *At Ease: Stories I Tell to Friends* (London, 1968), pp. 210–13; D.D. Eisenhower, *Public Papers of the Presidents, Dwight D. Eisenhower, 1960–61* (Washington, DC, 1961), pp. 1035–40; R. Griffith, "Dwight D. Eisenhower and the Corporate Commonwealth," *American Historical Review* (1982), pp. 87–122; F. Kaplan, *The Wizards of Armageddon* (Stanford, CA, 1983), pp. 126–7, 145–7, 176–8, 180–4.

18. Kennedy, *Freedom from Fear*, pp. 10–103; A.J. Badger, *The New Deal: The Depression Years, 1933–40* (New York, 2002), pp. 41–54.

19. Kennedy, *Freedom from Fear*, pp. 104–30; A. Brinkley, *The End of Reform* (New York, 1995), pp. 3–17.

20. Leuchtenburg, "New Deal and the Analogue of War," in Braeman, *Change and Continuity*, pp. 96–143; Schaffer, *America in the Great War*, pp. 109–26; Brinkley, *End of Reform*, pp. 31–47.

21. Kennedy, *Freedom from Fear*, pp. 131–77.

22. Ibid., pp. 177–89; Badger, *New Deal*, pp. 80–88.

23. W. Welk, "Fascist Economic Policy and the NRA," *Foreign Affairs* (1933), p. 98; FA, i, p. 642; K.K. Patel, *Soldiers of Labor: Labor Service in Nazi Germany and New Deal America, 1933–1945* (Cambridge, 2005); J.A. Garraty, "The New Deal, National So-

cialism, and the Great Depression," *American Historical Review* (1973), pp. 907–44; W. Schivelbusch, *Three New Deals: Reflections on Roosevelt's America, Mussolini's Italy, and Hitler's Germany, 1933–1939* (New York, 2007); T.E. Lifka, *The Concept of "Totalitarianism" and American Foreign Policy 1933–1949,* 2 vols. (New York, 1988), pp. 13–55; H. Hoover, *The Challenge to Liberty* (New York, 1934).

24. K. McQuaid, *Big Business and Presidential Power: From FDR to Reagan* (New York, 1982), pp. 11–61; E.W. Hawley, "The New Deal and Business," and M. Derber, "The New Deal and Labor," both in J. Braeman, R.H. Bremner and D. Brody (eds.), *The New Deal: The National Level* (Columbus, 1975), pp. 50–82, 110–32; M.W. Coulter, *The Senate Munitions Inquiry in the 1930s* (New York, 1997), pp. 35–65; R.F. Burk, *The Corporate State and the Broker State: The Du Ponts and American National Politics, 1925–1940* (New Haven, 1990), pp. 122–235.

25. D. MacArthur, *General Douglas MacArthur Reminiscences* (New York, 1964), pp. 99–103; Bendersky, "Jewish Threat," pp. 212–19.

26. S. Casey, *Cautious Crusade: Franklin D. Roosevelt, American Public Opinion and the War Against Nazi Germany* (Oxford, 2001), pp. 15–30; R. Dallek, *Franklin D. Roosevelt and American Foreign Policy 1933–1945* (Oxford, 1979), pp. 23–121; M.A. Butler, *Cautious Visionary: Cordell Hull and Trade Reform, 1933–37* (Kent, OH, 1998), pp. 1–45.

27. Kennedy, *Freedom from Fear,* pp. 126–9, 390; E.M. Bennett, *Franklin D. Roosevelt and the Search for Victory: American-Soviet Relations, 1939–45* (Wilmington, DE, 1993), pp. 1–24; FA, i, pp. 102, 109, 124–5; N.H. Hooker (ed.), *The Moffat Papers* (Cambridge, MA, 1956), p. 93.

28. Kennedy, *Freedom from Fear,* pp. 154–8; Steiner, *Lights That Failed,* pp. 690–5.

29. FRUS, 1933, i, p. 210; FA, i, pp. 375, 421; E. Roosevelt (ed.), *FDR: His Personal Letters 1928–1945,* 3 vols. (London, 1952), iii, p. 143.

CHAPTER 7: THE NAVAL ARMS RACES BEGIN

1. P. Schmidt, *Hitler's Interpreter* (London, 1951), pp. 32–6; DGFP, c, iv, no. 141.

2. N.A. Lambert, "Transformation and Technology in the Fisher Era: The Impact of the Communications Revolution," *Journal of Strategic Studies* (2004), pp. 272–97; J.T. Sumida, *In Defence of Naval Supremacy: Finance, Technology, and British Naval Policy, 1889–1914* (London, 1989).

3. R. O'Connell, *Sacred Vessels: The Cult of the Battleship and the Rise of the US Navy* (Boulder, CO, 1991), pp. 199–206, 234–47; J.R. Ferris, "The Symbol and the Substance of Seapower: Great Britain, the United States and the One-Power Standard, 1919–1921," in B.J.C. McKercher (ed.), *Anglo-American Relations in the 1920s* (London, 1991), pp. 55–80.

4. Ferris, "Symbol and the Substance of Seapower," in McKercher, *Anglo-American Relations,* pp. 76–95; J.T. Sumida, "British Naval Procurement and Technological Change 1919–1939," in P.P. O'Brien (ed.), *Technology and Naval Combat in*

the Twentieth Century and Beyond (London, 2001), p. 134; L. Johnman and H. Murphy, *British Shipbuilding and the State Since 1918* (Exeter, 2002), pp. 7–59.

5. Edgerton, *Warfare State*, pp. 35–41.

6. TNA, CAB 29/148, NCM (35) 23, 30 October 1934.

7. A.J. Marder, *Old Friends, New Enemies: Royal Navy and the Imperial Japanese Navy, 1936–1941* (Oxford, 1981) pp. 22–7.

8. R. Manheim (ed.), *Mein Kampf* (London, 1992), pp. 129–31; BA-MA, RM 6, 263, 1–33, "Feinde der Marine."

9. K.W. Bird, *Erich Raeder* (Annapolis, 2006), pp. 1–111; G. Schreiber, "Zur Kontinuität des Groß-und Weltmachtstrebens der deutschen Marineführung," *Militärgeschichtliche Mitteilungen* (1979), pp. 101–72; J. Dülffer, *Weimar, Hitler, und die Marine: Reichspolitik und Flottenbau, 1920 bis 1939* (Düsseldorf, 1973), pp. 98–203.

10. F. Spotts, *Hitler and the Power of Aesthetics* (London, 2002), p. 312.

11. M. Salewski, "Marineleitung und politische Führung, 1931–1935," *Militärgeschichtliche Mitteilungen* (1971), pp. 113–58; Dülffer, *Weimar, Hitler, und die Marine*, pp. 299–369; Maiolo, *Royal Navy*, pp. 19–37, 63–86.

12. J. Maiolo, "Deception and Intelligence Failure: Anglo-German Preparations for U-boat Warfare in the 1930s," *Journal of Strategic Studies* (1999), pp. 55–76.

13. Maiolo, *Royal Navy*, pp. 19–44; DGFP, c, iv, No. 275.

14. T.P. Mulligan, "Ship-of-the-Line or Atlantic Raider? Battleship Bismarck Between Design Limitations and Naval Strategy," *Journal of Military History* (2005), pp. 1013–44.

15. Maiolo, *Royal Navy*, pp. 87–110.

16. TNA, CAB 16/112, DRC 37, December 1936.

17. W.R. Braisted, "Charles Frederick Hughes," in R.W. Love (ed.), *The Chiefs of Naval Operations* (Annapolis, 1980), pp. 49–66; B.J.C. McKercher, "'A Certain Irritation': The White House, the State Department, and the Desire for a Naval Settlement with Great Britain, 1927–1930," *Diplomatic History* (2007), pp. 829–63; J. Gooch, "'Hidden in the Rock': American Military Perceptions of Great Britain 1919–1940," in L. Freedman (ed.), *War, Strategy and International Politics* (Oxford, 1992), pp. 115–74; W.M. McBride, "The Unstable Dynamics of a Strategic Technology: Disarmament, Unemployment, and the Interwar Battleship," *Technology and Culture* (1997), pp. 286–423; M.A. West, "Laying the Legislative Foundation: The House Naval Affairs Committee and the Construction of the Treaty Navy, 1926–1934" (PhD Thesis, Ohio State University, 1980), pp. 8, 12–15.

18. R.H. Levine, "The Politics of American Naval Rearmament, 1930–1938" (PhD Thesis, Harvard University, 1972), pp. 51–61.

19. C.L. Symonds, "William Veazie Pratt," in Love, *Chiefs of Naval Operations*, pp. 69–86; S.E. Pelz, *Race to Pearl Harbor: The Failure of the Second London Conference and the Onset of World War II* (Boston, 1984), pp. 67–76.

20. E.S. Miller, *War Plan Orange: The U.S. Strategy to Defeat Japan, 1897–1945* (Annapolis, 1991).

21. *New York Times,* December 5, 1932; Pratt, 27 March 1933, File 18, FDRL; K.S. Davis, *FDR: The Beckoning of Destiny 1882–1928* (New York, 1971); E.J. Marolda (ed.), *FDR and the U.S. Navy* (Basingstoke, 1998).

22. J.E. Cook, *Carl Vinson: Patriarch of the Armed Forces* (Macon, GA, 2004), pp. 18–191; Vinson to FDR, 28 December 1932, File 9501, FDRL.

23. J. Walter, "Admiral William H. Standley," in Love, *Chiefs of Naval Operations,* pp. 89–99; U.S. General Board, 1 October 1934, Box 36, Norman H. Davis Papers, Library of Congress, USA.

24. Pelz, *Race to Pearl Harbor,* pp. 125–9, 155–6; Hooker, *Moffat Papers,* pp. 90–3, 115–22; Memorandum by Davis, 28 April 1934, Box 9, Norman H. Davis Papers, Library of Congress, USA; FRUS, 1935, i, pp. 144–9, 23 November 1934.

25. Levine, *Naval Rearmament,* pp. 247–8, 251; *New York Times,* December 30, 1934; Commander R.E. Schuirmann, 28 June 1935, Box 36, Norman H. Davis Papers, Library of Congress, USA.

26. D.C. Evans and M.R. Peattie, *Kaigun: Strategy, Tactics and Technology in the Imperial Japanese Navy, 1887–1941* (Annapolis, 1997), pp. 370–83; S. Asada, *From Mahan to Pearl Harbor: The Imperial Japanese Navy and the United States* (Annapolis, 2006), p. 206.

27. Asada, *From Mahan to Pearl Harbor,* pp. 47–55.

28. Ibid., pp. 56–7.

29. Ibid., pp. 60–95.

30. I. Gow, *Military Intervention in Pre-war Japanese Politics: Admiral Kato Kanji and the Washington System* (London, 2003).

31. Asada, *From Mahan to Pearl Harbor,* pp. 99–125, 164–72; T. Kuramatsu, "Britain, Japan and Inter-war Naval Limitation 1921–1936," in I. Gow and Y.A. Hirama (eds.), *A History of Anglo-Japanese Relations 1600–2000* (London, 2003), pp. 109–26.

32. Asada, *From Mahan to Pearl Harbor,* pp. 126–57.

33. S. Asada, "The Japanese Navy and the United States," in D. Borg and S. Okamoto (eds.), *Pearl Harbor As History* (New York, 1973), p. 240.

34. T. Chida and P.N. Davies, *The Japanese Shipping and Shipbuilding Industries* (New York, 1990); Y. Katada, "Towards the Dismantling of Japan's Military Industrial Complex: The Navy and the Economy in the 1930s," *NUCB Journal of Economics and Information Science* (2005), pp. 21–34.

35. Asada, *From Mahan to Pearl Harbor,* pp. 192–205.

36. Pelz, *Race to Pearl Harbor,* p. 159.

37. *Documents of the London Naval Conference: December 1935–March 1936* (London, 1936), p. 54.

38. FRUS, 1936, i, pp. 94–101.

CHAPTER 8: "WE HAVE REACHED A PLATEAU"

1. *Vierteljahrshefte zur Konjunkturforschung,* vol. III a (1937), pp. 281–4; League of Nations, *Report of the Committee for the Study of Raw Materials,* A.27, 1937 II B, Official Journal (1937), LNDP.

2. Tooze, *Wages of Destruction,* pp. 207–12, 214–19; D. Petzina, *Autarkiepolitik im Dritten Reich* (Stuttgart, 1968), pp. 24–33; M. Thomas, *Britain, France and Appeasement: Anglo-French Relations in the Popular Front Era* (Oxford, 1997), pp. 115–37.

3. TBJG, I, 3/i, pp. 313–14; Geyer, *Aufrüstung oder Sicherheit,* pp. 445–7; Dülffer, *Weimar, Hitler, und die Marine,* pp. 315–16; Deist, "The Rearmament of the Wehrmacht," in *Germany and the Second World War,* i, pp. 434–7; Müller, *General Ludwig Beck,* pp. 469–77, and his *Beck: Eine Biographie,* pp. 186–236; Homze, *Arming the Luftwaffe,* pp. 103–12.

4. Petzina, *Autarkiepolitik,* pp. 26–8, 37–8; see Blomberg's fulsome comments to Hitler in BA-MA, RH 15, 70, August 15, 1936.

5. Kershaw, *Hitler,* i, pp. 529–42; Overy, *Goering,* pp. 37–47.

6. Overy, *Goering,* pp. 42–3; R.J. Overy, *War and Economy in the Third Reich* (Oxford, 1995), p. 187; Petzina, *Autarkiepolitik,* p. 43.

7. Tooze, *Wages of Destruction,* pp. 214–19; Petzina, *Autarkiepolitik,* pp. 45–8.

8. B.R. Kroener, *Der starke Mann im Heimatkriegsgebiet: Generaloberst Friedrich Fromm* (Paderborn, 2005), pp. 254–61; BA-MA, RH 15, 70, General Fromm, 1 August 1936; BA-MA, RH 15, 70, General Fritsch, 12 August 1936.

9. M. Harrison and R.W. Davies, "The Soviet Military-Economic Effort During the Second Five Year Plan (1933–37)," *Europe-Asia Studies* (1997), pp. 369–406.

10. L. Waddington, *Hitler's Crusade: Bolshevism and the Myth of the International Jewish Conspiracy* (London, 2007), pp. 79–121.

11. TBJG, I, 3/ii, p. 102.

12. J. Noakes and G. Pridham (eds.), *Nazism 1919–1945: State, Economy and Society 1933–1939* (Exeter, 2000), pp. 87–95.

13. Domarus, *Hitler,* ii, pp. 826–31; IMT, xxxvi, 416-EC.

14. G.L. Weinberg, *The Foreign Policy of Hitler's Germany,* 2 vols. (Chicago, 1970–81), i, pp. 337–48; T. Ōhata, "The Anti-Comintern Pact, 1935–1939," in J.W. Morely (ed.), *Deterrent Diplomacy: Japan, Germany, and the USSR, 1935–1940* (New York, 1976), pp. 9–37.

15. Weinberg, *Foreign Policy,* i, pp. 264–71, 331–6; Mallet, *Mussolini,* pp. 59–66.

16. R.H. Whealey, "Mussolini's Ideological Diplomacy," *Journal of Modern History* (1967), p. 435.

17. F. Minniti, "Le materie prime nella preparazione bellica dell'Italia, 1935–1943, Parte I e II," *Storia Contemporanea* (1986), p. 12; DDI, 8, iii, no. 561; OO, xxvii, pp. 241–8; *The Times,* March 24, 1936.

18. Zamagni, *Economic History,* pp. 253–5; Ristuccia, *Italian Economy,* pp. 51, 221–33; Sarti, *Fascism and the Industrial Leadership,* pp. 121–2; Minniti, "Aspetti organizzativi

del controllo," pp. 323–4; A. Curami and L. Ceva, "Industria bellica e Stato nell'imperialismo fascista degli anni Trenta," *Nuova Antologia* (1988), pp. 325–37.

19. G. Federico and R. Giannetti, "Italy: Stalling and Surpassing," in J. Foreman-Peck, and G. Federico (eds.), *European Industrial Policy* (Oxford, 1999), p. 135; G. Federico, "Italy's Late and Unprofitable Forays into Empire," *Revista de Historia Económica* (1998), pp. 377–402; G. Tattara, "External Trade in Italy, 1922–38," *Rivista di Storia Economica* (1988), p. 114.

20. Mallett, *Mussolini,* pp. 86–105; Bosworth, *Mussolini,* p. 317.

21. Zamagni, *Economic History,* pp. 253–4; M. Fratianni and F. Spinelli, *A Monetary History of Italy* (Cambridge, 1997), pp. 150–7; F. Guarneri, *Battaglie economiche tra le due grandi guerre,* 2 vols. (Milan, 1953), ii, pp. 84–100.

22. J. Wright and P. Stafford, "Hitler, Britain and the Hossbach Memorandum," *Militärgeschichtliche Mitteilungen* (1987), pp. 86–8; H. Meier-Welcker, "Zur deutsch-italienischen Militärpolitik und Beurteilung der italienischer Wehrmacht vor dem Zweiten Weltkrieg," *Militärgeschichtliche Mitteilungen* (1970), pp. 59–94.

23. CDP, pp. 42–8.

24. DDI, 8, v, appendix no. 1, pp. 785–9; ASMAE, AP 1931–1945, Germany, b. 33, f. 2, 21 September 1936; Gooch, *Mussolini and His Generals,* p. 347; CDP, pp. 50–1.

25. CDP, pp. 56–60; DGFP, c, v, nos. 618, 624; OO, xxviii, pp. 67–72.

26. DDI, 8, v, no. 277; OO, xxviii, pp. 48–54.

27. R. Mallett, *The Italian Navy and Fascist Expansionism, 1935–40* (London, 1998), pp. 48–91; ACS, Ministero della Marina, b.295, 13 January 1936; Ristuccia, *Italian Economy,* pp. 77–8, 81–2; A. Caracciolo, *La Banca d'Italia tra l'autarchia e la guerra, 1936–1945* (Rome, 1993), pp. 21–30.

28. LSMG, pp. 373–5.

29. OO, xxviii, pp. 175–81.

30. D. Ferrari, "Per uno studio della politica militare del Generale Alberto Pariani," *Studi storico militari* (1988), pp. 371–400; Gooch, *Mussolini and His Generals,* pp. 355–72; F. Minniti, "Piano e ordinamento nella preparazione italiana alla guerra degli anni trenta," *Dimensioni e Problemi della Ricerca Storica* (1990), pp. 140–60; LSMG, p. 379.

31. Bottai D, pp. 113–14.

32. Wright and Stafford, "Hitler, Britain and the Hossbach Memorandum," pp. 86–8; TBJG, I, 3/ii, pp. 249, 346–9.

33. Tooze, *Wages of Destruction,* pp. 223–30; Petzina, *Autarkiepolitik,* pp. 57–77.

34. CDP, pp. 80–91; DDI, 8, vi, no. 162; Mallett, *Mussolini,* pp. 108–13.

35. Tooze, *Wages of Destruction,* pp. 231–40; J. Dülffer, "Der Beginn des Krieges 1939: Hitler, die innere Krise und das Mächtesystem," *Geschichte und Gesellschaft* (1976), p. 458; Homze, *Arming the Luftwaffe,* pp. 144–5.

36. Geyer, *Aufrüstung oder Sicherheit,* p. 444; Gooch, *Mussolini and His Generals,* p. 329; T.P. Conwell-Evans, *None So Blind: A Study of the Crisis Years, 1930–1939, Based on the Private Papers of Group-Captain M. G. Christie* (London, 1947), pp. 78–81.

37. DDI, 8, vi, no. 201.

CHAPTER 9: GUNS AND BUTTER

1. *The Times,* 18 January 1936; CDL, iv, pp. 169–70.

2. G.C. Peden, *British Rearmament and the Treasury, 1932–1939* (Edinburgh, 1979), pp. 73–9; A. Booth, "Britain in the 1930s: A Managed Economy?" *Economic History Review* (1987), p. 509; TNA, CAB 16/112, DRC, 31 October 1935; Chamberlain diary, 2 August 1935, Birmingham University Library, UK; CDL, iv, pp. 119, 133, 143, 149, 165, 184; Self, *Chamberlain,* pp. 246–50.

3. Stewart, *Burying Caesar,* pp. 223–8; CDL, iv, p. 165; Williamson, *Baldwin,* pp. 305–13.

4. TNA, CAB 48/1, ICF/450, 1 April 1933; Wark, *Ultimate Enemy,* pp. 158–70; TNA, FO 371/18882, C8368/4887/18, "Industrial Mobilisation," December 1935; E. Ludendorff, *Der totale Krieg* (Munich, 1935).

5. TNA, CAB 60/3, Principal Supply Officers, 13 December 1932; CAB 53/4, Chiefs of Staff, 12 October 1933; TNA, CAB 16/123, DRC 37, 21 November 1935 and CAB 24/259, CP 36, 12 February 1936; see, for instance, Lloyd, *Experiments in State Control,* p. xi. "'Another great war will plunge the world into a sort of military communism,' Lloyd predicted in 1924, 'in comparison with which the control exercised during the recent war will seem an Arcadian revel. Personal freedom and private property are condemned by the exigencies of a modern war.'"

6. CDL, iv, p. 175; R.J. Overy, "Airpower and the Origins of Deterrence Theory Before 1939," *Journal of Strategic Studies* (1992), pp. 73–101.

7. R. Toye, *The Labour Party and the Planned Economy, 1931–1951* (London, 2003), pp. 9–33; D. Ritschel, *The Politics of Planning: The Debate on Economic Planning in Britain in the 1930s* (Oxford, 1997), pp. 1–17, 183–231 and 220–9; CRD 1/65/2, 25 October 1934, and CRD 1/65/2/19, "State and Industry," April 1935, Conservative Party Archives, Bodleian Library, Oxford, UK.

8. Imlay, *Facing the Second World War,* pp. 308–9; D.G. Anderson, "British Rearmament and the 'Merchants of Death': The 1935–36 Royal Commission on the Manufacture of and Trade in Armaments," *Journal of Contemporary History* (1994), pp. 18–19; TNA, CAB 23/80, Cabinet, 24 October 29 October 7 November 1934, and CAB 16/125, Royal Commission, 6 May 1936.

9. TNA, CAB 16/112, DRC 38, 17 October 1935.

10. D. Edgerton, "Technical Innovation, Industrial Capacity and Efficiency: Public Ownership and the British Military Aircraft Industry, 1935–1948," *Business History* (1984), pp. 247–79; S. Ritchie, *Industry and Air Power: The Expansion of British Aircraft Production, 1935–41* (London, 1997), p. 49.

11. M.S. Smith, *British Air Strategy Between the Wars* (Oxford, 1984), pp. 159–65.

12. UK House of Commons, Command Paper 5107, 3 March 1936; TNA, AIR 9/8, "Potential Dangers," 15 January 1936.

13. Alexander, *Republic in Danger,* pp. 1–55.

14. Ibid., pp. 34–42; DDF, 2, i, no. 83; H. Strachan, "War and Society in the 1920s and 1930s," in Chickering and Förster, *Shadows of Total War,* pp. 44–5.

15. T. Imlay, "Preparing for Total War: The Conseil Supérieur de la Défense Nationale and France's Industrial and Economic Preparations for War After 1918," *War in History* (2008), pp. 43–65; Serrigny, "L'Organisation de la nation pour," pp. 583–601.

16. Jackson, *Politics of the Depression,* pp. 101–11; Alexander, *Republic in Danger,* pp. 56–79; Frank, *Le prix du réarmement,* pp. 55–63, 96–125.

17. M.G. Gamelin, *Servir,* 3 vols. (Paris, 1946–7), ii, pp. 177–81.

18. Jackson, *Nazi Menace,* pp. 169–77; Alexander, *Republic in Danger,* pp. 259–60; Frank, *Le prix du réarmement,* p. 127; DDF, 2, i, nos. 83, 196, 202, 334, 392; Weinberg, *Foreign Policy,* i, p. 252; Thomas, *Britain, France,* pp. 24–46.

19. DDF, 2, ii, no. 357; SHD-DAT, 7N, 2521-6, 8 April 1936; Alexander, *Republic in Danger,* pp. 58, 66, 69–70, 110–13; J.J. Clarke, "The Nationalisation of the War Industries in France, 1936–37," *Journal of Modern History* (1977), p. 425; Gamelin, *Servir,* i, pp. 210–14.

20. J. Colton, "The Formation of the French Popular Front, 1934–36," in M. Alexander and H. Graham (eds.), *The French and Spanish Popular Fronts* (Cambridge, 1989), pp. 9–23; J. Jackson, *The Popular Front in France* (Cambridge, 1988), pp. 17–51, 85–112, 299–302.

21. J. Colton, *Léon Blum: Humanist in Politics* (Durham, NC, 1987), pp. 3–323; Jackson, *Popular Front,* pp. 52–61; Jackson, *Politics of the Depression,* pp. 137–66.

22. L. Blum, *Peace and Disarmament* (London, 1932), pp. 30–7, 102–3, 159; L. Blum, *L'Oeuvre de Léon Blum,* 8 vols (Paris, 1955–72), iii-2, pp. 544–7.

23. M. Alexander, "Soldiers and Socialists: The French Officers Corps and Leftist Government, 1935–37," in Alexander and Graham, *French and Spanish Popular Fronts,* pp. 62–78; Gamelin, *Servir,* ii, pp. 222–4.

24. S. Greenwood, "Caligula's Horse Revisited: Sir Thomas Inskip as Minister for the Coordination of Defence, 1936–39," *Journal of Strategic Studies* (1994), pp. 17–25; Roskill, *Hankey,* iii, pp. 202–11.

25. G. Best, *Churchill and War* (London, 2005), pp. 1–99.

26. P. Addison, *Churchill: Unexpected Hero* (Oxford, 2006), pp. 7–123; Stewart, *Burying Caesar,* p. 40; R. Toye, *Lloyd George & Churchill* (London, 2007), pp. 238–71; Stewart, *Burying Caesar,* pp. 45–199.

27. R.A.C. Parker, *Churchill and Appeasement* (Basingstoke, 2000), pp. 27–49, 64–91; Stewart, *Burying Caesar,* pp. 201–48; D.C. Watt, "Churchill and Appeasement," in R. Blake and W.R. Louis (ed.), *Churchill* (Oxford, 1994), pp. 199–214.

28. Stewart, *Burying Caesar,* pp. 214–18; R.A.C. Parker, *Churchill,* pp. 82–3.

29. D. Reynolds, "Churchill's Writing of History: Appeasement, Autobiography and the Gathering Storm," *Transactions of the Royal Historical Society* (2001), pp.

221–47; W.S. Churchill, *Marlborough: His Life and Times*, 4 vols. (London, 1933–8), ii, pp. 113–16.

30. HCDeb, 5, vol. 311, pp. 335–7, 433–5, vol. 315, pp. 115–16; Parker, *Churchill*, pp. 85–111.

31. M. Gilbert, *Winston S. Churchill: The Coming of War, 1936–39*, vol. V, part 3 (London, 1982), pp. 141, 157–8.

32. G.C. Peden, "Arms, Government and Businessmen, 1935–1945," in J. Tuner (ed.), *Businessmen and Politics* (London, 1984), pp. 132–5; W.J. Reader, *Architect of Air Power: The Life of the First Viscount Weir of Eastwood, 1877–1959* (London, 1968), p. 201.

33. Reader, *Architect*, pp. 235–7; S. Ritchie, *Industry and Air Power*, p. 262; TNA, CAB 16/123, Defence Policy and Requirements Committee, 13 January 1936.

34. N. Rollings, "Whitehall and the Control of Prices and Profits in a Major War, 1919–1939," *Historical Journal* (2001), pp. 517–40; R.P. Shay, *British Rearmament in the 1930s* (Princeton, 1977), pp. 97–9, 111, 125–30; TNA, CAB 24/259, DPR(DR)8, 23 January 1936; Lord Weir Papers, 19/16, 26 March 1936, Churchill College Cambridge, UK.

35. Ritchie, *Industry and Air Power*, 147–76; E. Lund, "The Industrial History of Strategy: Re-evaluating the Wartime Record of the British Aviation Industry in Comparative Perspective, 1919–1945," *Journal of Military History* (1998), pp. 75–99.

36. Lord Weir Papers, 17/10, 10 June 1936, Churchill College Cambridge, UK; TNA, CAB 16/136, DPR Committee, 11 June 1936.

37. TNA, PREM 1/193, 28 July 1936; TNA, T 161/720, S49175, October 1936; Williamson, *Baldwin*, pp. 294–335.

38. TNA, CAB 55/5, Chiefs of Staff, 25 March 1936; CAB 24/265, CP297, 30 October 1936; HCDeb, 5, vol. 317, pp. 743–4.

39. Colton, *Léon Blum*, pp. 198–210; Blum, *L'Oeuvre*, iv-1, pp. 364–70; Frank, *Le prix du réarmement*, pp. 65–71.

40. Alexander, *Republic in Danger*, pp. 80–113; DDF, 2, ii, no. 369; du Réau, *Daladier*, pp. 177–80.

41. Jackson, *Nazi Menace*, pp. 100–1, 178–87; du Réau, *Daladier*, pp. 180–9.

42. Gamelin, *Servir*, i, pp. 210–14.

43. DDF, 2, ii, no. 375; Clarke, "Nationalisation of the War Industries in France," pp. 423–6.

44. SHD-DAT, 7N 3434-1, 1 June and 25 August 1936; R. Jacomet, *L'armement de la France 1936–1939* (Paris, 1945), pp. 117–32.

45. Frank, *Le prix du réarmement*, pp. 71–4.

46. Jackson, *Nazi Menace*, pp. 125–30, 194–8.

47. S. Jansen, *Pierre Cot: Un antifasciste radical* (Paris, 2002), pp. 17–277; H. Chapman, *State Capitalism and Working-Class Radicalism in the French Aircraft Industry* (Berkeley, 1991), pp. 15–111; Facon, *L'armée de l'air*, pp. 70–7; Frank, *Le prix du réarmement*, pp. 79–81, 262–4; DDF, 2, ii, no. 369 and iii, no. 67; SHD-DAA, 1B4-1, 1 December 1936.

48. K. Mouré, "'Une eventualité absolument exclue': French reluctance to devalue, 1933–1936," *French Historical Studies* (1988), pp. 479–505; Frank, *Le prix du réarmement*, pp. 135–8; Schwarz, "Searching for Recovery," in Garside, *Capitalism in Crisis*, pp. 104–12.

49. Jackson, *Nazi Menace*, p. 107.

50. R. Girault, "The Impact of the Economic Situation," and R. Frank[enstein], "The Decline of France and French Appeasement, 1936–1939," both in W.J. Mommsen and L. Kettenacker (eds.), *The Fascist Challenge and the Policy of Appeasement* (London, 1983), pp. 209–23, 236–9; C. Maddison, "French Interwar Monetary Policy" (PhD Thesis, European University Institute, Florence, 1994), pp. 399–481; Eichengreen, *Golden Fetters*, pp. 348–83.

51. Archives du Ministère des Affaires Étrangères, Paris, Papiers Massigli, vol. 10, 3 November 1936.

52. R. Frank[enstein], "Le Front Populaire a-t-il perdu la guerre?" *L'Histoire* (1983), pp. 58–66; Colton, *Léon Blum*, pp. 181–97.

53. Parker, *Churchill*, p. 107; Thomas, *Britain, France*, pp. 89–108.

54. Paxton, *Anatomy of Fascism*, pp. 68–73; Jackson, *Popular Front*, pp. 174–7, 249–68; Imlay, *Facing the Second World War*, pp. 251–5; Alexander, *Republic in Danger*, pp. 92, 129.

55. TBJG, I, 3/ii, pp. 346–9; Jackson, *Nazi Menace*, p. 225; M. Dockrill, *British Establishment Perspectives on France, 1936–1940* (Basingstoke, 1999), pp. 39–53.

CHAPTER 10:
"NEXT TIME WE'LL URGE ON THE OTHER SIDE"

1. RGASPI, 558/11/447/130-44.

2. Davies, *Industrialisation of Soviet Russia*, p. 319.

3. Harris, "Encircled by Enemies," pp. 513–30; I. Stalin, *Works*, 13 vols. (Moscow, 1952–54), xii, p. 256.

4. Davies, *Industrialisation of Soviet Russia*, p. 324; Samuelson, *Stalin's War Machine*, pp. 143–5; Harrison and Davies, "Soviet Military-Economic Effort," p. 385; R.W. Davies, "Planning for Mobilization," in Harrison, *Guns and Rubles*, pp. 122–3; Samuelson, *Stalin's War Machine*, pp. 139, 165–80; Stone, *Hammer and Rifle*, pp. 207–8.

5. M. Habeck, *Storm of Steel: The Development of Armor Doctrine in Germany and the Soviet Union, 1919–1939* (New York, 2003), pp. 213–18, 226–32.

6. Samuelson, *Stalin's War Machine*, pp. 148–56; RGASPI, 588/11/447/97-123 (23 April 1934); also RGASPI, 558/11/447/124-6 (23 May 1934).

7. Samuelson, *Stalin's War Machine*, pp. 156–7.

8. Habeck, *Storm of Steel*, pp. 71–116; Samuelson, *Stalin's War Machine*, pp. 150–1; RGAE, 4372/91/2196/1. 1-5 (January 1934); RGAE, 4372/91/1824/41 (January 1934).

9. AVPRF 05/14/97/29/21-2 (28 January 1934); AVPRF 05/15/105/30/22-3 (3 April 1934); O.N. Ken, *Collective Security or Isolation? Soviet Foreign Policy and Poland, 1930–1935* (St. Petersburg, 1996), pp. 188–266.

10. Stalin, *Works,* xiii, pp. 282–312; Davies, *Industrialisation of Soviet Russia,* pp. 331–61, 475–6; RGASPI 558/11/374/1-6 (December 1933) .

11. S. Dullin, "Litvinov and the People's Commissariat of Foreign Affairs: The Fate of an Administration Under Stalin, 1930–39," in Pons and Ramano, *Russia in the Age of Wars,* pp. 121–46; D. Watson, *Molotov* (Basingstoke, 2005), p. 151; Davies, *Stalin-Kaganovich,* pp. 293–4.

12. Harris, "Encircled by Enemies," pp. 535–9; V.N. Khaustov, V.P. Naumov and N.S. Plotnikova (eds.), *Lubianka: Stalin i Glavnoe upravlenie gosbezopasnosti NKVD, 1937–1938: Dokumenty* (Moscow, 2004), pp. 533–41, 572–3.

13. AVPRF, 010/10/48/8/22 (22 January 1935).

14. Samuelson, *Stalin's War Machine,* pp. 159, 185–6; S. Pons, *Stalin and the Inevitable War* (London, 2002), pp. 88–9; RGASPI, 17/162/17/156-7; RGASPI, 17/162/17/159; N.V. Yakubovich, *Aviatsiia SSSR nakanune voiny* (Moscow, 2006), pp. 14–15; RGASPI, 17/162/18/10-11, 13-15; R.W. Davies, "Soviet Military Expenditure and the Armaments Industry, 1929–33," *Europe-Asia Studies* (1993), pp. 390–1.

15. Davies, *Economic Transformation,* p. 17; R.W. Davies and M. Harrison, "Defence Spending and the Defence Industry in the 1930s," in Harrison and Barber, *Soviet Defence-Industry Complex,* pp. 79–88; J.T. Greenwood, "The Aviation Industry, 1917–97," in R. Higham, J.T. Greenwood and V. Hardesty (eds.), *Russian Aviation and Airpower in the Twentieth Century* (London, 1998), pp. 137–8.

16. Lih, *Stalin's Letters to Molotov,* p. 235.

17. RGASPI, 17/162/17/157 and RGASPI, 17/162/18/5 (22 March 1935); Dullin, "Litvinov," p. 125.

18. J. Haslam, *The Soviet Union and the Struggle for Collective Security in Europe, 1933–39* (Basingstoke, 1984), p. 93; Watson, *Molotov,* p. 148; M. Tukhachevsky, *Sentinel of Peace* (New York, 1936), pp. 3–14.

19. S.G. Payne, *The Spanish Civil War, the Soviet Union, and Communism* (New Haven, 2004), pp. 124–73.

20. AVPFR, 05/16/114/1/195-8 (7 September 1936); Pons, *Stalin and the Inevitable War,* p. 46.

21. Pons, *Stalin and the Inevitable War,* pp. 47, 66–7; *Izvestiia* TsK 3 (1990), pp. 205–12.

22. Samuelson, *Stalin's War Machine,* pp. 159–61.

23. Pons, *Stalin and the Inevitable War,* pp. 60, 68; RVPRF, 05/16/11/6/65-76 (9 December 1936).

24. E.A. Rees, "Stalin As Leader, 1924–1937," and S.G. Wheatcroft, "From Team-Stalin to Degenerate Tyranny," both in Rees, *Nature of Stalin's Dictatorship,* pp. 19–58, 79–107.

25. M. Harrison, "The Dictator and Defence," in Harrison, *Guns and Rubles,* pp. 1–30; Davies and Harrison, "Defence Spending," in Harrison and Barber, *Soviet Defence-Industry Complex,* p. 73; M. Harrison and A. Markevich, "Hierarchies

and Markets: The Defence Industry under Stalin," in Harrison, *Guns and Rubles*, pp. 50–64.

26. Harrison and Markevich, "Hierarchies and Markets', pp. 65–77.

27 A. Markevich, "Planning the Supply of Weapons: The 1930s," in Harrison, *Guns and Rubles*, pp. 78–117; Samuelson, *Stalin's War Machine*, pp. 190–2; M. Harrison and A. Markevich, "The Soviet Market for Weapons," in Harrison, *Guns and Rubles*, pp. 156–79.

28. Davies, "Planning for Mobilization," in Harrison, *Guns and Rubles*, pp. 118–55.

29. M. Harrison, "Soviet Industry and the Red Army Under Stalin: A Military-Industrial Complex?" *Cahiers du monde russe* (2003), pp. 323–42; RGASPI 558/11/88/26-65 (19–27 August 1935); Markevich, "Planning the Supply of Weapons," in Harrison, *Guns and Rubles*, p. 108.

30. J. Maiolo, "Anglo-Soviet Naval Armaments Diplomacy Before the Second World War," *English Historical Review* (2008), pp. 351–78.

31. D. Priestland, *Stalinism and the Politics of Mobilization* (Oxford, 2007), pp. 244–403; Harrison, "Dictator and Defence," in Harrison, *Guns and Rubles*, pp. 4–16; E. van Ree, *Political Thought of Joseph Stalin* (London, 2001), pp. 126–54.

32. O.V. Khlevniuk, "The Objectives of the Great Terror, 1937–1938," in E.A. Rees (ed.), *Soviet History, 1917–53* (London, 1995), pp. 158–76; I. Banac (eds.), *The Diary of Georgi Dimitrov 1933–1949* (New Haven, 2003), p. 65; J.A. Getty and O.V. Naumov, *The Road to Terror: Stalin and the Self-Destruction of the Bolsheviks, 1932–1939* (New Haven, 1999).

33. J.R. Harris, "General Secretary," in S. Davies and J.R. Harris (eds.), *Stalin* (Cambridge, 2005), p. 64; O.V. Khlevniuk, *In Stalin's Shadow: Career of Sergo Ordzhonikidze* (New York, 1995), pp. 126–74.

34. S. Main, "The Arrest and 'Testimony' of Marshal of the Soviet Union M.N. Tukhachevsky (May–June 1937)," *Journal of Slavic Military Studies* (1997), pp. 151–95; R.R. Reese, "The Impact of the Great Purge on the Red Army," *The Soviet and Post-Soviet Review* (1992), pp. 198–214.

35. Davies, *Economic Transformation*, p. 17; Davies and Harrison, "Defence Spending," p. 83; J. Rohwer and M. Monakov, *Stalin's Ocean-going Fleet* (London, 2001), pp. 74–87.

36. Davies, "Planning for Mobilization," in Harrison, *Guns and Rubles*, pp. 125–49; Samuelson, "The Red Army's Economic Objectives," pp. 64–5. My emphasis.

37. M. Mukhin, "Market for Labor in the 1930s: The Aircraft Industry," in Harrison, *Guns and Rubles*, pp. 180–209.

38. S.W. Palmer, *Dictatorship of the Air: Aviation Culture and the Fate of Modern Russia* (Cambridge, 2006), pp. 204–19; M. Mukhin, "Employment in the Soviet Aircraft Industry, 1918–1940," *PERSA Paper no. 36* (2004), p. 12; J.T. Greenwood, "The Aviation Industry," and his "The Designers," both in Higham, Greenwood, and Hardesty, *Russian Aviation and Airpower*, pp. 134–9, 166–70.

39. Yakubovich, *Aviatsiia SSSR*, pp. 357–60.

40. AVPRF, 05/16/114/1/15, 57–9 (13 January and 22 February 1936).

41. R.R. Rader, "Anglo-French Estimates of the Red Army, 1936–1937," *Soviet Armed Forces Review Annual* (1981), pp. 265–80; J.S. Herndon, "British Perceptions of Soviet Military Capability, 1935–39," in Mommsen and Kettenacker, *Fascist Challenge and the Policy of Appeasement*, pp. 297–319.

42. Radar, "Anglo-French Estimates," pp. 270–6; Habeck, *Storm of Steel*, pp. 241–6; Jackson, *Nazi Menace*, pp. 200, 291; Alexander, *Republic in Danger*, pp. 293–302; P. Buffotot, "The French High Command and the Franco-Soviet Alliance 1933–1939," *Journal of Strategic Studies* (1982), pp. 46–59; Müller, *Ludwig Beck*, pp. 512–20, and his *Beck: Eine Biographie*, pp. 321–30; Watt, "Churchill and Appeasement," in Blake and Louis, *Churchill*, pp. 206–8.

43. Khaustov, *Lubianka: Stalin*, pp. 440–54; Coox, *Nomonhan*, pp. 93–119; J. Haslam, *The Soviet Union and the Threat from the East* (Basingstoke, 1992), pp. 89–90.

44. Coox, *Nomonhan*, pp. 120–41; Haslam, *Threat from the East*, pp. 90–121.

45. C. Andrew and V. Mitrokhin, *The Mitrokhin Archive: The KGB in Europe and the West* (London, 1999), pp. 107–9; R. Radosh, M. Habeck and G. Sevostianov (eds.), *Spain Betrayed: The Soviet Union in the Spanish Civil War* (New Haven, 2001), p. 426; Pons, *Stalin and the Inevitable War*, pp. 126–36; Z. Steiner, "The Soviet Commissariat of Foreign Affairs and the Czechoslovakian Crisis in 1938," *Historical Journal* (1999), pp. 751–79.

46. E. van Ree, *The Political Thought of Joseph Stalin* (London, 2001), pp. 230–54.

47. Pons, *Stalin and the Inevitable War*, pp. 137–144.

48. J. Degras, *Soviet Documents on Foreign Policy 1917–1941*, 3 vols. (London, 1953), iii, pp. 315–22.

49. D. Watson, "Molotov's Apprenticeship in Foreign Policy: The Triple Alliance Negotiations in 1939," *Europe-Asia Studies* (2000), pp. 695–722; S. Dullin, *Men of Influence: Stalin's Diplomats in Europe, 1930–1939* (Edinburgh, 2008), pp. 11–91.

50. Haslam, *Threat from the East*, pp. 128–34; Coox, *Nomonhan*.

51. C. Hill, *Cabinet Decisions on Foreign Policy: The British Experience, October 1938–June 1941* (Cambridge, 1991), pp. 48–84; Jackson, *Nazi Menace*, pp. 370–4; Alexander, *Republic in Danger*, pp. 306–10; DGFP, d, vii, no. 213.

52. Banac, *Dimitrov*, pp. 115–16. Emphasis in the original.

CHAPTER 11:
"THEY ARE SERIOUS, THE ENGLISHMEN"

1. *The Times*, February 17–20, 1937; TBJG, I, 2/ii, pp. 379–84.

2. DDI, 8, vi, no. 201; Tooze, *Wages of Destruction*, pp. 115–20, 225–30; Petzina, *Autarkiepolitik*, pp. 57–133; P. Hayes, *Industry and Ideology: IG Farben in the Nazi Era* (Cambridge, 1987), pp. 155–211.

3. Tooze, *Wages of Destruction*, pp. 231–4.

4. T. Sarholz, "Die Auswirkungen der Eisen- und Stahlkontingentierung auf die deutsche Aufrüstung oder Sicherheit 1933–1939" (PhD Thesis, Darmstadt University of Technology, 1983), pp. 219–34; BA-MA, RH 15/148, 4 May 1937; Kroener, *Der starke Mann*, pp. 306–14.

5. Homze, *Arming the Luftwaffe*, pp. 139–54, 180–204; Budraß, *Flugzeugindustrie*, pp. 471–503.

6. Tooze, *Wages of Destruction*, pp. 230–6; IMT, xxxvi, 286-EC.

7. Carroll, *Total War*, pp. 140–9; IMT, xxxvi, 244 and 408-EC; Overy, *Göring*, pp. 52–5.

8. Tooze, *Wages of Destruction*, pp. 99–134, 230–9; C. Buchheim and J. Scherner, "The Role of Private Property in the Nazi Economy: The Case of Industry," *Journal of Economic History* (2006), pp. 390–416; Overy, *Göring*, pp. 62–8.

9. DGFP, d, i, no. 1; DDI, 8, vii, no. 393; Ciano, p. 25.

10. Bottai D, p. 120; Ciano, pp. 11–13, 19, 21–2, 25, 28; R. Moseley, *Mussolini's Shadow: The Double Life of Count Galeazzo Ciano* (New Haven, 2000), pp. 36–8.

11. Gooch, *Mussolini and His Generals*, pp. 360–3; *The Times*, May 5, 1937.

12. Ristuccia, *Italian Economy*, pp. 28–32, 47–121; V. Zamagni, "Italy: How to Lose the War and Win the Peace," in Harrison, *Economics of World War II*, pp. 198–9.

13. *The Times*, July 5, 1937; Zamagni, *Economic History*, pp. 285–7; J. Cohen, "Was Italian Fascism a Developmental Dictatorship?" *Economic History Review* (1988), pp. 95–113.

14. A. Curami, "Tecnologia e modelli di armamento," in V. Zamagni (ed.), *Come perdere la guerra e vincere la pace: l'economia italiana tra guerra e dopoguerra, 1938–1947* (Bologna, 1997), pp. 166–71; L. Ceva and A. Curami, *La meccanizzazione dell'esercito fino al 1943*, 2 vols. (Rome, 1989), i, pp. 106–10, 202–9; Gooch, *Mussolini and His Generals*, p. 363.

15. G. Alegi, "Qualità del materiale bellico e dottrina d'impiego italiana nella seconda guerra mondiale: il caso della Regia Aeronautica," *Storia Contemporanea* (1987), pp. 1197–2019; F. Minniti, "La politica industriale del Ministero dell'Aeronautica: mercato, pianificazione, sviluppo (1935–1943), Parte I e II," *Storia Contemporanea* (1981), pp. 5–55, 271–312; Curami, "Tecnologia e modelli," pp. 172–6, and his "Piani e progetti dell'aeronautica italiana 1939–1943: Stato Maggiore e Industrie," *Italia Contemporanea* (1992), pp. 243, 247–9, 251–2; B.R. Sullivan, "Downfall of the Regia Aeronautica," in R. Higham and S.J. Harris (eds.), *Why Air Forces Fail* (Lexington, KY, 2006), pp. 139–42.

16. B. Sullivan, "Fascist Italy's Military Involvement in the Spanish Civil War," *Journal of Military History* (1995), pp. 697–727; G. Rochat, *Le guerre italiane 1935–1943* (Turin, 2005), pp. 98–126, 137–41; P. Preston, "Mussolini's Spanish Adventure," and C. Leitz, "Nazi Germany's Intervention into the Spanish Civil War and the Foundation of

HISMA/ROWAK," both in A. Mackenzie and P. Preston (eds.), *The Republic Besieged* (Edinburgh, 1996), pp. 21–51, 53–85; DGFP, d, i, no. 12.

17. Mallett, *Mussolini*, pp. 86–9, 101–27, 144–9, 159–60; Maiolo, "Deception and Intelligence," pp. 62–4.

18. TNA, FO 371/21157, R2183/R4908/1/22, 25 March and 3 May 1937, and FO 371/21160, R1612/1/22, 14 July 1937; Gooch, *Mussolini and His Generals,*pp. 328–9; OO, xxviii, pp. 186–7; FRUS, 1937, i, pp. 655–65.

19. Bottai D, p. 120; DGFP, c, iv, no. 368; DGFP, d, i, no. 84; Mallett, *Italian Navy,* pp. 55, 101–3, 148; USMM, DG, O-A, b.1, f.1, "Studio circa la Preparazione," 16 September 1937; DDI, 8, vii, no. 658; Ciano, pp. 32, 39, 42.

20. BA-MA, RW 19/1253, July 1937.

21. Dülffer, *Weimar, Hitler, und die Marine,* pp. 425–34, 446–7.

22. For instance: N. Below, *At Hitler's Side: The Memoirs of Hitler's Luftwaffe Adjutant 1937–1945* (London, 2001), pp. 19–21, and Wright and Stafford, "Hitler, Britain and the Hossbach Memorandum," pp. 102–3, 99; also see for instance Smith, *British Air Strategy,* p. 177.

23. IMT, xxxiv, 175-c; Geyer, *Aufrüstung oder Sicherheit,* pp. 419–33; Schäfer, *Blomberg,* pp. 160–72; DGFP, c, iv, no. 371.

24. Wark, *Ultimate Enemy,* pp. 174–87; TNA, CAB 55/9, JP186, 22 December 1936; Jackson, *Nazi Menace,* pp. 217–20.

25. DGFP, d, i, No. 19; Hoßbach, *Zwischen Wehrmacht,* pp. 188–94, 217–20; Dülffer, *Weimar, Hitler, und die Marine,* pp. 299, 446–51.

26. DGFP, d, i, nos. 21, 86, 93; Wright and Stafford, "Hitler, Britain and the Hossbach Memorandum," pp. 95–106.

27. Post, *Dilemmas of Appeasement,* pp. 247–96; CDL, iv, pp. 219–20, 246–8.

28. W.N. Medlicott, "Britain and Germany: The Search for Agreement, 1930–1937," in D. Dilks (ed.), *Retreat from Power* (London, 1981), pp. 78–101; TNA, FO 371/19787-20467, W18355/18355/50, C8998/8998/18, Vansittart, 16 and 31 December 1936; J.R. Ferris, "'Indulged in All Too Little'? Vansittart, Intelligence, and Appeasement," *Diplomacy and Statecraft* (1995), pp. 122–75.

29. TNA, CAB 55/8, JP155, 26 October 1936; Williamson, *Baldwin,* pp. 313–26.

30. L. Hollis, *One Marine's Tale* (London, 1956), pp. 48–51; Wark, *Ultimate Enemy,* pp. 195–201; Bond, *Chief of Staff,* i, p. 99; Gat, *Fascist and Liberal Visions,* pp. 13–42; Liddell Hart diary, 21 July 1936, LH 11/1936/26, King's College London, UK.

31. TNA, CAB 104/34, Hankey to Baldwin, 9 October 1936.

32. TNA, CAB 63/51, Hankey, 21 December 1936; CHT 3/1, Chatfield Papers, 25 December 1936, National Maritime Museum, Greenwich, UK.

33. Edgerton, *Warfare State,* pp. 33–41; Maiolo, *Royal Navy,* pp. 133–7; G.A.H. Gordon, *British Seapower and Procurement Between the Wars* (Basingstoke, 1988), pp. 258–65.

34. Smith, *British Air Strategy,* pp. 160–76; M.S. Smith, "Planning and Building the British Bomber Force," *Business History Review* (1980), pp. 35–62.

35. Ritchie, *Industry and Air Power*, pp. 7–105; Society of British Aircraft Manufacturers, "The Problem of Efficient Quantity Production," 1937, AC 70/10/55, Royal Air Force Museum, London, UK.

36. Wark, *Ultimate Enemy*, pp. 59–64; Smith, *British Air Strategy*, pp. 173–80.

37. Jackson, *Popular Front*, pp. 52–61; Jackson, *Politics of the Depression*, pp. 137–66.

38. Colton, *Léon Blum*, pp. 270–85; Jackson, *Popular Front*, pp. 179–85; Frank, *Le prix du réarmement*, pp. 145–61.

39. Frank, *Le prix du réarmement*, pp. 163–75; P. Jackson, "Naval Policy and National Strategy in France, 1933–1937," *Journal of Strategic Studies* (2000), pp. 130–59.

40. Jackson, *Nazi Menace*, pp. 207–20; SHD-DAT, 7N 2676, April 1937; Frank, *Le prix du réarmement*, pp. 222–38.

41. Jansen, *Cot*, pp. 278–307; Jackson, *Nazi Menace*, pp. 235–7; Alexander, *Republic in Danger*, pp. 291–303; Buffotot, "Franco-Soviet Alliance," pp. 546–59.

42. R.J. Overy, "The German Pre-war Aircraft Production Plans," *English Historical Review* (1975), p. 781; M. Mukhin, *Aviapromyéslennost' SSSR v 1921–1941 godach* (Moscow, 2006), p. 115; Ritchie, *Industry and Air Power*, p. 90; Zamagni, "Italy: How to Lose the War and Win the Peace," p. 196; Frank, *Le prix du réarmement*, pp. 238, 255–64, 317; Budraß, *Flugzeugindustrie*, p. 376; Chapman, *State Capitalism*, pp. 101–47.

43. Jackson, *Nazi Menace*, pp. 235–7; Jackson and Maiolo, "Strategic Intelligence," pp. 440–5; DDF, 2, vii, no. 325.

44. Jackson, *Nazi Menace*, pp. 222, 276.

45. CDL, iv, pp. 233, 239, 246–8, 259, 264, 286–7, 303; TNA, CAB 53/34, COS 639, 12 November 1937.

46. Peden, *British Rearmament*, pp. 62, 81; N.J. Crowson, *Facing Fascism: The Conservative Party and the European Dictators, 1935–40* (London, 1997), pp. 126–30; M.J. Daunton, *Just Taxes: The Politics of Taxation in Britain, 1914–1979* (Cambridge, 2002), pp. 169–74.

47. Gibbs, *Grand Strategy*, pp. 279–96; TNA, CAB 23/88, Cabinet, 30 June 1937; CAB 23/90A, 27 October 1937 and CAB 24/270, CP165(37), 25 June 1937.

48. TNA, CAB 24/273-4, CP316(37), 15 December 1937 and CP24(38), 8 February 1938.

CHAPTER 12: " . . . A DIFFERENT KIND OF NATION"?

1. Kershaw, *Hitler*, ii, pp. 51–60; Schäfer, *Blomberg*, pp. 95–7, 173–205.

2. W. Michalka (ed.), *Das Dritte Reich: Dokumente zur Innen- und Aussenpolitik* (Munich, 1985), pp. 246–7; W. Warlimont, "Der Einsatz der staatlichen Gewalten in der Führung des totalien Krieges," *Militärwissenschaftliche Rundschau* (1936), pp. 309–23; *The Times*, 4 February 1938.

3. Kershaw, *Hitler*, ii, pp. 64–86; Weinberg, *Foreign Policy*, ii, pp. 261–300.

4. DGFP, d, i, no. 31; Wright and Stafford, "Hitler, Britain and the Hossbach Memorandum," pp. 95–106; DGFP, d, i, no. 342.

5. Michalka, *Dritte Reich,* pp. 241–5; W. Michalka, *Ribbentrop und die Deutsche Welt-politik 1933–1940* (Munich, 1980), pp. 106–92; DGFP, d, i, no. 93.

6. Michalka, *Dritte Reich,* p. 244.

7. DGFP, d, ii, nos. 131-3; IMT, xxvi, 1780-PS; D.C. Watt, "Hitler's Visit to Rome and the May Weekend Crisis: A Study in Hitler's Response to External Stimuli," *Contemporary History* (1974), pp. 23–7.

8. Bosworth, *Mussolini,* pp. 329–31; Kershaw, *Hitler,* ii, pp. 78–80.

9. Ciano, pp. 53, 58, 68; Gooch, *Mussolini and His Generals,* pp. 386–407; USSME, H-6, r. 12, "Situazione Strategica Italiana," 29 June 1938.

10. Gooch, *Mussolini and His Generals,* pp. 386–8; Mallett, *Mussolini,* pp. 164–73.

11. Ciano, pp. 87–8; Watt, "Hitler's Visit to Rome," pp. 23–32, and his "An Earlier Model for the Pact of Steel: The Draft Treaties Exchanged Between Germany and Italy During Hitler's Visit to Rome in May 1938," *International Affairs* (1957), pp. 185–97; Schmidt, *Hitler's Interpreter,* pp. 82–3; M. Knox, *Hitler's Italian Allies: Royal Armed Forces, Fascist Regime, and the War of 1940–1943* (Cambridge, 2009), pp. 13–14; P. Baxa, "Capturing the Fascist Moment: Hitler's Visit to Italy in 1938 and the Radicalization of Fascist Italy," *Journal of Contemporary History* (2007), pp. 227–42.

12. Watt, "Hitler's Visit to Rome," pp. 29–30; L.E. Hill (ed.), *Die Weizsäcker Papiere 1933–1950* (Frankfurt, 1974), pp. 127–8.

13. Stewart, *Burying Caesar,* pp. 280–94; CDL, iv, pp. 294–303.

14. TNA, CAB 53/8, Chiefs of Staff, 19 January 1938; D.C. Allard, "Naval Rearmament, 1930–1941: An American Perspective," *Revue Internationale D'Histoire Militaire* (1991), p. 46; Gibbs, *Grand Strategy,* p. 308.

15. M. Muir, "Rearming in a Vacuum: United States Navy Intelligence and the Japanese Capital Ship Threat, 1936–45," *Journal of Military History* (1990), pp. 473–85; Pelz, *Race to Pearl Harbor,* pp. 167–211; Maiolo, *Royal Navy,* pp. 133–47; TNA, ADM 167/98-9 and 104, Admiralty Board, 17, 25 November 1937, 15 June 1938, and ADM 205/80, Captain T. Phillips, 4 April 1938.

16. CDL, iv, pp. 304–8.

17. TNA, CAB 23/93, Cabinet, 14 March 1938; Smith, *British Air Strategy,* pp. 198–206.

18. Smith, *British Air Strategy,* pp. 206–10; Parker, *Churchill,* pp. 138–59; Jackson, *Nazi Menace,* p. 165.

19. Gibbs, *Grand Strategy,* pp. 314–15; TNA, CAB 23/93, Cabinet, 22 March 1938.

20. R.A.C. Parker, "British Rearmament 1936–9: Treasury, Trade Unions and Skilled Labour," *English Historical Review* (1981), pp. 333–6; T. Imlay, "Democracy and War: Political Regime, Industrial Relations, and Economic Preparations for War in France and Britain up to 1940," *Journal of Modern History* (2007), pp. 10–20, 31–42.

21. Parker, "British Rearmament," pp. 93, 313; Peden, *Arms, Economics,* p. 127; Shay, *British Rearmament,* p. 297; Gibbs, *Grand Strategy,* pp. 570–82; Peden, *British Rear-*

mament, pp. 132–4; Ritchie, *Industry and Air Power,* pp. 50, 68–9, 94–5, 131; TNA, ADM 205/80, Chatfield, 1 April 1938; Gordon, *British Seapower,* pp. 179, 219; Maiolo, *Royal Navy,* pp. 133–47, 171–84.

22. Gibbs, *Grand Strategy,* p. 583; TNA, CAB 23/93, Cabinet, 6 April 1938.

23. Colton, *Léon Blum,* pp. 286–300; DDF, 2, vi, no. 446; see also DGFP, d, iii, no. 549.

24. Colton, *Léon Blum,* pp. 301–3; Frank, *Le prix du réarmement,* pp. 85–6, 180–6; Jackson, *Popular Front,* pp. 185–6.

25. J.M. Blum, *From the Morgenthau Diaries,* 3 vols. (Boston, 1959–67), i, pp. 498–501.

26. Colton, *Léon Blum,* pp. 303–7; R.F. Kuisel, *Capitalism and the State in Modern France* (Cambridge, 1981), pp. 124–7.

27. du Réau, *Daladier,* pp. 15–174.

28. Frank, *Le prix du réarmement,* pp. 176–80; FRUS, 1938, i, pp. 63–5; Girault, "The Impact of the Economic Situation," in Mommsen and Kettenacker, *Fascist Challenge and the Policy of Appeasement,* pp. 240–3.

29. du Réau, *Daladier,* pp. 175–212; Archives du Ministère des Affaires Étrangères, Paris, Papiers 1940: Fonds Daladier, vol. i, 29 March 1938.

30. Imlay, "Democracy and War," pp. 20–3; É. Daladier, *In Defence of France* (London, 1939), pp. 46, 53–60; Frank, *Le prix du réarmement,* pp. 188–93; Jackson, *Nazi Menace,* p. 286.

31. Frank, *Le prix du réarmement,* pp. 187–99.

32. Facon, *L'armée de l'air,* pp. 77–88; Chapman, *State Capitalism,* pp. 151–74; Jackson, *Nazi Menace,* pp. 268–79.

33. Frank, *Le prix du réarmement,* pp. 226–8; Alexander, *Republic in Danger,* pp. 121–4; Dutailly, *Les problèmes de l'armée de terre,* pp. 139–74.

34. Jackson, *Nazi Menace,* pp. 279–85; I. Pfaff, "Die Modalitäten der Verteidigung der Tschechoslowakei 1938 ohne Verbündete," *Militärgeschichtliche Mitteilungen* (1998), pp. 23–77; N. Jordan, "The Cut-Price War on the Peripheries," in R. Boyce and E.M. Robertson (eds.), *Paths to War* (London, 1989), pp. 128–66; Alexander, *Republic in Danger,* pp. 210–78; TNA, CAB 55/12, Chiefs of Staff, 19 March 1938.

35. Jackson, *Nazi Menace,* p. 276–7; DDF, 2, viii, no. 462 and ix, No. 230.

36. Dockrill, *British Establishment,* pp. 90–1; Gibbs, *Grand Strategy,* pp. 622–40; Maiolo, *Royal Navy,* pp. 149–58.

37. CDL, iv, p. 307; TNA, CAB 23/623, Foreign Policy Committee, 18 March 1938.

38. Jackson, *Nazi Menace,* pp. 294–5; J. Jackson, *France: The Dark Years 1940–1944* (Oxford, 2001), pp. 90–1.

39. DBFP, 3, i, no.164; CDL, iv, p. 318; FRUS, 1938, i, pp. 493–5; Jackson, *Nazi Menace,* p. 258.

40. Weinberg, *Foreign Policy,* ii, pp. 367–8.

41. DBFP, 3, i, no. 250; DGFP, d, ii, nos. 184–6; CDL, iv, pp. 324–5.

42. DGFP, d, ii, no. 221; Watt, "Hitler's Visit to Rome," pp. 23–32.

43. F. Wiedemann, *Der Mann der Feldherr werden wollte* (Velbert, 1964), pp. 125–7; Müller, *General Ludwig Beck*, pp. 512–20, and his *Beck: Eine Biographie*, pp. 321–30.

44. Dülffer, *Weimar, Hitler, und die Marine*, pp. 466–503; IMT, xxxiv, 023-c.

45. J. Heyl, "The Construction of the Westwall: An Example of National Socialist Policy-making," *Central European History* (1981), pp. 63–78; Jackson, *Nazi Menace*, pp. 257, 284–5.

46. DDF, 2, x, nos. 401, 444–5; Schmidt, *Hitler's Interpreter*, pp. 88–9; Jackson, *Nazi Menace*, p. 278; P. Facon, "La Visite du general Vuillemin en Allemagne (16–21 août 1938)," *Recueil D'articles et Études (1981–1983)* (Vincennes, 1987), pp. 221–62.

47. L. Budraß, "Unternehmer im Nationalsozialismus: Der "Sonderbevollmächtigte des Generalfeldmarschalls Göring für die Herstellung der Ju 88," W. Plumpe and C. Kleinschmidt (eds.), *Unternehmen zwischen Markt- und Macht* (Essen, 1992), pp. 74–89, and his *Flugzeugindustrie*, pp. 471–653; Overy, "Pre-war Production Plans," p. 780.

48. R. J. Overy, "From 'Uralbomber' to 'Amerikabomber': The Luftwaffe and Strategic Bombing," *Journal of Strategic Studies* (1978), pp. 154–78; Below, *At Hitler's Side*, pp. 21–2.

49. Tooze, *Wages of Destruction*, pp. 250–9; M. Geyer, "Rüstungsbeschleunigung und Inflation: Zur Inflationsdenkschrift des Oberkommandos der Wehrmacht vom November 1938," *Militärgeschichtliche Mitteilungen* (1981), pp. 121–86.

50. Müller, *Ludwig Beck*, pp. 502–62, and his *Beck: Eine Biographie*, pp. 307–33.

51. Müller, *Beck: Eine Biographie*, pp. 334–64.

52. BA-MA, RM 11/4, OKM Az. 66 K1c, 1 July 1938.

53. Tooze, *Wages of Destruction*, pp. 255–68, 289–91; DDF, 2, viii, no. 114 and x, no. 148; Wark, *Ultimate Enemy*, pp. 166–72; TNA, FO 371/21666, C542/C1432/C1801/65/18, Morton notes and correspondence, February–April 1938; TNA, CAB 23/93, Cabinet, 18 May 1938, and CAB 2/7, Committee of Imperial Defence, 21 July 1938.

54. TNA, C12179/36/17, FO 371/21596, ICF/62/F/1, October 1938; E. Kiesling, *Arming Against Hitler: France and the Limits of Military Planning* (Lawrence, KS, 1996), pp. 12–40.

CHAPTER 13: THE GREAT ACCELERATION, 1938–39

1. Domarus, *Hitler*, ii, pp. 1149–61; W. L. Shirer, *Berlin Diary* (Baltimore, 1941), pp. 126–31.

2. Weinberg, *Foreign Policy*, ii, pp. 314–425.

3. CDL, iv, p. 347.

4. Weinberg, *Foreign Policy*, ii, pp. 425–64; A. B. Zeman and A. Klimek, *The Life of Edvard Beneš, 1884–1948: Czechoslovakia in Peace and War* (Oxford, 1997), pp. 117–39.

5. Kershaw, *Hitler*, ii, pp. 113–25; DBFP, 3, ii, no. 1228.

6. TNA, PREM 1/236, R. Hopkins, 29 October 1938.

7. R.J. Overy, "Germany and the Munich Crisis: A Mutilated Victory?" in E. Goldstein and I. Lukes (eds.), *The Munich Crisis, 1938* (London, 1999), pp. 191–215; Maiolo, *Royal Navy*, pp. 117–19, 163–7, 220; DBFP, 3, iii, appendix no. 6, p. 659.

8. Tooze, *Wages of Destruction*, pp. 285–7; Kopper, *Schacht*, pp. 306–39; Domarus, *Hitler*, ii, p. 1223; *The Times*, 13 October 1938.

9. IMT, xxvii, PS-1301, pp. 160–4; also see his 8 July 1938 speech, in IMT, xxxviii, R-140.

10. Tooze, *Wages of Destruction*, 287–93; IMT, xxxii, PS-3572; M. Geyer, "Rüstungsbeschleunigung und Inflation," pp. 143–7.

11. Watt, *How War Came*, pp. 30–45; DGFP, d, iv, nos. 81, 411.

12. Dülffer, *Weimar, Hitler, und die Marine*, pp. 471–505; Maiolo, *Royal Navy*, pp. 63–86, 139–58.

13. Stewart, *Burying Caesar*, pp. 319–44; Self, *Chamberlain*, pp. 327–41.

14. TNA, CAB 23/95, Cabinet, 3 and 26 October 1938.

15. CDL, iv, pp. 358, 361–2; Smith, *British Air Strategy*, pp. 217–20; J.C. Slessor, *The Central Blue: The Autobiography of Sir John Slessor, Marshal of the RAF* (London, 1957), pp. 169–85, 203–9; TNA, CAB 27/648, CP218(38), 25 October 1938; TNA, AIR 8/227, air force staff, 2 November 1938.

16. TNA, CAB 24/279, CP234(38), 21 October 1938, and CAB 23/96, Cabinet, 31 October 1938.

17. Peden, *British Rearmament*, pp. 65, 97–8; TNA, T160/878, F16065, S.D. Waley, 16 November 1938.

18. TNA, CAB 23/96, Cabinet, 7 November 1938, and CAB 24/28, CP247(38), 6 November 1938; Gibbs, Grand Strategy, pp. 296–8, 583–600.

19. TNA, CAB 104/43, "Crisis and After," 14 November 1938, and FO 1096/86, "Factors, Aims," 2 January 1939.

20. TNA, CAB 27/624, Foreign Policy Committee, 14 November 1938, and CAB 23/96, Cabinet, 30 November 1938.

21. N.J. Crowson, "The Conservative Party and the Call for National Service, 1937–1939," *Contemporary Record* (1995), pp. 507–28; C.A. MacDonald, "Economic Appeasement and the German 'Moderates' 1937–1939," *Past and Present* (1972), pp. 105–35; D. Hucker, "Franco-British Relations and the Question of Conscription in Britain 1938–1939," *Contemporary European History* (2008), pp. 437–49; Maiolo, *Royal Navy*, pp. 44–51.

22. P. Stafford, "The Chamberlain-Halifax Visit to Rome: A Reappraisal," *English Historical Review* (1983), pp. 61–100.

23. Watt, *How War Came*, pp. 92–108; Hucker, "Franco-British Relations," pp. 447–9.

24. CDL, iv, p. 377.

25. M. Thomas, "France and the Czechoslovak Crisis," in Goldstein and Lukes, *Munich Crisis*, pp. 122–59; du Réau, *Daladier*, pp. 235–94.

26. Jackson, *Nazi Menace*, pp. 298–307, 320–1; SHD-DAT, 2N 224–1, 12 April 1938 and 5N 579–1, 25 October 1938.

27. Imlay, *Facing the Second World War*, pp. 243–58; Frank, *Le prix du réarmement*, pp. 197–201.

28. T. Imlay, "Paul Reynaud and France's Response to Nazi Germany, 1938–1940," *French Historical Studies* (2003), pp. 497–505; *Time*, 21 November 1938; Frank, *Le prix du réarmement*, pp. 201–6, 271.

29. M.P. Seidman, "The Birth of the Weekend and the Revolts Against Work 1936–1938," *French Historical Studies* (1981), pp. 270–6; Chapman, *State Capitalism*, pp. 175–211; Imlay, *Facing the Second World War*, pp. 262–71.

30. Imlay, *Facing the Second World War*, pp. 33–42; Jackson, *Nazi Menace*, pp. 314–25; DDF, 2, xii, no. 314.

31. DBFP, 3, iii, no. 325; DDF, 2, xii, no. 390; O.H. Bullitt, *For the President Personal & Secret: Correspondence Between Franklin D. Roosevelt and William C. Bullitt* (London, 1972), pp. 308–11; Jackson, *Nazi Menace*, pp. 339–40.

32. SHD-DAT, 7N, 3434-3, 29 December 1938 and 2N 224-1, 7 January 1939; DDF, 2, xiii, no. 234.

33. Jackson, *Nazi Menace*, pp. 325–8, 336.

34. Mallett, *Mussolini*, pp. 174–95; Gooch, *Mussolini and His Generals*, pp. 385–95, 423–39; Ciano, p. 128.

35. P. Einzig, *Economic Problems of the Next War* (London, 1939), p. 119; *The Times*, 22 October 1938.

36. M. Toscano, *The Origins of the Pact of Steel* (Baltimore, 1967), pp. 52–70; Ciano, pp. 148–9.

37. Gooch, *Mussolini and His Generals*, pp. 451–5; Mallet, *Italian Navy*, p. 138.

38. Toscano, *Pact of Steel*, pp. 85–106.

39. CDP, pp. 259–65; DBFP, 3, iii, no. 500; Ciano, pp. 176–7.

40. USMM, DC, O-A, b.1, f.1, "Pro-memoria sul Programma Anno XVII e Seguenti," January 1939; ACS, Ministero della Marina, Gabinetto, b. 86, f. Inghilterra, no. 135, "Costruzioni navali nel 1938," *Brivonesi*, 11 January 1939; Ristuccia, *Italian Economy*, pp. 122–79; Minniti, "Le materie prime nella preparazione," pp. 5–40, 245–76; Mallett, *Italian Navy*, p. 137; Bottai D, p. 139.

41. Bottai D, pp. 143–4.

42. DGFP, d, vi, nos. 205, 211.

43. OO, xxix, pp. 251–3; Ciano, pp. 225–7.

44. Toscano, *Pact of Steel*, pp. 307–70; CDP, p. 284; DDI, 8, xii, no. 59.

45. BA-MA, RW19/1285, "Vortrag gehalten am 1 Feb. 1939'; IMT, vii, EC-282; U. Hasell, *The Von Hassell Diaries, 1938–1944* (London, 1948), p. 39; A.M. Beck, *Hitler's Ambivalent Attaché: Lt. Gen. Friedrich Von Boetticher in America, 1933–1941* (London, 2005), pp. 108, 125–7, 130; DGFP, d, iv, no. 672; CDL, iv, p. 375.

46. IMT, xxxvi, 028-EC; Carroll, *Total War*, pp. 191–212.

47. Beck, *Hitler's Ambivalent Attaché*, p. 129; H. Groscurth, *Tagebücher eines Abwehroffiziers 1938–1940* (Stuttgart, 1970), p. 167; Hassell, *Diaries*, p. 39; DGFP, d, viii, no. 663 and d, ix, no.1.

48. Tooze, *Wages of Destruction*, pp. 293–9; Domarus, *Hitler*, iii, p. 1444; Homze, *Arming the Luftwaffe*, pp. 222–33; Budraß, *Flugzeugindustrie*, pp. 557–75; Tooze, *Wages of Destruction*, pp. 302–5, 314, pp. 311–17; Kroener, *Der starke Mann*, pp. 315–22; ACS, Ministero della Marina, Gabinetto, b. 88, f. Germania, no. 358, "Conversazione," 23 February 1939; Bird, *Erich Raeder*, pp. 122–7.

49. Ohata, "The Anti-Comintern Pact, 1935–1939," in Morely, *Deterrent Diplomacy*, pp. 51–111; Toscano, *Pact of Steel*, pp. 263–89; Watt, *How War Came*, pp. 188–98.

50. Maiolo, *Royal Navy*, pp. 176–85; TNA, CAB 2/7, Committee of Imperial Defence, 11 April 1939; Domarus, *Hitler*, iii, pp. 1522–35, 1561–96. The arms seized from the Czech Army probably amounted to enough to equip thirty divisions, but that did not mean that Germany suddenly had that many more units. Much of the Czech arsenal was sold to Balkan and Middle Eastern states. Probably ten German divisions were armed with Czech weapons, including several hundred tanks. See W. Murray, *The Change in the European Balance of Power, 1938–39* (Princeton, 1984), p. 292.

51. DGFP, d, vi, no. 433; Overy, *Goering*, pp. 76–92.

52. Kershaw, *Hitler*, ii, pp. 189–99; Watt, *How War Came*, pp. 430–46; H. Schwendemann, *Die wirtschaftliche Zusammenarbeit zwischen dem Deutschen Reich und der Sowjetunion von 1939 bis 1941* (Berlin, 1993), pp. 13–72.

53. Below, *At Hitler's Side*, pp. 24–5; Homze, *Arming the Luftwaffe*, pp. 248–51. The latest Luftwaffe intelligence study in fact described the aircraft industries of Britain and France as "inadequate to catch up with the major advance in the expansion of the air forces achieved by Germany during the next one to two years." See H. Boog, "German Air Intelligence and the Second World War," *Intelligence & National Security* (1990), pp. 250–425.

54. CDP, pp. 298–302; Moseley, *Mussolini's Shadow*, pp. 64–79.

55. Dülffer, "Der Beginn des Krieges 1939," pp. 443–70; Tooze, *Wages of Destruction*, pp. 316–25; DGFP, d, vii, nos. 192–3; Kershaw, *Hitler*, ii, pp. 206–11.

56. Müller, *Das Heer und Hitler*, pp. 394–421; Kroener, *Der starke Mann*, pp. 342–50; Watt, *How War Came*, pp. 479–528; Kershaw, *Hitler*, ii, pp. 211–30.

57. Kershaw, *Hitler*, ii, p. 230; Watt, *How War Came*, pp. 166–87; Self, *Chamberlain*, pp. 351–60.

58. *The Times*, March 17, 1939; TNA, CAB 23/98, Cabinet, 18 March 1939; CDL, iv, pp. 396–7.

59. Self, *Chamberlain*, pp. 356–7; Hill, *Cabinet Decisions*, pp. 30–47.

60. Gibbs, *Grand Strategy*, pp. 491–526; Hucker, "Franco-British Relations," pp. 447–56; Bond, *Chief of Staff*, i, pp. 183–202; Self, *Chamberlain*, pp. 362–3; TNA, CAB 23/99, Cabinet, 19 and 24 April 1939.

61. *The Economist*, March 25, April 29 and June 3, 1939; TNA, CAB 24/283, CP48(39), 21 February 1939, and CAB 24/285, CP84(39), April 1939; Imlay, *Facing the Second World War*, pp. 320–5, 206–16, 325–34; Stewart, *Burying Caesar*, pp. 353–73; Rollings, "Whitehall and the Control of Prices," pp. 531–6; TNA, CAB 24/287, CP118(39), 18 May 1939.

62. Imlay, *Facing the Second World War*, pp. 154–66, 278–81; Daladier, *Defence of France*.

63. Frank, *Le prix du réarmement*, pp. 209–17, 226–31, 306; Imlay, *Facing the Second World War*, pp. 271–2; Jackson, *Politics of the Depression*, p. 211; Facon, *L'armée de l'air*, pp. 85–92; J.M. Haight, *American Aid to France*, 1938–1940 (New York, 1970), pp. 69–102.

64. M. Alexander, "Preparing to Feed Mars: Anglo-French Economic Coordination" and W. Philpott, "The Benefit of Experience? The Supreme War Council and the Higher Management of Coalition War, 1939–40," both in W. Philpott and M. Alexander (eds.), *Anglo-French Defence Relations Between the Wars* (Basingstoke, 2002), pp. 186–208, 209–26; TNA, CAB 53/47, COS877, 11 April 1939; SHD-DAT 7N 3439–1, 15 April 1939.

65. Jackson, *Nazi Menace*, pp. 350–7; CDL, iv, p. 378; Wark, *Ultimate Enemy*, pp. 220–2; Imlay, *Facing the Second World War*, p. 43; SHD-DAT 7N 2524–1, 14 April 1939.

66. Wark, *Ultimate Enemy*, pp. 211–24; Jackson, *Nazi Menace*, pp. 298–336; FRUS, 1939, i, no. 270; CDL, iv, pp. 428, 431.

67. CDL, iv, pp. 412, 416–18, 428, 442; Jackson, *German Menace*, pp. 379–87; DDF, 2, xviii, no. 324.

68. Bond, *Chief of Staff*, i, p. 221.

69. Ciano, pp. 258–72; Moseley, *Mussolini's Shadow*, pp. 72–85.

70. DGFP, d, vii, nos. 271, 317, 341; Bottai D, pp. 156–7; Bottai D, pp. 154–6.

71. Watt, *How War Came*, pp. 530–604; Self, *Chamberlain*, pp. 370–82; Stewart, *Burying Caesar*, pp. 379–84.

72. Bottai D, p. 176.

CHAPTER 14: "THE ACID TEST . . .
IS WHETHER ANYONE IS READY TO DISARM"

1. Brinkley, *End of Reform*, pp. 15–30; Kennedy, *Freedom from Fear*, pp. 190–362; A.P.N. Erdmann, "Mining for the Corporatist Synthesis: Gold in American Foreign Economic Policy, 1931–1936," *Diplomatic History* (1993), pp. 171–200.

2. Adelstein, "'The Nation As an Economic Unit'," pp. 178–87.

3. Roosevelt, *Letters*, iii, pp. 147, 168–9, 209, 214; D. Tierney, *FDR and the Spanish Civil War* (Durham, NC, 2007), pp. 25–88; FA, ii, pp. 437–8, and iii, pp. 442–3; D.B. Schewe (ed.), *Franklin D. Roosevelt and Foreign Affairs 1937–39*, 10 vols. (New York, 1979), v, pp. 53–6; PPA, vi, p. 158; FA, ii, pp. 453–4.

4. FA, ii, pp. 323, 546; Levine, *Naval Rearmament,* pp. 299–300; Pelz, *Race to Pearl Harbor,* p. 42; M. Muir, "American Warship Construction for Stalin's Navy Prior to World War II: A Study in Paralysis of Policy," *Diplomatic History* (1981), pp. 337–51; McBride, "Unstable Dynamics of a Strategic Technology," p. 417; FA, ii, pp. 573–5.

5. "World Expenditures," 19 July 1935, no. 3492, George C. Marshall Papers, Lexington, VA; T.D. Biddle, *Rhetoric and Reality in Air Warfare: The Evolution of British and American Ideas about Strategic Bombing, 1914–1945* (Princeton, 2004), pp. 128–75; Johnson, *Fast Tanks and Heavy Bombers,* pp. 153–66; Biddle, *Rhetoric and Reality,* pp. 146–7; J.S. Underwood, *The Wings of Democracy: The Influence of Air Power on the Roosevelt Administration 1933–1941* (College Station, TX, 1991), pp. 85–102; M.S. Sherry, *The Rise of American Air Power* (New Haven, 1987), pp. 22–75.

6. Underwood, *Wings of Democracy,* pp. 27–84.

7. J. Vander Meulen, *The Politics of Aircraft* (Lawrence, KS, 1991), pp. 41–81; R. Schaffer, "The Politics of Aircraft," *Business History Review* (1993), pp. 490–1; Mukhin, "Market for Labor in the 1930s," in Harrison, *Guns and Rubles,* pp. 184–5; D.A. Daso, *Hap Arnold and the Evolution of American Airpower* (Washington, DC, 2001), p. 156.

8. A.W. Schatz, "The Anglo-American Trade Agreement and Cordell Hull's Search for Peace, 1936–1938," *Journal of American History* (1970–1), pp. 85–103; Blum, *Morgenthau Diaries,* iii, p. 524.

9. Dallek, *Roosevelt and American Foreign Policy,* pp. 144–9; H.L. Ickes, *The Secret Diary of Harold L. Ickes,* 3 vols. (New York, 1953–4), ii, p. 227.

10. B. Welles, *Sumner Welles: FDR's Global Strategist* (New York, 1997), pp. 196–208; C.A. MacDonald, *The United States, Britain and Appeasement, 1936–1939* (New York, 1981), pp. 16–75.

11. Casey, *Cautious Crusade,* pp. 5–15; Roosevelt, *Letters,* iii, pp. 162–3, 203; T.G. Mahnken, *Uncovering Ways of War: U.S. Intelligence and Foreign Military Innovation, 1918–1941* (New York, 2002), pp. 86–131.

12. Ickes, *Diary,* ii, pp. 296, 315; PPA, vii, pp. 68–9; Sherry, *Rise of American Air Power,* pp. 61–2.

13. MacDonald, *United States,* pp. 76–105; Watt, *How War Came,* pp. 124–34; Roosevelt, *Letters,* iii, pp. 232–4.

14. B.R. Farnham, *Roosevelt and the Munich Crisis* (Princeton, 1997), pp. 139, 173; D. Reynolds, *From Munich to Pearl Harbor: Roosevelt's America and the Origins of the Second World War* (Chicago, 2001), pp. 41–68.

15. Bullitt, *For the President,* p. 288; Hooker, *Moffat Papers,* p. 206.

16. J.P. Kennedy to Roosevelt, February 1938, PSF: Navy, and H.R. Wilson to Roosevelt, 11 July 1938, German files, I301, FDRL; Dallek, *Roosevelt and American Foreign Policy,* p. 172; M.S. Watson, *Chief of Staff: Pre-war Plans and Preparations* (Washington, DC, 1950), pp. 133–5.

17. Mr. Oliphant, "Meeting at White House," November 14, 1938, Morgenthau Diary, 150/338, and General Arnold, November 15, 1938, PPF1-P, Box 118, FDRL.

18. L. Bland (ed.), *The Papers of George Catlett Marshall: "We Cannot Delay"* (Baltimore, 1986), p. 651. M. Lowenthal, *Leadership and Indecision: American War Planning and Policy Process, 1937–1942* (New York, 1988), pp. 239–77.

19. Sherry, *Rise of American Air Power*, p. 80; Daso, *Hap Arnold*, p. 160; I.B. Holley, *Buying Aircraft: Materiel Procurement for the Army Air Forces* (Washington, DC, 1964), pp. 177–86.

20. Beck, *Hitler's Ambivalent Attaché*, pp. 108, 125.

21. Ickes, *Diary*, ii, pp. 469, 474.

22. PPA, viii, pp. 1–12; also Edison manuscript, September 2, 1939, recollection of FDR's reaction to outbreak of war in Europe, PSF: E, FDRL.

23. H.W. Baldwin, "America Rearms," *Foreign Affairs* (1938), pp. 430–44; H.J. Tobin and P.W. Bidwell, *Mobilizing Civilian America* (New York, 1940); Stromberg, "American Business," pp. 58–72; J. Doenecke, *Storm on the Horizon: The Challenge to American Intervention, 1939–1941* (New York, 2003), pp. 1–149; Lifka, *Concept of "Totalitarianism,"* pp. 91–121.

24. K.D. McFarland and D.L. Roll, *Louis Johnson and the Arming of America: The Roosevelt and Truman Years* (Bloomington, IN, 2005), pp. 33–56; K.D. McFarland, *Harry H. Woodring: A Political Biography of FDR's Controversial Secretary of War* (Lawrence, KS, 1976), pp. 138–59.

25. Brinkley, *End of Reform*, pp. 175–80; A.A. Blum, "Birth and Death of the M-Day Plan," in H. Stein (ed.), *American Civil-Military Decisions* (Tuscaloosa, 1963), pp. 67–83, and his "Roosevelt, the M-Day Plans, and the Military-Industrial Complex," *Military Affairs* (1972), pp. 44–6; Koistinen, *Planning War, Pursuing Peace*, pp. 305–16; Roosevelt, *Letters*, iii, pp. 241, 338–9.

CHAPTER 15: "MIRACLES CANNOT HAPPEN"

1. *New York Times*, January 21, 1940; also Crowther's articles of September 18, 1938, and April 27, 1941, and his *Ways and Means of War* (Oxford, 1940).

2. Alexander, "Preparing to Feed Mars," in Philpott and Alexander, *Anglo-French Defence Relations*, pp. 186–208; Haight, *American Aid to France*, pp. 132–231; J. Jackson, *The Fall of France* (Oxford, 2003), pp. 12–21; J.-L. Crémieux-Brilhac, *Les Français de l'an 40*, 2 vols. (Paris, 1990), ii, pp. 21–355; Frank, *Le prix du réarmement*, pp. 7–9, 281–319; W.K. Hancock and M.M. Gowing, *British War Economy* (London, 1949), pp. 83–178; Ritchie, *Industry and Air Power*, pp. 219–48; S. Broadberry and P. Howlett, "The United Kingdom: 'Victory at all Costs,'" in Harrison, *Economics of World War II*, pp. 43–63; Peden, *Arms, Economics*, pp. 184–94.

3. Philpott, "Benefit of Experience?" in Philpott and Alexander, *Anglo-French Defence Relations*, pp. 209–26; E. May, *Strange Victory: Hitler's Conquest of France* (London, 2000), pp. 306–22; F. Bédarida, *La stratégie secrète de la drôle de guerre: Le Conseil*

suprême interallié, septembre 1939–avril 1940 (Paris, 1980), pp. 79–106; TNA, CAB 65/1, War Cabinet, 13 September 1939.

4. For instance: TNA, FO 371/20727, IFC/322, 15 September 1937; M.J. Clark et al. (ed.), *Readings in the Economics of War* (Chicago, 1918); and Rosenbaum, "War Economics," pp. 64–94.

5. Müller, "Mobilization of the German Economy," in *Germany and the Second World War,* v, p. 410.

6. Self, *Chamberlain,* pp. 383–403; CDL, iv, pp. 445, 450–1, 456–7, 460–1, 467, 483, 514; Stewart, *Burying Caesar,* pp. 385–92.

7. Self, *Chamberlain,* pp. 389–90; and more generally TNA, PREM 1/384.

8. P. Howlett, "British Business and the State during the Second World War," in J. Sakudo and T. Shiba (eds.), *World War II and the Transformation of Business Systems* (Tokyo, 1994), pp. 133–6; Imlay, *Facing the Second World War,* pp. 334–53.

9. P. Howlett, "The Wartime Economy, 1939–1945," in R. Floud and P. Johnson (eds.), *The Economic History of Britain Since 1700: 1939–1992* (Cambridge, 2004), pp. 283–90.

10. W. Philpott and M. Alexander, "The French and the British Field Force: Moral Support or Material Contribution?" *Journal of Military History* (2007), pp. 743–72.

11. T. Imlay, "Mind the Gap: The Perception and Reality of Communist Sabotage of French War Production during the Phoney War 1939–1940," *Past and Present* (2005), pp. 179–224.

12. Imlay, *Facing the Second World War,* pp. 281–90; J.M. Sherwood, "Rationalization and Railway Workers in France: Raoul Dautry and Les Chemins de Fer de l'Etat, 1928–1937," *Journal of Contemporary History* (1980), pp. 443–74; R. Baudoui, *Raoul Dautry, 1880–1951: Le technocrate de la République* (Paris, 1992), pp. 187–208; Crémieux-Brilhac, *Les Français,* ii, pp. 105–14.

13. Imlay, *Facing the Second World War,* pp. 271–98.

14. Jackson, *Fall of France,* pp. 120–4; Imlay, "Paul Reynaud," pp. 497–515; R. Frank[enstein], "Le financement de la guerre et les accords avec les Britanniques (1930–1940)," in CNRS, *Français et Britanniques dans la Drôle de guerre* (Paris, 1979), pp. 461–87; Reynaud, 28 December 1939, in British House of Commons Command Paper 6159.

15. Alexander, *Republic in Danger,* pp. 314–77; May, *Strange Victory,* pp. 271–305.

16. Imlay, *Facing the Second World War,* pp. 51–4, 106–9; Bédarida, *La stratégie secrète,* pp. 115–98; D. Dilks (ed.), *The Diaries of Sir Alexander Cadogan, O. M., 1938–1945* (London, 1971), pp. 218, 238.

17. T. Munch-Petersen, *The Strategy of Phoney War: Britain, Sweden, and the Iron Ore Question, 1939–1940* (Stockholm, 1981); C. Richardson, "French Plans for Allied Attacks on the Caucasus Oil Fields, 1940," *French Historical Studies* (1974), pp. 130–56; B. Millman, "Toward War with Russia: British Naval and Air Planning for Conflict in the Near East, 1939–40," *Journal of Contemporary History* (1994), pp. 261–83.

18. T. Imlay, "A Reassessment of Anglo-French Strategy During the Phoney War, 1939–1940," *English Historical Review* (2004), pp. 343–57; May, *Strange Victory*, pp. 328–38.

19. Bédarida, *La stratégie secrète*, pp. 235–76; Jackson, *Fall of France*, pp. 125–9; Imlay, "Paul Reynaud," pp. 526–38.

20. R. Macleod and D. Kelly (eds.), *Ironside Diaries, 1937–1940* (London, 1963), pp. 235–9.

21. Self, *Chamberlain*, pp. 391–4; Stewart, *Burying Caesar*, pp. 392–404.

22. P. Salmon, "Churchill, the Admiralty and the Narvik Traffic, September–November 1939," *Scandinavian Journal of History* (1979), pp. 305–26; J.C. Cairns, "Reflections on France, Britain and the Winter War Prodrome, 1939–40," *Historical Reflections* (1996), pp. 269–95; Imlay, "A Reassessment of Anglo-French Strategy," pp. 348–62; Bédarida, *La stratégie secrète*, pp. 279–360.

23. Self, *Chamberlain*, pp. 411–16; CDL, iv, p. 514.

24. K.A. Maier and B. Stegemann, "Securing the Northern Flank of Europe," in K.A. Maier, H. Rohde, B. Stegemann and H. Umbreit (eds.), *Germany and the Second World War: Germany's Initial Conquests in Europe*, vol. 2 (Oxford, 1991), pp. 181–225; W.K. Wark, "Beyond Intelligence: The Study of British Strategy and the Norway Campaign 1940," in M.G. Fry (ed.), *Power, Personalities, and Policies* (London, 1993), pp. 233–57.

25. Self, *Chamberlain*, pp. 416–30; Stewart, *Burying Caesar*, pp. 404–20.

26. Wright and Stafford, "Hitler, Britain and the Hossbach Memorandum," p. 97.

27. Domarus, *Hitler*, iii, pp. 1829–48; Hill, *Cabinet Decisions*, pp. 100–45; Jackson, *Fall of France*, pp. 120–3.

28. K-H. Frieser, *The Blitzkrieg Legend: The Campaign in the West, 1940* (Annapolis, 2005), pp. 18–25.

29. Below, *At Hitler's Side*, pp. 40–1; C. Burdick and H.-A. Jacobsen (eds.), *The Halder War Diary 1939–1942* (New York, 1988), pp. 62–6; DGFP, d, ix, no. 1.

30. IMT, xxxvii, 052-L; Burdick and Jacobsen, *Halder War Diary*, pp. 69–72.

31. DGFP, d, viii, no. 384; Kershaw, *Hitler*, ii, pp. 275–9.

32. Burdick and Jacobsen, *Halder War Diary*, pp. 77–8; Müller, *Das Heer und Hitler*, pp. 471–573; G.R. Ueberschär, "General Halder and the Resistance to Hitler in the German High Command 1938–40," *European History Quarterly* (1988), pp. 321–47; C. Hartmann, *Halder: Generalstabschef Hitlers 1938–1942* (Paderborn, 1991), pp. 157–72.

33. Schwendemann, *Die wirtschaftliche Zusammenarbeit*, pp. 73–149.; Müller, "Mobilization of the German Economy," in *Germany and the Second World War*, v, pp. 453–62; Tooze, *Wages of Destruction*, p. 332.

34. Burdick and Jacobsen, *Halder War Diary*, p. 63; Tooze, *Wages of Destruction*, pp. 333–7.

35. B.H. Klein, *Germany's Economic Preparations for War* (Cambridge, MA, 1959); A.S. Milward, *War, Economy and Society, 1939–45* (London, 1987); T. Mason, *Social Pol-*

icy in the Third Reich: The Working Class and the "National Community" (Oxford, 1993), pp. 179–274.

36. Overy, *War and Economy*, pp. 177–256; Tooze, *Wages of Destruction*, pp. 333–67.

37. TBJG, I, 7, pp. 293–4; Müller, "Mobilization of the German Economy," in *Germany and the Second World War*, v, pp. 407–53, 474–563; Kroener, *Der starke Mann*, pp. 366–77; Tooze, *Wages of Destruction*, pp. 345–53; P. Erker, "Emergence of Modern Business Structures? Industry and War Economy in Nazi Germany," in Sakudo and Shiba, *World War II and the Transformation of Business Systems*, pp. 158–73.

38. Bird, *Erich Raeder*, pp. 134–52; Maiolo, "Deception and Intelligence," pp. 55–76.

39. Hartmann, *Halder: Generalstabschef Hitlers*, pp. 172–84; Frieser, *Blitzkrieg Legend*, pp. 59–74.

40. May, *Strange Victory*, pp. 240–68.

41. Jackson, *Fall of France*, pp. 25–59; May, *Strange Victory*, pp. 306–433.

42. Frieser, *Blitzkrieg Legend*, pp. 1–3, 100–290; W.S. Churchill, *The Second World War: Their Finest Hour* (London, 1949), pp. 38–42.

43. Jackson, *Fall of France*, pp. 125–42; Jackson, *Dark Years*, pp. 112–235.

44. Frieser, *Blitzkrieg Legend*, pp. 28–44; Jackson, *Fall of France*, pp. 14–17; Frieser, *Blitzkrieg Legend*, pp. 44–54; F.R. Kirkland, "The French Air Force in 1940: Was It Defeated by the Luftwaffe or by Politics?," *Air University Review* (1985), pp. 101–18; W. Murray, *Luftwaffe 1933–1945: Strategy for Defeat* (London, 1996), pp. 42–5.

45. D. Porch, "Military 'Culture' and the Fall of France in 1940," *International Security* (2000), pp. 157–80; Jackson, *Fall of France*, pp. 21–5. Contrast E. Kier, *Imagining War: French and British Military Doctrine Between the Wars* (Princeton, 1997), with G. Vardi, "The Enigma of German Operational Theory: The Evolution of Military Thought in Germany, 1919–1938" (PhD Thesis, London School of Economics and Political Science, 2009) and M. Strohn, "The German Army and the Conduct of Defensive Battle, 1918–1939" (DPhil Thesis, University of Oxford, 2007).

46. Jackson, *Nazi Menace*, pp. 117–18, 184–91, 324–6; J.P. Harris, "British Military Intelligence and the Rise of German Mechanized Forces, 1929–40," *Intelligence and National Security* (1991), pp. 395–417, and his *Men, Ideas and Tanks: British Military Thought and Armoured Forces, 1903–39* (Manchester, 1996), pp. 395–417; D. French, *Raising Churchill's Army: The British Army and the War against Germany 1919–1945* (Oxford, 2001), pp. 12–47; A. Gat, *British Armour Theory and the Rise of the Panzer Arm* (London, 2000); J.A. Gunsburg, "The Battle of Gembloux, 14–15 May 1940: The 'Blitzkrieg' Checked," *Journal of Military History* (2000), pp. 97–140; M. Alexander, "After Dunkirk: The French Army's Performance Against 'Case Red,' 25 May to 25 June 1940," *War in History* (2007), pp. 219–64.

47. Porch, "Military 'Culture'," pp. 164–9.

48. Jackson, *Fall of France*, pp. 197–227.

49. May, *Strange Victory*, pp. 448–52; Jackson, *Fall of France*, p. 28.

50. Hill, *Cabinet Decisions,* pp. 146–87; D. Reynolds, "Churchill and the British Decision to Fight on in 1940: Right Policy, Wrong Reasons," in R.T.B. Langhorne (ed.), *Diplomacy and Intelligence During the Second World War* (Cambridge, 1985), pp. 147–67.

51. S. Broadberry, and P. Howlett, "Blood, Sweat and Tears: British Mobilisation for World War II," in R. Chickering, S. Forster and B. Greiner (eds.), *A World at Total War: Global Conflict and the Politics of Destruction, 1939–1945* (Cambridge, 2004), pp. 157–76; M. Harrison, "Resource Mobilization for World War II: the USA, UK, USSR and Germany, 1938–1945," *Economic History Review* (1988), pp. 171–92; *New York Times,* June 2, 1940.

52. Beck, *Hitler's Ambivalent Attaché,* p. 158; TBJG, I, 8, pp. 42–3.

CHAPTER 16: WARS OF RAPID DECISION?

1. H. Trevor-Roper (ed.), *Table Talk 1941–1944* (New York, 2000), p. 172; J.P. Harris, "The Myth of Blitzkrieg," *War in History* (1995), pp. 335–52; W.J. Fanning, "The Origin of the Term 'Blitzkrieg': Another View," *Journal of Military History* (1997), pp. 283–302.

2. J. Förster, "Hitler's Decision in Favour of War Against the Soviet Union," in H. Boog, J. Förster, J. Hoffmann, E. Klink, R.-D. Müller and G.R. Ueberschär (eds.), *Germany and the Second World War: The Attack on the Soviet Union,* vol. 4 (Oxford, 1996), p. 13; Frieser, *Blitzkrieg Legend,* pp. 326–7.

3. Gooch, *Mussolini and His Generals,* pp. 465–72, 487–9; Ciano, pp. 293, 310, 357.

4. Gooch, *Mussolini and His Generals,* pp. 89–98; M. Knox, *Mussolini Unleashed, 1939–1941: Politics and Strategy in Fascist Italy's Last War* (Cambridge, 1982), pp. 54–8; Ciano, pp. 278, 288, 310, 357; DDI, 9, ii, appendix vii.

5. Moseley, *Mussolini's Shadow,* pp. 86–102.

6. DGFP, d, viii, no. 384; R.M. Salerno, "The French Navy and the Appeasement of Italy, 1937–39," *English Historical Review* (1997), pp. 66–104; Maiolo, *Royal Navy,* pp. 171–6.

7. Ristuccia, *Italian Economy,* pp. 72–3, 99–100; Minniti, "Le materie prime nella preparazione," pp. 5–40; Gooch, *Mussolini and His Generals,* pp. 498–9, 502–5; Bottai D, p. 176; Minniti, "Aspetti organizzativi," pp. 325–8.

8. A. Raspin, *The Italian War Economy 1940–43* (London, 1986), pp. 136–80; Knox, *Mussolini Unleashed,* pp. 71–3, 82–6; R. Mallett, "The Anglo-Italian War Trade Negotiations, Contraband Control and the Failure to Appease Mussolini, 1939–1940," *Diplomacy and Statecraft* (1997), pp. 137–67; Ciano, p. 307.

9. Bottai D, pp. 156–7; Bosworth, *Mussolini,* pp. 357–65; CDP, pp. 309–16; Ciano, pp. 284–6, 311.

10. TNA, FO 371/23798, R9301, WP (30) 100, October 24, 1939; Ciano, p. 311; DGFP, d, viii, no. 542; A. Pirelli, *Taccuini 1922–43* (Bologna, 1984), pp. 230, 233; DGFP, d, viii, nos. 663, 665, 667, 669–70; Ciano, p. 318.

11. DGFP, d, viii, no. 504; Bottai D, p. 175; Ciano, pp. 311, 315.

12. Ciano, pp. 307, 310–11.

13. Knox, *Mussolini Unleashed,* pp. 76–9; Gooch, *Mussolini and His Generals,* pp. 502–8; G. Schreiber, "Political and Military Developments in the Mediterranean Area, 1939–40," in G. Schreiber, B. Stegemann and D. Vogel (eds.), *Germany and the Second World War: The Mediterranean, South-east Europe and North Africa, 1939–41,* vol. 3 (Oxford, 1995), pp. 25–39; Bottai D, p. 176; Minniti, "Le materie prime nella preparazione," pp. 245–76; Ristuccia, *Italian Economy,* pp. 172–9.

14. J. Förster and E. Mawdsley, "Hitler and Stalin in Perspective: Secret Speeches on the Eve of Barbarossa," *War in History* (2004), p. 62; Ciano, pp. 414–15.

15. Knox, "Conquest, Foreign and Domestic," pp. 1–57; Ciano, p. 336.

16. DGFP, d, ix, no. 1; Bottai D, pp. 183–4, B.R. Sullivan, "'Where one man, and only one man, led': Italy's Path from Non-Alignment to Non-Belligerency to War, 1937–1940," in N. Wylie (ed.), *European Neutrals and Non-Belligerents During the Second World War* (Oxford, 2001), pp. 147–8; F. Minniti, "Profilo dell'iniziativa strategica italiana dalla non belligeranza alla guerra parallela," *Storia Contemporanea* (1987), pp. 1113–95.

17. R.J.B. Bosworth, *Mussolini's Italy* (London, 2005), p. 457; Ciano, pp. 352, 354; DDI, 9, iv, no. 642; Gooch, *Mussolini and His Generals,* pp. 508–18; Bosworth, *Mussolini,* pp. 365–74.

18. Moseley, *Mussolini's Shadow,* pp. 113–27; Ciano, pp. 390–1.

19. Knox, *Mussolini Unleashed,* pp. 231–85, and his *Hitler's Italian Allies;* F.W. Deakin, *The Brutal Friendship: Mussolini, Hitler and the Fall of Fascism* (London, 1962); V. Zamagni, "Italy: How to Lose the War and Win the Peace," in Harrison, *Economics of World War II,* pp. 177–223; D. Bigazzi, "The Production of Armaments in Italy, 1940–45," in Sakudo and Shiba, *World War II and the Transformation of Business Systems,* pp. 182–205; E. Agarossi, *A Nation Collapses: The Italian Surrender of September 1943* (Cambridge, 2000).

20. Maiolo, "Deception and Intelligence," pp. 55–76; M. Milner, *The Battle of the Atlantic* (London, 2003).

21. R.J. Overy, *The Battle* (London, 2000) and his *Why the Allies Won* (London, 1996), pp. 101–33.

22. Burdick and Jacobsen, *Halder War Diary,* p. 231; Toye, *Lloyd George and Churchill,* pp. 336–90.

23. Doenecke, *Storm on the Horizon,* pp. 125–64; D. Reynolds, *The Creation of the Anglo-American Alliance, 1937–1941* (London, 1981), pp. 96–132.

24. Beck, *Hitler's Ambivalent Attaché*, p. 150; Geyer, *Aufrüstung oder Sicherheit*, p. 162; H.-A. Jacobson, *Kriegstagebuch des Oberkommandos der Wehrmacht 1940–41* (Frankfurt, 1965), i, 107E-10SE.

25. In *Wages of Destruction*, pp. 9–12, 402–10, Tooze makes this point brilliantly. Also see H. Sirois, *Zwischen Illusion und Krieg: Deutschland und die USA, 1933–1941* (Paderborn, 2000), pp. 189–261; Tooze, *Wages of Destruction*, pp. 446–7; Budraß, *Flugzeugindustrie*, pp. 705–35.

26. Bird, *Erich Raeder*, pp. 154–68; Schreiber, "Political and Military Developments," in *Germany and the Second World War*, iii, pp. 209–46.

27. Burdick and Jacobsen, *Halder War Diary*, pp. 240–1; K. Schmider, "The Mediterranean in 1940–41: Crossroads of Lost Opportunities?" *War and Society* (1997), pp. 19–41; Hartmann, *Halder: Generalstabschef Hitlers*, pp. 207–24.

28. Michalka, *Ribbentrop und die Deutsche Weltpolitik*, pp. 269–94.

29. Burdick and Jacobsen, *Halder War Diary*, pp. 227–31, 242–5, 256–7, 279, 294–305, 310–11, 345–7; Förster and Mawdsley, "Hitler and Stalin," pp. 61–78.

30. Burdick and Jacobsen, *Halder War Diary*, p. 294; Tooze, *Wages of Destruction*, pp. 420–4; Schwendemann, *Die wirtschaftliche Zusammenarbeit*, pp. 194–229; R.-D. Müller, "From Economic Alliance to War of Colonial Exploitation," in *Germany and the Second World War*, iv, pp. 118–28; Schmidt, *Hitler's Interpreter*, pp. 209–20; DGFP, d, xi, nos. 325–6, 328–9.

31. J. Förster, "The German Army and the Ideological War Against the Soviet Union," in G. Hirschfeld (ed.), *The Policies of Genocide* (London, 1986), pp. 15–29; J. Hürter, *Hitlers Heerführer: Die deutschen Oberbefehlshaber im Krieg gegen die Sowjetunion 1941/42* (Paderborn, 2007), pp. 21–221; Kershaw, *Hitler*, ii, pp. 233–61, 317–24, 335–7, 348–60; C.R. Browning, *The Origins of the Final Solution: The Evolution of Nazi Policy 1939–42* (London, 2004).

32. Frieser, *Blitzkrieg Legend*, pp. 349–53; J. Klink and H. Boog, "The Military Concept of the War against the Soviet Union," in *Germany and the Second World War*, iv, pp. 225–85; G.R. Ueberschär, "Die militärische Planung für den Angriff auf die Sowjetunion," in G.R. Ueberschär and L.A. Bezymenskij (eds.), *Der deutsche Angriff auf die Sowjetunion 1941* (Darmstadt, 1998), pp. 21–37.

33. J. Förster, "The German Military's Image of Russia," in L. Erickson and M. Erickson (eds.), *Russia: War, Peace and Diplomacy* (London, 2005), pp. 117–29; E. Mawdsley, *Thunder in the East: The Nazi-Soviet War, 1941–1945* (London, 2005), pp. 41–54; Ciano, pp. 448–9.

34. Müller, "From Economic Alliance to War," in *Germany and the Second World War*, iv, pp. 142–54.

35. Tooze, *Wages of Destruction*, pp. 432–52.

36. Coox, *Nomonhan*; Haslam, *Threat from the East*, pp. 128–41.

37. R.R. Reese, "Lessons of the Winter War: A Study in the Military Effectiveness of the Red Army, 1939–1940," *Journal of Military History* (2008), pp. 825–52.

38. Banac, *Dimitrov*, pp. 127–8, 145; E.N. Kulkov and O.A. Rzheshevsky, *Stalin and the Soviet-Finnish War, 1939–40* (London, 2002), pp. 262–75.

39. S. Talbot and E. Crankshaw (eds.), *Khrushchev Remembers* (New York, 1971), p. 166; Davies, "Planning for Mobilization," and Mukhin, "Market for Labor in the 1930s," both in Harrison, *Guns and Rubles*, pp. 130–1, 138–9, 197–206; V.P. Naumov (ed.), *1941 god*, 2 vols. (Moscow, 1998), i-ii, nos. 7, 31, 68, 324, 438.

40. E. Mawdsley, "Crossing the Rubicon: Soviet Plans for Offensive War in 1941," *International History Review* (2003), pp. 824-6; Naumov, *1941 god*, i, nos. 41, 44, 92, 79, 98, 122; Yakubovich, *Aviatsiia SSSR*, pp. 365–78; Banac, *Dimitrov*, p. 138.

41. L. Bezymenski, "Wjatscheslaw Molotows Berlin-Besuch vom November 1940 im Licht neuer Dokumente," in B. Pietrow-Ennker (ed.), *Präventivkrieg? Der deutsche Angriff auf die Sowjetunion* (Frankfurt, 2000), pp. 113–27; Banac, *Dimitrov*, pp. 133–4, 136–7.

42. Mawdsley, "Crossing the Rubicon," pp. 827–30; Naumov, *1941 god*, i, nos. 272–3, 278; F. Chuev, *Molotov Remembers* (New York, 1993), pp. 22–6, 200–2; Schwendemann, *Die wirtschaftliche Zusammenarbeit*, pp. 151–94, 265–352; Naumov, *1941 god*, i, no. 162.

43. D.E. Murphy, *What Stalin Knew: The Enigma of Barbarossa* (New Haven, 2005), pp. 156–8; G. Gorodetsky, *Grand Delusion: Stalin and the German Invasion of Russia* (New Haven, 1999), pp. 52–7, 134–5, 231–6; Banac, *Dimitrov*, p. 149; Gorodetsky, *Grand Delusion*, pp. 155–78, 246–74; TNA, CAB 81/102, Joint Intelligence Committee (41)218, 23 May 41.

44. Förster and Mawdsley, "Hitler and Stalin," pp. 78–103; V.A. Nevezhin, "Stalin's 5 May 1941 Addresses: The Experience of Interpretation," *Journal of Slavic Military Studies* (1998), pp. 116–46.

45. Mawdsley, "Crossing the Rubicon," pp. 820–32; Naumov, *1941 god*, ii, no. 31.

46. G. Aselius, *The Rise and Fall of the Soviet Navy in the Baltic, 1921–1941* (London, 2005), p. 169; Naumov, *1941 god*, ii, no. 655; V. Anfilov, "Zhukov" in Skukman, *Stalin's Generals*, p. 346.

47. Mawdsley, "Crossing the Rubicon," p. 831.

48. Ibid., pp. 833–53; Naumov, *1941 god*, ii, no. 473.

49. D. M. Glantz, *Stumbling Colossus: The Red Army on the Eve of World War* (Lawrence, KS, 1998), pp. 102–7; Davies, "Planning for Mobilization," in Harrison, *Guns and Rubles*, p. 138.

50. A. Hill, "The Icebreaker Controversy and Soviet Intentions in 1941: The Plan for the Strategic Deployment of Soviet Forces of 15 May and Other Key Documents," *Journal of Slavic Military Studies* (2008), p. 116.

51. Mawdsely, *Thunder in the East*, pp. 18–37, 44–87; Burdick and Jacobsen, *Halder War Diary*, p. 446.

52. Burdick and Jacobsen, *Halder War Diary*, p. 506; K. Reinhardt and K.B. Keenan, *Moscow—The Turning Point? The Failure of Hitler's Strategy in the Winter of 1941–42*

(Oxford, 1992); D.M. Glantz, *Colossus Reborn: The Red Army at War, 1941–1943* (Lawrence KS, 2005).

53. Overy, *Why the Allies Won*, pp. 182–90; M. Harrison, "The USSR and Total War: Why Didn't the Soviet Economy Collapse in 1942?" in Forster and Greiner, *A World at Total War*, pp. 137–56.

CHAPTER 17: "IS TOTAL WAR, THEN, THE PATH TO FREEDOM?"

1. N. Takafusa, *Lectures on Modern Japanese Economic History 1926–1994* (Tokyo, 1994), pp. 87–101; A. Hara, "Japan: Guns Before Rice," in Harrison, *Economics of World War II*, pp. 233–9; Barnhart, *Japan Prepares for Total War*, p. 112.

2. Takafusa, *Lectures*, pp. 78–88; Barnhart, "Japan's Economic Security," pp. 112–13, and his *Japan Prepares for Total War*, pp. 71–114.

3. J.W. Garver, "China," in Boyce and Maiolo, *Origins of World War Two*, pp. 190–203; Y. Sun, *China and the Origins of the Pacific War, 1931–41* (New York, 1993), pp. 87–108.

4. Ōhata, "The Anti-Comintern Pact, 1935–1939," in Morely, *Deterrent Diplomacy*, pp. 1–111; Barnhart, *Japan Prepares for Total War*, pp. 136–61; Peattie and Evans, *Kaigun*, p. 358.

5. Hara, "Japan: Guns Before Rice," in Harrison, *Economics of World War II*, p. 238; A. Best, *British Intelligence and the Japanese Challenge in Asia, 1914–41* (Basingstoke, 2002), pp. 87–130.

6. Lifka, *Concept of "Totalitarianism,"* pp. 104–23; H. Hoover, "It Needn't Happen Here," *American Mercury* (1940), pp. 165–73, and *New York Times*, September 19, 1940; PPA, ix, p. 7. 7. "Air Force," May 15, 1940, PSF: Johnson, FDRL; PPA, ix, pp. 198–204.

8. Daso, *Hap Arnold*, p. 160; Sherry, *Rise of American Air Power*, pp. 91–9; Biddle, *Rhetoric and Reality*, pp. 204–8; DGFP, d, ix, no. 352.

9. B.M. Simpson, *Admiral Harold R. Stark: Architect of Victory, 1939–1945* (Columbia, SC, 1989), pp. 18, 21–8; Cook, *Carl Vinson*, pp. 129–53.

10. Watson, *Chief of Staff*, pp. 150, 154–6, 168–72, 176–7; Bland, *Papers of George Catlett Marshall*, pp. 123–4; T. Parrish, *Roosevelt and Marshall* (New York, 1989), pp. 15–157.

11. M. Matloff and E.M. Snell, *Strategic Planning for Coalition Warfare, 1941–1942* (Washington, DC, 1953), p. 14; Watson, *Chief of Staff*, pp. 107–12; R.M. Leighton, "The American Arsenal Policy in World War II: A Retrospective View," in D.R. Beaver (ed.), *Some Pathways in Twentieth Century History* (Detroit, 1969), p. 226.

12. D.G. Hauglund, "George C. Marshall and the Question of Military Aid to England, May–June 1940," *Journal of Contemporary History* (1980), pp. 745–60; M. Stoler, "From Continentalism to Globalism: General Stanley D. Embick, the Joint Strategic Survey Committee, and the Military View of National Policy during the

Second World War," *Diplomatic History* (1982), pp. 303–21; Reynolds, *Anglo-American Alliance,* pp. 95–150; Tooze, *Wages of Destruction,* pp. 396–425.

13. Casey, *Cautious Crusade,* pp. 24–7; Doenecke, *Storm on the Horizon,* pp. 100–49; Adelstein, "'The Nation As an Economic Unit,'" pp. 160–87.

14. R.D. Cuff, "Commentary," in J. Titus (ed.), *The Home Front and War in the Twentieth Century* (Washington, DC, 1984), pp. 111–18; Brinkley, *End of Reform,* pp. 175–80; Ickes, *Diary,* iii, pp. 193–6; Stromberg, "American Business," pp. 74–5; Blum, *Morgenthau Diaries,* ii, pp. 138–44, 146–8.

15. PPA, ix, pp. 230–45.

16. McQuaid, *Big Business and Presidential Power,* pp. 62–74; Brinkley, *End of Reform,* p. 180; P.A.C. Koistinen, *Arsenal of World War II: The Political Economy of American Warfare, 1940–1945* (Lawrence, KS, 2004), pp. 47–71; K.E. Eiler, *Mobilizing America: Robert P. Patterson and the War Effort, 1940–45* (Ithaca, NY, 1998), pp. 69–70; PPA, ix, pp. 201–2, 235–7, 290; G.T. White, *Billions for Defence: Government Finance by the Defence Plant Corporation During World War II* (Tuscaloosa, 1980), pp. 1–10.

17. Adelstein, "'The Nation As an Economic Unit,'" pp. 178–87.

18. Casey, *Cautious Crusade,* pp. 26–8; Kennedy, *Freedom from Fear,* pp. 454–64.

19. C.E. Kirkpatrick, *An Unknown Future and a Doubtful Present: Writing the Victory Plan of 1941* (Washington, DC, 1990), p. 41; Stark to Roosevelt, 12 November 1940, PSF: Navy, FDRL.

20. Reynolds, *Anglo-American Alliance,* pp. 145–68.

21. PPA, ix, pp. 633–44, 663–72.

22. Reynolds, *Anglo-American Alliance,* pp. 169–91; R.M. Hutchins, "The Proposition Is Peace," *Vital Speeches* (1941), p. 391.

23. H. Rockoff, "The United States: From Ploughshares to Swords," in Harrison, *Economics of World War II,* pp. 81–121; H.G. Vatter, *The U.S. Economy in World War II* (New York, 1985), pp. 7–11; Harry Hopkins to FDR, 22 August 1940, PSF: Hopkins, FDRL; PPA, ix, pp. 622–31, 679–702 and x, pp. 349–59; E. Janeway, *The Struggle for Survival: A Chronicle of Economic Mobilization in World War II* (New Haven, 1951), pp. 185–243; Brinkley, *End of Reform,* pp. 180–2.

24. McQuaid, *Big Business and Presidential Power,* pp. 74–7; Vatter, *U.S. Economy in World War II,* pp. 12–13.

25. McQuaid, *Big Business and Presidential Power,* pp. 77–85; S.A. Brandes, *Warhogs: A History of War Profits in America* (Lexington, KY, 2006), pp. 227–65; Vander Meulen, *Politics of Aircraft,* pp. 182–220; White, *Billions for Defense,* pp. 1–49. The big corporations of course did not have it all their own way. In April 1941 Missouri Senator Harry S. Truman came into the limelight by conducting hearings into the arms industry on behalf of the small manufacturers. See T. Wilson, "The Truman Committee," in R. Bruns and A. Schlesinger (eds.), *Congress Investigates: A Documented History, 1792–1974* (New York, 1975), pp. 3115–36.

26. Overy, *Why the Allies Won,* pp. 103–33; Biddle, *Rhetoric and Reality,* pp. 214–88.

27. W.F. Kimball, *The Juggler: Franklin Roosevelt As Wartime Statesman* (Princeton, 1994), pp. 21–41; W. Heinrichs, *Threshold of War: Franklin D. Roosevelt and American Entry into World War II* (Oxford, 1988), pp. 92–106; Watson, *Chief of Staff*, pp. 338–9, 347–8.

28. Kirkpatrick, *Unknown Future*, pp. 5–33; Bendersky, "'Jewish Threat'," pp. 227–86.

29. Kirkpatrick, *Unknown Future*, pp. 55–102; K.E. Eiler, *Wedemeyer on War and Peace* (Stanford, CA, 1988), pp. 1–26; Wedemeyer Interview, 1984, U.S. Army Military History Institute, Carlisle Barracks, Carlisle, PA.

30. Joint Board Estimate, September 11, 1941, PSF: Safe, FDRL; Reynolds, *Anglo-American Alliance*, pp. 202–19; W. Heinrichs, "President Franklin D. Roosevelt's Intervention in the Battle of the Atlantic, 1941," *Diplomatic History* (1986), pp. 311–32; Casey, *Cautious Crusade*, p. 405.

31. Heinrichs, *Threshold of War*, pp. 118–45; J.G. Utley, *Going to War with Japan, 1937–1941* (Knoxville, TN, 1985), pp. 102–37.

32. Y. Oka, *Konoe Fumimaro* (Tokyo, 1983), pp. 87–118; Berger, "Politics and Mobilization in Japan," in Duus, *Cambridge History of Japan*, pp. 126–45; Kerde, "The Ideological Background of the Japanese War Economy," in Pauer, *Japan's War Economy*, pp. 23–8.

33. Berger, "Politics and Mobilization in Japan," in Duus, *Cambridge History of Japan*, p. 143.

34. S. Hatano and S. Asada, "The Japanese Decision to Move South," in Boyce and Robertson, *Paths to War*, pp. 383–91; Asada, *From Mahan to Pearl Harbor*, pp. 212–39; J. Tsunoda, "The Navy's Role in the Southern Strategy," in J.W. Morely (ed.), *The Fateful Choice: Japan's Advance into Southeast Asia, 1939–1941* (New York, 1980), pp. 242–75; Barnhart, *Japan Prepares for Total War*, pp. 162–75.

35. Barnhart, *Japan Prepares for Total War*, pp. 162–75; Asada, *From Mahan to Pearl Harbor*, p. 223.

36. C. Hosoya "The Tripartite Pact, 1939–1940," in J.W. Morely, *Deterrent Diplomacy*, pp. 191–257; N. Ike, *Japan's Decision for War: Records of the 1941 Policy Conferences* (Stanford, CA, 1967), pp. 3–13.

37. Berger, "Politics and Mobilization in Japan," pp. 145–8; R. Sims, *Japanese Political History Since the Meiji Renovation, 1868–2000* (London, 2002), pp. 217–26.

38. P. Duus, "The Reaction of Japanese Big Business to a State-Controlled Economy in the 1930s," *International Review of Economics and Business* (1984), pp. 826–31; Samuels, *Machiavelli's Children*, p. 148; Takafusa, *Lectures*, pp. 102–4; Barnhart, *Japan Prepares for Total War*, pp. 200–1.

39. Takafusa, *Lectures*, pp. 93–4.

40. Barnhart, *Japan Prepares for Total War*, pp. 202–14, and his "Pacific War," pp. 118–20; Evans and Peattie, *Kaigun*, pp. 356–83, 447–86.

41. Asada, *From Mahan to Pearl Harbor,* pp. 240–60; P. Mauch, "A Bolt from the Blue? New Evidence on the Japanese Navy and the Draft Understanding Between Japan and the United States, April 1941," *Pacific Historical Review* (2009), pp. 55–79.

42. Ike, *Japan's Decision for War,* pp. 46–90; J.W. Morely (ed.), *The Final Confrontation: Japan's Negotiations with the United States, 1941* (New York, 1994), pp. 106–58.

43. Heinrichs, *Threshold of War,* pp. 146–214; Utley, *War with Japan,* pp. 138–82; Hatano and Asada, "Move South," pp. 394–403.

44. Ike, *Japan's Decision for War,* pp. 126–63; Takafusa, *Lectures,* pp. 106–11.

45. Morely, *Final Confrontation,* pp. 158–82; N. Kawamura, "Emperor Hirohito and Japan's Decision to Go to War with the United States Reexamined," *Diplomatic History* (2009), pp. 51–65.

46. Kawamura, "Emperor Hirohito," pp. 65–75; Oka, *Konoe Fumimaro,* pp. 119–59; R.J. Butow, *Tōjō and the Coming of the War* (Princeton, 1961), pp. 3–27, 133–309; Coox, *Nomonhan,* pp. 103–4.

47. Ike, *Japan's Decision for War,* pp. 184–239; Barnhart, *Japan Prepares for Total War,* pp. 250–62.

48. Kawamura, "Emperor Hirohito," pp. 75–9; Asada, *From Mahan to Pearl Harbor,* pp. 284–6; Ike, *Japan's Decision for War,* pp. 262–85.

CONCLUSION: THE RACE GOES ON

1. For a survey of the "economic fundamentals," see Mark Harrison, "The Economics of World War II: An Overview," in *Economics of World War II,* pp. 1–42; and more generally M. Beckley, "Economic Development and Military Effectiveness," *Journal of Strategic Studies* (2010), pp. 41–77.

2. Morely, *Final Confrontation,* p. 268.

3. Mawdsley, *World War II: A New History* (Cambridge, 2009), pp. 190–247, 267–73, 408–37; Evans and Peattie, *Kaigun,* p. 366; Overy, *Why the Allies Won,* p. 331.

4. Domarus, *Speeches,* iv, pp. 2531–51; Watson, *Chief of Staff,* p. 366; Kennedy, *Freedom from Fear,* p. 487.

5. M. Harrison, *Soviet Planning in Peace and War 1938–1945* (Cambridge, 1985), pp. 94–9; more generally M. Harrison and J. Barber, *The Soviet Home Front, 1941–5: A Social and Economic History of the USSR in World War II* (Cambridge, 1991); Mawdsley, *Thunder in the East,* pp. 185–223, 249–314.

6. Tooze, *Wages of Destruction,* pp. 507–655.

7. H.R. Trevor-Roper, *The Testament of Adolf Hitler: The Hitler-Bormann Documents* (London, 1961), pp. 29–109.

8. "Hoover Proposes Dictatorial Rule of War Economy," *New York Times,* May 21, 1942.

9. H. Rockoff, "The Paradox of Planning in World War II," unpublished draft paper dated June 2008; Vatter, *U.S. Economy in World War II*, pp. 67–101; Kennedy, *Freedom from Fear*, pp. 655–68; Overy, *Why the Allies Won*, pp. 190–8.

10. Kennedy, *Freedom from Fear*, pp. 621–31; Brinkley, *End of Reform*, pp. 182–200.

11. Kennedy, *Freedom from Fear*, pp. 631–47; Kirkpatrick, *Unknown Future*, pp. 103–114; Harrison, "Resource Mobilization for World War II," pp. 171–91.

12. C. Craig and S. Radchenko, *The Atomic Bomb and the Origins of the Cold War* (New Haven, 1998); D. Holloway, "Nuclear Weapons and the Escalation of the Cold War, 1942–1962," in M.P. Leffler and A.O. Westad (eds.), *The Cambridge History of the Cold War*, vol. 1 (Cambridge, 2010), pp. 376–377.

13. A.L. Friedberg, *In the Shadow of the Garrison State: America's Anti-Statism and Its Cold War Grand Strategy* (Princeton, 2000) pp. 9–62; Kaplan, *Wizards of Armageddon*, pp. 126–7, 145–7, 176–8, 180–4; Barber and Harrison, *Soviet Defence Industry Complex*, pp. 3–29, 118–94.

14. W. Burr and D.A. Rosenberg, "Nuclear Competition in an Era of Stalemate, 1963–1975," in M.P. Leffler and A.O. Westad (eds.), *The Cambridge History of the Cold War*, vol. 2 (Cambridge, 2010), pp. 88–111; Rhodes, *Arsenals of Folly*, pp. 306–9; M.S. Sherry, *In the Shadow of War: The United States Since the 1930s* (New Haven, 1995); R.H. Kohn, "The Danger of Militarization in an Endless 'War' on Terrorism," *Journal of Military History* (2009), 177–208.

INDEX